Ecuador

& the Galápagos Islands

Rob Rachowiecki

LONELY PLANET PUBLICATIONS
Melbourne • Oakland • London • Paris

ECUADOR

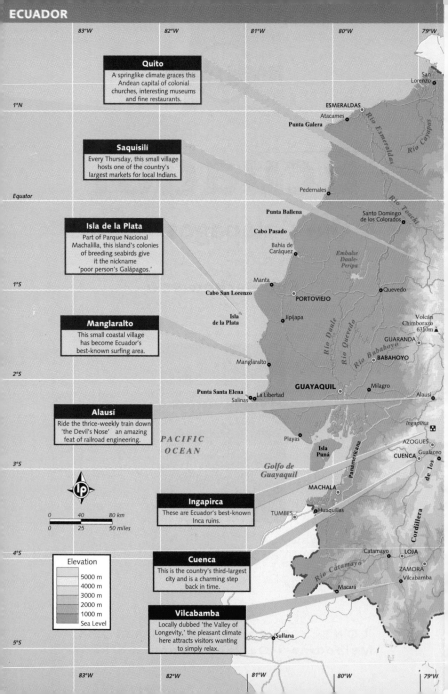

Quito
A springlike climate graces this Andean capital of colonial churches, interesting museums and fine restaurants.

Saquisilí
Every Thursday, this small village hosts one of the country's largest markets for local Indians.

Isla de la Plata
Part of Parque Nacional Machalilla, this island's colonies of breeding seabirds give it the nickname 'poor person's Galápagos.'

Manglaralto
This small coastal village has become Ecuador's best-known surfing area.

Alausí
Ride the thrice-weekly train down 'the Devil's Nose' — an amazing feat of railroad engineering.

Ingapirca
These are Ecuador's best-known Inca ruins.

Cuenca
This is the country's third-largest city and is a charming step back in time.

Vilcabamba
Locally dubbed 'the Valley of Longevity,' the pleasant climate here attracts visitors wanting to simply relax.

1°N

Equator

1°S

2°S

3°S

4°S

5°S

83°W 82°W 81°W 80°W 79°W

San Lorenzo
ESMERALDAS
Atacames
Punta Galera
Río Esmeraldas
Río Cayapas
Río Teaone
Pedernales
Punta Ballena
Santo Domingo de los Colorados
Cabo Pasado
Bahía de Caráquez
Embalse Daule-Peripa
Manta
Cabo San Lorenzo
Quevedo
Isla de la Plata
PORTOVIEJO
Jipijapa
Volcán Chimborazo 6310m ▲
Río Daule
Río Quevedo
Río Babahoyo
GUARANDA
BABAHOYO
Manglaralto
GUAYAQUIL
Milagro
Punta Santa Elena
La Libertad
Salinas
Alausí
Ingapirca
PACIFIC OCEAN
Playas
Isla Puná
AZOGUES
CUENCA
Gualaceo
Golfo de Guayaquil
Panamericana
Cordillera de
MACHALA
TUMBES
Huaquillas
Catamayo
LOJA
ZAMORA
Vilcabamba
Río Catamayo
Macará
Sullana
Río Sucio

N

0   40   80 km
0   25   50 miles

Elevation
5000 m
4000 m
3000 m
2000 m
1000 m
Sea Level

ECUADOR

COLOMBIA

Otavalo
Ecuador's most famous Indian-crafts market boasts bargains galore!

Flotel Orellana
This floating hotel staffed by naturalist guides gives visitors a comfortable look at Río Aguarico.

Jungle Lodges
Rustic but comfortable jungle hotels on Río Napo and other rivers offer guided wildlife-watching opportunities.

Parque Nacional Cotopaxi
The Andean scenery here is dominated by the cone-shaped Volcán Cotopaxi (5897m).

Tena
Not only a good base for jungle trips, Tena is fast becoming the nation's premier kayaking and river-rafting destination.

PERU

Galápagos Islands
The legendary fearlessness of the wildlife makes these islands a must for naturalists who can afford the trip.

PACIFIC OCEAN

Isla Pinta (Abingdon)
Isla Marchena (Bindloe)
Isla Genovesa (Tower)
Volcán Wolf 1646m
Isla San Salvador (Santiago or James)
Isla Fernandina (Narborough)
Isla Pinzón (Duncan)
Isla Baltra
Isla Santa Cruz (Indefatigable)
Isla Santa Fe (Barrington)
Isla San Cristóbal (Chatham)
Isla Isabela (Albemarle)
Puerto Villamil
Puerto Ayora
PUERTO BAQUERIZO MORENO
Isla Tortuga
Isla Santa María (Floreana or Charles)
Isla Española (Hood)

same scale as main map

Ecuador & the Galápagos Islands
5th edition – February 2001
First published – February 1986

Published by
Lonely Planet Publications Pty Ltd ABN 36 005 607 983
90 Maribyrnong St, Footscray, Victoria 3011, Australia

Lonely Planet Offices
Australia Locked Bag 1, Footscray, Victoria 3011
USA 150 Linden St, Oakland, CA 94607
UK 10a Spring Place, London NW5 3BH
France 1 rue du Dahomey, 75011 Paris

Photographs
All of the images in this guide are available for licensing from
Lonely Planet Images.
|W| www.lonelyplanetimages.com

Front cover photograph
Conolophus subcristatus on South Plaza Island, the Galápagos
Islands (Tom Ulrich/Tony Stone Images)

Title page photograph
Galápagos Wildlife Guide (Sally Dillon)

ISBN 0 86442 761 1

Printed by SNP SPrint (M) Sdn Bhd
Printed in Malaysia

Although the authors
and Lonely Planet try
to make the informa-
tion as accurate as
possible, we accept
no responsibility for
any loss, injury or
inconvenience sus-
tained by anyone
using this book.

Contents

THE WESTERN LOWLANDS 341

THE NORTH COAST 359

THE SOUTH COAST 399

THE GALÁPAGOS ISLANDS 436

4   Contents

GALÁPAGOS WILDLIFE GUIDE   449

LANGUAGE   501

GALÁPAGOS FAUNA CHECKLIST   508

ACKNOWLEDGMENTS   510

INDEX   518

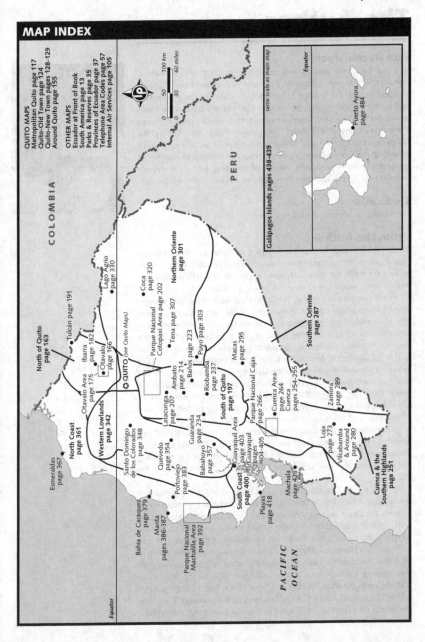

COLOMBIA

PERU

PACIFIC OCEAN

Galápagos Islands pages 438–439

same scale as main map

Puerto Ayora page 484

Equator

0 50 100 km
0 30 60 miles

North of Quito page 163
Tulcán page 191
Ibarra page 182
Otavalo page 166
Otavalo Area page 175
Lago Agrio page 330
Coca page 320
Northern Oriente page 301
QUITO (see Quito Maps)
Parque Nacional Cotopaxi Area page 202
Tena page 307
Latacunga page 207
Ambato page 214
Baños page 223
Puyo page 303
Riobamba page 237
Macas page 295
South of Quito page 197
Guaranda page 234
Parque Nacional Cajas
Southern Oriente page 287
Western Lowlands page 342
Santo Domingo de los Colorados page 348
Quevedo page 354
Cuenca Area page 264
Cuenca pages 254–255
Zamora page 289
North Coast page 361
Esmeraldas page 367
Portoviejo page 383
Babahoyo page 357
Guayaquil Area page 403
Guayaquil pages 404–405
Loja page 273
Vilcabamba & Around page 280
Cuenca & the Southern Highlands page 251
Bahía de Caráquez page 379
Manta pages 386–387
Parque Nacional Machalilla Area page 392
South Coast page 400
Machala page 428
Playas page 418

The Author

Rob Rachowiecki

Rob was born near London and became an avid traveler while still a teenager. He has visited countries as diverse as Greenland and Thailand. He spent most of the 1980s in Latin America – traveling, mountaineering and teaching English – and he now works in Peru and Ecuador part time as a leader for Wilderness Travel, an adventure-travel company. He is also the author of three other Lonely Planet guides – *Peru*, *Costa Rica* and the US guide *Southwest* – and he has contributed to LP's *South America on a shoestring* and *Central America on a shoestring*. In addition, he has worked on books by other publishers. When not traveling, he lives in Arizona with his wife, Cathy, and their three children – Julia, Alison and David.

Dedication

For JulsBaguls, because she is a real jewel!

From the Author

Three separate trips to Ecuador followed by innumerable emails and phone calls made this completely updated edition possible. Many people in Ecuador made my visits both more enjoyable and satisfyingly informative, and I would like to especially thank the following.

As always, the great staff at the Quito clubhouse of the South American Explorers set me straight on numerous issues. Jane Letham, a former South American Explorers manager, provided me with a seemingly inexhaustible stream of comments about anything to do with Quito. My friend Nancy Pelaez of Hostal Villa Nancy provided support, information and hospitality far and beyond the call of duty. Jean Brown of Safari Tours provided detailed information on the Galápagos and drove me around a dizzying number of lodges south of Quito and in the Mindo area, all the while dropping lovely tidbits of information from her encyclopedic knowledge of Ecuador. In Mindo, Tom Quesenberry helped with local information and followed up with several emails.

Steve Nomchong of Yacu Amu Rafting and Gynner Coronel of Ríos Ecuador are without any doubt the most knowledgeable river runners in Ecuador, and I greatly appreciate the time they both spent in educating me in the ways that river rafting and kayaking are growing rapidly in the country.

In the Oriente, Douglas McMeekin of Yachana Lodge invited me to a memorable Amazon-style Thanksgiving lunch and was a great source of information about the area. Arnaldo Rodriguez of Canodros provided me with scads of information about the Achuar people and the Kapawi Ecolodge. Kathy Kiefer kindly shared her knowledge of the Papallacta area with me. The Honorable Mayor of Zamora cordially mailed me a map of that town because the map was unavailable when I visited. I also enjoyed eye-opening conversations about the region with Randy Borman of Zabalo, geologist Mark Thurber, Lee Schel of the Sacha Lodge, director of the Eloy Alfaro Military College Coronel Luis B Hernández P, Santiago Herrera of Rain Forestur and Randy Smith of Coca – among many others.

In Otavalo, anthropologist Rodrigo Mora provided much information about the area. South of Quito, the delightful and charming Mignon Plaza told great stories at the Hacienda San Agustín de Callo. Owen Stevens accompanied me on hikes in Cotopaxi. Tom Walsh of Riobamba gave me a fantastic inside look at the lives of the *campesinos* in remote parts of Chimborazo Province. Eduardo Quito of Cuenca taught me much about that area, including Parque Nacional Cajas. In Vilcabamba, Orlando & Alicia Falco of the Rumi-Wilco Ecolodge were a great source of maps and information, especially about Parque Nacional Podocarpus, as was the friendly manager of the Hidden Garden. I also thank Avetur staff for a tour of many of the hotels in and around Vilcabamba.

On the coast, my thanks go to Jacob Santos, Daniel Proaño and Nicola Mears (all of Bahía de Caráquez), who gave me much insight into their local area. Director Eric Hortman personally guided me around the Bosque Protector Cerro Blanco. Peace Corps volunteer Rick Rhodes introduced me to the new Museo de Amantes de Sumpa, in the Santa Elena Peninsula. Helpful conversations with Clarisse Stong of Pro-Pueblo, Francisco Frias of Montañita, the folks at Tres Palmeras restaurant, ornithologist Nancy Hilgut and a host of others helped me pull this section together.

Have I forgotten somebody? I'm sure I have, and I apologize. To everyone who sent me reports and helped me gather information, a hearty *'Mil gracias!!'* Folks who wrote in are acknowledged at the end of the book.

Finally, I hug my dear and wonderful children – chess player and pianist Julia, soccer player Alison and Lego player David – for understanding that Dad has to work in Ecuador for weeks on end; and my wife, Cathy, for keeping things on an even keel while I'm on the road. Thank you all.

Readers can contact me with comments, criticisms or updates at robrachow@earthlink.net, but I regret that I am unable to plan your trip for you! I do acknowledge all emails.

This Book

FROM THE PUBLISHER

The 5th edition of *Ecuador & the Galápagos Islands* was edited by Wendy Taylor, under the enlightened guidance of senior editor Maria Donohoe and with the assistance of Amelia Borofsky, Susan Derby, Paul Sheridan, Vivek Wagle, and Suki Gear. The maps were created by workhorse Sean Brandt, under the direction of the ever vigilant senior cartographer Monica Lepe. Matt DeMartini helped Sean by drawing some maps, and Kat Smith and Chris Gillis helped edit a few maps. Ken DellaPenta indexed the book.

The colorwraps were designed by Jennifer Steffey. In addition to taming the wildlife guide and creating the cover, Wendy Yanagihara designed the book, with the help of Margaret Livingston and Joshua Schefers and under the leadership of design manager Susan Rimerman. Beca Lafore coordinated the illustrations, and Justin Marler and Alan Tarbell drew exciting new ones. Other illustrations were the work of Mark Butler, Hugh D'Andrade, John Fadeff, Hayden Foell, Beth Grundvig, Lara Sox Harrison, Pablo Sanaguano, Jim Swanson and Hannah Reineck.

Foreword

ABOUT LONELY PLANET GUIDEBOOKS

The story begins with a classic travel adventure: Tony and Maureen Wheeler's 1972 journey across Europe and Asia to Australia. Useful information about the overland trail did not exist at that time, so Tony and Maureen published the first Lonely Planet guidebook to meet a growing need.

From a kitchen table, then from a tiny office in Melbourne (Australia), Lonely Planet has become the largest independent travel publisher in the world, an international company with offices in Melbourne, Oakland (USA), London (UK) and Paris (France).

Today Lonely Planet guidebooks cover the globe. There is an ever-growing list of books, and there's information in a variety of forms and media. Some things haven't changed. The main aim is still to help make it possible for adventurous travelers to get out there – to explore and better understand the world.

At Lonely Planet we believe travelers can make a positive contribution to the countries they visit – if they respect their host communities and spend their money wisely. Since 1986 a percentage of the income from each book has been donated to aid projects and human-rights campaigns.

Updates Lonely Planet thoroughly updates each guidebook as often as possible. This usually means there are around two years between editions, although for more unusual or more stable destinations the gap can be longer. Check the imprint page (following the color map at the beginning of the book) for publication dates.

Between editions, up-to-date information is available in two free newsletters – the paper *Planet Talk* and email *Comet* (to subscribe, contact any Lonely Planet office) – and on our website at www.lonelyplanet.com. The *Upgrades* section of the website covers a number of important and volatile destinations and is regularly updated by Lonely Planet authors. *Scoop* covers news and current affairs relevant to travelers. And, lastly, the *Thorn Tree* bulletin board and *Postcards* section of the site carry unverified, but fascinating, reports from travelers.

Correspondence The process of creating new editions begins with the letters, postcards and emails received from travelers. This correspondence often includes suggestions, criticisms and comments about the current editions. Interesting excerpts are immediately passed on via newsletters and the website, and everything goes to our authors to be verified when they're researching on the road. We're keen to get more feedback from organizations or individuals who represent communities visited by travelers.

> Lonely Planet gathers information for everyone who's curious about the planet – and especially for those who explore it first-hand. Through guidebooks, phrasebooks, activity guides, maps, literature, newsletters, image library, TV series and website, we act as an information exchange for a worldwide community of travelers.

Research Authors aim to gather sufficient practical information to enable travelers to make informed choices and to make the mechanics of a journey run smoothly. They also research historical and cultural background to help enrich the travel experience and allow travelers to understand and respond appropriately to cultural and environmental issues.

Authors don't stay in every hotel because that would mean spending a couple of months in each medium-size city and, no, they don't eat at every restaurant because that would mean stretching belts beyond capacity. They do visit hotels and restaurants to check standards and prices, but feedback based on readers' direct experiences can be very helpful.

Many of our authors work undercover; others aren't so secretive. None of them accept freebies in exchange for positive write-ups. And none of our guidebooks contain any advertising.

Production Authors submit their raw manuscripts and maps to offices in Australia, the USA, the UK or France. Editors and cartographers – all experienced travelers themselves – then begin the process of assembling the pieces. When the book finally hits the shops, some things are already out of date, we start getting feedback from readers and the process begins again....

WARNING & REQUEST

Things change – prices go up, schedules change, good places go bad and bad places go bankrupt – nothing stays the same. So, if you find things better or worse, recently opened or long since closed, please tell us and help make the next edition even more accurate and useful. We genuinely value all the feedback we receive. Julie Young coordinates a well-traveled team that reads and acknowledges every letter, postcard and email and ensures that every morsel of information finds its way to the appropriate authors, editors and cartographers for verification.

Everyone who writes to us will find their name in the next edition of the appropriate guidebook. They will also receive the latest issue of *Planet Talk*, our quarterly printed newsletter, or *Comet*, our monthly email newsletter. Subscriptions to both newsletters are free. The very best contributions will be rewarded with a free guidebook.

Excerpts from your correspondence may appear in new editions of Lonely Planet guidebooks, the Lonely Planet website, *Planet Talk* or *Comet*, so please let us know if you *don't* want your letter published or your name acknowledged.

Send all correspondence to the Lonely Planet office closest to you:

Australia: Locked Bag 1, Footscray, Victoria 3011
USA: 150 Linden St, Oakland, CA 94607
UK: 10a Spring Place, London NW5 3BH
France: 1 rue du Dahomey, 75011 Paris

Or email us at: talk2us@lonelyplanet.com.au

For news, views and updates, see our website: www.lonelyplanet.com

HOW TO USE A LONELY PLANET GUIDEBOOK

The best way to use a Lonely Planet guidebook is any way you choose. At Lonely Planet, we believe the most memorable travel experiences are often those that are unexpected, and the finest discoveries are those you make yourself. Guidebooks are not intended to be used as if they provided a detailed set of infallible instructions!

Contents All Lonely Planet guidebooks follow the same format. The Facts about the Country chapters or sections give background information ranging from history to weather. Facts for the Visitor gives practical information on issues like visas and health. Getting There & Away gives a brief starting point for researching travel to and from the destination. Getting Around gives an overview of the transport options available when you arrive.

The peculiar demands of each destination determine how subsequent chapters are broken up, but some things remain constant. We always start with background, then proceed to sights, places to stay, places to eat, entertainment, getting there and away, and getting around information – in that order.

Heading Hierarchy Lonely Planet headings are used in a strict hierarchical structure that can be visualized as a set of Russian dolls. Each heading (and its following text) is encompassed by any preceding heading that is higher on the hierarchical ladder.

Entry Points We do not assume guidebooks will be read from beginning to end, but that people will dip into them. The traditional entry points are the list of contents and the index. In addition, however, some books have a complete list of maps and an index map illustrating map coverage.

There may also be a color map that shows highlights. These highlights are dealt with in greater detail later in the book, along with planning questions. Each chapter covering a geographical region usually begins with a locator map and another list of highlights. Once you find something of interest in a list of highlights, turn to the index.

Maps Maps play a crucial role in Lonely Planet guidebooks and include a huge amount of information. A legend is printed on the back page. We seek to have complete consistency between maps and text, and to have every important place in the text captured on a map. Map key numbers usually start in the top left corner.

Although inclusion in a guidebook usually implies a recommendation, we cannot list every good place. Exclusion does not necessarily imply criticism. In fact, there are a number of reasons why we might exclude a place – sometimes it is simply inappropriate to encourage an influx of travelers.

Introduction

Ecuador is the smallest of the Andean countries, and in many ways, it is the easiest and most pleasant to travel in.

From the beautifully preserved colonial capital of Quito, in the highlands at 2850m above sea level, you can travel by frequent buses to Andean Indian markets, remote jungle towns and warm Pacific beaches. In fact, starting from Quito, you can get to most points in this tropical country in less than a day by public transportation.

The highlands have many colorful Indian markets – some are world famous and deservedly so, others are rarely visited by foreigners but are no less interesting. Any journey in the highlands is dominated by magnificent volcanoes, including Cotopaxi, which at 5897m is one of the highest active volcanoes in the world. The area around

Volcán Tungurahua is closed because of constant volcanic eruptions, but there is a new tourism program for taking travelers to sites where they can safely watch the pyrotechnics.

Jungle travel in Ecuador is easier than in most countries because the distance between jungle sites and cities is far less – you can be in the jungle after only a day's bus travel from Quito. There are many exciting opportunities to hire local guides or to strike out on your own from jungle towns such as Tena, Macas or Coca, which is on Río Napo, Ecuador's main tributary of the Amazon.

The coast, too, has much to offer. You can go to a picturesque fishing village and watch the fishers expertly return their traditional balsa-wood rafts through the ocean breakers to the sandy shore, or help them

pull in their nets in return for some of the catch. You can also laze on the beach in the equatorial sun, swim in the warm seas and, in the evening, listen to salsa music in a local bar.

The Galápagos Islands, 1000km off the coast of Ecuador, are high on the list of destinations for travelers interested in wildlife. Here you can swim with penguins and sea lions or walk along beaches while pelicans flap by and huge iguanas scurry around your feet. The animals are so unafraid of humans that at times it's difficult to avoid stepping on them.

This book covers everything you'll need to know about traveling through this enchanting country, including the most interesting sights, the best-value hotels and restaurants and practical advice on all forms of public transportation, from air flights to dugout canoes. All this – set off by a host of background details on the country, its people and its culture – will make this guide an indispensable part of your trip.

Facts about Ecuador

HISTORY

Most histories of Ecuador begin with the Inca expansion from Peru in the 15th century. Archaeological evidence, however, indicates the presence of people in Ecuador for many thousands of years before then.

It is generally accepted that Asian nomads crossed the Bering Strait some 25,000 years ago and began reaching the South American continent by about 12,000 BC. It is believed that several thousand years later, trans-Pacific colonization by the island dwellers of Polynesia added to the population.

Although the Stone Age tools that were found in the Quito area have been dated to 9000 BC, the oldest signs of a more developed culture are burials found in Santa Elena that date to 6000 BC. The most ancient widespread artifacts date to 3200 BC (the Valdivia period) and consist mainly of ceramics (especially small figurines) found in the central coastal area of Ecuador. Examples of these can be seen in the major museums of Quito and Guayaquil.

Early Tribes

The history of pre-Inca Ecuador is lost in a tangle of time and legend. Generally speaking, the main populations lived on the coast and in the highlands. The earliest historical details we have date to the 11th century, when there were two dominant tribes: the expansionist Caras, who resided in the coastal areas, and the peaceful Quitus, who lived in the highlands.

The Caras, led by Shyri, conquered the Quitus, but it seems to have been accomplished by peaceful expansion rather than by bloody warfare. The Cara/Quitu peoples became collectively known as the Shyri nation and were the dominant force in the Ecuadorian highlands until about 1300, by which time the Puruhá, of the southern highlands, had also risen to power under the Duchicela lineage.

Conflict was avoided by the marriage of a Shyri princess, the only child of a king Caran of the Shyris, to Duchicela, the eldest son of the king of the Puruhás. This Duchicela/Shyri alliance proved successful, and the Duchicela line ruled more or less peacefully for about 150 years.

The Inca Empire

At the time of the Inca expansion, the descendants of Duchicela still dominated the north, and the south was in the hands of the Cañari people. The Cañari defended themselves bitterly against the Inca invaders, and it was some years before the Inca Tupac-Yupanqui was able to subdue them and turn his attention to the north. During this time, he fathered a son, Huayna Capac, by a Cañari princess.

The subjugation of the north took many years, and Huayna Capac grew up in Ecuador. He succeeded his father to the Inca throne and spent years traveling all over his empire, from Bolivia to Ecuador, constantly putting down uprisings from all sides. Wherever possible, he strengthened his position by marriage; his union with Paccha, the daughter of the defeated Cacha Duchicela, produced a son, Atahualpa.

The year 1526 is major in Ecuadorian history. The Inca Huayna Capac died and left his empire not to one son, as was traditional, but to two: Huáscar of Cuzco and Atahualpa of Quito; thus the Inca Empire was divided for the first time. In the same year, on September 21, the first Spaniards landed in northern Ecuador near what is now Esmeraldas. They were led south by the pilot Bartolomé Ruiz de Andrade on an exploratory mission for Francisco Pizarro, who remained farther north. Pizarro was not to arrive as conqueror for several years.

Meanwhile, rivalry between Huayna Capac's two sons worsened. The Inca of Cuzco, Huáscar, went to war against the Inca of Quito, Atahualpa. After several years of fighting, Atahualpa defeated Huáscar near Ambato and was thus the sole ruler of the weakened and still-divided Inca Empire when Pizarro arrived in 1532 with plans to conquer the Incas.

The Spanish Conquest

Pizarro's advance was rapid and dramatic. His horse-riding, armor-wearing, cannon-firing conquistadors were believed to be godlike, and although they were few in number, they spread terror among the Indians. In late 1532, a summit meeting was arranged between Pizarro and Atahualpa. Although Atahualpa was prepared to negotiate with the Spaniards, Pizarro had other ideas. When the Inca arrived at the pre-arranged meeting place (Cajamarca, in Peru) on November 16, the conquistadors captured him and massacred most of his poorly armed guards.

Atahualpa was held for ransom, and so incalculable quantities of gold, silver and other valuables poured in to Cajamarca. Instead of being released when the ransom was paid, the Inca was put through a sham trial and sentenced to death. Atahualpa was charged with incest (marrying one's sister was traditional in the Inca culture), polygamy, worship of false gods and crimes against the king, and he was executed on August 29, 1533. His death effectively brought the Inca Empire to an end.

Francisco Pizarro

Despite the death of Atahualpa, his general Rumiñahui continued to fight against the Spaniards for two more years. Pizarro's lieutenant Sebastián de Benalcázar finally battled his way to Quito in late 1534, only to find the city razed to the ground by Rumiñahui, who preferred to destroy the city rather than leave it in the hands of the conquistadors.

Quito was refounded on December 6, 1534, and Rumiñahui was captured, tortured and executed in January 1535. The most important Inca site in Ecuador that remains partially intact today is at Ingapirca, to the north of Cuenca.

The Colonial Era

From 1535 onward, the colonial era proceeded with the usual intrigues among the Spanish conquistadors, but with no major uprisings by the Ecuadorian Indians. Francisco Pizarro made his brother Gonzalo the governor of Quito in 1540. Hoping to conquer the Amazon and find more gold, Gonzalo sent his lieutenant Francisco de Orellana away from Quito to prospect in 1541. The lieutenant and his force ended up floating all the way to the Atlantic, becoming the first party known to descend the Amazon and thus cross the continent. This feat took almost a year and is still commemorated in Ecuador.

Lima, in Peru, was the seat of the political administration of Ecuador during the first centuries of colonial rule. Ecuador was originally known as a *gobernación* (province), but in 1563, it became the Audiencia de Quito, a more important political division. In 1739, the *audiencia* was transferred from the viceroyalty of Peru, of which it was a part, to the viceroyalty of Colombia (then known as Nueva Grenada).

Ecuador remained a peaceful colony during these centuries, and agriculture and the arts flourished. Various new agricultural products were introduced from Europe, including cattle and bananas, which still remain important in Ecuador today. There was prolific construction of churches and monasteries, which were decorated with unique carvings and paintings resulting from a blend of Spanish and Indian art influences. This so-called 'Quito School of Art,' still admired by visitors today, has left an indelible stamp on the colonial buildings of the time.

Life was comfortable for the ruling colonialists, but the Indians (and later, the *mestizos,* or people of mixed Spanish/Indian blood) were treated abysmally under their rule. A system of forced labor was not only tolerated but encouraged, and it is no surprise that by the 18th century there were several uprisings of the Indians against the Spanish ruling classes. Both poor and rich died in violent fighting.

One of the best-remembered heroes of the early revolutionary period is Eugenio Espejo, born in Quito in 1747 of an Indian father and a mulatto mother. Espejo was a brilliant man who obtained his doctorate by the age of 20 and became a major literary voice for independence. He wrote political satire, founded a liberal newspaper and spoke out strongly against colonialism. He was imprisoned several times and died in jail in 1795.

Independence

The first serious attempt to liberate Ecuador from Spanish rule was by a partisan group led by Juan Pío Montúfar on August 10, 1809. The group managed to take Quito and install a government, but this lasted only 24 days before royalist troops (loyal to the king of Spain) were able to regain control.

Independence was finally achieved by Simón Bolívar, the Venezuelan liberator who marched southward from Caracas, freed Colombia in 1819 and supported the people of Guayaquil when they claimed independence on October 9, 1820. It took almost two years before Ecuador was entirely liberated from Spanish rule. The decisive battle was fought on May 24, 1822, when one of Bolívar's best officers, Field Marshal Sucre, defeated the royalists at the Battle of Pichincha and took Quito.

Bolívar's idealistic dream was to form a united South America, and he began by amalgamating Venezuela, Colombia and Ecuador into the independent nation of Gran Colombia. This lasted only eight years, with Ecuador becoming fully independent in 1830. In the same year, a treaty was signed with Peru, drawing up a boundary between the two nations. This boundary was shown on all Ecuadorian maps prior to 1999. (In 1942, after a war between Ecuador and Peru, the border was redrawn but was not officially acknowledged by Ecuadorian authorities until a peace treaty with Peru in late 1998.)

Political Development

Independent Ecuador's internal history has been a typically Latin American turmoil of open political warfare between liberals and conservatives. Quito has emerged as the main center for the church-backed conservatives, while Guayaquil has traditionally been associated with liberal and socialist beliefs. This rivalry continues on a social level today; Quiteños have nicknamed Guayaquileños *monos* (monkeys), and the lively coastal people think of the highland inhabitants as very staid and dull.

The rivalry between the political groups has frequently escalated to extreme violence; conservative President García Moreno was shot and killed in 1875, and liberal President Eloy Alfaro was killed and burned by a mob in Quito in 1912. The military began to take control, and the 20th century saw almost as many military as civilian periods of rule.

Ecuador's most recent period of democracy began in 1979, when President Jaime Roldos Aguilera was elected. He died in an airplane crash in 1981, and his term of office was completed by his vice president, Osvaldo Hurtado Larrea.

In 1984, the conservative León Febres Cordero was elected to the presidency. In the elections of 1988, the people elected Rodrigo Borja, a social democrat, and the government then leaned to the left. The 1992 elections resulted in the victory of another conservative – Sixto Durán Ballén, a Quiteño and a member of the Partido Unidad Republicano (Republican Unity Party). President Durán's right-wing government attempted to tackle the deficit and reduce inflation, but it ran into strong opposition from trade unions, who opposed privatization proposals, and from indigenous and environmental groups, who opposed the destruction of their homelands and the flora and fauna of the Amazon rainforest by oil exploration. Widespread protests created major problems for the administration. The conservative government was also plagued with corruption scandals, one of which involved Vice President Alberto Dahik, who was accused of depositing state funds into private bank accounts. Dahik resigned in October 1995 and left the country.

Despite intense and bloody rivalry among liberals, conservatives and the military during the earlier part of this century, Ecuador has remained internally peaceful in recent years, although there are often demonstrations, marches and strikes that shut down public transportation for a day or two.

Recent Political Turmoil

The contenders in the July 1996 election were two firebrand politicians from Guayaquil, both known for their brash, macho attitudes. Neither had enjoyed much support in the staid political circles of Quito. The rightwing Jaime Nebot, a wealthy rancher and a former governor of Guayaquil Province, was known for parliamentary antics – including a drunken exchange in congress, during which he threatened to piss upon a political opponent. His opponent, Abdala Bucaram, a populist former mayor of Guayaquil, is remembered for alleging that a political opponent had inferior sperm.

The victor was the 44-year-old Bucaram, who received about 54% of the vote and was nicknamed 'El Loco' (the madman) for his fiery, curse-laden style of oration and his penchant for performing at rock concerts as part of his campaign. This was his third run for the Ecuadorian presidency. Bucaram's campaign promised cheap public housing, lower prices for staple food products and free medicine, which made him popular with the poor.

However, he promptly devalued the sucre and increased living costs while carousing with beautiful women in nightclubs. His government lasted barely half a year before massive strikes led by several important agencies, including trade unions and CONAIE (Confederation of Indigenous Nations of Ecuador), paralyzed the country. Congress responded by terminating Bucaram's presidency and declaring him mentally unfit to govern. Having lost the support of the entire nation, Bucaram fled to Panama in February 1997, where he still resides.

After Buacaram's ouster, the presidency was briefly assumed by his vice president,

Ecuador's recent presidents: Bucaram, Alarcón, Arteaga, Mahuad, Noboa

Rosalía Arteaga, who became Ecuador's first female president, albeit for less than two days. Normally, the vice president is the constitutionally accepted successor to a president who is unable to finish the term of office, but congress voted overwhelmingly to replace her with Fabián Alarcón, the head of congress. He led the government until elections were held again in 1998. In this hotly contested election, a former mayor of Quito, Jamil Mahuad of the Popular Democracy party, defeated businessman Alvaro Noboa by less than 5% of the popular vote.

Mahuad, educated at Harvard, was widely seen as an honest and hardworking man who could pull Ecuador out of what was beginning to be its worst economic crisis since the early 20th century. His reputation for honesty was badly tarnished by his involvement in a banking scandal, and by late 1999, his popularity ratings had dropped to single digits. The year 1999 also saw a drastic devaluation of Ecuador's currency, the sucre, which dropped from about 6000 to the US dollar in January 1999 to about 20,000 a year later. Mahuad announced that the only way to stop this downward economic spiral was to dollarize the economy, ie, abandon the national currency and use US dollars instead. (This has already happened in several other countries, including Panama.)

This announcement led to a national strike and a march of thousands of poor protesters on government buildings in Quito, led by the leaders of CONAIE and a contingent of mainly junior military officers. After the marchers took over the Congress building on January 20, 2000, Antonio Vargas, the leader of CONAIE, along with army Colonel Lucio Guiterrez and former supreme court president Carlos Solorzano, briefly formed a governing triumvirate. A few hours later, Mahuad resigned, and his vice president, Gustavo Noboa, backed by most of the military, assumed power, making him Ecuador's fifth president in fewer than three years.

Noboa is seen as one of the few honest politicians in a country where political corruption is the norm. He soon announced that plans for dollarization would continue.

Relations With Peru

After Peru's war with Ecuador in 1942, a treaty signed in Río de Janeiro gave Peru control of a huge chunk of the Amazon Basin. Before the war, Ecuador's borders reached as far south as Iquitos (in Peru). Since the treaty with Peru, which the Ecuadorians claimed was coerced while the world was occupied with WWII, there have been numerous border incidents, some escalating into deadly battles or minor wars. These usually flared up in January, the month during which the treaty was signed. The most recent serious incidents were in 1981 and 1995 and resulted in dozens of casualties among the armed forces on both sides.

In 1998, the presidents of Ecuador and Peru signed a new treaty that gave Ecuador a symbolic and face-saving 1 sq km of what had been formerly Peru. In return, Ecuador gave up its claim for land as far south as Iquitos, and relations between the two countries have improved dramatically.

GEOGRAPHY

Despite its small size, Ecuador is one of the world's most varied countries. At about 270,000 sq km, it is about the size of New Zealand or the US state of Nevada, and somewhat larger than the UK or the Australian state of Victoria. Ecuador straddles the equator on the Pacific coast of South America and is bordered by only two countries – Colombia to the north and Peru to the south and east.

The country is divided into three regions. The backbone of Ecuador is the Andean range, with Chimborazo (6310m) as its highest peak. The mountains run north to south, splitting the country into the western coastal lowlands and the eastern jungles of the upper Amazon Basin, known in Ecuador as the Oriente. Traversing only 200km as the condor flies, you can climb from the coast all the way to snowcaps over 6km above sea level and then descend down to the steaming rainforest on the eastern side.

The central highlands are composed of two somewhat parallel volcanic mountain ranges, each about 400km long, with a valley nestled between them. This valley was appropriately dubbed 'The Avenue of the Volcanoes' by the German explorer Alexander von Humboldt, who visited Ecuador in 1802. Within the valley is the capital, Quito (at 2850m above sea level, the second-highest national capital in the world after La Paz, Bolivia), as well as many other towns and tiny villages that are often of great interest to the traveler for their Indian markets and fiestas. This is the region with the highest population density in the country.

Ecuador's Coast

Unlike Peru to the south, Ecuador has warm water bathing its coast, and swimming is pleasant year-round. There are palm-fringed, sandy beaches that unfortunately suffered greatly during the 1982–83 and 1997–98 El Niño floods. Many of the beaches were destroyed – palm trees were uprooted, the sand was washed away and oceanfront buildings and streets were damaged – and the coastal highway was impassable for several months, but the region is now recovering.

According to Cárdenas and Greiner, who accomplished the noteworthy (if slightly mad) project of *Walking the Beaches of Ecuador* (see Guidebooks, in the Books section of the Facts for the Visitor chapter), the Ecuadorian coastline is approximately 2790km in length, of which less than one-third is beaches. The rest is a combination of mangroves, estuaries, river deltas and other geographic features.

There are two definite seasons on the coast. The rainy season lasts from December to May, and the dry season the rest of the year. The rainy season is hot and humid as well as wet, and the climate in the lowlands is uncomfortable. At this time, local people flock to the beaches. The beaches are especially popular from January to Easter, because the water temperature, influenced by El Niño currents, is warmer than the rest of the year – and that time period also coincides with regional school vacations.

The biggest problem during the wet months is that the rain can make roads slow or impassable. Generally, the main roads remain open year-round, but sometimes they're nothing but mud – rubber boots are the locally favored footwear. During the dry season, there are often fewer Ecuadorian tourists than during the wet, because they don't like the cooler water, but there are plenty of foreign visitors. The quietest months are September to November.

Having said all this, it should be noted that visiting Ecuador just for the beaches can be disappointing – they don't compare with the beaches of the Caribbean. The Andes, Amazon and Galápagos are all much more worthwhile destinations for foreign travelers. If you have some time on your hands and just love the coast, then by all means, go. But the beaches are not the highlight of a trip to Ecuador, although the interesting culture, archaeological sites, and good surfing of the coast make a visit worthwhile.

Traveling along the coast is varied and exciting. If you were to begin in the north and work your way southward, you could travel by motorized dugout, bus, *ranchera* (open-sided, flatbed truck), poled dugout and/or on foot.

Four provinces lie along the coast. Esmeraldas is the most northerly province in Ecuador. It is also the wettest and most humid of the coastal provinces – there are tropical rainforests in the northern coastal areas and in the inland regions of the province. The southern coastal areas of Esmeraldas and the coast of Manabí Province (south of Esmeraldas) become drier and less humid, and there are some remnants of tropical dry forest.

The south coast, which consists of the provinces of Guayas and El Oro, is generally much drier and more barren than the north coast. The weather pattern changes, and the rainy season, which in the north lasts from December to May, is only from January to April in Guayaquil. Further west

The western coastal lowlands used to be heavily forested, but most of the natural vegetation has now been destroyed for agriculture, and the mangroves have been hacked out in order to create shrimp ponds. The western provinces of Los Ríos, Manabí and El Oro are the most intensively farmed in Ecuador. The eastern lowlands of the Oriente still retain much of their virgin rainforest, but oil exploitation and colonization are beginning to seriously threaten this habitat. The population

Ecuador's Coast

and south, it becomes drier still, and just beyond the Peruvian border, the South American coastal desert begins.

The agriculturally important lowlands of Los Ríos Province (see the Western Lowlands chapter) continue into the provinces of Guayas and El Oro. Bananas are the most important crop, and irrigation in the dry south enables plantations to continue as far south as beyond Machala. Rice, coffee, cacao and African palm are other important crops in this region.

West of Guayaquil is the dry, infertile and scrubby Santa Elena Peninsula, which doesn't have enough rivers for irrigation. Archaeological investigation shows that the land used to be as wet and fertile as it is in the northern coastal areas now, but drought and deforestation over the last 5000 years have wrought severe changes. Decorations on pottery shards and other excavated remains indicate that farmers living in the area from 3000 to 1500 BC cultivated maize, manioc, avocado, beans, squash, chilies, papaya, pineapple, palms and the bottle gourd. Bananas, Ecuador's most important crop, were introduced after the Spanish conquest.

The heart of the south coast is Guayaquil, Ecuador's largest city. To the west are the popular beach resorts of Playas and Salinas, and to the south is another important port city, Machala, which is the common gateway to Peru.

The cuisine in the northern provinces is unique and tasty – but you have to seek it out to avoid the ubiquitous rice with fried fish or grilled chicken. Esmeraldas makes delicately flavored *encocado* (coconut-flavored) seafood dishes, but you have to ask around for them. *Cocadas* are sweet bars of grated coconut cooked in sugar and sold on bus journeys throughout the province. In Manabí, dishes are often deliciously flavored with peanut sauces; again, you need to ask around to find this. Further south, in the provinces of Guayas and El Oro, the food tends to be less unique, although Guayaquil has the gamut of cuisines. *Patacones* (fried plantain chips) are a favorite side dish all along the coast. Plantains are also served boiled whole, and taste rather stodgy. Raw seafood is often marinated to make ceviche, which is very good.

Lobster, served in some coastal seafood restaurants, is locally overfished and endangered. Restaurants are not legally allowed to serve lobster that was fished in Ecuador until the species recovers, but many places still have it on the menu. If you see it on a menu, it could have been imported, or it may have been caught during the few short weeks of lobster season, but it is probably being served illegally, so it's best avoided. Shrimp too is currently on a decline because of two diseases that have decimated the output of shrimp farms. Conservation agencies point out that shrimp farms contribute to the destruction of the coastal mangrove habitats, and shrimp are considered amongst the least ecofriendly of marine foods.

The ethnicity of the population also changes from north to south. Esmeraldas has the highest percentage of Afro-Ecuadorians of any province, and it also has several Indian tribes upriver from the coast. Further south, the population is more mestizo – the typical Spanish-Indian mix prevalent throughout Latin America.

The coast has a higher incidence of malaria than the Oriente, so come prepared, especially during the wet months, when mosquitoes abound.

of the Oriente has more than tripled since the late 1970s.

In addition to the mainland, Ecuador owns the Galápagos Islands, which straddle the equator and lie about 1000km west.

CLIMATE

Ecuador's climate follows a pattern different from what travelers from temperate regions are used to. Instead of the four seasons, there are wet and dry seasons, and weather patterns vary greatly among different geographical regions.

The Galápagos and the coastal areas of the mainland are influenced by ocean currents. The warm equatorial countercurrent from the central Pacific causes a hot and rainy season from January through April. It doesn't rain all the time, but you can expect torrential downpours that often disrupt communications, especially during El Niño years. Daytime high temperatures average about 30°C (86°F) but may be higher, and although the heat makes travel in the coastal regions unpleasant, this is when locals hang out at the beach to cool off. From May to December, both the cool Humboldt and Peru currents from the south keep temperatures a few degrees lower, and it rarely rains, although it is often gray, damp and overcast, especially in July and August.

The dry season in the highlands is from June through September, and a short dry season also occurs around Christmas. It doesn't rain daily in the wet season, however. April, the wettest month, averages one rainy day in two. Daytime temperatures in Quito average a high of 20°C to 22°C (68°F to 72°F) and a low of 7°C to 8°C (45°F to 48°F) year-round, although you should expect more extreme variations on occasion.

If you plan to travel in the Oriente, bring your rain gear, as it rains during most months, especially during the afternoon and evening. August and December through March are usually the driest months, and April through June are the wettest – with regional variations. It's usually almost as hot as the coast.

Despite all these statistics, remember the Ecuadorian adage that all four seasons can be experienced in one day. Without a doubt, the most predictable aspect of the weather in Ecuador is its unpredictability.

ECOLOGY & ENVIRONMENT

Deforestation is Ecuador's most severe environmental problem in all three of its major physiographic regions – the western

El Niño

At irregular intervals of every few years, the warm central Pacific currents of January through April are more pronounced and may flow for a longer period, causing the El Niño phenomenon. This is characterized by abnormally high oceanic temperatures during the coastal rainy season; much marine life (seaweed, fishes) is unable to survive. This in turn creates problems for other species – ranging from marine iguanas and seabirds to human beings – that rely on marine life for food.

A particularly extreme El Niño occurred from late 1982 through early 1983, causing severe problems for the wildlife of the Galápagos Islands and for the coastal fishing industry. This was repeated in 1997–98, with grave consequences for the Ecuadorian coast – landslides wiped out major roads and cut off villages for weeks on end.

The climatological phenomenon is named El Niño (The Baby Boy) because it usually gets under way at year's end, or about the time the Christ child was born. For all its disruptiveness, El Niño is still far from being fully understood by climatologists. However, the US National Oceanographic and Atmospheric Administration (NOAA) now has a Web site explaining what is known about the El Niño phenomenon and making some attempt at forecasting future events; you can find it at www.pmel.noaa.gov/toga-tao/el-nino/nino-home.html.

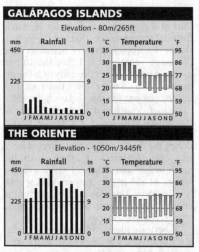

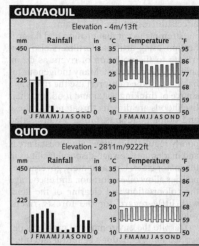

coastal lowlands, the central Andean highlands and the eastern Amazonian lowlands.

In the highlands, almost all of the natural forest cover has disappeared – only a few pockets remain protected, mainly in private nature reserves.

Along the coast, the once-plentiful mangrove forests have all but vanished too. These forests can harbor a great diversity of marine and shore life, but they have been cut down in order to make artificial ponds in which shrimp are reared for export. About 95% of the forests of the western slopes and lowlands have disappeared to become agricultural land, with banana plantations accounting for much of this. The ecological importance of this area has been identified only recently. The western lowlands are host to a greater number of different species than almost anywhere on the planet, and a large number of these species are endemic. Countless species have surely become extinct even before they have been identified. An effort is now being made to conserve what little there is left in both private and national reserves.

Although much of the rainforest in the Ecuadorian Amazon remains standing, it is seriously threatened by fragmentation. Since the discovery of oil, roads have been

built into the area, colonists have followed and the destruction of the forest has increased exponentially. The main drive behind the destruction is logging for short-term timber sales, followed by cattle ranching.

Clearly, these problems are linked tightly with Ecuador's economy. Oil, bananas and shrimp are the nation's top three exports. However, the serious environmental damage caused by the production of these and other products requires that their value be carefully examined. All of these products are subject to the whims of world markets, volatile economic pressures and other variables. Oil reserves are not expected to last more than a few decades. In 1999, whitespot disease wiped out most of Ecuador's shrimp exports, although solutions to this problem are being implemented. Banana crops could be wiped out by catastrophic diseases or climatic factors.

Apart from the direct loss of tropical forest and the plants and animals that depend on it (see the boxed text 'Why Conserve the Rainforest?' later in this chapter), deforestation also leads to severe environmental degradation in other ways. The loss of forest cover leads to erosion of the soil, which is then washed into rivers. The increased amount of silt in the rivers make them less able to support microorganisms, and this affects the rest of the food chain.

Attempts to combat erosion and desertification using artificial fertilizers also contribute to the pollution of rivers, as do oil spills in the rainforest. Many indigenous inhabitants of the rainforest use the rivers as a source of drinking water and food, and their livelihoods are directly threatened by these and other pollutants. Other water-related problems are caused by improper and poorly regulated mining in the coastal areas and inadequate sewage-disposal facilities in the major cities. Unfortunately, government policies allow oil exploration and encourage the colonization and clearing of the land, with little regard for the forests, rivers, wildlife or residents.

Despite the environmental problems described here, Ecuador's beautiful and often unique scenery and wildlife, combined with its fascinating people – particularly the Indians of the highlands – attract hundreds of thousands of international visitors annually. This makes tourism one of the country's top sources of revenue. The tourism industry is aware of the potential problems of uncontrolled tourism, and various successful efforts have been made to allow the country to benefit from the industry while controlling potential damage.

In the ever-popular Galápagos Islands, for example, attempts to build large resort hotels have been averted, and all visitors are accompanied by trained guides. On the mainland, various ecotourism operations provide lodge accommodations and guides in areas of protected forest. In 1990, the Asociación Ecuatoriana de Ecoturismo (ASEC) was founded, and it was officially recognized by the government in 1992. Today, several dozen travel agencies, outfitters and hotel and lodge operators are members of ASEC, and together they work to sustainably and responsibly develop the industry – both within their own operations and through public education and political pressure.

To read about how you can minimize your impact on Ecuador as a traveler, see Responsible Tourism in the Facts for the Visitor chapter.

FLORA & FAUNA

Part of the reason that Ecuador is among the most species-rich nations on the globe is that it is a tropical country. Scientists have for many years realized that the tropics harbor a much greater diversity of living organisms than do more temperate countries, but the reasons for this variation are still a matter of debate and research. The most commonly held belief is that the tropics acted as a refuge for plants and animals during the many ice ages that affected more temperate regions – in other words, the much longer and relatively stable climatic history of the tropics has enabled speciation to occur. This may well be part of the answer, but ecologists offer various other, more technical, theories.

A better-understood reason for Ecuador's biodiversity is simply that there are a great number of different habitats within the borders of the small country. Obviously, the cold, high Andes support species very different from the low tropical rainforests, and when all the intermediate areas are included and the coastal region added, the result is a wealth of habitats, ecosystems and wildlife. Ecologists have labeled Ecuador as one of the world's 'megadiversity hotspots.' This has attracted increasing numbers of nature lovers from all over the world.

Habitats

Ecologists use a system called Holdridge Life Zones to classify the type of vegetation found in a given area. Climatic data – such as temperature, rainfall and the variation of the two throughout the year – are analyzed and combined with information on latitudinal regions and altitudinal belts to give 116 life zones on earth. Some two dozen tropical life zones are found in Ecuador. These are often named according to forest type and altitude, and so there are dry, moist, wet and rainforests in tropical, premontane, lower montane, montane and subalpine areas. Within each life zone, several types of habitat may occur. Thus, Ecuador has many habitats, each with particular associations of plants and animals. Some of the most important or interesting are described here.

Mangrove Swamp The coastal lowlands have a variety of habitats; the mangrove swamp is one of the most extraordinary. Mangroves are trees that have evolved the remarkable ability to grow in salt water. The red mangrove is the most common in Ecuador, and like other mangroves, it has a broadly spreading system of intertwining stilt roots to support the tree in the unstable sandy or silty soils of the shoreline.

Mangroves form forests and are good colonizing species – their stilt roots trap sediments and build up a rich organic soil, which in turn supports other plants. In between the roots, a protected habitat is provided for many types of fish, as well as mollusks, crustaceans and other invertebrates. The branches provide nesting areas for seabirds, such as pelicans and frigatebirds. Mangroves are found primarily in the far northern and southern coastal regions of the country – the shrimp industry has extensively destroyed the mangroves on most of Ecuador's coastline, endangering the breeding grounds of many species. (See also the boxed text 'Maltreated Mangroves' in the North Coast chapter.)

Tropical Dry Forest This fast-disappearing habitat is found in hot coastal areas with well-defined wet and dry seasons. Tropical dry-forest trees lose their leaves during the dry season and tend to grow in a less concentrated pattern than those in the rainforest, creating a more open habitat. It is estimated that only about 1% of tropical dry forest remains undisturbed. The best and only extensive example in Ecuador is found on the central Pacific coast, in Parque Nacional Machalilla; see that section in the North Coast chapter for a more in-depth description of this type of forest.

Tropical Cloud Forest These types of tropical forests are found in remote valleys at higher elevations, and comparatively little is known about them. They are called cloud forests because they trap (and help create) clouds, which drench the forest in a fine mist, allowing some particularly delicate forms of plant life to survive. Cloud-forest trees are adapted to steep rocky soils and a harsh climate. They have a characteristically low, gnarled growth of dense, small-leaved canopies and moss-covered branches supporting a host of plants, such as orchids, ferns and bromeliads. These aerial plants, which gather their moisture and some nutrients without ground roots, are collectively termed epiphytes.

The dense vegetation at all levels of this forest gives it a mysterious and delicate fairy-tale appearance. It is the home of such rare species as the woolly tapir, the Andean spectacled bear and the puma. This habitat is particularly important as a source of freshwater and as an impediment to erosion.

Páramo These high-altitude grasslands and shrublands lie above the cloud forests. The páramo is the natural 'sponge' of the Andes – it catches and gradually releases much of the water that is eventually used by city dwellers in the highlands. The páramo covers over 10% of Ecuador's land area and is characterized by a harsh climate, high levels of ultraviolet light and wet, peaty soils. It is an extremely specialized highland habitat unique to the neotropics (tropical America) and is found only in the area starting from the highlands of Costa Rica at 10°N to northern Peru at 10°S. Similarly elevated grasslands in other parts of the world differ in their climates and evolutionary history and have different assemblages of plants and animals.

The páramo has a limited flora that is dominated by cushion plants, hard grasses and small herbaceous plants. These plants have adapted well to the harsh environment, and consequently, the vegetation looks strange and interesting. Major adaptations include small, thick leaves, which are less susceptible to frost; curved leaves with heavy, waxy skins to reflect extreme solar radiation during cloudless days; an insulating fine, hairy down on the plant's surface; a rosette leaf formation, which prevents the leaves from shading one another during photosynthesis and which protects the delicate center of the plant; and compactness, so the plant grows close to the ground, where the temperature is more constant and the wind less strong. Thus, many páramo plants sometimes resemble a hard, waxy, green carpet.

Not all páramo plants are so compact, however. The giant *Espeletia,* which are members of the daisy family, are a weird sight as their loosely arranged stands float into view in a typical páramo mist. They are as high as a person, hence the local nickname *frailejones,* meaning 'gray friars.' They are an unmistakable feature of the northern Ecuadorian páramo, particularly in the El Ángel region near Tulcán. Farther south, the páramo becomes drier, and the bromeliads called *puyas* are found – plants with a rosette of spiky leaves growing out of a short trunk.

Another attractive plant of the central and southern Ecuadorian páramo is the *chuquiragua,* which resembles a thistle topped with orange flower heads and has stems that are densely covered with tough, spiky leaves. This plant has medicinal properties – it is used locally to soothe coughs and to treat liver and kidney infections.

The páramo is also characterized by dense thickets of small trees. These are often *polylepis* species, or *quinua* in Quichua, members of the rose family. With the Himalayan pines, they share the world altitudinal record for trees. They were once considerably more extensive, but fire and grazing have pushed them back into small pockets. Instead, grasses are more common. A spiky, resistant tussock grass locally called *ichu* is commonly encountered. It grows in large clumps and makes walking uncomfortable.

Over half a million Ecuadorians live on the páramo, so it is of considerable importance to the inter-Andean economy. It has been used for growing a large variety of potatoes and other tubers for centuries, while the great increase in cattle grazing is a more recent phenomenon. In order to manage the land for cattle, burning is carried out to encourage the growth of succulent young shoots. This does not favor older growth, and combined with erosion caused by overgrazing, it poses considerable threats to this fragile habitat.

Rainforest Of all the tropical habitats found in Ecuador, the rainforest seems to attract the most attention from visitors.

A walk through any tropical forest shows that it is very different from the temperate forests that many Europeans or North Americans may be used to. Forests in temperate regions tend to have little variety (it's pines, pines and more pines, or interminable acres of oaks, beech and birch). Tropical forests, on the other hand, have great variety. If you stand in one spot and look around, you'll see scores of different species of trees, and you'll often have to walk only several hundred meters to find another example of any particular species.

Visitors to the rainforest are often bewildered by the huge variety of plants and animals. Useful field guides are few, with the exception of those for mammals and birds. For this reason, it is worth investing in a guided natural-history tour if you are particularly interested in learning about the fantastic flora and fauna – although no guide will be able to answer all your questions!

One thing that often astounds visitors is the sheer immensity of some trees. A good example is the ceiba tree (also called the kapok), which has huge, flattened supports around its base that can easily reach five or more meters across. The smooth gray trunk often grows straight up for 50m before the branches begin. The branches spread out into a huge crown with a slightly flattened appearance; the shape is distinctive, and the tree is often the last to be logged in a ranching area. When you see a huge, buttressed, flat-looking tree in a pasture in the Amazonian lowlands, very often it is a ceiba. This is also one of the few rainforest trees to shed its leaves, which it does before flowering, in order to enable the wind to better distribute the pollen. Most other trees in the rainforest are pollinated by animals and don't need to shed their leaves to allow the wind to do the job.

Some rainforest trees have strange roots that look like props or stilts. These trees are most frequently found in rainforest that is periodically flooded – the stilt roots are thought to play a role in keeping the tree upright during the inundation. Various types of trees use this technique – in the Oriente, palms are often supported by this kind of root system; on the coast, the mangroves have stilt roots.

In areas that have been cleared – often naturally, as by a flash flood, which may remove the trees on the riverbanks, or simply by an ancient forest giant falling during a storm – various fast-growing pioneer species appear. These may grow several meters a year in areas where abundant sunlight is suddenly available. Some of the most common and easily recognized of these are in the genus *Cecropia,* which has a number of species. Their gray trunks are circled by ridges at intervals of a few centimeters but are otherwise fairly smooth, and their branches tend to form a canopy at the top of the trunk rather than all along it. The leaves are very large and palmate (like a human hand with spread fingers), and their undersides are a much lighter green than their tops. This is particularly noticeable when strong winds make the leaves display alternately light and dark green shades in a chaotic manner.

The Galápagos Between 700 and 800 species of vascular plants have been recorded in the Galápagos, of which over 250 species are endemic. In addition, about 500 nonvascular plants (mosses, lichens and liverworts) have been described. There are six different vegetation zones, beginning with the shore and ending with the highlands. These zones are the littoral, arid, transition, Scalesia, Miconia and fern-sedge. Each zone supports different and distinctive plant species.

The **littoral zone** contains species such as mangroves, saltbush and sesuvium. These plants are characterized by their ability to tolerate relatively high quantities of salt in their environment.

Immediately beyond the littoral zone is the **arid zone**, where many of the islands' cactus species are found, including forests of the giant prickly pear cactus. Trees such as the ghostly looking palo santo, the palo verde, and the spiny acacias are found here,

as is the yellow cordia shrub (which has yellow flowers).

The **transition zone** has decreasing numbers of the arid zone trees and increasing numbers of lichens, perennial herbs and smaller shrubs. The vegetation is both varied and thick and no particular plants are dominant.

In the higher islands, the transition zone gives way to a cloud-forest type of vegetation, and the dominant tree is the endemic **Scalesia**. The trees are covered with smaller plants, such as mosses, bromeliads, liverworts, ferns and orchids.

Next is the treeless high-altitude Miconia zone, which is characterized by dense endemic shrub, liverworts and ferns. This zone is found only on the southern slopes of Santa Cruz and San Cristóbal.

Finally, the **fern-sedge zone** is the highest and contains mainly ferns and grasses, including the Galápagos tree fern, which grows up to 3m high.

It is beyond the scope of this book to delve more deeply into the many hundreds of plant species; the books by Schofield (1984), Jackson (1985) and Wiggins & Porter (1971) provide good additional reading (see the Books section in the Facts for the Visitor chapter).

Biodiversity

The species listed in this section are just a few of the most common sights in the forest. The incredible variety of plants correlates with the high biodiversity of the animals that live within the forests. Terry Erwin of the Smithsonian Institution has spent much time in Amazonian rainforests and reports that 3000 species of beetles were found in five different areas of rainforest – and each area was only 12 meters square! Erwin estimates that each species of tree in the rainforest supports over 400 unique species of animals. Given the thousands of known tree species, this means that there are millions of species of animals living in the rainforest, many of them insects and most of them unknown to science. These complex interrelationships and high biodiversity are among the reasons that many people are calling for a halt to the destruction of tropical forests. Despite this, Ecuador has one of the highest rates of deforestation in South America. For more information on rainforest conservation, see this chapter's boxed text 'Why Conserve the Rainforest?'

Flora

There are about 25,000 species of vascular plants in Ecuador, and new species are being discovered every year. This number is exceptionally high when compared to the 17,000 species found in the entire North American continent. An introduction to some of the most common plants of Ecuador is given in Habitats, earlier in this section.

Fauna

Birds Bird watchers from all over the world come to Ecuador because of the great number of species recorded here – over 1500, or approximately twice the number found in any one of the continents of North America, Europe or Australia. The South American continent has almost 3000 species of birds, although it is impossible to give a precise number, as new species are often reported.

Most birds added to the Ecuadorian list are already known from other South American countries. Occasionally, however, a species new to science is discovered – a very rare event in the world of birds. It is likely that bird species exist in Ecuador that have never been described by scientists.

Many visitors are less interested in observing a newly described species and are more interested in seeing the birds typical of Ecuador. One of these is the Andean condor, often called the largest flying bird in the world. With a wingspan of 3m and a weight of 10kg, it is certainly magnificent. In 1880, the British mountaineer Edward Whymper noted that he commonly saw a dozen on the wing at the same time. Today there are only a few hundred pairs left in the highlands, so you shouldn't expect to see them frequently. Condors are best recognized by the flat gliding flight with fingered wing tips (formed by spread primary feathers), the silvery patches on the upper wing surface (best seen when the bird

wheels in the sun), a white neck ruff and an featherless pinkish head. Otherwise, the bird is black.

Other birds of the highlands include the carunculated caracara, a large member of the falcon family. It has bright orange-red facial skin, yellowish bill and legs, and white thighs and underparts; it is otherwise black. This bird is often seen in the páramos of Parque Nacional Cotopaxi (see the South of Quito chapter). Also frequently sighted here is the Andean lapwing – unmistakable with its harsh and noisy call; its reddish eyes, legs and bill; and its brown/white/black-striped wing pattern, which is particularly noticeable in flight.

The well-known house sparrow of Europe, Asia, Australia and North America is a rarely seen recent arrival in South America. Instead, the similarly sized rufous-collared sparrow, readily identified by the chestnut collar on the back of the neck, takes the place of the house sparrow in Ecuador and most of the continent.

For many visitors, the diminutive hummingbirds are the most delightful birds to observe. About 120 species have been recorded from Ecuador, and their exquisite beauty is matched by extravagant names, such as green-tailed goldenthroat, spangled coquette, fawn-breasted brilliant and amethyst-throated sunangel.

Hummingbirds beat their wings in a figure-eight pattern up to 80 times per second, thus producing the hum for which they are named. This exceptionally rapid wingbeat enables them to hover in place while feeding on nectar, or even to fly backward. These tiny birds must feed frequently in order to gain the energy needed to keep them flying. Species such as the Andean hillstar, living in the páramo, have evolved an amazing strategy to survive a cold night; they go into a state of torpor – like a nightly hibernation – by lowering their body temperature by about 25°C, thus lowering their metabolism drastically.

For visitors interested in birds, a trip to the Galápagos Islands is very rewarding. This is partly because about half of the 58 resident species are endemic to the islands. Also, most of the Galápagos birds have either lost, or not evolved, a fear of humans. Therefore, travelers can walk among colonies of blue-footed boobies or magnificent frigatebirds without causing them to fly off. See the Galápagos Wildlife Guide in the Galápagos Islands chapter for more information.

Serious birders may want to spend time on the Ecuadorian coast. A local ornithologist claims that there are twice as many endemic species within 50km of Guayaquil than there are in the Galápagos Islands, but many of these are small and not visually exciting.

Some other exciting birds on the mainland include the brightly colored blue-and-yellow macaws and 44 other parrot species; 19 different toucans, with their incredibly large and hollow bills; the huge and very rare harpy eagle, which is capable of snatching monkeys and sloths off branches as it flies past; and a large array of other tropical birds, such as flycatchers (167 species), tanagers (133 species), antbirds (110 species) and cotingas (43 species).

Mammals Mammals, too, are well represented – there are some 300 species recorded in the country. These vary from monkeys in the Amazonian lowlands to the rare Andean spectacled bear in the highlands. The most diverse mammals are the bats, of which there are well over 100 species in Ecuador alone.

Visitors to protected areas of the Amazonian lowlands may see one or more of the several species of monkeys found in Ecuador, including the howler, spider, woolly, titi, capuchin and squirrel monkeys, as well as tamarins and marmosets. The monkeys of the New World (the Platyrrhini) differ markedly from the monkeys of the Old World, including ourselves (the Catarrhini). New World monkeys have been studied comparatively little, and their names are still under constant study and revision.

The male howler monkeys are heard as often as they are seen; their eerie vocalizations carry long distances and have been likened to a baby crying or to the wind moaning through the trees. Many visitors are

Squirrel monkey

unable to believe they are hearing a monkey when they first listen to the mournful sound.

Other tropical specialties include two species of sloths. The diurnal three-toed sloth is often sighted, whereas the two-toed sloth is nocturnal and therefore rarely seen. Sloths are often found hanging motionless from tree limbs, or progressing at a painfully slow speed along a branch toward a particularly succulent bunch of leaves, which are their primary food source. Leaf digestion takes several days, and sloths defecate about once a week. Sloths are most fastidious with their toilet habits, always climbing down from their tree to deposit their weekly bowel movement on the ground. Biologists do not know why sloths do this; one suggested hypothesis is that by consistently defecating at the base of a particular tree, the sloths provide a natural fertilizer that increases the quality of the leaves of that tree, thus improving the sloth's diet.

Mammals commonly seen in the highlands include deer, rabbits and squirrels. Foxes are also occasionally sighted. There are far fewer species of mammals in the highlands than in the lowlands. The mammals most commonly associated with the Andes are the Camelids – the llamas, alpacas, guanacos and vicuñas. Of these, only the llama is common in Ecuador, and there are far fewer there than in Peru or Bolivia. They can be seen occasionally on the outskirts of Quito, and there is a huge flock near the entrance of Parque Nacional Cotopaxi. Many are seen in and around remote Andean villages. Llamas are exclusively domesticated and are used primarily as pack animals, although their skin and meat is occasionally used in remote areas. Their wild relative, the lovely vicuña, has been reintroduced to the Chimborazo area and can quite easily be spotted there, although not elsewhere.

Other possible mammal sightings include anteaters, armadillos, agoutis (large rodents), capybaras (even larger rodents,

Leaf-cutter ant

some weighing up to 65kg), peccaries (wild pigs) and otters. River dolphins are occasionally sighted on Amazonian tributaries. Other exotic mammals, such as ocelots, jaguars, tapirs, pumas and spectacled bears, are very rarely seen.

Insects Many thousands of species of insects have been described from Ecuador; undoubtedly, many thousands more remain undiscovered.

Butterflies, of which there are some 4500 species, are among the first insects that the visitor to the tropics notices. Perhaps the most dazzling butterflies are the morphos. With their 15cm wingspan and electric blue upper wings, they lazily flap and glide along tropical rivers in a shimmering display. When they land, however, their wings close, and only the brown underwings are visible. In an instant their colors change from outrageously flaunting to modestly camouflaging.

Camouflage plays an important part in many insects' lives. Some resting butterflies look exactly like green or brown leaves; others look like the scaly bark of the tree on which they are resting. Caterpillars are often masters of disguise. Some species mimic twigs; another is capable of constricting certain muscles to make itself look like the head of a viper, and yet another species looks so much like bird droppings that it rarely gets attacked by predators.

Any walk through a tropical forest will almost invariably allow the observer to study many different types of ants. Particularly interesting are the leaf-cutter ants, which can be seen marching in columns along the forest floor, carrying pieces of leaves like little parasols above their heads. The leaf segments are taken into the ants' underground colony, and there, the leaves are allowed to rot into a mulch. The ants tend their mulch gardens carefully and allow a certain species of fungus to grow there. The fruiting bodies of the fungus are then used to feed the colony, which can exceed a million ants. The fungus has lost its ability to reproduce itself and relies on the ants to propagate it, which they do by taking some fungus with them when they start a new nest.

Other insect species are so tiny as to be barely visible, yet their lifestyles are no less esoteric. The hummingbird flower mites are barely half a millimeter in length and live in flowers visited by hummingbirds. When the flowers are visited by the hummers, the mites scuttle up into the birds' nostrils and use this novel form of air transportation to disperse themselves to other plants. Smaller still are mites that live on the proboscis of the morpho butterflies.

From the largest to the smallest insects, there is a world of wonder to be discovered in the tropical forests.

Poison-arrow frog

Amphibians & Reptiles These creatures form a fascinating part of the Ecuadorian fauna. The approximately 360 species of amphibians include tree frogs that spend their entire life cycle in trees. Some of them have solved the problem of where to lay their eggs by doing so into the water trapped in cuplike plants called bromeliads, which live high up in the forest canopy.

Perhaps more bizarre still are the marsupial frogs. The females carry their eggs in pouches under their skins – sometimes 200 or more at a time. The eggs are pushed into the pouches by the male immediately after fertilization. Hatching occurs in the pouches, and the tadpoles eventually emerge from under their mother's skin.

Dendrobatids, better known by their colloquial name of poison-arrow frogs, are among the most brightly colored of frogs. Some are bright red with black dots, others are red with blue legs and still others are bright green with black markings. Some species have skin glands exuding toxins that can cause paralysis and death in many animals, including humans. It is well known that dendrobatids have long been used by Latin American forest Indians to provide a poison with which to dip the tips of their hunting arrows. It should be mentioned that the toxins are most effective when introduced into the bloodstream (as with arrows), but they have little effect when a frog is casually touched.

There are nearly 350 species of reptiles recorded in Ecuador, which is about 100 more than are found in the whole of North America. Snakes – much talked about but seldom seen – make up roughly half of Ecuador's reptiles. Snakes usually slither away into the undergrowth when they sense that people are coming, so only a few fortunate visitors are able to catch a glimpse of one. Perhaps Ecuador's most feared snake is the fer-de-lance, which is very poisonous and sometimes fatal to humans. It often lives in overgrown, brushy fields, so the agricultural workers clearing these fields are the most frequent victims. Tourists are rarely bitten.

Fish Recent inventories of Amazonian fish have shown surprisingly high biodiversity. There are about 2500 species in the whole Amazon Basin, and roughly 1000 species in Ecuador. Some of them are fearsome. The electric eel can produce shocks of 600 volts; a school of piranha can devour a large animal in minutes; stingrays can deliver a crippling sting; and the tiny candirú catfish can swim up the human urethra and become lodged there by erecting its sharp spines. Despite these horror stories, most Amazonian rivers are safe to swim in. Follow the example of the locals: Shuffle your feet as you enter the water to scare off the bottom-dwelling stingrays; wear a bathing suit to avoid having a candirú swim up your urethra; and don't swim with open, bleeding cuts or in areas where fish are being cleaned, because piranhas are attracted to blood and guts.

Conservation

Various international agencies – such as Conservation International, The Nature Conservancy, Natural Resources Defense Council, the World Wildlife Fund and World Wide Fund for Nature – have provided much-needed expertise and economic support. They've developed programs such as 'debt for nature' swaps, whereby parts of Ecuador's national debt was forgiven in return for the government giving local groups funds for preserving crucial habitats. These swaps are not as popular or as successful as they used to be, and the focus of conservation work nowadays is financial support to train and equip local park rangers, educate the population, fund research and develop low-impact and sustainable practices, such as responsible tourism.

By far the biggest environmental NGO (nongovernmental organization) within Ecuador is the Fundación Natura. In the absence of a specific government department for the environment, the Fundación

Why Conserve the Rainforest?

The loss of tropical forests is a problem that has become acute in recent years. Deforestation is happening at such a rapid rate that most of the world's tropical forests will probably disappear within decades. Two important questions arise: Why are habitats such as the tropical rainforests so important, and what can be done to prevent their loss?

Much of Ecuador's remaining natural vegetation is tropical forest, and there are many reasons why this particular ecosystem is important. Roughly half of the 1.6 million known species on earth live in tropical rainforests such as those found in Parque Nacional Yasuní (see the Northern Oriente chapter). Scientists predict that millions more species remain to be discovered, principally in the world's remaining rainforests, which have the greatest biodiversity of all habitats. This incredible array of plants, animals and insects cannot exist unless the rainforest is protected; deforestation will result in countless extinctions.

Many medicines – ranging from anesthetics to antibiotics, from contraceptives to cures for illnesses such as heart disease and malaria – have been extracted from rainforest flora. Countless medicinal uses of plants are known only to the indigenous inhabitants of the forest. Much of this knowledge is being lost as the various indigenous cultures are assimilated into the Western way of life, or as tribal groups are destroyed by disease or genocide. Other pharmaceutical treasures remain locked up in tropical forests, unknown to anyone. They may never be discovered if these forests are destroyed.

Many tropical crops are monocultures that suffer from a lack of genetic diversity. In other words, all the plants are almost identical because agriculturalists have bred strains that are high yielding, easy to harvest, and that taste good. If these monocultures are attacked by a new disease or pest epidemic, they could be wiped out because resistant strains have been bred out of the population.

Plants such as bananas (Ecuador's most economically important agricultural product) are found in the wild in tropical forests. In the event of an epidemic, scientists could seek out disease-resistant wild strains to breed into the commercially raised crops. Deforestation leads not only to species extinction, but also to loss of the genetic diversity that may help species adapt to a changing world.

While biodiversity for esthetic, medicinal and genetic reasons may be important to us, the survival of tropical rainforests is even more important to the indigenous peoples who live within them. In Ecuador, there are Huaorani, Shuar, Cofan, Secoya, Cayapa and other Indian groups still living in a more or less traditional manner. These tribes rely on the rainforest to maintain a basic cultural way of life that has persisted in various forms for centuries. Accelerated deforestation has led to these important cultural practices having to negotiate with modernity.

has been most involved in improving the system of protected areas in the country and has developed its own cloud-forest reserve – Pasochoa, near Quito. The Fundación also has a large environmental-education program and arranges campaigns on specific conservation issues. Because it is Ecuador's biggest and best-known NGO, it tends to receive a large share of international funding and has been criticized by smaller, grassroots NGOs as having a top-heavy bureaucracy.

Local conservation groups have blossomed since the late 1980s. Groups on the coast are particularly concerned with the protection of the mangrove forests and have been forging cooperative links with shell and crab collectors, who are being affected by mangrove destruction. Some groups have been quite successful in providing legal protection for these forests. Other groups have concentrated on improving environmental data collection and training members in the disciplines needed to create

Why Conserve the Rainforest?

Rainforests are important on a global scale because they moderate climatic patterns worldwide. The destruction of rainforests is a major contributing factor to global warming, which, if left unchecked, could lead to disastrous changes to our world. These changes include the melting of ice caps, which would cause a rise in ocean levels and the flooding of major coastal cities – many of which are only a scant few meters above sea level. Global warming would also make many of the world's breadbasket regions unsuitable for crop production.

All of these are good reasons for the preservation of the rainforests and other habitats, but the reality of the economic importance of forest exploitation by developing nations that own the tropical forests must also be considered. It is undeniably true that rainforests provide resources in the way of lumber, pastureland and possible mineral wealth, but this is a shortsighted view.

The long-term importance of the rainforest as a resource of biodiversity, genetic variation and pharmaceutical wealth is recognized both by countries that contain forest and by the other nations of the world that would be affected by the destruction of these rainforests. Efforts are now under way to show that the economic value of the standing rainforest is greater than the wealth realized by deforestation.

One way of making a tropical forest an economically productive resource without cutting it down is by protecting it in national parks and reserves and making it accessible to tourists and travelers. Ecotourism is becoming increasingly important for the economy of Ecuador and other nations with similar natural resources.

People are more likely to visit Ecuador to see monkeys in the forest than cows in a pasture. Visitors spend money on hotels, transportation, tours, food and souvenirs. In addition, many people who spend time in the tropics become more understanding of the natural beauty within the forests and of the importance of preserving them. As a result, visitors return home and become goodwill ambassadors for tropical forests.

Other innovative projects for the sustainable development of tropical forests are being organized. The tagua nut is being harvested sustainably. This South American rainforest product is as hard as ivory and is being used to carve ornaments – and even to make buttons, which are bought by North American clothing manufacturers. Brazil nuts are also harvested. Debt-for-nature swaps have been initiated by conservation organizations. Iguana farms, orchid plantations, the export of tropical-butterfly pupae, wickerwork from aerial roots and the seed harvesting of ornamental plants are some of the other projects being explored. Whatever the methods used to preserve the rainforests, it is essential that they are protected.

a strong information base for national conservation research.

The Amazon region has been an important focus for small NGOs in recent years. They focus not only on the environment, but also on the protection of the rights of indigenous inhabitants. In the mid- and late 1990s, organizations protecting the fast-diminishing and unique forests on the western slopes of the Ecuadorian Andes have become important.

Several small groups have been established to protect specific natural areas. These groups go on to involve communities around the reserves through environmental education, agroforestry and community-development projects. Such community involvement at the grassroots level is essential for viable conservation in Ecuador.

The role of indigenous organizations should also be recognized as an effective voice in environmental protection. The struggle they have been engaged in to secure land rights, particularly in the Amazon regions, has gone a long way toward securing the future of the tropical forests in that area.

In the Galápagos Islands, the Charles Darwin Foundation is a long-established and tireless protector of the archipelago. Conservation, scientific research, and education of both locals and international visitors are among its main goals.

Most of these organizations rely on support from the public. Even large entities such as the World Wildlife Fund receive the bulk of their income not from government agencies or corporate contributions, but from individual members. The vital work of these and other agencies requires every assistance possible. Ecuadorian conservation groups are particularly in need of assistance. If you visit Ecuador and would like to help conserve it, please obtain more information from the following addresses and contribute whatever you can. These are a selection of the best-known organizations. Other local groups are listed in the text.

Acción Ecológica (☎ 02-230 676, ☎/fax 547 516, 527 583, red@hoy.net, www.ecuanex.net.ec/accion/)

Centro de Investigaciones de Los Bosques Tropicales (CIBT; ☎ 02-540 346, cibt@ecuanex.net.ec, www.forests.org/ric)

Charles Darwin Foundation (☎ 02-244 803, fax 443 935, cdrs@fcdarwin.org.ec, www.galapagos.org) 6 de Diciembre 4757, Quito, Ecuador; in the USA (☎ 703-538-6833, fax 538-6835) 100 N Washington St, Suite 232, Falls Church, VA 22046, USA

Consejo Ecuatoriano para Conservación y Investigación de Aves (CECIA; ☎ 02-464 359, cecia@uio.satnet.net) La Tierra 203 y Los Shyris, Quito, Ecuador

Conservation International (in the USA; ☎ 800-406-2306, 202-429-5660, www.conservation.org) 2501 M St NW, Suite 200, Washington, DC 20037, USA

Fundación Jatun Sacha (☎/fax 02-432 240, 432 173, 432 246, 453 583, www.jatunsacha.org)

Fundación Maquipucuna (☎ 02-507 200/1, fax 504 571, maqui@peachnet.campuscwix.net) Baquerizo 238 y Tamayo, Quito, Ecuador

Fundación Natura (☎ 02-446 081, natura@natura .org.ec, wwwpub4.ecua.net.ec/fnatura) Río Guayas 105 y Amazonas, Quito, Ecuador

Galápagos Conservation Trust (gct@gct.org, www .gct.org)

International Union for the Conservation of Nature and Natural Resources (☎ 02-466 622, fax 466 624, samerica@uicnsur.satnet.net, www .iucn.org/places/sur) Atahualpa 955 y República, 4th floor, Quito, Ecuador

Nature Conservancy (☎ 02-248 588, fax 462 217, cprogram@q.tnc.org.ec); in the USA (☎ 800-628-6860, www.tnc.org) The Latin America Division, 4245 N Fairfax Dr, Suite 100, Arlington, VA 22203, USA

World Wildlife Fund (☎ 202-293-4800, fax 293-9211) 1250 24th Street NW, Washington, DC 20037, USA

Note that several of these organizations have lodges and other facilities, which are listed in this book under the appropriate regional chapter.

National Parks

Ecuador's first *parque nacional* (national park) was the Galápagos, formed in 1959, but it was not until the mid- to late 1970s that a comprehensive national-park system began to be established on the mainland. The first mainland park was Cotopaxi, es-

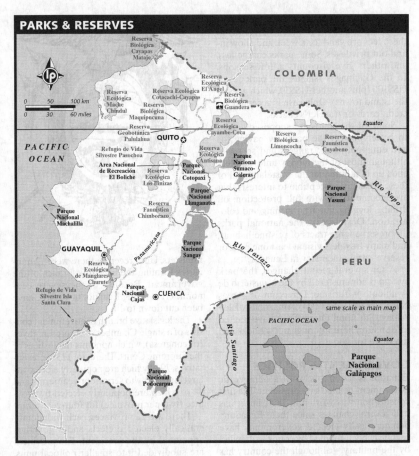

PARKS & RESERVES

Reserva Biológica Cayapas Mataje

COLOMBIA

Reserva Ecológica El Ángel

Reserva Ecológica Cotacachi-Cayapas

Reserva Biológica Guandera

Reserva Ecológica Mache Chindul

Reserva Biológica Maquipucuna

0   50   100 km
0   30   60 miles

Reserva Ecológica Cayambe-Coca

Equator

Reserva Geobotánica Pululahua

QUITO

Reserva Biológica Limoncocha

Reserva Faunística Cuyabeno

PACIFIC OCEAN

Refugio de Vida Silvestre Pasochoa

Reserva Ecológica Antisana

Parque Nacional Sumaco-Galeras

Área Nacional de Recreación El Boliche

Reserva Ecológica Los Ilinizas

Parque Nacional Cotopaxi

Parque Nacional Yasuní

Río Napo

Parque Nacional Llanganates

Reserva Faunística Chimborazo

Parque Nacional Machalilla

GUAYAQUIL

Parque Nacional Sangay

Río Pastaza

PERU

Panamericana

Reserva Ecológica de Manglares Churute

Refugio de Vida Silvestre Isla Santa Clara

Parque Nacional Cajas

CUENCA

same scale as main map

PACIFIC OCEAN

Equator

Río Santiago

Parque Nacional Galápagos

Parque Nacional Podocarpus

tablished in 1975, followed by Machalilla, Yasuní and Sangay in 1979 and Podocarpus in 1982. Several more have been added since then, as well as reserves of various kinds and a few national monuments and recreation areas. New reserves and parks are added regularly. In addition, local conservation organizations, such as Fundación Natura and Fundación Jatun Sacha, have begun to set aside private nature reserves. All of Ecuador's major ecosystems are partly protected in one (or more) of these areas.

The national parks do not have much of a tourist infrastructure. There are almost no hostels, drive-in campgrounds, restaurants, ranger stations, museums, scenic overlooks or information centers. Many are inhabited by native peoples who were living in the area for generations before it achieved park or reserve status. Some of the parks and reserves are remote, difficult to reach and lack almost all facilities.

Nevertheless, the adventurous traveler can visit most of them, and details are given in the appropriate sections of this book. Entrance fees vary, and Ecuadorians pay only a small fraction of the fee charged to foreign visitors. On the mainland, most highland parks charge US$10, and most lowland parks charge US$20 per visitor, but these fees are valid for a week and allow in-and-out privileges. Some parks charge less, and others give discounts in low seasons. In the Galápagos Islands, the park fee is US$100 (plus another US$30, which goes to the island towns). Only cash is accepted; no credit cards or traveler's checks.

Some of the funds are supposedly used to better protect the parks by paying for and equipping park rangers and so forth, although most of the money unfortunately ends up in a bureaucratic wasteland. All of these areas are susceptible to interests that are incompatible with full protection: oil drilling, logging, mining, ranching and colonization. Despite this, the national parks do preserve large tracts of pristine habitat, and many travelers visit at least one park or reserve during their stay in Ecuador.

After several recent changes, the park system is administered by the Ministerio de Ambiente y Turismo, Dirección de Areas Naturales (☎ 02-548-924), Amazonas y Eloy Alfaro, 8th floor, Quito. They have limited information here, although a few books and maps are for sale.

GOVERNMENT & POLITICS

Ecuador is a republic with a democratic government headed by a president. The first constitution was written in 1830, but it has had several changes since then. Ecuador's democratically elected governments have regularly been toppled by coups – often led by the military – although the country has been relatively democratic since 1979, with the exception of the crazy years beginning in 1997 (see History, earlier in this chapter). All literate citizens over 18 have the right to vote, and the president must receive over 50% of the vote to be elected. With about 15 different political parties, 50% of the vote is rarely achieved, in which case there is a second round between the top two contenders. A president governs for four years and cannot be reelected, though a change of this law has been considered.

The president is also the head of the armed forces and appoints his own cabinet ministers. Until recently, there were 12 ministries forming the executive branch of the government. Because of the severe economic crisis facing Ecuador now, these have been cut down to 10.

The legislative branch of government consists of a single Chamber of Representatives (or congress), which appoints the justices of the Supreme Court. There are 123 representatives, 79 of which are popularly elected at-large nationally to serve four-year terms, and 44 of which are popularly elected by province (two per province) for four-year terms.

There are 22 provinces, each with democratically elected prefects and a governor appointed by the president. The provinces are subdivided into smaller political units, called *cantones;* each canton has a democratically elected *alcalde,* or mayor.

The political parties change often; new ones are formed and old ones are abandoned on a regular basis. They have positions that include left-wing, center, populist and right-wing, the latter being the most frequently accepted by the voters. There are also a number of communist, socialist and revolutionary political movements that are not officially recognized. These groups do have a certain amount of political power, which they exercise by forming alliances with the official parties.

ECONOMY

Until recently, Ecuador was the archetypal 'banana republic.' Indeed, in the early 1970s, bananas were the single most important export, and almost all of Ecuador's exports were agricultural. This changed very rapidly with the discovery of oil. Petroleum exports rose to first place in 1973, and by the early 1980s, it accounted for well over half of the total export earnings.

The newfound wealth produced by oil export has improved the standards of living to some extent. Nevertheless, Ecuador remains a poor country. Distribution of wealth has been patchy, and much of the rural population continues to live at the same standard as in the 1970s. About 40% of the national income goes to the richest 5% of the population. However, education and medical services have improved.

Despite the income from oil exports, the 1980s was a difficult decade for the Ecuadorian economy. In 1982–83, El Niño floods caused severe disruptions in agriculture, and exports of bananas and coffee were roughly halved. This was followed by a drop in world oil prices in 1986. In that year, oil exports dropped from about US$1820 million in

PROVINCES OF ECUADOR

1985 to US$910 million in 1986. In 1987, a disastrous earthquake wiped out about 40km of the oil pipeline, severely damaging both the environment and the economy. Oil exports in 1987 totaled only US$645 million.

After oil was discovered, Ecuador began borrowing money with the belief that profits from oil exports would enable the country to repay its foreign debts. This proved impossible in the mid-1980s due to the sharp decline in Ecuador's oil exports. Although the pipeline has been repaired and oil exports have increased, their value (US$875 million in 1988, US$1030 million in 1989, US$1250 million in 1993, US$1050 million in 1997) is still well short of the levels of the early 1980s. Ecuador's foreign debt stands at about US$12.5 billion.

About 25% of the budget is used to pay for the foreign debt. In 1999, Ecuador became the first country to be unable to pay its Brady Bonds (international loans) and is currently experiencing its worst economic crisis since the early 20th century. Ecuador continues to rely on oil as its economic mainstay, but reserves are not as large as had been anticipated. Estimates range from 10 to 15 years until the remaining reserves are depleted at the current rates of extraction. Other major exports have also dropped; shrimp exports dropped by 80% in 1999 following devastating whitespot and yellowhead diseases.

In 1999, Ecuador's inflation was over 60% – the worst in Latin America. In March 2000, Ecuador replaced its currency (the sucre) with the US dollar upon approval of the US government and World Monetary Fund. The changeover is under way. While this measure should improve the economy in the long run, on a short-term basis, the country's poor and middle-class are likely to experience more economic hardship.

POPULATION & PEOPLE

The last census was in 1990, and with the current economic crisis, it's not known when the next one will be. Official population estimates for August 1998 (the latest available) approach 13 million (of which over seven million are living in poverty), which is approximately 11 times the number of Indians estimated to have been living in the area at the time of the Spanish conquest.

The population density of about 48 people per sq km is the highest of any South American nation. About 40% of this total are Indians, and another 40% are mestizos. It is difficult to accurately quantify how many pure-blooded Indians and how many mestizos there are – some sources give figures of 25% Indian and 55% mestizo. About 15% are white, and most of the remainder is black, with a small number of people of Asian descent.

Of the Indians, the majority are Quichua-speaking and live mainly in the highlands. Among the Quichua-speakers, various subgroups have been isolated from one another for centuries and, consequently, the language they speak varies markedly from province to province. Sometimes the Indians themselves have a difficult time understanding the dialects of the Indians of a different region.

The Quichua Indians of each region also have distinctive differences in clothing – it is possible to tell where an Indian is from by the color of a poncho or by the shape of a hat. Some of the best-known highland groups are the Otavaleños, Salasacas, Cañaris and Saraguros. Many Indians now live in towns and cities.

The province of Chimborazo has the largest population of rural Quichua Indians – there are some 270,000 living in over 400 legally recognized communities and villages in the páramo.

A few other small groups live in the Amazonian lowlands. These groups include about 65,000 Quichuas, about 40,000 Shuar (formerly called Jivaro), about 1000 Huaoranis and about 650 each of the Cofan and Siona-Secoya peoples. There are also about 5000 Chachi (formerly Cayapas) Indians living near the coast in the rainforests of northern Esmeraldas Province, and about 1000 Tsachilas (Colorado) Indians living near Santo Domingo de los Colorados, in the western lowlands. All these groups have their own languages, often completely unrelated to one another.

Approximately 48% of the Ecuadorian population live on the coast (and the Galápagos), and about 46% live in the highlands. The remainder live in the jungle region of the Oriente, and colonization of this area is slowly increasing.

The birth rate is 22.6 per 1000 inhabitants, and the annual population increase is 1.7%, which means that the population will double in about 40 years. This is significantly lower than the early 1990s (31 per 1000, 2.4% and 29 years). Life expectancy is 69.5 years for males and 74.9 years for females.

About 35% of the population is under the age of 15, or roughly twice as much as in Europe and North America.

The urban population is 60%. The rural population is mainly indigenous. People living in the country are often referred to as *campesinos* (peasants or farmers). An indigenous person is called an *indígena,* but not *indio,* which is considered insulting.

EDUCATION
Elementary education (two years of kindergarten and six grades of school) is mandatory, although about 50% of children drop out of school before completing elementary education. Of those continuing on to the six grades of secondary education, about a further 50% drop out.

A student must satisfactorily complete a grade (which normally takes a year) before being allowed to continue to the next grade. A diploma is issued to those students completing secondary education. The diploma is a basic requirement for higher education. There are about 20 universities and technical colleges in Ecuador.

In the highlands, the school year is from September to June. On the coast, however, the school year is from May to January.

The adult literacy rate is about 90%.

ARTS
A visit to any archaeology museum in Ecuador will testify to the artistic excellence of the pre-Columbian peoples. Their pottery shows fine painting and sculpture, and their metallurgy – particularly gold and silver work – was highly developed. Because the names of the artists have long been forgotten, their work is thought of as archaeology

rather than fine art. Nevertheless, some of this archaeological work formed the basis of what became known as the Quito school of art.

Colonial Art
The Spaniards arriving in the 16th century brought their own artistic concepts with them. These often revolved around Catholic religious themes. The Spaniards soon began to train the local indigenous artists to produce the colonial religious art that can now be seen in many churches and art museums. Religious statues were carved, painted then embellished with gold leaf – sculpture, painting and gold work were all techniques with which the Indians had long been familiar. Paintings, too, had liberal amounts of gold leaf included. And so arose the *Escuela Quiteña,* or Quito school of art: Spanish religious concepts as executed and heavily influenced by Indian artists.

The Quito school lasted through the 17th and 18th centuries. Some of the best-known artists of this period include the sculptor Manuel Chili, better known by his Quichua nickname, 'Caspicara,' meaning 'pockmarked.' Some of his work can be seen in the church of San Francisco in Quito. This church also contains a famous sculpture of the Virgin by Bernardo Legarda. Notable painters include Miguel de Santiago, whose huge canvases grace the walls of Quito's church of San Agustín, and Manuel Samaniego, Nicolás Goríbar and Bernardo Rodríguez.

Many of Quito's churches were built during this colonial period, and their architects were also somewhat influenced by the Quito school. In addition, churches often had Moorish (Arab) influences (Spain had been under the rule of the Moors for centuries). The overall appearance of the architecture of colonial churches is overpoweringly ornamental, and almost cloyingly rich – in short, baroque. The houses of the middle and upper class of that period were elegant and simple, often consisting of rooms with verandahs around a central courtyard.

Many of the houses had two stories, the upper floors bearing ornate balconies. The walls were whitewashed, and the roofs were of red tile. Quito's colonial architecture has been well preserved and led to UNESCO declaring old Quito *Patrimonio de la Humanidad* (Patrimony of Humanity) in 1978. Several other towns, notably Cuenca, have attractive colonial architecture.

Post-Colonial Art

The Quito school died out with the coming of independence. The 19th century is called the Republican period, and its art is characterized by formalism. Its favorite subjects are heroes of the revolution and important members of high society in the new republic. Rather florid landscapes are another popular theme.

The 20th century saw the rise of the indigenist school, which is characterized by subject matter rather than by style. The oppression and burdens of Ecuador's indigenous inhabitants are the unifying theme. Important indigenist artists include Eduardo Kingman (deceased 1998), Endara Crow, Camilo Egas (deceased 1962) and Oswaldo Guayasamín (deceased 1999). These and other artists have works in modern galleries and museums in Quito.

Music

Traditional Andean music has a distinctive and haunting sound that has been popularized in western culture by songs such as Paul Simon's version of *El Cóndor Pasa.*

Two main reasons contribute to the otherworldly quality of the traditional music of the Andes. The first is the scale: it is pentatonic, or consisting of five notes, as opposed to the seven-note octaves we are used to. The second is the fact that string and brass instruments were imported by the Spanish; pre-Columbian instruments consisted of wind and percussion, which effectively portray the windswept quality of páramo life.

Ancient traditional instruments include the *rondador,* or bamboo panpipe; the *quena* and *pingullo,* or large and small bamboo flutes; *conchas,* or conch shells played like a horn; and a variety of drums, rattles and bells. The Spanish brought stringed instruments (guitars, harps and violins). Some of these were incorporated into Andean music, and others were modified to produce the typical *charango,* a very small instrument with five double strings. The sounding box was often made of an armadillo shell, but fortunately for the armadillos, wood is being increasingly used.

Most traditional music today is a blend of pre-Columbian and Spanish influences. It is best heard in a *peña,* or *música folklórica* club (see Entertainment in the Facts for the Visitor chapter). Traditional music can also be heard on the streets during fiestas, but increasingly often, fiesta ensembles are cacophonous brass bands.

There are occasional symphony concerts, but it is the more traditional music, with pre-Columbian influences, that is of the greatest interest to many visitors.

Crafts

In Ecuador, indeed in much of Latin America, there is a bridge between fine arts and crafts: *artesanía.* This literally means artisanship and refers to textile crafts ranging from finely woven ponchos to hammocks, as well as well-made panama hats, basketwork, leatherwork, jewelry, woodcarving and ceramics.

These items are discussed in more detail under Shopping in the Facts for the Visitor chapter.

Literature

Ecuador has not produced any writers that have become household names outside the country. Nevertheless, there are several notable literary figures.

Juan Montalvo (1832–89) was a prolific essayist from Ambato who frequently attacked the dictatorial political figures of the time, particularly President Gabriel García Moreno. His best-known work is *Siete Tratados* (1882), or 'Seven Treatises,' which includes a comparison between Simón Bolívar and George Washington. Juan León Mera (1832–94), also from Ambato, is famous for his novel *Cumandá* (1891), which describes Indian life in the 19th century. English translations of these two works are hard to find, but the Spanish originals can be found in Ecuador.

Coracachi leather manufacturer

Perhaps the most notable Ecuadorian writer of the 20th century was Jorge Icaza (1906–79), a Quiteño. He was profoundly influenced by the indigenist school, and his most famous novel is *Huasipungo* (1934), translated as *The Villagers* (1973). This is a brutal story about Indians, the seizure of their land and the savage massacre of those who protested. The book is made all the more horrifying by the knowledge that this story is based on the real problems facing the Indians. Icaza was also known as a playwright, actor and writer of short stories.

There are many contemporary Ecuadorian writers. A good introduction to Ecuadorian literature is *Diez Cuentistas Ecuatorianos* (1990, Libri Mundi, Quito), a book of short stories by 10 Ecuadorian writers born in the 1940s. The stories are in Spanish with English translations. Pablo Cuvi's *In the Eyes of My People* has 121 superb color photographs, most taken by the author, and is available in Spanish or English. It is an informed and informal travelogue about Ecuador written in a distinctive and evocative style that seems like a cross between Kerouac's *On the Road* and

Steinbeck's *Travels with Charley*. These books were recently out of print, but new editions may be forthcoming.

Theater
The performing arts are important in Ecuador, although, as with literature, there are no artists whose names are known to most visitors. There are several theaters, especially in Quito, where performances include street theater, mime, political satire and more traditional plays.

SOCIETY & CONDUCT
Social Issues
Legally and morally, everyone is equal in Ecuador, irrespective of race or gender. In reality, blacks and indigenous people are discriminated against and treated as second-class citizens. This is particularly true of indigenous people. The term 'indio' (Indian), while having few negative connotations in English, is considered an insult in Spanish. A few popular nightclubs in Quito will not allow black people in – this was reported to me by black US Peace Corps Volunteers and embassy staff, not just by locals.

The Indian population frequently stages protests about their unfair and inhumane treatment. In 1990, Indians barricaded themselves into a church (Santo Domingo) and demanded their rights. Their demands ranged from autonomy of Indian groups to providing basic services, such as running water, to indigenous communities. While autonomy could be considered a debatable issue, the right to running water is basic. These kinds of issues continue to be problems as we enter the 21st century.

Graffiti of the *'Vayase Yanqui'* (Yankee, go home) type is seen in Ecuador. While many Ecuadorians display some anti-American sentiment, this is directed against the interventionist policy of the USA in Latin America, and not against the individual US traveler. Indeed, US citizens often remark how friendly the Ecuadorian people are. This is partly because of Ecuadorians' inherent politeness, and partly because US travelers are the second-most frequent visitors (after neighboring Colombians) to

Ecuador, and thus contribute an important amount to the nation's economy.

Dos & Don'ts

Greetings are important to Ecuadorians, especially in the highlands. Strangers conducting business will, at the minimum, exchange a cordial *'Buenos días, cómo está?'* before launching into whatever they are doing. Male friends and casual acquaintances meeting one another in the street shake hands at the beginning and end of even a short meeting; women kiss one another on the cheek in greeting and farewell. Men often kiss women decorously on the cheek, except in a business setting, where a handshake is more appropriate. Close male friends hug one another in the traditional *abrazo*. Indians, on the other hand, don't kiss; and their handshakes, when offered, are a light touch rather than a firm grip. In all situations, politeness is a valued habit.

Ecuadorians are used to less personal space than North Americans and Europeans. Conversations tend to take place face to face; streets and public transportation are very crowded, and homes have little individual space. Frequent kissing and hugging on a nonsexual basis, such as that described above, is an example of this. Noise seems part of the way of life. Radios and TVs in cheaper hotel rooms are turned on early in the morning and late at night without thought as to whether guests in neighboring rooms can hear. Don't expect anyone to take you very seriously if you ask to have the volume turned down; carry earplugs instead.

Clothing is important to Ecuadorians, and even poor people will try to dress their best. The casually unkempt look (except among teenagers) is out; the well-pressed suit or attractive skirt and blouse are in. That is not to say that Ecuadorians don't like to dress informally – they do – but a neat and conservative turnout is preferred, especially in the highlands. Shorts are not worn in the highlands except by athletes and gauche travelers. Wear long pants or a skirt.

Spitting is common, particularly in the lower socioeconomic classes; however, belching or burping in public is considered the absolute height of bad manners by everyone.

The concept of smoking being a health hazard is not very big in Ecuador. Nonsmoking areas are rare, and most restaurants allow diners to smoke wherever they please. The same applies to public transportation, including airplanes.

When calling someone over to you, don't crook your finger up and beckon, as people do in North America or Europe. This is rude. A better way to call someone over from a distance is to give a flat, downward swipe of the open hand. Body language using hands and facial expressions is hard to describe but is an important part of interpersonal communications. Watch to see how Ecuadorians do things.

Begging is a fact of life in Ecuador. If you drive on the back roads in the highlands at certain times, you may see campesinos lined up along the roads with their hands out in supplication. This is particularly true on Sunday and around Christmas. At those times, it's considered OK to give the people something, but please, do so in a manner that shows some basic human respect. I once saw a busload of tourists throw candy through the windows of the bus and onto the ground. They then filmed the ensuing scramble and roared off without any interaction with the people begging. It is difficult to say which were the more pathetic – the tourists or the beggars.

Begging children are becoming more common in the cities. Particularly sad is the sight of little girls, four or five years old, walking the main drag of Quito (Avenida Amazonas), trying to sell roses to tourists at all hours of the night. These kids are often forced to work the streets until the early hours of the morning. While giving them money may help them on an immediate level, the long-term problem of homeless kids working the streets and not receiving an education is exacerbated. Donations to one of the many charities (such as Save the Children) that help homeless children all over the world is a good alternative. You can specify that you wish the money to be spent in Ecuador. In Quito, ask at the South American Explorers about donating time or money to worthwhile causes.

Treatment of Animals

In common with most Latin American countries, bullfighting and cockfighting are considered acceptable sporting activities. Most Ecuadorians are either in favor of these traditional activities or hold no strong opinion on them. Few Ecuadorians oppose these blood sports, although most will politely hear reasonably presented opinions against them.

RELIGION

As is common with other Latin American countries, Ecuador's predominant religion is Roman Catholicism. Some of the older towns have splendid 16th- and 17th-century Catholic churches. Although churches of other faiths can be found, they form only a very small minority. The Indians, while outwardly Roman Catholic, tend to blend Catholicism with their traditional beliefs.

LANGUAGE

For the traveler in Ecuador, Spanish is the most useful language. Although Spanish is translated as *español*, the form used in Ecuador is more frequently and correctly called *castellano*. Most Indians are bilingual, with Quichua (or Quechua) being their preferred language and Spanish their second tongue. In addition to the Quichua-speaking Indians of the highlands, there are several small lowland groups that speak their own languages; some are dialects of Quichua and some completely unrelated to Quichua. In addition, Quichua speakers in Ecuador use a dialect very different from that spoken in Peru and Bolivia, so it's difficult for highland Indians from these different countries to communicate easily, although some words are the same. It is rare to encounter Indians who understand no Spanish at all, although they certainly exist in the remoter communities. Although English is understood in the best hotels, airline offices and tourist agencies, it is of little use elsewhere.

If you don't speak Spanish, take heart. It is an easy language to learn. Courses are available in Quito and other cities, or you can study books, records and tapes while you are still planning your trip. These study aids are available for free from many public libraries. You might want to consider taking a course. Once you have learned the basics, you'll find that you'll be able to travel all over Latin America, since apart from Brazil, where Portuguese is spoken, most of the countries use Spanish.

Spanish is easy to learn. It uses Roman script, and with few exceptions, it is spoken as it is written and vice versa. Imagine trying to explain to someone learning English that there are seven different ways of pronouncing 'ough.' This isn't a problem in Spanish. Also, many words are similar enough to English that you can figure them out by guesswork. For example, 'Instituto Geográfico Militar' means 'Military Geographical Institute.'

Even if you don't have time to take a course, bring a phrasebook and dictionary. A good phrasebook is Lonely Planet's *Latin American Spanish Phrasebook*. Don't dispense with the dictionary, however, because the phrasebook can't help you translate the local newspaper.

See the Language chapter in the back of this book for basic information on Latin American Spanish.

Facts for the Visitor

HIGHLIGHTS

Ecuador is a tiny country, yet it encompasses a huge variety of elevations and environments, from the Pacific coast, to glacier-clad Andean highlands, to the Amazonian lowlands, to the Galápagos Islands, 1000km off the coast. So the country's greatest highlight is simply the opportunity to see and experience many different regions in a short time.

Indian Markets

These are often a success story for everyone – gringos go home with beautiful souvenirs; artisans make a living selling their crafts; and local buses, hotels and restaurants benefit as well. There are plenty of great markets; Otavalo is the most famous, but markets at Saquisilí and many other highland towns and villages are well worth visiting.

Wildlife

Half of the birds in South America are found in Ecuador – and little Ecuador has twice as many birds as all of North America. See the Books section, later in this chapter, for listings of bird-watching guides. Refugio de Vida Silvestre Pasochoa (near Quito and operated by Fundación Natura) and the Mindo area are among the best places in the highlands to see many species of birds. The Galápagos Islands are fabulous if you want to see frigatebirds, boobies, pelicans, giant tortoises and sea lions face to face – literally. However, the islands are prohibitively expensive to visit – go if you are really interested, don't bother if wildlife is not your thing.

Various kinds of trips can be taken into the rainforest. Many areas of the Ecuadorian rainforest have been colonized, and you won't see jaguars in these areas (which are, of course, the easiest areas to get to). In the remoter areas, the luxuriant vegetation masks much of the wildlife. Nevertheless, Ecuador is as good a country as any in which to visit the rainforest. See the Oriente chapters for more details.

Finally, don't neglect the wildlife of the highlands – the *páramo* habitats of the Tulcán area, Parque Nacional Cotopaxi and Parque Nacional Las Cajas are all recommended.

Architecture

Many highland towns have Spanish colonial architecture dominating their city centers. Quito's and Cuenca's old towns have been especially well preserved since colonial times and have been designated World Cultural Heritage Sites by UNESCO. Many other highland towns have interesting colonial architecture.

Fiestas

From the capital's annual fiesta during the first week in December to the local festivities in small towns and villages, fiestas are a chance to mingle with local people and have fun. All Souls' Day (November 2) is particularly recommended in the highlands; Bolívar's Birthday (July 24) and the Founding of Guayaquil (July 25) are particularly recommended in Guayaquil. Carnaval time (the weekend preceding Ash Wednesday) is celebrated all over Latin America – in Ecuador, it takes the form of water-throwing in most areas, and there is a festival of fruit and flowers in Ambato.

Unusual Transportation

There are numerous interesting, unusual and fun ways to travel, but there's no guarantee of luxurious comfort! Ride on the roof of the train as it zigzags down El Nariz del Diablo (Devil's Nose) – a dizzying descent from Alausí in the highlands to Sibambe in the coastal lowlands. Voyage along a tropical river in a dugout canoe from Borbón on the coast or Misahuallí in the Oriente. Pack yourself into a bus full of locals and take the high road around Chimborazo. Cross Río Guayas by passenger ferry to see the busy traffic on Ecuador's widest river. Amble around the Vilcabamba area by horseback.

PLANNING
When to Go

Travelers can visit Ecuador year-round. Certain areas are better at certain times of the year, but there are no general cut-and-dried rules.

The high seasons are generally considered to be mid-December through January and June to August, as that is when the most foreign visitors arrive.

In the Galápagos, peak tourist periods are June to August, December to January and near Easter. The wildlife is always there, and birds of different species breed at different times, so you can see courting behavior and young in their nests during any month. The exception to this is the waved albatross, which leave en masse in mid-December and stay at sea until late March.

The islands have two seasons: The rainy season lasts from January to about June, and the dry season lasts from June to December. The rainy season has many warm, sunny periods interspersed with showers and an occasional downpour – it is generally pleasant. February is the hottest month; March and April are milder. Water temperatures are a balmy 23°C or 24°C and are great for snorkeling. The water is usually fairly calm. Temperatures drop to around 18°C to 20°C between May and July.

The dry season is generally cooler and often misty, and a fog (called *garúa*) sometimes envelopes the islands. A warm sweater may be needed at night. The ocean tends to be choppy in July and is often at its roughest August to October. Droughts or heavy rains can occur at unpredictable and irregular intervals – often associated with the El Niño climatic phenomenon. Rainfall can vary tremendously between the wettest and driest years – one report claims that the wettest year on record had 100 times as much rain as the driest.

The coast has a similar weather pattern – hot and wet from January to May (when tropical rainstorms may make some of the poorer roads impassable) and drier and cooler during the rest of the year. January to April, although rainy, coincides with coastal school vacations, and so the beaches are crowded. July and August are gray, damp and overcast. Locals don't visit the coast much then, but gringos do because those may be the only months during which they can get away!

The dry season in the highlands is normally June to August, which coincides with the wettest months in the Oriente, when roads may be closed.

Maps

Bookstores have a limited selection of Ecuadorian maps. The best selection can be found at the Instituto Geográfico Militar (IGM), on top of a hill at the end of Paz y Miño, off Avenida Colombia, in Quito's new town (IGM has a map of the Galápagos at 1:500,000 scale). The building can be recognized by the map of Ecuador painted on one of its outside walls. There are no buses; walk (maybe not on your first day at this altitude) or take a taxi. Permission to enter the building is given to you at the main gate in exchange for your passport. Hours are 8 am to 4 pm Monday to Thursday (closed 1 to 1:30 pm for lunch) and 1 pm Friday.

Few city maps are published, and except for detailed maps of the whole of Quito, Guayaquil and Cuenca, you'll find the city maps in this book are often the best available. The IGM does have some excellent large-scale maps of the whole country, ranging from a 1:1,000,000 one-sheet Ecuador map to 1:50,000 topographical maps. These occasionally go out-of-print, but most maps are freely available for reference, and B&W photocopies are available. Some areas, especially the Oriente and parts of the western lowlands, are inadequately mapped.

Bradt Publications (☎ 01753 894444, fax 892333, enquiries@bradt-travelguides.com) is at 19 High St, Chalfont St Peter, Bucks, SL9 9QE, England; it has Ecuadorian maps for sale. Bradt Publications and ITMB (Canada) jointly published a map of the Galápagos at 1:500,000 scale that is better than the IGM map of the same scale. It's called *Galápagos Islands Map 312*, and it is full of useful information about wildlife, history and tourism.

What to Bring

This is a tough issue. Bring as little as possible…but bring everything that's important to you! If you're interested in photography, you'll only curse every time you see a good shot (if only you'd brought your telephoto lens), and if you're a musician, you won't enjoy the trip if you constantly worry about how out of practice you are getting.

A good idea once you're in Quito is to divide your gear into two piles – one for what you'll need for the next section of your trip, the rest to stash in the storage room at your hotel (most hotels have one). Ecuador is a small country, so you can use Quito as a base and divide your traveling into, say, coastal, highland and jungle portions, easily returning to Quito between trips and picking up the gear you need for the next.

Traveling light is much less of a hassle, so don't bring things you can do without. Traveling on buses and trains is bound to make you slightly grubby, so bring one change of dark clothes that don't show the dirt, rather than seven changes of nice clothes for a four-week trip. Many people go overboard with changes of clothes, but one change to wash and the other to wear is the best idea. Bring clothes that wash and dry easily (jeans take forever to dry).

Remember that clothes can be bought cheaply in Ecuador. T-shirts are popular souvenirs, and heavy wool sweaters and long-sleeved cotton shirts can be bought inexpensively at Indian markets. A shopping mall will yield underwear and socks. In fact, you can outfit yourself quite well in Ecuador. This is very useful if you are arriving in the country on a cheap air-courier ticket, when you are allowed only carry-on luggage. You can buy clothes of almost any size, but shoes go up only to size 43 Ecuadorian (and European), which is about 10½ North American. This is true of most Latin American countries, so bring a spare pair if your feet are big and if you're planning a long trip.

Tampons are available in Ecuador, but only in the major cities and in regular sizes, so make sure you stock up with an adequate supply before visiting smaller towns, the jungle or the Galápagos. Some tampons are sold without applicators and are relatively expensive – sanitary pads are cheaper. Contraceptives are available in the major cities – condoms are widely sold, but their quality may be questionable. Spermicidal jelly is hard to find. The choice of oral contraceptives is limited, so if you use a preferred brand, you should bring it from home.

The highlands are often cold, so bring a windproof jacket and a warm layer to wear beneath, or plan on buying a thick sweater in Otavalo. A hat is indispensable; it'll keep you warm when it's cold, shade your eyes when it's sunny and keep your head dry when it rains (a great deal). A collapsible umbrella is great protection against sun and rain as well. Cheap highland hotel rooms often lack heat – usually, extra blankets are provided on request, but a sleeping bag is very useful but not essential.

In the Galápagos, you can purchase most things in Puerto Ayora, but at a price. Little or nothing is available aboard the boats. You should bring all the film, sunblock, insect repellent, books and medical supplies (including motion-sickness medication) that you need. Sunglasses and a shade hat are also recommended. If you plan on doing a lot of snorkeling, it is strongly suggested that you bring your own snorkel and mask. Likewise, avid birders should bring binoculars. Shipboard life is casual, so dress accordingly. Be prepared to get wet during landings – shorts are a good idea. Trails can be very rocky and the lava is extremely rough; sturdy shoes that can get wet are important (old tennis shoes are ideal). Bring a spare pair of footwear to keep dry and wear on the boat.

The following is a list of small items you will find useful and probably need:

- pocket flashlight with spare bulb and batteries
- travel alarm clock
- Swiss Army–style pocketknife
- sewing and repairs kit (dental floss makes strong, colorless emergency thread)
- a few meters of cord (useful for clothesline and spare shoelaces)
- sunglasses
- sealable plastic bags

- soap and dish, shampoo, toothbrush and tooth-paste, shaving gear, towel
- toilet paper (rarely found in cheaper hotels and restaurants)
- earplugs for sleeping in noisy hotels or buses
- insect repellent (containing a high concentration of deet)
- sunblock (30SPF or higher is recommended but hard to find in Ecuador)
- address book
- notebook
- pens and pencils
- paperback book (easily exchanged with other travelers when you've finished)
- water bottle
- first-aid kit (see Health, later)

Optional items include:

- camera and film
- Spanish-English dictionary and phrasebook
- small padlock
- large folding nylon bag to leave things in storage
- snorkeling gear (for the Galápagos)
- water-purification tablets or filter
- binoculars and field guides (highly recommended if you plan on visiting the Amazon)

Finally, you need something to carry everything around in. A backpack is recommended, because carrying your baggage on your back is less exhausting than carrying it in your hands, which are left free. On the other hand, it's often more difficult to get at things inside a pack, so some travelers prefer a duffel bag with a full-length zipper. Whichever you choose, ensure that it is a good, strongly made piece of luggage, or you'll find that you spend much of your trip replacing zippers, straps and buckles. Hard traveling is notoriously rough on your luggage, and if you bring a backpack, it's best to go with one that has an internal frame. External frames snag on bus doors, luggage racks and airline baggage belts, and are liable to get twisted, cracked or broken.

RESPONSIBLE TOURISM

Ecuador's tourism industry has been growing in recent years and is now a significant part of the economy. On the surface, inter-national tourists spending money are a positive force. But tourists and travelers need to look deeper than just spending their money. Hundreds of thousands of foreign visitors can create a negative impact on the society and environment of Ecuador.

Problems exist with the dichotomy between rich tourists (and even the most budget-oriented backpacker is rich by local standards) and the locals who work for sub-standard wages to provide services for tourists. For example, demands by groups of non-Spanish-speaking tourists can range from reasonable to rude and obnoxious. Some things that may not seem immediately wrong (taking a person's photograph, demanding toilet paper in a cheap restaurant, expecting the same amenities as you have at home, etc) are not reasonable by local standards.

So what can be done to promote responsible tourism? Here are some suggestions. Start by learning at least enough Spanish to be able to say 'hello,' 'thank you,' 'Ecuador is a beautiful country' and a few more phrases. Don't be afraid to use them! Interact with the local people – don't just take photos and run – and don't make promises you can't keep.

Accept and respect local customs and lifestyles rather than imposing your own. Support local artisans by buying locally made handicrafts and artwork, but don't buy illegal artifacts, such as pre-Columbian pieces or items made from endangered animals, such as cat skins or jewelry made from sea turtle or black coral.

Read the section on Society & Conduct in the Facts about Ecuador chapter, and act in a locally acceptable way. Remember the old proverb 'When in Rome, do as the Romans do' (but not to the point of throwing trash on the street or trail just because some Ecuadorians do it – use common sense). Use local services as much as possible so as to leave your money with the local economy. On outdoor expeditions, don't allow your guides to hunt, cut trees for bonfires, harass wildlife or litter. Try to set a good example, but be sensitive to local customs and beliefs.

TOURIST OFFICES

Because of Ecuador's severe economic problems of 1999 and 2000, there has not been an effective system of government-run tourist offices. Some local offices continue to operate in some cities, but their information is not always up-to-date.

VISAS & DOCUMENTS
Passport

All nationals entering as tourists need a passport that must be valid for at least six months after your arrival. Check the expiration date on your passport – it's easy to forget. If you run out of pages in your passport, new ones can be added more cheaply than getting a new passport. This can be done at your embassy if you are already traveling, or at your passport office at home. Allow several days at your embassy and several weeks at your home passport office.

You should always carry your passport, as there are occasional document checks on public transportation. You can be arrested if you don't have identification. Immigration checks go through periodic swings. You can be in Ecuador for three months without anyone asking to see your passport, or you can be stopped in the street for no reason and asked for your documents twice in one week. Failure to produce a visa or tourist card (see Travel Permits, later) can result in deportation.

Visas

Most travelers entering Ecuador as tourists do not require visas. Citizens of Cuba, a few Asian countries and some Central American countries currently require a tourist visa. These regulations are subject to change; it's worth checking with an Ecuadorian consular office for current requirements.

All travelers who do not wish to enter as tourists require visas. Nonimmigrant visas are available for diplomats, refugees, students, laborers, religious workers, businesspeople and cultural-exchange visitors. Various immigrant visas are also available. Obtaining a visa is time consuming, so commence the process as far ahead of your visit as possible. However, visas enable holders to apply for a *censo* (temporary residence card) and pay resident prices in national parks, as well as on trains and planes, which usually charge more for foreign visitors.

One traveler reports that he tried to obtain a six-month visa to teach English; the consul in San Francisco made this difficult by requiring police records and various other official letters and documents. He tried again at the Los Angeles consulate and was able to obtain a visa with no problem, just by presenting his airline ticket home and a valid passport. Obviously, the situation varies from consulate to consulate, so if at first you don't succeed, try again elsewhere. See Embassies, later in this chapter, for a partial list of Ecuadorian embassies.

Visa holders who apply for residency need to get an exit permit from the immigration authorities in Quito before they leave the country. Depending on their status, some residents may have to pay an exit tax.

See Visa Extensions under Quito for details on extending your visa.

Travel Permits

Tourists need a passport and a T-3 tourist card, which is obtainable upon arrival in Ecuador. There is no charge for this document, but don't lose it, as you will need it for stay extensions, passport checks and leaving the country. If you should lose it, you can get another at the immigration office in Quito or Guayaquil, or at the point at which you exit the country.

Upon arrival, if you show your outbound ticket, you should get as many days as you need. You are given an identical *entrada* (entrance) stamp on both your passport and T-3 tourist card, which indicates how long you can stay. The maximum is 90 days, but usually less is given. It's easy and quick to get a stay extension in Quito.

There are also T-1 and T-2 tourist cards. These are for short visits only and may be issued to travelers in transit through the country, or to those who are staying for less than 72 hours.

Onward Tickets

In addition to your passport and tourist card, you officially need a ticket out of the country and evidence of sufficient funds for your stay (US$20 per day). This is the law, and although it is not regularly enforced, if you turn up at the border stoned or looking as if you haven't washed or eaten for a week, it probably will be.

Most airlines flying to Quito want to see an onward ticket or a residence visa. If you're flying in, it's safest to buy an onward ticket. Make sure it can be refunded if you don't use it. In Ecuador, this can take a couple of weeks, but you'll get the money in dollars. Don't worry about an onward ticket at the land borders; it's very unlikely that the rule will be mentioned if you arrive looking reasonably respectable.

Travel Insurance

No matter how you're traveling, make sure you take out travel insurance. This should cover you not only for medical expenses and luggage theft or loss, but also for unavoidable cancellation or delays in your travel arrangements. Everyone should be covered for the worst possible case, such as an accident that requires hospital treatment and a flight home. Coverage depends on your insurance and type of ticket, so ask both your insurer and your ticket-issuing agency to explain the finer points. Some policies will not cover you if something happens to you while you are in a 'notorious' trouble spot. STA Travel (see the Getting There & Away chapter) offers a variety of travel-insurance options at reasonable prices. Ticket loss is also covered by travel insurance. Make sure you have a separate record of all your ticket details – or better still, a photocopy of the ticket itself. Also, make copies of your policy in case the original is lost.

Buy travel insurance as early as possible. If you buy it the week before you fly, you may find, for instance, that you're not covered for delays to your flight caused by strikes or other industrial action that may have been in force before you took out the insurance.

Driver's License

If you plan on renting a car, a valid driver's license from your home country is normally accepted if it is of the type that has a photograph on it. Otherwise, get an international driver's license.

Hostel Cards

Ecuador has a limited hostel system, and hostel cards get you a 10% discount. However, it is not worth getting a hostel card for the trip, because it won't save you much. If you already have one, you might as well bring it.

Student Cards

Students receive small discounts on flights to the Galápagos and pay only 50% of the US$100 Galápagos park-entrance fee. Other discounts may be available, but the Galápagos ones are the biggest. International student cards alone are not accepted, because false ones have been issued in Ecuador and officials no longer trust them. Bring both an ISIC card and the student card from your home school, college or university – and make sure that the photo on it looks like you and that it has not expired. Generally, student cards are less useful in Ecuador than in many other countries.

Vaccination Certificates

While these are not required by law, vaccinations are advisable. See the Health section, later in this chapter.

Copies

Before you leave home, you should photocopy all important documents (passport data page and visa page, credit cards, travel-insurance policy, air/bus/train tickets, driver's license, etc). Leave one copy with someone at home and keep another with you, separate from the originals.

It's also a good idea to store details of your vital travel documents in Lonely Planet's free online Travel Vault in case you lose the photocopies or can't be bothered with them. Your password-protected Travel Vault is accessible online anywhere in the world – create it at www.ekno.lonelyplanet.com.

EMBASSIES & CONSULATES
Ecuadorian Embassies & Consulates

Although some countries have Ecuadorian consular representation in several cities, the following are their main offices. Many countries other than the ones listed here have Ecuadorian embassies or consular representation; their addresses and telephone numbers can be found in telephone directories.

Australia (☎ 02-9223 3266, 9223 0041) 388 George St, 1702A, American Express Tower, Sydney, NSW 2000

Canada (☎ 613-563 8206, fax 235 5776) 50 O'Connor St, Suite 1311, Ottawa, Ontario K1N 6L2

Colombia (☎ 1-218 3526) Carrera 11 No 86-32, oficina 404

France (☎ 01-45 61 10 21, fax 42 89 22 09) 34 avenue de Messine, 75008 Paris

Germany (☎ 228-35 25 44) Koblenzerstrasse 37, 5300 Bonn 2

New Zealand (☎ 09-309 0229, fax 303 2931) Ferry Building, 2nd floor, Quay St, Auckland

Peru (☎ 01-440 9941, fax 422 0711) Las Palmeras 356, San Isidro

The Netherlands (☎ 70-3463753) Surinamestraat 11 2585 GG Den Haag

The UK (☎ 020-7584 1367, fax 823 9701) Flat 3B, 3 Hans Crescent, Knightsbridge, London SW1X OL5

The USA (☎ 202-234-7200, fax 667-3482) 2535 15th St NW, Washington, DC 20009

Embassies & Consulates in Ecuador

Many countries have embassies in Quito and consulates in Quito or Guayaquil. It is a good idea to register with your embassy, especially if you plan to stay in the country for any extended period. Their office hours are short, so call ahead to find out when they are open or if they have recently changed addresses. There are more than those mentioned here, so check in the yellow pages under 'Consulados' or 'Embajadas.'

Quito Both embassies and consulates are found in Quito. Dial 02 if calling from outside Pichincha Province.

Canada (☎ 232 114, 506 162, fax 503 108) 6 de Diciembre 2816 and P Rivet, 4th floor

Colombia (☎ 920 916, 458 012, fax 460 054) Atahualpa 955 and República, 3rd floor

France (☎ 543 101, fax 506 468) Diego de Almagro 1550 and Pradera

Germany (☎ 970 820, fax 970 815) Naciones Unidas and República de El Salvador, Edificio Citiplaza, 14th floor

Holland (☎ 525 461, 229 229, fax 567 917) 12 de Octubre 1942 and Cordero, World Trade Center, Tower 1, 1st floor

Ireland (☎ 451 577, fax 269 862) Antonio de Ulloa 2651 and Rumipamba

Panama (☎/fax 566 449) Diego de Almagro 1550 and La Pradera, 3rd floor

Peru (☎ 468 410, 468 389, fax 468 411) El Salvador 495 and Irlanda

The UK (☎ 970 800/1, fax 970 810, emergencies 09-723 021) Naciones Unidas and República de El Salvador, Edificio Citiplaza, 14th floor

The USA (☎ 562 890, fax 502 052) Patria and 12 de Octubre

Guayaquil Because this is Ecuador's major port and city, there are many consulates. Travelers heading for Peru may want to visit the Peruvian consulate – its hours were recently 8:30 am to 1 pm weekdays. Dial 04 if calling from outside Guayas Province.

Australia (☎ 680 823, 680 700, fax 682 008) Nahín Isaías and F de Orellana, Cuidadela Kennedy

Canada (☎ 563 580, 566 747, fax 314 562) Córdova 810, 4th floor

Colombia (☎ 563 308, fax 563 854) Córdova 812, 2nd floor

France (☎ 294 334, fax 295 267) Edificio Bayfordvesa, prolongación Avenida Menéndez Gilbert, vía Terminal Terrestre, Urbanización Sta Leonor

Germany (☎ 200 500, 206 867, fax 206 869) Avenidas Las Monjas and CJ Arosemena, Km2.5, Edificio Berlin

Peru (☎ 322 738, 327 639, fax 325 679) 9 de Octubre 411, 6th floor

The Netherlands (☎ 562 777, 563 857, fax 563 964) P de Icaza 454

The UK (☎ 560 400, 563 850, fax 562 641) Córdova 623

The USA (☎ 323 570, fax 325 286) 9 de Octubre and García Moreno

Your Own Embassy

It's important to realize what your own embassy – the embassy of the country of which you are a citizen – can and can't do to help you if you get into trouble. Generally speaking, it won't be much help in emergencies if the trouble you're in is remotely your own fault. Remember that you are bound by the laws of the country you are in. Your embassy will not be sympathetic if you end up in jail after committing a crime locally, even if such actions are legal in your own country.

In genuine emergencies, you might get some assistance, but only if other channels have been exhausted. If you need to get home urgently, a free ticket home is exceedingly unlikely – the embassy would expect you to have insurance. If all your money and documents are stolen, it might assist you with getting a new passport, but a loan for onward travel is out of the question.

Some embassies used to keep letters for travelers or have a small reading room with home newspapers, but these days, most of the mail-holding services have been stopped, and even newspapers tend to be out-of-date.

CUSTOMS

Each traveler is allowed to import a liter of spirits, 300 cigarettes and an unspecified 'reasonable' amount of perfume into Ecuador, all duty free. There is no problem with bringing in the usual personal belongings, but if you plan on bringing in several cameras, a computer or something else that might not be considered a 'usual personal belonging,' you should check with an Ecuadorian consulate.

Pre-Columbian artifacts are not allowed to be taken out of Ecuador or to be imported into most other countries. Bringing endangered-animal products home is also illegal.

MONEY
Currency

Until 2000, the currency in Ecuador was the sucre. This was exchanged at 6000 for US$1 in early 1999, but was valued at only 25,000 for US$1 in early 2000. In an attempt to stop this rampant inflation during Ecuador's worst economic crisis, the government decided to dollarize the economy, exchanging 25,000 sucres for US$1 (see the boxed text 'Ecuador's Dollarization'). US dollars will be standard Ecuadorian currency by late 2000. Ecuadorian sucre bills are being withdrawn, although it is difficult to predict when they will be completely out of circulation. New coins of 1, 5, 10, 25 and 50 cents are being minted. The coins will be identical in shape, size and color to their US equivalents but will bear images of famous Ecuadorians rather than US presidents. They are scheduled to appear in August 2000, and sucre bills exchanged for the coins will be destroyed by the treasury. There are no plans to print Ecuadorian versions of US dollar bills.

It is most important to know that cash bills are likely to be refused if they have tears in them, so bring a supply of bills in good condition. Also note that counterfeit US$1 bills have recently been brought into circulation; check carefully (see the boxed text 'Ecuador's Dollarization').

Exchanging Money

Banks are generally open 9 am to 1:30 pm weekdays. In some cities, banks may stay open later or may be open on Saturday, especially if Saturday happens to be market day. *Casas de cambio* (currency-exchange places) are usually open 9 am to 6 pm weekdays and until noon on Saturday. There is usually a lunch hour, which varies from place to place.

In Quito and Guayaquil, the international airport and major hotels have exchange facilities that are open past the usual hours.

Cash & Traveler's Checks US dollars are now the accepted Ecuadorian currency. Hard currencies of other nations, and pesos and nuevos soles from neighboring Colombia and Peru, can be exchanged for US dollars in casas de cambio and in banks. It is best to change money in the major cities of Quito, Guayaquil and Cuenca. Outside of these cities, traveling with US dollars is advised. Consider bringing US dollars with you on your trip in case you have trouble exchanging your home country's currency.

There is not a significant difference between the exchange rates for cash and traveler's checks. Traveler's checks are much safer because they are refunded if they are lost or stolen. I've had no difficulty exchanging major brands of traveler's checks in Ecuador. Don't bring all of your money in traveler's checks, however. It's always useful to have a supply of US cash for the occasions when only cash is accepted.

ATMs Ecuadorian ATMs are compatible with foreign credit cards. Holders of Visa cards will find that Banco de Guayaquil and Filanbanco have 24-hour ATMs, and holders of MasterCards should use Banco del Pacífico and Banco Popular. Many other banks offer ATM facilities – look at their logos to see if your credit/debit card is accepted. Make sure your PIN (Personal Identification Number) is four digits, as Ecuadorian ATMs don't normally recognize longer ones. If your PIN is a word, make sure to memorize the numeric equivalent before you leave, as letters may not always be given on Ecuadorian PIN pads.

To avoid getting stung with high interest rates on cash withdrawals from credit cards,

Ecuador's Dollarization

During 1999–2000, Ecuador suffered its most severe economic crisis of modern times. In early 2000, embattled President Jamil Mahuad pinned his political future and Ecuador's economic survival on dollarization, a process whereby Ecuador's unstable national currency, the sucre, would be replaced by the US dollar. This process has been used successfully in a few other economically hard-hit countries, including nearby Panamá (where the US dollar is called a Balboa).

The move met with bitter opposition from various Ecuadorian groups, one of which was the powerful CONAIE (Confederation of Ecuadorian Indian Nations). The organization argued that most of Ecuador's poorer populations would not be able to deal with a currency from another country. US dollars, printed in English, would be difficult to read and understand by people for whom Quichua is the first language, Spanish a second language and English a distant and rarely encountered third language.

Formidable protests by CONAIE, supported by a handful of lower-echelon military officials, led to the ouster of President Mahuad, who, after a few hours of political posturing by the protestors, was replaced by his constitutional successor, Vice President Gustavo Noboa. The new president vowed to continue with dollarization.

In March 2000, the Ecuadorian parliament approved the law to dollarize the economy, with September 2000 being the final date set for changing sucres to dollars. In April 2000, taxi drivers announced that they would be changing their meters to US dollars. In June, Ecuadorian banks announced they would issue checks only in US dollars, and a planned nationwide protest by CONAIE fizzled.

Various problems have come out of this change in currency. Both taximeters and phone booths need to be reconfigured. ATMs already pay out sums in US dollars, but because of Ecuador's low cost of living, most Ecuadorian ATM users want a small amount of money, so US$1 bills are needed. The ATMs often run out of the popular US$1 and US$5 dollar bills (although travelers wanting US$20 or more rarely have a problem). Recently, a rash of false one-dollar bills was reported. Genuine greenbacks have a few, very fine, 4mm-long blue or red silk threads embedded into the paper and scattered randomly throughout the bill. Counterfeit versions also have the blue and red threads, but they are printed on and aren't as fine as the silk threads.

The bottom line is that travelers will be using US dollars, but exactly how the sucre-to-US-dollar process will be completed remains up in the air.

you can do one of two things (and not get charged any interest). Firstly, you can use a debit card (but it must be in the form of a credit card; ask your bank if you don't already have one of these). Alternatively, use a credit card by paying your entire credit-card bill and adding enough money to cover your trip. Otherwise, using ATMs will be very expensive.

It's hard to say whether Visa or Master-Card is better. Generally, ATMs accepting Visa are more widespread, but in the Galápagos, only MasterCard is accepted.

Credit Cards Credit cards can be useful, and most major cards are accepted, particularly in 1st-class restaurants, hotels, gift shops and travel agencies. Cheaper hotels, restaurants and stores don't want to deal with credit cards. Even if an establishment has a credit-card sticker in the window, don't assume that credit cards are accepted. The sticker may be for embellishment only.

Visa, MasterCard and Diners Club are the most widely accepted. American Express is less popular. These companies have offices in Quito; see the Quito & Around chapter for their locations. If you use a different card, you have to call home (collect calls are usually accepted) to report its loss and arrange for another card to be sent to you. Find out what telephone number you need to call before you leave home.

Credit-card transactions usually cost a small percentage of the bill. In North America and Europe, this cost is borne by the merchant. In Ecuador, the merchant will often add 4% to 10% to the bill in order to cover the transaction fee. Check this carefully – paying cash is often a better value.

Another use for credit cards is getting cash from a bank or ATM (see ATMs, earlier). Note that cash advances on credit cards, either from a bank or through an ATM, are charged the normal rate of interest (usually 15% to 20%) from the day you obtain the money. One way of avoiding this is to overpay your credit-card bill, thus leaving a positive balance in your account.

Not all bank branches will give cash advances.

Filanbanco Merger

Filanbanco, with its reliable, nationwide system of ATMs that accept Visa credit or debit cards, is slated to merge with Banco La Previsora in December 2000. Readers may find that the name of Filanbanco, in the text and map keys, may have changed.

International Transfers If you run out of money, it is a simple matter to have more sent to you – assuming, of course, that there's someone at home kind enough to send you some. A bank transfer is most quickly done by fax, although this will take at least three days. All you need to do is pick an Ecuadorian bank that will cooperate with your bank at home (eg, Bank of America, Bank of London & South America, Banco del Pacífico) and fax your family, friend or bank manager to deposit the money in your name at the bank of your choice. Commissions are likely to be charged by the bank sending the money, so find out about this from your bank at home before you go.

Recently, Western Union offices have opened in major cities. They offer a faster and more convenient way of receiving cash, but it is also more expensive. For example, receiving US$1000 in Quito costs US$75.

Change

Don't expect to be able to pay for inexpensive services with large bills, because change is often not available. Cabdrivers may say they don't have change simply to try to make a bit of extra money. It's worth asking drivers *'¿Tiene cambio de diez dolares?'* ('Do you have change for US$10?' – or whatever the size of your bill), to make sure you're not stuck with this. If traveling to small towns, bring a supply of small-denomination bills.

Security

Pickpockets prey on easy targets, and unsuspecting tourists are a prime choice. Avoid losing your money by following a few basic precautions: Carry money in inside pockets, money belts or pouches beneath your clothes. Don't carry a wallet in a pocket or a purse, as these are the first places pickpockets look. Divide your money and carry it in several places, some in an inside pocket and some in a money pouch, for example, so that if you are pickpocketed you don't lose all your cash.

If you are traveling for many months, it's a good idea to carry an emergency packet somewhere separate from all your other valuables. This emergency packet could be sewn into a jacket (don't lose the jacket!) or even carried in your shoe. Aside from money, it should contain a photocopy of the important pages of your passport in case it is lost or stolen. On the back of the photocopy, list the serial numbers of all your traveler's checks, airline tickets, credit cards and bank accounts, as well as any important telephone numbers. Also keep one high-denomination bill in with this emergency stash. You will probably never have to use it, but it's a good idea not to put all your eggs into one basket. In most decent hotels, you can leave money and valuables in a safe-deposit box, although this is not very reliable in the most basic hotels.

Costs

Costs in Ecuador are among the lowest in Latin America. However, they can fluctuate widely – the price of travel basics such as hotels, meals and transportation can almost double or halve from year to year, but they are still cheap by Western standards. It is important to note that the prices given in this book were researched just before the dollarization process went into effect, and rates could change significantly and quickly.

During the past few years, Ecuador has developed a two-tier pricing system in which foreign visitors pay a lot more money than Ecuadorian residents for some services. Train rides are in the range of US$10 to US$20 for foreigners, compared to less than US$1 for residents. Some flights cost roughly twice as much for foreigners as for residents. National-park entrance fees are much higher for foreigners (per person, US$10 or

US$20 on the mainland, US$100 in the Galápagos; valid for a week or two weeks). Many top-end hotels charge foreigners as much as twice what they charge nationals.

Travelers on a budget can save money by using buses and by staying in budget and mid-range hotels, none of which are currently subject to the so-called 'gringo tax.' Restaurants should also provide meals at the same price for everyone.

If you're on a very tight budget, you'll find that you can easily manage on a bare-bones budget of US$10 per day, including the occasional luxury such as a bottle of beer or a movie. If you're really economical, you could manage on less if you stay in the very cheapest and most basic hotels and eat the meal of the day in restaurants.

If you can afford to spend a little more, however, you'll probably enjoy yourself more. The luxury of a simple room with a private hot shower and a table on which to write letters home can be had for as little as US$3 per person if you know where to go – this book will show you where.

Saving time and energy by flying back from a remote destination that required several days of land travel to reach is also recommended. At present, the most expensive internal flight on the Ecuadorian mainland is about US$53 (for foreigners flying from Quito to the Amazon), and most flights are much cheaper. A taxi, particularly when you're in a group, isn't expensive and usually costs less than US$1 for short but convenient rides. Even if you demand the very best available, in most parts of Ecuador it will cost much less than it would wherever home may be.

There are those travelers who spend most of their time worrying over how to make every penny stretch further. It seems they spend more time looking at their finances than looking at the places they're visiting. Of course, many travelers are on a grand tour of South America and want to make their money last, but a person can get so burned out on squalid hotels and bad food that the grand tour becomes an endurance test. Consider whether you'd like to spend eight months traveling comfortably and enjoyably or a full year of strain and sacrifice.

There is one major stumbling block for budget travelers, and that is the Galápagos. Getting there is expensive, and staying there isn't particularly cheap either. Read the Galápagos chapter before you decide whether you want to go.

Tipping & Bargaining

Better restaurants add a 10% tax and a 10% service charge to the bill. If the service has been satisfactory, you can add another 5% for the waitperson. Cheaper restaurants don't include tax or service charge. If you want to tip your server, do so directly – don't just leave the money on the table.

Tip porters at the airport about US$0.25 per bag and bellboys at a 1st-class hotel about US$0.50 per bag. Hairdressers receive US$0.50 or more for special services. Taxi drivers are not normally tipped, but you can leave them the small change from a metered ride.

If you go on a guided tour, a tip is expected. Unfortunately, some Ecuadorian tour companies pay guides low wages, so the guides make more in tips than in wages. If you are in a group, tip a top-notch guide about US$2 to US$3 per person per day – less for a half-day tour. Tip the driver about half as much as the guide. If you engage a private guide, tip about US$10 per day. These suggestions are for professional, bilingual guides – tip more if you feel your guide was exceptional and less if he or she wasn't that great.

If you're going on a long tour that involves guides, cooks, crew (eg, in the Galápagos), tip about US$25 to US$50 per client per week, and distribute among all the personnel.

If you are driving and decide to park your car on the street, boys or men will offer to look after your car. Give them about US$0.20 for several hours, a few cents for a short time.

Bargaining is accepted and expected in markets when buying crafts, and occasionally in other situations. If you're not sure whether bargaining is appropriate, try asking for a *descuento* (discount). These are often given at hotels, tour agencies, gift shops and other places where tourists spend money.

Taxes

A total of 20% (10% tax and 10% service charge) is added to bills in the best hotels and restaurants, although the cheapest hotels and restaurants don't add anything. Ask if you aren't sure. There is no system of rebates for international travelers.

POST & COMMUNICATIONS

Post offices often have a number of nearby kiosks, which are good places to buy postcards, aerograms, envelopes etc.

Postal Rates

Because of the incredible fluctuations in local currency values, it is not possible to give accurate mail rates. Expect to pay roughly US$0.50 to mail a letter overseas. Parcels are expensive to send (see Sending Parcels, later in this section).

For reasons that aren't clear, letters to the same destination but mailed from different towns are often charged different postage. Apparently, some post offices aren't sure what the correct postage is, or perhaps they don't have the correct denomination of stamps.

Sending Mail

Most letters and postcards from Ecuador should arrive at their destinations, sometimes in as little as a week to the USA or Europe, although closer to two weeks is normal. Aerograms are nice because they contain no enclosure and are more likely to arrive safely. For a few cents extra, you can send mail *certificado,* and although it's not likely to get lost this way, there isn't much you can do if it doesn't arrive.

Ask to see each letter postmarked at the post office – it's a good way to help ensure that your mail reaches its destination. A reader wrote in early 1999 that of 28 cards left in a Quito mailbox, only seven arrived. Dishonest postal workers will sometimes steam off the stamps to re-use them and throw away your mail.

Post offices are marked on the maps in this book. In some smaller towns, it is often just part of a house or a corner of a municipal office. In Quito and Guayaquil, there are several post offices dotted around town. Business hours are usually 9 am to 5 pm weekdays. In the bigger cities, they're open a half-day on Saturday.

Sending Parcels

Ecuadorian air-mail rates for parcels have soared in the last few years, so Ecuador is no longer a cheap place from which to mail your extra souvenirs home.

Parcels weighing less than 2kg can be sent from most post offices. Heavier parcels should be mailed from the Quito post office at Ulloa and Dávalos. Regulations change, so check in advance whether the parcel should be sealed or unsealed (for customs inspection) when you bring it to the post office. Recently, parcels had to be open and you had to seal it up in front of the postal official, so bring tape or strong string. The Quito clubhouse of the South American Explorers (see Useful Organizations, later) is usually up-to-date on this.

Courier companies in Quito and Guayaquil can send important parcels quickly to major airports around the world, but the addressee must come to the airport to pick up the parcel. This is a fast, reliable, but expensive service – about US$57 to the USA for a parcel weighing under 1kg.

Receiving Mail

Incoming mail is unreliable. A few letters may take as long as two months to arrive, and occasionally, some never make it. Ask your friends to photocopy important letters and to send two copies. Alternatively, use a courier service for important documents. FedEx charges about US$54 to send an 8oz document from the USA to Quito. For easy communication, see Fax, Email & Internet Access, later in this section.

Most travelers use either the post office's *lista de correos* (poste restante/general delivery) or American Express for receiving mail. Members of the South American Explorers can receive mail at the Quito club-

house (see Useful Organizations, later in this chapter).

Mail sent to the post office is filed alphabetically; so if it's addressed to John Gillis Payson, Esq it could well be filed under 'G' or 'E' instead of 'P.' It should be addressed in the following manner: John PAYSON, Lista de Correos, Correos Central, Quito (or town and province of your choice), Ecuador. Ask your loved ones to print your last name and avoid appending witticisms such as 'World Traveler Extraordinaire.'

American Express (☎ 02-560 488) will also hold mail for clients addressed in the following manner: John PAYSON, c/o American Express, Apartado 2605, Quito, Ecuador. The street address is Avenida Amazonas 339 (in the Ecuadorian Tours building), and hours are 8 am to 5 pm weekdays.

Receiving small packages is usually no problem. If the package weighs more than 2kg, however, you will have to go to customs to retrieve it and perhaps pay duty.

Telephone

Telephone service is erratic everywhere and expensive if calling abroad. Christopher Isherwood described the Quito telephone service as 'about as reliable as roulette' (*The Condor and the Cows*, 1949), and it still has a long way to go. With a little patience you can usually place calls to anywhere, although long-distance and international calls from small or remote towns can be a problem. The phone service on the Galápagos has improved recently, but it remains somewhat unreliable.

Andinatel (mainly in the highlands and Oriente) and Pacifictel (mainly in the coastal lowlands) are the places to go for long-distance national and international telephone services. The offices are officially open 8 am to 10 pm daily, except in small and remote towns, where there may be shorter hours. These government-run institutions may become privatized soon. In addition, the city of Cuenca uses Etapa, a private telephone service.

Phone numbers with '09' before the six-digit number indicate that the number belongs to a mobile phone. See Mobile

Phones, later in this section, for more details about calling these numbers.

Calls within Ecuador The number of public phone booths is increasing. Unfortunately, they can be irritatingly complicated to use. Some booths use only one of two kinds of phone cards – Porta or BellSouth, which can be bought for various denominations and are usually sold in places convenient to the phone booths. Others accept only coins, and still others accept only *fichas* (tokens). For local calls within a city, you can often borrow a phone in a store or use a private phone offered by entrepreneurs on the street – they will dial the call for you (to make sure you are not calling your mum in London) and will charge you a few cents for the call. All but the most basic hotels will allow you to make local city calls.

Intercity calls can be dialed directly or through the operator at Andinatel or Pacifictel offices. Street entrepreneurs will also help you place long-distance calls.

If you need a national operator, dial ☎ 105. If you need information, dial ☎ 104. Unfortunately, telephone companies change numbers frequently; residents have said that their number has changed without even receiving notification from the phone company! In most major cities, you can reach the police by calling ☎ 101 or ☎ 911; otherwise, follow instructions given in public phone booths or ask at your hotel or other operator.

Local numbers have six digits. Two-digit area codes are divided by province:

TELEPHONE AREA CODES

Azuay	07
Bolívar	03
Cañar	07
Carchi	06
Chimborazo	03
Cotopaxi	03
El Oro	07
Esmeraldas	06
Galápagos	05
Guayas (includes Guayaquil)	04
Imbabura	06
Loja	07
Los Ríos	05
Manabí	05
Morona-Santiago (except Palora 03)	07
Napo	06
Orellana	06
Pastaza	03
Pichincha (includes Quito)	02
Sucumbíos	06
Tungurahua	03
Zamora-Chinchipe	07

Dial ☎ 09 for mobile phones. Note that dialing 09 usually results in much higher charges from anywhere, so ask about this before dialing an 09 number. Don't use area codes unless you are calling a number outside of the area you are calling from. If you need to dial an area code, you have to dial both digits in-country, but drop the 0 when calling from abroad.

International Calls The country code for Ecuador is 593. To call a number in Ecuador from abroad, call the international access code (011 from North America, 00 from Britain, 0011 from Australia), the country code (593), the area code *without* the 0, and the six-digit local telephone number.

The cheapest way to make an international call from Ecuador is to use the 'Net to Phone' services found in Internet cafes in major cities (see Fax, Email & Internet Access, later in this section). Smaller towns and remote villages lacking Internet facilities can often (but not always) communicate with Quito and connect an international call. These cost about US$7 for three minutes to the US and about US$10 to Europe if you call from an Andinatel or Pacifictel office. Waiting time can sometimes be as short as 10 minutes, but it can also take an hour or more to get through. Rates are 20% cheaper on Sunday and after 7 pm on other days.

The best hotels can connect international calls to your room at almost any time, but these are often heavily surcharged by the hotel. Collect or reverse-charge calls are possible to a few countries that have reciprocal agreements with Ecuador; these agreements vary from year to year, so you should ask at the nearest telephone office. International calling cards from your country don't work very well, because the local telephone companies don't make any money from them and are reluctant to use them.

If you are calling from a private phone, you can call the international operator (☎ 116) to place a call. After you have given the operator the number you want to call, hang up. You will be called back when the call gets through – anywhere from five minutes to over an hour. You will also receive a call back to be informed of the charges. These operator-assisted calls are the most expensive.

Mobile Phones Also known as cell phones, these are quite popular in Ecuador mainly because there is a long wait to get lines installed into houses and businesses. When trying to reach someone on a mobile phone, you must dial ☎ 09 first. Few travelers will have any reason to carry a mobile phone with them, but they are available to rent for business travelers who need one. Ask the concierge or hotel desk what's available; this is a rapidly growing and changing facility.

International Phone Cards Subscribers to international phone cards from countries outside of Ecuador should check what their access number in Ecuador is. These calls may be more expensive than using local cards, but you get the advantage of an operator speaking your language. Some access numbers may require a local fee or may not be available from all phones.

Fax, Email & Internet Access

The phone offices and top-end hotels can send faxes for you, but they are expensive. Using the Internet to communicate is much cheaper.

Internet cafes have proliferated in the late 1990s. Quito is the main center, and there are dozens of places competing for your business. Rates are currently very cheap, at about US$1 an hour or less. Other cities are following suit, but still have only one or a few Internet cafes; Quito is definitely the place for the best choice and rates. In small towns with Internet access you need to place a long-distance call to get connected, which results in rates that are several times higher than in Quito. So if you want to surf, go to Quito. If you just want to check your email, you can find a pricey connection in most towns.

Some hotels allow you to connect your laptop to their telephone lines; just unplug the phone and plug in your laptop. The connections are the same as those used in the USA. Then you can either use a local access number with AOL or CompuServe (check with your provider for the most recent number); or, if you are traveling in Ecuador for a long time, sign up with a local Internet provider. Some hotels allow you to use the hotel computer to check your email.

Email access is available to members of the South American Explorers at the Quito clubhouse (see Useful Organizations, later in this chapter).

INTERNET RESOURCES

The World Wide Web is a rich resource for travelers. You can research your trip, hunt down bargain airfares, book hotels, check on weather conditions and chat with locals and other travelers about the best places to visit (or avoid!).

There's no better place to start your Internet explorations than the Lonely Planet Web site (www.lonelyplanet.com). Here you'll find succinct summaries on traveling to most places on earth, postcards from other travelers and the Thorn Tree bulletin board, where you can ask questions before you go or dispense advice when you get back. You can also find travel news and updates for many of our most popular guidebooks, and the subWWWay section links you to the most useful travel resources elsewhere on the Web.

There are several other Web sites to get you started learning about Ecuador before you get there or after you arrive. If you read Spanish, you can access several of Ecuador's newspapers at the sites listed under Newspapers & Magazines, later in this chapter. The South American Explorers has an excellent Web site: www.samexplo .org. Ecuador Explorer has general travel and tour information and a good overview of what the country has to offer: www .ecuadorexplorer.com. The Gourmet Club lists Ecuador's best restaurants and hotels, sells topographical maps, provides other information and allows you to make purchases and reservations online at www .bestdealecuador.com. A site containing news, directories, economic developments and historical background is maintained by the Ecuadorian embassy in Washington, DC, at www.ecuador.org. The Galápagos Coalition has a Web site with a comprehensive virtual library worth a peek: www.law .emory.edu/PI/GALAPAGOS/. For news with a strong ecotourism angle, check out www2.planeta.com/mader/ecotravel/south/ ecuador/ecuador1.html – if that doesn't work, start at www2.planeta.com/ and navigate.

Many other Web sites with a narrower focus are listed in appropriate parts of this book.

BOOKS

Most books are published in different editions by different publishers in different countries. As a result, a book might be a hardcover rarity in one country but readily available in paperback in another. Fortunately, bookstores and libraries can search by title or author, so they are the best place for advice on the availability of the following recommendations. For books published in Ecuador, the date and publishers are provided to aid you in tracking the book down.

There are two particularly well-known bookstores in Ecuador that sell a selection of new books in English, French, German and Spanish. In Guayaquil, go to the Librería Científica, at Luque 225. In Quito, there is Libri Mundi, the best-known bookstore in Ecuador; it is at JL Mera 851.

An excellent source of books about Latin America is the South American Explorers – contact the US office or Web site for a catalog, which may have books that are not easily available from your bookseller. The Quito clubhouse sells only to members. Some titles listed here can be found only in Ecuador.

Since the last edition, many books have unfortunately gone out-of-print, such as Tom Miller's *The Panama Hat Trail* (one of the best travelogues with a purpose in Ecuador) and Henri Michaux's quirky and mystical prose/poetry *Ecuador – a Travel Journal*. It's too bad – maybe these and many others will be reprinted, and your library may be a source of out-of-print books.

Lonely Planet

Other guidebooks can complement this one, especially if you are visiting South American countries other than Ecuador. *Read This First: Central & South America* is part of a new series of LP books that are specifically geared toward how to prepare and what to expect on your trip.

Lonely Planet's South American guides include the following titles: *Argentina, Uruguay & Paraguay; Bolivia; Chile & Easter Island; Colombia; Brazil; Peru* and *Venezuela*. Budget travelers planning to cover a large part of the continent should consider LP's *South America on a shoestring*.

LP's *Latin American Spanish phrasebook* is helpful for travelers without a good grasp of the most commonly used language in

Ecuador. *Healthy Travel – Central & South America* is an excellent, pocket-size book for tips on treating common illnesses, coping with high altitudes and avoiding dangerous encounters with wildlife; it has an illustrated guide to medicinal rainforest flora as well.

These and other Lonely Planet products can be found in bookstores worldwide or ordered online at www.lonelyplanet.com. Click on 'Propaganda' and you're on your way.

Guidebooks

The Ecotourist's Guide to the Ecuadorian Amazon, by Rolf Wesche et al (1995, CEPEIGE, Quito), is a practical guide to ecotourism in the Napo Province area. This was followed by *Defending Our Rainforest: A Guide to Community-based Ecotourism in the Ecuadorian Amazon,* by Rolf Wesche et al (1999, Acción Amazonia, Quito). Both are recommended. *Guía de Parques Nacionales y Reservas del Ecuador,* created by multiple agencies (1998, Quito), is a glossy book with information in Spanish about the national parks; a separate CD has an English version.

Climbing & Hiking in Ecuador, by Rob Rachowiecki & Mark Thurber, is a detailed guide to climbing Ecuador's mountains. It also describes many beautiful hikes, some of which are simple day hikes suitable for the beginner. There is also a series of climbing guides to Ecuador's more popular mountains by Jorge Anhalzer. These four-page guides have a sketch map of the *ruta normal* (normal route) on the back page and are available in Quito. They're lightweight, if nothing else.

If the Pacific coast intrigues you as much as Andean mountains, *Walking the Beaches of Ecuador,* by José-Germán Cárdenas & Karen Marie Greiner (1988, Quito), is for you. The authors walked or jogged the entire length of Ecuador's coastline. It's hard to find, but ask around.

Natural History

Robert Ridgely and Paul Greenfield are the authors of *A Guide to the Birds of Ecuador*. This book should be available from Cornell University Press in 2001. Although over a decade late, it is going to be a very good book! Meanwhile, ornithologists have to avail themselves of Hilty & Brown's *A Guide to the Birds of Colombia,* which covers many of Ecuador's species. For beginners looking for an introduction, *Common Birds of Amazonian Ecuador,* by Chris Canaday & Lou Jost (1997, Libri Mundi, Quito), is a good choice.

Birding Ecuador, by Clive Green, details the author's several long bird watching trips to Ecuador. The sketch maps, practical information and checklist are very useful to bird watchers. The book is available from the American Birding Association (ABA; ☎ 719-578-0607, 800-834-7736, fax 719-578-9705, abasales@abasales.com, PO Box 6599, Colorado Springs, CO 80934, USA); you can visit the association's Web site at www.americanbirding.org. The ABA also has *Birds of the High Andes,* by Fjeldsa & Krabb, an excellent, detailed, well-illustrated and indispensable guide for those interested in Andean avifauna (it costs around US$140). The ABA also sells several cassette tapes of Ecuadorian bird calls.

Neotropical Rainforest Mammals – A Field Guide, by Louise H Emmons, is essential for those seriously interested in tropical mammals. The book is detailed and portable, and almost 300 species are described and illustrated. Although some of the mammals included are found only in other neotropical countries, many of Ecuador's mammals, and certainly all the known rainforest inhabitants, are found within the book's pages.

Flora del Ecuador and *Fauna del Ecuador,* both by Erwin Patzelt and published in Ecuador in Spanish, are heavy encyclopedic tomes available in Ecuador. Ethnobotanists will want *A Field Guide to Medicinal and Useful Plants of the Upper Amazon,* by James L Castner et al.

There are several excellent books on South American natural history which contain some information on Ecuador. Michael Andrews' *Flight of the Condor* (1982, Little, Brown & Co) is a common favorite but may be out-of-print.

For the layperson interested in rainforest biology, try the entertaining and readable *Tropical Nature,* by Adrian Forsyth & Kenneth Miyata. Forsyth is also the author of the children's book *Journey Through a Tropical Jungle.* Other good natural-history books include *A Neotropical Companion,* by John C Kricher, and Catherine Caulfield's *In the Rainforest,* which emphasizes the problems of the loss of the rainforest.

A new recommendation is *Ecuador and Its Galápagos Islands: The Ecotraveller's Wildlife Guide,* edited by David L Pearson & Les Beletsky. It provides a general overview of both mainland and Galápagos wildlife.

Galápagos Islands

The excellent *A Traveler's Guide to the Galápagos Islands,* by Barry Boyce, is written by an expert tour operator to the islands. It has detailed and lengthy listings of the better boats and tour agencies.

The best general guide to the history, geology and plant and animal life of these islands is the thorough and highly recommended *Galápagos: A Natural History,* by Michael H Jackson, who is also Galápagos guide. This book was recently out-of-print, but a reprint is planned. Another good, more recent and more portable choice is *Galápagos Wildlife – A Visitor's Guide,* by David Horwell & Pete Oxford. Maps of the main visitor sites are included, and the main author runs Galápagos Adventure Tours in the UK and knows what he wrote about.

Avid birders will like *The Collins Field Guide to the Birds of Galápagos,* by Michael Harris et al. This excellent handbook illustrates and fully describes every Galápagos bird species. A good and more recent book is *A Guide to the Birds of the Galápagos Islands,* by Isabel Castro & Antonia Phillips.

Amateur botanists will want Eileen Schofield's booklet *Plants of the Galápagos Islands,* which describes 87 common plants and is much more convenient than the classic, encyclopedic *Flora of the Galápagos Islands,* by Wiggins & Porter. A newer choice is *Flowering Plants of the Galápagos,* by Conley K McMullen.

Snorkelers and divers should look for *Reef Fish Identification – Galápagos,* edited by Paul Humann et al. Dive and gift shops in oceanographical aquariums and museums in the US sell waterproof cards illustrating common fish of the Pacific. These can be taken underwater and help in identifying some of the Galápagos species. Unfortunately, these cards are not available in Ecuador.

Galápagos: Islands Born of Fire, by Tui de Roy, is a beautiful book illustrated by the Galápagos' premier photographer, Tui de Roy. She has had several other books published.

The most famous of the visitors to the Galápagos was Charles Darwin, who was there in 1835. You can read his *Origin of Species* or his journal *The Voyage of the Beagle.* These 19th-century texts are rather dated and make heavy reading today. There are numerous modern biographies – including *Charles Darwin – Voyaging: A Biography,* by Janet Browne, and *Darwin: The Life of a Tormented Evolutionist,* by Adrian Desmond et al. Readers interested in a layperson's introduction to evolutionary theory can try the amusingly written but roughly accurate *Darwin for Beginners,* by Jonathan Miller & Borin Van Loon. Jonathan Weiner's *The Beak of the Finch* describes current research on the evolution of Darwin's finches.

Floreana, by Margaret Wittmer (various editions and publishers), describes the life of one of the earliest colonists of the islands (Wittmer arrived in 1932 and still lives there).

No list of books about this fascinating laboratory of evolution is complete without mentioning Kurt Vonnegut's whimsical novel *Galápagos,* in which a group of vacationers are stranded on the islands and become the progenitors for a strange new twist in human evolution. It makes for a good read on the plane ride to the islands.

Indigenous People

Going back to the arrival of the Spanish conquistadors, the best book is undoubtedly John Hemming's excellent *The Conquest of the Incas.* Although this deals mainly with Peru (the heart of the Inca Empire), there are several sections on Ecuador. Serious students will be enlightened by *Costume and Identity in Highland Ecuador,* by Ann P Rowe et al.

In the Oriente, the Shuar are described by Michael Harner using their old name, *The Jivaro: People of the Sacred Waterfalls.* An eye-opening book about the Huaorani (formerly called the Aucas) is Joe Kane's *Savages.* Randy Smith, a Canadian who has worked with and for the Huaorani for over a decade, wrote *Crisis Under the Canopy: Tourism and Other Problems Facing the Present Day Huaorani* (available in Quito). Also of great interest is Mike Tidwell's *Amazon Stranger,* although the Cofan village chief, Randy Borman (a son of American missionaries who was raised in the rainforest), says that you should take it all with a pinch of salt. Other books about Ecuador's and South America's Indian peoples are available at Libri Mundi (see the beginning of the Books section).

Miscellaneous

Edward Whymper's *Travels Amongst the Great Andes of the Equator,* first published in 1891 and now reprinted, is an exceptional book describing the author's 1880 mountaineering expedition, which made eight first-ascents of Ecuadorian peaks, including the highest, Chimborazo. There are also fascinating descriptions of travel in Ecuador a century ago, and the woodcut engravings are pure delight.

Living Poor, by Moritz Thomsen, is a classic account of Peace Corps life in coastal Ecuador during the 1960s. Unlike most volunteers, who are in their 20s, Thomsen was 48 when he arrived for a four-year stint in one of Ecuador's poorest areas. He writes with eloquence and humor about a place and people he obviously grew to love.

Two Wheels & a Taxi: A Slightly Daft Adventure in the Andes, by Virginia Urrutia, is the author's story of her bicycling trip around Ecuador, accompanied by a local cabdriver for logistical support. Urrutia was 70 when she made the trip – an inspiration to us all.

Crafts of Ecuador is available in Ecuador and features fabulous photos and text by Pablo Cuvi. He also wrote *In the eyes of my people,* an excellent Ecuadorian photoessay, but it's now difficult to find. It's worth the effort though!

A Cloud Forest Kitchen, by Sandra Statz (a co-owner of the Intag Cloud Forest Preserve), describes how to cook delicious dishes simply with local ingredients, some of which you won't find in your local supermarket.

Finally, linguists should pick up the inexpensive booklet *Spanish Colloquialisms – Ecuador,* by Nick Crowder; it has a few words that you might not have come across.

FILMS

The Lonely Planet *Ecuador* video is a good way to get an understanding of the experience of traveling in Ecuador before actually going there; it's available in stores or on the LP Web site (www.lonelyplanet.com) under Propaganda. General travel videos about Ecuador, the Amazon and the Galápagos exist in various formats in Ecuador and in many other countries. If buying in Ecuador, make sure the film is compatible with the system in your country (most are compatible only with North American systems). Many libraries lend videos as well as books; check them out.

NEWSPAPERS & MAGAZINES

Although Ecuador is a small country, there are literally dozens of newspapers available. Most towns of any size publish a local newspaper, which is useful for finding out what's screening in the local cinemas or catching up on the local gossip, but has little national news and even less international news. A better selection is available in Quito and Guayaquil.

The best newspapers that are published in Quito are the independent *El Comercio* (www.elcomercio.com) and the more liberal *Hoy* (www.hoy.com.ec); published in Guayaquil are the independent *El Telégrafo* and *El Universo* (www.eluniverso.com). They are all inexpensive. Ecuador's best-known news magazine is *Vistazo,* which is published every two weeks. It is popular, widely read and covers most of what is going on in Ecuador – politics, sports, economy etc. All the above are in Spanish.

A locally printed, somewhat abbreviated but up-to-date English version of the *Miami Herald* is available in Quito and Ecuador and costs about US$0.50. Other international newspapers are more expensive and are available at Libri Mundi bookstore in Quito, the reading rooms of the luxury hotels in Quito and Guayaquil, and at the international airports. These tend to be a couple of days old. Latin American editions of *Time* and *Newsweek* are also readily available at about US$2 each, and *The Economist* can be bought for US$4. All foreign editions are in English, but they have more space devoted to Latin American news.

Current information about the continent is available through two quarterly newsletters: the *South American Explorer,* published by the South American Explorers, and *The Latin American Travel Advisor.* (See Useful Organizations, later in this chapter.)

Free English-language newspapers and magazines are available in Quito; basically, they provide lots of advertising for local hotels, restaurants, and travel agencies, with an occasional article of interest.

RADIO & TV
There are about 15 television channels in Ecuador, although not all can be picked up throughout the country. Some remote towns receive only one or two channels, and the programming leaves much to be desired.

A cable network offers US satellite stations such as CNN, but only a few of the more expensive hotels have them. Some cheaper hotels offer cable, but it is mainly limited to Spanish-language broadcasts from Ecuador and other Latin American countries. If it's important to you, ask when you are checking in.

If you carry a portable radio when you travel, you'll find plenty of stations to choose from. There is more variety on radio than on TV, and you can listen to programs in Quichua as well as in Spanish. There are

some 300 stations, including about 10 cultural and 10 religious ones. HCJB (89.3 FM in Quito and 102.5 FM in Guayaquil) is a missionary radio station with programming in English and a nightly world-news roundup at 8:50 pm. Owners of portable shortwave radios can easily pick up BBC World Service, Voice of America and Radio Australia.

PHOTOGRAPHY & VIDEO
Film & Equipment
Definitely bring everything you'll need. Camera gear is very expensive in Ecuador, and film choice is limited. Some good films are unavailable, such as Kodachrome slide film. However, Ektachrome and Fujichrome slide films are available. Ordinary print film, such as Kodacolor and Fujicolor, is the most widely available and reasonably priced (about the same as in the US) and is usually the best buy. Slide film is more expensive. If buying film in small towns, check the expiration date.

Developing
Don't have slide film developed in Ecuador if you can help it, as processing is mediocre (though amateur photographers should find print developing to be OK). On the other hand, carrying around exposed film for months is asking for washed-out results. It is best to send it home as soon as possible after it's exposed.

To avoid problems with the mail service, send film home with a friend. You'll often meet people heading back to whichever continent you're from, and they can usually be persuaded to do you this favor, particularly if you offer to take them out to dinner. By buying either process-paid film or pre-paid film mailers, you can place the exposed film in the mailer and not worry about the costs. The last thing you want to do on your return from a trip is worry about how you're going to find the money to develop a few dozen rolls of film.

Technical Tips
Equatorial shadows are very strong and come out almost black on photographs. A bright but hazy day often makes for better

photographs than a very sunny one. Photography in open shade or using fill-in flash will help. The best time for shooting is when the sun is low – the first and last two hours of the day. If you are heading into the Oriente, you will need high-speed film, a flash and a tripod to take photographs in the jungle. The amount of light penetrating the layers of vegetation is surprisingly low.

Photographing People

The Ecuadorian people make wonderful subjects for photos. From an Indian child to the handsomely uniformed presidential guard, the possibilities of 'people pictures' are endless. However, most people resent having a camera thrust in their faces, and people in markets will often proudly turn their backs on pushy photographers. Ask for permission with a smile or a joke, and if this is refused, don't become offended. Some people believe that bad luck can be brought upon them by the eye of the camera. Others are just fed up with seeing their pictures used in books, magazines and postcards; somebody is making money at their expense. Sometimes a 'tip' is asked. Be aware and sensitive of people's feelings – it is not worth upsetting someone to get a photograph.

It is worth bringing some photographs from home – of your family and the places where you live, work or go to school. They will be of interest to the Ecuadorian friends you make, and they're a great icebreaker if your Spanish is limited.

The Galápagos

Any kind of camera will enable amateur photographers to get satisfying pictures in the Galápagos – the animals will stay near the trails and can often be approached within 2m or 3m.

Advanced photographers will have their own favorite lenses and equipment. A few suggestions: First, nonprofessional photographers routinely use two 36-exposure rolls of film per day in the Galápagos – and then complain that they didn't bring enough. Film is rarely available on the boats, so make sure you bring enough.

Don't forget spare batteries for your camera and flash unit. If your camera battery goes dead, you may not find another in the islands. Also bring resealable plastic bags for wet panga rides. Specially designed waterproof camera bags are available from photography stores, but plastic bags are an adequate and much cheaper alternative. Lead foil bags are a good idea to protect your film from airport X-ray machines.

A zoom lens is very useful. You can change from a wide-angle landscape shot to a telephoto opportunity of a pelican flying over your head without having to change lenses.

Finally, remember to make note of what you photographed after each island excursion, and label each film canister. Otherwise, when you get home, you'll find you can't remember which island or bird is which.

TIME

The Ecuadorian mainland is five hours behind Greenwich Mean Time, and the Galápagos are six hours behind. Mainland time is equivalent to Eastern Standard Time in North America. Because of Ecuador's location on the equator, days and nights are of equal length year-round, and there is no daylight saving time.

It is appropriate to mention here that punctuality is not one of the things Latin Americans are famous for.

ELECTRICITY

Ecuador uses 110 volts, 60 cycles, AC (the same as in North America, but not compatible with Britain and Australia). Plugs have two flat prongs, as in North America.

WEIGHTS & MEASURES

Ecuador uses the metric system, and so does this book. For travelers who still use miles, ounces, bushels, leagues, rods, magnums, stones and other quaint and arcane expressions, there is a metric conversion table at the back of this book.

LAUNDRY

There are almost no self-service laundry machines in Ecuador. Almost all laundries

Spinning Otavaleña

Woven 'friendship' bracelets make great small, light gifts.

The most famous Ecuadorian souvenir - the panama hat

Handbags - handy while traveling

Stock up on Spanish vocabulary and healthy vitamins at a local produce market.

Memorable rooftop view from below Alausí

Clambering aboard for a rooftop adventure

Rancheras, a common, if uncomfy, way to travel

In the Oriente, hire someone to row, row, row you gently down Río Napo in a dugout canoe.

(lavanderías) only do dry cleaning, although there are a few in Quito, Guayaquil and some other towns popular with travelers where you can have your clothes washed and dried if you leave them for a few hours.

Many hotels will have someone to do your laundry; this can cost very little in the cheaper hotels (about US$1 for a change of clothes). The major problem is that you might not see your clothes again for two or three days, particularly if it is raining and they can't be dried. There are faster laundry services in the better hotels, but rates are charged by the piece and are often very expensive. Then tax is added!

If you want to wash the clothes yourself, ask the hotel staff (in budget hotels) where to do this. Most cheaper hotels will show you a huge cement sink and scrubbing board, which is much easier to use than a bathroom washbasin. There is often a well-like section next to the scrubbing board that is full of clean water. Don't dunk your clothes in this water, as it is often used as an emergency water supply in the case of water failure. Instead, use a bowl or bucket to scoop water out, or run water from a tap.

TOILETS

Ecuadorian plumbing is poor and has very low pressure. Putting toilet paper into the bowl may clog the system, so a waste receptacle is provided for the used paper. A basket of used toilet paper may seem unsanitary, but it is much better than clogged bowls and water overflowing onto the floor. A well-run cheap hotel will ensure that the receptacle is emptied and the toilet cleaned daily. The same applies to restaurants and other public toilets. The more expensive hotels have adequate flushing capabilities.

Public toilets are limited mainly to bus terminals, airports and restaurants. Lavatories are called *Servicios Higiénicos* and are usually marked 'SS.HH' – a little confusing until you learn the abbreviation. People needing to use the lavatory will often go into a restaurant and ask to use the *baño;* toilet paper is rarely available, so the experienced traveler carries a personal supply.

Note that some public lavatories in the better restaurants etc provide hand towels. If they are used and damp, you might be better off shaking your hands dry to avoid some possible infection.

Because of the lack of public lavatories, men tend to urinate outdoors much more than visitors may be used to, particularly in areas lacking restaurants or similar facilities. Behind trees, against walls, behind buses, up alleys – it is a common, discreet but unremarkable sight. Women in towns are likely to ask a restaurant if they can use the facilities, and in the country, local *campesino* (peasant or farmer) women may urinate outdoors simply by squatting down with their voluminous skirts around them.

HEALTH

It's true that most people traveling for any length of time in South America are likely to have an occasional mild stomach upset. It's also true that if you take the appropriate precautions before, during and after your trip, it's unlikely that you will become seriously ill.

There are two authoritative Web sites for travel health: the official site of the Centers for Disease Control and Prevention and the official site of the World Health Organization. Their Web sites are at www.cdc.gov and www.who.int, respectively.

Travel Health Guides

LP's new *Healthy Travel – Central & South America* is an excellent, inexpensive pocket-size guide to minimizing health risks while traveling in Latin America. Written by Dr Isabelle Young and a team of travel-health experts, the book includes tips on treating common travel illnesses, coping with high altitudes and avoiding dangerous encounters with wildlife, as well as a comprehensive first-aid section and an illustrated guide to useful rainforest plants.

Vaccinations

Vaccinations are the most important part of your pre-departure health preparations. The Ecuadorian authorities do not, at present, require anyone to have an up-to-date international vaccination card to enter the country, but you are strongly advised to read the following list and receive the ones appropriate for your trip. Pregnant women should consult with their doctor before taking these vaccinations.

The **yellow fever** vaccination is very important if you are planning a trip to the jungles of the Oriente or the coastal lowlands, but it's not necessary if you intend to stay in the highlands and Galápagos. This vaccination lasts 10 years.

The **typhoid** vaccination can be taken orally (in three or four doses; the vaccine lasts five years) or by a single injection (which lasts three years). The oral vaccine needs to be completed one week before you start malaria pills.

Hepatitis comes in five forms: A, B, C, D and E. Three of those (B, C and D) are spread by blood or sexual contact and can become long-term health problems; there is a vaccine for B. Latin America is not a particular hotspot for hepatitis B, but carrier rates in some parts of the Amazon region are high. Hepatitis C is mainly spread through blood transfusions and shouldn't be much of a worry for travelers. Hepatitis D only occurs in conjunction with hepatitis B. A and E are spread via contaminated food or water and are common in Latin America (especially A), but once you've had them, you're immune for life.

Protection from hepatitis A can be provided either with the antibody gamma globulin (this is not a vaccine, but it protects you for two to six months) or with the hepatitis A vaccine (there is no vaccine for hepatitis E). The vaccine provides long-term immunity after an initial course of two injections and a booster at one year. It may be more expensive than gamma globulin, but it certainly has many advantages, including length of protection and ease of administration. It takes about three weeks to provide satisfactory protection, so plan ahead. Gamma globulin is an antibody that reduces the chances of hepatitis infection. Because it may interfere with the development of immunity, it should not be given until at least 10 days after administration of

the last vaccine needed; it should also be given as close as possible to departure, as it is most effective during the first few weeks after administration (its effectiveness gradually lessens within three and six months).

Since the outbreak of **cholera** in Latin America in 1990, many travelers have expressed interest in a vaccine for the disease. These are available but are not very good. Protection is estimated at about 50% to 80% efficient and only lasts for a maximum of six months. The disease is best prevented by clean eating habits (see Cholera, later in this section).

In addition, most people in developed countries get a **diphtheria-tetanus** injection and oral **polio** vaccine while they are in school. You should get boosters for these every 10 years.

Medical Insurance

However fit and healthy you are, *do* take out a medical-insurance policy, preferably one with provisions for flying you home in the event of a medical emergency. Even if you don't get sick, you might be involved in an accident. Shop around for the best policy, and be sure to read the fine print. Some policies will not cover 'dangerous activities' such as scuba diving, climbing or motorcycle riding – try to avoid this type of policy. (See also Travel Insurance under Visas & Documents, earlier in this chapter.)

First-Aid Kit

The scope of your first-aid kit should depend on your knowledge of first-aid procedures, where and how far off the beaten track you are going, how long you will need the kit and how many people will be sharing it. The following is a suggested checklist that you should amend as required. A convenient way of carrying your first-aid kit so that it doesn't get crushed is in a small plastic container with a sealing lid, such as Tupperware.

Don't use medications indiscriminately, and be aware of their side effects. Some people may be allergic to things as simple as aspirin. Antibiotics such as tetracycline can make you extra sensitive to the sun, thus increasing the chance of severe sunburn. Antibiotics are not recommended for prophylactic use – they destroy the body's natural resistance to diarrhea and other diseases. Lomotil will temporarily stop the symptoms of diarrhea, but it will not cure the problem. Motion sickness or antihistamine medications can make you drowsy.

Although many drugs can be easily bought in Ecuadorian pharmacies, you should be aware that some drugs that have been banned in North America or Europe are still sold in third-world countries (including Ecuador) where regulations are lax. Make sure you buy the drug you need and not some strange mixture that may not be good for you. Check expiration dates on over-the-counter medicines.

Health Precautions

Several other things must be considered before leaving home. If you wear prescription glasses or contacts, make sure you have a spare pair and the prescription. The tropical sun is strong, so you may want to have a prescription pair of sunglasses made.

Also buy sunblock with a minimum SPF of 15, or 30 if you are fair or burn easily. High-SPF sunblock is hard to find in Ecuador outside of Quito.

Ensure that you have enough of the prescription medicines you use regularly. Have a recent dental examination rather than risk a dental problem in Ecuador.

Finally, frequent hand-washing with soap (especially before eating) goes a long way toward preventing the spread of infections and diseases; don't dry your hands afterward on a restaurant hand towel that looks damp and well-used – it might have the germs that you just washed off!

Water Purification

Tap water for drinking or washing fruits and vegetables must be purified. The most effective method is to boil it continuously for 20 minutes, which is obviously inconvenient.

Various water-purifying tablets are available, but most of them aren't wholly effective – the hepatitis virus may survive. The most effective have iodine in them, but they

Medical Kit Checklist

Following is a list of items you should consider including in your medical kit – consult your pharmacist for brands available in your country.

❑ **Aspirin or paracetamol** (acetaminophen in the USA) – for pain or fever

❑ **Antihistamine** – for allergies, eg, hay fever; to ease the itch from insect bites or stings; and to prevent motion sickness

❑ **Cold and flu tablets, throat lozenges and nasal decongestant**

❑ **Multivitamins** – consider taking for long trips, when dietary vitamin intake may be inadequate

❑ **Antibiotics** – consider including these if you're traveling well off the beaten track; see your doctor, as they must be prescribed, and carry the prescription with you

❑ **Loperamide or diphenoxylate** –'blockers' for diarrhea

❑ **Prochlorperazine or metaclopramide** – for nausea and vomiting

❑ **Rehydration mixture** – to prevent dehydration, which may occur, for example, during bouts of diarrhea; particularly important when traveling with children

❑ **Insect repellent, sunscreen, lip balm and eye drops**

❑ **Calamine lotion, sting relief spray or aloe vera** – to ease irritation from sunburn and insect bites or stings

❑ **Antifungal cream or powder** – for fungal skin infections and thrush

❑ **Antiseptic (such as povidone-iodine)** – for cuts and grazes

❑ **Bandages, Band-Aids (plasters) and other wound dressings**

❑ **Water purification tablets or iodine**

❑ **Scissors, tweezers and a thermometer** – note that mercury thermometers are prohibited by airlines

❑ **Sterile kit** – in case you need injections in a country with medical hygiene problems; discuss with your doctor

make the water taste strange and are not recommended for frequent or long-term use. A saturated iodine solution of iodine crystals placed in a small vial of water works fine; about four drops will treat a liter of water.

A variety of portable filters have recently come on the market. They are available from camping stores and tend to be expensive but are worthwhile for an extended trip.

Tooth-brushing and iced drinks are subjects of frequent debate. The safest way is to use bottled or purified water for brushing teeth and to avoid drinks with ice in them. However, if you are on an extended trip, you will tend to build up resistance over the months, and the minute amount of tap water ingested in tooth-brushing becomes increasingly less likely to hurt you. In 1st-class hotels and restaurants, the waiter may tell you that the water used for ice has been purified. This may be true, but you can never really be sure. It's a risk you either decide to take or not – depending on how much you want ice in your drink.

Diarrhea

Drastic changes in diet experienced while traveling can often make you susceptible to minor stomach ailments such as diarrhea. After you've been traveling in South America for a while, you seem to build up some sort of immunity, which just goes to show that most of the stomach problems you get when you first arrive aren't serious.

The major problem when you have diarrhea is fluid loss, which can lead to severe dehydration – you can actually dry out to the point of death if you go for several days without replacing the fluids you're losing – so drink plenty of liquids. Caffeine is a stomach irritant and a diuretic, so the best drinks are weak herbal tea, mineral water and caffeine-free soft drinks. Avoid milk, and stick to a light, bland diet, such as crackers, toast, rice and noodle soup. Cultured yogurt helps repopulate your intestine with beneficial organisms; other dairy products are not recommended. By giving your body plenty of fluids and bland food, you can often get rid of diarrhea naturally in about 24 to 36 hours. Rest as much as you can.

If you need to make a long journey, you can stop the symptoms of diarrhea by taking Lomotil or Imodium. These pills will not cure you, however, and it is likely that your diarrhea will recur after the drug wears off. Pepto-Bismol helps some people. Resting and drinking plenty of fluids is the most benign treatment.

Most people get diarrhea during a trip, but in most cases, it lasts only a few hours or a day and is a mild inconvenience rather than a major problem. You never know when it may hit you though, so it's worth carrying some toilet paper with you – many Ecuadorian toilets lack it just when you need it the most.

If you have recurring diarrhea, a course of antibiotics may help, but get a stool sample checked and talk to a doctor first.

Dysentery

If your diarrhea continues for several days and is accompanied by nausea, severe abdominal pain, gas and fever, and you find blood or mucus in your stool, it's likely that you have contracted dysentery. Although many travelers suffer from an occasional bout of diarrhea, dysentery is fortunately not very common. There are two types: amoebic and bacillary. It is not always obvious which kind you have. Although bacillary responds well to antibiotics, amoebic – which is rarer – involves more complex treatment. If you contract dysentery, you should seek medical advice.

Hepatitis

Most serious diseases are relatively uncommon. A depressingly common disease is hepatitis A, which is caused by ingesting contaminated food or water. Salads, uncooked or unpeeled fruit, unboiled drinks and dirty hands are the worst offenders. Infection risks are minimized by using bottled drinks, washing your own salads with purified water and paying scrupulous attention to your toilet habits.

If you get the disease, you'll know it. Your skin and especially the whites of your eyes will turn yellow, and you will literally feel so tired that it takes all your effort to go to the toilet. There is no cure except bed rest. If you're lucky, you'll be on your feet in a couple of weeks; if you're not, expect to stay in bed for months.

If you do get hepatitis A, it's not the end of the world. You may feel deathly ill, but people almost never suffer from permanent ill effects. If you're on a long trip, you don't have to give up and go home. Find a hotel that has a decent restaurant and get a room that isn't two flights of stairs and three hallways away from the nearest bathroom. Arrange with the hotel staff to bring you meals (high in calories and protein, but low in fat) and drinks as you need them, and go to bed. Chances are that you'll be fit enough to travel again within a month. Definitely avoid alcohol for several months, and don't take any medications (even over-the-counter) unless you check with a doctor.

Hepatitis B and hepatitis C are more serious, less common, and are transmitted via bodily fluid (by using a dirty syringe, by having unprotected sex etc). These forms of hepatitis are more likely to lead to long-lasting ill effects, and you'll need a blood test to identify which kind you have.

Cholera

Cholera is transmitted orally, by the ingestion of impure water or contaminated food. It is suggested that drinking only bottled drinks or purified water and avoiding all uncooked food is the best prevention – better than taking vaccinations. Talk to your physician if you are concerned about this. The bacteria that causes cholera is easily killed by boiling.

Cholera symptoms appear one to three days after infection, beginning with an extremely sudden, explosive onset of diarrhea that rapidly empties the gastrointestinal tract. The patient continues to produce a watery, mucuslike diarrhea, which is often accompanied by severe bouts of vomiting. Blood is not normally found in the stool. The main problem is rapid dehydration, which, if left untreated, can lead to death in a few days. Treatment is by oral or intravenous replacement of fluids and is simple and very effective.

Although thousands of cholera victims died in Latin America during the outbreak in the early 1990s, they were generally extremely poor people who either could not afford or were too far away from medical treatment. Very few cases of cholera have been reported in travelers, and of those, few if any resulted in death. If you maintain clean toilet and eating habits, you are more likely to get killed in a transportation accident than die from cholera.

Malaria

This is another disease to think about before leaving. Malarial mosquitoes don't live above 2500m, so if you plan on staying in the highlands, you needn't worry about malaria. (I've been told they don't live much above 500m in the Oriente and that they don't live in the Galápagos.) If you plan on visiting the lowlands, you should purchase antimalarial pills in advance, because they have to be taken from two weeks before until six weeks after your visit. Dosage and frequency of pill-taking varies from brand to brand, so check this carefully.

Chloroquine (called Aralen in Ecuador) is recommended for short-term protection. Long-term use of chloroquine *may* cause side effects, and travelers planning a long trip into the lowlands should discuss this risk against the value of protection with their physician. Recently, chloroquine-resistant strains of malaria have been found in Ecuador – the new recommended drug is mefloquine (Lariam), but this is less widely available and more expensive than chloroquine. Pregnant women are at a higher risk when taking antimalarials and should discuss this with their doctor. Fansidar is now known to cause sometimes fatal side effects; this drug should be used only under medical supervision.

The main symptoms of malaria are cold sweats and chills, alternating (with alarming rapidity) with high fevers and disorientation. One moment you are shivering under a pile of blankets and a few minutes later you are desperate for a cold sponge bath. If you do get malaria, the treatment is to begin by taking roughly a quadruple dose of antimalarial tablets, but this again varies with the brand, and medical advice should be sought.

Protection Against Mosquitoes If you are going to spend a great deal of time in tropical lowlands and prefer not to take antimalarial pills on a semipermanent basis, remember that malarial mosquitoes bite at night. You should wear long-sleeved shirts and long trousers from dusk till dawn, apply insect repellent frequently and sleep under a good mosquito net. Sleeping under a fan is also effective; mosquitoes don't like wind. Also, keep in mind that only some *Anopheles* species carry the disease, and they generally bite standing on their heads with their back legs up – mosquitoes that bite in a position horizontal to the skin are not malarial mosquitoes.

A woman traveler suggests that changing into a skirt or dress for dinner is not a good idea in mosquito-prone areas, as dusk is a particularly bad time for mosquitoes, and a skirt does little to keep the insects away. Keep the long pants and bug repellent on!

Mosquitoes that carry dengue fever and yellow fever can bite during the day. Most people don't worry too much about yellow fever because they should have been inoculated. However, in areas where dengue fever has been reported (often in some areas of the coast in the rainy season), it is worth covering up and using insect repellent during the day.

Dengue Fever

There is no prophylactic available for this mosquito-borne disease; the main preventative measure is to avoid mosquito bites (see Malaria, earlier in this section). The carrier is *Aedes aegypti* – a different species from that which carries the malarial parasite, but it is avoided in the same way.

A sudden onset of fever, headaches and severe joint and muscle pains are the first signs before a pink rash starts on the trunk of the body and spreads to the limbs and face. After about three or four days, the fever will subside, and recovery will begin. A shorter, less severe second bout may occur about a day later. There is no treatment except for bed rest and painkillers. Aspirin should not be taken. Be sure to remain hydrated and drink plenty of fluids.

Serious complications are not common, but full recovery can take up to a month or more. Although it is quite common in some Latin American countries, dengue fever is less common in Ecuador. Less than 3% of cases in the Americas are the more dangerous, hemorrhagic dengue fever, which may be lethal. It's not easy to tell the difference, so medical help should be sought.

Sexually Transmitted Diseases

Male and female prostitutes are quite active in the major cities, and the incidence of sexually transmitted diseases (including AIDS) is increasing among them. There are two effective ways to avoid contracting an STD: Have a monogamous relationship with an uninfected partner or abstain from sexual activity.

Travelers who are without an exclusive sexual partner and who are unwilling to abstain are strongly advised against using prostitutes. Having sex with a person other than a prostitute is somewhat safer, but is still far from risk-free. The use of condoms minimizes, but does not eliminate, the chances of contracting an STD. Condoms are widely available in Ecuadorian pharmacies, but they may be of poor quality – consider bringing your own.

Diseases such as syphilis and gonorrhea are marked by rashes or sores in the genital area and burning pain during urination. Women's symptoms may be less obvious than men's. These diseases can be cured relatively straightforwardly by antibiotics. If

Insect Repellent

The most effective ingredient in insect repellents is diethyl-metatoluamide, also known as deet. You can buy repellent with 90% or more of this ingredient; many brands (including those available in Ecuador) contain less than 15%, so buy it ahead of time. The rub-on lotions seem to be most effective, and pump sprays are good for spraying clothes – especially at the neck, wrist, waist and ankle openings.

Some people find that deet is irritating to the skin – they should use lower strengths. Everyone should avoid getting deet in the eyes, on the lips and in other sensitive regions. This stuff can dissolve plastic, so keep it off plastic lenses etc. If you put deet on your face and forehead, make sure to keep sweat out of your eyes.

Deet is toxic to children and shouldn't be used on their skin. Instead, try Avon's Skin So Soft, which has insect-repellent properties and is not toxic – get the oil, not the lotion. Camping stores sometimes sell insect repellents with names such as 'Green Ban' – these are made with natural products and are not toxic, but they seem to be less effective than repellents with deet.

Mosquito coils can sometimes be bought in Ecuador. They work like incense sticks and are fairly effective at keeping mosquitoes away.

not treated, they can become dormant, only to emerge a few months or years later in forms that are much more difficult to treat. Ecuadorian doctors know how to treat most STDs – if you have a rash, discharge or pain, go see a doctor. Herpes and AIDS are incurable as of this writing. Herpes is not fatal.

HIV/AIDS

HIV, the Human Immunodeficiency Virus, may develop into AIDS, Acquired Immune Deficiency Syndrome (SIDA in Spanish). HIV is a significant problem in Brazil, and the virus is spreading in other South American countries, particularly among prostitutes of both sexes. Any exposure to blood, blood products or other bodily fluids may put the individual at risk.

Ecuador is one of a growing number of countries where HIV is transmitted predominantly through heterosexual sex. Apart from abstinence, the most effective preventative is to always practice safe sex using latex barriers, such as condoms and dams. Condoms (preservativos) are available in some Ecuadorian pharmacies, although they may be of low quality, so bring your own if you are unable to abstain. It is impossible to detect the HIV-positive status of an otherwise healthy-looking person without a blood test.

HIV/AIDS can also be spread through transfusions of infected blood; if you need a transfusion, go to the best clinic available, and make sure they screen blood for transfusions. It can also be spread by dirty needles – vaccinations, acupuncture, tattooing and ear or nose piercing can potentially be as dangerous as intravenous drug use if the equipment is not clean. If you do need an injection, ask to see the syringe unwrapped in front of you, or better still, buy a needle and syringe pack from a pharmacy – it is a cheap insurance package against infection with HIV. Fear of HIV infection should never preclude treatment for serious medical conditions. Although there may be a risk of infection, it is very small indeed.

Altitude Sickness

This occurs when you ascend to high altitudes quickly – for example, if you fly from sea level to Quito (2850m). The best way to prevent altitude sickness (locally called soroche) is to spend a day or two traveling slowly to high altitudes, thus allowing your body time to adjust. Even if you don't do this, it is unlikely that you will suffer greatly in Quito, because it is still relatively low. A few people do become seriously ill, but most travelers experience no more than some shortness of breath and headache. If, however, you travel higher than Quito, you may experience more severe symptoms, including vomiting, fatigue, insomnia, loss of appetite, a rapid pulse and irregular breathing during sleep.

The best thing you can do upon arriving at a high altitude is to take it easy for the first day and avoid cigarettes and alcohol. This will go a long way to helping you acclimatize. If you feel sick, the best treatment is rest, deep breathing, an adequate fluid intake and a mild painkiller such as Tylenol to alleviate headaches. If symptoms are very severe, the only effective cure is oxygen. The best way to obtain more oxygen is to descend to a lower elevation.

Heat & Sun

The heat and humidity of the tropics make you sweat profusely and can also make you feel apathetic. It is important to maintain a high fluid intake and to ensure that your food is well salted. If fluids and salts that are lost through perspiration are not replaced, heat exhaustion and cramps frequently result. The feeling of apathy that some people experience usually fades after a week or two.

If you're arriving in the tropics with a great desire to improve your tan, you've certainly come to the right place. The tropical sun will not only improve your tan, it will also burn you to a crisp. An effective way of immobilizing yourself is to cover yourself with sunblock, walk down to the beach, remove your shoes and badly burn your feet, which you forgot to put lotion on and which are especially untanned.

The power of the tropical sun cannot be overemphasized. Don't spoil your trip by trying to tan too quickly; use strong sunblock lotion frequently, and put it on all exposed skin. It is hard to find strong sunblock in Ecuador – bring it from home. Wearing a wide-brimmed hat is also a good idea.

Bites & Stings

Insects Insect repellents go a long way in preventing bites, but if you do get bitten,

avoid scratching. Unfortunately, this is easier said than done. To alleviate itching, try applying hydrocortisone cream or calamine lotion, or try soaking in a baking-soda bath. Antihistamine tablets also help. Scratching will quickly open bites and cause them to become infected. Skin infections are slow to heal in the heat of the tropics, and all infected bites, as well as cuts and grazes, should be kept scrupulously clean, treated with antiseptic creams or iodine solution, and covered with dressings on a daily basis.

Another insect problem is infestation by lice (including crabs), which crawl around in your body hair and make you itch. To get rid of them, wash with a shampoo that contains benzene hexachloride (available in local pharmacies), or shave the affected area. To avoid reinfection, wash all your clothes and bedding in hot water and the shampoo. It's probably best to just throw away your underwear. Lice thrive on body warmth; clothing that isn't worn will cause the beasties lurking within to die in about 72 hours.

Arachnids Scabies are mites that burrow into your skin and cause it to become red and itchy. To kill scabies, wash yourself with a benzene benzoate solution, and wash your clothes too. Benzene benzoate is obtainable from pharmacies in Ecuador.

Scorpions and spiders can give severely painful – but rarely fatal – stings or bites. A common way to get bitten is to put on your clothes and shoes in the morning without checking them first. Develop the habit of shaking out your clothing before putting it on, especially in the lowlands. Check your

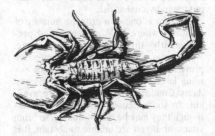

Scorpion stings are painful but rarely fatal.

bedding before going to sleep. Don't walk barefoot, and look where you place your hands when reaching to a shelf or branch. It's extremely unlikely that you will get stung, so don't worry too much about it.

Reptiles Being bitten by a snake is also extremely unlikely. Should someone be bitten, the snake may be a nonvenomous one. In any event, follow this procedure: First, kill the offending creature for identification, if you can do so safely. If not, make note of the snake's markings, size etc, and try to keep the snake away from other people. Second, don't try the slash-and-suck routine. One of the world's deadliest snakes is the fer-de-lance, and it has an anticoagulating agent in its venom. If you're bitten by a fer-de-lance, your blood coagulates twice as slowly as the average hemophiliac's, so slashing at the wound with a razor is a likely way to help someone bleed to death. The slash-and-suck routine does work in some cases, but this should be done only by someone who knows what they are doing.

Third, get the victim to a doctor as soon as possible. Fourth, reassure the victim and keep calm. Even the deadly fer-de-lance only succeeds in killing a small percentage of its bite victims. Fifth, while reassuring and evacuating the victim, apply a tourniquet just above the bite if it is on a limb. Release pressure for 90 seconds every 10 minutes, and make sure that the tourniquet is never so tight that you can't slide a finger underneath it. If circulation is cut off completely, worse damage will result.

Mammals Rabid dogs are more common in Latin America than in more developed nations. If you are bitten by a dog, try to have it captured for tests. If you are unable to test the dog, you must assume that you have rabies, which is invariably fatal (if untreated), so you cannot take the risk of hoping that the dog was not infected. Treatment consists of a series of injections. Rabies takes from five days (exceptionally) to several weeks to develop, so if you are bitten, don't panic. You've got plenty of time to get treated. Ensure that any bite or scratch is cleaned immediately and thoroughly with soap and running water (or that it is swabbed with alcohol) to prevent potential infections or tetanus.

Rabies is also carried by vampire bats, who actually prefer to bite the toes of their sleeping human victims rather than necks, as in popular folklore. So don't stick your toes out from your mosquito net or blanket if you're sleeping in an area where there are bats. Other carriers are monkeys, cats…in fact, many mammals. A rabies vaccine is now available and should be considered if you are in a high-risk category, for example if you intend to explore caves (with bats) or work with animals.

Medical Attention

If you've taken the precautions mentioned in the previous sections, you can look forward to a generally healthy trip. Should something go wrong, however, you can get good medical advice and treatment in the major cities – addresses and directions are given in the appropriate city sections. Guayaquil and Quito have the most comprehensive medical facilities in Ecuador. For straightforward procedures, costs are lower than in the USA. You will be expected to pay for services when you receive them; you can file a claim with your insurance company later (keep your receipts and other paperwork).

Many towns have hospitals, but often, they are short on medicine, equipment and staff; they should sometimes be a last resort. Better care can usually be received in private clinics, many of which are identified in the text and maps of this book. Better clinics will open over the life of this book; if you need medical attention, always ask locally for the name of the best hospital, clinic, doctor or specialist.

WOMEN TRAVELERS

A supplementary book that may be useful is *Handbook for Women Travelers*, by Maggie & Jemma Moss. There are other books devoted to this topic as well, ask at your local bookstore. Any practical advice for women from women travelers is much appreciated.

Attitudes Toward Women

Generally, women travelers will find Ecuador safe and pleasant to visit. This is not to say that machismo is a thing of the past. On the contrary, it is very much alive and practiced. Ecuadorian men generally consider *gringas* to be more liberated (and therefore easier sexual conquests) than their Ecuadorian counterparts. Local men often make flirtatious comments, whistle and hiss at single women – both Ecuadorian and foreign. Women traveling together are not exempt from this attention. Ecuadorian women usually deal with this by looking away and completely ignoring the man, which works reasonably well for gringas, too. Women who firmly ignore unwanted verbal advances are often treated with respect.

Women who speak Spanish find that it is easier to deal with traveling and with the persistent (and often well-meant) questions: 'Where are you from? How old are you? What do you study/do for work? Are you married/do you have a boyfriend?' The pattern is always the same. Some single women claim to be married or have steady boyfriends. Some wear a wedding ring and carry a photo of their 'husband.' A useful phrase in Spanish is *¡No me molestes!* (Don't bother me).

Safety Precautions

Traveling with another woman gives you some measure of psychological support. Traveling with a man tends to minimize the attention that Ecuadorian men may direct toward you. Increasing numbers of Ecuadorian men are becoming sensitive to the issue of machismo – they may practice it with their buddies, but won't hassle every gringa they see.

Occasionally, you hear of a woman traveler being raped. A rape-prevention counselor who works with women in the US Peace Corps suggests that a lone woman should never wander around poorly lit areas at night or remote places (empty-looking beaches) at any time. Don't assume that a deserted tropical beach is really deserted – walk with friends. Other suggestions include carrying a metal whistle (in your hand, not in your backpack). This produces a piercing blast and will startle off most would-be rapists long enough for a woman to get away.

There are many women who have traveled safely, and alone, throughout Ecuador. Just because machismo exists does not mean that all single women travelers are going to have their entire trip ruined by unwanted advances or worse. Many women have made friends with Ecuadorian men and found them charming and friendly. However, unless you are attracted to a local man, you should avoid going somewhere with him alone, as that indicates that you are interested in sleeping with him, and you will be pressured to do so. Friendships are best developed in public group settings.

Macho behavior is often exacerbated when men are with their buddies and have been drinking. This is particularly true at fiestas, especially the kind that have lots of street dancing and drinking. Single women are definitely perceived as available and will be subject to harassment or worse. Women accompanied by a man at a fiesta will experience much less of a hassle. Women travelers have reported that they have been bothered in the port town of Esmeraldas (see the North Coast chapter) more than in other places in Ecuador.

Organizations

There are a few local organizations promoting women's rights, especially in the underclass indigenous communities. CEPAM (☎ 02-546 155), Los Ríos 2238 and Gandar, in Quito, runs an emergency shelter for women (☎ 02-625 316), but this is designed mainly for local women – gringas are expected to be able to afford their own shelter.

The South American Explorers' clubhouse in Quito is often staffed by women – these friendly and wonderful people can tell you like it is. Safari Tours in Quito has opened a women-only hostal (see the Quito & Around chapter); its co-director Jean Brown can provide no-nonsense information if needed (although her primary position is as the repository of an awesome brain-bank of travel information).

GAY & LESBIAN TRAVELERS

Gay rights in a political or legal context don't even exist as an issue for most Ecuadorians. Homosexuality was illegal within the country until late 1997, when this law was repealed as anticonstitutional. However, there is still much antigay bias. As in most Latin countries, sexuality is more stereotyped than it is in Europe or North America, with the man playing a dominant macho role and the woman tagging along with that. This attitude spills over into the perception of homosexuality. A straight-acting macho man will seldom be considered gay, even if he is, while an effeminate man, regardless of his sexual orientation, will be called a *maricón,* a mildly derogatory term for a homosexual man. Relatively few gay men in Ecuador are exclusively homosexual; bisexuality is more common.

Ecuadorian gay and lesbian groups seldom promote themselves as such in order to avoid any organized backlash. Police harassment of individual homosexuals, although illegal, is a regular occurrence. Lesbians, often unwilling to associate themselves with larger, less politically compromised activist groups, are an almost ignored segment of the population. Same-sex couples traveling in Ecuador should be wary of showing affection in public. I've heard reports of a small underground social scene, mainly in Quito and Guayaquil, but no significant movement has developed. The various gay-oriented travel guides rarely have much information about Ecuador.

On the other hand, several fiestas in Ecuador have parades with men cross-dressing as women. This is all meant in fun, rather than as an open acceptance of sexual alternatives, but it does provide the public at large (both gay and straight) a popular cultural situation in which to enjoy themselves in an accepting environment. On New Year's Eve, puppets representing the old year are burned at midnight. Meanwhile, men dressed as women (posing as the puppets' widows) walk the streets, asking passersby for spare change that will later be used for the year-end party. More entertaining still, Latacunga's incredible Mama Negra festival, in late September, features cross-dressing men brandishing whips!

In Quito, you can see roaming bands of transvestites on the streets of the tourist district. Some of these are dangerous prostitutes; others are out for fun. There are also a few backdoor cabarets where you can drink a toast to men performing in drag.

Organizations

The Lesbian, Gay, Bi, Trans Community Center and AIDS Activist organization (FEDAEPS; ☎ 02-223 298) is at Baquerizo Moreno 166 and Tamayo, in Quito. It opens to the public Thursdays at 3 pm; gay and lesbian literature is available, and there are often discussions at 6 pm.

In the USA, Matthew Seats (☎ 757-220-9427, vacations@erols.com) is an IGLTA-certified gay-travel specialist who can arrange tours and travel to Ecuador (and anywhere else) for all travelers, regardless of sexual orientation.

DISABLED TRAVELERS

Unfortunately, Ecuador's infrastructure for disabled travelers is virtually nonexistent, as is the case with most third-world countries. Wheelchair ramps are few and far between, and pavements are often badly potholed and cracked. Bathrooms and toilets are often barely large enough for an able-bodied person to walk into, and very few indeed are accessible to wheelchairs. Signs in Braille or telephones for the hearing-impaired are practically unheard of.

Nevertheless, there are disabled Ecuadorians who get around, mainly through the help of others. It is not particularly unusual to see disabled travelers being carried to a seat on a bus, for example. Buses are (legally) supposed to carry disabled travelers for free. Local city buses, which are already overcrowded, won't do that, but long-distance city buses sometimes will. Disabled travelers are also eligible for 50% discounts on domestic airfares. One reader wrote that the best resource for disabled travelers is the disabled people in Ecuador. If you take the time to learn Spanish, you will find they can be very helpful.

SENIOR TRAVELERS

Seniors may be able to arrange discounts for flying into Ecuador, but once there, options are limited. People over 65 are legally allowed to travel at half-price on buses, but this is mainly for locals; foreign travelers can ask about it. Also ask about 50% discounts on domestic airfares; these should be available.

TRAVEL WITH CHILDREN

Children pay full fare on buses if they occupy a seat, but they often ride for free if they sit on a parent's knee. The fare for children under 12 is halved for domestic flights (and they get a seat), while infants under two cost 10% of the fare (but they don't get a seat). In hotels, the general rule is simply to bargain. The charge for children should never be as much as that for an adult, but whether they stay for half-price or free is open to discussion. While 'kids meals' (small portions at small prices) are not normally offered in restaurants, it is perfectly acceptable to order a meal to split between two children or an adult and a child. Foreigners traveling with children are still a curiosity in Ecuador (especially if they are gringos) and will meet with extra (generally friendly) attention and interest.

For more advice and suggestions, read Lonely Planet's *Travel with Children,* by Maureen Wheeler.

USEFUL ORGANIZATIONS
South American Explorers

Formerly called the South American Explorers Club, this organization was founded in 1977 in Lima, Peru, and now has clubhouses in Quito and Cuzco, Peru, as well as a head office in Ithaca, New York. The clubhouses function as information centers for travelers, adventurers, scientific expeditions etc and provide a wealth of advice about traveling anywhere in Latin America. Anyone considering a trip to Ecuador would do well to join.

The clubhouses have an extensive library of books, maps and trip reports left by other travelers, all indexed by region and date. Many maps and books are for sale. Useful current advice can be obtained about travel conditions, currency regulations, weather conditions and so on. The Quito clubhouse is open 9:30 am to 5 pm weekdays (until 8 pm on Thursday).

The SAE is an entirely member-supported, nonprofit organization. Annual membership dues are US$40/70 per individual/couple and include four quarterly issues of the informative and enjoyable *South American Explorer* magazine. (Membership dues and donations are tax deductible in the US. Members from other countries must add US$10 for postage.)

Members receive full use of the Quito, Lima and Cuzco clubhouses, which have the following facilities: an information service and library; introductions to other travelers and notification of expedition opportunities; storage of excess luggage (anything ranging from small valuables to a kayak); storage or forwarding of mail addressed to you at the club; use of the club's computer (including sending and receiving email); a relaxing place in which to read and research, or just to have a cup of tea and a chat with the friendly staff and other members; a book exchange; the buying and selling of used equipment; a notice board; discounts on the books, maps and gear sold at the club; extra activities, such as the Thursday-night talks presented in Quito; and other services. One area of the clubhouse is dedicated to volunteer programs within Ecuador. The storage facilities are particularly useful if you plan on returning to Ecuador; you can leave heavy camping/climbing gear here from year to year.

Services for nonmembers are limited: the staff is happy to answer a few quick questions about Ecuador and show you around the clubhouse. But staff are volunteers, and members' needs come first. Much of the clubhouse is designated for members only, although there is a room for visitors with a limited amount of free handouts and information about volunteer opportunities; you are encouraged to join. Paid-up members can stay all day.

You can join when you get to Ecuador, or you can join in advance by contacting the US office (see the following list for all contact information) or online at www .samexplor.org.

Quito (☎/fax 225 228, explorer@saec.org.ec) Jorge Washington 311 and Leonidas Plaza, postal address: Apartado 21-431, Quito, Ecuador

Lima (☎/fax 01-425 0142, montague@amauta .rcp.net.pe) Avenida Portugal 145, Breña, postal address: Casilla 3714, Lima 100, Peru

Cuzco (☎/fax 084-22 3102, saec@wayna.rcp.net .pe) Avenida Sol 930, postal address: Casilla 500, Cuzco, Peru

New York (☎ 607-277-0488, 800-274-0568, fax 277-6122, explorer@samexplo.org) 126 Indian Creek Rd, Ithaca, NY 14650, USA

Latin American Travel Advisor

You can get up-to-date information on safety, political and economic situations, health risks and costs for all the Latin American countries (including Ecuador) from *The Latin American Travel Advisor*. This is an impartial, 16-page, quarterly newsletter published in Ecuador (fax 02-562 566, fax in North America 888-215-9511, lata@pi .pro.ec, PO Box 17-17-908, Quito, Ecuador). Four issues are US$39, the most recent issue is US$15 and back issues are US$7.50 sent by airmail.

DANGERS & ANNOYANCES

Although rip-offs are a fact of life in Latin America, you'll find Ecuador safer than its northern neighbor, Colombia. Unfortunately, Ecuador is not as safe to travel in now as it was in the early 1980s. This is probably related to the recently depressed economic situation combined with the increase in tourism over the past couple of decades. You should, therefore, take some simple precautions to avoid being robbed.

Theft Armed robbery is still rare in Ecuador, although parts of Quito, Guayaquil and some coastal areas do have a reputation for being dangerous (specific information is given in the appropriate regional chapters of this book). Sneak theft is more common, and you should remember that crowded places are the haunts of pickpockets. This

means poorly lit bus stations, crowded city streets or bustling markets. What often happens is that travelers get so involved in their new surroundings and experiences that they forget to stay alert, and that's when something is stolen. It could happen in New York City or London as well.

Thieves look for easy targets. Tourists who carry a wallet or passport in a hip pocket are asking for trouble. Leave your wallet at home; it's an easy mark for a pickpocket. Carrying a roll of bills loosely wadded under a handkerchief in your front pocket is as safe a way as any of carrying your daily spending money. The rest should be hidden. Always use at least an inside pocket – or preferably, a body pouch, money belt or leg pouch – to protect your money and passport. Leaving money in hotel safe deposits is usually reliable, but make sure that it is in a sealed, taped envelope – don't just turn over a money belt or wallet. A few readers have reported a loss of money from deposits in cheaper hotels. Separate your money into different places so that if you are robbed, you won't lose it all.

Thieves often work in pairs or groups. While one distracts you, another is robbing you. This can happen in a variety of ways: a bunch of kids fighting in front of you, an old lady 'accidentally' bumping into you, someone dropping something in your path or spilling something on your clothes, several people closing in around you on a crowded city bus…the possibilities go on and on. The only thing you can do is try, as much as possible, to avoid very tight crowds and stay alert, especially when something out of the ordinary happens.

To worry you further, there are the razor-blade artists. No, they don't wave a blade in your face and demand 'Your money or your life!' They simply slit open your luggage with a razor when you're not looking. This includes a pack on your back or luggage in the rack of a bus or train – or even your trouser pocket.

Many travelers carry their day packs in front of them to avoid having them slashed during trips. Some travelers buy large grain sacks from hardware stores or markets and put their packs or luggage in them when they travel. This makes their bag look less obviously like a tourist's bag – many locals use grain sacks to transport their belongings. Also, the sacks will keep your luggage clean and more protected.

When walking with a large pack, move fast and avoid stopping – this makes it difficult for anyone intent on cutting the pack. If you have to stop (at a street crossing, for example), gently swing from side to side and look around a lot. Taking a taxi from the bus station to a hotel is a safer alternative in some cities (this is mentioned in the text under the appropriate city). Never put your bag down unless you have your foot firmly on it.

One of the best solutions to the rip-off problem is to travel with a friend and to watch out for one another. An extra pair of eyes makes a lot of difference. There are often shifty types eyeing baggage at bus stations or pockets in busy markets, but they'll notice if you are alert and are far less likely to bother you if you are. They'd rather pick the wallet from some gawker who isn't paying attention.

Drugs Definitely avoid any conversation with someone who offers you drugs. In fact, talking to any stranger on the street can hold risks. It has happened that travelers who have talked to strangers have been stopped soon after by plainclothes 'police officers' and were accused of talking to a drug dealer. In such a situation, never get into a vehicle with the 'police,' but insist on going to a bona fide police station on foot.

Scams Be wary of false or crooked police who prey on tourists. Plainclothes 'policemen' may produce official-looking documents – always treat these with suspicion, or simply walk away with a smile and a shrug. On the other hand, a uniformed official who asks to see your passport in broad daylight in the middle of a busy street is probably just doing the job – a few friendly words and a compliment on how you are enjoying this beautiful country will usually ensure that your passport will be examined quickly and returned politely.

Also, don't accept food from strangers; occasional reports surface of travelers eating cookies offered by some smooth-talking 'friends' on a bus and waking up two days later in an alley with everything robbed. Unopened packages of cookies and other foods are injected with horse tranquilizers using hypodermic syringes. It may sound weird, but it's true.

Robbery Every year or so, you hear of a couple of nighttime bus robberies in the Guayaquil area. Night buses are simply held up at a road block and robbed by armed men. These are always long-distance buses, so you should avoid taking night buses that go through Guayas Province unless you have to. It happens to one bus in many thousands, so don't get paranoid if your schedule demands a night bus through the area.

If you are driving a car, never park it unattended. Never leave any valuables in sight in the car – even attended cars will have their windows smashed by hit-and-run merchants.

There has been a rash of recent problems for climbers and hikers. Armed gangs have robbed tourists hiking up Quito's backyard volcano, Pichincha. Others have robbed and raped small groups staying in some of the remoter mountain huts, such as on Iliniza and Tungurahua. Never leave gear unattended in a mountain hut while you are hiking. Some huts, eg, on Cotopaxi or Chimborazo, have guardians and a place to lock up gear when you climb, and these are relatively safe. Inquire at the South American Explorers clubhouse (see Useful Organizations, earlier in this chapter) for up-to-date information on these problems. Also, climb and hike in a sizable group in questionable areas.

Take out traveler's insurance if you're carrying really valuable gear, such as a good camera. But don't get paranoid – Ecuador is not an extremely dangerous country; there are people who have made dozens of trips to Ecuador without ever being robbed.

If you are robbed, you should file a police report as soon as possible. This is a requirement for any insurance claims, although it is unlikely that the police will be able to recover the property. Normally, only the main police station in a town will deal with this.

EMERGENCIES

The telephone system is not very good, and there is no nationwide emergency system. In major cities, dialing ☎ 101 or ☎ 911 will get you the police. Otherwise, follow instructions given in public phone booths or ask at your hotel or other operator.

LEGAL MATTERS

If you get into legal trouble and are jailed, your embassy can offer only limited assistance. This may include an occasional visit from an embassy staff member to make sure that your human rights have not been violated, letting your family know where you are and putting you in contact with an Ecuadorian lawyer (whom you must pay yourself). Embassy officials will not bail you out, and you are subject to the laws of Ecuador, not to the laws of your home country.

Drug penalties in Ecuador for possession of even small amounts of illegal drugs are much stricter than in the USA or Europe. Defendants often spend many months in jail before they are brought to trial, and if convicted (as is usually the case), they can expect sentences of several years in jail.

Businesspeople should be aware that a legal dispute that may be of a civil nature in their home countries may be handled as a criminal proceeding in Ecuador. This may mean that you are not allowed to leave Ecuador while your dispute is being settled, and that it could possibly lead to arrest and jailing until the case is settled.

Drivers should carry their passports as well as their driver's licenses. In the event of an accident, unless extremely minor, the vehicles should stay where they are until the police arrive and make a report. This is essential for all insurance claims. If the accident results in injury and you are unhurt, you should take the victim to obtain medical help, particularly in the case of a pedestrian accident. You are legally responsible for the pedestrian's injuries and will be jailed unless you pay, even if the accident was not your fault. Drive defensively.

BUSINESS HOURS

Banks are open 9 am to 1:30 pm weekdays. Many stay open later, but money-changing facilities stop around 1:30 pm.

In Quito and Guayaquil, most stores, businesses, exchange houses and government offices are open from about 9 am to 5:30 pm weekdays, with an hour off for lunch. In smaller towns, lunch breaks of two hours are not uncommon. On Saturday, many stores and some businesses are open 9 am to noon. Stores in major shopping malls are open until about 8 pm.

Restaurants tend to remain open late in the big cities, where 10 pm is not an unusual time to eat an evening meal. In smaller towns, restaurants often close by 9 pm; in villages, much earlier. Restaurants are often closed on Sunday, so the selection of eating places can be quite limited then.

PUBLIC HOLIDAYS & SPECIAL EVENTS

Many of the major festivals are oriented toward the Roman Catholic liturgical calendar. They are often celebrated with great pageantry, especially in highland Indian villages, where a Catholic feast day is often the excuse for a traditional Indian fiesta, which includes drinking, dancing, rituals and processions. Other holidays are of historical or political interest. On major holidays, banks, offices and other services are closed, and transportation is often very crowded, so book ahead if possible.

The following list describes the major holidays, but they may well be celebrated for several days around the actual date. Those marked by an asterisk (*) are official public holidays, when banks and businesses are closed; others are more local holidays. If an official public holiday falls on a weekend, offices may be closed on the nearest Friday or Monday. If an official holiday falls midweek, it may be moved to the nearest Friday or Monday to create a long weekend.

New Year's Day* January 1
Epiphany* January 6
National Community Spirit Day February 27

Carnaval* February, March or April – Held the last few days before Lent, Carnaval is celebrated with water fights. Ambato has its fruit and flowers festival.

Easter* March or April – Palm Sunday, Holy Thursday, Good Friday, Holy Saturday and Easter Sunday are celebrated with religious processions. Holy Saturday is a public holiday, but many businesses close earlier in the week.

Labor Day* May 1 – This day is celebrated with workers' parades.

Mother's Day May, 2nd Sunday – Expect restaurants to be crowded with families taking mom out to dinner.

Battle of Pichincha* May 24 – This national holiday celebrates the decisive battle of independence from the Spanish in 1822.

Corpus Christi June – This is a movable religious feast day combined with a traditional harvest fiesta in many highland towns. Usually the 9th Thursday after Easter, it features processions and street dancing.

St John the Baptist June 24 – In the Otavalo area, this day is celebrated with a fiesta.

Sts Peter and Paul June 29 – In the Otavalo area and in other northern highland towns, this day is celebrated with a fiesta.

Simón Bolívar's Birthday* July 24

Founding of Guayaquil July 25 – This is a major festival for the city of Guayaquil; it combines with the national holiday of July 24, and the city closes down and parties.

Quito Independence Day* August 10

Guayaquil Independence Day* October 9 – This combines with the October 12 national holiday and is an important festival in Guayaquil.

Columbus Day* October 12 – This is a national holiday to celebrate the 'discovery' of America; it's also known as Americas Day or *Día de la Raza*.

Fiesta del Yamor September 1–15 – This is Otavalo's annual festival.

All Saints' Day* November 1

All Souls' Day* November 2 – This is celebrated by flower-laying ceremonies in cemeteries. It's especially colorful in rural areas, where entire Indian families show up at the cemeteries to eat, drink and leave offerings in memory of their departed relatives. The atmosphere often becomes festive rather than somber.

Cuenca Independence Day* November 3 – This combines with the national holidays of November 1 and 2 to give Cuenca its most important fiesta of the year.

Founding of Quito* December 6 – This is celebrated in Quito throughout the first week of December with bullfights, parades and street dances.

Christmas Eve* December 24

Christmas Day* December 25

End-of-year celebrations December 28–31 – Parades and dances culminate in the burning of life-size effigies in the streets on New Year's Eve.

In addition to these major festivals, there are many smaller ones. Most towns and villages have their own special day, as well as a weekly market day (see the Shopping section, later in this chapter).

ACTIVITIES

Where to begin? There are so many exciting activities to experience in Ecuador that any list of suggestions will certainly be inadequate. The following are the main outdoor activities that are possible. Where a place name is mentioned, refer to that section for more information.

Bird Watching

Ecuador has some of the best birding in the world. The Galápagos Islands have 28 endemic species; and an ornithologist in Guayaquil says that within 50km of that city, you can find over 50 Ecuadorian mainland endemic species. Most of these tend to be of the small and easily overlooked variety, but serious birders with a good local guide or with a professional birding tour can certainly rack up their life lists in Ecuador.

Hiking & Mountaineering

Tents, sleeping bags and other gear can be rented in Quito and some other towns. Adventures in Parque Nacional Cotopaxi, Area Nacional de Recreación Las Cajas (near Cuenca); the Inca site of Ingapirca, around Chimborazo (Ecuador's highest mountain); and Parque Nacional Machalilla are all worthwhile and are described in this book. Guided treks are available.

Topographical maps are available from the Instituto Geográfico Militar (IGM) in Quito. Dedicated adventurers should read *Climbing & Hiking in Ecuador* (see the

Books section, earlier in this chapter). A useful Web site is www.cotopaxi.com. If you understand Spanish, you can obtain updated volcano information at http://geofisico.cybw.net/.

Many of Ecuador's volcanoes are not too difficult to climb and make ideal destinations for those who want to get some real high-altitude experience. Of Ecuador's 10 peaks over 5000m in elevation, several are regularly climbed, including the two highest in the country, Chimborazo (6310m) and Cotopaxi (5897m), both of which can be climbed in one long day from their respective climbers' refuges, usually leaving at midnight to avoid potentially dangerous soft-snow conditions in the late afternoon. Others, such as Tungurahua, are currently off-limits because of volcanic activity. Potential climbers *must* take the time to acclimatize before attempting an ascent – several days in Quito or another highland town is a minimum. Cotopaxi is probably the most frequently climbed high peak in Ecuador.

Mountaineers will require standard snow and ice gear: a rope, crampons, ice axe, high-altitude sun protection and cold-weather clothing as a minimum. Climbers can rent equipment in Quito, Ambato, Riobamba and Baños (if and when it returns to normal), but be sure to check it carefully. Unless you are very experienced, hiring a guide from one of these towns is recommended. Several agencies offer both rental gear and guides. If you are inexperienced, you should find a guide who will spend some time teaching you how to use your equipment. Ice axes are used as emergency brakes if you fall down a glacier – if you don't know how to self-arrest with an ice axe, make sure you find a guide who will take a day before the climb to teach you some basics. This will cost extra.

The weather can turn bad quickly in the Andes, and both experienced and inexperienced climbers have been killed. Some 'guides' have climbed a mountain a couple of times, and then offer their services for very low prices – these people are not listed in this book. Hire an experienced climbing guide and climb in safety. Expect to pay very roughly US$100 per person to climb a major peak – this is for a group of three climbers with one guide without lessons. Climbs of minor peaks not requiring technical equipment are cheaper partly because the climb is easier and partly because a guide can take a larger group, so the cost can be split more ways. Good guides should have a card accrediting them to ASEGUIM, the Ecuadorian Mountain Guide Association.

You can climb year-round, but the best months are considered to be June to August and December to February.

There is no skiing in Ecuador, but a few experienced mountaineers have carried mountain-skis up some peaks and skied back down.

Horseback Riding

Unfortunately, the standards of care for horses used for tourist trails has been very low over the years, and several travelers have written to say that the horses are old, overworked and underfed and have sores. There are, however, some agencies that do look after the animals, but they charge more for tours. Those travelers looking for the cheapest rates are going to get a hack and contribute to its misery. Go with a reputable company, even if it costs more.

An expensive but fully reputable company is Ride Ecuador (☎ 09-738 221, ☎/fax 02-437 644, in the UK ☎/fax 1780 740 220, ridecuador@travelecuador.net). Nine-day tours featuring either a combination of hotels and camping or stays in rural haciendas and riding between them are offered for experienced riders. Shorter tours can be custom-made for both experienced and inexperienced riders. Horses and guides are top notch. You can visit www.travelecuador.net/ride for more information.

Mountain Biking

Mountain biking is still a relatively new sport, although a couple of outfitters in Quito have been around for years and offer adequate bikes and knowledgeable guides. If you plan on getting around by bicycle, see the Getting Around chapter.

Most outfitters will prefer to send a guide with you, as riders of rental bikes are notorious for trashing the bike. (One coastal bike-rental agency said that travelers frequently would ride bicycles into the surf for fun. Salt water and sand obviously didn't do the machines any good.) The guides know all the best routes, and in the mountains, van support takes riders to the tops of spectacular long rides down the Andes. These are frequently recommended trips by travelers.

River Running

Both rafters and kayakers will find superb white water in Ecuador. This fact has only recently become internationally recognized, and river running is Ecuador's fastest-growing outdoor activity. Rafting can be done year-round, and even complete beginners can enjoy the activity, as rafts are captained by seasoned and qualified experts. Kayakers tend to be more experienced, and often will bring their own state-of-the-art kayak with them to enjoy a few weeks of world-class kayaking.

The best-known river is Río Blanco, and others are in the same watershed, about 2½ hours west of Quito. It's a year-round possibility as a day trip from the capital, although conditions are wildest from February to about June. Two-day trips are also available.

On the eastern side of the Andes, Ríos Napo and Misahuallí, near Tena, are the best known, with the latter including an exciting portage around a waterfall. Water levels fluctuate during the year, but something can be found to run at any time, usually as a day trip returning to overnight in Tena. North, Río Quijos provides good rafting from October to February, and farther south, Río Upano, near Macas, is good from about September to February but requires a commitment of several days, with camping on the beach or in Indian villages. Río Pastaza and Río Patate, near Baños, have also been run commercially, but it should be noted that inexperienced 'guides' caused four Belgians to drown in an accident here in 1998, and the Patate is very polluted. There are many other rivers that

are being discovered, but they are not run commercially with any regularity.

Outfitters operate mainly in Quito and Tena, although some activity is found near Baeza and (perhaps) Baños. A good operator will have insurance and highly experienced guides with certified first-aid training; they will carry a well-stocked and up-to-date medical kit (especially on multiday trips), serve hygienically prepared food (enduring the runs while running a river is a definite bummer for you and your raftmates) and provide top-notch equipment: self-bailing rafts, US Coast Guard–approved life jackets, 1st-class helmets, dry bags in good condition (to make sure your sleeping bag and other gear stays dry throughout the trip), rain- and insect-proof tents, splash jackets or wetsuits for the colder rivers, and high-quality lightweight paddles and spares.

While it's possible to run rivers more cheaply with less-than-state-of-the-art equipment or with inexperienced or untrained guides, you have to decide where your priorities lie – saving money or saving your skin if the river turns rough. Many good companies raft rivers accompanied by a kayaker who is experienced in river rescue. There is a fledgling river guide association (AGAR), and travelers should check guide's credentials. Only a few river guides have passed AGAR testing, and only reputable companies are listed in this book.

Surfing

Not yet a well-developed sport in Ecuador, surfing nevertheless has its aficionados. The best spot in Ecuador for meeting a few other surfers and swapping stories is Montañita; it's not unduly crowded.

Snorkeling

If you're planning on a trip to the Galápagos, make sure to include snorkeling on your list of things to do. Donning a mask and snorkel will expose you to a completely new world. Baby sea lions may come up and stare at you through your mask, various species of rays come slowly undulating by, and penguins dart past you in a stream of bubbles. The hundreds of species of fish are spectacularly colorful, and you can watch the round, flapping shapes of sea turtles as they circle you. This won't, of course, happen immediately after you enter the water, but you do stand a good chance to see most of these things if you spend, say, half an hour per day in the water during a week of cruising the islands.

A mask and snorkel also gives you the opportunity to observe more sedentary forms of life. Sea urchins, starfish, sea anemones, algae and crustaceans all colorfully combine in an exotic display of underwater life. You may be able to buy them in sporting goods stores in Quito or Guayaquil, and they can sometimes be borrowed in the Galápagos, but if you definitely plan to visit the islands, you should bring a mask from home to ensure a good fit and to enable you to snorkel when you feel like it.

The water temperature is generally around 22°C from January to April and about 18°C during the rest of the year. If you plan on spending a lot of time in the water, you may want to bring a 'shorty' wetsuit with you.

Scuba Diving

This activity is becoming increasingly popular in the Galápagos, and there were recently five dive operators in Puerto Ayora; not all have a good reputation. Conditions for diving in the islands are difficult for beginners, and Lonely Planet received one tragic report of a pair of novice divers drowning in 1997, although it is unclear who or what was responsible for the deaths. Remember that there is no decompression chamber in the Galápagos. Don't plan on flying to Quito for at least 12 hours – some experts advise waiting 24 hours – after your last dive.

Diving in the islands provides excellent opportunities of seeing some really dramatic underwater wildlife – hammerhead and other sharks, a variety of rays (occasionally a manta ray), turtles, penguins, sea lions, moray eels, huge numbers of fish of many kinds and, if you're very lucky, dolphins or even whales.

See the Galápagos chapter for information on dive centers.

COURSES

Various colleges and organizations in the USA can provide you with information on studying in Ecuador. Most of these courses are available for academic credit, and some have both cultural and linguistic elements. You have to pay for tuition, room and board, but student grants, awards and other financial aid can often be arranged. Students should talk to their college advisors to see if their institution has more information. Students wishing to make a long-term commitment (ie, more than the three months allowed for a tourist visa) should get a student visa ahead of time in their home country, as getting one in Ecuador is very difficult.

Most foreign students come simply to learn Spanish, and there is a plethora of schools to help them at any level. With many courses, accommodations with local families can be arranged, and they sometimes also include intensive one-on-one instruction for several hours a day. Costs are reasonable. Most schools are found in Quito, but there are also schools in Cuenca, Otavalo, Baños and other towns; these are listed under the specific towns.

There is a dance school (see Dancing Lessons, under Quito, in the Quito & Around chapter) that teaches salsa. Other cultural activities (music, weaving) can also be learned, but not usually from school. Ask around for artists who would like to tutor you.

WORK

Officially, you need a worker's visa to be allowed to work in Ecuador.

Teaching

Tourists have obtained jobs teaching English in language schools, usually in Quito. Schools often advertise for teachers on the bulletin boards of hotels and restaurants. You are expected to be a native English speaker or the equivalent. Pay is low, but it's enough to live on if you're broke. It's best to start looking soon after you arrive, because it's not easy to get a work visa, and you may have to leave in 90 days.

If, in addition to speaking English like a native, you actually have a bona fide teaching credential, so much the better. Schools such as the American School in Quito will often hire teachers of mathematics, biology and other subjects, and may help you get a work visa if you want to stay on. They also pay much better than the language schools. Members of the South American Explorers may use the organization to find contacts with schools that are looking for teachers. Also check ads in local hotels and newspapers.

If you want to look in advance, a useful Web site is www.teachabroad.com/search .cfm, which lists both paying and voluntary positions.

Volunteer Work

Numerous organizations look for volunteers. Most want a minimum commitment of several weeks or months, and many charge a small amount to cover board and lodging (this may be as high as US$10 a day, but it's often less). Volunteers can work in conservation programs, help street kids, teach, build nature trails, construct Web sites, do medical or agricultural work – possibilities are varied.

The Quito clubhouse of the South American Explorers has a volunteer desk where current offerings are posted. Melani Martinod is the current representative there. Contact the clubhouse (see Useful Organizations, earlier in this chapter) for a listing in advance. The clubhouse itself often needs volunteers.

EcoEcuador (contact Marta Aucancela, Melani Martinod, or Carly Mattes at ☎ 09-714 154 or EcoEcuador@hotmail.com) is a nonprofit group developing long-term solutions for the conservation of natural features in Ecuador. They are supported by local businesses, private institutions and the general public and need volunteers to work in many fields and areas.

It's also worth searching the Internet for voluntary work. An organization that can provide you with long lists of voluntary positions in Ecuador (and elsewhere) for a fee is Voluntary Work Information Service (VWIS; ☎/fax 41-22-366 1651, Case Postal 90, 1268 Begnins, Vaud, Switzerland); its Web site is www.workingabroad.com.

Several organizations and places that accept volunteers are listed in appropriate parts of the text – see the index under 'Volunteering.' Finally, if you are already in Ecuador, ask around. Word-of-mouth contacts are often the best.

Other Work

Some enterprising travelers make money selling jewelry or art in crafts markets. Most other jobs are obtained by word of mouth (eg, bartenders, jungle guides), but the possibilities are limited. If you are a professional river or mountaineering guide, try contacting the outfitters listed in this book.

Another way of making money – if you're in that unfortunate position of needing it – is by selling good-quality equipment such as camping and climbing gear or camera items. Good used gear can be sold for about 50% to 60% of its new price.

ACCOMMODATIONS

There is no shortage of places to stay in Ecuador. It is virtually unheard of to arrive in a town and not be able to find somewhere to sleep, but during major fiestas or on the night before market day, accommodations can be rather tight. For this reason, as many places to stay as possible are marked on the town maps. Most of the time, many of them will be superfluous, but every once in a while you'll be glad to have the knowledge of as many lodgings as possible.

Reservations

The telephone numbers for many hotels are included in this book, but the cheaper ones may not accept phone reservations, and even if they do, they may not honor them if you arrive late in the day. The best use of the telephone in these cases is to call from the bus station to see if they have a room available; if you then intend to stay, head over right away. Better hotels will tell you what time you have to arrive by; others may want a prepayment by means of a deposit to their bank account.

Also included where appropriate are the email addresses or Web sites. These are convenient tools, but expect to pay for them. Rates secured by email are guaranteed, but walk-in rates off the streets can be much lower – but if the hotel has no room, you are out of luck.

Camping

There are no campgrounds catering to recreational vehicles (RVs). Camping in tents is allowed on the grounds of a few rural hotels, in the countryside and in some national parks. There are no campgrounds in towns; the constant availability of cheap hotels makes them superfluous.

There are climbers' refuges *(refugios)* on some of the major mountains; you need to bring your own sleeping bag. Backcountry campers should refer to *Climbing & Hiking in Ecuador* (see the Books section, earlier in this chapter).

Hostels

A youth-hostel system has recently appeared, and holders of youth-hostel cards often get a small (10%) discount. The cheapest hostels start around US$5 per person in dorms, but they are clean and well run. Most have more expensive private rooms as well. Cheaper hotels can, however, be found, and so hostels aren't necessarily a better deal. Details are given in the text under individual cities. *Hostales* are different from hostels; see Hotels, later in this section, for information on them.

B&Bs

The B&B (Bed & Breakfast) system as known in North America and Europe is not well developed in Ecuador. However, many hotels provide breakfasts, and some call themselves B&Bs.

Hotels

Hotels go by a variety of names. A *pensión* or a *hospedaje* is usually an inexpensive boarding house or place of lodging, often family run. A *hostal* (as opposed to a youth hostel) can vary from inexpensive to moderately priced, depending on whether the

owner thinks of the place as a cheap hostel or an upmarket inn. A *hostería* tends to be a mid-priced, comfortable country inn. *Cabañas* are cabins found both on the coast and in the Oriente. They can range from basic and cheap little boxes to pleasant, mid-priced bungalows. *Hotel* is a catch-all phrase for anything from a flea-ridden brothel to the most luxurious place in town. A *lodge*

Hotel Pricing Problems

During 1999 and 2000, Ecuador experienced extreme economic problems, with the value of its currency in January 2000 worth only about 25% of what it was worth in January 1999 (see also Economy, in the Facts about Ecuador chapter). A hotel rate of US$20 on one night could have been as cheap as US$10 the next (as happened on an infamous day in April 1999, when the value of the sucre dropped 50% in 24 hours). Obviously, 1999 and 2000 were cheap years to travel in Ecuador, especially for budget travelers, who found hotel rates to be sometimes half of what they were listed as in the last edition of this book.

The prices given in this edition are what were available at research time. In each town, hotels are listed in roughly ascending order of cost, so readers will be able to find something in their desired price range after adjusting for any further economic change.

tends to be in remote rural areas and usually provides complete service (meals, guides and transportation arrangements), as well as lodging, which is often rustic, but comfortable enough if kerosene lanterns and cold showers aren't a deterrent.

Price Categories In small towns, accommodations are grouped into one section. In larger towns, they are separated into groups.

'Budget' hotels are the cheapest, but not necessarily the worst. Although rooms are usually basic, with just a bed and four walls, they can nevertheless be well looked after, very clean and an amazing value. These hotels are often good places to meet other travelers, both Ecuadorian and foreign. Prices in this category range from US$2 to approximately US$10 per person. Every town has hotels in this price range, and in smaller towns, hotels aren't any more expensive. Although you'll usually have to use communal bathrooms in the cheapest hotels, you can sometimes find rooms with a private bathroom for as little as US$4 or US$5 per person.

Rooms in 'mid-range' hotels usually cost from about US$8 to US$30 per person (depending on the city), but they are not always better than the best hotels in the budget price range. On the whole, however, you can find some very good bargains here. Even if you're traveling on a budget, there are always special occasions (your birthday?) when you can indulge in comparative luxury for a day or two.

'Top end' hotels are absent from many towns. In major cities, hotels in this price category may be luxurious and may have a two-tiered pricing system. In Guayaquil and Quito, for example, a luxury hotel may charge a foreigner well over US$100 for a double, but an Ecuadorian might get the room for half the price or less. This system stinks, but it is legal, and there's not much you can do about it other than avoid staying in luxury hotels. Apart from the expensive luxury hotels, included in this category are some nice hotels with rates that are still very cheap by Western standards – about US$50 a double and up.

Budget Hotels The fact that a hotel is marked on a city map does not necessarily imply that it is recommended. Some are listed because they may be all that is available in the shoestring price range, and they may be barely adequate. If you are going to a town specifically for a market or fiesta, try to arrive a day early, or at least by early afternoon the day before – otherwise, you might not find a vacancy.

Sometimes it's difficult to find single rooms, and you may get a room with two or even three beds. In most cases, however, you are only charged for one bed and won't have to share unless the hotel is full (Atacames is a notable exception to this). Ensure in advance that you won't be asked to pay for all the beds or share with a stranger if you don't want to. This is no problem 90% of the time. Some of the cheapest hotels will ask you to take a bed in a room with other travelers. These 'dormitory-style' accommodations may save you a little money, but don't leave your valuables lying around unattended, and don't assume that every traveler is honest.

If you are traveling as a couple or in a group, don't automatically presume that a room with two or three beds will be cheaper per person than a room with one bed. Sometimes it is, and sometimes it isn't. If a price is given per person, then usually a double or triple room will cost two or three times a single, respectively. If more than one price is given, this indicates that double and triples are cheaper per person than singles.

Couples sharing one bed (*cama matrimonial*) are sometimes charged less than two people in a room with two beds.

Look around the hotel if possible. The same prices are often charged for rooms of different quality. Even in the US$3-a-night cheapies, it's worth looking around. If you are shown a horrible airless box with just a bed and a bare light bulb, you can ask to see a better room without giving offense simply by asking if there is a room with a window, or explaining that you have to write some letters home and need a room with a table and chair. You may be amazed at the results.

Never rent a room without looking at it first. In most hotels, even the cheapest, the person working there will be happy to let you see the room. If he or she isn't, then it usually means that the room is filthy anyway. Also ask to see the bathroom, and make sure that the toilet flushes and the water runs if you want a wash. If the shower looks and smells as if someone threw up in it, the staff obviously don't do a very good job of looking after the place. There's probably a better hotel at the same price nearby.

Bathroom Facilities In budget hotels, bathrooms are rarely what you may be used to at home. The cheapest hotels don't always have hot water, or it may be turned on only at certain hours of the day, or it may be available upon request with an hour's notice. Ask about this before checking in.

Some showers are heated electrically, where a single cold-water showerhead is hooked up to an electric heating element that is switched on when you want a hot (more likely, tepid) shower. Although these may look and sound dangerous, they are usually safe, although mild electric shocks are very occasionally reported.

Some hotels charge extra for hot showers, and a few simply don't have showers at all. At the other end of the spectrum, the better mid-range hotels and all top-end hotels have modern bathrooms.

Security Most hotels will give you a key to lock your room, and theft from your hotel room is not as frequent as it is in some other countries. Nevertheless, carrying your own padlock is a good idea if you plan on staying in the cheapest hotels (but otherwise, it is not necessary). Once in a while, you'll find that a room doesn't look very secure – perhaps there's a window that doesn't close, or the wall doesn't come to the ceiling and can be climbed over. It's worth finding another room. This is another reason why it's good to look at a room before you rent it.

You should never leave valuables lying around the room. It's just too tempting for a maid who earns only US$2 a day for her work. Money and passports should be in a secure body pouch; valuables can usually be kept in the hotel strongbox. (Some cheaper hotels might not want to take this responsibility.) Don't get paranoid though – things are rarely stolen from rooms.

Many small hotels lock their doors at night, which may make it difficult for late-night revelers to return to their rooms. Usually, there is a doorbell, but it is often located in some not-very-obvious position. Normally, there is a night guard who will let you in, but if the guard is asleep, it may take several minutes of ringing, knocking or yelling to get attention. It's worth asking what time the hotel locks up (and where the night bell is) if you are planning on a night out – then at least someone might expect you.

Cable TV Many hotels advertise cable TV. This is often local cable, which brings in about 10 local channels; or, it may be Spanish-language cable, which brings in about 20 Spanish-language channels. Few hotels have international cable with CNN or similar English-language channels.

Homestays
These are normally organized by Spanish schools to enable the traveler to practice Spanish in a home environment and eat meals with the family. Great. The downside is that you might not get to sample many of the local restaurants, and young women may find that the family they stay with are overly concerned about their going out alone at night.

Staying in Villages
If you're traveling really far off the beaten track, you may end up in a village that doesn't have even a basic pensión. You can usually find somewhere to sleep by asking around, but it might be just a roof over your head rather than a bed, so carry a sleeping bag or at least a blanket.

The place to ask at first would probably be a village store – the store owner usually knows everyone in the village and would know who is in the habit of renting rooms or floor space. If that fails, you can ask for the *alcalde* (mayor) or at the *policía* (police). You may end up sleeping on the floor of the schoolhouse, the jail or the village community center, but you're likely to find someplace if you persevere. People in remote areas are generally hospitable.

FOOD

If you're on a tight budget, food is the most important part of your trip expenses. You can stay in rock-bottom hotels, travel 2nd-class and never consider buying a souvenir, but you've got to eat well. This doesn't mean expensively, but it does mean that you want to avoid spending half your trip sitting on the toilet.

The worst culprits for making you sick are salads and unpeeled fruit. With the fruit, stick to bananas, oranges, pineapples and other fruit that you can peel yourself. With unpeeled fruit or salads, wash them yourself in water that you can trust (see Health, earlier in this chapter). As long as you take heed of the salad warning, you'll find plenty of good things to eat at reasonable prices. You certainly don't have to eat in a fancy restaurant; the kitchen facilities there may not be as clean as the white tablecloths. A good sign for any restaurant is if the locals eat there – restaurants aren't empty if the food is delicious and healthy.

You can eat cheaply from street and market stalls if the food looks freshly cooked, but watch to see if your plate is going to be 'washed' in a bowl of cold, greasy water and wiped with a filthy rag – try food that can be wrapped in paper, such as *llapingachos* (see the list under Local Food, next). A *comedor* is literally a dining room, but the name is often applied to a cheap restaurant where the locals eat. Comedores are good places for an inexpensive meal. Having said that, Ecuador's current economic crisis means that you can eat well for much less than in the past.

If you're not on a tight budget or if you want to splurge a little, cities big enough to have 1st-class hotels also have good but expensive (by Ecuadorian standards) international restaurants, often right in the hotels themselves.

For breakfast, the usual eggs and bread rolls or toast are available in restaurants. *Huevos fritos* are fried eggs, *revueltos* are scrambled, and *pasados* or *a la copa* are boiled or poached. These last two are usually runny, so ask to have them *bien cocidos* (well cooked) or *duros* (hard) if you don't like your eggs that way. *Tostadas* are toast and *panes* are bread rolls, which go well with *mantequilla y mermelada* (butter and jam). A good local change from eggs is sweet-corn tamales, called *humitas*, which are often served for breakfast with coffee (mainly in the highlands). If you want inexpensive luxury, go for breakfast at the fanciest hotel in town (assuming it has a restaurant or cafeteria). You can relax with coffee, rolls and the morning paper, or get a window seat and watch the world go by. Despite the elegant surroundings and the bow-tied waiter, you are only charged an extra few cents for your coffee. It makes a nice change, and the coffee is often very good.

Lunch is the biggest meal of the day for many Ecuadorians. If you walk into a cheap restaurant and ask for the *almuerzo*, or lunch of the day, you'll get a decent meal for US$1 to US$2. An almuerzo always consists of a *sopa* (soup) and a *segundo* (second dish), which is usually a *seco* (stew) with plenty of rice. Sometimes, the segundo is *pescado* (fish) or a kind of lentil or pea stew *(lenteja, arveja)*, but there's nearly always rice. Many, but not all, restaurants will give you a salad (often cooked), juice and a *postre* (dessert) in addition to the two main courses.

The supper of the day is usually similar to lunch. Ask for the *merienda*. If you don't want the almuerzo or merienda, you can choose from the menu, but this is always more expensive. However, the set meals do tend to get repetitious, and most people like to try other dishes.

Local Food

The following is a list of local dishes worth trying at markets, street stands and restaurants.

Caldos – These soups are very popular and are often served in markets for breakfasts. Soups are known as *caldos, sopas* or *locros*. Chicken soup, or *caldo de gallina,* is the most popular. *Caldo de patas* is soup made by boiling cattle hooves; it's as bad as it sounds.

Cuy – This is a whole roasted guinea pig and is a traditional food dating back to Inca times. It tastes rather like a cross between rabbit and chicken. The sight of the little paws and teeth sticking out and eyes tightly closed is a little unnerving, but cuy is supposed to be a delicacy, and some people love it.

Lechón – This is suckling pig; they are often roasted whole and are a common sight at Ecuadorian food markets. Pork is also called *chancho*.

Llapingachos – These fried potato-and-cheese pancakes are often served with *fritada* – scraps of fried or roasted pork.

Locro – This is a thick soup, usually made of potatoes and corn and with an avocado or cheese topping.

Seco – This is meat stew and is usually served with rice. It can be *seco de gallina* (chicken stew), *de res* (beef), *de chivo* (goat) or *de cordero* (lamb). The word literally means 'dry' (as opposed to a 'wet' soup).

Tortillas de maíz – Tasty fried corn pancakes.

Yaguarlocro – Potato soup with chunks of barely congealed blood sausage floating in it. If you happen to like blood sausage, you'll find this soup very tasty.

A *churrasco* is a hearty plate that comes with a slice of fried beef, one or two fried eggs, vegetables (usually boiled beet slices, carrots and beans), fried potatoes, a slice of avocado and tomato and the inevitable rice. If you get *arroz con pollo,* you'll be served a mountain of rice with little bits of chicken mixed in. If you're fed up with rice, go to a *Pollo a la Brasa* restaurant, where you can get fried chicken, often with fried potatoes on the side. *Gallina* is chicken that has usually been boiled, as in soups, while *pollo* is more often spit-roasted or fried. Pollo tends to be underdone, but you can always send it back to have it cooked longer.

Parrilladas are steak houses or grills. These are recommended if you like meat and a complete loss if you don't. Steaks, pork chops, chicken breasts, blood sausages, liver and tripe are all served on a grill, which is placed on the table. If you order a parrillada for two people, you might find there's enough for three (you can get a plastic bag for the leftovers). If you don't want the whole thing, choose just a chop or a steak. Although parrilladas aren't particularly cheap, they are reasonably priced and are a very good value.

JOHN MAIER, JR

Seafood is very good, even in the highlands, as it is brought in fresh from the coast and iced. The most common types of fish are a white sea bass called *corvina* and trout *(trucha)*. *Ceviche* is popular throughout Ecuador; this is seafood marinated in lemon and served with popcorn and sliced onions – it's delicious. Unfortunately, improperly prepared ceviche has recently been identified as a source of the cholera bacteria. However, most restaurants in Ecuador are aware of this and prepare the ceviche under sanitary conditions, so if the restaurant is popular and looks clean, the ceviche will most likely be both delicious and safe. Ceviche can be *de pescado* (fish), *de camarones* (shrimp) or *de concha* (shellfish).

Most Ecuadorian meals come with *arroz* (rice), and some travelers get fed up with it. Surprisingly, one of the best places to go for a change from rice is a Chinese restaurant. These are known as *chifas* and are generally inexpensive and a good value. Apart from rice, they serve *tallarines*, which are noodles mixed with your choice of pork, chicken, beef or vegetables *(legumbres, verduras)*. Portions tend to be filling.

Vegetarian

Vegetarians won't have major problems in Ecuador. Some towns have vegetarian restaurants, and in other places, something can easily be found. *Chifas* (Chinese restaurants) are found in most towns and usually can do a noodle and vegetables dish or something similar. Note that telling wait-staff that you don't want meat doesn't always get the message across – meat usually refers to red meat, so chicken-noodle soup might be suggested as a vegetarian choice! Pizza is also popular – it doesn't have to have meat on it – or you can go to a *cevichería* if you don't consider seafood to be meat. If you are a vegan, you may need to exercise a little more imagination, but dedicated vegans have said that they have gotten by OK.

DRINKS
Nonalcoholic Drinks

Drinking tap water anywhere in Latin America is not recommended. *Agua potable* means that the water comes from the tap, but it's not necessarily healthy. Even if it comes from a chlorination or filtration plant, the plumbing is often old, cracked and full of crud. You can buy bottled water very cheaply in almost any grocery store. It comes in plastic bottles of 500ml, 1l, 2l and 4l and is either carbonated *(con gas)* or noncarbonated *(sin gas)*.

These come in glass or plastic bottles and in cans. Glass bottles require a deposit, but you can drink the contents in the store to avoid paying it. Plastic bottles don't require deposits, but are disposable and contribute to the litter problem. Cans are expensive.

All the usual soft drinks are available, as are some local ones with such endearing names as Bimbo or Lulu. Soft drinks are collectively known as *colas,* and the local brands are very sweet. 7-Up is simply called *seven,* so don't try calling it *siete arriba,* as no one will have any idea what you're talking about. You can also buy Coca-Cola, Pepsi Cola, Orange Fanta or Crush (called 'croosh') and Sprite – the latter is pronounced 'essprite'! Diet soft drinks are less common, but diet cola can often be found.

Ask for your drink *helada* if you want it out of the refrigerator or *al clima* if you don't. Remember to say *sin hielo* (without ice) unless you really trust the water supply.

Juices *(jugos)* are available everywhere, but they cost more than soft drinks. Most juices are either *pura* (with no water) or made with *agua purificada* (boiled or bottled water), although you may want to avoid juices from roadside stands or cheap restaurants, where the water quality is questionable. The most common kinds are *mora* (blackberry), *naranja* (orange), *toronja* (grapefruit), *piña* (pineapple), *maracuya* (passion fruit), *sandía* (watermelon), *naranjilla* (a local fruit that tastes like a bitter orange) or papaya.

Coffee is available almost everywhere, but may be disappointing. Coffee beans may be roasted and ground fine, then compacted into a small perforated metal cup over which boiling water is slowly poured. The result is a thick syrup, which is then poured into cruets and diluted with hot milk or water. Sometimes it tastes OK, but sometimes it's poor. It looks very much like soy sauce, so always check before pouring it into your milk (or over your rice)! Instant coffee is also served. 'Real' filtered coffee is becoming more available. Espresso is available only in the better restaurants. *Café con leche* is coffee with milk, and *café con agua* or *café negro* is black coffee.

Tea, or *té*, is served black with lemon and sugar. If you ask for tea with milk, British style, you'll get a cup of hot milk with a tea bag to dunk in it. Herb teas and hot chocolate are also popular.

Alcoholic Drinks

Finally, we come to those beverages that can loosely be labeled 'libations.' The selection of beers is limited, but they are quite palatable and inexpensive. Pilsner usually comes in large 650ml bottles and is often the cheapest. Club is slightly more expensive, has a slightly higher alcohol content and comes in small 330ml bottles. Other beers are imported and available only in

the more expensive restaurants or at some specialty liquor stores.

Local wines are truly terrible and should not be experimented with. Imported wines from Chile, Argentina or Peru are good but cost much more than they do in their country of origin – nevertheless, they are the best deals for wine drinkers. Californian and European wines are available, but are more expensive still, and Australian wines haven't made it to Ecuador yet.

Spirits are expensive if imported and not very good if made locally, with some notable exceptions. Rum is cheap and good. The local firewater, *aguardiente*, or sugarcane alcohol, is an acquired taste but is also good. It's very cheap; you can get a half bottle of Cristal aguardiente for about US$1. A popular fiesta drink that is made and sold on the streets is a *canelita* or *canelazo* – a hot toddy made with hot water, aguardiente, lemon and *canela* (cinnamon). If you're desperate for reasonably priced gin, vodka or whiskey, try the Larios brand – probably the best of a bad bunch.

Quiteños drinking local brew, Parque El Ejido

ENTERTAINMENT

The most typical nightlife is a peña, or Ecuadorian *música folklórica* club (see Music, in the Facts about Ecuador chapter, for a description of traditional folkloric music). This is a popular form of entertainment for all Ecuadorians, from cabinet ministers to campesinos. Concerts are informal affairs that are usually held late on a weekend night and are accompanied by plenty of drinking. They are not held everywhere – Quito and Otavalo often have good ones.

Apart from peñas, there are the usual nighttime activities in Quito and Guayaquil, but they are limited elsewhere. Cinemas are popular and cheap, but they are losing their audience to the world of video rental. There are theater productions and symphonies in the main cities. Discos and dance clubs are popular in the main cities too. Some of these are great fun if you like dancing to Latin rhythms such as salsa or merengue. In the smaller towns, there isn't much to do. On the whole, Ecuador is not a major destination for those who seek entertainment of the nightlife variety.

SPECTATOR SPORTS

The national sport is *fútbol* (soccer), which is played in every city, town and village. Major-league games are played in Quito and Guayaquil on Saturday afternoons and Sunday mornings. People in Ecuador, as in all of Latin America, can be quite passionate about soccer, and going to a game is usually exciting.

Volleyball is popular, but more as an amateur game played in parks and parking lots than as a professional sport. Golf and tennis are becoming increasingly popular, and Ecuadorian tennis players are becoming increasingly known world-wide. Ecuadorian tennis player Andres Gómez won the US Open Men's Doubles (with Slobodan Zivojinovic) in 1986, as well as the French Open in 1990. He has been followed by Nicolás Lapentti, who was ranked No 8 in the world by the ATP during 1999. Another notable sporting achievement was Jefferson Perez' gold medal in the 20km walk during the 1996 Atlanta Olympics.

Typically, Latin American activities such as bullfighting and cockfighting are popular here. The main bullfighting season is during the first week in December in Quito, when bullfighters from Mexico and Spain may take part. Other highland towns have occasional bullfights, but this sport is less popular in the lowlands. Cockfighting is popular nationwide, and most towns of any size will have a *coliseo de gallos* (cockfighting arena). A variety of strange ballgames are also played. One of these is a sort of paddleball called *pelota de guante,* where players hit a rubber ball with large, spiked paddles.

SHOPPING

Souvenirs are good, varied and cheap. Although going to villages and markets is fun, you won't necessarily save a great deal of money. Similar items for sale in the main cities are often not much more expensive, so if you're limited on time, you can shop in Quito or Guayaquil. If you only have the time or inclination to go on one big shopping expedition, you'll find that the Saturday market at Otavalo is one of the largest in South America, has a wide variety and is convenient – this makes it very popular. Many other markets are colorful events for locals rather than tourists.

In markets and smaller stores, bargaining is acceptable, indeed expected, but don't expect to reduce the price by more than about 20%, unless you are buying in quantity. In 'tourist stores' in Quito, prices are usually fixed. Some of the best stores are quite expensive; on the other hand, the quality of their products is often superior. Shopping in markets is more traditional and fun – but remember to watch your pockets.

Watch out not to buy more things than you can handle – it's expensive to send things home (see Sending Parcels, under Post & Communications, earlier in this chapter).

Clothing

Woolen goods are popular and are often made of a pleasantly coarse homespun wool. Otavalo is good for sweaters, scarves, hats, gloves and vests. The price of a thick sweater will begin under US$10, depending on size and quality; fashionable boutique sweaters can fetch US$50. If you're planning trips high into the mountains, these make good, warm additions to your wardrobe. Wool is also spun into a much finer and tighter textile that is used for making ponchos. Otavaleño Indian ponchos are amongst the best anywhere.

Clothing is also made from Orlon, which is cheaper than wool. Some can tell the difference just by looking, but if you're not sure, try the match trick: Take a tiny piece of lint from the material and set fire to it. If it melts, it's Orlon; if it burns, it's wool. (Perhaps the match trick is not the wisest idea – storekeepers may not appreciate it.) Many people think that only woolen items are traditional, earthy, cool, ethnic etc. While that may be true, if you see an Orlon sweater that you like, there's nothing to stop you buying it, and it'll be one of the cheapest sweaters you've ever bought.

Hand-embroidered clothes are also attractive, but it's worth getting them from a reputable shop; otherwise they may shrink or run. Cotton blouses, shirts, skirts, dresses and shawls are available.

Ecuadorian T-shirts with designs featuring Galápagos animals are very popular; many other bold and distinctive motifs are available. If you're a T-shirt collector, you'll find all sizes and colors to choose from.

Panama hats are worth buying. A good panama is so finely made that it can be rolled up and passed through a man's ring, but it's unlikely that you'll find many of that quality. They are made from *toquilla*, a palmlike bush that grows abundantly in the coastal province of Manabí. Montecristi and Jipijapa are major centers. The hat's name dates back to the 1849 California gold rush, when prospectors traveling from the eastern US to California through the Isthmus of Panama bought the hats, but they are originally Ecuadorian.

Weavings

A large variety of mainly woolen weavings are to be found all over the country, with Otavalo, as usual, having a good selection. They range from sq-foot weavings that can

Main Market Days

The more important markets are asterisked.

Saturday
Otavalo*, Latacunga*, Riobamba*, Cotacachi, Guano, Azoguez

Sunday
Sangolquí*, Machachi*, Pujilí*, Peguche, Cuenca, Santo Domingo de los Colorados, Salcedo, Tulcán

Monday
Ambato*

Tuesday
Latacunga, Riobamba, Guano

Wednesday
Pujilí

Thursday
Saquisilí*, Cuenca, Riobamba, Tulcán

be sewn together to make throw cushions or shoulder bags, to weavings large enough to be used as floor rugs or wall hangings. Designs range from traditional to modern; MC Escher styles are popular.

Bags

Apart from bags made from two small weavings stitched together, you can buy *shigras*, or shoulder bags made from agave fiber, that are strong, colorful and eminently practical. They come in a variety of sizes and are expandable. Agave fiber is also used to make macramé bags.

Leather

A famous center for leatherwork is Cota-cachi, north of Otavalo. Prices are cheap in comparison to those in more developed countries, but quality is very variable, so examine possible purchases carefully. Although the best leatherwork in Ecuador is supposedly done in the Ambato area, it's much easier to find leather goods for sale in Cotacachi. Leatherwork items range from full suits to coin purses and from wide-brimmed hats to luggage.

Products from Trees

The major woodworking center of Ecuador is San Antonio de Ibarra, and any items bought elsewhere are likely to have been carved there. Items range from the utilitarian (bowls, salad utensils, chess sets, candlesticks) to the decorative (crucifixes, statues, wall plaques). Again, prices are very low, but quality varies.

Balsa-wood models are also popular. They are made in the jungles of the Oriente and are sold in many of Quito's gift stores. Brightly painted birds are the most frequently seen, but other animals and boxes are also sold.

Tagua-nut carvings are common souvenirs. The nut is actually the seed of a coastal palm (*Phytelephas macrocarpa*). The egg-sized seed is hard enough to be called 'vegetable ivory' and is carved into small animal figurines, as well as a variety of novelty items, such as napkin rings and chess pieces.

Jewelry

Ecuador isn't famous for its gemstones, but it does have good silverwork. Chordeleg, near Cuenca, has beautifully filigreed silver items. The Amazon area produces necklaces made from nuts and other rainforest products.

Bread Figures

Painted and varnished ornaments made of bread dough are unique to Ecuador and are best obtained in Calderón, a village just north of Quito. Some of the most inexpensive ones are designed as (and make) great Christmas tree ornaments. Designs are imaginative and fun – Christmas stockings with a mouse peeking out, giant green cacti vaguely suggestive of a Christmas tree, animals, candles…the designs go on and on. For a few dollars, you can buy decorations for everyone on your gift list.

Other Items

Baskets made of straw, reeds or agave fibers are common everywhere. Onyx (a pale, translucent quartz with parallel layers of different colors) is carved into chess sets and other objects. Miniature blowpipes modeled after those used by Amazonian Indians are also popular, and you'll find plenty of other choices.

Getting There & Away

There are three ways of getting to Ecuador: by air from anywhere in the world, by land (from either Colombia or Peru) and by sea. However, very few people even consider the ocean route these days, as it is more expensive and less convenient than flying.

AIR
Airports & Airlines

There are two major international airports serving Ecuador: one in Guayaquil and one in Quito. A flight between these two cities only costs about US$50 if you buy the ticket in Ecuador, but it's US$100 when bought in other countries. Contact information for the Quito and Guayaquil offices of international airlines is given in the Getting There & Away sections under those cities.

Ecuatoriana flies to and from New York, Mexico City, Panama City and several Brazilian cities. TAME has service from

---

Volcanic Activity

Since late 1999, Volcán Pichincha has been erupting on a regular basis. So far, these eruptions have been confined to huge clouds of gas, steam and ash shooting several kilometers into the air – major lava flows have not yet occurred. Pichincha is close to Quito, but because of the geographical lay of the land, it would be impossible for lava flows to reach the capital. However, occasional eruptions have covered Quito with a light sprinkling of volcanic ash, and this has forced the international airport to close several times for periods ranging from a few hours to a few days. Arriving international flights have been diverted to Guayaquil, from where passengers are either bused to Quito (which takes about seven hours) or flown up the next day if conditions have improved. Domestic flights could be diverted to Latacunga (a 90-minute drive from the capital).

Quito and Guayaquil to Cuba and Santiago, Chile; from the Ecuadorian town of Tulcán to Cali, in southern Colombia; and is planning on flights to Piura, Peru, in the near future. TAME's Web site is at www .tame.com.ec. Saeta, which was once a major international Ecuadorian airline, has shut down indefinitely.

American Airlines has the most frequent services to Ecuador from the USA, with the most gateway cities. Continental flies to Ecuador from Houston, Texas. Both airlines stop in, or continue on to, other Latin American cities. Several major Latin American carriers fly from Ecuador to Latin America and the USA.

Major carriers from Europe include Air France, Iberia, KLM and Lufthansa; they usually stop in Miami or somewhere in the Caribbean or Latin America en route to Ecuador. Other European carriers provide flights that connect with North and Latin American airlines.

If you plan to fly to Ecuador, bear in mind that the main hub for flights to and from western South America is Lima, Peru. You may be able to fly more cheaply to Lima and finish your journey to Ecuador by land. Bus travel from Lima to the Ecuadorian border takes about 24 hours and costs about US$20. If you prefer to travel directly to Ecuador, frequent international flights arrive and depart from either Quito or Guayaquil.

If, because of a late flight (though not a rescheduled one) you lose a connection or are forced to stay overnight, the carrier is responsible for providing you with help in making the earliest possible connection and paying for a room in a hotel of their choice. They should also provide you with meal vouchers. If you are seriously delayed on an international flight, ask for these services.

Buying Tickets

The high season for air travel to and within Ecuador is mid-June through early September and December through mid-January. Lower fares may be offered at other times.

Remember that roundtrip fares are always cheaper than two one-way tickets. They are also cheaper than an 'open jaw' fare, which enables you to fly into one city (say Lima) and leave via another (say Río de Janeiro).

The ordinary tourist- or economy-class fare is not necessarily the most economical way to go. It is convenient, however, because it enables you to fly on the next plane out, which you can't do when you buy an advance purchase excursion (APEX) ticket. Also, an economy-class ticket is valid for 12 months. The Internet also has a wealth of resources for finding cheap fares.

Taxes There is also a 12% tax on all international flights originating in Ecuador (this is on top of the US$25 departure tax that has to be paid by everyone leaving the country, no matter where the flight originated). This 12% tax must be paid before boarding the aircraft. For example, if you purchase a Miami-Caracas ticket and a Quito-Miami ticket (intending to travel overland from Caracas to Quito), you will be charged 12% of the Quito-Miami fare at the airport because this flight originates in Ecuador. This does not apply to the return portion of a Miami-Quito-Miami ticket, because it does not originate in Ecuador. Check this carefully if you are buying a ticket originating in Ecuador.

Student & Youth Fares Students with international student ID cards and anyone under 26 can get discounts with most airlines. Although student and youth fares can be arranged through most travel agents and airlines, it is a good idea to go through agents that specialize in student travel – several are listed in the country sections of this chapter. Note that student fares are not only cheap, but often include free stopovers, don't require advance purchase and may be valid for up to a year – a great deal if you are eligible.

Airline Deals No matter what age you are, if you can purchase your plane ticket well in advance and stay for a minimum length of time, you can buy a ticket that's usually about 30% or 40% cheaper than the full economy fare. These are often called APEX, excursion, or promotional fares, depending on the country you are departing from and the rules and fare structures that apply there.

Often, the following restrictions apply: You must purchase your ticket at least 21 days (sometimes more or fewer) in advance; you must stay a minimum period (about 14 days on average); and you must return within 180 days (sometimes fewer, for example, passengers from the USA must return within 30 days to qualify for the lowest APEX fares). Individual airlines have different requirements, and these change from time to time. Most of these tickets do not allow stopovers, and there are extra charges if you change your destinations or dates of travel. These tickets are often sold out well in advance, so try to book early.

Warning

The information in this chapter is particularly vulnerable to change: Prices for international travel are volatile, routes are introduced and canceled, schedules change, special deals come and go, and rules and visa requirements are amended. Airlines and governments seem to take a perverse pleasure in making price structures and regulations as complicated as possible. You should check directly with the airline or a travel agent to make sure you understand how a fare (and ticket you may buy) works. In addition, the travel industry is highly competitive and there are many lurks and perks.

The upshot of this is that you should get opinions, quotes and advice from as many airlines and travel agents as possible before you part with your hard-earned cash. The details given in this chapter should be regarded as pointers and are not a substitute for your own careful, up-to-date research.

Get your sundries and then some in one of Quito's many outdoor markets.

Old Town Quito holds many spectacular colonial buildings.

Quito plaza (no swimming!)

Monasterio de San Francisco, with the eerie glow of the sun through Pichincha's volcanic ash

North of Ibarra is the lovely Río Chota valley, home to many Ecuadorians of African descent.

Tulcán's cemetery has a striking topiary garden.

Sampling the greens at the market in Otavalo

Air Travel Glossary

Cancellation Penalties If you have to cancel or change a discounted ticket, there are often heavy penalties involved; insurance can sometimes be taken out against these penalties. Some airlines impose penalties on regular tickets as well, particularly against 'no-show' passengers.

Courier Fares Many businesses often need to send urgent documents or freight securely and quickly. Courier companies hire people to accompany the package through customs and, in return, offer a discount ticket which is sometimes a phenomenal bargain. However, you may have to surrender all your baggage allowance and take only carry-on luggage.

Full Fares Airlines traditionally offer 1st class (coded F), business class (coded J) and economy class (coded Y) tickets. These days there are so many promotional and discounted fares available that few passengers pay full economy fare.

Lost Tickets If you lose your airline ticket an airline will usually treat it like a traveler's check and, after inquiries, issue you with another one. Legally, however, an airline is entitled to treat it like cash and if you lose it then it's gone forever. Take good care of your tickets.

Onward Tickets An entry requirement for many countries is that you have a ticket out of the country. If you're unsure of your next move, the easiest solution is to buy the cheapest onward ticket to a neighbouring country or a ticket from a reliable airline which can later be refunded if you do not use it.

Open-Jaw Tickets These are return tickets where you fly out to one place but return from another. If available, this can save you backtracking to your arrival point.

Overbooking Since every flight has some passengers who fail to show up, airlines often book more passengers than they have seats. Usually excess passengers make up for the no-shows, but occasionally somebody gets 'bumped' onto the next available flight. Guess who it is most likely to be? The passengers who check in late.

Promotional Fares These are officially discounted fares, available from travel agencies or direct from the airline.

Reconfirmation If you don't reconfirm your flight at least 72 hours prior to departure, the airline may delete your name from the passenger list. Call to find out if your airline requires reconfirmation.

Restrictions Discounted tickets often have various restrictions on them – such as needing to be paid for in advance and incurring a penalty to be altered. Others are restrictions on the minimum and maximum period you must be away.

Round-the-World Tickets RTW tickets give you a limited period (usually a year) in which to circumnavigate the globe. You can go anywhere the carrying airlines go, as long as you don't backtrack. The number of stopovers or total number of separate flights is decided before you set off and they usually cost a bit more than a basic return flight.

Transferred Tickets Airline tickets cannot be transferred from one person to another. Travelers sometimes try to sell the return half of their ticket, but officials can ask you to prove that you are the person named on the ticket. On an international flight tickets are compared with passports.

Travel Periods Ticket prices vary with the time of year. There is a low (off-peak) season and a high (peak) season, and often a low-shoulder season and a high-shoulder season as well. Usually the fare depends on your outward flight – if you depart in the high season and return in the low season, you pay the high-season fare.

Discounted Tickets The cheapest way to go is with a ticket sold by companies specializing in air travel ('consolidators' or 'bucket shops'). These companies are legally allowed to sell discounted tickets to help airlines and charter companies fill their flights. These tickets often sell out fast, and you may be limited to a few available dates and other restrictions. While APEX, economy and student tickets are available directly from the airlines or from a travel agent, discounted tickets are available only from the discount ticket agencies themselves. Most of them are good, reputable, legalized and bonded companies, but once in a while, a fly-by-night operator comes along and takes your money for a super-cheap flight and gives you an invalid or unusable ticket, so check what you are buying carefully before handing over your money. Paying by credit card gives you the greatest protection against this.

Discount ticket agencies often advertise in newspapers and magazines; there is much competition, and a variety of fares and schedules are available. Fares to South America have traditionally been relatively expensive, but ticket agencies have recently been able to offer increasingly economical fares to the continent.

Courier Travel If you are flexible with dates and can manage with only carry-on luggage, you can fly to Ecuador as a courier. This is most practical between major US gateways and Guayaquil or Quito. Couriers are hired by companies that need to have packages delivered to other countries, and they will give the courier exceptionally cheap tickets in return for using his or her baggage allowance. These are legitimate operations – all baggage that you are to deliver is completely legal. And it is amazing how much you can bring in your carry-on luggage. A few couriers boarding an aircraft have worn two pairs of trousers and two shirts under a sweater and rain jacket and stuffed the pockets with travel essentials. Bring a folded plastic shopping bag, and once you have boarded the aircraft, you can remove the extra clothes and place them in the plastic bag! (Try not to have metal objects in inside pockets when you go through the metal detector at the airport! Also bear in mind that most courier companies want their couriers to look reasonably neat, so you can't overdo the 'bag lady' routine.) Remember, you can buy things such as T-shirts, a towel and soap after you arrive at your destination, so traveling with just carry-on luggage is certainly feasible.

Another possibility (at least for US residents) is to join the International Association of Air Travel Couriers (IAATC). The membership fee of $45 gets members a bimonthly update of air-courier offerings, access to a fax-on-demand service with daily updates of last minute specials and the bimonthly newsletter *Shoestring Traveler*. For more information, contact IAATC (☎ 561-582-8320) or visit its Web site, www .courier.org. However, be aware that joining this organization does not guarantee that you'll get a courier flight.

Second-Hand Tickets You'll occasionally see advertisements on youth hostel bulletin boards and in newspapers for 'second-hand tickets.' That is, somebody purchased a roundtrip ticket or a ticket with multiple stopovers and now wants to sell the unused portion of the ticket.

The prices offered look very attractive indeed. Unfortunately, these tickets, if used for international travel, are usually worthless, as the name on the ticket must match the name on the passport of the person checking in. Some people reason that the seller of the ticket can check you in with his or her passport, and then give you the boarding pass – wrong again! Usually the immigration people want to see your boarding pass, and if it doesn't match the name in your passport, you won't be able to board your flight.

What happens if you purchase a ticket and then change your name? It can happen – some people change their names when they get married or divorced; some people change their names because they feel like it. If the name on the ticket doesn't match the name in your passport, you could have problems. In this case, be sure you have documents such as your old passport to prove that the old you and the new you are the same person.

Ticketless Travel Ticketless travel, whereby your reservation details are contained within an airline computer, is becoming more common. On simple roundtrip flights, the absence of a ticket can be a benefit – it's one less thing to worry about. However, if you are planning a complicated itinerary that you may wish to amend en route, there is no substitute for the good old paper version.

Travelers with Special Needs

Most airlines can accommodate travelers with special needs, but only if requested some days in advance. On flights with meals, a variety of special cuisine can be ordered in advance at no extra charge. These may include most of the following: vegetarian, low fat, low salt, children's, kosher and others.

Airlines can easily accommodate travelers requiring physical assistance. Wheelchairs designed to fit in aircraft aisles, plus an employee to push the chair if necessary, are available with advance notice. Passengers can check their own wheelchairs as luggage. Blind passengers can request to have an employee take them through the check-in procedure and all the way to their seats. Again, ask if you have special needs – airlines usually work to oblige.

Departure Tax

There is a departure tax is US$25 for international flights originating in Quito or Guayaquil. Short cross-border hops, such as Tulcán-Cali (Colombia) or Puyo-Piura (Peru), are not taxed.

The tax is payable in US cash only. Traveler's checks are not accepted; if you only have plastic, use an airport ATM to obtain cash. This tax is always paid on departure and is not included in the cost of your ticket.

The USA

From the USA, there are direct flights nonstop to Quito or Guayaquil from New

York, Houston and Miami. American Airlines and Continental are the US carriers, and some Latin American carriers stop in Ecuador en route to somewhere else.

Generally speaking, the USA does not have such a strong discount-ticket tradition as Europe or Asia, but in recent years, 'consolidators' (as discount ticket agencies in the US are called) have begun to appear. Sometimes the Sunday travel sections in the major newspapers (the *Los Angeles Times*, the *San Francisco Examiner,* the *Chicago Tribune* and the *New York Times*) advertise cheap fares to South America, although these are sometimes no cheaper than APEX fares. Newspapers of smaller cities often have one or two consolidators advertising as well. Several useful books about this have been published; a large bookstore with a good travel section (or a travel bookstore) will advise you of recent publications.

A good place to start for students is STA Travel (☎ 800-777-0112, 781-4040), which has offices in many towns; the 800 number automatically connects you to the nearest. STA's Web site is at www.statravel.com. A travel agency with great deals for all age groups is Council Travel, a subsidiary of the Council on International Educational Exchange (CIEE; ☎ 212-661-1414, 800-226-8624, fax 212-972-231), 205 E 42nd St, New York, NY 10017. You can find local addresses and telephone numbers for Council Travel in the telephone directories of many North American cities, particularly those with universities; the company's Web site is at www.counciltravel.com.

Another excellent source for cheap tickets is eXito Latin America Travel Specialists (☎ 800-655-4053, fax 510-655-4566, exito@wonderlink.com), 1212 Broadway, Suite 910, Oakland, CA 94612. They specialize in Latin America only and can do both short- and long-term tickets with multiple stopovers if desired. The company's Web site is at www.exitotravel.com.

Courier flights are more common from the USA than from Europe and are a good option for people flying from New York or Miami. For up-to-date information, contact Travel Unlimited, PO Box 1058, Allston,

MA 02134, which publishes monthly listings of courier and other cheap flights to Ecuador and many other countries. A year's subscription costs US$25 in the USA and US$35 elsewhere. You can get a single issue for US$5. Also contact the Association of Air Travel Couriers at ☎ 561-582-8320 or visit its Web site at www.courier.org.

Canada

From Canada, American Airlines and Continental have connections from Toronto and Montreal via New York or Miami and on to Guayaquil or Quito. Canadian Airlines and Air Canada fly to US gateways and connect with other carriers. Travel CUTS (☎ 416-614-2887, 800-667-2887, fax 416-614-9670), 200 Ronson Dr, Suite 300, Toronto, ON M9W-5Z9, has about 60 offices nationwide and is a good choice for student, youth and budget airfares. You can visit its Web site at www.travelcuts.com.

See The USA, earlier in this section, for eXito, which can arrange discounted fares from Canada. Also see the Sunday travel sections of major newspapers for advertising by consolidators offering cheap fares.

The UK

There are no direct flights from the UK to Ecuador. Discount ticket agencies generally provide the cheapest fares from the UK to South America. Fares from London are often cheaper than from other European cities, even though your flight route may take you from London through a European city! Many European (especially Scandinavian) budget travelers buy from London ticket agencies, as cheap fares are difficult to find in their own countries. Although the discounted tickets sold by these ticket agencies are often several hundred dollars cheaper than official fares, they usually carry certain restrictions – but they are valid and legal.

In London, competition is fierce. Discount flights are often advertised in the classifieds. There have been consistently good reports about Journey Latin America (JLA; see The UK under Organized Tours, later in this chapter, for contact information). JLA spe-

cializes in cheap fares to South America in addition to arranging itineraries (by phone or fax) for both independent and escorted travel; ask for the free magazine *Papagaio*. Flightbookers (☎ 020-7757 2611), 177 Tottenham Court Rd, London W1P OLX, recently had some of the cheapest flights from the UK; its Web site is at www.flightbookers.net. Another recommended agency is Trailfinders (☎ 020-7983 3939), 194 Kensington High St, London W8 7RG.

Specializing in flights for students and people under 26 is Council Travel (☎ 020-7437 7767), 28A Poland Street, London W1V 3DB; you can visit its Web site at www.counciltravel.com. STA Travel (☎ 020-7361 6161) is at 86 Old Brompton Rd, London SW7 3LQ; it also has other offices throughout the UK. You can visit its Web site at www.statravel.com. Usit Campus (☎ 020-7730 3402), 52 Grosvenor Gardens, London SW1W 0AG, has branch offices throughout the UK; its Web site is at www.usitcampus.com.

The cheapest fares from London may start at under £500, which is an incredible deal, considering the distance. Restrictions are usually that the flights may leave only on certain days, the tickets may be valid for only 90 days, and there may be penalties for changing your return date. A £10 departure tax is added.

Australia & New Zealand

There is no real choice of routes between Australia/New Zealand and South America, and there are certainly no bargain fares available. The most convenient air route is the twice-a-week Sydney-Auckland-Buenos Aires flight with Aerolíneas Argentinas, continuing to Quito with Ecuatoriana. However, some travelers prefer longer routes via Honolulu and/or Los Angeles because there are more departures.

Students should check with STA Travel (☎ 131 776 Australiawide, 09-309 0458 in New Zealand), which has dozens of offices in Australia and New Zealand. STA's Web site is at www.statravel.com.au. Also try Flight Centre (☎ 131 600 Australiawide, 09-309 6171 in New Zealand); there are many branches in both countries. Flight Centre's Web site is at www.flightcentre.com.au.

Check the ads in the travel pages of papers such as Melbourne's *The Age* or the *Sydney Morning Herald*.

Continental Europe

There are few direct flights from Europe to Ecuador; most involve a change of plane and airline in Miami or in a South American capital other than Quito. Iberia has a nonstop flight to Quito from Madrid, and KLM has a flight from Amsterdam to Quito via Curacao and Guayaquil (no change of planes is required).

Across Europe, many travel agencies have ties with STA Travel, where cheap tickets can be purchased and STA-issued tickets can be altered (usually for a US$25 fee). Visit the Web site at www.statravel .com for information on STA worldwide partners. Also visit the Web site of Council Travel at www.counciltravel.com for information on its partners in Europe.

France has a network of student travel agencies that can supply discount tickets to travelers of all ages. OTU Voyages (☎ 01 44 41 38 50) has a central Paris office at 39 Ave Georges Bernanos (5e) and 42 offices around the country, its Web site is at www .otu.fr. Acceuil des Jeunes en France (☎ 01 42 77 87 80), 119 rue Saint Martin (4e), is another popular discount travel agency.

There are two general travel agencies in Paris that offer some of the best services and deals. They are Nouvelles Frontières (☎ 08 03 33 33 33), located at 5 Ave de l'Opèra (1er), www.nouvelles-frontieres .com; and Voyageurs du Monde (☎ 01 42 86 16 00), 55 rue Sainte Anne (2e).

Belgium, Switzerland, the Netherlands and Greece are also good places for buying discount air tickets. In Belgium, Acotra Student Travel Agency (☎ 02-512 86 07), at Rue de la Madeline in Brussels, and WATS Reizen (☎ 03-226 16 26), at de Keyserlei 44 in Antwerp, are both well-known agencies. In Switzerland, SSR Voyages (☎ 01-297 11 11) specializes in student, youth and budget fares. In Zurich, there is a branch at Leonhardstrasse 10, and there are others in most major Swiss cities. SSR's Web site is at www.ssr.ch.

In the Netherlands, NBBS Reizen is the official student travel agency. You can find it in Amsterdam (☎ 020-624 09 89) at Rokin 66, and there are several other agencies around the city. Another recommended travel agent in Amsterdam is Malibu Travel (☎ 020-626 32 30), at Prinsengracht 230.

In Athens, check the many travel agencies in the back streets between Syntagma and Omonia Squares. For student and nonconcessionary fares, try Magic Bus (☎ 01-323 7471, fax 322 0219).

Latin America

Flights from Latin American countries are usually subject to high tax and good deals are less frequent.

Many Latin American airlines fly to Ecuador, including Aerolíneas Argentinas; Aerolíneas Centrales de Colombia; Avensa and Servivensa (Venezuela); Avianca (Colombia); Copa (Panama); Cubana de Aviación (Cuba); Ecuatoriana (Ecuador); Grupo Taca (Central America); LanChile; and Varig (Brazil). In addition, several US companies have flights between some Latin American cities and Lima.

Asia

The normal route is to fly from Asia to the US and connect to Ecuador from there. Again, fares are not cheap. Council Travel (www.counciltravel.com) is at Cosmos Aoyama, Gallery Floor, 5-53-67 Jingumae, Shibuya-ku, Tokyo 150, Japan (☎ 3-5467-5535, fax 3-5467-7031).

STA Travel (www.statravel.com) has offices or representatives in Japan, Singapore, Malaysia, India and Thailand. Hong Kong has many travel agencies, of which Hong Kong Student Travel Bureau (☎ 2730 3269), 8th floor, Star House, Tsimshatsui has been recommended.

Africa

Most travelers will need to make lengthy and expensive connections via Europe. The main exception is South Africa, which has flights from Johannesburg to Brazil with

Varig, from where connections to Ecuador are easily made. STA Travel has offices in Cape Town, Johannesburg and Pretoria. Its Web site is at www.statravel.com.

LAND

If you live in the Americas, it is possible to travel overland by bus. However, if you want to start from North or Central America, the Carretera Panamericana stops in Panama and begins again in Colombia, leaving a 200km roadless section of jungle known as the Darien Gap. This takes about a week to cross on foot and by canoe in the dry season (January to mid-April) but is much heavier going in the wet season. This overland route has become increasingly dangerous because of banditry and drug-related problems, especially on the Colombian side. Most overland travelers fly or take a boat around the Darien Gap.

Once in South America it is relatively straightforward to travel by public bus from the neighboring Andean countries (Colombia and Peru) although this is a fairly slow option. See Lonely Planet Guides to those countries for full details. There is no departure tax for leaving Ecuador overland.

SEA

Occasionally you can find a ship going to Guayaquil, Ecuador's main port, though this is a very unusual way to arrive in Ecuador. It's certainly cheaper and more convenient to fly, but the 'romance' of crossing the world the old way is still a draw to some.

Very few cruise ships use Guayaquil as a port of call as they head down the Pacific coast of South America. A few cargo lines will carry passengers.

The standard reference for passenger ships is the *OAG Cruise & Ferry Guide,* published by Reed Travel Group (☎ 0158-2600 111), Church St, Dunstable, Beds LU5 4HB, UK. Another choice is the *Berlitz 2000 Complete Guide to Cruising & Cruise Ships.*

It is possible to arrive in Ecuador on your own sailing boat or, if you don't happen to have one, as a crew member. Crew members don't necessarily have to be experienced because many long ocean passages involve standing watch and keeping your eyes open. You should be able to get along with people in close quarters for extended periods of time, as this is the most difficult aspect of the trip. If you get fed up with someone, there is nowhere else to go. Crew members are often (but not always) asked to contribute toward expenses, especially food. Still, this is usually much cheaper than traveling overland. Check the notice boards around marinas for vessels looking for additional crew members. In Ecuador, Salinas is the port most frequented by international yachts. For information, read the *World Cruising Handbook* by Jimmy and Doina Cornell.

RIVER

Since 1998, when the long-awaited Peace Treaty was signed with Peru, it has technically been possible to travel down Río Napo from Ecuador to Peru, joining the Amazon near Iquitos. The problems are that border facilities are minimal (though they are expected to expand in 2000 and 2001), and the boats doing the trip are infrequent.

It is also geographically possible to travel down Río Putumayo into Colombia and Peru, but this is a dangerous region because of drug smuggling and terrorism and is not recommended.

ORGANIZED TOURS

Many kinds of organized tours are available. These range from hotel-based visits of the highlands to strenuous mountaineering expeditions, from camping in the rainforest to staying at a luxurious jungle lodge and, of course, tours to the Galápagos.

Many tours can be arranged within Ecuador and are described in the main body of the book. Other tours can be arranged in advance from home (especially if you live in the USA). There are many operators to choose from. You can find their addresses in advertisements in outdoor and travel magazines such as *Escape* and *Outside,* as well as more general magazines such as *Natural History, Audubon* and *Smithsonian.* The following are some of the best and most well established companies, but there are certainly others.

The USA

Backroads 801 Cedar St, Berkeley, CA 94710-1800 (☎ 510-527-1555, 800-462-2848, fax 510-527-1444, www.backroads.com). This agency offers a combination of mountain biking, hiking and other adventure trips combined with top-end accommodations.

Earthwatch Institute 3 Clocktower Place, Suite 100, Box 75, Maynard, MA 01754 (☎ 978-461-0081, 800-776-0188, fax 978-461-2332; info@earthwatch.org). 'Volunteers' pay approximately US$2000 to assist scientists carrying out research; a variety of trips are offered and all are tax deductible.

Elderhostel 75 Federal St, Boston, MA 02110-1941 (☎ 877-426-8056, 978-323-4141, network @elderhostel.org, www.elderhostel.org). Excellent educational tours for travelers over 55 (younger companions permitted).

Field Guides 9433 Bee Cave Rd, Building 1, Suite 150, Austin, TX 78733 (☎ 512-263-7295, 800-728-4953, fax 263-0117, fgileader@aol.com). These tours are for dedicated bird watchers.

Galápagos Travel 783 Río Del Mar Boulevard, Suite 47, Aptos, CA 95003 (☎ 831-689-9192, 800-969-9014, fax 831-689-9195, galapagostravel@compuserve.com). Galápagos uses the better type of small boat.

INCA, International Nature & Cultural Adventures, 1311 63rd St, Emeryville, CA 94608 (☎ 510-420-1550, fax 420-0947, info@incafloats .com). This agency mainly arranges Galápagos tours on small boats, in addition to some mainland tours.

International Expeditions One Environs Park, Helena, AL 35080 (☎ 205-428-1700, 800-633-4734, fax 205-428-1714, www.ietravel.com).

High-quality natural history tours with excellent guides and accommodations.

Wilderness Travel 1102 Ninth St, Berkeley, CA 94710-1211 (☎ 510-558-2488, 800-368-2794, fax 510-558-2489, info@wildernesstravel.com). One- and two-week Galápagos tours on the best small boats, Amazon tours and combinations.

Wildland Adventures 3516 NE 155th St, Seattle, WA 98155 (☎ 206-365-0686, 800-345-4453, fax 206-363-6615, info@wildland.com). This agency offers general tours with an emphasis on responsible tourism.

The UK

Galápagos Adventure Tours Dept SB, 37-39 Great Guildford St, London SE1 0ES (☎/fax 020-7261 9890, david@galapagos.co.uk). Fully escorted tours to the Galápagos on the best boats. Scuba diving and jungle excursions are available.

Journey Latin America 12 & 13 Heathfield Terrace, Chiswick, London W4 4JE (☎ 020-8747 3108 for flights, 8747 8315 for tours, fax 8742 1312, sales@journeylatinamerica.co.uk). Flight and tour specialists to Latin America with many years of experience.

South American Experience 47 Causton St, London SW1P 4AT (☎ 020-7976 5511, fax 7976 6908, sax@mcmail.com). Similar to Journey Latin America.

Australia

Adventure Associates 197 Oxford Street Mall, Bondi Junction, Sydney NSW 2022; PO Box 612 Bondi Junction, NSW 1355 (☎ 02-9389 7466, fax 02-9369 1853, www.adventureassociates.com). Various tours.

Contours 1/84 William St, Melbourne, VIC 3000 (☎ 03-9670-6900, fax 03- 9670-7558; contours@compuserve.com). Good variety of Latin American tours at mid- to lower-top-end prices.

Getting Around

Ecuador has a more efficient transportation system than most Andean countries. Also, because of its small size, you can usually get anywhere and everywhere quickly and easily. The bus is the most frequently used method of transportation; you can take buses from Tulcán, on the Colombian border, to Huaquillas, on the Peruvian border, and arrive in only 18 hours. Airplanes and boats (especially in the Oriente and in the Galápagos) are also frequently used, but trains are less used.

Whichever form of transportation you use, remember to have your passport with you – do not leave it in the hotel safe or packed in your luggage. To board many planes and boats, you need to show your passport.

Buses may go through a transit police check upon entering any town and, although your passport is not frequently asked for, it's good to have it handy for those times when you are asked to show it. Passport controls are more frequent when traveling by bus in the Oriente. If your passport is in order, these procedures are no more than cursory.

AIR

Even the budget traveler should consider the occasional internal flight. With the exception of flying to the Galápagos Islands, internal flights are comparatively cheap. There is a two-tier pricing system on a few flights, on which foreigners pay more than Ecuadorians. These include flights to and from the Oriente towns of Macas, Lago Agrio and Coca (US$53 one way to or from Quito for foreigners; about half of that for locals) and to the Galápagos (US$333/377 roundtrip from Guayaquil/Quito, which is about twice what Ecuadorians pay and four times what island residents pay). Flights between Quito and Guayaquil are around US$50 if bought in Ecuador with TAME. Despite the extra costs, foreigners are not treated to any better in-flight service. Other

flights cost the same for Ecuadorians and foreigners, but this may change in the future.

The main airports are shown on the accompanying Internal Air Services map. Most flights originate or terminate in Quito or Guayaquil, so a useful way for the traveler to utilize these services is by taking a long overland journey from one of these cities and then returning quickly by air.

Ecuador's most important domestic airline is TAME, which flies to almost all destinations in the country. SAN-Saeta was TAME's main competitor, but it has shut down indefinitely. Other, smaller airlines include Aerogal, which flies between Quito and Coca, and Austro Aeréo, which flies from Cuenca to Guayaquil and Macas (with possible expansion in the future).

There are also various small companies, most of which fly along the coast in light aircraft carrying five to nine passengers. Chartered flights can be arranged into the Oriente. The military has been known to provide flights, as have the missions and the oil companies; however, this is becoming less common. These days, with improving air services, it's usually easier to pay a few extra dollars for a scheduled flight than to spend several days lining up a flight with someone else.

TAME flies from Quito to most major cities (see the Internal Air Services map) with the exception of Coca, which is served by Aerogal. There may be seasonal TAME flights from Guayaquil to Salinas; the airline sometimes suspends or cancels flights if aircraft need maintenance or if there aren't enough passengers, but this has not been happening as much as it did a few years ago. See the Galápagos Islands chapter for information on getting there from the mainland.

Flights are frequently late, but not by very much. Flights that depart first thing in the morning are more likely to be on time, but by the afternoon, things tend to have slid half an hour behind schedule. You should show up about an hour early for domestic flights, as baggage handling and check-in procedures tend to be rather chaotic. It's best to travel light and avoid having to check your baggage. Some major towns now offer advance check-in for travelers with carry-on luggage.

If you show up early for your flight between Quito and Guayaquil, you can often get on an earlier flight if there is room.

There are usually no seating assignments on domestic flights – you choose your seat aboard, on a first-come, first-served basis. There are no separate sections for smokers and nonsmokers. Many flights give extraor-dinary views of the snowcapped Andes; it is worth getting a window seat even if the weather is bad, as the planes often rise above the clouds, allowing spectacular views of volcanoes riding on a sea of cloud (see the boxed text 'Ecuador from Above').

If you need to fly, don't despair if you can't get a ticket. Go to the airport early and get yourself on a waiting list; often, passengers don't show up. If you do have a reservation, confirm flights both 72 and 24 hours in advance, as well as when you arrive in Ecuador. If it's impossible for you to do so, tell them beforehand so that they know. Try

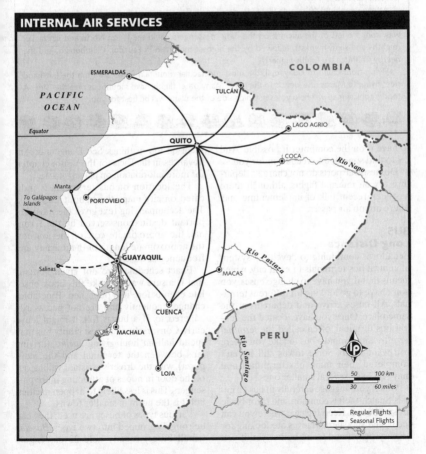

INTERNAL AIR SERVICES

Ecuador from Above

Once in a while, you may be treated to a special mountain flyby when flying in Ecuador. This happened to me on the flight from Macas to Quito. We flew by Cotopaxi, and the pilot decided to give us a closer look. Banking sharply, he did a complete circuit of the volcano. For over a minute, we enjoyed a wonderful view of the top of the mountain and a rare look directly into the crater.

I also remember a spectacular Quito-Cuenca flight I chanced to take one cloudless morning in June. As we took off, Cayambe (Ecuador's third-highest peak) was briefly visible behind the aircraft. Almost immediately, the majestic bulk of Antisana (the fourth-highest) appeared, its four lumpy peaks rising from the edge of the Amazon Basin. After a few minutes, we passed the ice-cream cone of Cotopaxi (second-highest), and then Tungurahua (10th-highest), which is currently erupting. Soon after, the jagged peaks of El Altar (fifth-highest) appeared, with a sulfur-yellow lagoon in the middle of the blown-away crater, followed by the smoking volcano, Sangay (seventh-highest).

After a wonderful 40-minute flight, we descended, flying low over the red-tiled colonial roofs of Cuenca, with a good look at the blue-domed cathedral in the central plaza. The view I describe was from the left of the aircraft; on the right, passengers could see Iliniza Norte and Iliniza Sur (eighth- and sixth-highest), followed by the highest mountain in Ecuador, Chimborazo, and the nearby Carihuairazo (ninth-highest).

Flying from Quito to Guayaquil, the most spectacular mountain views are from the left-hand side; flying to Macas, the view is to the right. Many other flights have mountains on either side. A topographical map will help you see which side of the plane will be best for you.

to have it on the computer if possible. And try to find someone to reconfirm for you.

Domestic airports do not charge a departure tax on internal flights, although there has been recent talk of implementing one. There are no air passes.

BUS
Long Distance
Ecuador is continuing to develop a system of central bus terminals in each city, which means that if you have to change buses, you don't have to go looking for different terminals. All buses arrive and depart from the same place. Once you have located the central bus terminal, often called the *terminal terrestre*, simply find a bus to take you where you want to go. Some towns still haven't completed their main bus terminals and may still have several smaller ones.

Watch your luggage carefully in bus terminals. Snatch-theft is common, and razor-blade artists abound. Keep luggage where you can see it, and stay alert. Thieves are looking for an easy rip-off and won't bother you if you

seem on top of things. See Dangers & Annoyances, in the Facts for the Visitor chapter, for more information on playing it safe.

The location of bus terminals is indicated on city maps throughout this book. The accompanying text gives the most important destinations served by the terminal, the approximate cost of the journey, the approximate length of the journey and frequency of buses.

Exact schedules are not given here, as that is a sure way to make this book obsolete even before it is published. Timetables change frequently and are not necessarily adhered to. If a bus is full, it might leave early. Conversely, an almost empty bus may spend half an hour giving *vueltas* (driving laps between the terminal and the main plaza), with the driver's assistant yelling out of the door in hopes of attracting more passengers. This is less likely to happen in cities, but it is the norm in smaller towns.

Various types of buses are used; they can be roughly grouped into two types. *Busetas* (small buses) usually hold 22 passengers and are fast and efficient. Although standing passengers are not normally allowed, the seats can be rather cramped. Larger coaches, called *autobuses* or *buses grandes,* have more space but often allow standing passengers, so they can get rather crowded. These are generally slower than the busetas, because they drop off and pick up so many standing passengers. Increasing numbers of buses have installed video players, and so if the passing countryside is not enough to entertain you, you might be able to watch a film.

There are no bus-pass systems in Ecuador, and there aren't any classes either. Some buses are more expensive but offer faster service or maybe an on-board bathroom; but it's not always clear what you get until you are on the bus.

If you're traveling very light, it's best to keep your luggage inside the bus with you. For a short trip, leave excess luggage at the South American Explorers clubhouse (see Useful Organizations, in the Facts for the Visitor chapter) or in a hotel's storage room, and travel with a bag small enough to fit under the seat or between your legs. Local people get away with taking fairly large pieces of luggage aboard, so you don't have to put yours on the outside luggage rack, even if the driver tells you to.

If your luggage is too big to fit in your seat, it will have to go on top or in a luggage compartment. Sometimes the top is covered with a tarpaulin, but not always; so pack your gear in large plastic bags (garbage bags are good) in case of rain. The luggage compartment is sometimes filthy, and your luggage can get covered with grease or mud. Placing your luggage in a large protective sack is a good idea. Many locals use grain sacks as luggage; you can buy them for a few cents in general stores or markets. There are a few stories of theft from luggage inside luggage compartments, and even of whole pieces of luggage being stolen. This is not a frequent occurrence, but minimize the risk by securely locking checked luggage and keeping your eye on it as it is loaded into the luggage compartment. Check on it during stops.

Often when a bus stops on main routes, vendors selling fruit, rolls, ice cream or drinks suddenly appear, so you won't starve. Long-distance buses usually stop for a 20-minute meal break at the appropriate times. The food in the terminal restaurants may be somewhat basic, so if you're a picky eater you should bring food with you.

On remote routes, full buses allow passengers to travel on the roof. This can be fun, with great views but minimal comfort!

Reservations Getting around Ecuador by bus is easy, but here are some tips to make your travels more enjoyable. If you go to the terminal the day before your bus trip, you can usually buy tickets in advance. This means you can choose your approximate time of departure, and often you can choose your seat number too. If you're tall, especially if you're over 6 feet (or 180cm) tall, you can avoid being squished in the tiny back seat of a bus this way. It's worth buying tickets in advance to get a front-row seat, which generally means more leg room, much better views and a more exciting trip.

Riders get a chance to stretch their legs as a flat tire is repaired.

Some people prefer second-row seats, to avoid being jostled by passengers getting on and off. In the event of a serious accident, the front row is usually the most lethal (though it's probably not as dangerous as some people make out.) Try to avoid those rows over the wheels – usually the third row from the front and the third from the back in the busetas, and the fourth or fifth rows from the front and back in larger buses. Ask about the position of the wheels when buying your ticket. Also remember that the suspension at the back of a bus is usually far worse than anywhere else, so try to avoid the back rows.

Some bus companies don't sell tickets in advance. This is usually when they have frequent departures (twice an hour or more). You just arrive and get on the next bus that's going your way. If the next bus out has only uncomfortable seats, you can miss it and be first on the next one (assuming the wait is not too long).

If traveling during long holiday weekends or special fiestas, you may find that buses are booked up for several days in advance, so book early if you can.

Fares for tickets bought in bus terminals are a set price. The larger terminals often have traveler information booths that can advise you about this, but normally you get charged the correct fare. The booths can give you information on all the routes available from the larger terminals.

If you're only going part of the way, or you get on a bus in a small town as it comes by between larger towns, the bus driver will charge you appropriately. About 90% of the time you are charged honestly, although once in a while they try to overcharge you.

If you want to travel somewhere immediately, just go to the terminal and you'll usually find the driver's assistant running around trying to hustle up some passengers for his bus. Often, on frequently served routes, you'll be on a bus going your way within a few minutes of arriving at the terminal. Before boarding a bus, make sure it's going where you want to go.

Occasionally drivers will say that they are going where you want to go and then take you only part of the way and expect you to change buses. If you want a direct bus, make sure you ask for it. Also, make sure that it is leaving soon, and not in two hours.

Trucks In remote areas, trucks often double as buses. Sometimes they are flatbed trucks with a tin roof, open sides and uncomfortable wooden plank seats. These curious-looking buses are called *rancheras* and are seen on the coast and in the Oriente.

In the remoter parts of the highlands, ordinary trucks or pickups *(camionetas)* are used to carry passengers; you just climb in the back. If the weather is OK, you get fabulous views and can feel the refreshing wind (dress warmly). If the weather is bad, you hunker down underneath a dark tarpaulin with the other passengers. It certainly isn't the height of luxury, but it may be the only way of getting to some remote rural areas, and if you're open-minded about the minor discomforts, you may find that these rides are among the most interesting you have in Ecuador.

Payment for these rides is usually determined by the driver and is a standard fare depending on the distance. You can ask other passengers how much they are paying; usually you'll find that the trucks double as buses and charge almost as much.

Local

There are no underground or surface trains in Ecuadorian cities. Local transportation is by bus or taxi.

Local buses are usually slow and crowded, but they are also very cheap. You can get around most towns for about US$0.10. Local buses often travel to nearby villages, and riding along is a good, inexpensive way to see the area. Just stay on the bus until the end of the line, pay another US$0.10 and head back again. If you make friends with the driver, you may even end up with an entertaining tour director who points out the local sights while collecting fares.

When you want to get off a local bus, yell *¡Baja!* which means 'Down!' (as in 'The passenger is getting down'). Telling the driver to stop will make him think you're trying to be a backseat driver, and you will be ignored. He's only interested if you're getting off the bus. Another way of getting him to stop is to yell *¡Esquina!* (which means 'corner'). He'll stop at the next one. Adding *por favor* doesn't hurt and makes everyone think you speak excellent Spanish. If you don't actually speak Spanish and someone tries to converse with you after your display of linguistic brilliance, a smile and a sage nod should suffice until you get down from the bus.

TRAIN

Ecuador's rail system was severely damaged by landslides and flooding during the extremely heavy rains of the 1982-83 El Niño wet season. It was not until the 1990s that parts of the system reopened again, including the dramatic descent from Alausí along *El Nariz del Diablo* (the devil's nose), a spectacular train ride made famous by a British TV series on the world's greatest train journeys.

At this time, a train runs three times a week from Riobamba Alausí, down El Nariz del Diablo and then back up to Alausí again. There is a weekly train between Quito and Riobamba and another weekly excursion train from Quito to Area de Recreación El Boliche, near Cotopaxi. Passengers are allowed to ride on the roof of some carriages, and this is a very popular trip. In the north an *autoferro* (looks like a bus on a railway chassis) runs most days between Ibarra and halfway to San Lorenzo.

ENAFER is the government-run national train company, but there is no central telephone number to reach them. You must go to individual towns to buy tickets and get information. Departure times and other rail-service information are given under the appropriate town headings. Note that a two-tier fare system applies. Foreigners pay about US$15 for any of the train trips outlined in this section, regardless of how far they travel on it. Locals pay about US$1. There are no classes.

CAR & MOTORCYCLE
Road Rules

Driving is on the right side of the road. Bear in mind that Ecuador's system of road signs is very poor. A sign may point to your destination several kilometers before the turnoff, then when you reach the turnoff there may be no sign at all. Large potholes, narrow roads and drivers passing on curves, speeding or going too slow are all part of the adventure. Even so, a car does allow you the freedom to choose where you go *if* you can figure out how to get there!

Because of poor road conditions and dangerously fast local drivers, driving in Ecuador is not recommended – unless you are a confident and experienced driver.

Rental

Renting a car in Ecuador is more expensive than full-price car rental in Europe or the US. Cheap car rentals just aren't found. If the price seems reasonable, check to see for what extras you have to pay; often there is a per kilometer charge and you have to buy insurance. Some cars are not in very good condition.

It is difficult to find car rental outside of Guayaquil, Quito, Cuenca and a few other towns. You need a credit card to rent, as a cash deposit is not accepted. Renters normally have to be 25 years old (a few companies may accept 23- or 21-year-old drivers). A valid driver's license from your home country is usually accepted if it has your photograph on it. Some companies require an international driver's license, so if you know that you will be driving, it's best to apply for one in your home country before you leave. If you already have a standard driver's license, this is normally a straightforward process.

Typical rates start close to US$40 per day for a subcompact car but can go over US$100 for a large 4WD vehicle. Weekly rentals are the best deals. Weekly rates – including insurance, tax and unlimited distance allowances – range from under US$300 for a three-door subcompact to about US$550 to US$800 for a 4WD sport utility vehicle. It's

Driving Distance (in kilometers)

	Ambato	Bahía de Caráquez	Baños	Cuenca	Esmeraldas	Guayaquil	Huaquillas	Ibarra	Loja	Macará	Macas	Manta	Otavalo	Quito	Riobamba	Tena
Bahía de Caráquez	406															
Baños	40	446														
Cuenca	306	530	309													
Esmeraldas	390	392	430	667												
Guayaquil	288	280	288	250	472											
Huaquillas	440	533	445	242	670	253										
Ibarra	251	455	291	557	433	535	693									
Loja	511	695	514	205	832	415	233	762								
Macará	701	682	704	395	819	402	195	952	190							
Macas	230	642	190	231	620	432	473	479	436	626						
Manta	404	120	444	446	442	196	449	505	611	598	628					
Otavalo	231	435	271	537	413	515	673	20	742	932	459	485				
Quito	136	340	176	442	318	420	578	115	647	837	366	390	95			
Riobamba	52	464	55	254	442	233	390	303	459	649	245	456	283	188		
Tena	180	586	140	449	497	428	585	271	598	788	208	584	251	186	195	
Tulcán	376	580	416	682	558	660	818	125	887	1077	604	630	145	240	428	396

worth shopping around for the best price, but beware of a poor car if the price is low. Both Budget and Localiza have received mainly favorable reports.

Automobile insurance policies can carry a hefty deductible – as much as US$1000, depending on the company. Some international rental agencies (Budget, Avis, Hertz) will make reservations for you from your home country.

Generally, car rental places are honest, though there are warnings and complaints from time to time. Have everything put into writing to avoid confusion or misunderstandings. This document should include prices; distance allowances (kilometraje); any applicable discounts, taxes or surcharges; and the place and time of vehicle return. Make sure any existing damage to the vehicle (scratches etc) are noted on the rental form. Rental cars are often rather old and beat-up but reasonably well serviced. Make sure there is a spare tire and jack (if only to know where they are stored in case of a flat tire).

Rental cars are targets for thieves. Don't leave your car parked with bags or other valuables in sight. When leaving your car for any period, especially overnight, park in a guarded lot.

Ecuador is an oil-producing country and it keeps down the price of gasoline (petrol) for domestic consumption. Depending on the grade, gas is approximately US$1 or less per gallon (for some reason gas is not dispensed in liters).

Motorcycle rental is hard to find in Ecuador.

Purchase

Santiago, Chile, is the best place in South America to buy your own vehicle, be it motorcycle or car, new or used. People who prefer to drive a vehicle of their own might consider buying one in Santiago and continuing from there.

Shipping a Vehicle

Few travelers arrive with their own vehicle. However, if you want to ship a vehicle (or any other large item), a company with representatives worldwide and an office in Ecuador is Ecu-Line (www.eculine.be). The world headquarters (☎ 32-3-541 24 66, fax 541 79 61, info@eculine.be) are at Schouwkensstraat 1, B 2030, Antwerpen, Belgium. The Ecuador branch (☎ 04-292 075, 286 743, fax 397 066, 286 743, flde@gu.pro.ec) is at Avenida Quito 806 and 9 de Octubre, in Guayaquil. There are also offices in most other countries.

TAXI

Reasonable gas prices combined with low wages means that taxis in Ecuador are very cheap.

Ecuadorian taxis come in a variety of shapes and sizes, but they are all yellow. Most have a lit sign on top reading 'Taxi' – those that don't have a taxi sticker in the windshield. Taxis often belong to cooperatives; the name and telephone number of the cooperative is usually printed on the door.

The main rule for taking taxis is to ask the fare beforehand, or you'll be overcharged more often than not. Meters are rarely seen, except in the capital, where they are obligatory. Even if there is a meter, the driver may not want to use it. This can be to your advantage, because with the meter off the driver can avoid interminable downtown traffic jams by taking a longer route. This saves both you and him time and the extra cost in gas is negligible. A long ride in a large city (Quito or Guayaquil) shouldn't go over US$3 and short hops cost well under US$1. In smaller towns fares vary from about US$0.50 to US$2. Fares from international airports (Quito and Guayaquil) can be exorbitantly high – see those towns for tips on how to avoid getting gouged. On weekends and at night, fares are always about 25% to 50% higher. Taxis can be hard to flag down during rush hours.

You can hire a taxi for several hours. A half day might cost about US$10 to US$15 if you bargain. You can also hire pickup trucks that act as taxis to take you to remote areas (such as a climbing hut or a refuge). If you hire a taxi to take you to another town, a rough rule of thumb is about US$1 for every

10km. Remember to count the driver's return trip, even if you're not returning. If you split the cost between four passengers, you'll each be paying between two and three times the bus fare for a roundtrip.

Hiring a taxi for a few days is comparable to renting a car, except that you don't have to drive, and you have to pay for the driver's food and room. Some tour companies in Quito specialize in renting 4WD vehicles with experienced drivers who will get you to some remote areas.

BICYCLE

Each year a handful of cyclists attempt to ride from Alaska to Argentina, or any number of shorter long-distance rides, and manage to get through Ecuador OK. They report that coastal areas are flat and relatively boring, while cycling in the Andes is more fun and visually rewarding, though strenuous. Mountain bikes are recommended, as road bikes don't stand up to the poor road quality.

Renting bikes has only recently become an option in Ecuador, and is mainly for short tours (see Organized Tours under Quito, in the Quito & Around chapter, for information on mountain-biking tours). Otherwise, rental is uncommon and the quality of the bicycles is poor. Bikes for sale tend to be of the one-speed variety, so dedicated bikers are probably better off bringing their own. Most airlines will allow bikes to be checked at no extra cost if they're in boxes. However, boxes give baggage handlers little clue as to the contents and the box is liable to be roughly handled, possibly damaging the bike. An alternative is wrapping your bike in heavy-duty plastic. Airlines' bicycle-carrying policies vary, so shop around.

Bicycle shops are scarce in Ecuador and their selection of parts is often inadequate. Bring important spare parts from home.

HITCHHIKING

Hitchhiking is never entirely safe in any country in the world, and we don't recommend it. Travelers who decide to hitchhike should understand that they are taking a small but potentially serious risk. People who do choose to hitchhike will be safer if they travel in pairs and let someone know where they are planning to go.

Hitching is not very practical in Ecuador for three reasons: There are few private cars, public transportation is relatively cheap and trucks are used as public transportation in remote areas, so trying to hitch a free ride on one is the same as trying to hitch a free ride on a bus. Many drivers of *any* vehicle will pick you up but will also expect payment. If the driver is stopping to drop off and pick up other passengers, ask them what the going rate is. If you are the only passenger, the driver may have picked you up just to talk with a foreigner, and he may wave aside your offer of payment. If you do decide to try hitching, make sure in advance of your ride that you and the driver agree on the subject of payment.

WALKING

Ecuador has several options for adventurous treks in the Andes, although the trails are not as well known as those in Peru. Some excellent hiking and climbing guidebooks have been published specifically for foot travelers; see Books, in the Facts for the Visitor chapter, for a listing of the better ones.

Walking around cities is generally safe, even at night, if you stick to the well-lit areas. Always be on the alert for pickpockets, though, and make inquiries before venturing into an area you don't know.

BOAT

Boat transportation is common in Ecuador and can be divided into four types. The most common is the motorized dugout canoe, which acts as a water taxi or bus along the major rivers of the Oriente and parts of the coast. In the Galápagos there are medium-sized motor cruisers and sailboats that are used by small groups to move between the islands of the archipelago. Third, there are large vessels used either for carrying cargo and a few passengers, or as cruise ships for many passengers.

Finally, many rivers are crossed by ferries that vary from a paddled dugout taking one passenger at a time to a car ferry capable of moving half a dozen vehicles. These are sometimes makeshift transportation to replace a bridge that has been washed out, is being repaired or is still in the planning stages.

Dugout Canoes

Dugout canoes often carry as many as three dozen passengers and are the only way to get around many roadless areas. If you hire one as a personal taxi, it is expensive. However, taking a regularly scheduled ride with other passengers is quite affordable, though not as cheap as a bus for a similar distance. An outboard engine uses more fuel per kilometer than a bus engine and dugouts travel more slowly than a bus.

The only places between which you are likely to travel any distance in dugouts are on jungle tours in the Oriente and a few parts of the northwest coast.

Most of these boats are literally dugouts, with a splashboard sometimes added to the gunwales. These are long in shape and short on comfort. Seating is normally on hard, low, uncomfortable wooden benches which accommodate two people each. Luggage is stashed forward under a tarpaulin, so carry hand baggage containing essentials for the journey. You will be miserable for hours if you don't take the following advice, which alone is worth the cost of this book: *Bring seat padding.* A folded sweater or towel will make a world of difference on the trip.

On the smaller boats, the front seats give better forward views but are the narrowest, the middle seats are wider and more comfortable, and the back seats are closest to the noise and fumes of the engine.

Pelting rain and glaring sun are major hazards, and an umbrella is excellent defense against both. Bring suntan lotion or wear long sleeves, long pants and a sun hat – people have been literally unable to walk because of second-degree burns on their legs after a six-hour exposure to the tropical sun. The breeze as the boat motors along tends to keep insects away and cool you, so that you are not likely to notice the burning effect of the sun. If the sun should disappear or the rain begin, you can become quite chilly, so bring a light jacket.

Insect repellent is useful during stops along the river. A water bottle and something to snack on will complete your hand baggage. Don't forget to stash your spare clothes in plastic bags, or they'll get soaked by rain or spray.

A final word about dugout canoes: They feel very unstable! Until you get used to their motion, you might worry about the whole thing just rolling over and tipping everybody into the shark-, piranha- or boa constrictor-infested waters. Desperately gripping the side of the canoe and wondering what madness possessed you to board in the first place doesn't seem to help. Dugouts are much more stable than they feel, so don't worry about a dunking.

Yachts

The idea of sailing your own yacht to the Galápagos sounds romantic. Unfortunately, to sail around the Galápagos, you need a license, and licenses are all limited to Galápagos boats. If you arrive at the islands in your own boat, you will have to moor the boat in Puerto Ayora and hire one of the local boats to take you around. The Ecuadorian authorities give transit permits of seven days for sailors on their own boats (this is a recent ruling and is subject to change; previously, it was only 72 hours). Longer stays may be possible if you are moored and not sailing.

Other Boats

In the Galápagos, you have a choice of traveling in anything from a small sailboat to a cruise ship complete with air-conditioned cabins and private baths. More information on these boats is given in the Galápagos chapter.

In addition to the dugout canoes of the Oriente, one cruise ship, *Flotel Orellana*, makes relatively luxurious passages down Río Aguarico; it's described in the Northern Oriente chapter.

A few boats travel between the Galápagos and Guayaquil, but it's easier to fly there and sail between the islands once you arrive. Again, there is more information under the appropriate coastal towns.

ORGANIZED TOURS

Many kinds of tours are available, from hotel-based excursions to the highlands to strenuous mountaineering expeditions, from camping in the rainforest to staying at a luxurious jungle lodge – and, of course, there are the tours to the Galápagos.

Many tours can be arranged within Ecuador and are described in the main body of the book under the appropriate cities. Others can be arranged in advance from home, especially if you live in the USA. See the Getting There & Away chapter for more details.

Quito & Around

Highlights

- The Monastery of San Francisco – Ecuador's oldest church and one of many stunning colonial buildings in the old town
- Checking email, surfing the Web, sipping a coffee and hanging out in one of Quito's many cybercafes, which have formed a trendy subculture of their own
- Dancing, sweating and mingling in one of Mariscal's many nightclubs
- Being a total tourist and straddling the hemispheres at the Mitad del Mundo monument

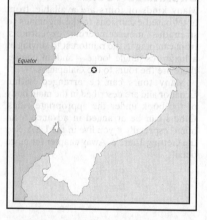

Ecuador's capital has enough attractions to keep visitors busy for a few days. Once they are ready for a break from the city, there are several interesting nearby areas that can be visited on day trips.

Quito

☎ 02

Quito has a wonderful springlike climate despite the fact that it is only 22km south of the equator. At about 2850m above sea level, it is in a valley flanked by majestic mountains, and on a clear day, several snow-capped volcanoes are visible from the capital. As well as being in a beautiful location, it is rich in history, and much of the old colonial town is well preserved.

In 1978, UNESCO declared Quito's colonial center a world cultural heritage site. Now, development and other changes in Quito's old town are strictly controlled. This is not to say that progress has stopped – on the contrary, the new sections of town are modern, and the old center bustles with life. But the buildings in the old center are unchanged, and to walk down colonial Quito's streets late on Sunday, when traffic is reduced, is to step into a bygone era. There are no modern buildings discordantly built next to centuries-old architecture, and no flashing neon signs to disrupt the ambience of the past.

HISTORY

The site of the capital dates from pre-Columbian times. Early inhabitants of the area were the peaceful Quitu people, who gave their name to the city. The Quitus integrated with the coastal Caras, giving rise to the Indian group known as the Shyris. Around AD 1300, the Shyris joined with the Puruhás through marriage, and their descendants fought against the Incas in the late 15th century.

By the time the Spanish arrived in Ecuador (1526), Quito was a major Inca city. Rather than allowing it to fall into the hands of the Spanish conquerors, Rumiñahui, a general of Atahualpa, razed the city shortly before their arrival. There are no Inca remains. The present capital was founded atop the ruins by Spanish lieutenant Sebastián de Benalcázar on December 6, 1534. Many colonial-era buildings survive in the old town.

ORIENTATION

Quito's population of over 1,600,000 makes it the second-largest city in Ecuador (Guaya-

Addresses in Quito

Quito's addresses are given by placing the building number after the street name, eg: Jorge Washington 311. At time of writing, Quito was changing to a new address system based on N, S, W, E quadrants, so an address might be Amazonas N22-62. Many buildings have the old address, some have both and a few have just the new address, so it can be confusing. Both are used in this chapter, depending on the information received from each place.

Taxi drivers know all the main thoroughfares and most cross streets, but they only have the vaguest notion of a numbered street address, especially now that Quito is introducing a completely new street-numbering system. It is important to tell a taxi driver your cross street, as well as your street address, unless you are visiting a well-known landmark. Check the maps for the nearest cross street, and be prepared to help direct the taxi driver.

quil is the largest). It lies along the central valley in a roughly north-south direction and is approximately 17km long and 4km wide. It can conveniently be divided into three segments.

The center (El Centro) is the site of the old town, with its whitewashed, red-tiled houses and colonial churches. This is the area of greatest historical interest to travelers, but it is also a poor area with few good hotels (although travelers can stay here comfortably).

The north is modern Quito, the new town, with its major businesses, airline offices, embassies, shopping centers and banks. Most hotels and restaurants are found here. The north end contains the airport and the middle- and upper-class residential areas. Amazonas is the best-known street, although Avenida 10 de Agosto and Avenida 6 de Diciembre are the most important thoroughfares.

The south consists mainly of working-class residential areas.

Maps

The best maps are available from Instituto Geográfico Militar (IGM; ☎ 545 090), which is on top of a hill at the end of Paz y Miño, a small street a few blocks southeast of Parque El Ejido, in the new town. There are no buses, so you have to walk or take a taxi. The map sales room is open 8 am to 1 pm and 1:30 to 4:30 pm Monday to Thursday

and 7 am to 3 pm Friday. You need to leave your passport at the gate to be allowed in. Go in the morning to buy maps – it can take a while. There is a good selection of country and topographical maps to look at or buy, but the selection of city maps is very limited, and you'll often be better off with this book's city maps. The most useful map of Quito is one of the blue-covered ones by Nelson Gómez, published every year or two and available at most bookstores. Empresa del Centro Histórico (☎/fax 583 827/33, ech@ech .com.ec), Venezuela 976 and Mejía, publishes free or nominally priced maps of walks with detailed information on the sights of Quito (see the Old Town map for its location).

INFORMATION
Tourist Offices

Camara Provincial de Turismo de Pichincha (CAPTUR; ☎ 224 074), Avenida 6 de Diciembre N22-02, at Carrión, provides information about Quito and its province of Pichincha. Hours are 8 am to 6 pm weekdays (see the New Town map).

South American Explorers

The SAE clubhouse (☎ 225 228) is at Jorge Washington 311, near Leonidas Plaza Gutiérrez, in the new town. Hours are 9:30 am to 5 pm weekdays. The mailing address is Apartado 21-431, Avenida Eloy Alfaro, Quito. See the Facts for the Visitor chapter for details on the organization.

Foreign Embassies

Virtually all foreign embassies are in Quito (consulates are in either Quito or Guayaquil). See the Facts for the Visitor chapter for their addresses and other contact information.

Visa Extensions

There are several immigration offices, and all are closed weekends and holidays. Jefatura Provincial de Migración (☎ 247 510, 450 573), Isla Seymour 1152, at Río Coca (see the Metropolitan Quito map) is for T-3 tourist-card extensions of up to 90 days for tourists who received only 30 or 60 days upon arrival. Hours are 8:30 am to noon and 3 to 5 pm weekdays.

Oficina de Migración (☎ 456 249), Amazonas 2639 at República (see the New Town map), is for tourists who have already stayed 90 days and want 30 more (a process that can be performed only three times, for a maximum of 180 days per year). Normally, this is only done when your time has expired, not in advance, and only at the immigration officer's discretion. Most applicants have been successful. Hours are 8 to 11:45 am and 3 to 5 pm weekdays.

For visas longer than 180 days, you need to apply at the Ecuadorian embassy nearest your home address for a student, volunteer, cultural-exchange, work, business or other visa. These need to be registered within 30 days at Dirección de Extranjería (☎ 561 010), at Carrión and Páez (see the Mariscal Sucre inset on the New Town map). Visa holders then need to go to Oficina de Migración (previously mentioned) to purchase an ID called a *censo,* which then enables them to get discounted resident rates on train tickets and airfares and in national parks. If visa holders wish to leave the country and return, they need a *salida* (exit) form from the Jefatura Provincial de Migración (previously mentioned), which can be used for multiple exits and reentries.

It's best to go earlier in the day for the most efficient service. Also read the Visas & Documents section of the Facts for the Visitor chapter for more information.

Money

Banks are open 9 am to 1:30 pm (later in some branches) weekdays and sometimes on Saturday mornings. They can receive money wired from your home bank and pay you in US dollars. Many banks also have 24-hour ATMs, which also pay out US dollars. There are several banks in the new town along Amazonas between Patria and Orellana, and there are dozens more throughout town – ask at your hotel for the nearest one. The following are some banks with ATMs in the Mariscal Sucre area of the new town:

Filanbanco (Visa), Amazonas and Roca

Banco de Guayaquil (Visa), Colón and Reina Victoria

Banco del Pacífico (MasterCard), Amazonas and Veintimilla

For changing traveler's checks, there are *casas de cambio* (currency-exchange places) on Amazonas and a few in other parts of town. They are usually open until 6 pm weekdays and on Saturday mornings.

For weekend casas de cambios, the Multicambios airport office is open for all flight arrivals in the international arrival area. If you aren't an arriving passenger, try Producambios, in the domestic lounge; it's open 6 am to 9 pm daily. Centro Comercial El Jardín is another option; it's open 10 am to 6 pm daily.

Credit cards are widely accepted in 1st-class restaurants, hotels, travel agencies and stores. Make sure you are getting a good exchange rate. Some places charge a 4% to 10% commission to cover their banking costs; ask before signing. Visa is the most widely accepted card, followed by MasterCard. The main credit-card offices are:

American Express (☎ 560 488), Amazonas 339

MasterCard (☎ 262 770), Naciones Unidas 825

Visa (☎ 459 303), De Los Shyris 3147

Diners Club (☎ 981 300), Amazonas 4560 (not mapped)

Western Union (☎ 565 059) is at Avenida de la República 433, near Almagro, as well as

METROPOLITAN QUITO

To Nono
To La Mitad del Mundo
To Cayambe & Otavalo

Av Diego de Vásquez
Av De La Prensa
Av 6 de Diciembre
Av General Eloy Alfaro
Av Occidental

Tufiño
Aeropuerto Mariscal Sucre
Av 10 de Agosto

PLACES TO STAY
1 Hostería San Jorge
16 Hotel Four Points Sheraton
15 Holiday Inn Crowne Plaza

PLACES TO EAT
10 Swiss Corner
20 San Thelmo
21 Café Tequila
25 Sató

OTHER
2 Airport Terminal
3 Women's Prison
4 Centro Comercial El Bosque
5 Plaza de Toros
6 Jefatura Provincial de Migración
7 Visa Office; Filanbanco
8 Clínica de la Mujer
9 Quasar Nautica
11 Cinemark
12 Hospital Voz Andes
13 MasterCard Office;
   Banco del Pacífico
14 Fundación Octaedro
17 UK & German Embassies;
   Centro Comercial Quicentro
18 Estadio Atahualpa
19 Centro Comercial Iñaquito;
   Multicines & Supermaxi
22 Hospital Metropolitano;
   Centro Meditropoli
23 Centro Comercial El Jardín
24 Museo de Ciencias Naturales
25 Centro Cultural Mexicano
26 La Cima de la Libertad
27 Monastery of San Diego
28 Train Station

De Las Palmeras
Av El Inca
Estación Norte
Río Coca
De Los Shyris
Av Oriental
Amazonas
La Y (Iñaquito)
Estadio
Naciones Unidas
La Carolina
Floron
Mariana de Jesús
República de El Salvador
Mariana de Jesús
Cuero y Caicedo
Vía a Tumbaco
Orellana
Colón   Colón
Mariscal   Santa Clara
Av América
Av 6 de Diciembre
Av De La República
Río Machángara

see Quito - Old Town map

Banco Central
Teatro Sucre
Plaza Grande
Santo Domingo
Ejido
La Alameda
Hermano Miguel
Marín
Cumandá
Recoleta
Machángara
Colina
Chimbacalle
Cardinal de la Torre
Villaflora
Estación Sur

see Quito - New Town map

Av Simón Bolívar
Av Pichincha
Av General Rumiñahui
Av Napo

0   1.5   3 km
0   1   2 miles

Av Occidental
Av Alonso de Angulo
Av Simón Bolívar

To Latacunga

at Colón 1333. A US$1000 transfer from the USA costs US$55.

Post & Communications

The central post office is at Espejo 935, in the old town. Hours are 7:30 am to 5:30 pm weekdays and 8 am to 2 pm Saturday. Currently, this is where you pick up your *lista de correos* (general delivery) mail. A branch post office (☎ 508 890) in the new town is on Colón near Reina Victoria; it has the same hours. If you are mailing a package of over 2kg, use the office at Ulloa 273, near Dávalos (☎ 521 730).

American Express (☎ 560 488) clients can receive mail sent to them c/o American Express, Apartado 2605, Quito, Ecuador. The office's street address is Amazonas 339, 5th floor; it is open 8 am to 5 pm weekdays.

There are several air courier services: DHL (☎ 485 100), at Avenida Eloy Alfaro and Los Juncos; FedEx (☎ 569 356), Amazonas 517, near Santa María; IML (☎ 567 112), 9 de Octubre 1114, near Colón; and UPS (☎ 256 790, 460 469), Iñaquito N35-155, near Santa María de Vela. Rates are high: a package weighing less than 1kg costs US$38 to send to the USA and US$57 to send to Europe.

The main Andinatel office for international calls is in the new town at Avenida 10 de Agosto and Colón (☎ 507 691, 509 025). The old town office (☎ 612 112) is on Benalcázar at Mejía. Other offices are the bus terminal, in old town – Terminal Terrestre de Cumandá (☎ 580 582) – and at the airport (☎ 451 858). These offices are open 8 am to 10 pm (last call at 9:30 pm) daily. Cheap rates for international calls are after 7 pm. See Email & Internet Access, next, for cheaper options.

Email & Internet Access

There are literally dozens of cybercafés where you can read or send email, surf the Web or use the net-to-phone services. The latter allows you to call any phone for less than 25% of what it costs on a regular phone. The downsides of net-to-phone are poor connections and time lag, which means you have to get used to waiting a few seconds

after you finish speaking to get a spoken reply – but it works, and it's cheap!

The cybercafés vary from smoky places serving beer, coffee and snacks to relatively sedate places where the computer is king. Rates don't vary much from place to place (about US$1 per hour), but computer quality and modem speeds do vary. Most cybercafés are in the center of the new town (there are about eight on Calamá, which is only four blocks long!). The office of the South American Explorers has a long list of cybercafés that members have recommended. If you are in Quito for a while, you'll find one that suits you.

Travel Agencies

Most of the well over 100 travel agencies in Quito will sell you both domestic and international airline tickets (adding the obligatory 12% tax); make hotel reservations; and arrange guided trips to hike in the mountains, climb the snowcapped volcanoes, explore the jungle or visit the Galápagos. But be warned – most guide services are not cheap. It is usually better to deal directly with the agency supplying the services you want.

Note that it is often cheapest to book a tour close to where you will be touring. Therefore, some travelers try to arrange a tour in the Galápagos or in the Oriente upon arrival in these destinations. This works, but there are several problems. During the Galápagos' high seasons, many boats are full, and it may be difficult to find one available. During the low seasons (and at any time in the Oriente), it may take several days to get a group of people together who are interested in doing the same thing. This is OK if you have a week or two to kill, but if you want to be sure of leaving on a trip soon after you arrive, you should book in advance – especially for the Galápagos. (Several readers have written that they have been able to get on a Galápagos tour within two or three days at a good price, but a few waited more than a week.) See the Galápagos Islands chapter for more general information on island tours.

If you're a budget traveler who's not much limited by time and you want to take a trip to the Oriente, a good tactic is to gather a group of budget travelers by advertising in your hotel or at the South American Explorers clubhouse. Then go to the Oriente together, as a group, to find a guide. If you are on a short trip, by all means book a tour in Quito. Good guides and tours are available, and you can leave quickly, although you'll pay a bit more for this convenience.

The agencies that are mentioned in this section can generally be found on the New Town map.

Affiliated with American Express, Ecuadorian Tours (☎ 560 488, ecuadorian@ accessinternet.net), Amazonas 339, near Jorge Washington, is a good all-purpose travel agent.

The biggest and best-known travel agency is Metropolitan Touring (☎ 464 680, 464 470, fax 464 702, info@metropolitan.com.ec), República de El Salvador N36-84; it also has a branch (☎ 560 651, fax 560 807) at Amazonas N20-39. This agency runs medium-priced to luxury tours in the Galápagos on both yachts and cruise ships, and the naturalist guides that work with this company are very good. Metropolitan also runs the 1st-class (by Oriente standards) *Flotel Orellana* on Río Aguarico (see the Northern Oriente chapter) and operates expensive but luxurious train trips in specially modified coaches. Ecuador's best-known mountaineer, Marco Cruz, heads the agency's climbing program. Metropolitan's preset itineraries are good, but the company is not as good at customized, tailor-made travel (according to two readers who tried this).

Nuevo Mundo Expeditions (☎ 564 448, 509 431, fax 565 261, nmundo@interactive .net.ec), Coruña 1349 (N26-207), at Orellana, is a small but very professional outfit with strong conservation interests (English-speaking owner Oswaldo Muñoz is a founding member and past president of the Ecuadorian Ecotourism Association). The company has top-end prices, but it also has top-end tours and guides (it's the only company whose equator tour includes a visit to the unique and fascinating Solar Museum). Nuevo Mundo also organizes Galápagos tours, arranges visits to Reserva Producción

Faunística Cuyabeno (in the Oriente) and offers a variety of Andean horseback-riding and trekking trips. Of particular interest are the company's cultural tours, one of which features shamanism and natural healing. You can find the company's Web site at www.nuevomundotravel.com.

A top-end ecotourism company that also features cultural tours and bird watching expeditions is Viajes Orion (☎ 462 004, fax 432 891, vorion@uio.satnet.net), Atahualpa 955 at Avenida de la República. The general manager, Myriam Burneo, speaks English and French fluently. You can visit the company's Web site at www.vorion.com.

A company that offers a variety of day tours in the Quito area and is aimed at the budget traveler is Sangay Touring (☎ 550 176, 550 180, fax 560 428, mslater@accessinter .net), Amazonas 1188 at Cordero. Jeep trips, hiking excursions and visits to cloud forests and erupting volcanoes are among the day tours offered at rates ranging from US$26 to US$58 per person, depending on the distance covered (most are under US$40). The staff also arranges economically priced Galápagos tours. English is spoken by managers Martin Slater and Jonathan Hall – second-generation Ecuadorians whose fathers were among the early pioneers of Ecuadorian volcano exploration.

The Cultura Reservation Center (☎/fax 558 889, info@ecuadortravel.com), in the hotel Café Cultura (see Places to Stay, later) makes reservations for a dozen hotels and lodges around the country.

A company that offers expensive but very good luxury yacht trips in the Galápagos is Quasar Nautica (☎ 257 822, fax 436 625, qnautic1@ecnet.ec), Shyris 2447 at Gaspar de Villaroel; see the Metropolitan Quito map. Slightly cheaper, but still at the top end of the market, is Angermeyer's Enchanted Expeditions (☎ 569 960, fax 569 956, angermeyer@accessinter.net), Foch 769, between JL Mera and Amazonas. This agency runs some of the best, most popular small boats in the Galápagos, and there is sometimes a discount of several hundred dollars for passengers booking less than a week before a cruise. Angermeyer's also arranges excursions to the Oriente and the Andes. Another agency with Galápagos tours is Etnotur (☎ 564 565, 230 552, fax 502 682, etnocru@uio.satnet.ec), Cordero 1313 at JL Mera. Mainland and Galápagos tours alike are offered, and English, German, French and Spanish are spoken. Galasam (☎ 507 079/080, fax 567 662, galasam@accessinter.net), Amazonas 1342 and Cordero (head office in Guayaquil) has a variety of boats, mostly at mid-range prices.

The following are reputable adventure-travel and climbing agencies. Safari Tours (☎ 552 505, 223 381, fax 220 426, admin@safari.com.ec), Calamá 380 and JL Mera, provides in-depth information and services ranging from volcano climbs to jungle trips to local jeep tours to personalized off-the-beaten-track expeditions. The agency's mountain guides are among the best in Quito, and the owner, Jean Brown, is a walking encyclopedia of travel information. Safari Tours provides 4WD transportation to just about anywhere and has a database of available Galápagos trips, as well as contacts at a host of hotels and lodges. There is a paperback-book exchange, too.

Sierra Nevada (☎ 553 658, fax 554 936, snevada@accessinter.net), Pinto 637 at Amazonas, does climbing, river rafting and mountain biking. Pamir (☎ 220 892, fax 547 576, htorres@pi.pro.ec), JL Mera 721, has very experienced climbing and trekking guides. Others to try are Sur Trek (☎ 561 129, fax 561 132, surtrek@surtrek.com), Amazonas 897, which has years of experience doing trekking and climbing excursions and offers mountain biking as well; Andinismo (☎ 223 030), 9 de Octubre 479 and Roca; and Compañía de Guías (☎ 504 773, guias-montania@accessinternet.net), Jorge Washington and Avenida 6 de Diciembre, whose guides speak several European languages.

For buying or renting climbing and camping equipment, check out Andinismo (mentioned in the previous paragraph); Alta Montaña (☎ 558 380, fax 504 773), Jorge Washington 425 and Avenida 6 de Diciembre; The Explorer (☎ 550 911), Reina Victoria 928 and Pinto; and Moggely Climbing (☎ 554 984), Pinto E4-225 and Amazonas.

Yacu Amu Rafting (☎ 236 844, fax 226 038, yacuamu@ecnet.ec), Baquedano E5-27 and JL Mera, has some of the most experienced river-rafting guides and top-class equipment. There are daily departures for the 'Lo...ng Run,' which has 42 rapids in 27km of river and is supposedly the longest day trip for a river run in Ecuador. Rates are US$60 per person – this includes a three-hour bus ride from Quito down the western slopes of the Andes, several hours of rafting, lunch, and a couple of cold beers (or soft drinks) waiting for you when the fun is done. Additionally, there are trips ranging from two to eight days, as well as a kayaking school for beginners. The warm waters of Ecuador and the experienced guides make this a great option for beginning kayakers. Owner Steve Nomchong is a professional kayaker who has competed internationally and who also works as a judge and safety inspector on the international circuit, so you are in good hands. He has strong ties with Angermeyer's Enchanted Expeditions (previously mentioned) and can put together excellent river/Galápagos packages, as well as packages with other areas. The company's Web site is at www.yacuamu.com.ec.

Also well recommended and experienced, Ríos Ecuador, based out of Tena (see the Northern Oriente chapter for details), has an office at (☎/fax 558 264, info@riosecuador.com), Guizpucoa 210 and Cadiz (in La Floresta district). Adventour (☎ 820 848, fax 223 720, info@adventour.com.ec), Calamá 339 and JL Mera, also has one certified river-running guide and arranges mountain- and motor-biking trips as well.

For mountain biking, try Biking Dutchman (☎ 542 806, fax 567 008, dutchman@ecuadorexplorer.com), Foch 714 and JL Mera. It has good bikes and guides and offers one- to five-day tours.

The following companies offer jungle trips and strive to be environmentally and culturally responsible. Tropic Ecological Adventures (☎ 225 907, fax 560 756, tropic@uio.satnet.net), Avenida de la República 307 and Almagro, shares an office with the cultural and conservation organization Acción Amazónica and works closely with Indian communities in the northern Oriente. Emerald Forest Expeditions (☎ 526 403, ☎/fax 541 543), Amazonas 1023 and Pinto, is another good company (see Coca, in the Northern Oriente chapter). Another jungle outfitter with a good reputation and several reader recommendations is Native Life (☎ 550 836, 505 158, fax 229 077, natlife1@natlife.com.ec), Pinto 446 and Amazonas. It specializes in Cuyabeno, among other areas. Rain Forestur (☎/fax 239 822, rainfor@interactive.net.ec), Amazonas 420, near Roca, has trips to Cuyabeno and elsewhere (for details, see Baños, in the South of Quito chapter). The staff there also arranges trekking and Indian market tours in the Quito area. Kem Pery Tours (☎ 226 583, 226 715, fax 568 664, kempery@ecuadorexplorer.com), Pinto 539, does trips to Bataboro Lodge, on the edge of Huaorani territory (see Coca, in the Northern Oriente chapter). Neotropic Turis (☎ 521 212, 09-930 778, fax 554 902, info@neotropicturis.com), Amazonas N24-03, near Wilson, runs the comfortable Cuyabeno Lodge in the Reserva Producción Faunística Cuyabeno (see the Northern Oriente chapter). The agency has a Web site at www.neotropicturis.com.

Fundación Golondrinas (☎ 226 602), Isabel La Católica 1559, is a conservation project with volunteer opportunities. The organization arranges four-day walking tours in the *páramo* and forests west of Tulcán (see the boxed text 'The Cerro Golondrinas Project,' in the North of Quito chapter).

Bookstores

Libri Mundi (☎ 234 791), JL Mera 851, is Quito's best bookstore, with a good selection of titles in English, German, French and Spanish. It has books about Ecuador, as well as those of a more general nature. Hours are 8:30 am to 7 pm weekdays, and 9:30 am to 1:30 pm and 3:30 to 6:30 pm Saturday. Ask about locations. Libro Express (☎/fax 548 113), Amazonas 816 and Veintimilla, is good for maps, magazines and some books. Some new bookstores on Amazonas also offer guidebooks in English. Abya Yala (☎ 506 247, 562 633), Avenida 12 de Octubre 1430 and Wilson, has books on Indian culture and anthropology (mainly in Spanish).

If all you want is a novel for that long bus trip or flight home, your best bet is Confederate Books (☎ 527 890), Calamá 410, which has Ecuador's best selection of used books in English and several other languages. It also has used guidebooks and other reference works. Everything is less than cover price, and you can sell books there too.

Cultural Centers

The British Council (☎ 540 225, 508 282), Amazonas 1646, is open 7 am to 9 pm weekdays and 9 am to 5 pm Saturday. It has British newspapers and a café that is open 7 am to 8 pm weekdays.

The Alianza Francesa (☎ 249 345/50) is at Avenida Eloy Alfaro 1900 and Avenida 6 de Diciembre. The Asociación Humboldt (☎ 548 480), Vancouver at Polonia, is the German cultural center and hosts lectures, exhibitions and films.

Centro Cultural Afro-Ecuatoriano (☎ 522 318), Tamayo 985, is an information source on black Ecuadorian culture and sometimes has events. El Centro Cultural Mexicano (☎ 255 149), Suiza 343 and República de El Salvador, sometimes features the works of Ecuadorian and Latin American artists.

Laundry

At the following places, you can have your clothes washed, dried and folded within 24 hours:

Opera de Jabón/Soap Opera (☎ 543 995), Pinto 325 and Reina Victoria

Blanquita Laundry, Tamayo 257 and Robles

Rainbow Laundry (☎ 237 128), JL Mera 1337 and Cordero

Superlavado (☎ 09-459 922 for pickup and delivery), Pinto 305 and Reina Victoria

Wash and Go (☎ 230 993), Pinto 340 and JL Mera

Usually, clothes must be left in the morning and picked up in the evening. Opera de Jabón allows you to wash clothes yourself. Most hotels will wash and dry your clothes, but this gets quite expensive in the 1st-class hotels (less so in more modest establishments). Most cheaper hotels provide facilities for hand-washing laundry.

Photography

Cameras are expensive in Quito. If yours breaks, a recommended repairman is Gustavo Gómez (☎ 230 855), Edificio Molino, Asunción 130 and 10 de Agosto, Office 1.

There are several places along Amazonas in the new town and around Plaza Santo Domingo in the old town where print film is processed within a day. The results are usually satisfactory but not top quality. Fotomania (☎ 520 346), Avenida 6 de Diciembre 921 and Patria, has been recommended for good-quality processing and instant passport photos. (See also Photography & Video, in the Facts for the Visitor chapter.)

Medical Services

See the Metropolitan Quito map for the locations of the following three hospitals. An American-run hospital with an outpatient department and emergency room is Hospital Voz Andes (☎ 262 142), Juan Villalengua 267, near the Iñaquito trolley stop. Fees start at about US$8 for an office visit. A newer hospital that has been recommended as the best is Hospital Metropolitano (☎ 261 520, 269 030, 265 020), at Mariana de Jesús and Occidental. A private clinic specializing in women's medical problems is Clínica de la Mujer (☎ 458 000), Amazonas 4826 and Gaspar de Villarroel.

In the new town, Clínica Pichincha (☎ 562 408/296), Veintimilla 1259 and Páez, does lab analysis for parasites, dysentery etc.

The following individual doctors have been recommended. Dr Steven Contag, a gynecologist (☎ 267 972, 555 000), Centro Meditropoli, office 109, at Mariana de Jesus and Occidental (near the Hospital Metropolitano) speaks English. Dr John Rosenberg, an internist who specializes in tropical medicine (☎ 521 104 ext 310, 227 777, 09-447 237), Foch 476 and Almagro, speaks

English and German and makes house calls. Dr José A Pitarque, an ophthalmologist, (☎ 268 173), Centro Meditropoli, office 211, speaks English. Your embassy or the South American Explorers can recommend others.

There are many dentists in Quito. Some recommended ones include English-speaking Dr Jorge Cobo Avedaño (☎ 256 589, 463 361 ext 222), Centro Meditropoli, office 004; English- and German-speaking Dr Roberto Mema (☎ 569 149), Coruña E24-865 and Isabel La Católica; and orthodontists Sixto and Silvia Altamirano (☎ 244 119), Amazonas 2689 and Avenida de la República.

Note that foreign medical insurance, if it covers your hospital visit, normally does not reimburse the hospital. You must pay your own medical fees directly to the doctor or hospital and then bill your insurance company for reimbursement of the covered portions. Doctors and hospitals normally accept credit-card payments. (See also Health, in the Facts for the Visitor chapter.)

Women Travelers

La Casa de Mujer (☎ 546 155), Los Ríos 2238 and Gándara, is near La Parque Alameda. It provides emergency beds, showers and kitchen facilities for women for about US$1 per night; it is geared toward Ecuadorian women, but it might be of some assistance to other women in an emergency. Hostal Eva Luna (see Places to Stay, later) is a hostal for women only. The Carcel de Mujeres (Women's Prison), on Calle de Las Toronjas off Avenida El Inca (see the Metropolitan Quito map), has several foreign women imprisoned for drug offenses. Women from the USA, Italy, Austria, Sweden, Jamaica and Tanzania have all requested visitors to chat with. Inexpensive care packages – shampoo, tampons (especially hard to get in prison), fruit, audio cassettes, magazines etc – are welcomed. Visiting hours are 10 am to 3 pm (last entry at 2:30 and no entry or exit from noon to 1 pm) Wednesday, Saturday and Sunday.

Emergency

Some helpful numbers to have in an emergency are:

Police	☎ 101
Fire department	☎ 102
Red Cross ambulance	☎ 131

Dangers & Annoyances

The elevation of about 2850m will make you feel somewhat breathless if you first arrive from sea level. This is a mild symptom of altitude sickness and will disappear after a day or two. It is best to take things easy upon arrival. To minimize the symptoms, don't overexert yourself, eat light and avoid cigarettes and alcohol.

Quito is a safer city than Bogotá, but unfortunately, crime has been on the rise over the last few years. Be aware that pickpockets work crowded areas, such as buses, markets and plazas. (See also Dangers & Annoyances in the Facts for the Visitor chapter.)

The old town, where there are plenty of camera-laden tourists, is becoming increasingly attractive to groups of thieves. Plaza San Francisco in particular has recently had a rash of thefts, and the old town as a whole is a place in which to be careful. You might want to consider going on a tour or in a group to take photographs. If you dress inconspicuously and don't carry a valuable camera, you can wander around freely. After you have identified the areas you want to photograph, return with some friends and your camera.

One place you should definitely avoid is the steps of García Moreno heading from Ambato to the top of El Panecillo – there have been repeated reports of armed thieves there. Take a taxi or a tour to the top, and once there, stay within the paved area around the statue of the Virgin. You won't have any problem there, and you can take good photos of Quito and the surrounding mountains. Don't wander off down the grassy slopes, or you'll stand a good chance of being robbed. It's also been known to happen that a taxi with tourists is stopped by robbers on the drive up – the driver was probably in cahoots with the thieves, so take a taxi from a taxi stand.

Generally, the new town is safer than the old town, but you should still stay alert, especially at night. The area bounded by Avenidas Patria, Amazonas, Colón and 12 de Octubre contains many of the better hotels, restaurants, gift shops and travel agencies. It is, therefore, popular with tourists and is becoming the haunt of pickpockets. The most dangerous area in the new town is unfortunately Mariscal Sucre, which is where most of the budget hotels, bars, cybercafés and restaurants are. Transvestite prostitutes (who can be dangerous) often hang out at the corner of Reina Victoria and Foch late at night. Knife and gun holdups have been reported in Mariscal Sucre.

Should you be unfortunate enough to be robbed, you should file a police report, particularly if you wish to make an insurance claim. The place to go is the police station at Mideros and Cuenca, in the old town, between 9 am and noon. In the new town, you can report a robbery at the police station at JL Mera and Carrión. For insurance purposes, the report should be filed within 48 hours of the theft.

Despite these warnings, Quito is not particularly dangerous. If you avoid attracting undue attention, it's very unlikely that you'll have any problems at all.

THINGS TO SEE & DO

Although opening hours for colonial churches and museums are given throughout this book, these hours are rarely firm. Museums change their hours for reasons varying from a national holiday to staff sickness, so the opening hours in the following sections are meant only as guidelines. If possible, call ahead to verify hours. Monday is generally the worst day to visit museums, as many of them are closed.

Churches are open every day but are crowded with worshippers on Sunday. Hours are variable. Early morning seems to be a good time to visit churches. They sometimes remain open until after 6 pm, but they are often closed for parts of the day. It's unpredictable. Good luck!

QUITO & AROUND

QUITO - OLD TOWN

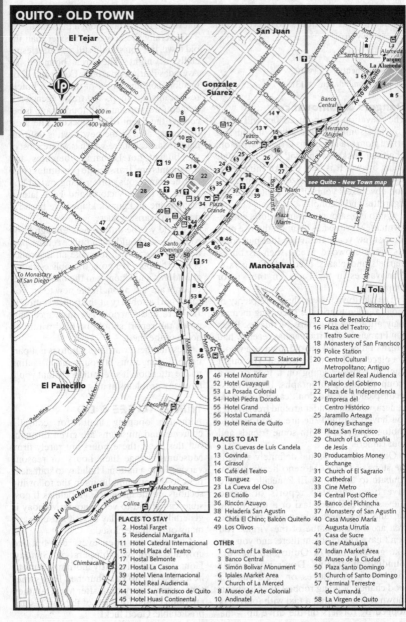

see Quito - New Town map

Staircase

12 Casa de Benalcázar
16 Plaza del Teatro;
   Teatro Sucre
18 Monastery of San Francisco
19 Police Station
20 Centro Cultural
   Metropolitano; Antiguo
   Cuartel del Real Audiencia
21 Palacio del Gobierno
22 Plaza de la Independencia
24 Empresa del
   Centro Histórico
25 Jaramillo Arteaga
   Money Exchange
28 Plaza San Francisco
29 Church of La Compañía
   de Jesús
30 Producambios Money
   Exchange
31 Church of El Sagrario
32 Cathedral
33 Cine Metro
34 Central Post Office
35 Banco del Pichincha
37 Monastery of San Agustín
40 Casa Museo María
   Augusta Urrutia
41 Casa de Sucre
43 Cine Atahualpa
47 Indian Market Area
48 Museo de la Ciudad
50 Plaza Santo Domingo
51 Church of Santo Domingo
57 Terminal Terrestre
   de Cumandá
58 La Virgen de Quito

46 Hotel Montúfar
52 Hotel Guayaquil
53 La Posada Colonial
54 Hotel Piedra Dorada
55 Hotel Grand
56 Hostal Cumandá
59 Hotel Reina de Quito

PLACES TO EAT
9 Las Cuevas de Luís Candela
13 Govinda
14 Girasol
16 Café del Teatro
18 Tianguez
23 La Cueva del Oso
26 El Criollo
36 Rincón Azuayo
38 Heladería San Agustín
42 Chifa El Chino; Balcón Quiteño
49 Los Olivos

PLACES TO STAY
2 Hostal Farget
5 Residencial Margarita I
11 Hotel Catedral Internacional
15 Hotel Plaza del Teatro
17 Hostal Belmonte
27 Hostal La Casona
39 Hotel Viena Internacional
42 Hotel Real Audiencia
44 Hotel San Francisco de Quito
45 Hotel Huasi Continental

OTHER
1 Church of La Basílica
3 Banco Central
4 Simón Bolívar Monument
6 Ipiales Market Area
7 Church of La Merced
8 Museo de Arte Colonial
10 Andinatel

Walking Tour

All sights mentioned in this section are described in more detail later in this chapter. Note that the Empresa del Centro Histórico (☎/fax 583 827/33, ech@ech.com.ec), Venezuela 976 and Mejía, publishes free or nominally priced maps of walks with detailed information on the sights seen; the staff may arrange guided walks as well (see the Old Town map).

The area of the old town bounded by Calles Flores, Rocafuerte, Cuenca and Manabí has most of the colonial churches and major plazas – including **Plaza de la Independencia**, which has the **Palacio del Gobierno** and the **cathedral**. There is no set route to recommend, but if you are short on time, at least see the Plaza de la Independencia and continue southwest on García Moreno two blocks to the **church of La Compañía**. From here, the **plaza and monastery of San Francisco** are one block along Sucre to the northwest. Be alert for pickpockets. Two blocks to the southeast of the church of La Compañía brings you to Calle Guayaquil; head southwest (right) for one block to see the **plaza and church of Santo Domingo**.

Stroll along the old-town streets, and you'll pass an interesting sight on almost every block. It is well worth spending several hours walking around this historic area, if not several days. It's also a bustling commercial area, full of yelling street vendors, ambling pedestrians, tooting taxis, belching buses, and whistle-blowing policemen trying to direct traffic in the narrow, congested one-way streets. Sunday is a good day to walk around the old center for some peace and quiet.

From the old town, head northeast along Calle Guayaquil toward the new town. Guayaquil runs into the important Avenida 10 de Agosto – turn left, and you will pass the **Banco Central** on your left. At the southernmost point of the triangular **Parque La Alameda** is an impressive **monument to Simón Bolívar**. As you head north through the park, you pass the **Quito Observatory**. As you leave the park, continue north on Avenida 6 de Diciembre.

After three blocks, you'll pass the modern **Palacio Legislativo** (Legislative

JANE SWEENEY

Plaza de la Independencia

Congress Building) on your right. Continuing on Avenida 6 de Diciembre takes you past the popular **Parque El Ejido** on your left and the huge, circular, mirror-walled **Casa de la Cultura** (see Museums – New Town, later in this section) on your right. Past the Casa de la Cultura, turn left for three blocks along Patria, with Parque El Ejido to your left, and you reach the small stone arch that is the beginning of Quito's most famous modern street, **Amazonas**.

It is about 3km from the heart of the old town to the beginning of Amazonas. Walk along Amazonas for banks, boutiques, souvenir stands and sidewalk cafés. On the parallel street of JL Mera, you will find the best bookstores and craft stores. There is much more to see, but it is scattered around Quito; you can walk, but many people take a bus or taxi to the places they are most interested in.

Museums – Old Town

Many churches have associated museums – see the Churches section, later.

Antiguo Cuartel de la Real Audiencia
This museum (☎ 214 018, 210 863), at
Espejo 1147 and Benalcázar, is in an old
building in the center. It used to be a Jesuit
house until 1767, when it became an army
barracks (which is what *cuartel* means). The
present museum contains a wealth of early
colonial art dating from the 16th and 17th
centuries, as well as more modern art. The
basement has gory waxworks showing the
assassination of local patriots by royalist
forces in 1810, over a decade before independence was achieved.

The building is just off the Plaza de la Independencia, and is a little difficult to find
because the sign is not obvious.

Casa de Benalcázar This building (☎ 288
102), Olmedo 968 and Benalcázar, dates
from 1534 and was restored by Spain in
1967. Entrance is free and hours are 9 am
to 1 pm and 2 to 6 pm weekdays. Sometimes classical piano recitals are held
here – it's a delightful site for such entertainment. Check the newspapers or inquire
at the house.

Casa de Sucre Several historical buildings
in the center are now museums. A good one
to visit is Casa de Sucre (☎ 952 860), Venezuela 573 and Sucre, which is well restored
with period (1820s) furniture; it also has a
small museum. Mariscal (field marshal)
Antonio José de Sucre, the hero of Ecuadorian independence (and the man after
whom the former Ecuadorian currency was
named), lived here. Hours are 8:30 am to
4 pm Tuesday to Friday and 9:30 am to 4 pm
Saturday – but they change frequently (as
with many of these places). Admission is
US$0.50. There is a small gift shop with
books about Ecuador.

Casa Museo María Augusta Urrutia This
restored house (☎ 580 107), García Moreno
760 and Sucre, is named after and was the
home of a distinguished philanthropist. It is
a typical example of a late-19th-century aris-
tocrat's house and has period furnishings.
Hours are 9 am to 5 pm Tuesday to Saturday; admission is free.

La Cima de la Libertad This museum is
housed in a modern building on the flanks
of Volcán Pichincha, west of the old town
(see the Metropolitan Quito map). It is
best reached by taxi. The museum was built
on the hill where Marshal Sucre fought the
decisive battle for independence on May
24, 1822. There is a collection of historical
and military artifacts and a huge and impressive mural by Kingman. Upon surrender of your passport, a soldier will guide
you around. Photography is prohibited
inside the museum. Outside, however, photography is recommended – there are great
views of the city below. Hours are 8:30 am
to 1 pm and 2 to 5:30 pm Tuesday to
Friday; admission is US$0.25.

Museo de Arte Colonial This museum
(☎ 212 297), on the corner of Cuenca and
Mejía, is in a restored 17th-century building.
It houses what many consider to be
Ecuador's best collection of colonial art
from the 16th to the 18th centuries. Many
famous sculptors and painters are represented, and there is also a collection of
period furniture. Hours are 10 am to 6 pm
Tuesday to Friday and 10 am to 2 pm Saturday. Admission is US$0.50.

Museo de la Ciudad Dating from 1563,
this beautifully restored building (☎ 283
882) at García Moreno and Rocafuerte
housed the San Juan de Dios hospital until
1973. Now a museum, its well-conceived exhibits depict daily life in Quito through the
centuries. Some of the exhibits feature in-
teractive computers. Hours are 9:30 am to
5:30 pm Tuesday to Sunday; admission is
US$4.

Museums – New Town
Casa de la Cultura Ecuatoriana This
large, circular glass building (☎ 223 392) at
the corner of Patria and Avenida 12 de
Octubre has a large art collection of contemporary Ecuadorian work and 19th-
century pieces. The contemporary exhibit
includes canvases by Ecuador's most
famous artists, including Guayasamín and
Kingman. Hours are 9 am to 5 pm Tuesday

to Friday and 10 am to 3 pm weekends. Admission is US$1/0.50 for adults/students.

There is also a movie theater that often shows international movies of note, as well as an auditorium where classical and other kinds of music are performed – check the newspapers or the posters on the front of the building.

Fundación Sinchi Sacha This nonprofit organization (☎ 230 609, 527 240), Reina Victoria 1780 and La Niña, exhibits the artwork and utensils of the peoples of the Oriente; in addition, it supports Amazonian cultures and publishes a variety of literature about the rainforest and its peoples. (Sinchi Sacha is Quichua for 'powerful forest.') The museum and the gift shop are open 8 am to 6:30 pm weekdays; the gift shop is also open 10 am to 6 pm Saturday.

Museo Amazónico This museum (☎ 432 915), Avenida 12 de Octubre 1436, is run by the Salesian Mission and has a small display of Indian artifacts collected by the missionaries in the jungle. Indian cultural publications (in Spanish) are sold. Hours are 9 am to 12:30 pm and 2 to 6 pm weekdays. Admission is US$0.50.

Museo de Ciencias Naturales This museum (☎ 449 824) houses a natural-history collection that has previously been exhibited in a military college and at the Casa de la Cultura Ecuatoriana. The current display is at Parque La Carolina, on the Los Shyris side, opposite República de El Salvador (see the Metropolitan Quito map). This is the best natural-history museum in Ecuador and is worth a visit if you want to acquaint yourself with Ecuador's flora and fauna.

Hours are 8:30 am to 4 pm weekdays, 9 am to 1 pm Saturday and 9 am to 2 pm Sunday. Admission is US$1/US$0.20 for adults/students.

Museo de Jacinto Jijón y Caamaño Across the traffic circle from the Casa de la Cultura Ecuatoriana and northeast along Avenida 12 de Octubre is the Universidad Católica, which has an interesting private

archaeology museum (☎ 521 834, 529 240) on the 3rd floor of the library. The museum is named after an Ecuadorian archaeologist, and much of the collection was donated by his family after his death. The entrance to the museum is on Avenida 12 de Octubre, near the intersection with Carrión.

Hours are 9 am to 4 pm weekdays (although they have, in the past, closed for lengthy lunch breaks). Admission is US$0.40, and you can get a guided tour (sometimes available in English) of the small archaeological collection. There is also a collection of colonial art exhibiting some of the masters of the Quito school.

Museo del Banco Central This is Quito's best archaeology museum (☎ 223 259) and is now housed in the Casa de la Cultura Ecuatoriana (previously mentioned). It features well-displayed pottery, gold ornaments (including the gold mask that is the symbol of Museo del Banco Central), skulls showing deformities and early surgical methods, a mummy and many other objects of interest. There is also a display of colonial furniture and religious art.

Entrance is US$1 (US$0.50 for students). Hours are 9 am to 5 pm Tuesday to Friday and 10 am to 3 pm weekends.

Museo Guayasamín Modern art can be seen at this museum (☎ 465 265, 446 455), Calle Bosmediano 543, which is the home of the late Oswaldo Guayasamín (1919–99), an Ecuadorian Indian painter who is now famous throughout the world. Guayasamín's collection of pre-Columbian and colonial pieces can also be seen.

The museum is in the residential district of Bellavista, northeast of downtown. You can walk uphill or take a bus along Avenida 6 de Diciembre to Avenida Eloy Alfaro, then a Bellavista bus up the hill (make sure the bus has a Bellavista placard, or ask the driver). The bus can drop you about a block from the museum. Hours are 9 am to 1:30 pm and 3 to 6:30 pm weekdays; entrance costs US$1. You can buy original artwork here – it's beautiful and not cheap. Posters are available at a reasonable cost.

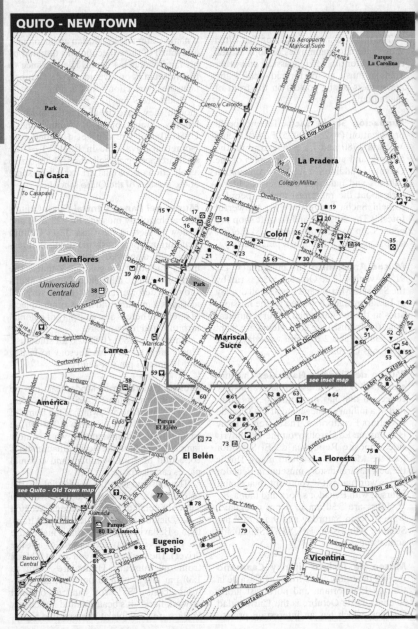

QUITO - NEW TOWN

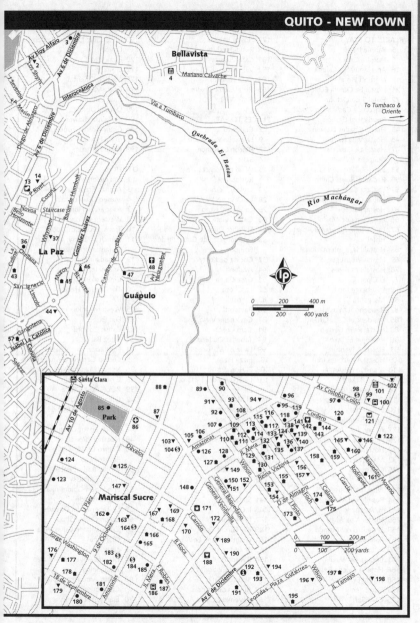

QUITO – NEW TOWN

PLACES TO STAY
5   Parque Italia
6   Nuestra Casa
16   Apartamentos Calima
19   Marriott Hotel
21   Hostal La Quinta Ecológica
22   Hotel 9 de Octubre
40   Rincón de Castilla
41   Residencial Carrión
43   Hostal Charles Darwin
45   Hostal Villa Nancy
47   Hostal La Casa de
     Guápulo
53   Swissôtel
55   Radisson Royal Quito
57   La Casa de Eliza
60   Hilton Colón Internacional
62   Hostal Raices
65   La Casona de Mario
67   La Cartuja; Amaranta Apart
     Hotel
68   Hostal Plaza Internacional
69   Hostal Villantigua
70   Hostal Los Alpes
75   El Ciprés
78   L'Auberge Inn
81   Margarita II
82   Residencial Marsella
85   Residencial Casa Oriente
88   Hostal Palm Garten
90   Albergue El Taxo
93   Hostal Adventure
109   Hostal Amazonas Inn
110   Mansión del Ángel
111   Hotel Pickett
114   Tortuga Verde
117   Orange Guesthouse
120   El Cafecito
122   Hotel Sebastián
127   Allston Inn Hotel
129   Hostelling International
130   Hostal Mundo Net
132   Magic Bean
135   Crossroads
138   Daguis
143   Alberto's House
144   Posada del Maple 2
153   El Vagabundo
155   Hostal Alpa Aligu
158   El Centro del Mundo
159   Loro Verde
160   Antinea Apart Hotel
161   Posada del Maple
166   Hotel Alameda Real
168   Hostal Eva Luna
173   Gan Eden
175   Casa Sol

177   Hostal Bavaria
178   Residencial Italia
187   Café Cultura
191   Villa Nancy B&B
193   Casa Helbling
195   Hotel Sierra Madre
197   Hotel Viena

PLACES TO EAT
2   Capuleto
9   La Paella Valenciana
12   Rincón La Ronda
14   Sake
15   Windmill Vegetarian
     Restaurant
23   Cielo y Tierra
28   La Casa de Mi Abuela
29   La Vieja Castilla
30   Café Galleti
31   El Pobre Diablo
33   La Bodeguita de Cuba; Ile de
     France
37   Cocina de Kristy
44   Avalon
51   Casa China
52   La Choza
53   Tanoshi
56   Pavarotti
87   Cevichería Viejo José
91   Café Colibri
94   Taberna Quiteña
99   La Jaiba Mariscos
102   Pizza Pizza
103   El Hornero
105   La Terraza del Tartaro;
     Las Redes
116   El Marqués
120   El Cafecito
127   Super Papa
130   Old El Paso
132   Magic Bean
133   Texas Ranch
134   El Maple
136   Adam's Rib
139   Café Sutra
140   La Creperie
141   Su Cebiche
145   Il Grillo
147   I Manantial
149   Art Forum Café
151   Grain de Café; Le Arcate
152   Tex Mex
154   Il Risotto
156   Mama Clorindas
157   Shorton Grill
163   Rincón de Francia
167   Pavement Cafes

169   Ch' Farina; La Guarida del
     Coyote
170   Pizza Hut
172   El Arabe
176   Mágico Oriental
179   Costa Vasca
187   Café Cultura
189   Double Dutch
190   Chifa Mayflower
194   Churrascaría Tropeiro
196   Chifa Hong Kong
198   Mare Nostrum

OTHER
1   Migraciones
3   Alianza Francesa
4   Museo Guayasamín
7   Asociación Humboldt
8   Western Union
10   Tropic Ecological Tours
11   French Embassy;
     Panamanian Embassy
13   Canadian Embassy
17   Andinatel
18   Cine Colón
20   The Turtle's Head
24   IML
25   Western Union
26   Fed Ex
27   British Council
32   Ghoz Bar
34   Fundación Sinchi Sacha
35   Centro Comercial Multicentro
36   Nuevo Mundo Expeditions
38   Cine Universitario
39   Parcel Post Office
42   Olga Fisch's Folklore Shop
46   Statue of Francisco de
     Orellana
48   Sanctuary of Guápulo
49   Ñucanchi Peña
50   Centro Cultural Afro-
     Ecuatoriano
54   World Trade Center;
     Dutch Embassy
57   Fundación Golondrinas
58   Bus to Mindo
59   La Taberna del Duende
60   Colón Coffee Shop
61   Compañía de Guías; Alta
     Montaña
63   Seseribó
64   Librería Abya Yala; Museo
     Amazónico
66   South American Explorers
     Clubhouse
70   Blanquita Laundry

QUITO – NEW TOWN

Aerial view over the old quarter, Quito

ALFREDO MAIGUEZ

Vivarium This museum (☎ 210 863), Reina Victoria 1576 and Santa María, is part of a herpetological research and education center. Exhibits include a number of live animals, including the highly poisonous fer-de-lance snake, boa constrictors, iguanas, turtles and tortoises. Hours are 9:30 am to 12:45 pm and 2:30 to 5:45 pm Tuesday to Saturday and noon to 6 pm Sunday. Call ahead to arrange a tour. Admission is US$1.

Churches – Old Town

There is a wealth of churches, chapels, convents, monasteries, cathedrals and basilicas in Quito. The old town especially has so many of them that you can hardly walk two blocks without passing a church. Photography is not normally permitted, because the intensity of the flash has a detrimental effect on the pigment in the many valuable religious paintings. Slides and postcards can be bought at the post office. There are signs asking tourists not to wander around during religious services – at such times, you can enter and sit in a pew.

This section highlights just a selection of Quito's most interesting and frequently visited churches. There are dozens more.

Cathedral Although not as rich in decoration as some of the other churches, Quito's cathedral, on the Plaza de la Independencia, has several points of historical interest. Plaques on the outside walls commemorate Quito's founders, and Marshal Sucre, the leading figure of Quito's independence, is buried in the cathedral. To the left of the main altar is a **statue of Juan José Flores**, Ecuador's first president. Behind the main altar is the smaller altar of Nuestra Señora de los Dolores; the plaque there shows where President Gabriel García Moreno died on August 6, 1875. He was shot outside the Palacio del Gobierno (just across the plaza) and was carried, dying, to the cathedral. The cathedral contains paintings by several notable artists of the Quito school. Visiting hours are erratic but are supposedly 8 to 10 am and 2 to 4 pm daily except Sunday. Admission is free.

Church of La Basílica High on a hill on Calle Venezuela, in the northeastern part of the old town, is this new church. It is still unfinished, although work on it began in 1926 (obviously, the tradition of taking decades to construct a church is still alive). However, the **tower** can be climbed and gives one of the best views of old Quito anywhere.

Church of La Compañía de Jesús Looking out across the plain, cobblestoned plaza of San Francisco, you see the ornate green-and-gold domes of the church of La Compañía de Jesús, just two blocks away. The construction of this Jesuit church began in 1605, the year that San Francisco was completed, and it took 163 years to build. The church is famous as the most ornate in Ecuador; it has been claimed that seven tons of gold were used to gild the walls, ceilings and altars. Quiteños call La Compañía the most beautiful church in the country, although some visitors find its splendor a little too rich. Note the Moorish influence in the intricate designs carved on the magnificent red-and-gold columns and ceilings. There is a beautiful cupola over the main altar. The remains of Santa Mariana de Jesús, a Quiteña who died in 1645, are kept here.

This church has suffered some settling of the foundations and was one of the most severely damaged in the 1987 earthquake. Interior restoration is scheduled for completion in December 2000; the exterior should be completed in 2001. A sign just inside the door gives visiting hours as 9:30 to 11 am and 4 to 6 pm daily, but don't rely on that. A small fire (apparently arson) caused minor damage in early 1996, which made the hours even less predictable. The church normally opens for services at 7 am. Admission is free.

Church of La Merced One of colonial Quito's most recently built churches is that of La Merced (at Cuenca and Chile), which was begun in 1700 and completed in 1742. Its **tower** has the distinction of being the highest (47m) in colonial Quito, and it contains the **largest bell** of Quito's churches.

The church has a wealth of fascinating art. Paintings show volcanoes glowing and erupting over the church roofs of colonial Quito, the capital covered with ashes, Marshal Sucre going into battle and many other scenes. The stained-glass windows also show various scenes of colonial life, such as early priests and conquistadors among the Indians of the Oriente. It is a surprising and intriguing collection. Hours change frequently.

Church of El Sagrario The construction of El Sagrario began in 1657 as the main chapel of the cathedral; it was finished 49 years later, but is now a separate church. This church was being renovated by Poland's University of Warsaw before the 1987 earthquake; but it was damaged by that quake. Renovation continues, and it is interesting to visit if you want to see how restoration work is done. El Sagrario is on García Moreno, next to the cathedral.

Church of Santo Domingo This church, on the plaza at the southwest end of Flores, is especially attractive in the evening, when its domes are floodlit. It too dates back to early Quito – construction began in 1581 and continued until 1650. An exquisite statue of the Virgen del Rosario, a gift from King Charles V of Spain, is now one of the church's main showpieces – you can find it in an ornately carved baroque-style side chapel. In the busy Plaza Santo Domingo there is a statue of Mariscal Sucre. In it, Sucre is pointing toward Pichincha, where he won the decisive battle for independence on May 24, 1822. The church is under restoration, and hours are unpredictable.

Monastery of San Agustín Two blocks away from the Plaza de la Independencia (at Chile and Guayaquil) is this church (locally referred to as a monastery), which is another fine example of 17th-century architecture. Many of the heroes of the battles for Ecuador's independence are buried here, and this is also the site of the signing of Ecuador's declaration of independence on August 10, 1809.

Museo de San Agustín (☎ 515 525, 580 263), at Chile and Flores is in the convent. It houses many canvases of the Quito school, including a series depicting the life of Saint Augustine, painted by Miguel de Santiago. Hours are 9 am to 1 pm and 3 to 6 pm.

Monastery of San Diego This monastery, to the northwest of El Panecillo and between Calicuchima and Farfán, is an excellent example of 17th-century colonial architecture; the building (including the monks' living areas) can be toured. There is a treasure of colonial art, including a pulpit by the notable Indian woodcarver Juan Bautista Menacho; it is considered to be one of the country's finest pulpits. The cemetery, with its numerous tombs, mausoleums and other memorials, is also worth a visit. The monastery, recently restored, should be visited with a guide, who is available 9:30 am to 1 pm and 2:30 to 5:30 pm daily – ring the doorbell. Entrance is US$0.60. There is an onsite museum as well.

Monastery of San Francisco This is Ecuador's oldest church and is on the plaza of the same name. Construction began only a few weeks after the founding of Quito in 1534, but the building was not finished until 70 years later. It is the city's largest colonial structure. The founder was the Franciscan missionary Joedco Ricke, who is credited with being the first man to sow wheat in

La Virgen de Quito

Ecuador. He is commemorated by a **statue** at the far right of the raised terrace in front of the church.

Although much of the church has been rebuilt because of earthquake damage, some of it is original. Go to the **chapel of Señor Jesús del Gran Poder**, to the right of the main altar, to see original tilework. The main altar itself is a spectacular example of baroque carving, and the roof and walls are also wonderfully carved and richly covered in gold leaf. Much of the roof shows Moorish influence.

The church contains excellent examples of early religious art and sculpture; unfortunately, it is often too dark to see them properly. Tour guides turn lights on periodically, so keep your eyes open for this. The bells are rung every hour, and often on the quarter hour. You can see the bell ringer at work in his cubbyhole just to the right of the main door. To the left of the monastery is the **Cantuña chapel**, which houses an excellent collection of Quito-school art. Visiting hours are 7 am to 11 am daily and 3 to 6 pm Monday to Thursday; admission is free.

To the right of the main entrance of the Monastery of San Francisco is **Museo Franciscano** (☎ 282 545), which contains some of the monastery's finest artwork. Here you can see paintings, sculpture and furniture dating back to the 16th century. One of the oldest signed paintings is a Mateo Mejía canvas that is dated 1615. Some of the woodcarvings are even older and are covered with gold leaf, paint, period clothing or a fine porcelain finish. Some of the furniture is fantastically wrought and inlaid with literally thousands of pieces of mother-of-pearl. Admission is US$0.50, and Spanish-speaking guides are available. Hours are 9 am to 6 pm Monday to Saturday and 9 am to 1 pm Sunday.

Churches – New Town

See Churches – Old Town, earlier, for the etiquette of visiting churches.

Church of El Belén At the north end of Parque La Alameda is this small church, which was built on the site of the first Catholic mass to be held in Quito.

Sanctuary of Guápulo In a precipitous valley on the east side of town is this sanctuary, which was built between 1644 and 1693. The best views of this delightful colonial church are from the **statue of Francisco de Orellana**, on Larrea just east of González Suárez. In the statue, Francisco de Orellana is looking down into the valley that was the beginning of his epic journey from Quito to the Atlantic – the first descent of the Amazon by a European. From the statue, there is a steep footpath that leads down to Guápulo, and it's a pleasant walk, although its somewhat strenuous coming back. The local No 21 Santo Domingo-Guápulo bus goes there.

The sanctuary's hours are 8 to 11 am and 3 to 6 pm Monday to Saturday. If it is closed, try asking at the caretaker's house, next to the church, to have it opened up. There is an excellent collection of colonial art and sculpture of the Quito school, and the pulpit, carved by Juan Bautista Menacho in the early 18th century, is particularly noteworthy.

Other Things to See – Old Town

El Panecillo The small, rounded hill that dominates the old town is called El Panecillo ('the little bread loaf') and is a major Quito landmark. It is topped by a huge statue of **La Virgen de Quito**, with a crown of stars, eagle's wings and a chained dragon atop the world. Read the Bible (Revelations 12) for some ideas about why the Virgin was built as she is.

From the summit, there are marvelous **views** of the whole city stretching out below, as well as views of the surrounding volcanoes. The best time for volcano views (particularly in the rainy season) is early morning, before the clouds roll in.

Definitely don't climb the stairs at the end of Calle García Moreno on the way to the statue – there have been numerous reports of travelers being robbed on the climb. The thieves may work in gangs and are sometimes armed. A taxi from the old town costs about US$2 or US$3, including wait time and return trip.

Markets At the bottom of El Panecillo is 24 de Mayo. This used to be a major open-air **Indian market**. An indoor market was opened in 1981 at the upper end of 24 de Mayo. Nonetheless, some outdoor selling still takes place, especially on Calle Cuenca and on the streets to the northwest of it, and at the intersection with 24 de Mayo. Saturday and Wednesday are the main market days, but the area is busy on other days as well. Nearby is the **Ipiales Market**, up the hill from Imbabura along Chile. Anything from stolen cameras to smuggled Colombian goods to underwear can be bought here. This is a fascinating area to visit, but there are many pickpockets and bag/camera snatchers, so go to look rather than photograph.

Parque La Alameda On the edge of the old town, you'll see the long, triangular Parque La Alameda, with its impressive **monument to Simón Bolívar** at the apex. There are several other interesting monuments in the park. On the southeast side, there is a **relief map of Ecuador**, and farther in toward the center are **statues** of the members of the 1736–44 French Académie des Sciences expedition that surveyed Ecuador and made the equatorial measurements that gave rise to the metric system of weights and measures.

In the center of the park is the **Quito Observatory** (☎ 570 765), which was opened by President García Moreno in 1864 and is the oldest in the continent. It is used both for meteorology and astronomy and can be visited 8 am to noon and 3 to 6 pm weekdays and 8 am to 1 pm Saturday. Admission is US$0.20. There are sometimes nighttime lectures and public viewing sessions.

At the north end of the park are a pair of ornamental **lakes**, where rowboats can be hired. Nearby is a small monument with a spiral staircase and a view of the **church of El Belén**. This part of the park is filled with picnicking families on weekends.

Don't walk around this (or any) park after dark.

Plaza de la Independencia While wandering around the churches of colonial Quito, you'll probably pass through the Plaza de la Independencia several times. Apart from the cathedral, you can see the **Palacio del Gobierno** (the Presidential Palace) – it is the low white building on the northwest side of the plaza, and the national flag is flying atop it. The entrance is flanked by a pair of handsomely uniformed presidential guards.

The president does indeed carry out business in this building, so sightseeing is limited to the entrance area. Inside, you can see a mural depicting Francisco de Orellana's descent of the Amazon. Ask the guard at the gate for permission to view the mural (it's not often given, but you can see inside from the gate).

The **Archbishop's Palace**, now a colonnaded row of small shops, can be seen on the northeast side of the Plaza. The interior patios can be visited.

Plaza del Teatro At the junction of Calles Guayaquil and Flores is the tiny Plaza del Teatro, where you'll find **Teatro Sucre**, which was built in 1878. Teatro Sucre is Quito's most sophisticated theater. Performances have been suspended while the theater is restored; completion is scheduled for the beginning of 2001.

Other Things to See – New Town
Avenida Amazonas From the center of the north end of Parque El Ejido runs modern Quito's showpiece street, Avenida Amazonas. Modern hotels, airline offices, banks and restaurants line this wide avenue, and there is plenty of room for pedestrians. Trucks and most buses are prohibited (except for a few buses bound for the airport and for the north end of the city). There are a number of outdoor restaurants where you can have a coffee or a snack and watch modern Quito go by.

Palacio Legislativo The legislative palace, on Calle Montalvo just off Avenida 6 de Diciembre, is the equivalent of the Houses of Parliament or Congress – it is where elected members of congress carry out the nation's affairs. A huge sculpted panel stretching across the north side of the building represents the history of Ecuador and is worth a quick look.

Parque El Ejido The pleasant, tree-filled Parque El Ejido is the biggest park in downtown Quito. It is a popular venue for ball games, and you can see impromptu games of soccer and volleyball, as well as a strange, giant marbles game typical to Ecuador. It is played with steel balls the size of golf balls. Open-air art shows are held on weekends at the north end of the park.

Produce Market The most popular produce market in the new town is the Santa Clara market on Ulloa and Versalles, just south of Colón.

LANGUAGE COURSES

Teaching Spanish as a second language is a large and growing industry in Quito. There are dozens of schools for learning Spanish – new ones open every month, while others fold. Classes are available at various levels; courses are offered for almost any length of time you want; classes can be private or group; accommodations with local families can be arranged. With so many possibilities, it is easy to take classes once you arrive in Quito. Make sure you get what you want by visiting several schools to see which is best for you. Schools advertise everywhere – flyers abound in popular hotels, restaurants, bars and cybercafés. Word of mouth from other travelers is always a sure bet on up-to-date information. Rates vary from about US$4 to US$8 per hour. The South American Explorers clubhouse is also a good source of recommendations.

DANCING LESSONS

Ritmo Tropical (☎ 227 051), Avenida 10 de Agosto 1792, office 108, in Mariscal Sucre (see the New Town map) has one-on-one or group dancing lessons specializing in salsa, merengue and cumbia.

WORK

Teaching English is the most usual way for travelers to earn money in Ecuador. The best

jobs are for bona fide teachers who obtain work in advance – see Work in the Facts for the Visitor chapter. If you have no job lined up, the best bet is at one of the local 'English as a second language' schools. These places advertise in the gringo hotels or in the newspapers when they need teachers.

PLACES TO STAY

As befits a capital city, Quito has over 200 hotels, and it is impossible to list them all. The following selection will give you plenty of choices.

As a general guideline, hotels in the old town tend to be less comfortable and older than those in the new town, but they offer the most rock-bottom rates. Guests here get to stay in a more historic area, but it lacks nightlife and is not very safe at night. International visitors are increasingly flocking to the new town, where many new hotels catering to all budgets have opened in recent years.

The more expensive hotels add a 12% or 22% tax – the rates given here include taxes, but ask the better hotels whether the tax is included in the rates they give you.

December is a busy month in Quito. The founding of Quito is celebrated on the 6th, and the Christmas/New Year period is also busy. Try not to arrive in the evening without a reservation if you wish to stay in a particular hotel during that time. July and August are busy months with vacationers from North America and Europe – hotel prices may go up a bit then.

Budget

Old Town Many cheap hotels are at the south end of the old town, on the streets heading toward Terminal Terrestre de Cumandá. In this area, you'll find a score of cheap hotels within a few blocks of one another. Some foreign budget travelers and many locals stay in the area, but watch your belongings on the streets, and make sure your room is always locked. Some travelers (particularly single women) do not feel comfortable staying in this area. Many budget hotels were quoting extremely low rates recently – this may be because of the economic woes of the sucre, so prices could change dramatically as dollarization kicks in.

International budget travelers like *Hotel Grand* (☎ 959 411, 280 192, grandhotelquito@ hotmail.com, Rocafuerte 1001). Basic but clean rooms are US$2/3 for singles/doubles, or US$3/4 with private bath. The hotel is family run and has hot water, a laundry service and a restaurant. Note: a theft was reported in early 1999. A block away, the friendly *La Posada Colonial* (☎ 282 859, fax 505 240, Paredes 188) is also a popular choice and has facilities similar to Hotel Grand. Rates are US$2 per person, or US$3 for a room with private bath. The rooms upstairs have good views. *Hotel Guayaquil* (Maldonado 3248) has hot water and varied doubles – some quite spacious – for US$2.50, or a tad more for rooms with bath. The best budget hotel in this area is *Hotel Piedra Dorada* (☎ 957 460, Maldonado 3210), which charges US$4/6 for clean rooms with TV and private bath with reliable hot water.

The best hotel near Terminal Terrestre de Cumandá is *Hostal Cumandá* (☎ 516 984, 513 592, Morales 449). Clean, carpeted rooms with bathrooms and hot water are US$5 per person; some rooms have a TV and a telephone. Avoid rooms on the terminal side, as it can get noisy – otherwise, it's a good value. Also close to the terminal, *Hotel Reina de Quito* (☎/fax 950 347, Maldonado 2648) boasts a Jacuzzi and sauna, as well as a restaurant and kitchen privileges. Their terraces sport good city views. Rates are about US$3 per person for rooms with bath.

Going from Plaza Santo Domingo along Flores, there's the friendly *Hotel Huasi Continental* (☎ 957 327, Flores 332), which has spartan but clean rooms for US$1.50 per person, or US$2 with private hot bath. The nearby and similarly priced *Hotel Montúfar* (☎ 211 419, 281 417, Sucre 160) is also basic but clean and quiet (although the rooms at the front are noisy); it has warm showers as well.

Hotel Plaza del Teatro (☎ 952 980, Guayaquil 1373), in a nice old house by the Plaza del Teatro, charges about US$3 per person for rooms with private hot bath. Nearby, the pleasant old *Hostal La Casona* (☎ 957 923, Manabí 255) has clean rooms for US$2 per person.

Hotel Catedral Internacional (☎ 955 438, fax 583 119, Mejía 638) is another reasonable choice. Rooms with private showers and TV are a good value at US$3/5. *Hotel San Francisco de Quito* (☎ 287 758, fax 951 241, hsfquito@impsat.net.ec, Sucre 217) is in an attractive colonial building surrounding a courtyard. Comfortable rooms with TV and hot shower are a good deal at US$4.50/7. *Hotel Viena Internacional* (☎ 954 860, fax 954 633, Flores 600) is popular with travelers wanting comfort in the old town. Large carpeted rooms – some with balconies and all with telephones, TV, bathrooms and hot water – are US$6 per person.

In the northeastern part of the old town, *Hostal Belmonte* (☎/fax 956 235, hbelmonte@waccom.net.ec, Antepara 413) has a TV lounge and café and offers kitchen privileges. Small, simple rooms with shared bath are US$3 per person; rooms with private bath are US$4. Just east of Parque La Alameda, the popular *Residencial Margarita I* (☎ 235 564, 548 080, 950 441, Elizalde 410) and *Margarita II* (☎ 952 599, Los Ríos 1995) have clean rooms at US$3/5 with private bath and TV.

New Town For clean rooms, hot water and a roof with a view, you can try *Residencial Marsella* (☎/fax 955 884, Los Ríos 2035), about a block south of Parque La Alameda. But there have been reports that everything is fine until you have a complaint, and then the management becomes unhelpful. Rates are about US$4 to US$6 per person; rooms vary widely in quality.

In Mariscal Sucre, the small, family-run *Residencial Italia* (☎ 224 332, 9 de Octubre 237) has plenty of kids running around. Basic rooms (some with bath) are US$2 to US$4 per person; this place is often full. *Hostal Mundo Net* (☎ 230 411, Pinto E6-32) is only US$2 per person for basic rooms and has an Internet café. The Israeli-run *Gan Eden* (☎ 223 480, Pinto E8-24) has a café and rooms with shared baths for US$2.25.

Doubles with a private bath are US$6. **Daguis** (☎ 228 151, davidcando@hotmail .com, Calamá E6-05) also charges about US$2 per person. **Rincón de Castilla** (☎/fax 224 312, Versalles 11-27) has basic but clean rooms for US$3 per person. Kitchen privileges, laundry facilities and Spanish lessons are offered. **Hostal Alpa Aligu** (☎ 558 202, 564 012, Pinto 240) is good and clean and has an accommodating staff. Rates are US$4 per person for rooms with shared baths. **Hostal Adventure** (☎ 226 340, fax 504 713, Pinto E4-225) has kitchen privileges and rooms with shared bath for US$4 per person, or US$6 for rooms with private bath.

The women-only **Hostal Eva Luna** (☎ 234 799, fax 220 426, admin@safari.com.ec, Roca Pasaje 405) is down a little alley off Roca near Amazonas. It has a TV/VCR lounge and a balcony. Rates are US$4 per person, and the place is owned by Safari Tours. The clean **Hotel Viena** (☎ 235 418, Tamayo 879) has small private showers with hot water and TVs in each room. It's a good value at US$3 per person. **Residencial Carrión** (☎ 234 620, fax 505 406, Carrión 1250 (OE2-58)) has a restaurant and rooms with phone, TV, and private bath. Rates are US$5/7.

Casapaxi (☎ 542 663, fax 508 633, Pasaje Navarro 364), near Avenida La Gasca, is about 1km north of Avenida América, up a hill; the No 19 bus passes by. It is clean, and the staff is helpful and friendly. Rates are US$3 to US$5 per person, and discounts are given for longer stays (as is true of most hostales). The rate at **La Casa de Eliza** (☎ 226 602, manteca@uio.satnet.net, Isabel La Católica 1559) is US$5 per person. Eliza, the owner, arranges excellent treks through northern Ecuador in association with the Cerro Golondrinas Cloudforest Conservation Project (see the boxed text in the North of Quito chapter). Her cheerful sister, Luisa, runs the comfortable **Nuestra Casa** (☎ 225 470, De Las Casas 435), which has rooms for singles, couples and groups at US$5 to US$7 per person. There's plenty of hot water in the communal shower, and you can make meals in the kitchen or hang out in the TV lounge or garden.

La Casona de Mario (☎ 544 036, fax 230 129, lacasona@punto.net.ec, Andalucía 213 (N24-115)) charges US$6 per person and is in an attractive old house with a garden. Guests hang out in the TV lounge and have laundry and kitchen privileges. **El Centro del Mundo** (☎/fax 229 050, centrodelmundo@ hotmail.com, García 569 (E7-22)) is run by travelers (an Ecuadorian/French-Canadian couple) for travelers and features cable TV, home cooking and a party reputation. Rates are US$5, including breakfast, for dorm rooms and US$9/16 for rooms with private bath. **Tortuga Verde** (☎ 556 829, fax 227 882), at the corner of JL Mera and Pinto, has a TV lounge and a travel agency. Clean rooms with bunk beds sleeping up to six are US$5 per person. **El Vagabundo** (☎ 226 376, Wilson E7-45) is clean and has a pizzeria. Rates are US$7 per person, and baths are shared.

El Cafecito (☎ 234 862, cafecito@ ecuadorexplorer.com, Cordero 1124), over the restaurant of the same name (see Places to Eat, later) has a few doubles and several rooms with four or six beds. It is very popular with young budget travelers. Rates are US$6 per person; bathrooms are shared. **El Ciprés** (☎/fax 549 558/561, turisavn@ ecuamex.net.ec, Lérida 381) is in a quiet neighborhood and has dorm and private rooms, a big garden, a TV lounge, Internet access and complimentary continental breakfast. Rates are US$5 per person for rooms with shared baths, and rooms with private bath cost US$7. You can be picked up at the airport if you plan to stay a few nights.

Albergue El Taxo (☎/fax 225 593, acordova@ramt.com, Foch 909 (E4-116)) is run by artists who charge US$3 per person for beds in a dorm and US$7/14 for private rooms with shared bath. The **Hostelling International** youth hostel (☎ 543 995, fax 508 221, Pinto 325 (E16-12)) has spotless rooms with one to four beds at US$6 (private bath) or US$4 (shared bath) per bed. Breakfast is included.

Parque Italia (☎ 462 823, fax 224 393, parque.italia@ibm.net, Narvaez 802 (OE5-12)) is a pleasant B&B that is operated by an

Ecuadorian/Austrian couple. Rooms with terraces and shared baths for one to three people go for US$8 per person, or US$24 for a double with private bath. The café here is a good one. The centrally located *Hotel Pickett* (☎/fax 541 453, 551 205, Wilson 712) charges US$12/16 for basic rooms with telephone and bath; there is plenty of hot water.

Loro Verde (☎ 226 173, Rodríguez 241 (E7-66)) has a great central location and spacious rooms with bath for US$10/16. Nearby, *Posada del Maple* (☎ 544 507, fax 504 404, mgallego@pi.pro.ec, Rodríguez 148 (E8-49)) is a pleasant and friendly little hotel that charges US$8 per bed in a dorm, US$10/15 for singles/doubles with shared bath and US$16/18 with private bath. A buffet breakfast is included, and it's on a quiet street. The new *Posada del Maple 2* (Cordero E5-48) provides similar services at slightly higher prices. Readers have recommended the cozy *Hostal Amazonas Inn* (☎ 225 723, 222 666, Pinto 471 (E4-324)). The helpful manager speaks English, and there's a café connected to the hotel. Rooms with private baths (some with street balcony or TV) are US$8/10/13/15 for one/two/three/four people.

Crossroads (☎/fax 234 735, crossrds@uio.satnet.com, Foch 678 (E5-23)) has been completely renovated and is popular. Facilities include a good café, cable TV, kitchen privileges and a patio with a fireplace. The American owner is helpful. Rates are US$5 for dorm beds, US$9/14 for singles/doubles with shared bath and US$12/20 with private bath. *Hostal La Quinta Ecológica* (☎ 230 723, 551 269, fax 558 857, came@uio.satnet.net, Cordero 1951) is an attractive house converted into a 10-bedroom hotel with a garden. Rooms have private baths and cost US$8/12/15 for singles/doubles/triples. The clean *Hotel 9 de Octubre* (☎ 552 424/524, 9 de Octubre 1047) has had a recent paint job and is a reasonable value at US$12 for a double with private bath and ample hot water. Some of the staff speak English.

Several readers have recommended *L'Auberge Inn* (☎ 552 912, fax 569 886, auberge@uio.satnet.com, Avenida Colombia 1138 (N12-200)). It has a kitchen, garden, fireplace and game room; rates are US$8/12 for singles/doubles with shared bath and US$10/15 with private bath. You can arrange to be picked up from the airport. Also very popular is *Villa Nancy B&B* (☎ 563 084, fax 547 657, villa_nancy@ecuatorianos.zzn.com, Carrión 335), which has a grassy garden and seven spacious, clean rooms with big shared bathrooms for US$15/20. A buffet breakfast is included. The friendly, multilingual owners offer airport pickup.

Magic Bean (☎ 566 181, magic@ecnet.ec, Foch 681 (E5-08)), above the popular restaurant of the same name (see Places to Eat, later), is a great meeting place. Rates are US$8 for clean dorm rooms or US$22/26/32 for singles/doubles/triples with bath. *Hostal Raices* (☎ 234 355, 236 432, Tamayo 459 (N21-255)) is a small, attractively decorated hotel with a cable TV lounge. Rates are US$14/22 for singles/doubles with private bath; breakfast is included.

In the eastern part of the new town is the quiet, historical residential district of Guápulo. The clean *Hostal La Casa de Guápulo* (☎ 220 473, guapulo@mailexcite .com, Leonidas Plaza Gutiérrez 257) gives guests the opportunity to stay in a colonial neighborhood away from the hustle and bustle of Quito. French, English and Spanish are spoken. Rates are US$8 per person for rooms with shared bath (singles pay US$10), and rooms with private bath start at US$12. Breakfast is included.

Mid-Range

Old Town The clean Hostal Farget (☎ 570 066, fax 570 557, Santa Prisca at Farget 109) has nice rooms with private bath for US$13/20, including breakfast.

Hotel Real Audiencia (☎ 950 590, fax 580 213, realaudi@hoy.net, Bolívar 220), near the northern corner of Plaza Santo Domingo, is the best hotel in the old town. It has large clean rooms with bath, phone and TV for US$26/37. Many rooms have good views, as do the bar and restaurant on the top floor.

New Town In Mariscal Sucre, *Casa Helbling* (☎ 226 013, fax 500 952, casahelbling@ accessinter.net, Veintimilla 531 (E18-166)) is in a comfortable, homey, colonial-style house. The friendly staff allow guests to use the kitchen and washing machine. Rates are US$12/20 for singles/doubles with shared baths and US$16/28 with private baths.

The centrally located *Allston Inn Hotel* (☎ 229 955, fax 508 956, JL Mera 741 (N23-41)) has been recommended for clean, comfortable rooms with private hot showers for US$17/24. The similarly priced *Hostal Bavaria* (☎ 509 401, fax 222 858, atrios@ ramt.com, Páez 232) looks quite pleasant and comfortable; rooms have a TV and phone. The recommended *Casa Sol* (☎ 230 798, fax 223 383, casasol@ecuadorexplorer .com, Calamá 127 (E8-66)) is a clean B&B with a helpful staff and rooms surrounding an airy garden/courtyard. Rates are US$17/29, including breakfast. *Hostal Plaza Internacional* (☎ 524 530, fax 505 075, Leonidas Plaza Gutiérrez 150) is a friendly place in a lovely older house. It's often full – especially with overland tour groups. The rates are US$20/30, and the staff speaks English.

Hostal Charles Darwin (☎ 234 323, fax 592 384, chdarwin@ecuanex.net.ec, La Colina 304) is a small, friendly and intimate hotel on a quiet side street. A garden invites sitting out. Rooms with private bath are US$30/40, including breakfast and kitchen facilities.

The small and pleasant *Hostal Palm Garten* (☎ 523 960, 526 263, fax 568 944, 9 de Octubre 923), in a converted mansion, has comfortable and attractive rooms with TV and telephone for US$25/37. The small *Hostal Villantigua* (☎ 227 018, 528 564, fax 545 663, Jorge Washington 237) has rooms with colonial-style furniture ranging in price from US$22 to US$40 for singles and US$35 to US$55 for doubles; all have private bath, and some have fireplaces and minibars. A breakfast room is open 7:30 to 9:30 am.

Orange Guesthouse (☎ 556 960, fax 569 956, angermeyer@accessinter.net, Foch 726) is associated with Angermeyer's Enchanted Expeditions (see Travel Agencies, under Information, earlier) and has eight pleasant rooms, each with private bath for US$24/30, including breakfast. *Hotel Sierra Madre* (☎ 505 687/8, 224 950, fax 505 715, htsierra@ hoy.net, Veintimilla 464) has very clean rooms (some with a balcony), and the helpful staff speak English. Rates are about US$40/60, and breakfast is included. *La Cartuja* (☎ 523 577, fax 226 391, Leonidas Plaza Gutiérrez 180) is a small, prettily decorated hotel in an older mansion. A dozen rooms, all different, cost US$40/50, and an American breakfast is an extra US$5. Room service is available, and some staff speak English.

Hostal Los Alpes (☎ 561 110, fax 561 128, alpes@accessinter.net, Tamayo 223) is in a beautiful old house. Comfortable carpeted rooms with spotless bathrooms and a telephone are US$42/58, including American breakfast. The restaurant is excellent. The hotel enjoys a lot of repeat business, so reservations are advised. A charming hotel in a converted mansion with a garden is *Café Cultura* (☎/fax 224 271, info@ cafecultura.com, Robles 513). It is above the restaurant of the same name (see Cafés, under Places to Eat, later). The beautifully painted public areas feature three fireplaces. The rooms are very comfortable and are attractively and individually decorated – look around to find one that appeals. Rates are US$46/58. The onsite travel office makes reservations for 12 other unique hotels throughout Ecuador.

The recommended *Hostal Villa Nancy* (☎ 550 839, 562 473, fax 562 483, npelaez@ pi.pro.ec, Muros 146) is in a mid-upper-class residential area east of Mariscal Sucre. The staff is superb, and there is always a helpful, English-speaking person on duty at the front desk who will assist you with any problem or question. The hotel features a sundeck, a Scandinavian sauna, a small garden, a lobby bar with free coffee and a breakfast room. Current issues of the *Miami Herald* and *Newsweek* are in the lobby. The 13 rooms are spotless and have plenty of hot water and private showers, a hairdryer, minifridge, writing desk, phone, cable television and a morning newspaper. Rates are

US\$50/70, including airport transfers and a self-serve buffet continental breakfast. The friendly owner, Nancy, was born in Manabí and educated in the USA – she speaks impeccable English and French and has extensive experience in the hospitality industry. She's normally there during breakfast, chatting with guests and making sure everything is 100% satisfactory.

Finally, if you want to stay in an old hacienda on a mountain overlooking Quito, try the 25-room *Hostería San Jorge* (☎/fax 565 964, 239 287, 494 002/43, info@hostsanjorge .com.ec). The hostería, once owned by 19th-century Ecuadorian President Eloy Alfaro, is 4km west of Avenida Occidental, on the road to Nono. It's situated at an altitude of 3200m and is on the flanks of Rucu Pichincha (see the Metropolitan Quito map). The hacienda has over 30 hectares and is suitable for hiking, horseback riding, bird watching and mountain biking – all of which can be arranged for a fee. The hiking is good acclimatization for folks wanting to climb Ecuador's major peaks. There is an indoor heated pool, sauna, whirlpool and steam room, as well as pleasant gardens. A restaurant serves local and international food, and a bar features a pool table, darts and other games for relaxing after an active day. All rooms have rustic fireplaces and hot showers. Rates are about US\$50/60, and large suites cost US\$80. Airport pickup costs US\$10, and all meals are available at moderate rates. You can visit the hostería's Web site at www.hostsanjorge.com.ec.

Under Places to Stay, Budget, see Magic Bean – it has rooms with mid-range prices as well. If you want to stay near but not in Quito, see the Around Quito section for several other mid-range suggestions.

Top End

All top-end hotels are in the new town. These hotels are very good and compare well with 1st-class hotels anywhere in the world. However, many suffer from the habit of charging non-Ecuadorian guests approximately twice as much as residents of Ecuador. (The higher rates are given in this book.) Although luxury hotels are popular with businesspeople and tour groups, their inflated rates place them beyond the price range of most independent travelers.

Among the best luxury hotels for independent travelers is *Hotel Sebastián* (☎ 222 400/300, fax 222 500, hsebast1@hsebastian .com.ec, Almagro 822), because foreigners are charged almost the same rate as Ecuadorians. There are about 50 good-sized rooms and seven suites – many with balconies and some with great views. Apart from the usual features – including cable TV, direct-dial phones, room service, desks, attractive furnishings – there are several thoughtful touches: Water has been filtered, so you can drink it out of the tap, and ozone-purified water is available at the cafeteria. Towels and sheets are washed upon request using environmentally safe soap (a rarity in Ecuador). The fruits and vegetables served in the coffee shop and restaurant are organically grown. There is a cozy bar with a fireplace and two meeting rooms. Rates are US\$85/96, or about US\$20 more for suites. The hotel has a Web site at wwwpub4 .ecua.net.ec/sebastian.

An intimate and attractive small boutique hotel in a refurbished colonial-style home is *Mansión del Ángel* (☎ 557 721, fax 237 819, Wilson E-29). Rooms are elegantly furnished with curtained four-poster brass beds, and there is a rooftop garden. Rates are US\$60/100, including continental breakfast.

Two large luxury hotels are on Amazonas in the heart of the new town. *Hotel Alameda Real* (☎ 562 345, fax 565 759, apartec@ uio.satnet.net, Roca 653) has 150 very large rooms – many with balconies, wet bars or kitchenettes – for US\$95/115. It has a good restaurant, a bar, a coffee shop and a casino.

The biggest hotel in town is *Hilton Colón Internacional* (☎ 561 333, 560 666, fax 563 903, reserv@hcolon.com), at Amazonas and Patria. This hotel has everything you might need for a luxurious stay – a pool, sauna, massage parlor, exercise room, discotheque, casino, salons, a small shopping mall, a 24-hour coffee shop, several cafés and restaurants, two bars and numerous meeting rooms. The Colón is one of the capital's main social centers, and this is where many visiting dignitaries stay. Its central location also makes it one of upper-class Quito's most lively meeting places. Almost all of the 450 rooms have good views of Quito – head up to the 20th floor and walk out onto the roof for a great view. Rooms here vary in size, but all have cable TVs, telephones, desks and spacious bathrooms. Rates are US$214, single or double.

The 240-room *Swissôtel* (☎ 567 600, 566 497, 569 189, fax 568 080, Avenida 12 de Octubre 1820) also has all the amenities you could possibly want (including pool, gym, excellent restaurants and a casino) for US$185. More expensive suites are available, and special rates as low as US$110 are sometimes offered. The hotel's Web site is at www.swissotel.com.

Several new large and luxurious chain hotels have recently opened and are aimed primarily, but not exclusively, at business travelers. These include *Radisson Royal Quito* (☎ 233 333, fax 235 777, radisson@ impsat.net.ec, Cordero 444), at US$100 a room, and *Marriott Hotel* (☎/fax 972 000, anamarriott@hotmail.com), at Orellana and Amazonas, with rooms and suites for US$133 to US$214.

Others are away from the center (see the Metropolitan Quito map), such as *Hotel Four Points Sheraton* (☎ 970 002, fax 433 906, sheraton@uio.satnet.net), at República de El Salvador and Naciones Unidas. Rooms cost about US$145. *Holiday Inn Crowne Plaza* (☎ 251 666, 445 305, fax 251 958, 445 180, admihote@accessinter.com, Los Shyris 1757) charges US$107.

Apartments

Visitors wanting to stay for a longer time may want to rent a room, apartment or suite with a kitchen. Often, apartments require a one-month minimum stay, and they are often full. All of the apartment buildings in this section can be found on the New Town map.

One of the least expensive is *Apartamentos Calima* (☎ 524 036, Cordero 2028), which charges US$46/67 per month for

pretty beat-up rooms. *Residencial Casa Oriente* (☎ 546 157, Yaguachi 824) charges US$100/125 per month for simple rooms. Daily rates are US$5 per person, and there are kitchen privileges and a rooftop terrace overlooking the city. *Alberto's House* (☎ 224 603, albertohouse@hotmail.com, García 648) charges US$35 per week or US$100 per month. Facilities include shared hot showers, a laundry room, kitchen privileges, a TV lounge, a pool table and a garden with a barbecue area.

The following places charge by the day. The well-equipped but small apartments at *Amaranta Apart Hotel* (☎ 543 619, fax 560 586, amaranta@impsat.net.ec, Leonidas Plaza Gutiérrez 194) cost US$36/50 a day. *Antinea Apart Hotel* (☎ 506 838, fax 504 404, hotelant@access.net.ec, Rodríguez 175) has lovely furnished apartments for US$55/65.

Homestays

For those who would like to stay in a local home, families interested in hosting travelers can be found through the South American Explorers (see Useful Organizations, in the Facts for the Visitor chapter) or by reading the local classifieds. If you are taking Spanish courses, ask at your school. Prices average between US$5 and US$13 per person per day, and sometimes include meals and laundry service. Prices may be negotiable if you are staying a long time or are in a group. Most families have only one or two rooms available; single rooms may cost a bit more. English is not always spoken.

PLACES TO EAT

Budget travelers often eat the *almuerzos* and *meriendas* (set lunches and dinners) that are sold in many restaurants, particularly those used by workers and businesspeople. These set meals often cost about US$1 and may not be on the menu – you have to ask for them. Almuerzos and meriendas are more difficult to find on weekends, because these meals are aimed at working people. Many restaurants are closed Sunday.

The fancier restaurants add 12% tax plus a 10% service charge to the bill. This does not necessarily happen in the cheaper places. In even the most expensive restaurants, however, two people can dine well for about US$30 or US$40 (not including wine, which would add at least US$10 per bottle).

Old Town

There are few restaurants of note in the old town, although this is where the cheapest places are found.

Recommended cheap places include *Rincón Azuayo (Espejo 812)*, which has Ecuadorian food, and the good Chinese restaurant *Chifa El Chino*, on Bolívar near Guayaquil. *Los Olivos*, on Rocafuerte just off Plaza Santo Domingo, is perhaps the best of several cheap Ecuadorian restaurants in the area. For a snack, *Café del Teatro*, by Teatro Sucre, is a good place to relax. *Heladería San Agustín*, on Guayaquil near the Monastery of San Agustín, has been serving ice cream for six decades. *Govinda (Esmeraldas 853)* does vegetarian lunches served by the Hare Krishna folks. Another vegetarian place is *Girasol (Oriente 581)*. *Tianguez*, under the Monastery of San Francisco, is run by Fundación Sinchi Sacha (see Museums – New Town, earlier) and has snacks, juices, Ecuadorian food and an art shop. In good weather, there are tables outside.

The more expensive *El Criollo (☎ 289 811, Flores 825)* has good Ecuadorian food in pleasant surroundings. *La Cueva del Oso (☎ 583 826, 572 783/6, Chile 1046)* looks upscale but is reasonably priced and has Ecuadorian specialties, as well as musicians at times. The high, old-fashioned, pressed-tin ceilings and photos of old Quito add a touch of the past to your repast. It is one of the best places in the old town for lunch and dinner. Another top-notch place is *Las Cuevas de Luís Candela (☎ 287 710)*, a Spanish restaurant at Benalcázar and Chile. It is more expensive than the other places. Also try *Balcón Quiteño (☎ 512 711)*, on top of Hotel Real Audiencia, for decent dining with good city views.

New Town

Just because you are in the new town doesn't mean you can't eat economically. The trick to finding cheap meals in the new town is to avoid eating on Amazonas, where most restaurants are expensive. Look for little places tucked away on side streets and offering set meals for local workers – the food is usually unexciting but a good value.

If you want inexpensive fast food, walk down Carrión east of Amazonas. This block has earned the nickname 'Hamburger Alley' and has about a dozen places serving burgers etc. It is very popular with students. Make sure that your burger is thoroughly cooked and hot – the hygiene is questionable in these joints.

Cafés Avenida Amazonas is a good place to watch the world go by. There are four or five popular *pavement cafés* on the 400 and 500 blocks of Amazonas (near Roca). They serve a decent cup of coffee and don't hassle you if you sit there for hours. These are extremely popular meeting places and are not very expensive.

Magic Bean (☎ 566 181), Foch 681 (E5-08), remains very popular (see Places to Stay, earlier). The bean in question is coffee, and the place serves excellent Colombian coffee and good breakfasts. It opens around 7 am and stays open all day, serving a variety of meals and snacks in an outdoor patio or indoor dining room – both are usually packed with international travelers. Above the café is a budget hotel (see Places to Stay). *Art Forum Café (JL Mera 870)*, opposite the Libri Mundi bookstore, is recommended for a light snack out of doors with less of the hustle and bustle of Amazonas or Magic Bean. The place serves good cappuccino and has an art gallery. The British-run Café Cultura (see Places to Stay), on Robles between JL Mera and Reina Victoria, has excellent breakfasts and serves lunch and English afternoon tea. The German-run *Café Colibri (☎ 564 011, Pinto 619)* also has excellent breakfasts, as well as German-style meals during the day. You can eat inside or in the garden. *Café Sutra (Calamá 380)* is an attractive place with a good variety of light meals and drinks. It is a popular evening gathering spot.

Colón Coffee Shop, at Amazonas and 18 de Septiembre, is reasonably priced, considering that it is in one of the capital's most luxurious hotels. It is open 24 hours and serves meals and snacks – great if you get 3 am munchies after a hard night of partying.

El Pobre Diablo (☎ 224 982, Santa María 338) is a café by day and a bar with (recorded) jazz in the evening. There is an interesting changing art exhibition, and it's a lively place to snack and chat. The classy *Café Galleti* (☎ 237 881, Amazonas 1494) boasts three dozen different kinds of well-prepared coffee, as well as a wide tea selection and delicate snacks. *Swiss Corner* (☎ 468 007, Los Shyris 2137) is probably Quito's best pastry shop, with quiches and cakes as well. Take it out or eat in; coffee and fresh juices are available. There is a buffet breakfast on weekends. *Mr Bagel* (☎ 240 978, Portugal 948) is the place for bagels.

Sató (☎ 256 172, República de El Salvador N34-51) is a gourmet café and art gallery. A hairdressing salon occupies the same building, so you can get your hair done, browse the art, and then enjoy a special meal, such as a smoked trout salad. Everything is freshly prepared. The owner, Sara, is a potter, and the small but exquisite menu is served on unique plates made by her. You can buy the plate you ate on if you want. It's slightly expensive for a café, but worth it.

Grain de Café (☎ 565 975, Baqueadano 330) is a café/restaurant where you can have just a coffee or order a full meal. It's a laid-back place in the best sense and has friendly staff and good food.

Chinese Chifas (Chinese restaurants) are popular in Ecuador, and Quito has several good, medium-priced places. The following are only a few. *Chifa Mayflower* (☎ 540 510, Carrión 442) is good, and meals start at about US$3. A little more expensive, but very good, is *Chifa Hong Kong* (☎ 223 313, Wilson 246). *Casa China* (☎ 522 115,

Cordero 613) is also good and reasonably priced. *Mágico Oriental* (☎ 116 767, Páez 243) is considered authentic and a little upscale.

Ecuadorian Budget travelers should check out *Mama Clorindas* (☎ 544 362, Reina Victoria 1144). It is a good, cheap place to try traditional local food, particularly at lunchtime – meals are about US$2 to US$3.

Good Ecuadorian food served in elegant surroundings can be found at *La Choza* (☎ 230 839, Avenida 12 de Octubre 1821). Expect to pay about US$15 for a complete meal. A little more expensive is *Rincón La Ronda* (☎ 540 459, 545 176, Bello Horizonte 400). There is often live music in the evenings. This place is popular with international tour groups, as well as with rich Ecuadorians. The interior is beautifully decorated, and the service is good, although the waiters encourage you to order expensive wines. Another place to try Ecuadorian food is at *Taberna Quiteña* (☎ 549 092, Amazonas 1259). This is a low-roofed cellar bar with musicians wandering around at night – the food is OK, but check the prices before you order. Meals should be around US$6.

Cocina de Kristy (☎ 501 209/10, Whymper 184) serves both upscale Ecuadorian and international food. This place has a superb balcony view over Quito and is a nice place to have a drink while watching the sun set and the city lights turn on. Bring a sweater.

French These restaurants are rather pricey, but they serve fine cuisine in elegant surroundings. Reservations are recommended, and although tourists can get by with good informal wear, expect the locals to be very dressed up.

The best known is *Rincón de Francia* (☎ 225 053, Roca 779), which has been around for decades. A full meal will cost US$20 or more – expensive by local standards. A local critic says the standard dishes are excellent but finds that the more complicated dishes are disappointing. Other places to try are *Le Saint Tropez* (☎ 277 558,

Reina Victoria N-26), near Santa Maria, and **Ile de France** *(☎ 553 1747, Reina Victoria 1747).*

Italian There are many Italian restaurants, but most are not very cheap. A popular and reasonably priced one is **Ch' Farina** *(☎ 434 481, Carrión 619).* A variety of pastas, pizzas and lasagnas are served, and carryout service is available. **Il Risotto** *(☎ 220 400, Pinto 209)* is run by an Italian couple and is a favorite for fans of Italian cuisine. Pasta meals start at around US$5.

Cheaper Italian food is available at the many pizza restaurants. **Pizza Hut** *(☎ 526 453, JL Mera 566)* is fairly standard. **Pizza Pizza** *(☎ 228 251, Santa María 126)*, in the northeastern part of Mariscal Sucre, has good, reasonably priced pizza and cable TV. **El Hornero** *(☎ 542 518, Veintimilla 1149)* does takeout and delivery. **Buon Giorno** *(☎ 801 488)* does deliveries to your hotel (not mapped). The best pizzería might be **Le Arcate** *(☎ 237 659, Baqueadano 358)* – it has over 50 kinds of pizza!

For upscale Italian dining, in ascending order of price, **Il Grillo** *(☎ 225 531, Baquerizo Moreno 533)* is very popular and has a variety of freshly made pasta dishes. **Capuleto** *(☎ 550 611, Avenida Eloy Alfaro 1732 (N32-544))* combines a good Italian café with a delicatessen for takeout and is open 8 am to midnight every day. Outdoor dining is possible, and service is good. **Pavarotti** *(☎ 566 668, Avenida 12 de Octubre 1955)* is near the swank Swissôtel and has sophisticated Italian dishes aimed at business diners and well-heeled tourists. Reservations are recommended.

Japanese The chef has incorporated some Ecuadorian food elements at the trendy Japanese sushi place **Sake** *(☎ 524 818, Rivet N30-166).* It's slightly pricey but good – and open until midnight every day. **Tanoshi** *(☎ 567 600)* is in the Swissôtel and has commensurate quality and prices; it is also open late.

Mexican A few Mexican restaurants have opened in recent years. Note that Mexican food tends to be spicy and hot – it is nothing like Ecuadorian food. One of the oldest and priciest places is **La Guarida del Coyote** *(☎ 503 292, Carrión 619)*; another is **Tex Mex** *(Reina Victoria 235).* Meals at Tex Mex are cheaper and are of the 'Americanized' version of Mexican cuisine ('Tex' is for Texas), but that doesn't detract from their tastiness. **Café Tequila** *(☎ 446 288, Avenida Eloy Alfaro 2897)* is a trendy Tex-Mex restaurant and bar. **Old El Paso**, on Reina Victoria, is good and has low prices and a cable TV (so you can watch a Mexican soap opera).

Seafood Ecuador is justly famous for its *ceviche* (marinated seafood). One of the best cevicherías is **Las Redes** *(☎ 525 691, Amazonas 845).* Have the *ceviche mixta;* it's huge and delicious and costs about US$6.

Other excellent seafood restaurants (in ascending order of price) are **La Jaiba Mariscos** *(☎ 543 887, Colón 870),* **Su Cebiche** *(☎ 526 380, JL Mera 1232)* and the popular **Mare Nostrum** *(☎ 237 236, 563 639, Foch 172).* Expect to pay about US$6 to US$12 for a main course at these restaurants.

There are several cheaper, but less elegant, seafood restaurants. **Cevichería Viejo José** *(☎ 540 187, Veintimilla 1254)* is just 1½ blocks from Amazonas. Despite the name, meat dishes are served in addition to seafood. The restaurant is run by people from the coastal province of Manabí. It is open every day, and you can get a decent meal and friendly service for about US$3.

Spanish Excellent Spanish food is served in a number of restaurants – as with the French places, they tend to be elegant, pricey and popular with the upper class and well-dressed businesspeople on expense accounts. One of the best is **La Vieja Castilla** *(☎ 566 979, La Pinta 435).* **Costa Vasca** *(☎ 564 940, 18 de Septiembre 553)* is also excellent and has intriguing and unusual decor. Another good choice is **La Paella Valenciana** *(☎ 228 681, Almagro 1727),* which has pricey but big portions and emphasizes seafood; it is popular with businesspeople for lunch.

Meat A good place to go if you are hungry – especially for meat – is the Brazilian *Churrascaría Tropeiro* (☎ 548 012, *Veintimilla 546*). US$6 buys an 'all-you-can-eat' meal. Waiters keep coming around with beef, pork, lamb, chicken and other goodies, and there is a self-serve salad bar.

La Casa de Mi Abuela (☎ 565 667, *JL Mera 1649*) is locally popular. Steaks are huge and not too expensive. The moderately priced *Shorton Grill* (☎ 523 645, *Calamá 216*) and *Texas Ranch* (☎ 557 642, *JL Mera 1140*) are also good. *Adam's Rib* (☎ 563 196, *Calamá 329*) is good for barbecued meats and steaks; it also has a bar and pool table.

Dedicated carnivores should know that although these are all good choices by Ecuadorian standards, their best cuts cannot compare to a tender steak from the US Midwest. For the highest-quality imported Argentine beef, try *San Thelmo* (☎ 434 128, *256 739, Portugal 570*). It is more expensive, but it has the best steaks in town. Other meats, fish and kid's portions are also served, and there is a small play area.

Vegetarian Quito is probably the best place in Ecuador for a choice of vegetarian food. *Double Dutch* (☎ 522 167, *Reina Victoria 600*) serves filling international vegetarian food – Indonesian, Indian, Dutch, Japanese etc. Meals are generally well reviewed, although a couple of readers were disappointed.

Windmill Vegetarian Restaurant (☎ 222 575, *Colón 2245*) has good set lunches and adjoins a health-food store. *El Maple* (☎ 251 503, *Calamá 369*) is organic as well as vegetarian and is popular. *El Marqués* (*Calamá 443*) has good set vegetarian lunches for under US$2 – a good price in a pricey area of town. It's relaxing, with simple but clean surroundings enhanced by classical music. Also good for cheap set lunches are *Manantial* (☎ 227 569, *9 de Octubre 599*) and *Cielo y Tierra* (☎ 230 590, *Cordero 1838*).

El Cafecito (☎ 234 862), Cordero 1124, under the popular budget hotel of the same name (see Places to Stay), serves inexpensive, mainly vegetarian meals and snacks all day long. There is also a bar with a fireplace – it's a relaxing place for an evening drink.

Other On the top floor of the Edificio Amazonas is *La Terraza del Tartaro* (☎ 527 987, *Veintimilla 1106*) – an elevator at the back of the lobby takes you up. This is a classy place serving a variety of international food. The food is good, but the view is excellent.

Super Papa (☎ 508 956, *JL Mera 741*) serves breakfast and hot baked potatoes stuffed with delicious hot or cold fillings 7 am to 9:30 pm daily. This small restaurant is popular with travelers and is a good meeting place. One wall is covered with notices ranging from personal notes to recommendations for new places to stay, eat, drink or visit.

La Bodeguita de Cuba (☎ 542 476, *Reina Victoria 1721*) has good Cuban meals. The bar comes alive at night, when live Cuban bands perform to a standing-room-only crowd – great music!

La Creperie (☎ 226 780, *Calamá 362*) serves both dinner and dessert crepes, as well as other dishes, such as goulash and steak. Meals cost around US$6. *El Arabe* (☎ 549 414, *Reina Victoria 627*) is the place to go for falafel and hummus.

Avalon (☎ 229 993, *509 875, Orellana 155*) is a pricey but excellent international restaurant that features an extensive menu, including homegrown oysters, called the best in Ecuador by a local restaurant reviewer (who is a fine cook himself).

In-the-know local foodies head out to *Muckis* (☎ 861 789, *09-720 211*), in El Tingo, about 30 minutes southeast of Quito. Cab-drivers know it. A changing international menu is presented on a chalkboard, and many vegetables and herbs are grown in the restaurant's garden. You can dine inside by a log fire or outside. The owner, Helge, is known as one of Quito's best chef's, and you should make a reservation for Sunday, when the place is absolutely packed. Muckis is expensive but worth it.

Quito's luxury hotels have excellent international restaurants. The Hilton Colón

Internacional serves a delicious and varied all-you-can-eat lunch buffet in the lobby every Sunday from noon until 2:30 pm. It costs US$12 and is well worth it if you are looking for a luxurious splurge. Gan Eden (see Places to Stay, earlier) has Israeli food and good breakfasts. Also check out the bars under Entertainment, later – some serve good food.

ENTERTAINMENT

Check the local newspapers *El Comercio* and *Hoy* for movie listings and other events.

Fiestas

Entertainment reaches its height during the various fiestas. Throughout the first week of December, the founding of Quito is celebrated with bullfights at the Plaza de Toros, just beyond the intersection of Avenidas América and 10 de Agosto. There is also street-dancing on the night of December 6.

New Year's Eve is celebrated by the burning of elaborate life-sized puppets (often representing politicians) at midnight. Carnaval (held the weekend before Ash Wednesday) is celebrated by intense water fights – no one is spared. Colorful religious processions are held during the Easter week.

The devil came down to Quito.

Cinemas

Films provide cheap (US$2 or under) and good entertainment. Some cinemas show popular English-language films with Spanish subtitles, while cheaper places resort to kung-fu and porno flicks. The best cinemas are the eight-screen US-style *Cinemark* (☎ 260 301), at Naciones Unidas and Avenida América, and *Multicines* (☎ 259 677), at the Centro Comercial Iñaquito, which show recent Hollywood hits and do the popcorn thing (see the Metropolitan Quito map for both). For arty or alternative movies, try Casa de la Cultura Ecuatoriana (see Museums – New Town, earlier) and *Fundación Octaedro* (☎ 469 170, 464 261, El Zuriaga E-28).

Many other cinemas advertise their films in the daily newspapers; a few of the better ones are mapped (Cines Colón and Universitario are on the New Town map, and Cines Atahualpa and Metro are on the Old Town map).

Performances

Metropolitan Touring, along with the Ministerio de Turismo, has organized a spectacular *ballet folklórico* called *Jacchigua*. It is presented at Teatro Aeropuerto at 7:30 pm Wednesday and Friday. Contact any travel agency for tickets. Admission is US$5 to US$15, depending on the seat.

If your Spanish is up to it, you can see a play at *Teatro Sucre*, in the old town's Plaza del Teatro – this is the oldest of Quito's cultural spots, and part of the fun is seeing the elegant building. Classical music is performed at this theater – sometimes, the National Symphonic Orchestra plays for no charge. This theater is being renovated with state-of-the-art stage equipment and is due to reopen by January 2001. Check the newspapers for schedules and information.

Other possibilities include the new town's *Teatro Prometeo* (☎ 226 116, Avenida 6 de Diciembre 794), which is inexpensive and sometimes has modern-dance performances and mime shows that anyone can understand. *Patio de Comedias* (☎ 561 902, 18 de Septiembre 457) has also been recommended for plays, which are often presented Sunday night.

Contemporary dance is presented at *Humanizarte* art gallery (☎ 523 319, *Amazonas 1167*). Interesting modern plays are performed at *Casa de Al Lado* (☎ 226 398, *Valladolid 1018*) – it is a dinner-theater place that also shows innovative films and may have live jazz or Latin music. The cover is US$6 to US$10.

These cultural events are advertised in the daily newspapers and on posters at the venues themselves. There is usually more going on in the rainy season.

Bars & Clubs

Peñas are bars that usually have traditional *música folklórica* shows and are often quite expensive. *Ñucanchi Peña* (☎ 540 967, *Universitaria 496*), in the new town, is a fairly inexpensive place with a US$4 cover. It's popular with students and families and is probably the best choice for travelers wanting to see a peña show. There are performances Tuesday to Saturday. *La Taberna del Duende* (☎ 544 970, *Páez 141*) is a cozy local bar with traditional music Thursday to Saturday.

Dancing is also popular; there is often a cover charge or a drink minimum. For dancing to Latin American music, try one of the *salsatecas*, which are especially popular with Ecuadorians and Latin American tourists, although there's usually a sprinkling of adventurous gringos. The best-known salsateca is *Seseribó*, in Edificio El Girón, at Veintimilla and Avenida 12 de Octubre. The smaller *Mayo 68* (*García 662*) is another good option.

Other dance clubs feature a mix of everything from rock to reggae and are favored by international travelers and Ecuadorians who can afford them. Many are found in the area bounded by Orellana and Calamá, and Amazonas and Almagro.

Arribar (☎ 228 545), at JL Mera and García, is a good dance club. *Zulu Bar*, at Calamá and Almagro, features techno until the wee hours. *Tijuana*, at Reina Victoria and Santa Maria, is good for a mix of Latin and Western pop.

If your idea of a night out is a drink and a chat in a pleasant bar, you'll find plenty of good places. Several are British or American bars that have a publike atmosphere. *La Reina Victoria* (☎ 233 369, *Reina Victoria 530*), owned and managed by friendly US/British couple Dorothy and Gary, is a real home away from home for the homesick British traveler. There is a fireplace, dartboard, bumper pool and excellent pub ambience suitable for all ages. Good food and a couple of microbrews are available. A newer British pub that is popular with the younger set is *The Turtle's Head* (☎ 565 544, *La Niña 626*). It has a great selection of beers (including some new and good microbrews), a gregarious Scottish landlord and a pool table. British bar food, designed to quell massive appetites, is served.

La Cascada Mágica (☎ 527 190, *Foch 476*) was recently opened by the managers of Magic Bean (see Places to Stay, New Town, earlier). It features pool, foosball, hockey and snacks, along with the drinks. *Ghoz Bar* (*La Niña 425*) is another choice for playing games and drinking.

The gay and lesbian scene in Quito is muted by antigay sentiments. The venues often change location in order to avoid harassment. Some gay-friendly places to try include the trendy *Matrioshka* (☎ 552 669, *Pinto 376*) and *Dionisios* (☎ 557 759, *Manuel Larrea 550*), which is behind Edificio Benalcázar and has live theater and dance performances on weekends. A reader wrote enthusiastically about the all-night party bar *Solomons*, on the two-block street of Moreno Bellido, just northwest of Avenidas Eloy Alfaro and La República.

El Pobre Diablo (see Places to Eat, Cafés, earlier) has a nice ambience, a fireplace, jazz music, beer, tea and coffee.

Note: Many readers and locals have reported that some bars have a racist policy whereby blacks are not admitted. These include the No-Bar, Tequila Bar and Papillón – all of these are popular with travelers who enjoy the lively music, dancing and action, but are probably unaware of the club's racist policies.

SHOPPING

There are many good stores for souvenir hunters in the new town along and near

Avenida Amazonas. If buying on the streets (there are street stalls and ambulatory vendors), you should bargain. In the fancier stores, prices are normally fixed, although bargaining is not out of the question – particularly if you are buying several things. The better stores are usually more expensive but not necessarily exorbitant, and the items for sale are often top quality.

Some stores sell pre-Columbian ceramics and colonial antiques. It is legal only for Ecuadorian residents to buy these items. You are not allowed to export archaeological or antique items, and they will be confiscated at customs upon departure from Ecuador or upon arrival at your home country. Another thing to avoid buying is anything made from animals – this includes black-coral jewelry and mounted butterflies, as well as the more obvious things, such as animal skins. These are protected, and it is illegal to import animal products into most countries.

The following is a list of stores that sell a wide selection of goods at a variety of price levels. Folklore, at Colón 260, is the store of legendary designer Olga Fisch (who died in 1991). This is the place to go for the very best and the most-expensive items. The Productos Andinos Indian cooperative, at Urbina 111 (near the intersection of Colón and Avenida 6 de Diciembre), has much cheaper but still highly recommended goods.

Most other stores' prices lie between those of the aforementioned places, yet they maintain a decent quality. The following are all reliable. Galería Latina (☎ 540 380), next to the Libri Mundi bookstore, has superb Andean textiles. Nearby is the Centro Artesanal (☎ 548 235), JL Mera 804, which is known for canvases painted by local Indian artists and other products. A block away is La Bodega (☎ 225 844), JL Mera 614, which has a wide and wonderful selection of souvenirs. MCCH, at JL Mera and Robles, is a women-artisan cooperative store with a fine selection.

Other recommended places nearby include El Aborigen (☎ 508 953), Jorge Washington 614, and Ecuafolklore (☎ 524 315), Robles 609. There are many other stores in the area, and their exclusion does not imply that they aren't any good! Wander around, and remember that many are closed Sunday.

Excellent Amazonian crafts are sold at Fundación Sinchi Sacha, which also has a museum. Profits benefit indigenous groups. For expensive modern art, go to Museo Guayasamín (see Museums – New Town for both places).

Note that souvenirs are a little cheaper outside Quito if you have the time and inclination to search them out – but it is more convenient to shop in the capital.

To buy groceries, batteries, stationery, soap and other essentials, try El Globo, at Avenida 10 de Agosto and Roca. There are many supermarkets. Supermaxi is good – there are branches at several shopping centers, including Centro Comercial Iñaquito. Shopping centers are similar to North American shopping malls – they feature many small stores selling all kinds of things. They are often called *centros comerciales,* abbreviated to CC. Most stores and shopping centers are closed Sunday, but the following malls are open every day.

Centro Comercial El Jardín (☎ 980 928), Amazonas and Avenida de la República

Centro Comercial El Bosque (☎ 456 333), Avenida Occidental at Carvajal

Centro Comercial Iñaquito (CCI; ☎ 259 444), Amazonas and Naciones Unidas

Centro Comercial Quicentro (☎ 464 512), Avenida 6 de Diciembre and Naciones Unidas

GETTING THERE & AWAY
Air
There is one airport, with a domestic and international terminal side by side. You can walk from one terminal to the other in about 60 seconds.

Services at the terminal include tourist information, money exchange, ATMs, a post office, a cafeteria/bar, an Andinatel office (8 am to 10 pm only – it's very difficult to call at other times unless you have a local calling card) and gift shops. For airport information, call ☎ 440 090.

The airport is about 10km north of the city center. See Getting Around, later, for bus and taxi information.

Domestic There is no departure tax for internal flights, most of which are run by TAME. Internal flights are fairly inexpensive (except for flights to the Galápagos) – prices and schedules change frequently, and the following price information is approximate and subject to change.

Flights to most cities cost US$25 to US$55. The most expensive mainland flights are to the Oriente, where foreigners must pay twice as much as locals.

Flights to Guayaquil are operated mainly by TAME (about US$30 to US$50 one way) and leave as many as 14 times a day on weekdays, about half that on weekends. Quito-Guayaquil flights are the most important air link in Ecuador and are rarely full; just show up at the airport and get on the next available flight.

Flights to Cuenca (US$30 with TAME) leave one to three times a day. TAME flies to the following:

destination	departures from Quito
Cuenca	three times daily
Esmeraldas	weekday mornings and Friday and Sunday afternoons
Lago Agrio	Monday to Saturday mornings and weekday afternoons
Loja	Monday to Saturday at 6 am
Macas	Monday, Wednesday and Friday afternoons
Manta	Monday to Saturday mornings and Sunday afternoons
Portoviejo	Monday, Wednesday and Friday afternoons
Tulcán	weekdays at 9:30am

Machala can be reached from Quito weekdays, with connections at Guayaquil. Aerogal operates flights to Coca (US$53) one or two times Monday to Saturday mornings.

A broken-down airplane can cause a city to be removed from the itinerary for a week or more until a needed part is obtained and replaced. Lack of passenger demand may also lead to canceled flights. But despite these frustrations, flying from Quito is generally straightforward and economical. Return flights to Quito are usually on the same planes that flew out.

Isla Baltra, in the Galápagos, is reached from Quito by TAME flights every morning. There may be a change at Guayaquil, but your luggage is transferred. The round-trip fare is US$378 for non-Ecuadorian residents (US$322 in the low season). These flights are the normal way to go for travelers heading to the main port of Puerto Ayora on Isla Santa Cruz. TAME also has morning flights to Isla San Cristóbal (sometimes changing at Guayaquil) daily except Thursday and Sunday (same price).

There are TAME offices at the following locations:

Colón 1001, near La Rábida (☎ 554 900)

Avenida 10 de Agosto 239, near La Parque Alameda (☎ 583 939, 510 305)

Avenida 12 de Octubre 1402, near Wilson (☎ 546 037)

The least crowded office seems to be the one on Avenida 12 de Octubre. You can also buy tickets through local travel agents (same price). AeroGal (☎ 257 202/3), Amazonas 7797, is near the airport. South of the airport are several companies that charter small planes.

International Several international airlines have offices in Quito. There is an international departure tax of US$25 payable in cash only. If you are flying internationally, confirm 72 hours in advance, reconfirm 24 hours in advance and arrive at the airport two hours before your flight. You might take off late, but at least you'll be on the flight. Flights are frequently overbooked, so if you don't reconfirm, you'll get bumped – 'Sorry, you're not on the computer.'

The following major airlines fly into Ecuador and have offices in Quito; there are others. These addresses change frequently.

Air France (☎ 224 818/57), World Trade Center, Avenida 12 de Octubre 1942, office 710

American Airlines (☎ 260 900), Amazonas 4545

Avianca (☎ 264 392), Edificio Twin Towers, República de El Salvador 780

British Airways (☎ 540 000/902), Amazonas 1429

Continental Airlines (☎ 557 170), World Trade Center, Avenida 12 de Octubre 1942, office 1106

Iberia (☎ 556 009), Edificio Filandes, Avenida Eloy Alfaro 939, 5th floor

KLM (☎ 986 828), Edificio Torre, Avenida 12 de Octubre 1492, office 1103

Lacsa/Grupo Taca (☎ 923 170), República de El Salvador N35-67

LanChile (☎ 508 396), 18 de Septiembre 238

Lufthansa (☎ 541 300, 508 396), 18 de Septiembre 238

Varig (☎ 437 137, 260 730), Portugal 794

A service via Loja or Machala to Piura, Peru, is to be inaugurated sometime in late 2000. Ask at travel agencies.

Bus

Quito's bus station, Terminal Terrestre de Cumandá, contains the offices of several dozen bus companies. It is a few hundred meters south of Plaza Santo Domingo, in the old town. The terminal can be reached by walking down the steps from Maldonado (see the Old Town map). The trolley will drop you off nearby. Taxi drivers often take an alternate route that enters the terminal from the south side.

The terminal serves most destinations from Quito. There is an information window, where staff will tell you which company goes where, although it's fairly obvious. Walk around and compare departures. For comfortable buses to Guayaquil from the new town, avoiding the trip to the terminal, you can go with Panamericana (☎ 553 690, 551 839), on Colón near Reina Victoria, or with Transportes Ecuador (☎ 226 267), JL Mera N21-44, near Jorge Washington. Panamericana also has long-distance buses to several other towns, including Machala, Loja, Cuenca, Manta and Esmeraldas. Its prices are higher than com-

panies at the bus terminal, but the buses are good and the service is convenient.

At the bus terminal, several companies often serve the same destination at different times. For the most-popular towns, you'll find ticket sellers yelling out their destinations, even though each window is clearly labeled. Only buses departing within a few minutes are allowed to park outside the terminal, so you can often be on your way within minutes of arriving. Usually, it is easy enough to get onto the bus you want, but if you plan on traveling during holiday periods or just before the weekend, it's best to go to the terminal and book in advance. If you do find you have to wait, there are several snack bars. There is also a post office, an Andinatel office, ATMs and small stores. Watch your luggage carefully inside the terminal.

All major towns are served from this terminal. Fares vary, depending on whether you get a comfortable bus with movies and a bathroom (only to the major cities) or an older bone-shaker. Prices change often because of inflation combined with fluctuation in gas prices. However, most destinations can be reached for less than US$1 per hour of travel. Approximate travel times to some major cities are listed below.

Ambato	2½
Bahía de Caráquez	8
Baños	3½ (if the town is open)
Coca	13
Cuenca	8
Guayaquil	8
Ibarra	3
Lago Agrio	10
Latacunga	1½
Machala	11
Manta	8
Otavalo	2¼
Portoviejo	8
Puyo	8 (if the road through Baños is open)
Riobamba	4
Santo Domingo	2½
Tena	6
Tulcán	5½

For other destinations, you may have to go to the nearest major city and change. Inquire at the bus offices.

Since hundreds of buses depart during the day, it is impossible to give accurate timetables. There are several buses per day to most destinations, and there may be several departures per hour to popular places such as Ambato or Otavalo. There is a US$0.10 departure tax from the bus terminal.

With several companies serving most destinations, you have a choice, so ask around. Companies serving the same destination are clustered together in one part of the terminal. Also, find out whether the bus will be a slow old one, which may give a more interesting ride, or a newer fast one, which may be small and cramped but will get you there faster. If the bus isn't almost full, the ticket seller will often show you which seats are available so you can choose where you sit.

A few buses leave from other places for some destinations in the province of Pichincha. Cooperativa Flor de Valle (☎ 527 495)

goes to Mindo (2½ hours) daily at 3:20 pm and also at 8 am Friday, Saturday and Sunday. The bus leaves from Larrea just west of Ascunción, near Parque El Ejido. Get there early, as the bus fills up.

Companies also sell tickets for direct rides to Lima, but these are two or three times more expensive than just going to the border and changing buses.

Train

If you are in a hurry or short on money, take a bus. There is one train to Riobamba that leaves 8 am Saturday. On Sunday, there is a roundtrip from Quito to Area Nacional de Recreación El Boliche, adjoining Parque Nacional Cotopaxi (see the South of Quito chapter). This train leaves at 8 am and returns at 5 pm, allowing several hours to hike and picnic. These are old-fashioned and uncomfortable trains with primitive bathroom facilities. Many passengers ride on the roof of the boxcar – a unique experience with great views, but very cold. The journey to Riobamba costs US$16 one way,

By Train Through the Valley of the Volcanoes

The trip to Riobamba takes about nine to 10 hours, but if there are problems, 12- or 13-hour journeys are possible. At the Quito train station, vendors sell snacks, drinks, gloves, hats and cushions for the journey. Snacks are also available en route. Tickets come with assigned seats, but so many travelers rush to climb up onto the top of the boxcar that the seats are often empty, while the boxcar roof is unbelievably crowded. Travelers can sit only on the flat roof of the boxcar; the roofs of the passenger cars are sloped, so no one is allowed there.

The following stops are usually made, but they can be very brief, so don't get left behind if you get off. See the South of Quito chapter for more details on these towns. **Machachi** (1¾ hours) has a hotel by the train station, where a brief stop is made upon request. **Area Nacional de Recreación El Boliche** (2¼ hours) is the destination for the Sunday trip. Saturday travelers to Riobamba get 15 minutes to stretch their legs and to buy snacks from the little store at the El Boliche stop. A brief stop is made on request at the main entrance to **Parque Nacional Cotopaxi** (three hours), although there is no station there. The village of **Lasso** (3¼ hours) also gets a brief stop, but **Latacunga** (3¾ hours) gets a five- or 10-minute stop. On clear days, there are great views of Cotopaxi, the Illinizas and other mountains in the section between Machachi and Latacunga. A brief stop is made at San **Miguel de Salcedo** (4½ hours), and a few minutes are spent in **Ambato** (5½ hours) picking up passengers. The area around Ambato tends to be extremely dusty, but views of Tungurahua are good. **Mocha** (seven hours) has a simple restaurant at the station, and 20 minutes may be spent there while the crew eats. **Urbinas** (eight hours) is a train station on the flanks of Chimborazo that has been converted into a hostal. **Riobamba** is reached after nine hours or so.

and the roundtrip El Boliche fare is US$20 (residents pay about US$2 for these trips). Partial, one-way fares are US$10 to El Boliche or Parque Nacional Cotopaxi and US$15 to Ambato.

The Quito train station (☎ 656 142) is on Sincholagua and Vicente Maldonado, about 2km south of the old town. The train-station booking office is open the day before trains depart, but there is normally no problem obtaining tickets from 7 am onward on travel days.

See also the boxed text 'By Train Through the Valley of the Volcanoes.'

GETTING AROUND
To/From the Airport

The Quito international airport (Aeropuerto Mariscal Sucre) is at the north end of Avenida Amazonas where it intersects Avenida de la Prensa, about 11km north of the center of old town. Many of the northbound buses on Amazonas and Avenida 10 de Agosto go to the airport. Some have *Aeropuerto* placards, and others say *Quito Norte*. A taxi from Quito should be US$3 to US$4. From the airport into town, taxi drivers try to overcharge – bargain hard unless you get a cab with a meter.

If you are going from the airport into town, you will find bus stops on Avenida 10 de Agosto, about 150m away from the front entrance of the terminal.

Bus

The crowded local buses have a flat fare that you pay as you board. They are safe enough and rather fun, but watch your bags and pockets. Generally speaking, buses run north-south and have a fixed route. There are various buses, and they are identified by the color of their stripe. *Popular* (light-blue) buses are the cheapest and most crowded. The *ejecutivo* (dark-blue) and *selectivo* (red) buses are less crowded, and some don't allow standing passengers. Fares vary from about US$0.10 to US$0.25. Pink-striped buses go out of Quito into nearby towns (but they are not long distance), and green-striped buses are feeders into the trolley (see that section, later). Buses have

destination placards in their windows, and drivers are usually helpful and will tell you which bus to take if they are not going to your destination. Traffic in the old town is very heavy, and you may often find it faster to walk than to take a bus, especially during the rush hours.

The narrow streets of downtown are usually one way. Calles Guayaquil and Venezuela are one way into the old town toward El Panecillo, and Calles García Moreno and Flores are one way out of the old town and away from El Panecillo. There are about 40 different bus routes. If you have a specific place you want to get to by local bus, ask your hotel's staff, bus drivers or passersby. The locals know where the buses go. It's not difficult to get around if you ask and are prepared to put up with very crowded buses and watch your belongings carefully.

Trolley

El Trole is Quito's most comfortable and useful transportation system. Trolleybuses run along Avenida 10 de Agosto, through the old town to the north end of the southern suburbs. The trolleys have designated stations and car-free lanes along the streets they travel, so they are speedy and efficient. They also are modern and designed to minimize pollution. The line runs between the Estación Sur, on Maldonado south of Villaflora, and the Estación Norte, on Avenida 10 de Agosto just north of Avenida de la Prensa. Trolleys run along Maldonado and Avenida 10 de Agosto about every 10 minutes from 6 am to 12:30 am (more often in rush hours), and the fare is US$0.25. Some trolleys only serve part of the route, but your ticket is valid for onward travel if you get dropped off before you reach your final destination. In the old town, southbound trolleys take the west route (along Guayaquil), while northbound trolleys take the east route (along Montúfar and Pichincha).

A new system, called the Ecovía, is being built along Avenida 6 de Diciembre between Río Coca in the north and La Marin in the south. Parts of this should be open by 2001.

Car

Car rental in Quito, as elsewhere in Ecuador, is expensive – taxis and buses are much cheaper and more convenient than renting a car.

A rental car is a possibility for getting around the country. However, if you plan on visiting the main towns and travelers' destinations, you will find the buses to be fast, efficient and reliable in most cases – and very cheap. Rental vehicles are useful for visiting some out-of-the-way areas that don't have frequent bus connections (in which case, a more expensive 4WD vehicle is a good idea).

The following companies are found in Quito. Ecuacar and Localiza have been recommended as particularly reliable and competitively priced.

Avis (☎ 440 270), at the airport

Budget (☎ 240 763, 459 052), at the airport

Ecuacar (☎ 247 298), at the airport

Hertz (☎ 254 257), at the airport

Budget (☎ 237 026), Amazonas 1408, near Colón; (☎ 525 328), Hilton Colón International

Ecuacar (☎ 529 781, 540 000), Colón 1280, near Amazonas

Hertz (☎ 569 130), at the Swissôtel

Localiza (☎ 505 974, 505 986), Avenida 6 de Diciembre 1570, near Wilson

See the Getting Around chapter for more car rental information.

Taxi

Cabs are all yellow and have red 'TAXI' stickers in the window. Usually, there are plenty available, but rush hour can leave you waiting 10 or 15 minutes for an empty cab. Rainy afternoons are particularly difficult times to hail a cab.

Cabs are legally required to have meters, and almost all drivers now use them, although occasionally they will ask to arrange a price with you beforehand. Sometimes this is to your advantage, as it enables the driver to take a roundabout route to avoid traffic, thus saving both of you time. But generally you should have

the driver use the meter. Late at night, they will ask for a higher fare, which is fair enough, but it shouldn't be more than twice the metered rate. Some drivers will say the meter is broken – you can always flag down another cab.

Taxis can be hired for several hours or for a day. If you bargain hard and don't plan on going very far, you could hire a cab for a day for about US$50. Cabs hired from the better hotels have set rates for long trips and are a bit more expensive but are more reliable. Short journeys downtown start at about US$1 and go to about US$5 for a long trip. From Amazonas to the top of El Panecillo is about US$10, including a one-hour wait and the return trip.

Unless you are visiting a well-known landmark, you will probably have to tell the driver the nearest cross street of your destination (use the maps in this chapter for reference).

Around Quito

☎ 02

Many excursions can be made from Quito using the city as a base. The destinations in this section are meant for day trips rather than as part of an overnight tour. In addition, the thermal baths of Papallacta (see the Northern Oriente chapter) can be a day trip from Quito.

POMASQUI

This village is passed about 16km from Quito on the way to Mitad del Mundo. Two churches on Plaza Yerovi (the main plaza), two blocks east of the gas station on the main highway, are worth a look.

On the plaza's south side, the **church of El Señor del Árbol** (the Lord of the Tree) has a noted sculpture of Christ in a tree – the branches of the tree look like Christ's arms raised above His head in a boxing champion's salute. Various miracles have been ascribed to this image by devotees.

On the plaza's east side, the **parish church** contains religious paintings – some of which are slightly bizarre (eg, the miracu-

AROUND QUITO

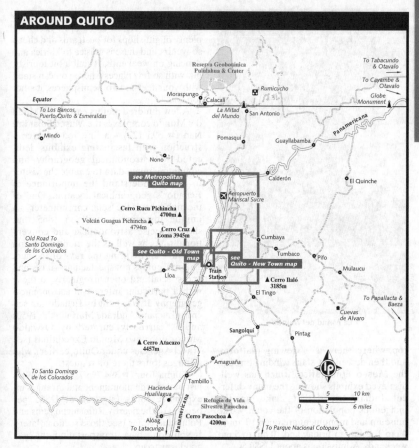

lous intervention of the Virgin to save a believer from certain death) – and various statues, including a carved and polychromed Santa Clara, who is the patron saint of Pomasqui.

The fiesta of El Señor del Árbol is normally the first Sunday in July. Día de Santa Clara is July 27, and so the whole month is a busy one for the citizens of Pomasqui, who have processions, games, bullfights etc.

LA MITAD DEL MUNDO
The most famous local excursion is to the equator at La Mitad del Mundo ('the middle

of the world'), in the village of San Antonio, about 22km north of Quito. This is the place where, in 1736, Charles-Marie de La Condamine's expedition made the measurements that showed that this was indeed the equator. The measurements also gave rise to the metric system and proved that the world is not perfectly round, but that it bulges at the equator.

The center of the Mitad del Mundo complex is a 30-meter-high stone trapezoidal **monument** topped by a brass globe that is 4.5m in diameter; it is built right on the equator. Visitors take an elevator to the

ROB RACHOWIECKI

La Mitad del Mundo

top, where there is a viewing platform, and then descend by stairs winding through the **Museo Etnográfico**, which has well-displayed exhibits showing the many different Indian tribes that make up the indigenous population of the country. The museum and monument are open 10 am to 4 pm Tuesday to Friday and 10 am to 5 pm weekends. Admission is about US$0.50.

Also at Mitad del Mundo is a realistic 1:200 scale **model of colonial Quito**. This is housed in a building to the left (west) of the monument and costs US$0.75 to visit. Visitors watch the scale model during a recorded talk (in Spanish), accompanied by lights to take you from dawn until late night; it's fun and impressive when you consider it was the brainchild of one enthusiastic man. Nearby, there is a **planetarium** run by the IGM with a variety of shows dealing with astronomy. Admission is inexpensive. To the southeast of the monument is a 'colonial village,' with plazas, buildings and a

bullring – all of which are used occasionally but are often closed and empty. There are plenty of gift shops for postcards and cheap souvenirs, and there is música folklórica and dancing on weekends. It's all a bit touristy, but with so few places where you can stand with your feet in two hemispheres, it's not too bad.

A few hundred meters east of the Mitad del Mundo complex is the **Museo Solar Inti Ñan** (☎ 395 122) – a tiny, red-brick construction with fascinating exhibits dedicated to astronomical geography and containing much data to enable the visitor to better understand the importance of Ecuador's geographical location. One of the highlights is the 'solar chronometer' – a unique instrument made in 1865 that shows precise astronomical and conventional time, as well as the month, day and season – all by using the rays of the sun. This museum is not spectacular – it is small and special and open irregularly to those with a particular interest in astronomical geography. It was built by Ecuadorian scientist Luciano Andrade Marín in the 1950s and is currently curated by Oswaldo Muñoz of Nuevo Mundo Expeditions (see Travel Agencies under Quito, earlier), who arranges tours there on request.

Calima Tour (☎ 394 796/7, fax 398 849) is just outside the monument and arranges inexpensive tours (starting at US$5 per person) of the nearby Rumicucho ruins and Pululahua crater (see those sections, later). If you don't have transportation, this is a good way to go.

Places to Stay & Eat

Hostería Aleman (☎ 394 243) is on the west side of the highway from Quito, almost 1km south of Mitad del Mundo. It has pleasant gardens and 11 rooms with hot showers and a small balcony. Rates are about US$16 for a double. The restaurant is presided over by an excellent German chef who prefers to work in the countryside rather than in a city – it's worth checking out. Standard breakfasts are about US$2, but it's best to call ahead and arrange lunch or dinner.

Southeast of the monument, the road goes to San Antonio. Along this road is the basic *Mitad del Mundo Hostal*, which has six rooms for US$4 per person. Opposite is the nicer-looking *Hostal Sol y Luna* (☎ 394 979), but it may be closed. Continuing into the village, about 1.5km from the monument, is *Rancho Alegre* (☎ 395 552), which has a pool, sauna, Jacuzzi, children's playground and café, in addition to 10 clean rooms with hot showers and TV. The facilities are locally popular on weekends for day use (US$2 for adults and US$1 for children under 12), and rooms are US$30 for singles or doubles, including use of the facilities.

Of several restaurants, *Equinoccio* (☎ 394 741), near the entrance to Mitad del Mundo, is the best known (and the most expensive). There are cheaper *comedores* on the road leading from Mitad del Mundo into the village center.

Getting There & Away

Catch a pink-striped bus signed 'Mitad del Mundo' running along Avenida América in Quito. They run several times an hour; the intersection with Colón is as good a place as any to wait. Buses tend to be crowded on Sunday.

Depending on how well you bargain, a taxi will cost about US$20 roundtrip, including waiting time at the monument.

Tours with bilingual guides are available from most of the major travel agencies. They all go to the Mitad del Mundo complex, except for Nuevo Mundo, which will take you to the solar museum if you wish. Tours cost about US$20 per person (depending on your group size) and last about three hours.

RUMICUCHO

This small, pre-Columbian archaeological site is about 3km north of San Antonio. The site is officially open 9 am to 3 pm weekdays and 8 am to 4 pm weekends, but you can walk in anytime. Entrance is about US$0.40, but it's not always collected. It's not Ecuador's most impressive site, but there are good views of Quito in the dis-

tance, and there probably won't be anyone else there. Walk all the way through; the best views are from the side farthest from the entrance.

Taxis to Rumicucho are available in San Antonio; the roundtrip fare, including wait time, should be about US$2 or US$3.

RESERVA GEOBOTÁNICA PULULAHUA

This small, 3383-hectare reserve lies about 4km northwest of Mitad del Mundo. The most interesting part of the reserve is the **volcanic crater** of the extinct Pululahua. This was apparently formed in ancient times, when the cone of the volcano collapsed, leaving a huge crater some 400m deep and 5km across. The crater's flat and fertile bottom is used for agriculture. Within the crater, there are two small cones – the larger Loma Pondoña (2975m) and the smaller Loma El Chivo.

The crater is open to the west side, through which moisture-laden winds from the Pacific blow dramatically. It is sometimes difficult to see the crater because of the swirling clouds and mist. The moist winds, combined with the crater's steep walls, create a variety of microclimates, and the vegetation on the fertile volcanic slopes is rampant and diverse. Because the walls are much too steep to farm, the vegetation grows undisturbed and protected. There are many flowers and a variety of birds.

The crater can be entered on foot by a steep trail from the Mirador de Ventanillas viewpoint, on its southeast side. There is also an unpaved road on the southwest side. The steep trail is the best way to see the birds and plants, because most of the flat bottom is farmed.

Information

The official entrance fee is US$5, but this is charged only if you enter by vehicle through Moraspungo; there are no charges for viewing or hiking in from the Mirador de Ventanillas viewpoint.

The Green Horse Ranch, inside the crater, owned by multilingual Astrid Muller, offers good horseback-riding trips.

Near Moraspungo are some cabins in the upper-budget price range. On the road between the viewpoint at the Moraspungo turnoff, signs point to *El Crater Restaurant* (☎ 439 254), which has good food but is usually open only on weekends.

The Texaco station near **Calacalí** is the last place for gas before Los Bancos if you are heading west. In Calacalí, the (much smaller) original equatorial monument can be seen. The Mitad del Mundo monument is an enlarged replica.

Getting There & Away
From Mitad del Mundo, a paved road continues to the village of Calacalí, about 7.5km away. There are occasional buses from San Antonio to Calacalí, particularly on weekends. About 4km beyond Mitad del Mundo on the road to Calacalí is the first paved road to the right. Ask the driver to drop you off there. About 1km along this road, there is a small parking area at the viewpoint.

Continuing on the road to Calacalí for 3km brings you to a sign for Moraspungo to the right. It's 3km to Moraspungo and about 12km more into the crater. There is an entry fee of US$5 per person entry fee at Moraspungo.

Taxis from San Antonio or Quito will take you to the rim, and tours can be arranged from Quito in combination with a visit to Mitad del Mundo.

CALDERÓN
This village is about 10km northeast of Quito on the Panamericana (not the road to Mitad del Mundo). Calderón is a famous center of a unique Ecuadorian folk art: The people make bread-dough decorations ranging from small statuettes to colorful Christmas tree ornaments, such as stars, parrots, Santas, tortoises, candles and tropical fish. The ornaments make practical gifts, as they are small, unusual and cheap (buy a handful for US$1). These decorative figures are inedible – preservatives are added so that they'll last many years. There are many stores on the main street.

Buses heading to Cayambe or Otavalo can take you there from Quito; flag one down on Avenida 10 de Agosto at a main intersection, such as Colón.

SANGOLQUÍ
The Indian market nearest the capital is Sangolquí's Sunday-morning market. There is a smaller market there on Thursday. Local buses go there frequently from Plaza Marín

---

Las Cuevas de Alvaro

About 32km east of Quito on the road to the Oriente, and about 10km past the village of Pifo, a dirt road goes to the right for a few kilometers to Alvaro's caves. Created by Ecuadorian eccentric Alvaro Bustamente, these caves were excavated by hand from a grassy hill in the middle of nowhere. Eventually, they became a series caves joined by underground passageways large enough for a tall person to walk through. It isn't clear why Alvaro built this structure – something about 'man's ties and dependence on the land.'

Now they have been turned into a seven-room underground hotel with shared hot showers and a restaurant serving homemade food. The rooms are comfortable and have electricity, but there are no TVs or telephones to intrude into the experience. Travelers can visit and inspect the complex for a small fee or eat lunch underground. A children's play area, an artificial lake with a rowboat and lookout towers are on the grounds around the hotel, and horseback riding and hiking are ideal activities. *Cuevas del Alvaro Lodge* (☎ 547 403, fax 228 902, birdecua@hoy.net, Carrión 555C, Quito) has an office in Quito. Rates are about US$25 per night, including breakfast, or about US$50 for two nights, including breakfast and a horseback-riding trip.

(also known as 'La Marín'), in Quito's old town. Sangolquí is about 20km southeast of the old town.

Places to Stay & Eat

Hostería Sommergarten (☎/fax 330 315, 332 761, reservations in Quito ☎/fax 221 480, rsommer@uio.satnet.net, Chimborazo 248, Sangolquí) is a quiet, 20-room hotel with a pool, sauna, steam bath and whirlpool (these facilities can be used by nonguests for US$5). Large, clean, unpretentious rooms are US$49/61, including American breakfast; suites are US$85.

Hostería La Carriona (☎ 331 974, 332 004, fax 332 005, lacarriona@accessinter.net) is 2.5km southwest of Sangolquí on the road to Amaguaña. This 200-year-old colonial hacienda is a delightful place to stay and is just a 30-minute drive from Quito. The old architecture is fronted by a cobbled courtyard and is surrounded by flower-filled gardens. A pool, sauna, steam bath, Jacuzzi, games area and meeting rooms are featured, and there is a large restaurant. About 30 units vary distinctly in character, from cozily rural rooms to lavishly ornate suites. All have private bath, TV and phone. Two simple singles are US$22 each, four larger singles are US$43, and doubles range from US$55 to US$73.

Not far from La Carriona is the area's best restaurant, *El Viejo Roble (☎ 334 036, Vía Amaguaña, Km2.5, Avenida Rumiñahui)*, with Ecuadorian and international cuisine served daily from 11 am until late. In Sangolquí itself are a number of cheap local places as well.

REFUGIO DE VIDA SILVESTRE PASOCHOA

Formerly a private reserve operated by Fundación Natura (☎ 447 341/4), this refuge became part of the Ecuadorian system of protected areas in 1996, although Fundación Natura still plays a part. The refuge is roughly 30km southeast of Quito and has one of the last remaining stands of undisturbed humid Andean forest left in the central valley. Over 100 species of birds have been recorded there.

Hacienda Hualilagua

Hualilagua de Jijón was built in 1718 on a hill with fabulous views of the central valley some 30km south of Quito. One of its outstanding features is a small stand of original Andean forest, which originally covered much of the sides of the central valley. The hospitable owners delight in showing you around the elegant hacienda and talking about the period furniture and artwork found throughout.

Normally, it is open Thursday and Sunday, when a breakfast (US$12) or lunch (US$23) of organic food is offered, thus making this a stopping point on the day trip to the Thursday Saquisilí market or Sunday Machachi market. Reservations at the hacienda can be made with Metropolitan Touring (see Travel Agencies under Quito, earlier), which offers a 'Hacienda, Chagras and Rodeo' package for US$55 – an all-day affair including the market, lunch at the hacienda and transportation. *Chagra* is the Ecuadorian term for a typical Andean cowboy, dressed in a heavy wool poncho, sheepskin chaps and a fedora against the cold. During a short rodeo, they show off their riding abilities and their skills with a lasso – a photogenic spectacle.

The forest is luxuriant and contains a wide range of highland trees and shrubs. These include the Podocarpaceae, which are the only conifers native to the Ecuadorian Andes (the pines seen elsewhere are introduced); various species of mountain palm trees; the Andean laurel; and the huge-leaved *Gunnera* plant (nicknamed 'the poor folks' umbrella'). Orchids, bromeliads, lichens, ferns and other epiphytic plants contribute to the forest's attractions. The prolific birdlife includes hummingbirds, of which at least 11 species are present. Various other tropical birds – such as furnarids, tapaculos, honeycreepers and tanagers – may be seen along the nature trails. Mammals such as rabbits, squirrels and deer are sometimes observed; foxes and even pumas more rarely so.

The reserve is a small one (only 500 hectares in size) and is located on the northern flanks of the extinct volcano of Pasochoa at elevations of 2900m to 4200m. The area is within the collapsed volcanic caldera (crater), and there are good views of other peaks. There are several trails, ranging from easy half-hour loops to fairly strenuous all-day hikes. The shorter trails are self-guiding; guides are available for the longer walks. One trail leads out of the reserve and to the summit of Pasochoa (4200m) – this hike takes about eight hours.

Information

A daily entrance fee of US$10 is charged to foreigners. Overnight camping is permitted in designated areas and costs US$3 per person. There are latrines, picnic areas, barbecue grills and water. There is also a simple hostal with 20 bunk beds for US$5 per person. You need to bring a sleeping bag. Hot showers and kitchen facilities are available. On weekends, when the place is usually crowded with locals, a small restaurant is open; otherwise, bring your own food. The reserve is open every day from dawn to dusk. Check with Fundación Natura about sleeping space on weekends – or better still, go midweek.

Getting There & Away

Buses leave from La Marín in Quito about twice an hour for the village of Amaguaña, an hour away from Quito. Ask the driver to let you off near El Ejido. From the church nearby, there is a signed cobblestone road to the reserve, which is about 7km away. You have to walk. Alternately, you can go all the way into Amaguaña (about 1km beyond El Ejido) and hire a truck to the reserve's entrance and information center for about US$7 (the truck can take several people).

Taxis from Quito will take you for about US$30 roundtrip, but make sure they know the way. Arrange a driver on the day before you visit to get there early – the best birding is in the early hours. Safari Tours arranges

tours as well (see Travel Agencies under Quito, earlier).

VOLCÁN PICHINCHA

Quito's closest volcano is Pichincha, looming over the western side of the city. The volcano has two main summits – the closer, dormant Rucu Pichincha (about 4700m) and the higher Guagua Pichincha (4794m), which is currently very active and is monitored by volcanologists. A major eruption in 1660 covered Quito in 40cm of ash; there were three minor eruptions in the 19th century. A few puffs of smoke occurred in 1981, but in 1999, the volcano rumbled into serious action (see the boxed text 'Volcanic Activity,' in the Getting There & Away chapter).

Climbing either of the summits is strenuous but technically straightforward, and no special equipment is required. By heading west on one of the streets leaving Quito and continuing upward, an ascent of Rucu Pichincha can be done in a long day, returning to the city by nightfall. Unfortunately, this is easier said than done. One main access street, 24 de Mayo, has been the scene of frequent attacks and robberies, and this route is strongly discouraged. Another main access, through the El Tejar neighborhood of Quito, does not have as many robbery problems – but vicious dogs have often bitten hikers. Once out of the city, the route goes past the TV antennas on the hill named Cruz Loma – several attacks, robberies and rapes have been reported in this area in recent years.

These warnings should not be taken lightly – walking through some of the poor suburbs on the western edges of the city is not a good idea if you are laden with good warm clothes and camera gear. The best solution is to go in a large group and check for the latest information before you go. The staff of the South American Explorers are always an excellent source of up-to-date information. The climbing guides listed earlier under Quito in Travel Agencies can also be of assistance. Guides will usually have a jeep available to drive you past all the problem areas and to a point high up on the mountain (even so, the shortened climb to the summit is a strenuous affair, taking most of a day). Many people continue to climb Rucu Pichincha because the views are superb, but get information before you go, and plan your trip with care to avoid having a problem.

Climbing the smoking Guagua Pichincha is a longer trip, but less beset with non-mountainous hazards, although reaching the crater is currently not permitted. Again, check with the South American Explorers or with a climbing guide for the latest information before you go.

North of Quito

Highlights

- Haggling in Otavalo, home of the most famous crafts market in South America
- Eating well and sleeping well at one of many upscale colonial haciendas outside of Otavalo
- Hiking through the eerie fog-bound scenery in the Páramos de El Ángel
- Strolling through the lovely topiary cemetery of Tulcán

Equator

The Andean highlands north of Quito are one of the most popular travel destinations in Ecuador. Few people spend any time in the country without visiting the famous Indian market in the small town of Otavalo, where you can buy a wide variety of weavings, clothing and handicrafts. Though many travelers limit their visit to just Otavalo, there is much more to see in this region.

The dramatic mountain scenery is dotted with shining white churches set in tiny villages and includes views of Volcán Cayambe, the third-highest peak in the country, as well as a beautiful lake district. Several small towns are noted for specialty handicrafts, such as woodcarving or leatherwork.

Ibarra is a small, charmingly somnolent colonial city worth visiting, both in its own right and as the beginning of the Ibarra-San Lorenzo route to the north coast. If you are traveling overland to or from Colombia, you will most likely travel through this region.

NORTH TO CAYAMBE
☎ 02

About 10km north of Quito on the Panamericana is the village of Calderón (see Around Quito, in the Quito & Around chapter). Beyond Calderón, the road descends in a series of magnificent sweeps toward the village of **Guayllabamba**, set in a fertile river valley of the same name that is famous for its produce. Roadside stalls offer huge avocados and that strangely reptilian-looking Andean fruit, the *chirimoya;* it's comparable to the sweetsop. The knobbly green skin is discarded, and the custardlike white pulp inside is eaten. The chirimoya definitely tastes better than it looks or sounds.

Guayllabamba is the site of the new **Quito Zoo**. It's actually about 3km out of Guayllabamba, but bus drivers to Otavalo know where to drop you off. From the zoo, pickups charge about US$0.20 to go to Guayllabamba and leave whenever they have a load; of course, you can opt to hike the 3km. Zoo admission is about US$1, and most exhibits are Ecuadorian animals, although there are a few African and Asian species. One reader comments that it's fun to

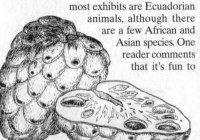

Cherimoya – strange fruit

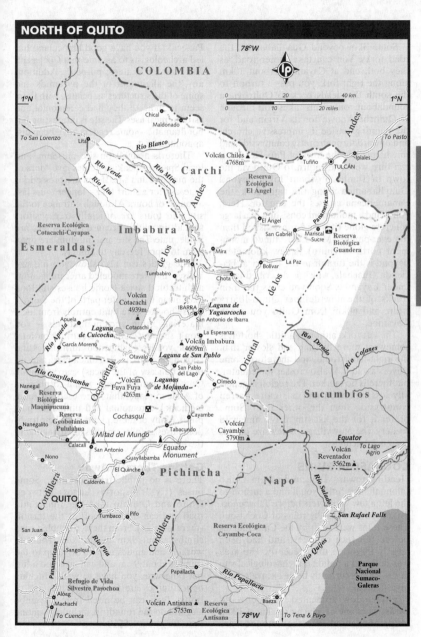

NORTH OF QUITO

go on weekends and watch Ecuadorian families picnicking and enjoying themselves.

Some 3km beyond Guayllabamba, the road forks. You can take either road, as they both end at Cayambe. About 10km along the right fork, you pass a turnoff to the south that leads back to Quito via a roundabout route. This takes you through **El Quinche**, known for its Virgin and for the paintings inside its impressive church, and onward through pretty countryside and tiny hamlets to the town of Pifo. Here, you can turn west and return to Quito via the town of Tumbaco. About 15km beyond Guayllabamba along the right fork, the Panamericana crosses the equator. Here, you'll find a **monument** consisting of a large concrete globe (it is by far less visited than the ever-popular Mitad del Mundo monument north of Quito). A few kilometers beyond is the turnoff to the historical Hacienda Guachala, which is described later, under Cayambe. Soon you cross the train tracks of the now-defunct Quito-Ibarra train, and 60km from Quito you reach Cayambe.

The left fork, although a little shorter, is somewhat more twisting and slower than the right-hand route, and therefore, some drivers avoid it. It also crosses the equator, but there is no marker. The region is generally less inhabited and has more barren countryside than the other road. Some prefer it for the exciting drive and wild scenery. The only village of any size on this road is Tabacundo.

COCHASQUÍ RUINS

Heading toward Tabacundo from Quito (along the left fork), you'll find a turnoff to the left a few kilometers before Tabacundo. That road leads to the ruins of Cochasquí. These ruins were built by the Cara Indians before the Inca conquest and had been largely forgotten until recently. The area was declared a national archaeological site in 1977 and is currently being excavated and investigated.

Fifteen low, truncated, grass-covered pyramids (some of which are almost 100m long) and about 30 other mounds are

visible. The remarkable panoramic view from the site (you can see the Quito hill El Panecillo if you have good binoculars) has led archeologists to assume that Cochasquí was built for strategic purposes. Additionally, the alignment of the pyramids and some of the structures associated with them seem to indicate they had ceremonial and astronomical uses. The site is interesting but not dramatic – some readers have been disappointed by it.

There is a small on-site museum, and local Spanish-speaking guides give tours of the museum and site. If you are pressed for time, ask for a short tour – longer tours last a couple of hours. Although entrance to the site and tours are officially free, visitors should tip guides, because their wages are inadequate. The site and museum are open 9 am to 4 pm Tuesday to Sunday.

The guides can also show you life-size houses that were modeled after indigenous architectural styles (some houses still look like this in the remoter parts of the Sierra). These houses were built entirely from local materials using ancient methods – you won't see any nails or electrical outlets! Inside, you'll see indigenous furnishings and cooking utensils, while guinea pigs (a traditional delicacy of the Incas) scurry around. Outside, a garden teems with a cornucopia of Andean plants that were used for food, medicinal, ceremonial and utilitarian purposes. Many of these plants and their traditional uses as folk remedies are dying out in the highlands.

Getting There & Away

There is no public transportation. Some buses (try Transportes Lagos) between Quito and Otavalo take the Tabacundo road and can drop you off at the turnoff (there is a sign). From there, a cobbled road climbs about 9km to the site. The site workers and guides usually drive up to the ruins at about 9 am and can give you a lift, but otherwise, you have to walk. Hitching opportunities are few due to the lack of traffic. Taxis can be hired from Cayambe and will do the roundtrip, including waiting time, for about US$10.

CAYAMBE
☎ 02

Cayambe, about 64km north of Quito along the Panamericana, has a population of about 15,000 and is the most important town on the way to Otavalo. It is famous for its dairy industry, and there are many stores and restaurants selling a variety of local cheeses and cheese products. Salt crackers called *bizcochos* are also produced here. The local Salesian monastery reportedly has an excellent library on indigenous cultures.

Places to Stay & Eat

Although this is the only town of any size so close to the equator, few people stay here, preferring instead to buy some cheese and continue on to Otavalo.

The centrally located **Youth Hostal Cayambe** (☎ *360 007, Bolívar 23*) is the cheapest place to stay. Bunks cost about US$5 per person. The clean **Hostería Mitad del Mundo** (☎ *360 226*), at the south end of town, charges about US$6 per person.

Hostería Napoles (☎ *360 231*) is about 1km north of town on the Panamericana. Cheese products are sold there, and it has one of the best restaurants in Cayambe. There is also a garden with a miniature 'zoo' (a few caged parrots etc). Cabins with private bath, hot water and TV cost US$9/15 for singles/doubles.

A few kilometers south of Cayambe is **Hacienda Guachala**, founded in 1580 and said to be the oldest hacienda in Ecuador. The place has housed Ecuadorian presidents and visiting luminaries during its four centuries in existence. In 1993, it opened as a hotel and now offers 14 comfortable rooms with private bath. There is a swimming pool, and two colonial chapels are on the landscaped grounds. Horseback riding, hiking and jeep tours are available. There is a restaurant and bar, and the main building contains many artifacts and antiques. Rates are about US$40, and reservations can be made in Quito (☎/fax 563 748, Reina Victoria 1138 and Foch, Office 4). The hacienda is about 1.5km along the Cangahua road, which heads southeast from the Panameri-

cana about 7km south of Cayambe. Several readers have recommended this place.

Getting There & Away

Any bus between Quito and Otavalo can drop you in Cayambe.

FROM CAYAMBE TO OTAVALO

From Cayambe, it is 31km along the Panamericana to Otavalo. The snowcapped mountain east of the road is the extinct **Volcán Cayambe**. At 5790m, it is Ecuador's third-highest peak. Trivia buffs: It is also the highest point in the world through which the equator directly passes – at about 4600m on the south side. There is a climbing refuge (refurbished in 1994) that costs US$10 to stay in, but you need a 4WD to reach it. From the refuge, the climb is more difficult than the more frequently ascended peaks of Cotopaxi and Tungurahua, but climbing guides in Quito can get you up there.

The Panamericana climbs from the Pichincha Province to the Imbabura Province, a region known for its indigenous inhabitants and pretty lake district. Soon you see the largest of these lakes, Laguna de San Pablo, stretching away to your right, with the high peak of Volcán Imbabura (4609m) behind it. The area is dotted with villages inhabited by the Otavaleño Indians.

OTAVALO
☎ 06

This small town, at 2550m and with some 26,000 inhabitants, is justly famous for its friendly people and their Saturday market. The market dates back to pre-Inca times, when jungle products were brought up from the eastern lowlands and traded for highland goods. Today's market serves two different groups: locals who buy and barter animals, food and other essentials; and tourists looking for crafts.

The goods sold at the market are undeniably oriented toward the tourist market, and this has led to complaints from travelers. But it's important to keep in mind the well-being of the weavers – their prosperity in this ever-changing and difficult world is quite a feat.

OTAVALO

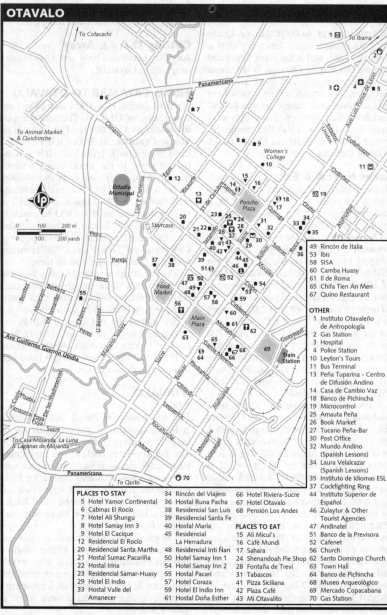

To Cotacachi
To Ibarra
To Animal Market & Quichinche
Panamericana
Women's College
Estadio Municipal
Staircase
Food Market
Main Plaza
Poncho Plaza
Train Station
To Casa Mojanda, La Luna & Lagunas de Mojanda
To Quito

49 Rincón de Italia
53 Ibis
58 SISA
60 Camba Huasy
61 Il de Roma
65 Chifa Tien An Men
67 Quino Restaurant

OTHER
1 Instituto Otavaleño de Antropología
2 Gas Station
3 Hospital
4 Police Station
10 Leyton's Tours
11 Bus Terminal
13 Peña Tuparina - Centro de Difusión Andino
14 Casa de Cambio Vaz
18 Banco de Pichincha
19 Microcontrol
25 Amauta Peña
26 Book Market
27 Tucano Peña-Bar
30 Post Office
32 Mundo Andino (Spanish Lessons)
34 Laura Velalcazar (Spanish Lessons)
35 Instituto de Idiomas ESL
37 Cockfighting Ring
44 Instituto Superior de Español
46 Zulaytur & Other Tourist Agencies
47 Andinatel
51 Banco de la Previsora
52 Cafenet
56 Church
62 Santo Domingo Church
63 Town Hall
64 Banco de Pichincha
68 Museo Arqueológico
69 Mercado Copacabana
70 Gas Station

PLACES TO STAY
5 Hotel Yamor Continental
6 Cabinas El Rocío
7 Hotel Ali Shungu
8 Hotel Samay Inn 3
9 Hotel El Cacique
12 Residencial El Rocío
20 Residencial Santa Martha
21 Hostal Sumac Pacariña
22 Hostal Irina
23 Residencial Samar-Huasy
29 Hotel El Indio
33 Hostal Valle del Amanecer
34 Rincón del Viajero
36 Hostal Runa Pacha
38 Residencial San Luis
39 Residencial Santa Fe
40 Hostal María
45 Residencial La Herradura
48 Residencial Inti Ñan
50 Hotel Samay Inn 1
54 Hotel Samay Inn 2
55 Hostal Pacari
57 Hotel Coraza
59 Hotel El Indio Inn
61 Hostal Doña Esther

66 Hotel Riviera-Sucre
67 Hotel Otavalo
68 Pensión Los Andes

PLACES TO EAT
15 Ali Micui's
16 Café Mundi
17 Sahara
24 Shenandoah Pie Shop
28 Fontaña de Trevi
31 Tabascos
41 Pizza Siciliana
42 Plaza Café
43 Mi Otavalito

NORTH OF QUITO

But an even truer measure of their success is their continuing sense of tribal identity and tradition. One of the most evident features of the Otavaleños' cultural integrity is their dress. Traditional attire is worn on normal workdays in homes, villages and fields – what you see them wearing is not just for tourists at the Saturday market. Otavaleño men are immediately distinctive with their long ponytails, calf-length white pants, rope sandals, reversible gray or blue ponchos, and dark felt hats. The women too are very striking in their beautifully embroidered blouses, long black skirts and shawls, and interesting folded head cloths. The women also wear bright jewels, the most obvious being the many strings of golden blown-glass beads around their necks and the long strands of red beads around their wrists and arms.

Most of the 26,000 inhabitants of Otavalo are whites or mestizos. Of the 40,000 Indians in the area, most live in the many nearby villages and come into Otavalo for market day. However, quite a few Indians own stores in Otavalo, where you can buy most items if you are unable to come for the market.

For detailed cultural information about the people of Otavalo, read Lynn Meisch's *Otavalo: Weaving, Costume and the Market* (Libri Mundi, Quito, 1987), available only in Ecuador.

Information

Tourist Offices There is no official tourist information office, but there are travel agencies (listed under Travel Agencies, later) that are helpful with local information. The town also has its own official Web site, www.otavalo.com.ec.

Money Casa de Cambio Vaz, on the Poncho Plaza, gives good rates and also changes traveler's checks. The casa de cambio under Zulaytur looks the fanciest but has the worst rates. The Banco de la Previsora, on Sucre between Colón and Calderón, gives cash advances on credit cards and has an ATM, but it rarely works. Banco de Pichincha, on Sucre between Quito and Quiroga, may be open on Sunday. You can sometimes buy souvenirs with US cash.

Post & Communications The post office is on Sucre at Salinas, on the 2nd floor. The Andinatel office is on Calderón between Jaramillo and Sucre. Internet access is available at Cafenet, Sucre 10-14, (with net-to-phone service; see Email & Internet Access under Information in the Quito & Around chapter for an explanation of this service) and at Microcontrol, Bolívar 14-22. New cybercafés continue to open and close.

Travel Agencies Zulaytur (☎ 921 176, fax 922 969), at the east corner of Sucre and

---

Otavalo's Weavings – A Phenomenal Success

The story of the phenomenal success of the Otavaleño weavers is an intriguing one. The backstrap loom has been used in the area for some 4000 years. The Indians' proficiency as weavers was harshly exploited by the colonialists beginning in 1555, and later by Ecuadorian landowners, who forced them to labor in *obrajes* (sweatshops), often for 14 or more hours a day. Miserable though this was, it did have the effect of instilling a great knowledge of weaving in the Otavaleño people.

In 1917, a local weaver had the idea of copying the Scottish tweeds that were then in vogue, and this was so successful that it again led to recognition of the skill of the Otavaleño weavers. This ability, combined with the Agrarian Reform of 1964 and the people's shrewd business sense, has made the Otavaleños the most prosperous Indian group in Ecuador – perhaps on the continent. It is difficult to find a town of any size that does not have an Otavaleño store. The Otavaleños also make frequent business trips to neighboring countries, and even to North America and Europe.

Colón, 2nd floor, is run by the knowledge-able, English-speaking Señor Rodrigo Mora. This agency has had many recommendations from readers. The people at Zulaytur are known to give tourist information even if you don't go on one of their tours.

A variety of inexpensive guided tours enable you to visit local Indian homes, learn about the entire weaving process, buy products off the loom and take photographs. Señor Mora's emphasis on anthropology and sociology makes his tours very worthwhile (although most other agencies are now following suit).

The most popular tour visits several local villages and lasts all day. Tours cost about US$10 per person with a maximum of ten passengers – it costs more if there are fewer passengers. Transportation is included, but lunch is extra. More expensive tours take travelers to visit the beautiful Andean lakes around Otavalo or to trek in the local countryside. If you have a reasonably large group, an informative slide presentation of the area can be arranged with Señor Mora. At appropriate times of year, visits to some of the local fiestas may be possible (although not all fiestas are open to outsiders).

There are several other agencies on the same block as Zulaytur. Each agency provides similar tours at competitive prices; visit them and choose the one that most appeals to you. Some agencies have horses for rent for about US$20 per half-day. Leyton's Tours (☎ 922 388), on Quito at Jaramillo, has horse and bike rentals.

Bookstores Book Market, Jaramillo 6-28, buys, sells and trades books in English, German, French and other languages; maps, posters, postcards and music cassettes are also for sale.

Medical Services The following doctors have been locally recommended. Dr Patricio Buitrón (☎ 921 159, 921 678), on Roca near Quiroga, speaks some English. Dr Klaus Fay (☎ 921 203), on Sucre near Morales, speaks German and English and is

available Tuesday through Saturday. The hospital (☎ 920 444, 923 566) is on Sucre, about 400m north of downtown.

Emergency There is a police station at the northeastern end of town on Avenida Luis Ponce de Leon.

Dangers & Annoyances Several rapes and armed robberies have been reported by readers and travelers hiking in the Lagunas de Mojanda area. Some of the attackers appeared to be well-dressed, affluent Ecuadorians. Check locally before venturing to this area, or go on a guided tour.

Markets

The main market day is Saturday. There are three main plazas, with the overflow spilling out onto the streets linking them. **Poncho Plaza** is where the items of most appeal to tourists are sold. Here, you can buy woolen goods such as ponchos, blankets, scarves, sweaters, tapestries and gloves, as well as a variety of embroidered blouses and shirts, shawls, string bags, rope sandals, jewelry etc.

Bargaining for each purchase is normal. If you buy several items from the same person, you can expect a discount of 20% or even more if you are good at bargaining. Some people are not good at it and feel uncomfortable trying to knock a few cents off an already cheaply priced item. Just remember that it is expected and make an offer a little below the first asking price.

This market gets under way in the early morning and continues until mid-afternoon. You are advised to spend Friday night in Otavalo and get to the market early. It can get rather crowded in mid-morning, when the big tour groups arrive and prices are higher. If you come in the early morning, you'll find a greater selection at better prices. Note that there are increasing numbers of pickpockets and bag snatchers at the market – keep your eyes open and your valuables hidden.

The **food market** sells produce and household goods for the locals, and there is an **animal market** that begins in the predawn hours (5 to 9 am) on the outskirts of town. These are not oriented toward tourists, but you are welcome to visit them; many people find the sight of poncho-clad Indians quietly bartering for a string of screaming piglets much more interesting than the scene at Poncho Plaza. The animal market is over by early morning, so plan on an early arrival. It lies over a kilometer out of town; cross the bridge at the end of Colón and follow the crowds to get there.

The popularity of the market is such that there is a smaller market held on Wednesday (mainly for tourists), and selling goes on every day during the peak visitor months of June to August. During these months, some travelers prefer the Wednesday market, which is less crowded and has as good a selection of crafts as the Saturday market. Even in the low season, some stalls are open every day, and stores selling crafts are open daily year-round.

Museums
The **Instituto Otavaleño de Antropología**, just off the Panamericana north of town, houses a small archaeological and ethnographical museum of the area, a library and a bookstore selling books (in Spanish) about the anthropology and culture of Otavalo. There are plans to expand it and add a cinema. It is open 8 am to noon and 2 to 6 pm Tuesday to Friday and 8am to noon Saturday; admission is free.

There is a small **Museo Arqueológico**, in Pensión Los Andes, on Montalvo near Roca. This is free for guests of the pensión, and there is a modest admission charge (about US$1) for others. The elderly owner/curator has a fund of stories about the pieces and gives guided tours in Spanish.

Language Courses
Mundo Andino (☎ 921 864, espanol@ interactive.net.ec), Salinas 4-04, has been warmly recommended for personable service and good teachers. The charge is about US$4 per hour for individual tuition, and homestays with local families can be arranged for about US$10 a day, including

meals. Mundo Andino also arranges hikes, dinners and other activities for students, including long-term volunteer activities.

The Quito-based Instituto Superior de Español (☎ 922 414), Sucre 11-10, also offers Spanish lessons. One reader suggests Instituto de Idiomas ESL (☎ 09-813 442), Roca 8-02, and recommends the hiking tours offered by the director, Washington Villamarin. Laura Velalcazar (☎ 921 741) gives private lessons and offers discounts for guests of the Rincón del Viajero B&B.

Special Events
Some small village fiestas date back to pre-Columbian rituals and can last as long as two weeks. Drinking and dancing are a big part of the festivities. They are not much visited by outsiders, and in some cases, it would be dangerous for tourists just to show up. One little-known annual event involves ritual battle between rival villages at which locals are sometimes killed. The authorities turn a blind eye, and outsiders are not tolerated.

June 24 is St John the Baptist Day (which is especially celebrated in the San Juan suburb, around the intersection of Cisneros with the Panamericana), and June 29 is the Day of Sts Peter and Paul. These and the intervening days are an important fiesta for Otavalo and the surrounding villages. There is a bullfight in Otavalo and a boating regatta on Laguna de San Pablo, as well as celebrations in nearby Ilumán.

A few kilometers southeast of Otavalo, on the southern shores of Laguna de San Pablo, in the villages around San Rafael, there is a fiesta called Corazas on August 19. Also in some of the south-shore villages is the Pendoneros Fiesta on October 15.

Otavalo's best-known fiesta is held in the first two weeks of September. The Fiesta del Yamor has plenty of music, processions and dancing, as well as fireworks displays, cockfights and an election of the Queen of the Fiesta.

The precise dates of these celebrations vary from year to year, but they are usually well publicized, and you can find out what's going on from posters in the area. In addition, there are the usual feast days that are celebrated throughout the land.

Places to Stay

Because Otavalo is such a popular destination, there are many more places to stay than in other bigger but less interesting towns. Despite this, it can get rather crowded on Friday night, so arrive early for the best selection. Most places are quite cheap, and new hotels open regularly. The new ones often have great promotional rates, so seek them out; also, remember that the current economic crisis may lead to wild fluctuations in the prices given in this chapter. If you arrive midweek and plan to stay a few days, you can often negotiate a cheaper price and have time to check out several places to find what's the best deal for you. Conversely, late Friday night isn't a good time to expect any favors. Prices may rise on weekends, especially during the high season or for one-night stays.

Note that the best hotels are in country haciendas outside of town (see Places to Stay under Otavalo Area, later). A car or taxi is the most convenient way to get to these.

There have been several reports of theft from hotel rooms in Otavalo. Keep your room door locked, even if leaving for just a little while.

Budget Currently, the most popular choice for budget travelers is *Hostal Valle del Amanecer* (☎ 920 990, fax 921 819, amanacer@ uio.satnet.net), on the corner of Roca and Quiroga. The charge is about US$4 per person, or US$5 with bath and hot water. The 26 rooms are small, and it gets very crowded, but it remains popular with young gringos. There's a café, restaurant and tour facilities.

For a quieter scene, *Residencial El Rocío* (☎ 920 584, Morales 11-70) is very clean and friendly and charges US$4 per person. It has a couple of rooms with private bath for US$10 a double. Hot water is available, and the view from the roof is nice. The owner has a vehicle and arranges lake tours. *Cabinas El Rocío* (same phone

and owners) is a quiet place in the San Juan neighborhood, just beyond the Panamericana; it has good views and a pleasant garden. The rooms are comfortable, clean and worth the price of US$6 per person if you want to get away from the town center.

Hotel Riviera-Sucre (☎ 920 241, García Moreno 3-14) is a clean place in an old house with a courtyard. It has hot water and is popular with budget travelers. Rates are about US$3 per person for rooms with shared hot showers and US$4 with private showers. *Hostal Sumac Pacariña* (Colón 6-10) has a game room and a decent, inexpensive café. Rooms with shared showers cost under US$3 per person. Other OK places at US$3 to US$4 per person, with hot water in shared baths, include *Residencial Santa Fe* (☎ 920 161, Colón 5-07); the family-run *Residencial San Luis* (☎ 920 614, Calderón 6-02); and the friendly little *Residencial Inti Ñan* (☎ 921 373, Montalvo 6-02), which is often full.

Pensión Los Andes (Montalvo 3-75) is the cheapest at about US$2 per person, and it is very basic but friendly. It has cold water, but it has a private archaeology museum! For about US$3 per person, *Residencial Samar-Huasy* (Jaramillo 6-11) has clean, small rooms. Hot showers are available at times. Other adequate places for around US$3 include *Residencial Santa Martha* (☎ 920 568, Colón 7-04) and *Residencial La Herradura* (☎ 920 304, Bolívar 10-05).

Of the newer hotels, *Hostal Irina* (☎ 920 864, Jaramillo 5-69) is a bargain at US$2 per person with shared hot showers and helpful staff. *Hostal María* (☎ 920 672, fax 920 858), on Jaramillo near Colón, is also a bargain and is always full on weekends. It charges under US$3 per person and has 12 clean rooms with private bath. *Rincón del Viajero* (☎/fax 921 741, Roca 11-07) is newly remodeled and has rooms with shared and private baths. The American and Ecuadorian owners charge about US$3 to US$5 per person, and Spanish lessons are available. A kitchen is planned.

Hostal Runa Pacha (☎ 921 730, fax 921 734), on Roca near Quiroga, has a brightly painted facade and is convenient to both the bus terminal and Poncho Plaza. A hardworking staff provides good service. Rooms vary from US$3 to US$6 per person, depending on the season and whether or not you want to share a bath. A reader recommends *Hostal Pacari* (☎ 922 169), which is just off the Panamericana. It is friendly and has rooms with cable TV and private hot showers for just US$4 per person. Kitchen privileges and a game room are offered.

Hotel El Cacique (☎ 921 740) and *Hotel Samay Inn 3* (☎ 922 438, samay@otavalo-web .com), opposite one another on the north end of 31 de Octubre, have nice carpeted rooms with TV for about US$5 per person. The private bathrooms have hot water in the morning. *Hotel Samay Inn 1* (☎ /fax 922 871, Calderón 10-05) and *Hotel Samay Inn 2* (☎/fax 922 995), on Colón near Roca, are fairly similar in quality and price. *Hotel El Indio* (☎ 920 060, Sucre 12-14) is similarly priced, centrally located and often full by Wednesday afternoon; the guests stay for the rest of the week. It also has rooms with TV, private hot showers and a restaurant. Don't confuse this place with Hotel El Indio Inn, which is listed under the mid-range accommodations section.

Hotel Otavalo (☎ 920 416, Roca 5-04) is very clean and has hot water and a restaurant. There are plans for an on-site Internet café by the end of 2000. Rooms vary widely – some have balconies and private baths; some are interior, and therefore quiet but dark; some share showers. Midweek rates are about US$6/10 for singles/doubles with private bath (less for a shared bath); weekend rates are higher.

Mid-Range If you're looking for a clean, mid-range place, *Hotel El Indio Inn* (☎ 922 922, fax 920 325, Bolívar 9-04) has nice large rooms with TV and telephone, as well as a good restaurant downstairs. There are 40 rooms, and they cost about US$14/20. Don't confuse this place with the budget Hotel El Indio, mentioned earlier. *Hotel Coraza* (☎ 921 225, fax 920 459, h.coraza@ uio.satnet.net), on Sucre near Calderón, has over 50 modern carpeted rooms with TV

and telephone. There is a decent restaurant, a bar, a coffee shop, a gift shop and a parking garage, and it is a good value for about US$10 per person. The small but personable *Hostal Doña Esther* (☎ /fax 920 739, Montalvo 4-44), which has a good Italian restaurant and attractively painted colonial-style rooms with private bath, makes a nice change from the standard furnishings in most hotels; it charges US$19/26/31 for singles/doubles/triples.

Hotel Yamor Continental (☎ 920 451), on Avenida Luis Ponce de Leon, has clean and spacious rooms in a hacienda-like building set in flower-filled gardens at the northeast end of town. There is a pool, a restaurant and a bar. Rooms with private bath, TV and phone are about US$15 for either one or two people, but this rate rises on weekends.

The prettiest hotel in town is *Hotel Ali Shungu* (☎ 920 750, alishngu@uio.telconet .net), at the northwest end of Quito. This nonsmoking hotel with a large and attractive patio and flowery garden has fine views of Volcán Imbabura. The rooms are appealingly decorated with local crafts and flowers, and there are plenty of lights. The 16 spacious and comfortable rooms with private bath and plenty of hot water go for about US$31/43. There are no triples, but a child's cot can be added for US$10. There

---

Volcano Folklore

Two extinct volcanoes can be seen from Otavalo on clear days: the massive bulk of Volcán Imbabura (4609m) to the east and the sharper, more jagged Volcán Cotacachi (at 4939m, Ecuador's 11th-highest mountain) to the northwest. The locals refer to these peaks as Taita ('Daddy') Imbabura and Mama Cotacachi. Legend has it that when it's raining in Otavalo, Taita Imbabura is pissing in the valley. Another legend suggests that when Mama Cotacachi awakes with a fresh covering of snow, she has been visited by Taita Imbabura during the night.

are two apartments, complete with VCR and stereo system, that cost US$85 to US$134 for two to six people. Credit cards are not accepted. Most readers recommend the hotel; a few have complained about problems with reservations and payments. The American owners require a two-night minimum during weekends, especially in the high season. A good restaurant (open 7:30 am to 8:30 pm) serving upscale vegetarian and meat dishes is on the premises, and it has live *música folklórica* on weekends (when a donation is requested). The hotel also has a fireplace, book exchange and laundry service.

Around Otavalo The *Casa Mojanda* (☎/*fax 09-731 737, fax 06-922 969, mojanda@uio.telconet.net)* is a family-run country hotel and organic farm about 4km south of Otavalo on the road to Lagunas de Mojanda; the setting is lovely. The Ecuadorian and American owners speak perfect English and are enthusiastic about their projects, which include low-impact tourism to benefit education, and cultural and health awareness in local indigenous communities. Visits to projects can be arranged. A useful library is on the premises. Casa Mojanda is built using rammed-earth construction, and various rooms are available. For budget travelers, a 10-bed cottage with a kitchen and bath is US$18 per person, including breakfast. Near the main lodge, a comfortable 10-bed dormitory with two bathrooms is designed for groups and costs US$43 per person, including a full breakfast, afternoon tea, and a three-course dinner. A private cottage with a terrace overlooking the mountains is US$67/110 for a single/double, including meals. Rentals of mountain bikes, kayaks and horses can be arranged with advance notice.

La Luna (☎/*fax 09-737 415)* is 4.5km south of Otavalo on the way to Lagunas de Mojanda. Run by two friendly Argentineans who speak English, this quiet place with a kitchen, dining room and fireplace has been recommended by several readers. There is a dorm with 12 bunks, three shared toilets and

two hot showers for US$3 per person, or US$4.50 with breakfast. For two or three people, four smaller rooms with shared bath are US$6 per person, including breakfast; two rooms with a double bed, private bath and fireplace are US$16 per couple, including breakfast. Or you can camp for US$1.50 per person, including the use of hot showers and the dining/bar area with videos and games. The owners can arrange mountain-bike and hiking tours and will make packed lunches or dinners with advance notice. Call them to ask about the three-bus-a-day schedule or to get picked up in Otavalo. A taxi will cost about US$3.

Places to Eat

There are many restaurants with a variety of cuisine aimed at the ever-present gringo visitor to Ecuador's most famous market. On the Poncho Plaza, *Shenandoah Pie Shop* is perennially popular for its homemade pies, though service can be casual to the point of indifference. *Ali Micui's*, on the north corner of the Poncho Plaza, serves inexpensive vegetarian food and has been around for decades under different owners and gets mixed reviews; the most recent have been favorable. Across the street, the more upmarket *Café Mundi* is popular as well.

Just off the Poncho Plaza on Salinas, *Tabascos* has slightly pricey Mexican and Italian food, decent breakfasts and a 2nd-floor patio overlooking the plaza, which is perhaps the best reason to eat there. *Sahara*, northeast of the plaza on Sucre, has Middle Eastern food and aromatic hookahs with fruit-flavored tobacco, while southwest of the plaza on Sucre, *Fontaña de Trevi* has good Italian food. *Il de Roma*, in the Hostal Doña Esther, also has good Italian food. Also recommended is *Rincón de Italia*, on Sucre near Calderón, and *Pizza Siciliana*, on Morales between Jaramillo and Sucre. *Quino Restaurant*, by Hotel Otavalo, is popular and has good, if pricey, food.

SISA, on Calderón next to Hotel Coraza, is mid-range in price. It has a wide variety of dishes and is one of the better restaurants in town. It also has the best coffee in town and good artwork on the walls. *Plaza Café*, on Sucre between Morales and Colón, has good coffee, food and ambience. Nearby, *Mi Otavalito* is also good for a variety of national and some international dishes at reasonable prices. *Ibis*, on Bolívar at Colón, is an art gallery-cum-coffee house; it has limited food but is a good place just to sit and write.

Chifa Tien An Men, on García Moreno just off the Main Plaza, is a reasonable choice for filling Chinese food. If you're after fried chicken, try *Camba Huasy*, on Bolívar just off the Main Plaza.

Hotel El Indio serves good local food, particularly fritada (not always available). Hotel Ali Shungu has some of the best food in town, and it's worth the extra few dollars, but get there early – it closes by 8:30 pm.

Entertainment

Otavalo is a quiet place during the week, but it gets livelier on the weekend.

On Friday and Saturday nights, there's the popular *Amauta Peña* (☎ 920 967, *Jaramillo 6-14*), near the west corner of the Poncho Plaza. It opens around 8 pm, but music doesn't begin until after 10 pm; there's a US$1 cover. The music and ambience can vary from abysmal to enjoyable. *Peña Tuparina – Centro de Difusión Andino*, on Morales near 31 de Octubre, is similar and has received several recommendations from travelers – the cover is about US$0.50. *Tucano Peña-Bar* (*Morales 5-10*) has both folklórica and salsa music. Several of the restaurants are popular hangouts as well.

Finally, the weekly cockfight is held in the ring at the southwest end of 31 de Octubre every Saturday afternoon at about 3 pm. Admission is US$0.60.

Getting There & Away

Bus Getting from Quito to Otavalo is straightforward. There are several companies at the main Terminal Terrestre, and buses leave frequently. They all charge under US$2 for the two- to three-hour ride. Transportes Otavalo and Transportes Los Lagos are the only ones allowed into Otavalo's bus terminal. Other companies will drop you off on the Panamericana, forcing you to walk into town.

From the northern towns of Ibarra or Tulcán, you'll find buses leaving for Otavalo every hour or so from their respective terminals.

For door-to-door van service, Hotel Ali Shungo has a shuttle that goes back and forth between Quito and the hotel for US$12 per person one way.

In Otavalo, the main bus-terminal area is at the north end of town. There is a taxi rank if you need it; you can take a taxi to most hotels for well under US$1. From this bus terminal, Transportes Otavalo or Transportes Los Lagos will take you to Quito or Ibarra. There are currently no direct buses to Tulcán; this may change. Transportes Otavalo also has buses to the towns of Apuela and García Moreno. You can also catch old local buses to some of the villages south of Otavalo, such as San Pablo del Lago. Cooperativa Imbaburapac has buses from Otavalo to Ilumán, Agato, San Pablo del Lago and Cayambe every hour or so. Transportes Cotacachi goes to Cotacachi via the longer route (through Quiroga), and Transportes 6 de Junio takes the shorter route (via the Panamericana). Transportes Cotacachi has some buses continuing on to Apuela and García Moreno. Transportes 8 de Septiembre is a local bus that also goes to Ilumán.

There is no strict schedule for services to any of these towns, and prices are low. Adventurous travelers might just want to get aboard and see what happens, but leave enough time to get back to a hotel, as most of the small villages have no formal accommodations.

For the villages of Calderón, Guayllabamba and Cayambe, take an Otavalo-Quito bus; just board the bus as it leaves and pay the driver for where you want to go. (On a busy Saturday afternoon, however, this might be a bit difficult.) You'll be dropped off at the turnoff from the main road and will have to walk several hundred meters to the village.

Train There is a train station, but no trains have run since the mid-1990s.

Taxi You can always hire a taxi from Quito for a few hours and have the driver take you exactly where you want to go. A taxi for the day can be hired for under US$50 if you have any bargaining ability – not too bad if you split it three or four ways.

OTAVALO AREA
☎ 06

Many of the Indians live and work in the nearby villages of Peguche, Ilumán and Agato. These are loosely strung together on the east side of the Panamericana a few kilometers northeast of Otavalo and can be reached by bus or taxi, on foot or with a tour. There are several other Otavaleño villages in the area, and a visit to the tourist agencies in Otavalo will yield much information. The villages southwest of Laguna de San Pablo are known for the manufacture of fireworks, as well as for *tortora* mats and other reed products.

Although people are generally friendly, bear in mind that on Saturday afternoon after the market, as well as on Sunday, some of the Indians get blind drunk (as happens throughout the Andes); you may, therefore, find this an inopportune time to visit.

Occasional reports of robberies trickle in, but they are not frequent. Many travelers enjoy walking around the area. When hiking around the region, ask locally for advice, go with friends or a group and avoid carrying all your valuables.

North along the Panamericana
About 3km north of Otavalo on the west side of the Panamericana is the new *Vista del Mundo Hotel, Resort & Spa* (☎ 946 333, 946 112). This is a unique project in Ecuador – it consists of a huge spa providing an array of computer-assessed health treatments; a resort with a spacious convention center, Japanese meditation garden, pool, and small golf course; and a hotel, where each bungalow is dedicated to an individual country (the roof of each is the shape of a hat typical of the country, and

murals within depict scenes from that country). A restaurant with room service is part of the plan. This luxurious, unusual and expensive spa is slated to open in 2000. Call for more information, or check the Web site at www.spavistadelmundo.com.

On an unpaved road west of the Panamericana and 4km north of Otavalo, *Cabañas Troje Cotama* (☎/fax 946 119) is in an isolated but panoramic location and has 10 rooms, all with private hot shower and fireplace, at US$24/29. Meals are available at about US$4 each, and the owner speaks English, Dutch and German. There are mountain bikes for rent, and it's a nice place to quietly hang out.

Near the turn to Cotacachi just off the Panamericana, the 210-year-old *Hacienda Pinsaqui* (☎/fax 920 387, 946 116/7, info@pinsaqui.com) is an elegant country home with 16 lovely guest rooms and a renowned horse stable. Simón Bolívar overnighted here during trips between Ecuador and Colombia. A photo in the hotel shows the owner leading his favorite stallion through the French doors of the lounge to the fireplace to meet the guests! (He doesn't do that any more.) The public areas include a reading room with a fireplace, a chapel and a cozy bar with barstools topped by saddles (emphasizing the rustic horsey feel of the place). The manmade lake and the 200-year-old gardens are very pretty and relaxing. Both horses and mountain bikes are available for hire. Rooms, some of which have a Jacuzzi, are US$72 to US$120 for one to four people, and suites are US$144, including American breakfast. Lunch or dinner is US$14.

Ilumán
This village, just off the Panamericana about 7km northeast of Otavalo, is a place to see weavers at work. The Conterón family runs a small handicrafts store, Artesanías Inti Chumbi, on the 2nd floor of their house on Parque Central. Apart from weavings and embroidered work, one of their specialties is very attractive Otavaleño dolls. Weaving demonstrations can be arranged. Cuy is prepared here if you order

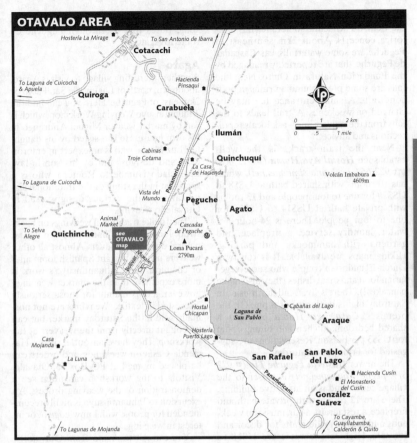

OTAVALO AREA

Hostería La Mirage
To San Antonio de Ibarra
Cotacachi
To Laguna de Cuicocha & Apuela
Hacienda Pinsaquí
Quiroga
Carabuela
Ilumán
Cabinas Troje Cotama
La Casa de Hacienda
Quinchuquí
To Laguna de Cuicocha
Vista del Mundo
Peguche
Volcán Imbabura 4609m
Agato
Animal Market
Cascadas de Peguche
To Selva Alegre
Quichinche
see OTAVALO map
Loma Pucará 2790m
Hostal Chicapan
Laguna de San Pablo
Cabañas del Lago
Araque
Casa Mojanda
Hostería Puerto Lago
San Rafael
San Pablo del Lago
La Luna
Hacienda Cusín
El Monasterio del Cusín
Panamericana
González Suárez
To Lagunas de Mojanda
To Cayambe, Guayllabamba, Calderón & Quito

Panamericana

0 1 2 km
0 .5 1 mile

NORTH OF QUITO

it a day in advance. This village can be a good destination during Otavaleño fiesta times because there are few tourists.

The easiest way to get to Ilumán from Otavalo is to take the Transportes 8 de Septiembre bus. You can also walk along the Panamericana or along the train tracks past Peguche.

Peguche

A popular walk heads out of Otavalo to the north and then east off the main highway – you'll be in Peguche in about an hour. Some people go in the hopes of being invited into the Indians' houses and buying the best weavings direct from the loom at bargain prices. That's wishful thinking. Prices aren't much (if at all) lower than in Otavalo, and the people have better things to do than invite curious gringos into their houses. On the other hand, the locals are friendly, and you might be lucky – especially if you speak Spanish (or better, Quichua).

One place that may allow visits is Tejidos Mimahuasi, which is the home of weavers José María Cotacachi and Luz María Ficha-bamba – they also sell their wares there. On Saturday, you can find the two at stall No 61 in Otavalo. On the central plaza of Peguche, the Centro Pachacutic sometimes has folk-lórica concerts. About 2km southeast of Peguche are some waterfalls, **Las Cascadas de Peguche**, that are reportedly managed by the Fundación Natura in Quito. Near the falls are some pre-Columbian ruins in poor condition. A small entrance fee may be charged on weekends. A trail leads to the falls from the railway line – ask locals for directions and advice.

Near the train tracks is the well-established ***Hostal Aya Huma*** (☎ 922 663, fax 922 664, ayahuma@imbanet.net), which has 10 rooms with shared bath at US$8 to US$20 for one to four people and 13 rooms with private bath at US$14 to US$36 for one to four people. There is 24-hour hot water, laundry service, a fireplace, and gardens with hammocks and parking. Hiking maps are available. It is run by a Dutch-Ecuadorian couple who serve vegetarian food and meat dishes (they also make pancakes!). There's live Andean music on Saturday nights beginning at 8 pm. On the premises, ***Casa Aya Huma*** provides a shared bedroom, kitchen and dining room for US$3 per person. Reservations are suggested for Friday and Saturday.

The newer ***Hostería Peguche Tío*** (☎ 922 619, pegtio@uio.satnet.net) is closer to the village center and is an attractive building. There are 12 rooms with private bath and fireplace, a restaurant, a bar, music on weekends and locally made crafts for decor and for sale. High-season rates are US$8 to US$26 for one to four people, but discounts are offered when the place isn't full.

About a kilometer north of Peguche is ***La Casa de Hacienda*** (☎ 946 336, fax 923 105), a modern but peaceful and rustic-looking small hotel. There are two double rooms for US$40 and three quad rooms (each with two bedrooms) at US$60 for four people. Rooms have a fireplace, and there are pleasant mountain views and a restaurant. More rooms are planned.

Another way of reaching Peguche from Otavalo is simply by walking northeast along the train tracks for about 3km; you can also walk to Ilumán or Agato from

Peguche. Cooperativa Imbaburapac has some buses that go through Peguche en route to Agato.

Agato

Another interesting village to visit is Agato, about 3km north of Laguna de San Pablo or 2km east of Peguche. Here you can find the Tahuantinsuyo Weaving Workshop, which is run by master weaver Miguel Andrango in his own house. He is assisted by his daughter, Luz María, who is an expert in embroidery and designs, and by his son-in-law, Licenciado Humberto Romero, who is a specialist in the study of the traditional significance of the various designs used in Otavaleño weaving.

They make traditional weavings on backstrap looms using handspun wool and natural dyes and products. Almost all other weavers use the upright Spanish loom and/or chemical dyes. Tahuantinsuyo's work is more expensive than the market weavings, however, and is mainly for those seriously interested in textiles. Weavings are not normally sold in the Saturday market but can be bought directly from the weavers at the workshop. They have an outlet at the Hacienda Cusín on weekends, and orders can be placed by mail at PO Box 53, Otavalo. Visitors to the workshop can often see a demonstration of the weaving process. An excursion to Tahuantinsuyo is highly recommended for people with knowledge of or interest in weaving.

You can get to Agato from Otavalo by bus using Cooperativa Imbaburapac. There are two routes – the northern one through Peguche passes by the workshop; the southern one doesn't. The workshop has a sign. A taxi will cost about US$1.50 from Otavalo, or you can walk (about 7km via Peguche), but it is easier to take a bus there and walk back.

Laguna de San Pablo

From Otavalo, the easiest way to reach the lake on foot is to head roughly southeast on any of the paths heading over the hill behind the train station. When you get to the lake, you'll find a (mostly paved) road

Miguel Andrango of Tahuantinsuyo Weaving Workshop

ROB RACHOWIECKI

encircling it, with beautiful views of Volcán Imbabura to the northeast; on this road, going clockwise around the lake, you'll pass through the village of San Pablo del Lago and end up on the Panamericana.

Cabañas del Lago (☎ *918 001, 918 108, in Quito* ☎ *435 936, fax 461 316, efernando@ uio.satnet.net)* is on the east side of Laguna de San Pablo. There are some 15 modern and comfortable cabins with private bath, and there's a restaurant on the premises. Small boats are available for rides or for hire, and horseback riding and miniature golf are also offered. Rates are about US$40 for a double room with TV, breakfast included.

The very popular *Hacienda Cusín* (☎ *918 013, 918 316, fax 918 003, in the USA 800-683-8148, hacienda@cusin.com.ec)* is a beautiful converted 17th-century hacienda with all the trimmings – it's on the southern outskirts of San Pablo del Lago (about 10km southeast of Otavalo). The oldest part of the hacienda dates to 1602, although it was completely remodeled in 1990. There is a cozy bar with a roaring fireplace, a game room (snooker, darts, table tennis), a well-stocked video room, a reading room, beau-

tiful gardens including an active farm, a squash court and horses and mountain bikes available for guests. Two exclusive craft shops, including the one run by the Andrango family from Agato (see that section, earlier), are on the premises. The hacienda is usually booked well in advance for weekends, but it is less busy midweek. It costs US$85 to US$195 (one to four people) for attractively furnished rooms with bath, and many have fireplaces. Continental breakfast is included. Some rooms are in the main building, while other rooms are in smaller cottages on the grounds. Complete packages, including three delicious homemade meals and two hours of horseback riding or mountain biking, are US$110 per person. Lunches are especially good – the traditional soups and local dishes attract day-trippers from Quito. Discounts can be negotiated for extended stays or by email.

El Monasterio de Cusín is under the same ownership as the hacienda and is similarly priced. There are 20 large rooms or cottages with fireplaces and beamed ceilings set around two attractive courtyards. A tower reading room offers lovely views, and the extensive gardens are filled with perennial flowers. There is a dining room and a conference room – the monastery is used for meetings and conferences. The owner, Nik Millhouse, is British, and the managers are Ecuadorian; one or both are always on the premises, and English is spoken. The Cusín also has information about and can make reservations for several other highland haciendas; extended hacienda stays and special trips – including weddings and honeymoons, overnight horse expeditions and Spanish or weaving courses – can be arranged.

Right on the lake, about 5km southeast of Otavalo on the Panamericana, is *Hostería Puerto Lago* (☎ 921 901/2, fax 920 900). There is a good restaurant with fine lake views, and boats are available. Rates are about US$55 per double.

On the western shores of Laguna de San Pablo is *Hostal Chicapan* (☎ 920 331), which has rooms with a hot shower for about US$7 to US$10 per person. Some rooms have balcony views of the lake. There is a restaurant, and horse and bike rentals can be arranged.

Lagunas de Mojanda

These beautiful lakes are set in high páramo scenery about 17km south of Otavalo. Camping is possible on the south side of the biggest lake (Laguna Grande de Mojanda), and there is a basic stone refuge (bring a sleeping bag and food). Fuya Fuya, a jagged, extinct volcano (4263m), is nearby. You can walk to the lakes or get there by taxi; there is a dirt road from Otavalo, and a taxi charges about US$10 roundtrip. You can make a good day trip by taking a taxi first thing in the morning and hiking back.

From the lakes, it is possible to hike across the páramo about 20km due south to the ruins of Cochasquí. The views are fantastic on clear days. A useful 1:50,000 topographical map of the Mojanda area, numbered ÑII-F1, 3994-III, is available from the IGM in Quito (see Maps, under Planning, in the Facts for the Visitor chapter).

Note the earlier warning about rapes and robberies in the Lagunas de Mojanda area (see Dangers & Annoyances under Otavalo, earlier).

COTACACHI
☎ 06

This small village, some 15km north of Otavalo and just west of the Panamericana, is famous for its leatherwork. Stores are strung out all along the main street (10 de Agosto), and you can find almost anything you might want in the way of leather goods. Market day is Saturday. Most tourists just pay a quick visit to the stores and return to Ibarra or Otavalo, but if you wander around to the right of the main street, you'll find an attractive main plaza.

Information

Organicafe-net (☎ 916 525), Modesto Penaherrera 15-78, near the Parque Central, has information about local ecotourism and provides Internet access.

Places to Stay & Eat

Budget travelers will find *Hostal Plaza* (☎ 915 327, Bolívar 12-26 at 10 de Agosto). The hostal is on the 3rd floor, and offers rooms with private hot showers for about US$3 per person. The owners are friendly and helpful.

On the western outskirts of town, the new *Hostería La Banda* (☎ 915 873, fax 915 176) looks like a nice place with 10 rooms, all with private baths, fireplaces and sitting rooms, and spacious gardens with Andean animals. The plan is to open in 2000, call for rates, which will be mid-range.

The hotel *El Mesón de las Flores* (☎ 915 264, fax 915 828), at García Moreno and Sucre, is in a lovely building over two centuries old. There is a good bar and restaurant. Rates are difficult to pin down – they can be anywhere from US$25 a double to twice that.

The elegant and romantic *Hostería La Mirage* (☎ 915 237, 915 077, fax 915 065; in the USA 800-327 3573; mirage1@mirage .com.ec) is in pleasant gardens almost a kilometer out of town. This lovely country hotel has antique furniture, bar, restaurant, fireplace, spa amenities including exercise room, sauna, indoor swimming pool, massage center, tennis court, horseback riding and tame birds. The hotel restaurant is the only one in Ecuador to achieve membership in the exclusive Relais & Chateaux association. These features have attracted various distinguished guests, including the Queen of Spain. Twenty three spacious rooms and suites all have a fireplace (the staff will light a fire on request) and attractively carved furniture; each unit is different. Rates range from are US$215 to US$342 for a double, including taxes, dinners and breakfasts (served in bed, if you wish). The hotel is often full on weekends, so reservations are recommended. The renowned restaurant is packed for lunch on Saturday with shoppers from the Otavalo market.

Getting There & Away

From the Otavalo bus terminal there are buses at least every hour. In Cotocachi, *camionetas* (pickups or light trucks) can be hired from the bus terminal by the market at the far end of town to take you to various local destinations, such as Laguna de Cuicocha.

RESERVA ECOLÓGICA COTACACHI-CAYAPAS

This huge reserve protects western Andean habitats ranging from Volcán Cotacachi down to the northwestern coastal lowlands. One cannot travel from the highland to lowland part of the reserve except by very difficult bushwhacking. Most visitors either visit the lowlands from San Miguel on Río Cayapas (see the North Coast chapter) or the highlands around Laguna de Cuicocha, which are described here.

LAGUNA DE CUICOCHA

Driving west some 18km from the town of Cotacachi, you reach an ancient, eroded volcanic crater famous for the deep lake found within. The crater is on the lower southern flanks of Volcán Cotacachi. Just before arriving at the lake, you will pass the entrance to the Reserva Ecológica Cotacachi-Cayapas. In the past, a nominal entrance fee was charged, but this may not be the case anymore.

At the lake, boats can take you on a cheap half-hour trip around the islands in the middle. On sunny weekends, this is often popular with the locals, but at other times, this facility may not be operating. Just watching everyone hanging around waiting for a boat can be more interesting than the ride itself. The view of the 3km-wide deep blue lake and the extinct Volcán Cotacachi behind it is quite impressive. There is a simple restaurant here, but nowhere to stay.

A path follows the edge of the lake, sometimes along the shore and sometimes inland because of cliffs. A profusion of flowers, including orchids, attracts hummingbirds. Views of the lake and the mountains surrounding it are excellent when the weather is good. The trail begins near the reserve's entrance booth and circles the lake counterclockwise. Ask the guards at the booth for details. Allow about six slow hours for the complete circuit, and bear in mind that the path becomes faint in places, particularly on the far side of the lake. Consider going as far as the trail is easy to follow and backtracking.

There have been occasional reports of hikers being robbed on this walk. Ask locally for the latest details and avoid carrying valuables. Also note that the blue berries growing around the lake are poisonous.

Getting There & Away

A group can hire a taxi or pickup from Cotacachi for under US$10, including a short waiting time at the lake and the return trip. One-way fares by taxi or truck cost about US$4 from Cotacachi. Buses pass the lake en route to Apuela from Otavalo.

You can avoid the main roads (the Panamericana from Otavalo to the Cotacachi turnoff and then the paved road through Cotacachi to the lake) either by hiking along the more direct, unpaved road between the lake and Cotacachi or by taking the old road between the lake and Otavalo (a long day hike). The 1:50,000 Otavalo map numbered ÑII-F1, 3994-IV is recommended for this region; this map should be available at IGM in Quito.

APUELA
☎ 06

West of Laguna de Cuicocha, the road reaches its highest point and begins to drop down the western slopes of the Andes. The scenery is splendidly rugged, and this is an opportunity to see some of the remoter, less-visited parts of the highlands. Some 40km (by road) west of Cuicocha, you reach the village of Apuela, set in subtropical forests at about 2000m above sea level. The people in Apuela are very friendly and will direct you to the thermal springs, about an hour's walk away from the village along the main road to the west. The three pools are about 35°C, and one is at 18°C; it's an untouristed, relaxing place. Admission is US$0.25.

Places to Stay & Eat

Accommodations are basic in town. *Hostal Veritas* is on the plaza, and the clean and friendly *Residencial Don Luis* is a couple of blocks away up the hill – both have cold showers and charge about US$2 per person. There is a simple restaurant across the street from Residencial Don Luis.

Outside of town, there are better places to stay. *Cabañas Río Grande (in Otavalo* ☎ *920 548, 920 442)* has rustic but clean cabins that sleep four for about US$4 per person. Private hot showers are available, and it's about an hour's hike to the springs. Get off the bus before Apuela – ask the driver. Zulaytur in Otavalo can make a reservation. Another hostal is under construction. You can also ask about *Hostal Gualima*, which provides meals and has shared hot showers.

Getting There & Away

There are several buses a day from Otavalo (four hours), more on Saturday, and they are often crowded. Try Transportes Otavalo and Transportes Cotacachi. Beyond Apuela, there are remoter villages, including Santa Rosa; inquire in Apuela about transportation between them.

INTAG CLOUD FOREST RESERVE

This private, 500-hectare reserve is in part a working 200-hectare farm and in part

primary and secondary forest. It lies between 1850m and 2800m in the western Andes near Apuela, a two-hour ride followed by a one-hour hike from Otavalo. The surrounding subtropical cloud forest is rich in flora and fauna, and birdlife is prolific; a list of the most common species is available at the reserve lodge. Orchids bloom during the dry season (July to September). The rainy season – Intag gets about 2.5m of rain annually – is October to May. Most rain falls in the afternoons and evenings; mornings are usually sunny. Much of the surrounding forest is threatened, and some has already been logged. The owners of the reserve, who are active in the local conservation movement, can fill you in on the details.

A rustic lodge provides clean, simple rooms (no electricity) that may have to be shared. Bathrooms are separate, and the showers are solar heated. The meals have a vegetarian emphasis and consist mainly of local produce, although chicken and dairy products are also available.

Up to 12 guests can be accommodated at a cost of US$45 per person per day with a minimum of six people. Smaller groups are charged US$67 per person per day. There is a two-night minimum stay. All meals and the services of a bilingual guide are included. Activities include horseback riding, fishing and hiking. Reservations are essential and should be made two months in advance with Carlos Zorrilla and Sandy Statz, Intag Cloud Forest Reserve, Casilla 18, Otavalo, Imbabura, Ecuador. Alternately, Safari Tours, in Quito, can help by forwarding reservations. Most guests have strong interests in conservation and natural history.

SAN ANTONIO DE IBARRA
☎ 06

This village is on the Panamericana about 20km north of Otavalo, just before the town of Ibarra (see that section, next). Although this place is famous for woodcarving, there's little wood found in the Ibarra area – most of it comes from the Ecuadorian jungles. Cedar and walnut are among the more frequently used woods. The village has a pleasant main square, around which stands a number of stores that are poorly disguised as 'workshops' or 'factories.' The most famous is the Galería Luis Potosí, which has some of the best carvings.

Señor Potosí is famous throughout Ecuador, and his work sells all over the world. Some of his best pieces – which sell for hundreds of dollars – are on display in the upstairs section of his gallery. The atmosphere is totally relaxed; no high-pressure salesperson breathes down your neck while you inspect the work.

A warning: Should you decide to purchase a large carving and have it shipped home, it's best to arrange for the shipping yourself. Some travelers have bought a carving, left a deposit for it to be shipped back, and found out many months later that their carving had been sold to someone else a few days later. They received their deposit back, but were very disappointed – their once-in-a-lifetime art investment had been sold to someone who paid cash and carried it out.

Not all the pieces are expensive, and you can buy small, mass-produced carvings for a couple of dollars. Various subjects are depicted, but the favorites seem to be beggars, religious statues and nude women.

Some say the best deals and selections are to be found on the streets away from the main square.

Places to Stay & Eat

The only accommodations are at *Hostería Los Nogales* (☎ 932 000), which has basic rooms starting at US$2 per person. Most visitors stay in Ibarra or Otavalo. There are no proper restaurants in San Antonio de Ibarra; one place, a block off the main plaza, serves greasy hamburgers and hot dogs.

Getting There & Away

Transportation from Ibarra is frequent during daylight hours; buses drop you off at the main plaza. The 15-minute ride costs just a few cents. Also, you can walk the few kilometers or so south on the Panamericana from Ibarra.

IBARRA
☎ 06

Just 22km north of Otavalo and 115km north of Quito is the charming colonial town of Ibarra. With about 140,000 inhabitants, it is the provincial capital of Imbabura. The 2210m elevation makes Ibarra lower than most highland cities, and it therefore has a pleasant climate. It's certainly less touristed than Otavalo, and some travelers prefer staying here.

There's not much to do in Ibarra itself, but parts of the town center bring visitors back to the 19th century. Horse-drawn carts clatter along cobbled streets flanked by colonial buildings, dark-suited old gentlemen sit in the shady parks discussing the day's events, and most good folks are in bed by 10 pm. It's a relaxing sort of place. Many of Ibarra's houses are in the colonial style. Red-tiled and whitewashed, they have given Ibarra the nickname of *la ciudad blanca* (the white city).

Market day is Saturday, and because most tourists go to Otavalo on Saturday, the Ibarra market is full of locals. After the market, the local men play *pelota de guante,* a strange Ecuadorian paddleball game played with a small, soft ball and large, spiked paddles that look like medieval torture implements.

Ibarra's annual fiesta is held during the last weekend in September, so the hotels are often full then; book in advance if you plan to stay there at that time.

Formerly, the main reason to overnight here was to take the daily train to San Lorenzo on the coast. Since a new road to San Lorenzo has opened, the train no longer runs there, and buses run several times a day, so fewer tourists stay overnight in Ibarra.

Orientation

Ibarra can be roughly divided into two areas. The southeast area around the train station is the busiest and has many cheap hotels, while to the north are the main plazas and the older buildings – it's a generally quieter and more pleasant area.

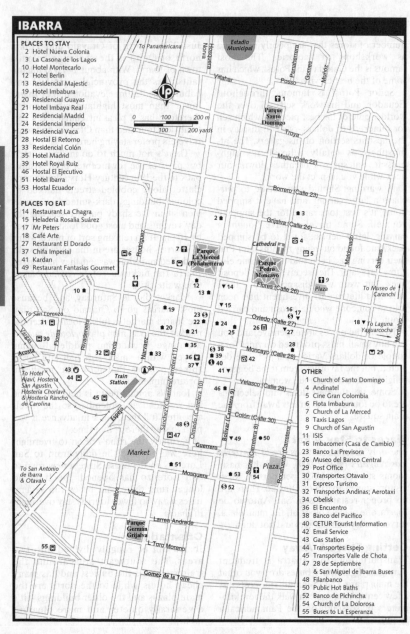

IBARRA

PLACES TO STAY
2 Hotel Nueva Colonia
3 La Casona de los Lagos
10 Hotel Montecarlo
12 Hotel Berlin
13 Residencial Majestic
19 Hotel Imbabura
20 Residencial Guayas
21 Hotel Imbaya Real
22 Residencial Madrid
24 Residencial Imperio
25 Residencial Vaca
28 Hostal El Retorno
33 Residencial Colón
35 Hotel Madrid
39 Hotel Royal Ruiz
46 Hostal El Ejecutivo
51 Hotel Ibarra
53 Hostal Ecuador

PLACES TO EAT
14 Restaurant La Chagra
15 Heladería Rosalia Suárez
17 Mr Peters
18 Café Arte
27 Restaurant El Dorado
37 Chifa Imperial
41 Kardan
49 Restaurant Fantasías Gourmet

OTHER
1 Church of Santo Domingo
4 Andinatel
5 Cine Gran Colombia
6 Flota Imbabura
7 Church of La Merced
8 Taxis Lagos
9 Church of San Agustín
11 ISIS
16 Imbacomer (Casa de Cambio)
23 Banco La Previsora
26 Museo del Banco Central
29 Post Office
30 Transportes Otavalo
31 Expreso Turismo
32 Transportes Andinas; Aerotaxi
34 Obelisk
36 El Encuentro
38 Banco del Pacífico
40 CETUR Tourist Information
42 Email Service
43 Gas Station
44 Transportes Espejo
45 Transportes Valle de Chota
47 28 de Septiembre
    & San Miguel de Ibarra Buses
48 Filanbanco
50 Public Hot Baths
52 Banco de Pichincha
54 Church of La Dolorosa
55 Buses to La Esperanza

Streets in Ibarra are both numbered and named. Roughly, north-south streets are numbered carreteras, and east-west streets are numbered calles. Both numbers and names appear on the street signs, but names seem to be more widely in use. Names are used in the text of this section.

Information
Tourist Offices CETUR (☎ 958 547, 958 759) is at Olmedo 9-56, but was closed at the time of this writing.

Money There are several banks, some with ATMs, although they are sometimes out of order or out of money. Filanbanco, on the southernmost block of Olmedo, has a Visa ATM, as does Banco La Previsora, at Olmedo and Oviedo. Banco del Pacífico, which is at Olmedo and Moncayo, has a Mastercard ATM. There are several others, such as Banco de Pichincha, in the same area, as well as a couple of casas de cambio – including Imbacomer, at Oviedo 7-13.

Post & Communications The post office is at Salinas 6-64. Andinatel is at Sucre 4-48. Internet connections are limited and expensive, but this will improve; ask around. Expensive email service is available at Moncayo 5-59, or try Hostal El Ejecutivo (☎ 956 575), Bolívar 9-69, which reportedly has public email service.

Things to See & Do
Also known as Peñaherrera, **Parque La Merced** has a church topped with a huge statue of the Virgin – **Virgin de La Merced**. Inside the church, there is an ornate altar. In the middle of the park, there is a bust of Victor Manuel Peñaherrera (1865–1930), the Ibarra-born professor who was deacon of the Faculty of Law in the Central University, as well as a judge on the Supreme Court during his lifetime.

The larger, tree-filled **Parque Pedro Moncayo** is dominated by the nearby **cathedral**. Pedro Moncayo (1807–88) was an Ibarra-born journalist and diplomat.

Out at the north end of Bolívar is the quaint little **Parque Santo Domingo**, which has a monument dedicated to Simón Bolívar to commemorate his victory at the Battle of Ibarra on July 17, 1823. It depicts the incongruous scene of an Andean condor attacking an African lion. A small zoological exhibit is planned.

Behind this small park, the modern concrete-block **church of Santo Domingo** is topped by a huge statue of Saint Dominic with a giant rosary swinging in the wind. Some people may enjoy viewing the paintings in the rather garish interior. A few of the paintings seem rather tongue-in-cheek: An old-fashioned representation of Jesus throwing the moneylenders out of the temple depicts one of the throng clutching a bag marked '$1000 Petroleo' (a jab at the rapacious oil-extraction process). The church also has a museum of religious art (open 9 am to noon and 3 to 6 pm Monday to Saturday; there is a small admission charge).

Also of interest is the **church of La Dolorosa**, on Sucre and Mosquera. It was built in 1928, but the domed roof collapsed completely during the earthquake of 1987. It has since been rebuilt.

The **Museo del Banco Central** is at Oviedo and Sucre. The **Museo de Caranchi** is a small archaeological museum almost 3km southeast of town along Montalvo. Hours are 9 am to 1 pm and 3 to 6 pm Tuesday to Sunday.

Language Courses
The Imbabura Spanish Center (☎ 959 429), directed by Miguel and Bernarda Ponce, Apartado 1001505, Ibarra, Imbabura, arranges one-on-one tuition for US$3 an hour and homestays with meals for US$15 a day. Study-tour packages are also available. Call them for directions to their school, which is in a private house away from the town center, at Urbanización La Victoria, Manzana 33, Casa 10.

Places to Stay
Budget There are many cheap hotels in Ibarra. The highest concentration of places to stay is near the train station. Many cost only about US$2, but they are basic, noisy

and usually only have cold water; not all are listed here. There are a few decent budget hotels, however. Generally speaking, Ibarra has some of the cheapest accommodations in Ecuador.

Hotel Imbabura (☎ 950 155, 958 522, fax 958 521, pepedavila@edoramail.com, Oviedo 9-33) is friendly and is one of the best budget choices. It has a pretty little flowery courtyard and a good café. The best rooms are on the quiet street; interior rooms can be dark. There are warm showers. Rates are a decent value at US$2.50 per person.

The popular (but often full by 3 pm) **Residencial Colón** (☎ 950 093, Narvaez 8-62) is clean and friendly and has basic rooms along a flower-filled patio. Rooms with private hot showers are under US$3 per person, and rooms with a shared bath cost a little less. There is also laundry service. Similar prices are found at the clean **Residencial Vaca** (Bolívar 7-53) and at **Residencial Majestic** (☎ 950 052, Olmedo 7-63) – both have fairly reliable hot water and some rooms with private bath.

Cheaper places abound. **Hotel Berlin**, by Parque La Merced, is very basic and rundown, but rooms cost well under US$2 per person, and some have plaza views. Others under US$2 worth trying include **Residencial Guayas**, on Moncayo near Narvaez, and **Residencial Imperio** (☎ 952 929, Olmedo 8-62).

Residencial Madrid (☎ 951 760, Olmedo 8-57) has carpeted rooms with TV for about US$4 per person. **Hostal El Retorno** (☎ 957 722, Moncayo 4-32) has fair-size rooms (some with TV) with private bath and 24-hour warm showers at about US$4 per person – a good deal. There are rooms with shared bath for about US$3 a person. There is a restaurant. The similarly priced **Hostal Ecuador** (☎ 956 425, Mosquera 5-54) also has a restaurant, as well as large, clean rooms with private hot shower.

For something a bit more upmarket, try **Hotel Madrid** (☎ 956 177, 959 017, fax 955 301, Moncayo 7-41), which has an attached restaurant; opposite is **Hotel Imbaya Real** (☎ 953 993, 959 729, Moncayo 7-44). Both have rooms with cable TV and private hot showers for about US$5.50 per person. A similar choice at about this price is **Hostal El Ejecutivo** (☎ 956 575, Bolívar 9-69).

The nice-looking **Hotel Nueva Colonia** (☎ 952 918, fax 955 543, Olmedo 5-19) charges about US$6/10 for singles/doubles with carpeted rooms, private bath, TV and telephone. There is a restaurant and an attractive roofed patio. **La Casona de los Lagos** (☎ 957 844, fax 951 629, Sucre 3-50) has a nice-looking restaurant and recently joined Hostelling International. Simple, but clean, pleasant rooms with bath are about US$6.50 per person and include an American breakfast. **Hotel Ibarra** (☎ 955 091, Mosquera 6-158) has adequate rooms with private bath and telephone for US$6 per person, and it has a restaurant.

Mid-Range The **Hotel Royal Ruíz** (☎ /fax 641 999, Olmedo 9-40) is bright and cheery and offers a sauna and café for guests. Singles/doubles with cable TV and private hot showers are about US$8/14. **Hotel Montecarlo** (☎ 958 266, fax 958 182, Rivadeneira 5-61) is also clean and bright and has rooms with TV, telephone and bath for US$12/16. Also advertised are a small indoor pool, a Jacuzzi, a sauna and a steam room – free for guests or US$2 per person for nonguests.

The better hotels are west of town, on or just off of the Panamericana and south toward Otavalo. The 1st-class (by Ibarra standards) **Hotel Ajaví** (☎ 955 221/787/555, fax 952 485) is just under 1km west of the town center. The hotel is modern and boasts a restaurant, bar, swimming pool, and sauna. Rooms are clean and spacious but unexciting. Doubles with TV, telephone and minifridge cost about US$30. A little over 2km west of town is the similarly priced **Hostería San Agustín** (☎ 955 888), in a pretty site 200m or 300m off the Panamericana. It has a decent restaurant.

Almost 4km west of Ibarra is the best hotel in the area, **Hostería Chorlaví** (☎ 955 777, fax 956 311, in Quito 522 703). With plenty of Old World charm, it is in a converted hacienda and has pretty gardens, a (cold) swimming pool and an excellent restaurant/bar. It also has a famous buffet lunch with folklórica on weekends, which is very popular with well-off Ecuadorians and tour groups after the Otavalo market – making it perhaps a bit too touristy for some travelers' tastes. There are rooms in the old hacienda building and cabins on the grounds. Rates are about US$35/45, depending on the room. Meals are about US$8. If this hotel is full, the smaller and similarly priced *Hostería Rancho de Carolina* (☎ *953 215*, ☎/fax *955 215*) is almost next door and has been recommended as clean and comfortable.

The good hotels are often booked well in advance, particularly on weekends. Make reservations if possible.

Places to Eat

For large helpings and reasonable prices, try *Restaurant La Chagra* (*Olmedo 7-48*). It is popular with the locals, maybe because it has a large-screen TV. There are also several good and cheap chifas on this street – look around and take your pick. *Chifa Imperial* (*Olmedo 9-47*) is a clean, brightly lit Chinese restaurant. *Restaurant El Dorado* (*Oviedo 5-45*) is mid-range in price and is a decent choice, with white tablecloths and good seafood (and other) dishes. Locals say the wishfully named and new *Restaurant Fantasías Gourmet* (☎ *959 815, Bolívar 10-90*) is good and inexpensive. *Mr Peters* (*Oviedo 7-30*) is good for hamburgers, pizza etc and is open until 10 pm or later on weekends. *Kardan*, on Bolívar near Velasco, serves vegetarian food and coffee.

Locals say that the best ice cream is in the traditional *Heladería Rosalia Suárez* (*Oviedo 7-82*). Doña Rosalia reportedly started the ice-cream shop when she was 16 and was reputedly 105 years old when she died in 1985. Her granddaughter runs it now, using the old-fashioned *helados de paila* technique, in which cream is spun in a copper pail on a bed of straw and ice. *Café Arte* (☎ *950 806, Salinas 5-43*) is open 4 to 10 pm, or later on weekends. Various snacks, especially Mexican ones, are served, as well as cocktails. There are also art shows and occasional musical performances in the evening.

Also, many of the mid-range hotels (listed earlier) serve excellent meals.

Entertainment

Ibarra is a quiet city and, even on Saturday night, there is little going on. There are a couple of cinemas. A popular bar to hang out in is *El Encuentro* (*Olmedo 9-35*). It has a rustic ambience (old leather saddles and strange implements hang from the walls) and occasional musical performances. Café Arte (see Places to Eat, earlier) is another place to hang out. *ISIS* is a disco club on the Oviedo circle; it's open 9 pm until late on Friday and Saturday. *Cine Gran Colombia*, near the cathedral, occasionally has performances, and occasional peñas are advertised, but locals are more likely to go into Otavalo for weekend nightlife.

Getting There & Away

Bus Buses to Ibarra depart from Quito's Terminal Terrestre all day, once or twice an hour. The trip can take 2½ to four hours, depending on the company. The fastest is Transportes Andinas, but the buses are small and frighteningly speedy. Other companies – such as Expreso Turismo, Flota Imbabura, Transportes Otavalo and Aerotaxi (to Quito from 3 am until late) – will take you more slowly and safely. They all charge about US$2. There are also frequent buses to and from Tulcán (US$2, three hours) with these companies, with the exception of Transportes Otavalo.

In the southwestern part of town, you can catch a bus to the village of La Esperanza (see that section, later in this chapter); these buses are crowded on weekends and sometimes continue farther south through Olmedo to Cayambe.

Ibarra's bus terminal is west of town, but it has been closed since 1994 and appears unlikely to reopen, so buses leave from various private terminals in town; see the Ibarra map to find their locations. Several times a day, there is direct bus service to several other major towns. These trips usually involve a stop in Quito but save you from having to look for another bus terminal in the capital. Towns served include Esmeraldas, Santo Domingo and Guayaquil.

In the late 1990s, a new road opened between Ibarra and San Lorenzo. Transportes Espejo and Transportes Valle de Chota, both near the train station, serve that coastal town about eight times a day.

Train Since the road opened to San Lorenzo, train service to that coastal town near the Colombian border has been suspended. Instead, *autoferros* (buses mounted on a train chassis) run as far as Río Blanco, about one-third of the way from Ibarra to San Lorenzo. In late 1999, the service ran daily at 7 am (US$7) but this was stopped again in early 2000 because of heavy rains. This is likely to continue to change. The train station can be reached at ☎ 950 390. Note that if you ask about a train *(tren)*, you'll be told there isn't one. Ask for the autoferro instead.

The section as far as Río Blanco is quite spectacular. You drop from Ibarra, at 2210m, to below 1000m within about 60km. Thus you see a good cross-section of Ecuador's western Andean foothills as you descend along the Río Mira valley, and there are good white-water views on the right side of the train.

If the autoferro is running, try making a reservation on the previous day, although this might not be possible; show up at least an hour early to get a ticket. There are always thieves working the crowds – keep valuables well hidden on your body.

The journey to Río Blanco is scheduled to take about four hours, but in reality, landslides, breakdowns and cows on the track are the norm, resulting in delays. In short, it can be an exciting or a frustrating trip, depending on your point of view.

Once in Río Blanco, there are places to stay, or you can continue to San Lorenzo or return to Ibarra by bus.

Taxi If you are in a real hurry to get back to Quito, you could use Taxis Lagos (☎ 955 150), Flores 9-24. It costs about US$5.50 per person, and six passengers are crammed

into a large taxi, but the taxis will deliver you to your hotel (or wherever you want). The taxis leave 10 times a day on weekdays, seven times on Saturday and from 8 am and 2 pm on Sunday for the 2¼-hour ride.

Getting Around
Local buses with the companies 28 de Septiembre and San Miguel de Ibarra (see the Ibarra map for their locations) provide service around town, and some continue to San Antonio de Ibarra. Different buses leave from the same street for several other local destinations. One exception is the bus to La Esperanza (30 minutes), which leaves about once an hour beginning at 6 am from Gomez de la Torre (see the Ibarra map). A La Esperanza bus terminal is being built on the north side of Parque Germán Grijalva. La Esperanza buses continue on to Olmedo and Cayambe.

LA ESPERANZA
☎ 06
This is a pretty little village in the country and is 6km to 7km due south of Ibarra. It is a good place for budget travelers looking for peace and quiet. There's nothing to do except talk to the locals and take walks in the surrounding countryside. It's supposed to be a good area to look for the **San Pedro cactus**, which contains mescaline and has hallucinogenic properties. Visit the Web site at www.mescaline.com/sanpedro for more information on the plant.

Volcán Imbabura (4609m) is about 9km to the southwest as the crow flies. It is easier to climb this mountain from La Esperanza than from the Laguna de San Pablo side. From La Esperanza, the volcano looks deceptively close – remember that you are not a flying crow, and that the summit is about 2000m higher than La Esperanza. There is a maze of tracks heading toward the summit, but you'll have to scramble the last bit – ask the locals for directions. Allow about 10 hours for the roundtrip, including time at the top for photographs of Laguna de San Pablo way below you.

If Imbabura seems like too ambitious of a climb, try **Loma Cubilche** (3836m). This hill is about 8km almost due south of La Esperanza. It's an easier climb and also offers good views. If climbing doesn't appeal to you at all, you can take the cobbled road through pretty countryside to the south – buses go along there occasionally.

Places to Stay & Eat

There is only one hotel – *Casa Aida*. It is very basic but friendly and costs about US$2 per person. You can get good, simple and cheap meals here, as well as a warm shower. This is a good place to get information and directions for local walks. There is also the small *Restaurant María*, which rents a basic room.

Getting There & Away

Buses from Ibarra serve the village frequently along a cobbled country road and irregularly continue farther south through Olmedo to Cayambe. Buses are crowded on weekends.

RÍO BLANCO AREA
☎ 06

This rural area is home to many of Ecuador's black farmers. The elevation is a subtropical 1000m, and the people are friendly. In the village of Limonal, you can stay at *Hostería Martyz (☎ 06-648 693)*, which has rooms with shared bath for about US$5 per person. Or you can stay at the slightly more expensive *Hostal Limonal (☎ 06-648 688)*, which has private baths. Both places have a swimming pool.

Limonal can be reached by the daily autoferro from Ibarra (if it is running!). Get off at the last station – San Juan de Lachas. Limonal is a 15-minute walk away. The village can also be reached by the several buses a day between Ibarra and San Lorenzo.

On the outskirts of Limonal is *Bospas Forest Farm (bospas@hotmail.com)*. The place is run by Piet Sabbe, a Belgian, as an example of a sustainable farm in an area that has suffered substantial deforestation. His idea is to teach the locals by example. He accepts volunteer assistants who have a basic knowledge of Spanish and who are familiar with the fields of permaculture, agroforestry, erosion control, organic pest control, fruit-tree grafting and related fields. Assistants are required to contribute US$150 per month for meals and accommodations (there are showers, but there is no electricity, and the nearest phone is in Limonal), and a two-month minimum stay is suggested. Exceptionally qualified people may be able to negotiate lower costs. Piet can arrange interesting hikes and horseback rides in the hills.

NORTH OF IBARRA
☎ 06

As you drive north from Ibarra on the Panamericana, you soon pass the highly touted tourist site of Laguna de Yaguarcocha (in Quichua, Yaguarcocha means 'blood,' so this can be translated as 'lake of blood'). It was so called after a battle between the Incas and the Caras, when the latter's bodies were supposedly thrown into the lake, turning the water red. There's not much to see except for a racetrack around the lake; it is used for auto racing during the annual fiesta at the end of September. A reader reports that boats are available for rent. You can walk to the lake in a couple of hours from Ibarra – head east on Oviedo to the edge of town, cross the river, and head north – or take a taxi (the fare should be about US$2 or US$3).

The Panamericana soon drops quite steeply to the Río Chota valley, at about 1565m, before beginning the long climb to San Gabriel, at almost 2900m. The warm and dusty town of Chota is inhabited by reserved but friendly black people whose ancestors were originally brought in as slaves in the 17th century. They now make their living growing fruit. Chota is less than an hour from Ibarra and can be visited on day trips. Fiestas and concerts there may occasionally be advertised in Ibarra. The music is a weird and wonderful mix of plaintive Andean and driving African sounds – it's worth hearing if you get the chance.

After leaving Chota, the Panamericana crosses the provincial line from Imbabura into Carchi. The road passes the little town of **Bolívar**, capital of the canton of the same name, and a few kilometers farther by the village of **La Paz**. Near La Paz are thermal springs and waterfalls, as well as a grotto containing stalactites and a famous statue of the Virgin. There are buses to the springs from Tulcán, or you can walk about 5km southeast of the Panamericana from La Paz on a road signed for 'Las Grutas.' The complex (thermal springs, pool and grotto) is open Thursday to Sunday. The road in this area is steep, winding and rather slow, and the scenery is wild.

About 90km north of Ibarra and 38km south of Tulcán is the small town of **San Gabriel**, which has a couple of basic hotels with cold water only. Five kilometers east is **Bosque de los Arreyanes**, which has many huge myrtle trees and other trees; it's a good place for birding. It's open 8:30 am to 4:30 pm daily; take a taxi or walk. There are two waterfalls – **Las Cascadas de Paluz** – on Río San Gabriel 3km and 4km north of San Gabriel (head north on Calle Bolívar and keep going). One of the falls is about 60m high.

EL ÁNGEL
☎ 06

This village is about 20km west of the Panamericana at San Gabriel. It's an entrance point to the Páramos de El Ángel, a wild area of highland vegetation and mists. Among the most notable plants in the páramo are the *frailejones,* a giant member of the daisy family that can grow to 2m in height – an amazing sight. The páramo is one of the few areas in Ecuador where Andean condors are seen, and there are many other intriguing plants and animals. In 1992, this area became protected by the formation of

In the páramo, keep your eyes peeled for a glimpse of the spectacular Andean condor.

the **Reserva Ecológica El Ángel**, which covers almost 16,000 hectares of páramo. Day tours (about US$10 per person, depending on the group's size) reportedly can be arranged at Grijalva 04-26 in El Ángel. The best way to visit the páramo is with the Cerro Golondrinas Project (see the boxed text).

Market day, on Monday, enlivens El Ángel, which is otherwise a very quiet little town.

Places to Stay & Eat
Ofelia López Peñaherrera rents *basic rooms* (Grijalva 02-59, there is no sign). There are no showers and the water is cold, but the family is friendly. Also try the basic *Residencial Viña del Mar*, on the main plaza; rooms are OK, but the bathrooms are grubby. Nearby, *Restaurant Los Faroles* (☎ 937 144) also offers basic rooms for US$2 per person.

Getting There & Away
Transportes Espejo, on the main plaza, goes to Quito via Ibarra about once an hour during the day. Buses to Tulcán leave only in the early morning.

RESERVA BIOLÓGICA GUANDERA
This 400-hectare, tropical, wet, montane forest reserve was founded in 1994 by the Fundación Jatun Sacha (see the Northern Oriente chapter). The reserve lies between 3100m and 3600m on a transitional ridge (forest to páramo) about 11km east of San Gabriel, near the village of Mariscal Sucre (which is not found on most maps). Andean spectacled bears (rarely glimpsed) and high-altitude parrots and toucans are among the attractions. From the village of San Gabriel, it is 90 minutes on foot to the reserve, where you can stay for US$25 a day in a bunk bed; simple meals and a guided walk are included in the price.

In Mariscal Sucre, ask for the reserve guard, José Cando Rosero. Mariscal Sucre is reached from San Gabriel's Plaza Central by school bus at 6 am and 1 pm when school is in session. Otherwise, there are buses on Saturday morning in San Gabriel for the

The Cerro Golondrinas Project

The Cerro Golondrinas area lies west of the Reserva Ecológica El Ángel and encompasses various ecosystems, including páramo and, in its lower elevations, temperate and subtropical montane cloud forest. There are areas of primary forest and páramo interspersed with small local farms. Similar forests on the western slopes of the Ecuadorian and Colombian Andes have been deforested at an alarming rate. The Cerro Golondrinas Project aims to conserve some of the remaining forests while improving the living standards of the farmers who reside in the area.

The project is one of the more successful grassroots conservation undertakings in Ecuador. It involves the cooperation of local campesinos and a small local NGO called Fundación Golondrinas, headquartered in a popular budget travelers' hostal in Quito, La Casa de Eliza (see Places to Stay under Quito).

Fundación Golondrinas promotes sustainable agricultural techniques – including (but not limited to) tree nurseries, orchid farms, bee keeping, reforestation projects and seed banks – as an alternative to the prevalent and highly destructive logging/cattle-ranch cycles (see Ecology & Environment, in the Facts about Ecuador chapter). They advocate protecting essential watersheds, which is best done by leaving standing forest to prevent erosion. Tourists are encouraged to trek through the area, enjoy the plants and animals, and visit with local families. The local families, in turn, work in sustainable agriculture and as hosts, guides and interpreters for visitors. This ecologically, environmentally and socially responsible form of tourism benefits the locals, protects the forests and provides visitors with an in-depth immersion into this remote region of Ecuador.

Travelers can become involved both as tourists and as volunteers or researchers. Four-day treks on foot or horseback led by local guides traverse a cross-section of Andean habitats and offer excellent opportunities for bird watching and nature study, as well as interaction with local families. The treks cost US$50 per person per day, including all food, accommodations and guiding services. During the wet months of October to May, the trails can get very muddy; the best time to go is during the dry season, when departures occur weekly.

More information about treks and volunteering is available by contacting Fundación Golondrinas (in Quito ☎ 02-226 602, manteca@uio.satnet.net), c/o La Casa Eliza, Isabel La Católica 1559, Quito. You can also visit the Web site at www.ecuadorexplorer.com/golondrinas.

Mariscal Sucre Saturday market, or you can take a taxi for about US$8 one way. Volunteers (who must pay US$300 a month for food and accommodations) and researchers are needed, and natural-history buffs are welcome. Reservations should be made at the Jatun Sacha office in Quito (☎/fax 250 976, 441 592, 253 266), Río Coca 1734, Casilla 17-12-897.

TULCÁN
☎ 06

This small city of about 53,000 inhabitants is the provincial capital of Carchi, the northernmost province of the Ecuadorian highlands. Driving north, you see plenty of farms and ranches, particularly as you get close to Tulcán, which is an important market town. For most travelers, its main importance is as the gateway into Ecuador from Colombia, some 6km away. Tulcán is not a particularly interesting town, but there are some interesting trips in the vicinity, described at the end of this chapter.

Tulcán is very popular for Colombian weekend bargain hunters. There is a Sunday street market (with few tourist items), and the hotels are often filled with Colombian shoppers on Saturday night.

At almost 3000m above sea level, Tulcán has a cold climate and is the highest provincial capital and town of its size in the country.

Abdón Calderón – Hero of Independence

Parque Isidro Ayora has a rather striking white statue of Abdón Calderón riding a horse. Calderón was a battle-hardened 18-year-old lieutenant fighting against the Spanish Royalists at the decisive Battle of Pichincha, which cemented Ecuador's independence on May 24, 1822. Abdón Calderón is famous not only for his youth, but also for his tenacity during the battle. Historians report that he was shot in the right arm, causing him to wield his sword with his left hand. A second bullet in the left arm made him drop his sword, but he continued fighting after having one of his soldiers tie the sword to his arm. A third shot in the left leg didn't stop him either. Finally, a bullet tore apart his right leg just as the battle was ending victoriously. He died the next day and was promoted to captain posthumously.

Orientation
The town is long and narrow, with most activity happening on or near the parallel streets of Bolívar and Sucre. A new numbering system for addresses has been developed, but many places still have or use the old numbers. To avoid confusion, the nearest intersections, rather than the numbers, are used here.

Information
Tourist Offices CETUR (☎ 983 892) is at Pichincha 4-69, near Bolívar, but was closed recently. Limited information is available at the border crossing.

Colombian Consulate The consul is on Bolívar near the post office, but hours are sporadic, so check the consulate in Quito for visa requirements.

Money Money exchange is better in Tulcán than at the border, except on weekends, when you are at the mercy of the street changers. (The bus running between Tulcán and the border accepts both Colombian currency and dollars.) Filanbanco, on Sucre near 10 de Agosto, has a Visa ATM, and Banco de Pichincha, on the same block, changes US dollars and traveler's checks. There are several other banks nearby, or try Casa Paz, on Ayacucho west of the central plaza.

Street changers with little black attaché cases full of money hang out around the border, the banks and the bus terminal.

Because there is no real black market, you won't get better rates from them than from the exchange houses, but they are useful when the other places are closed.

Post & Communications The post office is on Bolívar near Junín. The main Andinatel telephone office is on Olmedo near Junín, and there are branches at the terminal terrestre and at the border. Public Internet connections were unavailable in 1999; but this can change quickly, so ask around.

Emergency Clínica Metropolitana, at Bolívar and Panamá, is open 24 hours. There is a better hospital in Ipiales, 2km north of the border.

Things to See & Do
The big tourist attraction in town is the **topiary garden** that makes up the cemetery. The Tulcán cemetery is the most striking example in Ecuador of this form of gardening work, in which bushes and trees are trimmed and sculpted into animal or geometrical shapes, and it is one of the best in Latin America.

Behind the cemetery, the locals play a strange Ecuadorian paddleball game called pelota de guante (see the description under Ibarra, earlier) on weekends.

Weekend excursion buses with Cooperativa 11 de Abril make day trips to nearby **thermal springs**, departing from in front of the cathedral. These buses go to La Paz hot springs, 5km from the village of that name,

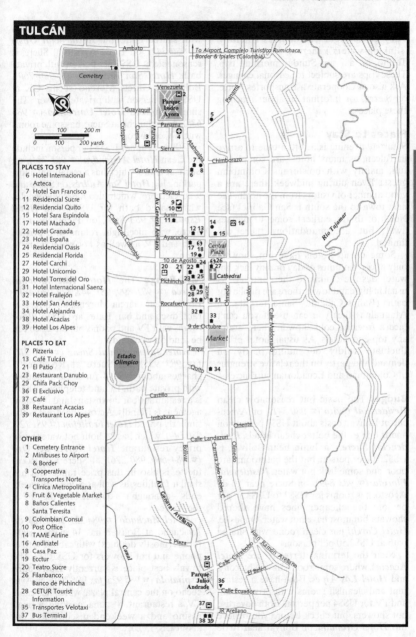

TULCÁN

Ambato

Cemetery

To Airport, Complejo Turístico Rumichaca,
Border & Ipiales (Colombia)

Guayaquil

Venezuela

Parque
Isidro
Ayora

Panama

Sierra

Garcia Moreno

Chimborazo

Boyaca

Junin

Ayacucho

10 de Agosto

Pichincha

Rocafuerte

9 de Octubre

Tarqui

Quito

Castillo

Imbabura

Calle Landazuri

Bolivar

Av. General Arellano

L Plaza

Parque
Julio
Andrade

Calle Ecuador

JR Arellano

Atahualpa

Central
Plaza

Cathedral

Sucre

Olmedo

Colon

Calle Maldonado

Rio Tajamar

Estadio
Olimpico

Market

Oriente

Carrera Julio Robles

Calle Carchi

Calle Carchi

Juan Ramon Arellano

El Belen

Av. General Arellano

Cuenca

Manabi

Cotopaxi

Calle Gran Colombia

Scale:
0   100   200 m
0   100   200 yards

PLACES TO STAY
- 6 Hotel Internacional Azteca
- 7 Hotel San Francisco
- 11 Residencial Sucre
- 12 Residencial Quito
- 15 Hotel Sara Espindola
- 17 Hotel Machado
- 22 Hotel Granada
- 23 Hotel España
- 24 Residencial Oasis
- 25 Residencial Florida
- 27 Hotel Carchi
- 29 Hotel Unicornio
- 30 Hotel Torres del Oro
- 31 Hotel Internacional Saenz
- 32 Hotel Fraileján
- 33 Hotel San Andrés
- 34 Hotel Alejandra
- 38 Hotel Acacias
- 39 Hotel Los Alpes

PLACES TO EAT
- 7 Pizzeria
- 13 Café Tulcán
- 21 El Patio
- 23 Restaurant Danubio
- 29 Chifa Pack Choy
- 36 El Exclusivo
- 37 Café
- 38 Restaurant Acacias
- 39 Restaurant Los Alpes

OTHER
- 1 Cemetery Entrance
- 2 Minibuses to Airport & Border
- 3 Cooperativa Transportes Norte
- 4 Clinica Metropolitana
- 5 Fruit & Vegetable Market
- 8 Baños Calientes Santa Teresita
- 9 Colombian Consul
- 10 Post Office
- 14 TAME Airline
- 16 Andinatel
- 18 Casa Paz
- 19 Ecctur
- 20 Teatro Sucre
- 26 Filanbanco; Banco de Pichincha
- 28 CETUR Tourist Information
- 35 Transportes Velotaxi
- 37 Bus Terminal

on Saturday excursions leaving at 8 am. They go to Aguas Hediondas (literally, 'stinking waters') thermal baths, beyond Tufiño, on a 7 am Sunday morning trip. These trips are subject to seasonal changes. Ask also at Cooperativa Transportes Norte, on Sierra, for information about reaching these places.

Places to Stay

Saturday evening is a rotten time to arrive in Tulcán, as many hotels are completely full, mainly with boisterous Colombian guests. Even during midweek, there are a good number of visitors from the north. The next town to the south is San Gabriel (see North of Ibarra, earlier), some 40 minutes away, but accommodations there are limited.

Some cheap hotels have hot showers only at certain times of day or may lack hot water despite claims to the contrary. As usual in highland towns, there are public hot baths (Baños Calientes Santa Teresita, on Atahualpa) that you can use if you can't face a freezing cold shower. There aren't any top-end hotels. As usual, hotel prices fluctuate wildly depending partly on demand and partly on the relative strengths of Colombian and Ecuadorian currencies.

Budget The basic but reasonably clean *Residencial Quito* (☎ 980 541), on Ayacucho at Bolívar, costs about US$2 per person and is one of the better cheap hotels. *Residencial Sucre*, on Junín near Bolívar, is US$2.50 per person, but the bathrooms are poor, and some lack hot water. *Residencial Florida* (☎ 983 849), on Sucre near 10 de Agosto, has rooms for US$2 to US$3.50 per person; the cheaper ones have shared showers, but most have hot water. Opposite, *Hotel Carchi* has clean rooms with shared bath at US$2.50 per person.

Near the terminal terrestre are *Hotel Acacias*, where some rooms have a balcony, and *Hotel Los Alpes*. Both have a restaurant and cleanish rooms with private bath and TV for US$4 per person. Both advertise hot showers, but check before you believe this. *Hotel Granada*, on Bolívar near 10 de Agosto, is just OK for US$3.50 per person with shared bath, and *Residencial Oasis* (☎ 980 342), on 10 de Agosto at Sucre, is reasonable at US$4 per person with private bath. *Hotel San Francisco* (☎ 980 760), Bolívar at García Moreno, seems OK at US$4 per person with private showers. The similarly priced *Hotel Unicornio* (☎ 980 638), on Pichincha at Sucre, has some rooms with TV or balcony.

Others at under US$5 per person include the clean *Hotel Alejandra* (☎ 981 784), on Sucre at Quito, which has a restaurant and a parking lot; *Hotel San Andrés*, on Sucre and 9 de Octubre, which also has some singles with shared bath for US$4; and *Hotel España* (☎ 983 860), on Pichincha near Sucre, with nice, light rooms with private bath and TV, as well as hot water 6 am to noon.

Mid-Range The *Hotel Internacional Azteca* (☎ 981 899, 981 447, fax 980 481), Bolívar near García Moreno, has a restaurant, disco and bar. Rates are US$6/10 for rooms with TV and phone, but the disco can be loud on weekends.

Hotel Internacional Saenz (☎ 981 916, fax 983 925), on Sucre at Rocafuerte, charges about US$14 for a clean double with private bath, TV and telephone. There is a restaurant/bar downstairs, and the management is friendly. Across the street is the similarly priced *Hotel Frailejón* (☎ 981 129, 980 149), which has 24-hour hot water and a pricey restaurant. *Hotel Torres del Oro* (☎ 984 660, 980 226), at Sucre and Rocafuerte, is also in this price range and has similar facilities, as well as a disco on weekends – although it's quieter than the one at the Azteca.

Hotel Machado (☎ 984 221, 984 810), on Ayacucho at Bolívar, has 14 clean, bright rooms (mostly doubles) with cable TV, telephone and hot showers for US$10/17. The town's best place is currently *Hotel Sara Espindola* (☎ 985 925, fax 986 209), on Ayacucho on the central plaza, which has cable TV, a restaurant, a sauna, parking, a small casino and a weekend disco. Rates are about US$15/20.

The priciest place to stay in the Tulcán area is *Complejo Turístico Rumichaca* (☎ 980 372, 980 276, fax 982 893) about 300m away from the border, 6km from town. It offers a swimming pool, restaurant, bar and a disco (if you can find someone to open it). Prices are US$18/24 with bath, TV and phone. Rooms are no better than the ones in town, but it's a bit quieter out there.

Places to Eat

Tulcán isn't one of this planet's culinary centers. Many restaurants are only open for lunch and supper and close in mid-afternoon. Monday night is a particularly poor night to go out in search of gastronomic adventures, as most of the restaurants are closed.

El Patio, on Bolívar between Pichincha and 10 de Agosto, has large portions and good breakfasts – it's one of Tulcán's best restaurants. *Café Tulcán*, on Sucre at Ayacucho, serves pastries and coffee.

In the town center, there are the usual chifas, of which *Chifa Pack Choy*, beneath Hotel Unicornio, is the best according to several travelers. There is a pizzeria in Hotel Internacional Azteca, and *Restaurant Danubio*, at Hotel España, has cheap Ecuadorian food.

There is a basic café in the bus terminal, but it's not always open. In case it's not, head for the not-very-exclusive *El Exclusivo*, on Bolívar near Calle Ecuador; it's at least clean and seems to have a reasonable selection of food. Both *Restaurant Acacias* and *Restaurant Los Alpes* are simple inexpensive restaurants in the hotels of the same names.

Check out the fruit and vegetable market near Panamá and Sucre, where horse-drawn carts unload produce every day.

Out by the border, a bunch of stalls sell snacks, but there are no restaurants, except in Complejo Turístico Rumichaca (listed under Mid-Range Places to Stay, earlier).

Entertainment

Teatro Sucre shows occasional movies, and there is dancing in the hotel discos on weekends (see Places to Stay, earlier).

Getting There & Away

Air The airport is 2km northeast of the center. TAME has an office on Sucre near Junín (☎ 980 675) and another at the airport (☎ 982 850). TAME flights from Quito to Tulcán leave at 9:30 am weekdays and return to Quito at 10:30 am Monday, Wednesday and Friday and at 12:50 pm Tuesday and Thursday. The 30-minute flight saves you five or six hours on the bus and costs about US$20. There are also flights to Cali, Colombia, at 10:30 am Tuesday and Thursday, returning from Cali at 11:40 am (US$68, plus a US$25 international departure tax).

Note that flights from Tulcán to Quito are often full and are also among the first to be canceled when TAME is having aircraft problems.

Ecctur (☎ 980 468, fax 980 368), on Sucre at 10 de Agosto, sells airline tickets and arranges tours.

Bus Buses to and from Ibarra (US$2.20, three hours) and Quito (US$4, 5½ hours) leave and arrive via the terminal terrestre, on the southwestern end of town. There are frequent departures, but the selection of times is better in the mornings. Transportes Velotaxi, two blocks north of the terminal, has small, fast buses to Quito at least every hour from 2:25 am to 10:30 pm. There are also eight daily direct departures for Guayaquil, if you enjoy the slow form of torture provided by cramped Ecuadorian buses during journeys taking 12 to 14 hours. Note that there can be a very thorough customs/immigration check between Tulcán and Ibarra.

If you wish to travel west of Tulcán along the border to Tufiño, Maldonado and Chical, take the Cooperativa Transportes Norte buses leaving from Sierra between Arellano and Manabí. There is a bus to Tufiño (US$0.50, one hour) every one or two hours until mid-afternoon. There is also one bus that departs every day at about 11 am and goes to Maldonado (US$2, 4½ hours) and Chical via Tufiño. There may be more buses to Maldonado; check with Cooperativa Transportes Norte.

Cooperativa 11 de Abril buses leave from a stop in front of the cathedral – these buses go to the thermal springs (see Things to See & Do, earlier in this section) as well as other nearby destinations.

Getting Around
To/From the Airport To get to the airport, take the border-crossing bus (see Crossing the Colombian Border, next), which will leave you by the entrance of the airport for the same price as going to the border. A taxi will cost about US$1.50, or it's a 2km walk from the city center. If flying into Tulcán, you have to take a taxi or walk, because there are no buses to take you from the airport into town.

Bus The terminal terrestre is inconveniently located 2.5km southwest of the town center. City buses (US$0.10) run southwest from the center along Bolívar and will deposit you at the terminal. If arriving at Tulcán, cross the street in front of the terminal and take the bus to get to the town center.

Crossing the Colombian Border
You don't need to obtain an exit or entry stamp in the town of Tulcán. All formalities are taken care of at the Ecuador-Colombia border, 6km away at Rumichaca. Fourteen-seat minibuses to the border leave as soon as they are full all day long starting at 6 am from Parque Isidro Ayora. The fare is about US$0.60 (Colombian currency or dollars).

Return buses from the border will charge the same to the town center, but you can usually persuade the driver to charge double and take you to the Tulcán bus terminal some 1.5km away if you are in a hurry to head south. Taxis between the bus terminal and the border are about US$3.

The border is open daily 6 am to 9 pm. With the heavy traffic from Colombia, entrance formalities (into Ecuador) are usually no problem. Almost nobody needs a visa, and tourist cards (which you must keep until you leave) are issued at the border. Unless you look like a bum, an exit ticket and sufficient funds are rarely requested.

You might not be given the full 90 days that you are allowed, but extensions in Quito are normally fast and straightforward. Make sure that both your tourist card and passport are correctly stamped and dated.

If leaving Ecuador, you must get a *salida* (exit) stamp in your passport and turn in your tourist card. Try not to lose your tourist card, but if you do, you should get another one free if your passport is in order. If your documents aren't in order, several things might happen. If you've merely overstayed the allowed time by a few days, you can pay a fine that is usually about US$10 – this really is a fine, not a bribe. If you've overstayed by several months, you may well have to pay a hefty fine or be sent back to Quito. And if you don't have an *entrada* (entrance) stamp, you will also be sent back.

On the Colombian side, entrance formalities are straightforward, as long as your passport and visa are in order. Most citizens of First World countries don't need a visa, but check with a Colombian consulate to make sure. From the border, there is frequent transportation to Ipiales, the first town in Colombia, 2km away. There you'll find plenty of hotels and onward connections; see Lonely Planet's *Colombia* or *South America on a shoestring*.

WEST OF TULCÁN
☎ 06

Right on the border to the west of Tulcán, the small villages of **Tufiño**, **Maldonado** and **Chical** are rarely visited by gringos.

At Tufiño, there are several **thermal springs**, most of them on the Colombian side of the border. It is easy enough to cross over the border to Colombia on a day pass to soak in the pools, but you are sent back to Tulcán if you want to enter Colombia properly. However, regulations change, so look into it. There is a basic *restaurant* in the village, but no hotels. If you ask around, you could probably find someone who will rent you a bed or floor space, but it's probably easiest to visit Tufiño in the morning and return to Tulcán on an afternoon bus.

The drive beyond Tufiño takes you over the Páramos de El Ángel, famous for their strange highland vegetation, especially the giant frailejones. The dirt road climbs to well over 4000m as it crosses the wild country at the base of Volcán Chiles (4768m), an extinct volcano on the border. The summit is about 4km away from the road, and the mountain can be climbed in a day with no technical equipment, although it is not a climb for beginners. The bus drivers know where to drop you off; the mountain is the obvious volcano to the north.

From the high mountain pass, it is a long descent down the western slopes of the Andes through wild and ever-changing scenery into the cloud forests below. Maldonado is in the Río San Juan valley, at just over 2000m above sea level and almost 90km west of Tulcán by road. The climate is reportedly pleasant, and swimming in the river is invigorating. There are a couple of small pensiones. Camping is possible in Chical, about 10km west of Maldonado and at the end of the road.

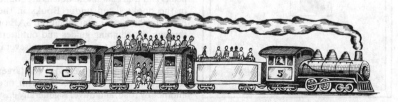

South of Quito

A glance at a relief map of Ecuador shows the Panamericana heading almost due south of Quito through a long valley flanked by two parallel ranges of high mountains. These two ranges consist for the most part of volcanoes, and several of them are still active. It was this feature that prompted Alexander von Humboldt, the German explorer who visited the country in 1802, to name Ecuador's central valley 'The Avenue of the Volcanoes' – a name that is still used today.

The central valley is only a tiny fraction of Ecuador's land surface, yet it contains almost half of its population. Traditionally, Ecuador's Andean Indians farmed the valley's rich volcanic soils, and after the conquest, the Spanish found that the central valley made a good communication route between the north and south. Today, the same route is used for the Panamericana, and a string of towns stretches south from the capital to Cuenca, Ecuador's third-largest city, some 300km south of Quito by air or 442km by road.

In between lies some of Ecuador's wildest scenery, including nine of the country's 10 highest peaks and scores of tiny villages of indigenous Andeans leading lives little changed in centuries. Many of these villages are so remote that access is only on foot; some are easier to get to and provide a fascinating glimpse of Andean life. The farther south one goes, the larger and remoter are the Indian populations. In Chimborazo Province, for example, there are approximately 250,000 Indians living in over 400 small legal communities and villages. Most villages have minor differences in dress that are immediately recognizable to the local people – the pattern, color or shape of a poncho, hat, dress, blouse, trousers or waistband can all indicate where an Indian is from.

Ecuador's most popular mountain climbs take place in this region, and a handful of local climbers and visiting mountaineers make attempts at scaling these giants year-round. In terms of weather and snow conditions, December and January are considered the best months, and March to May the worst. Some climbing and hiking information is given here for the most important peaks and trails, and more details are found in the books listed under Books in the Facts for the Visitor chapter, at the SAE or through the climbing guides and outfitters mentioned under Quito and under several towns in this chapter.

Most travelers, however, visit the larger towns that are well connected with one another by road, and travel is generally easy

Highlights

- Watching the lively sale of livestock, guns and all sorts of other items in Saquisilí, home of Ecuador's best and largest Indian market
- Getting a close look Andean life and beautiful mountain scenery in the remote villages west of Latacunga
- Peering at the pyrotechnics of the active Volcán Tungurahua from one of several villages in the Baños area
- Ascending toward the most distant point from the center of the Earth – the peak of Volcán Chimborazo

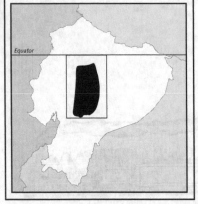

Equator

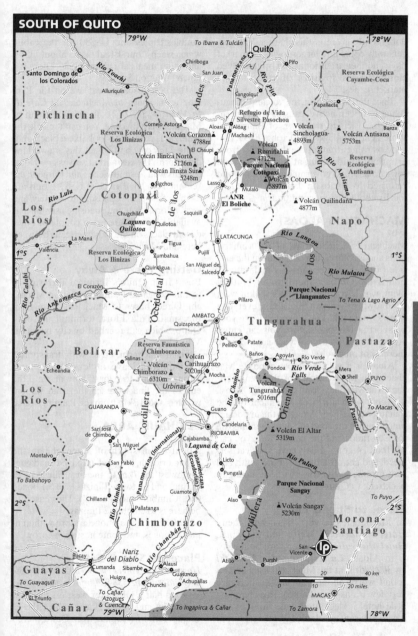

SOUTH OF QUITO

79°W   To Ibarra & Tulcán   **Quito**   78°W

Chiriboga   Pifo

San Juan   Río Pita

Santo Domingo de los Colorados   Río Toachi   Sangolquí   **Reserva Ecológica Cayambe-Coca**

Alluriquín   Papallacta   Baeza

Pichincha   **Refugio de Vida Silvestre Pasochoa**   Volcán Sincholagua▲ 4893m   **Volcán Antisana** 5753m

Cornejo Astorga   Aloasí   Aláag   Machachi

Reserva Ecológica Los Ilinizas   **Volcán Corazón** 4788m   **Volcán Rumiñahui▲** 4712m   **Reserva Ecológica Antisana**

El Cháupi   **Parque Nacional Cotopaxi**

Volcán Iliniza Norte 5126m   **Volcán Iliniza Sur▲** 5248m   **Volcán Cotopaxi** 5897m

Sigchos   Lasso   Mulaló   **Napo**

Río Lulu   **Cotopaxi**   **ANR El Boliche**   ▲ **Volcán Quilindaña** 4877m

Chugchilán   Saquisilí   Río Langoa

Laguna Quilotoa   Quilotoa   **LATACUNGA**   Río Mulatos

Los Ríos   La Maná   Tigua   **Parque Nacional Llanganates**

1°S   Valencia   Zumbahua   Pujilí   1°S

Reserva Ecológica Los Ilinizas   San Miguel de Salcedo   To Tena & Lago Agrio

Quindigua

Río Calabi   El Corazón   Píllaro

Río Angamarca   **AMBATO**

Quizapincha   **Tungurahua**   **Pastaza**

Bolívar   Salasaca

Reserva Faunística Chimborazo   Peílleo   Patate

Salinas   **Volcán Carihuairazo** 5020m   Baños   Agoyán   Río Verde

Echeandía   **Volcán Chimborazo▲** 6310m   Mocha   Pondoa   **Río Verde Falls**   Mera   **PUYO**

Urbinas   Shell

Los Ríos   **Volcán Tungurahua** 5016m   To Macas

GUARANDA   Penipe

San José de Chimbo   Guano   Candelaria

Montalvo   San Miguel   **RIOBAMBA**   ▲ **Volcán El Altar** 5319m

To Babahoyo   San Pablo   Cajabamba   **Laguna de Colta**

Chillanes   Licto   Río Palora   To Puyo

Pallatanga   Pungalá

2°S   Guamote   Alao   **Parque Nacional Sangay**   2°S

Chimborazo   ▲ **Volcán Sangay** 5230m   **Morona-Santiago**

Bucay   **Nariz del Diablo**   San Vicente

Cumandá   Sibambe   Atillo   Purshi

Guayas   Huigra   Alausí   Guasuntos   0   20   40 km

El Triunfo   Chunchi   Achupallas   0   10   20 miles

Cañar   To Cañar, Azogues & Cuenca   To Ingapirca & Cañar   MACAS   To Zamora

79°W   78°W

and accompanied by superb views. Visiting smaller villages is possible, and details for doing so are given in this chapter. Villagers generally come into larger towns on market days, and their traditional and brightly dyed clothing adds splashes of color to the market scenes.

Since the last edition, the volcano Tungurahua has been active, causing the government to evacuate the town of Baños and some nearby villages in October 1999. Despite warnings that a potentially disastrous eruption could occur at any time, some townsfolk defied government warnings and returned to Baños in January 2000. Ask locally about current conditions in the area.

MACHACHI & ALOASÍ
☎ 02

Machachi is a small town of 7000 inhabitants and is 35km south of Quito, on the east side of the Panamericana. Its main attraction is the Güitig mineral water bottling plant, which you can visit. It's a 4km walk from town, or you can take a taxi; everyone knows where it is. You'll need to leave your passport at the gate before you can enter. Apart from a cold pool you can swim in, there's not much else.

Aloasí is a village almost opposite Machachi, on the west side of the Panamericana. The Machachi train station is in Aloasí.

About 6km north of Machachi on the Panamericana (near Alóag) is the important junction with the road to Santo Domingo de los Colorados and the coast. Here, you can get food 24 hours a day, have your car serviced, and get off a bus from the south and wait for one to the coast without having to backtrack to Quito.

Places to Stay & Eat
In Machachi, the very basic and cheap *Hotel Residencial Mejía* and the worse *Hotel Miravalle* (no water!) are both dirty. In Aloasí, *La Estación de Machachi* (☎ 309 246) is at the Machachi train station (don't worry about train noise; there are very few trains from Quito). This charming little hotel is decorated with antiques and has a pleasant garden, a good restaurant

and 10 rooms and a cabin – all with private bath. Rates are US$12/15/18 for singles/doubles/triples and US$30 for the cabin, which sleeps four. Breakfast is about US$3, and other meals are about US$6. There is a lunch buffet on Sunday.

The best places to eat are on the Panamericana south of Machachi. *El Café de la Vaca* (☎ 315 012), about 3km south of Machachi, is a favorite. You can't miss it; the building is painted to look like a black-and-white dairy cow, and in fact, this is a working dairy farm. The restaurant serves good local food, as well as sandwiches and burgers; the set lunch is a good value at US$3. Hours are 8 am to 5:30 pm Wednesday to Sunday, and local information and roadside assistance is available here. There are a couple of other decent places on the Panamericana between here and Machachi.

Getting There & Away
Buses from Quito's Terminal Terrestre go to Latacunga and can drop you in Machachi. Direct buses to Machachi leave from the small Villa Flora terminal in south Quito, which can reached by city buses for Villa Flora.

From Machachi, buses with Transportes La Dolorosa leave at least every hour during the day to Aloasí. Stay on until the end of the line to reach the train station, which is about 3km from the Panamericana.

EL CHAUPI AREA
☎ 02

About 10km south of Machachi on the Panamericana, a signed, unpaved road goes southwest for 7km to the tiny village of El Chaupi and on to the Ilinizas (see the boxed text 'Climbing the Ilinizas'). The reason to be here is to climb the Ilinizas.

El Chaupi has a phone, a store with minimal supplies, and some hostales nearby.

Places to Stay & Eat
Hostal Casa Nieves (☎ 315 092, 09-582 639, in Quito ☎/fax 02-558 889, info@ecuadortravel .com) is half a kilometer west off the Panamericana and about 2km north of the El Chaupi turnoff. (Coming from Quito, there's

Climbing the Ilinizas

The Ilinizas are two mountains about 25km southwest of Machachi as the condor flies. Iliniza Sur (5248m), Ecuador's sixth-highest peak, is a difficult ice climb for experienced mountaineers with technical equipment. Iliniza Norte (5126m), Ecuador's eighth-highest peak, is a rough scramble that is suitable for fit, acclimatized and experienced hikers.

To reach the Ilinizas, take the unsigned turnoff from the Panamericana to El Chaupi; it's about 8km south of Machachi, and taxi drivers know it. There are hourly buses from Machachi. The road is cobbled for 7km to El Chaupi and continues another 9km as a dirt road to a parking area (identified by a small shrine to the Virgin), which can be reached by hired pickups (ask in the Machachi plaza for Don Tello, who will take you to the parking area for about US$30). Don't drive a rental car and leave it here; break-ins are frequent.

Many climbers elect to stay in one of the several simple accommodations in the El Chaupi area, then continue on foot to the parking area. It may be possible to hire a truck in El Chaupi to take you to the parking area.

From here, it is a three- to four-hour climb to a refuge where you can spend the night. Fit hikers could leave Quito at dawn, catch an early bus from Machachi to El Chaupi and walk hard to reach the refuge by nightfall. Part of the climb is up a steep ramp of volcanic scoria. The bulls you see along the way are bred for the bullring – imagine the strength they attain living up here at 4200m! The locals all tell you ¡Cuidado! (beware).

The refuge is at 4650m, just east of and below a saddle between the two mountains, and has bunks (bring a sleeping bag), cooking facilities, a fireplace (though not much fuel), a guardian and a fee of US$10 per night. A generator provides lighting. Water has to be carried from a nearby stream and purified. You could camp for free, but campsites are exposed to the weather and have no facilities, and you should not leave gear unattended. From the refuge, it is a two- or three-hour climb to Iliniza Norte along a fairly well-defined – but at times narrow, steep and slippery – trail.

a sign; from the south, look for a miniature Eiffel Tower-like structure by the turnoff.) This old farmhouse has a dormitory with bunks for US$9.60 per person, including breakfast. There are two triple rooms with shared bath for US$18 per person and two triple rooms with private bath for US$21.60 per person; the bunks are a better value. Showers are tepid, and some are hotter than others. You can visit the place's Web site at www.ecuadortravel.com. **Tambo Chisinchi** (☎ 315 041) is signed to the east shortly before the El Chaupi turnoff. It's about a kilometer off the Panamericana and has beds at US$7 per person; call ahead.

In El Chaupi, signs point to the Ilinizas and to places to stay. About half a kilometer away on the road to Ilinizas is a new **hostal** (☎ 09-699 068) with four beds (more are planned) and a kitchen; it's owned by Vladimir Gallo, who is also the manager of the Ilinizas climbers' refuge. Unfortunately, there have been several negative reports of Vladimir's entrepreneurial activities, so treat him with caution. However, be aware that he has a long-term contract to manage the Ilinizas refuge; he offers 'discounts' for climbers using his hostal, but be aware that they aren't always discounts. About 3km from El Chaupi on the road to Ilinizas is **Hacienda Nieves** (☎ in Quito 02-330 872, 342 808), which offers day trips from Quito, including horseback riding, for US$45. There is a six-bed cabin with kitchen for US$8 per person; call ahead to arrange accommodations.

Hacienda San José (☎ 09-713 986) is 3km from El Chaupi by another road. Owned by Rodrigo Peralva, who is friendly and helpful, this farm has two cabins with bunks, fireplaces and hot showers. In the main house, there's a kitchen and a sitting room. Maps are available, and the climbers' refuge can be reached in a few hours of walking. Very fit hikers could reach Iliniza Norte (5126m) and return in one long day. When Rodrigo is gone (usually on weekends), he leaves a key with the caretaker behind the house. Rates are US$10 per person, including breakfast when Rodrigo is there. This place has been recommended by climbers.

Getting There & Away

From Machachi, blue-and-white buses signed 'El Chaupi' leave about every hour during the day.

PARQUE NACIONAL COTOPAXI AREA

☎ 03

Established in 1975, the 33,393-hectare Parque Nacional Cotopaxi is mainland Ecuador's most popular and frequently visited national park. That is not to say it is crowded – indeed, it can be almost deserted midweek. Weekends are busier.

The park gives you a good look at the *páramo*. The pine forests on the lower slopes are not Ecuadorian; they are imported trees grown for forestry purposes.

The centerpiece of the park is the beautifully cone-shaped, snowcapped volcano Cotopaxi (5897m), Ecuador's second-highest peak. Present volcanic activity is limited to a few gently smoking fumaroles (the highest in the world) that cannot be seen except by mountaineers who climb up to the icy crater and peer within. There have, however, been many violent eruptions in the past few centuries – three of them wiped out the town of Latacunga. There are also several other peaks within the park, of which Rumiñahui (4712m) is the most important.

The wildlife is unusual and interesting. The Andean condor is present, though rarely seen. More frequently spotted birds include the carunculated caracara (a falcon with a distinctive orange face); the Andean lapwing; the Andean gull (this 'seagull' is at home 4000m above sea level); highland hummingbirds, such as the Andean hillstar and sparkling violetear; the great thrush (a common black thrush with a bright orange bill and feet and yellow eyes); a number of

Climbing Volcán Cotopaxi

duck and shorebird species; and other birds, the names of which are less recognizable to most gringo visitors (eg, cinclodes, solitaires, spinetails, canasteros).

The most frequently seen mammals in the park are white-tailed deer and rabbits. Little red brocket deer are also present; they are only about 35cm high at the shoulder. Their predators are rarely seen, but with luck, you may catch a glimpse of the *colpeo* (Andean fox) or puma. The rare Andean spectacled bear lives in the remote and infrequently visited eastern slopes of the park. Near the park entrance, a captive herd of llamas is being studied.

Although this park has the most well-developed infrastructure of the mainland parks – there are rangers, a small museum and information center, a climbers' refuge and camping and picnicking areas – facilities are basic, and most nonmountaineering visitors come on day trips.

The park entrance fee is US$10 per foreign visitor (US$0.60 for residents), but this doesn't include the overnight refuge fees (US$10) or camping fees (about US$1). Bring US$10 cash, as traveler's checks aren't accepted. Area Nacional de Recreación El Boliche also charges US$10, but the ticket is valid for both Cotopaxi and El Boliche, and it remains valid until you leave. To some extent, the elevated fees for foreign visitors help to fund the costs of running the park. The main problems facing the park are litter, poaching and inadequate staff.

The main entrance gate is open 7 am to 3 pm, but you can leave until about 6:30. Hikers can get in or out anytime, because the 'gate' is only a heavy, padlocked chain. Drivers can usually find a park guard happy to let them through at odd hours for a tip.

Altitude sickness is a very real danger; acclimatize for several days in Quito before attempting to walk in. Do not attempt to visit the park immediately after arriving in the highlands from a low elevation.

Hiking & Climbing

There are excellent hiking and mountaineering possibilities within the park; camping areas are shown on the map, and some places have simple shelters (a roof and walls, but no facilities). Another popular camping place is in the **Area Nacional de Recreación El Boliche**, which abuts the national park to the west. You can camp for a night, or bring plenty of food and hike all the way around Cotopaxi – this takes about a week. Information is available at the entrance booth, and finding these places is straightforward. A popular place to hike is around **Laguna de Limpiopungo**, a large Andean lake at 3880m above sea level, a few kilometers beyond the small museum/information center.

Mountaineers and the curious like to go up to **Refugio José Rivas**, at about 4800m above sea level on the northern slopes of the mountain. Sleeping in the refuge costs US$10; bunk beds and cooking facilities are available, but bring a warm sleeping bag. There is a guardian on duty who can show you where you can leave your gear if you need to do so; bring a padlock. Climbing beyond the refuge requires stamina, experience and snow- and ice-climbing gear; it's not a climb for the beginner, although it is a relatively straightforward climb for those who know what they are doing. See Travel Agencies & Guides under the Ambato section, later in this chapter, for information on hiring mountaineering guides.

Places to Stay

Apart from camping opportunities (see Hiking & Climbing, earlier in this section), there are more comfortable accommodations in the area surrounding the park.

The wonderful *Hacienda San Agustín de Callo* is a few kilometers west of the park and east of the Panamericana via signed dirt roads. Within the hacienda buildings are well-preserved Inca walls; the dining room and the private chapel are almost entirely Inca. These are the most northerly well-preserved remains of the Inca empire (others, farther north, are poorly maintained). After the conquest, the Augustine friars of Quito built a country house here, and the chapel is attributed to them. Several famous expeditions used San Agustín de Callo as a base, including the French Geodesic mission to

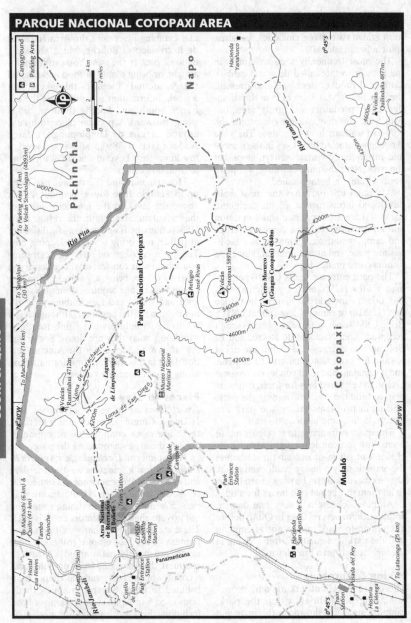

PARQUE NACIONAL COTOPAXI AREA

measure the equator in 1748 and the expeditions of Alexander von Humboldt in 1801 and Edward Whymper in 1880.

In 1921, the hacienda was sold to the Plaza family, who, at once time, owned most of the land between Quito and Cotopaxi. Today, the owner is the warmhearted Mignon Plaza, whose grandfather and uncle were once presidents of Ecuador. She relates interesting stories about the history of the hacienda, and you can eat dinner in the same dining room where Peruvian President Fujimori and Ecuadorian President Mahuad were entertained. In 1998, *National Geographic* funded research on the site, and excavations and investigations are slowly ongoing.

The hacienda has only recently been opened to guests. There are three double rooms and two suites, and a few more rooms are planned – they are currently being excavated. Three bedrooms have some Inca walls. All the rooms have at least two fireplaces, one in the bedroom and one in the bathroom. It gets cold during the night, but the staff always lights both fires, so you can take a hot shower by firelight. A guest sitting room boasts an Inca wall, two fireplaces and superb Cotopaxi views. Rates with all meals and activities – such as horseback riding, mountain biking and fishing – are US$115 per person per day, plus taxes. Day tours can be arranged. Reservations can be made in Quito (☎ 02-242 508, fax 269 884, mplaza@access.net.ec) or at the hacienda (☎/fax 719 160).

The hacienda can arrange transportation from Quito, or travel agencies can drop you off after a Cotopaxi visit. If driving or busing, look for signs on the north side of Lasso; the hacienda is about 5km northeast of the Panamericana on unpaved roads. A truck from Lasso can be hired for about US$2.

A good budget choice is *Cuello de Luna* (☎ 09-700 330, in Quito ☎ 02-242 744, fax 464 939, latitud0@accessinter.net), which is almost 2km west of the Panamericana opposite the Clirsen entrance to the national

Where Have All the Frogs Gone?

In the 1980s, *Atelopus* frogs, which have a distinctive orange belly and black back, were frequently seen around Limpiopungo. In the 1990s, sightings were few and far between. Herpetologists (scientists who study reptiles and amphibians) have noted that a puzzling loss has been occurring in frog and toad species all over the world during the past decade. Amphibians that once were common are now severely depleted in number or are simply no longer found at all. The scientists have been unable to agree upon an explanation for the sudden demise of so many amphibian species in so many different habitats.

One of several theories holds that worldwide air quality has degenerated to the extent that amphibians, which breathe both with primitive lungs and through their perpetually moist skin, are exposed to lethal doses of airborne toxins because of the gas exchange through their skin. Another theory is that frog skin gives little protection against UV light, and that the increasing UV-light levels of recent years have proven deadly to amphibians. Perhaps they are like the canaries that miners once used to warn them of toxic air in the mines. When the canary keeled over, it was time for the miners to get out! Are our dying frogs and toads a symptom of a planet that is becoming too polluted?

park. At 3125m, it is a good place to acclimatize and hike before heading into Cotopaxi. Rates start at US$11 for dorm beds; there are a few singles/doubles/triples with shared hot showers for US$20/26/36 and 16 rooms with private hot shower (many with fireplaces) at US$23/34/45/53 for one/two/three/four people. Breakfast (US$3.50) and other meals (US$6.50 to US$11) are available. Several readers have recommended this pleasant and friendly place.

Some 30km south of Machachi or 20km north of Latacunga is *Hostería La Ciénega* (☎ 719 052, 719 093, fax 719 182, in Quito ☎ 02-549126, 541 337, fax 02-549 126, hcienega@uio.satnet.net, Cordero 1442). This 400-year-old hacienda was converted into a hotel in 1982 and has 16 old rooms with walls several feet thick and colonial or 19th-century furnishings. The restaurant/bar is a popular stopping place for lunch and is often crowded with tour groups. Lunch reservations are advised. A new annex with 18 modern rooms is less attractive, though priced the same. Try to confirm that your reservation is in the original house, and get there early to avoid losing your space. Recently, the surrounding grounds were filled with plastic greenhouses, detracting from the beauty of the setting, though the flower-filled interior courtyard and side chapel remain delightful.

Rates are about US$33 to US$55 for one to three people; all rooms have a private bath, hot water and a heater. There is a huge honeymoon suite for US$77. The hotel is popular and often full, especially on weekends. Service is leisurely – it can take the receptionist half an hour to prepare your bill, and the restaurant is not a fast-food joint. Early morning departures are difficult; if you want to leave earlier than 8 am, skip breakfast and try to settle your bill the day before. The hostería is 1.5km west of the Panamericana and a short distance south of the village of Lasso; there is a sign. Bus drivers will drop you at the sign, and from there you can walk. You can also hire a car or taxi from Quito or Latacunga.

Just before La Ciénega is the newer *La Posada del Rey*, which has a swimming pool and perfectly adequate modern rooms with private baths for around US$20. Less known than La Ciénega, it makes a good cheaper or overflow choice.

Farther south, near Km 75 on the Panamericana, the centuries-old *Hostería San Mateo* (☎ 719 015, fax 719 471, san_mateo@yahoo.com) is in attractive rural surroundings with distant views of Cotopaxi. Five comfortable doubles with private hot bath cost about US$30, and a private cottage costs a little more. The owners are hospitable and run a good restaurant.

Beyond the far east side of the park is the remote *Hacienda Yanahurco*. It has seven rooms with private bath and affords you the opportunity to visit some of the lesser-known eastern slopes of the Andes. Visit the Web site at www.yanahurco.com.ec for more information.

Getting There & Away

You can drive, walk or hitchhike into the park. There are two main roads that lead in from the Panamericana, about 16km and 22km south of Machachi (or roughly 36km and 30km north of Latacunga), respectively. You can ask any Quito-Latacunga bus driver to let you off at either entrance.

The more northerly entrance is shortly after the Panamericana crests its highest point between Quito and Latacunga (at about 3500m). The entrance road has a sign for the park and another for Clirsen Satellite Tracking Station. The road is paved as far as Clirsen (which was previously operated by NASA), about 2km from the Panamericana. Near here is a llama-breeding facility and the Cotopaxi train station, where the Sunday train excursion from Quito stops. From here, the road then becomes dirt and soon passes the Río Daule campsite in Area Nacional de Recreación El Boliche, eventually reaching the entrance station to Cotopaxi; this dirt road is reportedly closed to vehicles, though it makes a good walk. It is about 3km shorter than driving along the road from the more important southerly entrance, which also has a national-park sign. Follow the main dirt roads (also signed) through the entrance point (about 8km or 10km from the Panamericana) to the park museum (about 15km from the Panamericana).

The Limpiopungo area for camping and picnicking is about 4km beyond the park museum, and the refuge is 12km farther. The lake is at 3880m, and the refuge is almost 1000m higher – a hard walk at this altitude if you aren't acclimatized.

On weekends, local tourists visit the park, and there is a good chance of getting a lift. Midweek, the park is almost deserted, and you'll probably end up walking.

Rides in pickups from Latacunga cost about US$20 to US$30, but you should bargain. Mountaineers wishing to reach the refuge must clearly specify that they want to go up the steep dirt road to the parking lot under the refuge at the end of the road. Most pickups will make it; a few can't. You can arrange for the pickup to return for you on a particular day for another US$20 to US$30. It is almost an hour's walk uphill from the parking lot (at 4600m) to the refuge, which looks as if it's about a 10-minute stroll away. This is not flat walking at sea level! Any car will get you into the park to visit the museum, see the llamas and picnic by Limpiopungo (about US$10 from Lasso), where excellent views of the mountain are possible, weather permitting. You could camp here and continue on foot.

It is also possible to reach the park from the north, such as from Machachi or Sangolqui, but you need to hire a vehicle and a guide who knows the route. Many of the major travel agencies in Quito can arrange tours to Cotopaxi, normally via the Panamericana. A day tour including a picnic lunch, driver and bilingual guide will visit the park as far as Limpiopungo but not necessarily as far as the parking lot below the refuge. A two-day tour will combine a day trip to Cotopaxi with an overnight at Hostería La Ciénega (see Around Cotopaxi, later in this chapter) or elsewhere on request and a visit to local Indian markets. Costs depend on the number of people in your group and the agency you book with. Bicycle tours with the Biking Dutchman are also available in Quito.

SAQUISILÍ
☎ 03

For many people, the Thursday morning market of Saquisilí is the main reason for going to Latacunga. Ecuadorian economists consider Saquisilí to have the most important Indian village market in the country, and many travelers rate it as the best they've seen in Ecuador. It is not a tourist-oriented market, although there are the usual few Otavaleño Indians selling their sweaters and weavings. This market is for the inhabitants of remote Indian villages who flood into town to buy or sell everything from bananas to homemade shotguns and from herbal remedies to strings of piglets. The majority of the Indians from the area wear little felt porkpie hats and red ponchos.

There are eight different plazas, each of which sell specific goods. Especially interesting is the animal market, a cacophonous affair, with screaming pigs playing a major role. Cattle, sheep and a few llamas are also common. The animal market is almost a kilometer out of town – go early and ask for directions.

Along with the travelers, there are thieves – one scenario is that a woman and child stumbles in front of an unsuspecting person, and in the ensuing apologies and confusion, another woman lifts a wallet using her long poncho as a cover for her activities.

The bus from Latacunga drops you off near the Plaza La Concordia, with its many trees surrounded by an iron railing. On Thursday, this becomes a market plaza.

Places to Stay & Eat
On the Plaza La Concordia, at Bolívar and Sucre, near where the bus drops you off, is the rundown *Pensión Chavela* and, reportedly, a new and cheap hotel. It is likely to be full the night before the market, and most travelers find it best to stay in Latacunga; the bus service begins at dawn, so you won't miss anything.

The German-run *Hostería Rancho Muller* (☎ 721 380, fax 721 103) is on the outskirts of town. Rates for clean, plain rooms with bath start at US$15, and the owner helps with your local arrangements. There is also a slightly pricey international restaurant; it has the best food in town.

Otherwise, there are no restaurants, but there are plenty of hole-in-the-wall places to eat. One plaza seems to be nothing but food stalls – if you stick to cooked food and don't have a delicate stomach, you'll enjoy it.

Getting There & Away

There are buses returning to Latacunga several times an hour after the market; there are also trucks and buses going to many of the remote villages farther west, such as Sigchos and Chugchilán. On market day and sporadically on other days, slow and crowded old buses go directly to and from Quito (US$1.50, two to three hours). Buses leave from near Plaza La Concordia, more or less from where you arrived.

People unwilling to travel by public transportation can hire a taxi in Quito (about US$40 for a half day, allowing a couple of hours at the market) or from Latacunga. The bigger tour companies organize one- or two-day tours to Saquisilí and other places. Overnights are usually at La Ciénega (see Around Cotopaxi, earlier).

LATACUNGA
☎ 03

The drive from Quito to Latacunga is magnificent in clear weather. Like a mammoth ice-cream cone, Cotopaxi looms to the left of the Panamericana as you travel south, and the two Ilinizas, also snowcapped, are on your right. Several other peaks are visible during the 90km drive, including distant Chimborazo if you are lucky. On exceptionally clear days, nine of Ecuador's 10 highest peaks can be seen.

Latacunga (population 54,000, elevation 2800m) is the capital of Cotopaxi Province. Although not an exciting town, it has an interesting history and is a good base for several excellent excursions. The town's name originates from the Indian words *llacta cunani*, which translate rather charmingly into 'land of my choice.' It became an important colonial center immediately after the conquest, but today, there is little evidence of its long and varied history.

Cotopaxi, which dominates the town on a clear day, erupted violently in 1742 and destroyed the town, which was rebuilt. Another eruption 26 years later wiped it out again, but the indomitable (or foolhardy) survivors rebuilt it a second time. An immense eruption in 1877 destroyed it a third time, and yet again it was rebuilt on the same site. At present, the volcano's activity is minor, and it is unlikely that an eruption will occur within the next several years.

Information

There is no tourist office, but some hotels provide local tours, guides and information. Filanbanco, on Quito near Guayaquil, has a Visa ATM. Banco Popular has a MasterCard ATM, and Banco del Austro and Banco de Pichincha change money; all three are near Parque Vicente León.

Andinatel and the post office are on Quevedo near Maldonado. Expensive Internet connections can be made from a place on the pedestrian mall off Parque Vicente León.

The town closes down early, and most restaurants stop serving by 8 or 9 pm.

Things to See

Latacunga is a good center for excursions to Cotopaxi (see earlier) and to the nearby villages that are described at the end of this section. In the town itself, there is little to see, partly because most historic buildings have been wiped out by volcanic eruptions. A small ethnography and art museum, Molinos de Monserrat, is run by the Casa de la Cultura Ecuatoriana; it is on Vela near Maldonado and is open Tuesday to Saturday (hours are changeable).

There are several plazas – Parque Vicente León is the most attractive, with its well-tended garden and topiary work. At the southeast corner of this plaza is the town hall, topped by a pair of stone condors, and on the south side is the cathedral. Behind the cathedral is a little arcade (Pasaje Catedral) that includes an art gallery. Many of the buildings are light gray and have been built from local volcanic rock.

Near the south end of town on Quevedo is an old hospital that is a historic landmark. The modern hospital is a block away.

Special Events

Latacunga's major annual fiesta is La Virgen de las Mercedes, held September 23 and 24. This is more popularly known as the Fiesta de la Mamá Negra, and there are processions, costumes, street dancing, Andean music and fireworks. This is one of those festivals that, although outwardly Christian, has much pagan Indian influence and is well worth seeing. A big parade in honor of La Mamá Negra is held during the Independence of Latacunga, which is celebrated on November 11 with parades and a bullfight.

There is also a weekly market Saturday and a smaller one Tuesday. The markets are colorful and fun but of no special interest, although a few crafts are sold, especially the small string bags known as *shigras*.

Places to Stay

Many people stay in Latacunga Wednesday nights for the Thursday-morning Indian market at Saquisilí. Hotels are often full by mid-afternoon Wednesday, so try to get

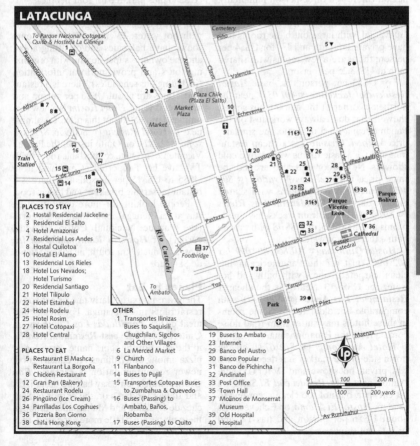

LATACUNGA

PLACES TO STAY
2   Hostal Residencial Jackeline
3   Residencial El Salto
4   Hotel Amazonas
7   Residencial Los Andes
8   Hostal Quilotoa
10 Hostal El Alamo
13 Residencial Los Rieles
18 Hotel Los Nevados;
    Hotel Turismo
20 Residencial Santiago
21 Hotel Tilipulo
22 Hotel Estambul
24 Hotel Rodelu
25 Hotel Rosim
27 Hotel Cotopaxi
28 Hotel Central

PLACES TO EAT
5   Restaurant El Mashca;
    Restaurant La Borgoña
8   Chicken Restaurant
12 Gran Pan (Bakery)
24 Restaurant Rodelu
26 Pingüino (Ice Cream)
34 Parrilladas Los Copihues
36 Pizzería Bon Giorno
38 Chifa Hong Kong

OTHER
1   Transportes Ilinizas
    Buses to Saquisilí,
    Chugchilan, Sigchos
    and Other Villages
6   La Merced Market
9   Church
11 Filanbanco
14 Buses to Pujilí
15 Transportes Cotopaxi Buses
    to Zumbahua & Quevedo
16 Buses (Passing) to
    Ambato, Baños,
    Riobamba
17 Buses (Passing) to Quito
19 Buses to Ambato
23 Internet
29 Banco del Austro
30 Banco Popular
31 Banco de Pichincha
32 Andinatel
33 Post Office
35 Town Hall
37 Molinos de Monserrat
    Museum
39 Old Hospital
40 Hospital

SOUTH OF QUITO

there early if you're arriving on that day; prices may be a little higher then. Prices can double during the hugely popular Fiesta de la Mamá Negra and seem to vary tremendously from day to day, so the following is just a rough guide. It's worth bargaining for the best rates.

A recommended budget hotel with large clean rooms and hot water in communal showers is the friendly *Hotel Estambul* (☎ *800 354, 801 293, Quevedo 6-46*). Rooms cost about US$4 per person, or US$5.50 with private bath. The hotel also arranges tours to Cotopaxi for about US$20 per person (there is a three-person minimum). Also good is the helpful *Residencial Santiago* (☎ *800 899, 802 164*), at 2 de Mayo and Guayaquil, with large but basic rooms that have private hot bath and TV for US$4 per person; there are a few rooms with shared bath at US$3.25 per person.

For US$3 per person, the basic *Hostal Residencial Jackeline* (☎ *801 033*), near the northeast corner of the market, has shared showers that don't always work. Just off the Panamericana on 5 de Junio, the similarly priced *Hotel Turismo* has a cheap restaurant and very basic rooms with shared cold showers. Next door and also around the same price is *Hotel Los Nevados* (☎ *800 407*), which has basic rooms with shared electric showers. *Residencial Los Rieles* (☎ *801 254*), by the train tracks, has simple rooms at US$3.50/5, or US$7/8 with private bath – there is hot water.

Hostal Quilotoa (☎ *801 866, 800 099, fax 802 090*), just off the Panamericana, has clean, carpeted rooms with bath and hot water for US$8/13. Nearby is the cheaper *Residencial Los Andes* (☎ *800 933*), with comparable but older rooms. Some rooms in these hotels may suffer from road noise coming from the Panamericana.

Hotel Amazonas (☎ *812 673*), on the north side of the market, has decent rooms with private hot shower and TV for US$7/13. Almost next door, *Residencial El Salto* is a bit cheaper, but not too clean according to readers. *Hostal El Alamo*, on Echeverría, is about US$6 per person and has TV and private hot showers.

Hotel Cotopaxi (☎ *801 310*), on the northeastern corner of Parque Vicente León, used to be Latacunga's best hotel but has been eclipsed by several better ones. On a recent visit, it was full of climbers and backpackers. Rates are US$5.50 per person in old but adequate rooms with private bath and hot water. Some of the rooms have pretty views of the park, but they may be a little noisy. There is a simple restaurant. Around the corner, the similarly priced and friendly *Hotel Central* (☎ *802 912*) has clean rooms with hot water. There is a restaurant, and day tours to Cotopaxi are offered (US$80 plus park fee for four people).

Hotel Tilipulo (☎ *802 130*), at Guayaquil and Quevedo, has clean, good-sized rooms with hot water, TV and telephone. Some rooms have balconies and/or sitting areas, and the owner is super helpful with organizing tours and providing local information (including bus schedules). There is a restaurant. Rates are about US$6 per person and are a good value. *Hotel Rosim* is a new recommendation at about this price. It's almost next to *Hotel Rodelu* (☎ *800 956, 811 264, ☎/fax 812 341*), on Quito just off the Parque Vicente León. Quite comfortable rooms with TV have been reported as anything from US$5 to US$15 per person, and there is a restaurant serving breakfast and Italian food.

People looking for more comfort often stay at La Ciénega, about 20km to the north (see Parque Nacional Cotopaxi Area, earlier), or *Hostería Rumipamba de las Rosas*, about 13km south, near San Miguel de Salcedo.

Places to Eat

There are no particularly fine or expensive restaurants in Latacunga. For steaks and meat dishes, *Parrilladas Los Copihues*, on Quito, is one of the best. *Restaurant Rodelu*, in the hotel of the same name, serves great pizza among other things. An equally good, newer recommendation is *Pizzería Bon Giorno*, which some say has the best pizzas and Italian food; it's on the corner of Sanchez de Orellana and Maldonado. Although these places are a little more expensive, they certainly won't break the bank.

For those on a tight budget, reasonable choices are **Restaurant La Borgoña** for simple Ecuadorian food and **Restaurant El Mashca** for grilled chicken; they are near each other on Valencia. Also cheap and good, **Chifa Hong Kong**, on Amazonas, does Chinese. **Pingüino**, on Quito, is the place to go for ice cream, and the bakery **Gran Pan**, on the corner of Guayaquil and Quito, is good for bread for picnics.

Many restaurants close by 8 pm during the week. **Chicken restaurants** on the Panamericana are open late. It's hard to find a restaurant for early breakfasts, unless you eat in one of the better hotels.

The Latacunga area is famous for its *allullas*, which are sold by local women at every bus stop or checkpoint. The women's high-pitched cries of *'Aziuuuuzia!'* become quite familiar. Allullas are rather dry biscuits made of flour, pork fat and a local unpasteurized cheese, and unfortunately, they taste no better than they sound.

Getting There & Away

Air There is a Latacunga airport, but it is not used for regularly scheduled flights. On rare occasions, a plane may be diverted here if it cannot land at Quito.

Bus There is no main bus terminal in Latacunga. Long-distance buses from Quito usually drop you on the Panamericana at Avenida 5 de Junio before continuing on to Ambato. However, this stretch of the Panamericana was recently under repair, and buses were using Subia, to the west. The 5 de Junio area is a good place to stand to catch any northbound or southbound buses; they pass every few minutes. Ask locals for the best place to wait. Flagging down a bus may be difficult on holiday weekends, as many buses are full and tend to do the Quito-Ambato-Riobamba run without picking up passengers at Latacunga. Be patient, and avoid leaving town on holiday weekends.

Slower buses leave from Quito's terminal direct for Latacunga. The bus stop for Quito-bound buses originating in Latacunga is in the Plaza Chile (also popularly known as Plaza El Salto). There is also a bus stop on the Panamericana (or Subia) just south of 5 de Junio for buses originating in Latacunga and going to Ambato. Quito (US$1.30) is about two hours away; Ambato is one hour; Riobamba is 2¼ hours.

Just half a block from the Panamericana on Avenida 5 de Junio is the bus stop for westbound buses. The road is paved as far as Pujilí, beyond which it deteriorates. This is one of the roughest, least-traveled and perhaps most spectacular bus routes joining the highlands with the western lowlands. If you're not pressed for time and don't mind the discomfort, riding a beat-up, crowded old bus on this dirt road may be the most interesting way of leaving the highlands. The bus climbs to Zumbahua, at 3500m (US$1.50, two hours), and then drops to Quevedo (US$3.30, 4½ hours), at only 150m above sea level. Transportes Cotopaxi runs this route, with departures every two hours all day long. Buy tickets on the bus. Near here, Transportes 14 de Octubre has a departure around 10 am for Zumbahua, Quilotoa and Chugchilán, but only Friday and Saturday. You can also find daily buses with Transportes Ilinizas to Saquisilí, Chugchilán, Sigchos and other villages on Benavídez north of the market. They leave at about 11 am.

The buses most frequently used by travelers are the one to Saquisilí (US$0.25, 30 minutes). Departures are every few minutes on market-day mornings, and every hour or so at other times. The buses leave from Benavídez one long block north of the market. Buses departing for various other nearby villages leave from this street or from the Plaza Chile; ask around. The bus for the village of Pujilí leaves at frequent intervals from Subia and 5 de Junio, a block west of the Panamericana.

Train The train station is on the west side of the Panamericana, 1km from the town center. The Riobamba-Quito train passes through Latacunga about three hours after leaving Riobamba or two hours after leaving Quito; see those towns for further details.

Taxi Plaza Chile (Plaza El Salto) is the place to go to hire taxis and pickup trucks for visits to Parque Nacional Cotopaxi and remote villages (pickups double as taxis on many of the rough roads in the highlands). Rates depend on your bargaining ability.

WEST OF LATACUNGA
☎ 03

The following circuit gives the adventurous traveler a close look at Andean life in some of the remote villages west of Latacunga. Public transportation is infrequent but available – be prepared for extremely crowded buses (or you can ride on the roof if the weather permits). All these places have basic accommodations. You can do this circuit in reverse with no problem.

The scenery around all the areas described in this section is quite splendid, and the Andean Indian inhabitants are somewhat withdrawn and not used to seeing strangers, although they are friendly and helpful once the ice has been broken, especially if you speak Spanish (though many of the Indians speak only Quichua). Transportation cannot be relied upon, and you may have to walk for long distances or wait for hours, so always carry warm clothes, a water bottle, some snacks and maybe even a sleeping bag. Hiring a car is an option, but it limits your contact with the locals. The area is photogenic, but please don't be obnoxious with your camera. The people are not keen on being photographed by strangers.

Pujilí

This village, with an elevation of 2900m, is 10km west of Latacunga and is easily visited by frequent public buses. It has a basic cheap hotel just off the main plaza and a couple of simple restaurants. The main market day is Sunday, and there is a smaller market Wednesday. All Souls' Day festivities (November 2) are quite traditional, as are the Corpus Christi celebrations (a movable date in June), when the colorful *El Danzante* festival takes place and dancers parade around on stilts wearing costumes.

Zumbahua & Tigua

Some 57km farther west, the tiny village of Zumbahua (3500m) has an unspoiled, interesting local market Saturday. Inhabitants often use llamas to transport goods to and from the market. There is traditional Andean music, dancing and heavy drinking Friday night, which spills over to market day – this is not a tourist event. There are a few small and very basic residenciales that fill up fast Friday, so get there early. The best is *Condor Matzi*, named after a peak to the south that is so steep that, locals say, only condors can reach the top. Simple rooms are about US$4 per person, and electric showers, meals and local guides are available. Buses from Latacunga leave several times a day. Buses from Zumbahua to either Latacunga or Quevedo run until about dusk.

Some 15km east of Zumbahua is Tigua (no services), a community known for the bright paintings of Andean life that are locally made on sheepskin canvases mounted on wood frames. Originally used to decorate drum skins, this indigenous art form is now known beyond the Tigua region but still takes its name from the village. At Km 53 on the Latacunga-Zumbahua road, you'll find the paintings of Alfredo Toaquiza, whose father, Julio, was a progenitor of the Tigua art form. Several other family members are involved in Tigua art, as is Humberto Latacunga (see Laguna Quilotoa, next). The paintings are sold in Quito, but prices are better in Tigua and in the village of Quilotoa.

Laguna Quilotoa

About 14km north of Zumbahua is the famous volcanic crater lake of Quilotoa. From the top of the crater, there are beautiful views of the green lake below and the snowcapped Cotopaxi and Iliniza Sur (5248m) in the distance. The lake has no inflow or outlet, and the water is very alkaline and impossible to drink. A recent expedition measured it at a depth of 250m, and although evaporation is slowly exceeding precipitation, the lake won't dry up anytime soon.

On the southwest side of the crater lake is the tiny village of Quilotoa. *Hostal Cabañas Quilotoa* is operated by artist Humberto Latacunga, who first settled the area around

SOUTH OF QUITO

1990; the place sleeps up to 40 people (about US$3 per person) in basic dorm rooms (private rooms are planned). Blankets are provided, but not linen. There's a fireplace, latrines and an electric shower; meals are available on occasion, including *cuy* (guinea pig). You can hire a mule or guide to visit the lake or other areas. Performances of Andean music and dancing can be arranged for groups, and Humberto's Tigua landscapes can be purchased at reasonable prices.

In 1999, a daily bus from Latacunga – via Pujilí, Zumbahua and Quilotoa – to Chugchilán began operating (see Getting There & Away under Latacunga, earlier). It passes at around 2 or 3 pm en route to Chugchilán and at around 6 am en route from Chugchilán to Latacunga. There is crowded transportation from Zumbahua after the Saturday market. You can hire a taxi in Latacunga or a truck or van in Zumbahua. It's about a four-hour walk from Zumbahua along the unpaved road, but carry water, as none is available.

Chugchilán

Continuing another 22km north of the lake on a terrible road, you reach the small village of Chugchilán, which at 3200m is surrounded by wild Andean scenery. In town, you can stay in *Pensión Popular*, which is extremely basic and run by the local priest, mainly for local indigenous travelers with little money. A small step up is the cold-water *Pensión La Dolorosa*, which translates as 'the painful pension' and has four beds. Much better is the friendly, locally run *Casa Mama Hilda*, on the northern edge of town, which has 10 beds and a shared hot shower for about US$2.50 per person, plus US$1.50 for a simple meal. This place is recommended by shoestring travelers.

If you have a few more dollars and you are interested in ecotourism, the best place is *Black Sheep Inn* (☎ 814 587, blksheep@ interactive.net.ec), barely a kilometer north of town on the road to Sigchos. Owned by a North American couple who have lived there since 1994, it's a simple but friendly

Hiking from Laguna Quilotoa to Chugchilán

It takes about four to five hours to hike around the rim of Laguna Quilotoa, at about 3850m above sea level. The lake itself is about 400m below the rim, and steep trails will take you down to the water in about 30 minutes – allow an hour to climb back up. From the parking area by the village, look for a precipitous cut to the left, which leads down to these trails.

A good hike is from Quilotoa to Chugchilán, which takes five hours with breaks. From the parking area, look left across the crater for the lowest, widest and biggest sandy spot, about a quarter of the way around. You will walk 45 to 60 minutes to that spot. As you walk around the rim, it is the third low sandy spot. The most common mistake is to leave the crater's rim too early, which is why you should identify the low sandy spot before starting the hike.

From the low sandy spot, looking just west of north, you can see the village of Huayama and, across a canyon, Chugchilán beyond. Follow a row of eucalyptus trees down and head toward Huayama. Eventually, you'll walk along or cross the road to Huayama (go to Huayama and not Huayama Grande, which is actually smaller). In Huayama, you may be able to buy a drink if you ask.

Huayama to Chugchilán is about two more hours. Leaving Huayama, walk past the cemetery. The first right is next to the cemetery. The second right goes to a small house. The third right follows the top of a gully. Don't drop into the gully; follow the path above it. After 15 to 20 minutes, you'll reach the edge of the canyon. A tunnel-like trail leads all the way to Chugchilán. You'll cross two footbridges as you drop down a narrow switchback trail. Cross a cement footbridge over the Río Sihui and then climb to Chugchilán for about an hour.

– Directions courtesy of Black Sheep Inn

place that practices high-altitude perma-culture and has composting toilets, an organic vegetable garden and a combina-tion chicken/greenhouse for fresh eggs and salads. Meals are mainly vegetarian (eggs aren't quite veggies, but that's about as far as it goes) and are good. The inn provides local tourist information (especially for hikers) and arranges horseback-riding trips with local people (US$10 for a half day) and jeep trips. There is a good collection of music of most genres and a lending library. Free pu-rified water is always available for a cold drink or hot tea/coffee. Animal lovers will find three large but friendly dogs, a cat, sev-eral chickens and ducks, a few llamas and, of course, some black sheep. It's a good place to unwind for a few days if you are seeking a simple, tranquil Andean setting (although you can send emails if you need to).

Rates are US$17 per person in a bunk-house sleeping eight, or US$34/40/57/72 for singles/doubles/triples/quads. All bathrooms are shared and have hot showers. Rates include breakfast and dinner, and small dis-counts for longer stays, students, seniors and SAE members are given, but credit cards are not accepted. The inn has a Web site at www.blacksheepinn.com.

Sigchos
This bigger village is 23km north of Chug-chilán, or 52km west of Saquisilí; it has an elevation of 2800m. There are a couple of basic places to stay and a small Sunday market. The best hotel is the four-story building above a store called **Comercial Gomez**, half a block from the bus stop; it charges US$1.50 per person and reportedly has a hot shower. There is also the cheaper **La Casa Campesino**.

Getting There & Away From Latacunga, there are several buses a day to Sigchos. One bus leaves at 10:30 am from Latacunga with Empresa La Iliniza to Chugchilán (four hours), passing through Sigchos at about 12:30 pm. On Thursday, you need to catch this bus in Saquisilí. The same bus leaves Chugchilán for Latacunga at 3 am daily except Sunday, when it leaves at 4 am.

Buses from Sigchos return to Latacunga several times a day; the last bus is at 2:30 pm.

Buses from Latacunga leave at least every two hours during the day for Zum-bahua. Return buses leave during the day about every two hours. Note that not all buses go into Zumbahua; some drop you off on the Latacunga-Quevedo road, and you have to walk about 2km into Zumbahua.

The stretch between Zumbahua and Chugchilán (and back), via Quilotoa, is served by buses Wednesday to Sunday. The most frequent schedules are Saturday and Sunday, when there are two or three buses, mainly in the morning. Wednesday to Friday see very early morning departures. Monday and Tuesday have little, if any, transporta-tion. This is a remote region; ask locally for updates and schedules.

SAN MIGUEL DE SALCEDO
☎ 03
This small town, usually called Salcedo, is 14km south of Latacunga on the Panameri-cana. It has a Sunday market and a lesser market Thursday. In mid-March, it hosts an important Agricultural and Industrial Fair, and there's a big fiesta around November 1. Otherwise, it's of little interest except to ice-cream aficionados, who say that Salcedo has some of the best ice cream in the area.

Places to Stay & Eat
There are a couple of cheap and basic hotels in the town center. On the northern out-skirts of town is **Hostería Rumibamba de las Rosas** (☎ 726 128, 726 306, 727 309, fax 727 103), a fairly modern hotel with com-fortable 'log cabin' bungalows furnished with antiques. There is a small private zoo, a duck pond, pony rides (and a saddled llama for children), a swimming pool, tennis courts and game rooms. The whole place has a Disneyland atmosphere. It's rather corny, but it's clean and well run, and the management is very friendly and anxious to please. Rooms are about US$50 for a double. The hostería's restaurant and bar are very good and are popular with Ecuadorians on family outings.

AMBATO
☎ 03

Some 47km south of Latacunga (136km south of Quito) is the important town of Ambato, the capital of Tungurahua Province. It was badly damaged in a 1949 earthquake, but a modern city was soon rebuilt. It is prosperous and growing and has a population of about 175,000. Its altitude is 2800m above sea level.

The city is proud of its cultural heritage, and nicknames itself 'Tierra de Los Tres Juanes' (Land of the Three Juans). The 'three Juans' were writers Juan Montalvo and Juan León Mera (see Arts, in the Facts about Ecuador chapter), and lawyer/journalist Juan Benigno Malo. All three are immortalized in Ambato's parks, museums and buildings.

Apart from the festivals described under Special Events in this section, later, most travelers just pass through Ambato on their way to Baños, which is one of the more popular destinations in the country. However, since the volcano Tungurahua started erupting in October 1999, many visitors use Ambato as a base for seeing the eruptions, as Baños is currently unsafe. Note that the downtown area is in a bowl surrounded by a loop of Río Ambato, and Tungurahua cannot be seen from there; however, climbing above the center (see the southeastern part of the Ambato map) will bring you high enough for volcano views. Don't bring an expensive camera – some of the streets aren't very safe.

The Monday market is a huge affair – the biggest in Ecuador.

Information
Tourist Offices This office (☎ 821 800), by Hotel Ambato, on Guayaquil and Rocafuerte, is open 8:30 am to noon and 2 to 5 pm weekdays. City maps are for sale here and in local bookshops.

Money Cambiato (☎ 821 008), Bolívar 686, will change both US traveler's checks and cash at rates close to those in Quito. Several banks (see the Ambato map) change foreign currency, but Cambiato is quicker. Filanbanco has a Visa ATM.

Post & Communications Andinatel and the post office are both on Castillo by Parque Juan Montalvo.

Ciudad Andina (☎ 822 242), Castillo 528, offers Internet connections 9 am to 1 pm and 3 to 8 pm weekdays, 9am to 1 pm and 3 to 6 pm Saturday, and 9 am to 1 pm Sunday. You can also use the Internet at Casa de Cultura until 7 pm weekdays, as well as in the Colegio Bolívar (next to Museo de Ciencias Naturales) from 8:30 am to 12:30 pm and 2:30 to 6:30 pm weekdays.

Travel Agencies & Guides Travel and 1st-class tour arrangements can be made at Metropolitan Touring (☎/fax 824 084), Rocafuerte 1401, near Montalvo; this company has a head office in Quito.

A recommended adventure-tour operator is Surtrek, just over 2km south of the city center, in La Casa Blanca (see Places to Stay, later). German, English and Spanish are spoken – ask for Frank Alte. Climbing equipment for clients is rented out, Aseguim-certified mountaineering guides for climbing the local snow peaks are provided, and trips to the new Parque Nacional Llanganates (see Around Ambato, later) and to difficult-to-reach volcanoes such as Sangay and Reventador are arranged. Trips range from one to eight days, and costs are at their best value for groups of three or more.

Since Volcán Tungurahua became active, various new outfitters in Ambato arrange day and overnight tours to ridges with campsites that have good views of the volcano. Ask around in Ambato; your hotel or the tourist office would be a good place to start.

Things to See
Las Quintas Because of reconstruction since the 1949 earthquake, most of the buildings in the center are new and of no great interest. A recommended walk is along Bolívar, southwest of the center, to the pleasant modern suburb of Miraflores, on the banks of Río Ambato (note that Calle Bolívar changes into Avenida Miraflores). The river can be crossed about 2km away from town on Avenida Los Guaytambos,

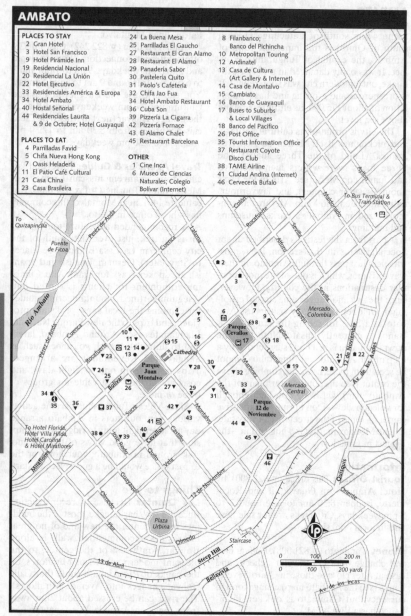

AMBATO

PLACES TO STAY
2 Gran Hotel
3 Hotel San Francisco
9 Hotel Pirámide Inn
19 Residencial Nacional
20 Residencial La Unión
22 Hotel Ejecutivo
33 Residenciales América & Europa
34 Hotel Ambato
40 Hostal Señorial
44 Residenciales Laurita
     & 9 de Octubre; Hotel Guayaquil

PLACES TO EAT
4 Parrilladas Favid
5 Chifa Nueva Hong Kong
7 Oasis Heladería
11 El Patio Café Cultural
21 Casa China
23 Casa Brasileira

24 La Buena Mesa
25 Parrilladas El Gaucho
27 Restaurant El Gran Alamo
28 Restaurant El Alamo
29 Panadería Sabor
30 Pastelería Quito
31 Paolo's Cafetería
32 Chifa Jao Fua
34 Hotel Ambato Restaurant
36 Cuba Son
39 Pizzería La Cigarra
42 Pizzería Fornace
43 El Alamo Chalet
45 Restaurant Barcelona

OTHER
1 Cine Inca
6 Museo de Ciencias
    Naturales; Colegio
    Bolívar (Internet)

8 Filanbanco;
    Banco del Pichincha
10 Metropolitan Touring
12 Andinatel
13 Casa de Cultura
     (Art Gallery & Internet)
14 Casa de Montalvo
15 Cambiato
16 Banco de Guayaquil
17 Buses to Suburbs
     & Local Villages
18 Banco del Pacífico
26 Post Office
35 Tourist Information Office
37 Restaurant Coyote
     Disco Club
38 TAME Airline
41 Ciudad Andina (Internet)
46 Cervecería Bufalo

which soon leads to **La Quinta de Juan Montalvo**, where that writer's villa stands (*quinta* means country house). It's in the suburb of Ficoa and can be visited 9 am to noon and 2 to 6 pm.

Several other famous Ambateños had country houses that survived the earthquake and are worth visiting; call ☎ 821 024 for information. **La Quinta de Juan León Mera** can be visited 9 am to noon and 2 to 6 pm. The house is set in an attractive botanical garden on Avenida Los Capulíes, in the suburb of Atocha. Close by is **La Quinta de la Liria**, the country home of the mountaineer Nicolás Martínez; this quinta is also set in a pleasant garden. Next to this home, **Centro Cultural de la Liria** was built in 1995 and contains an art museum and photography gallery of old and new photographs of Ambato.

The suburb of Atocha is on the far side of Río Ambato, about 2km northeast of the city center. It can be reached on foot by walking northwest out of town on Montalvo, which soon crosses the river, and then by turning right on Capulíes, about 200m beyond the river. La Quinta de Juan León Mera is about 1.5km to the northeast, and La Quinta de la Liria just beyond it. Local buses and taxis go to all these places.

Museo de Ciencias Naturales This natural-history museum (☎ 827 395) is in the Colegio Bolívar, on Sucre and Lalama, on the northwest side of the Parque Cevallos. There are hundreds of stuffed birds, mammals and reptiles; some are quite well done, but others are rather ratty. In the absence of comprehensive field guides to Ecuadorian wildlife, this is a good museum to visit if you wish to identify species you may have seen in the wild. There's also a rather gruesome display of freaks, such as two-headed calves and six-legged lambs.

Apart from the natural history, particularly enjoyable is the fine display of photographs taken around 1910 by Nicolás Martínez (see Las Quintas, earlier), who lived in Ambato. There are street and countryside scenes, as well as photographs of early mountaineering expeditions and Co-

topaxi in eruption. Museum curator Señor Héctor Vásquez is also a mountaineer, with ascents of the highest peaks of Argentina, Peru and Ecuador to his credit. He is knowledgeable and helpful, but is not always at the museum. Other displays include a fine geological collection of carefully labeled rocks and semi-precious stones, an archaeological collection with Inca pieces, traditional Ecuadorian clothing, a numismatic collection and other displays.

Entrance is US$2, and hours are 8:30 am to 12:30 pm and 2:30 to 6:30 pm weekdays.

Parque Juan Montalvo This attractive park features a statue of Montalvo and is Ambato's most important plaza. On the northwest side of the plaza, you can visit his house, **Casa de Montalvo** (☎ 821 024), which has some of his original manuscripts, as well as photos of old Ambato. The house is open 9 am to noon and 2 to 6 pm weekdays and 10 am to 1 pm Saturday; admission costs US$0.40. Next door is **Casa de Cultura** (☎ 820 338, 824 248), which has an art gallery and Internet café. Hours are 8 am to noon and 2 to 7 pm; admission is free. On the northeast side of this plaza is the modern and rather bleak **cathedral**, which has some good stained-glass windows.

The Market The huge weekly market is held Monday, and there are smaller ones Wednesday and Friday. Established in 1861, the Monday market is the largest city market in the country. Although it has been modernized (it takes place in buildings rather than outdoors), it is still a huge, bustling affair, attracting Indians from many nearby communities. The main spot for produce is the modern Mercado Central, at the southeastern end of Lalama, but there are many other markets scattered around town and in the suburbs (these are generally not aimed at tourists). Walking along Cevallos will bring you past Mercado Colombia (also called Modelo), and as you go farther northeast along Cevallos, you will pass some stalls selling local handicrafts – the best area is about 10 blocks from the center. As always, watch for pickpockets.

Special Events

Ambato is famous for its annual Fiesta de Frutas y Flores, which is supposed to co-incide with Carnaval but is usually held during the last two weeks in February. Hotels tend to be full at this time, so plan ahead. The festival's 50th anniversary will be in 2001. Apart from fruit and flower shows, the festivities include bullfights, parades, late-night street dancing and general fun. Travelers unable to find suitable accommodations during this time should look for rooms in Latacunga, Baños or Riobamba and take the one-hour bus journey into Ambato.

It is worth noting that Carnaval – held nationwide in the week before the beginning of Lent – is unique in Ambato in that the traditional 'sport' of water-throwing has been banned throughout the city. (Enterprising fiesta-goers may use foam instead.)

Places to Stay

Budget The place for basic, cheap hotels is around Parque 12 de Noviembre and Mercado Central. For about US$2, you can stay at *Residencial Laurita* (☎ 821 377, Mera 333), which is basic but adequate and has hot water. The cheapest rooms are on the top floor, with bathrooms below. The similar *Hotel Guayaquil* (☎ 821 194, 823 886, Mera 311), is a few doors away and is also OK. *Residencial 9 de Octubre* (☎ 820 018, Mera 325) has cold water, even though rooms also cost about US$2. There are several other very basic and rather grungy hotels in the US$2 to US$3 price range in this general area.

For about a US$2.50 per person, you can stay in *Residencial América* (Vela 737), which has shared hot showers and is reasonably clean and friendly. Next door is the similarly priced *Residencial Europa*, which claims to have hot water but sometimes doesn't. *Residencial Nacional* (☎ 823 820), on the corner of Vela and Lalama, charges US$2.75 and has hot water in the morning – sometimes. *Residencial La Unión* (☎ 824 215), on the corner of Espejo and 12 de Noviembre, is also OK and has hot water.

Hotel San Francisco (☎ 821 739, 840 148, 821 064, Egüez 837) is quite clean and

friendly. Reasonably large rooms with private hot bath cost US$4.50 per person. *Hotel Ejecutivo* (☎ 840 370, 825 866, fax 825 506, 12 de Noviembre 1230) has reasonable rooms with shared hot baths for about US$3 per person, or dark, small rooms with private bath, TV and telephone for US$7/11 singles/doubles.

La Casa Blanca (☎ 844 448, fax 844 512, adventures@ecuaworld.com, Cordero 2-10), near Los Shyris, is 2km from the center and a bit hard to find. This is the headquarters of Surtrek (see Travel Agencies & Guides, earlier in this section) and provides simple but clean hostal-style accommodations with shared hot showers, kitchen privileges, an outdoor terrace, and indoor fireplace and expedition planning. Rates are US$7/10, including breakfast; there are discounts for stays of a week or more.

Mid-Range Rooms at *Hotel Pirámide Inn* (☎ 842 092, fax 854 358), on the corner of Cevallos and Egüez, are US$10/16. Each room has one bed, decent carpeting, bath, a telephone and cable TV; it seems like a fair value.

Gran Hotel (☎ 824 119, ☎/fax 824 235), at Lalama and Rocafuerte, has carpeted rooms with private hot bath, telephone and TV for about US$11/16. A restaurant and parking are available. *Hostal Señorial* (☎ 825 124, 826 249, fax 829 536), on the corner of Cevallos and Quito, has 14 clean, carpeted rooms with bath, telephone and cable TV for US$12/18.

Out on Avenida Miraflores, in the suburb of the same name, are four quiet and pleasant hotels, all of which have been recommended. They all have restaurants (with limited menus or set meals) and double rooms with private baths and hot water for approximately US$20. The closest is *Hotel Florida* (☎ 843 040/74, Miraflores 1131), almost 1km southwest of where Bolívar becomes Avenida Miraflores on the map. An American breakfast is included in the rates. Farther along Miraflores is the German-run *Hotel Villa Hilda* (☎ 845 014, 840 700, fax 845 571), which is set in pleasant gardens and has a pool (though it wasn't working recently). The quality of rooms varies, as do prices, so look around. Next comes the cheapest of the four, *Hotel Carolina* (☎ *821 539)*, which has a pool and includes breakfast. Finally, you might try the clean and modern *Hotel Miraflores* (☎ *843 224, fax 844 395, hmflores@hmiraflores.com.ec, Miraflores 227)*. The hotel has Internet access, a restaurant and rooms with telephones and cable TV. Rates are US$16/20 for standard rooms, US$25 for minisuites and US$50 for the 'presidential suite,' all including an American breakfast.

By far the best hotel in the town center is *Hotel Ambato* (☎ *847 020, 847 068, fax 827 197, hambato@hotmail.com, Guayaquil 0108)*, on the corner with Rocafuerte. There is a casino; a good restaurant and bar (room service is available); and cozy rooms with private bath and hot water, telephone and cable TV. A café and terrace allow you to enjoy a snack outside. Rates for the 58 modern rooms are a very reasonable US$20/28, and a suite is US$35. (These prices are about half of what they were in the last edition.)

Places to Eat

Numerous chifas have filling inexpensive meals and are locally popular. Among them are *Chifa Jao Fua* (☎ *829 306)*, on Cevallos; *Chifa Nueva Hong Kong* *(Bolívar 768)*; and *Casa China*, at the corner of Espejo and 12 de Noviembre. You can also get super-cheap meals around the market.

Restaurant Barcelona, on 12 de Noviembre at Mera, is a brightly lit, cheap place that stays open until the wee hours.

For breakfast, the best bet is one of the cake shops for coffee, juice and rolls or sandwiches. Try *Panadería Sabor*, on Cevallos at Montalvo, or *Pastelería Quito*, on Mera near Cevallos.

El Patio Café Cultural is almost next to Casa de Montalvo and – apart from serving light meals and coffee – features cultural events, including poetry readings, musical evenings and art openings. Stop by and see what's happening. *Paolo's Cafetería*, on Cevallos at Mera, is a quiet place for a sandwich or snack, and *Oasis Heladería*, on Sucre near Egüez, is another popular café.

For good medium-priced steak, try eating at *Parrilladas El Gaucho* (☎ *828 969)*, on Bolívar near Quito, or the slightly cheaper *Parrilladas Favid*, on Bolívar near Mera. *Pizzería La Cigarra*, on José Rodo, a little street between Sucre and Cevallos, makes a reasonable pizza. *Pizzería Fornace* (☎ *823 244)*, on Cevallos near Montalvo, has a wide range of pizzas and other good Italian food in an upscale setting; prices are reasonable.

There are three Swiss-run El Alamo restaurants in Ambato: *Restaurant El Gran Alamo* (☎ *820 706, Montalvo 520)*, between Cevallos and Sucre, is quite fancy and comparatively expensive; *Restaurant El Alamo* (☎ *821 710, Sucre 660)*, near Mera, has interesting photos of old Ambato on the walls and is lower in price and good; and *El Alamo Chalet* *(Cevallos 612)*, near Montalvo, is in between the other two in value.

Hotel Ambato has the best hotel restaurant; some say it's the best restaurant in town. Its most obvious competitor is the nearby *La Buena Mesa* (☎ *822 330)*, on Quito near Rocafuerte. This is a good French restaurant recommended for its very

Artwork of indigenous artist Pablo Sanaguano

pleasant atmosphere. Other international restaurants worth a try are **Cuba Son**, on Guayaquil near Bolívar, which has a bar serving Cuban meals and snacks; and **Casa Brasileira**, on Rocafuerte near Castillo, which features Brazilian food, wood paneling and a pool table.

Entertainment

There is some nightlife in Ambato, but not much. **Restaurant Coyote Disco Club**, on Bolívar near Quito, is a restaurant that has dancing in the evenings. It's popular with young people and a bit more upscale than the funkier **Cervecería Bufalo**, at Olmedo and Mera, where there is beer and dancing. Also check out El Patio Café Cultural (see Places to Eat, earlier) for somewhat more intellectual pursuits. There are a few cinemas (some dedicated to porno flicks), but the Casa de Cultura sometimes has something better showing. Consult the local newspaper, *El Heraldo,* for what's playing. There is a casino at Hotel Ambato.

Getting There & Away

Air There is a small airstrip nearby for emergency and military use only. TAME (☎ 826 601, 820 322, 822 595), Sucre 331, near Guayaquil, only makes reservations for flights from other cities.

Bus The bus terminal (☎ 821 481) is 2km away from the town center, and buses to all destinations leave from there. Get there by heading north on 12 de Noviembre to the traffic circle and then turn right on Avenida de las Américas. The most frequent departures are for Quito (US$2, three hours), Baños (US$0.60, 45 minutes – check to see if Baños is safe), Riobamba (one hour) and Guayaquil (US$5, six hours). There are several buses a day to Cuenca (US$6, seven hours) and Guaranda (US$1.60, two hours), some of which continue to Babahoyo and a couple of which continue on to Chillanes. Several companies run a bus to Tena, in the Oriente (six hours, depending on road conditions; note that the road may be closed – see Baños, later in this chapter). There are buses for many other destinations.

For destinations that are north of Quito, it's usually best to take a bus to Quito and change at the terminal there.

Train The train station is near the main bus terminal, 2km away from the town center. There are services to Quito (US$15) Friday and Riobamba (US$12) Saturday. Most passengers pick up the train in either Quito or Riobamba and do the entire trip, which costs only US$16!

Getting Around

Bus The most important local bus service for the traveler is the route between the bus terminal and the town center. From the terminal, climb the exit ramp to Avenida de las Américas, which crosses the train tracks on a bridge. On this bridge is a bus stop, where a westbound (to your right) bus, often signed 'Centro,' will take you to Parque Cevallos for US$0.10.

Parque Cevallos is the center for many buses out of town into the suburbs, so it's a good place to ask around if you need to get somewhere. Buses marked 'Terminal' leave from the Martínez side of Parque Cevallos – if in doubt, ask. Buses to the suburb of Ficoa also leave from this park. A block away is Bolívar, which has buses to the suburb of Miraflores running along it. Buses to the Atocha suburb (more quintas) leave from 12 de Noviembre and Sevilla or Espejo. Buses for several surrounding villages also depart from the Parque Cevallos area.

Taxi Taxis from the bus terminal to the center cost under US$1. There are fixed rates for most runs around Ambato and surrounding villages, although attempted overcharging has been reported. There are many taxis at Parque 12 de Noviembre and Parque Cevallos.

AROUND AMBATO
☎ 03

Salasaca and Pelileo are the most frequently visited villages near Ambato, because they lie on the good main road to Baños. Other villages are off the main road but are interesting to visit on day trips. With the exception of Patate, none of these villages off the road to Baños have accommodations, and travelers are a rarity. In Ambato, ask at the bus terminal or at Parque Cevallos about buses to these places.

Quizapincha & Píllaro

Quizapincha, about 10km west of Ambato, is known for its leatherwork. It can be reached by buses crossing the Puente de Ficoa (bridge), at the northwest end of Montalvo.

Píllaro, some 20km to the northeast, is in a cereal- and fruit-growing area. July to August are big months for fiestas celebrated with bullfights, highland food and parades. July 15 is the fiesta of Apostolo Santiago (St James), and July 25 is Cantonization Day. August 10, Quito's Independence Day, is also vigorously celebrated with a bullfight and a bull run, in which the bulls charge through the streets; everybody participates.

Píllaro is the entry point for the new **Parque Nacional Llanganates**, a very remote and difficult-to-reach mountain range in which Atahualpa's treasure is supposedly buried. Many bona fide expeditions have searched for the treasure using ancient maps and documents from the time of the conquest, but nobody has found it yet!

Salasaca

As you head southeast from Ambato on the Baños road, the first place of interest is Salasaca, about 14km away. The village and its environs are inhabited by some 2000 Salasaca Indians, who are famous for their tapestries. They are less well known for their history, which is particularly interesting. Originally, they came from Bolivia, but they were conquered by the Incas in the 15th century.

One of the ways in which the Incas controlled the peoples they had conquered was to move them en masse to an area that the Incas had long dominated, and where there was less chance of an uprising. Apparently this is what happened to the Salasacas, who were moved from Bolivia. After the Spanish conquest, they remained where they were but retained an unusually high degree of independence and were almost unknown by outsiders until the middle of the 20th century.

The villagers are recognizable by their typical dress – especially the men, who normally wear broad-brimmed white hats, black ponchos, and white shirts and trousers. Traditionally a farming community, they raise their own sheep to obtain wool for their weavings, which are a secondary source of income. Their tapestries are all handmade and are different from work done by other Indian groups (although it's difficult to see the difference unless you have spent time examining Ecuadorian weaving).

There is no local produce market in Salasaca; the villagers use the nearby Pelileo Saturday market, or they go to Ambato. There is a **craft market** held every Sunday morning near the church on the Ambato-Baños road (both the church and the market are in Salasaca). Also along this road are several craft stores that are open daily. One of these is a women artisans' cooperative. Nearby is **Alonso Pilla's house** (☎ 09-840 125; as you arrive from Baños, it's on the left, about 100m past the Evangelical church in the center of the village). His house is open 11 am to 6 pm daily, and he gives weaving demonstrations on a backstrap loom using traditional techniques – his work has been highly recommended. Salasacan tapestries are also sold in craft stores in Quito and Cuenca.

The many Indian **fiestas** in the Salasaca area are worth looking out for. May and June are good months for fiestas all over the highlands. On the Sunday after Easter, there is a street dance between Salasaca and Pelileo. On June 15, the Salasaca dress up in animal costumes for Santo Vintio. Corpus Christi (which takes place on a movable date in June) is celebrated in Salasaca and Pelileo. The feast of St Anthony is celebrated at the end of November. All the usual annual holidays (Christmas, Easter etc) also offer interesting fiesta possibilities.

Pelileo

Some 6km beyond Salasaca on the Baños road is the larger village of Pelileo. Despite its 400-year history, the Pelileo of today is a very modern village. It was founded by the colonialist Antonio Clavijo in 1570 but was destroyed by earthquakes in 1698, 1797, 1840 and 1949. The present site is about 2km away from the ruins of the old town. It was among the places evacuated in 1999 following Tungurahua's eruptions, and although residents have returned now, it is still likely that ashfall could affect the town in the event of a major eruption. Pelileo is the market town for nearby villages, including Salasaca (Saturday is market day). Pelileo could be dubbed the 'Blue Jeans Capital of Ecuador' – there is an amazing variety of brands and sizes of jeans for sale, especially on market day.

Pelileo celebrates its cantonization on July 22 with the usual highland festivities: bullfights, parades and plenty of food and drink.

Baños is only 24km away, but the road drops some 850m from Pelileo. The descent along Río Pastaza gorge is spectacular, and some of the best views of the erupting volcano Tungurahua are to be seen on this drive. At 5016m (pre-eruption height), Tungurahua is Ecuador's 10th-highest peak and gives its name to the province.

Patate & Around

Patate, 25km from Ambato and 5km northeast of Pelileo, is a pretty village known for its picturesque locale on Río Patate, for its grapes and for its *aguardiente* (sugarcane alcohol), which is allegedly some of the best in the highlands. There are buses from Pelileo to Patate. Although it may suffer from light ashfall in the event of a major eruption, it is considered safer than Pelileo and Baños.

Hotel Turístico Patate (☎ 870 177, in Quito 02-590 657) offers 15 double rooms with private bath and hot water for US$12. There is a restaurant, bar and recreation area, and the management can arrange tours to the Llanganates and local ruins. The cheaper *Viña del Mar Hotel* (☎/fax 870 139) is the current favorite for volcano watchers hoping to see a Tungurahua eruption. For folks on a weekend day visit, stop by *Complejo Turiístico Valle Dorado* (☎ 870 253),

which has hot and cold swimming pools, a sauna and a restaurant.

At 2900m in the mountains northeast of Patate, and about 15km away by road, is *Hacienda Manteles* (☎/fax 870 123). This family farm was converted into a delightful country inn in 1992. From the hacienda, there are pretty views of the Río Patate valley below and Volcán Tungurahua and other mountains in the distance. The valley is covered by fields spread out like a checkered tablecloth – hence the name 'manteles,' which is Spanish for 'tablecloths.' Above the inn is an area of cloud forest that can be explored on foot or by horse (US$5 per hour). Guides can be hired to take you to a nearby waterfall, up into the páramo and across the Llanganates, or to visit pre-Columbian remains. Bird watching, hiking and fishing are other possible activities.

There are seven good-sized rooms; all have private hot showers and can sleep up to three or four people. Rates are US$57/69/81/93 for one/two/three/four people in a room. Fresh homemade meals are served buffet style and are all-you-can-eat. Breakfast is US$6, and lunch or dinner is US$13. Box lunches are also available. The restaurant/bar has a fireplace and is attractively decorated with Salasacan weavings. Reservations can be made at the hacienda itself, or in the Quito office (☎/fax 02-505 230, Humboldt 269), near San Ignacio, in the Gonzalez Suárez district. Discounts for residents and multiple days can be arranged. Guests with reservations can arrange to be picked up from the bus station in Patate at no extra charge.

BAÑOS
☎ 03

Before the volcanic danger announced in 1999 (see the boxed text 'Tungurahua Comes Back to Life'), there were almost 20,000 inhabitants and close to 100 places to stay in this small town and its outskirts. It was one of the most important tourist spots in the country and was popular with Ecuadorians and foreigners alike. Now, because of the volcanic action, the situation is on a day-to-day basis, and you must keep yourself apprised of potential dangers. Undeniably,

Tungurahua Comes Back to Life

Baños, an idyllically placed small town of 18,000 inhabitants living in a lush green valley on the slopes of Volcán Tungurahua, has for decades been synonymous with relaxation and tourism. Several dozen small hotels catered to Ecuadorian and foreign tourists alike, offering them vacations ranging from relaxing dips in hot springs after a night of dancing to strenuous climbs to peer into the gently active crater of the snowcapped volcano – which at 5016m is the 10th-highest peak in the country.

Although the volcano erupted in 1918, it was afterward considered semidormant and unthreatening. This suddenly changed in 1998, when increased seismic activity was detected. The volcano was placed on yellow alert (on a scale running from white to yellow to orange to red) – meaning that the volcano was being monitored and showing signs of activity, but that dangers of a major eruption were not imminent. This was changed to an orange alert after an Australian climber and his Ecuadorian guide were burned by a gaseous eruption on October 5, 1999. (An orange alert means that there is a 90% chance of a major eruption over the coming weeks or months, and that minor eruptions could occur at any time.)

Over the next two weeks, Tungurahua pumped clouds of steam and ash into aerial columns many kilometers in height, and ashfall was a regular occurrence in the surrounding area. At night, streams of glowing lava could be seen cascading down the sides of the volcano. By October 17, the authorities ordered the evacuation of over 20,000 inhabitants of Baños and nearby villages, saying that a major eruption could pose a deadly threat to the population. The roads between Ambato and Puyo and between Riobamba and Puyo were also closed. With the volcano erupting almost daily, tour operators in Quito and Ambato began offering trips to see the volcanic wonders from a safe distance.

Weeks turned into months, and by January 2000, there still had not been an eruption large enough to cause substantial damage to Baños. The inhabitants, desperate to return to their homes and their livelihoods, defied government orders and clashed with troops at a military checkpoint, resulting in several injuries and the death of one woman. Soon afterward, an agreement was reached, and about 3000 people were allowed back into Baños, and the road between Ambato and Puyo was reopened.

Slowly, curious day-trippers and tourists began to trickle into Baños, and week after week, more residents began to return and reopen their tourism businesses. By July 2000, an estimated 60% to 70% of businesses were operating in Baños, and tourism was beginning to recover.

The ambience of the town is a strange one – a mixture of an attempt at normalcy with an awareness of knowing that the volcano is still on orange alert. The volcano continues to shake and blow on a regular basis, but the situation could shift to a disastrous eruption within a matter of a few days or even hours. To keep the public apprised of the situation, *El Comercio* posts daily online updates (in Spanish) at www.elcomercio.com and in its daily printed edition. Spanish-speakers can also visit the Web site of Instituto Geofísico, at http://geofisico.cybw.net.

Baños is in a beautiful, if unpredictable, natural area. Ironically, the town itself is not the best vantage point from which to view volcanic eruptions, because it is right at the base of the mountain, and foreshortening prevents views of the crater. However, tours to good vantage spots are offered by all the tour companies.

Baños means 'baths,' which is precisely what the town is famous for. Some of them are fed by thermal springs from the base of the active Volcán Tungurahua, which means 'little hell' in Quichua. Other baths have meltwater running into them from Tungurahua's icy flanks. Locals swear that the baths are great for your health. While that is a debatable point, it is true that the casual atmosphere of this pretty resort town has made it a place to unwind after some hard traveling. Baños' elevation of 1800m gives it an agreeable climate, and the surroundings are green and attractive.

Baños is also the gateway town into the jungle via Puyo and Misahuallí. East of Baños, the road drops spectacularly, and there are exceptional views of the upper Amazon Basin stretching away before you. In the town itself, there are more attractions: an interesting basilica, a small museum, a little nightlife and restaurants featuring local cuisine.

Information

There is no tourist office, but (slightly biased) information can be obtained from the tour operators in town. Owners of hotels and restaurants are used to answering questions.

Money Banco del Pacífico, at Ambato and Halflants, has a MasterCard ATM.

Post & Communications The post office (☎ 740 901) and Andinatel (☎ 740 411) are both on the Parque Central. Internet access can be found at Cafe.com, on 12 de Noviembre near Oriente, and at Internet Café, on Reyes near Ambato.

Travel Agencies & Guides There are many guides – some of which are dishonest or inexperienced. If you hire a guide, make

sure that he or she has recommendations – listen to what other travelers have to say, and ask to see an up-to-date official guiding license. The best professional white-water guides should be certified by AGAR, and climbing guides should be certified by Aseguim. Jungle guides with 'Naturalista' licenses have received some training in explaining the flora and fauna.

When going on a tour, find out if any national park will be visited and whether the entrance fees (possibly up to US$20) are included in the cost. Specific agencies and guides are mentioned later in this section under the appropriate activity.

Medical Services The small local hospital (☎ 740 443/301) is on Montalvo near Pastaza. There are several pharmacies along Ambato.

Emergency The police station (☎ 740 251, or ☎ 101) is on Oriente near Mera. Visitors should ask at their hotels about emergency-evacuation procedures in the event of an eruption. Familiarize yourself with the street layout and where to go if an emergency evacuation is announced.

Things to See & Do

For a tour of the town, contact Cordova Tours, by the bus terminal. The company arranges 'party tours,' with open-sided buses and music at night and regular tours during the day. Car and jeep rentals are available through this company.

Basilica Within the town itself, the basilica, with the Dominican church of **Santuario de Nuestra Señora de Agua Santa**, is worth seeing. The church is dedicated to the Virgin of the Holy Water, who is credited with several miracles in the Baños area. The annual October celebration in her honor has much street music and many Indian bands playing, but generally, she is the object of devout admiration, as exemplified by the many offerings to her and the paintings depicting her miracles.

These paintings are simple but charming, with explanations in Spanish along the lines

BAÑOS

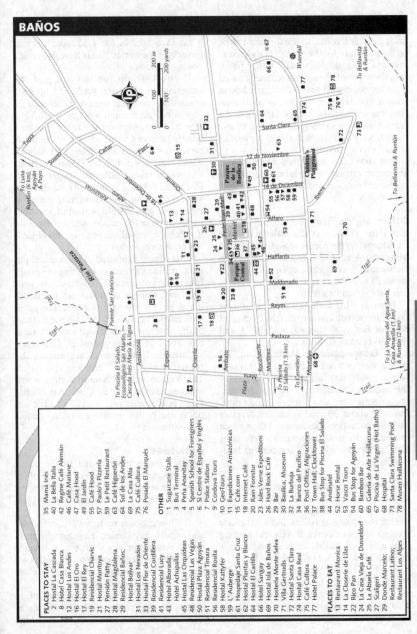

PLACES TO STAY
2   Hostal La Cascada
8   Hotel Casa Blanca
12 Hostal Los Andes
16 Hostal El Oro
17 Hostal El Rey
19 Residencial Charvic
21 Hostal Montoya
27 Pensión Patty
28 Hostal Magdalena
29 Residencial Baños;
    Hostal Bolívar
31 Hostal Los Nevados
33 Hostal Flor de Oriente
39 Residencial Cordillera
41 Residencial Lucy
43 Hotel Alborada;
    Hotel Achupallas
45 Hostal Las Orquídeas
48 Residencial Las Vegas
50 Hostal Plaza Agoyán
51 Residencial Timara
56 Residencial Rosita
58 Hostal Kattyfer
59 L'Auberge
61 Hospedaje Santa Cruz
62 Hostal Plantas y Blanco
64 Hostal El Castillo
66 Hotel Sangay
69 Hostería Isla de Baños
70 Hostería Monte Selva
71 Villa Gertrudis
72 Hostal Santa Clara
74 Hostal Casa Real
75 Café Cultura
77 Hotel Palace

PLACES TO EAT
13 Restaurant Monica
14 La Closerie de Lilas
22 Rico Pan
24 La Casa Vieja de Dusseldorf
25 La Abuela Café
27 Scaligeri
29 Donde Marcelo;
    Restaurant Latino;
    Restaurant Los Alpes

35 Mamá Inés
40 La Bella Italia
42 Regine Café Alemán
46 Café Mariane
47 Casa Hood
49 El Jardín
55 Café Hood
57 Paolo's Pizzería
59 Le Petit Restaurant
63 Café Higuerón
64 Sol de los Andes
69 La Casa Mía
75 Café Cultura
76 Posada El Marqués

OTHER
1   Sugarcane Stalls
3   Bus Terminal
4   Peña Ananitay
5   Spanish school for Foreigners
6   Si Centro de Español y Inglés
7   Police Station
9   Cordova Tours
10 GeoTours
11 Expediciones Amazónicas
15 Cafe.com
18 Internet Café
20 Rain Forestur
23 Jules Verne Expeditions
26 Hard Rock Café
29 Bar
30 Basílica; Museum
32 La Burbuja
34 Banco del Pacífico
36 Post Office; Migraciones
37 Town Hall; Clocktower
38 Bus Stop for Piscina El Salado
44 Andinatel
52 Horse Rental
53 Vasco Tours
54 Bus Stop for Agoyán
60 Bamboo Bar
65 Galería de Arte Huillacuna
67 Piscina de La Virgen (Hot Baths)
68 Hospital
73 Santa Clara Swimming Pool
78 Museo Huillacuna

of 'On January 30, 1904, Señor X fell off his horse as he was crossing the Río Pastaza bridge. As he fell 70m to the torrents below, he yelled "Holy Mother of the Holy Water" and was miraculously saved!' Other paintings show people being miraculously saved from exploding volcanoes, burning hotels, transit accidents and other misfortunes. Reading the explanations is amusing and a great way to practice your Spanish. Please remember, however, that this is a place of worship, so act accordingly.

Just above the church is a **museum** with an eclectic display of taxidermic animals, religious paintings, church vestments and local handicrafts.

Other Sights Browse (and buy if you want) the exhibits at the **Galería de Arte Huillacuna**, on the corner of Santa Clara and Montalvo. A couple of blocks away, **Museo Huillacuna** is erratically open and charges visitors a few cents to see its exhibits of local archaeology and culture.

There is a big **waterfall** at the southeast end of town. You can see the falls from most parts of Baños. Admission is US$0.75, and the falls open at 4:30 am.

The **Ecozoológico San Martín** (☎ 740 552) is 1km west of town and was built in a canyon that has been artfully used to display the animals. During the town's evacuation, the animals were also removed, and unfortunately, about 30 died from the stress of sudden evacuation. The animals (all of which are native Ecuadorian species) were later returned to the zoo. Call for current business hours.

Hot Baths There are three baths – two are in Baños (only one is hot), and the third is out of town. All charge a modest entrance fee for the changing rooms and for the safe storage of your clothes. Towels and bathing suits may be available for rent, and soap is for sale. Nude bathing is prohibited.

The best-known bath is La Piscina de La Virgen, which has hot showers and three concrete pools of different temperatures. You can't miss them – they're right under the waterfall.

A cold swimming pool that charges US$0.30 is nearby at Santa Clara. There is a sauna available for US$2 per person. Several of the better hotels have swimming pools or saunas.

If you walk up the hill and past the cemetery on Martínez, you'll end up on a track that crosses a stream (Quebrada de Naguasco) on a small wooden footbridge. The trail continues on the other side to a road in front of Cabañas Bascun, where you turn left to reach the Piscina El Salado, which also open at 4:30 am. (There are buses too, which take a different, longer route.) Piscina El Salado has hot and cold showers, several concrete pools of varying temperatures and an ice-cold waterfall to stand under if you're the masochistic sort. Because it is 2km or 3km of out of town, this place is not quite so crowded.

Everyone is supposed to shower and put on a bathing suit before entering the pools. However, you should avoid putting your head under or getting water in your mouth if you have a sensitive stomach. The pools look murky because of the mineral content of the water, which is touted for its restorative and healthful properties. Chlorates, sulfates and magnesium are among the principal chemicals found in the baths. The Virgen and El Salado waters reach temperatures of over 50°C, while the Santa Clara pool is normally about 24°C. The hot pools are better used for soaking rather than swimming.

Activities

Hiking Once you've visited all the pools, there are many walks to take. Plenty of information about walks is available in Baños. The following are some suggestions, but you should seek updates locally.

The walk down to Río Pastaza is easy and popular. Just behind the **sugarcane stalls** by the bus station is a short trail that leads to the **Puente San Francisco**, which crosses the river. You can continue on trails up the other side as far as you want.

Going south on Maldonado takes you to a footpath that climbs to **Bellavista**, where there is a building with a white cross high

How the Otavaleño chicken crossed the road

Whiling away the market day in Otavalo

Otavaleña in traditional attire preening produce

Otavaleño wearing a traditional dark felt hat

CHRIS BEALL

This sleeping giant, Volcán Tungurahua, is stirring once again.

WOODS WHEATCROFT

Herding sheep on the flanks of Volcán Cotopaxi

WOODS WHEATCROFT

Land carved by lava, Parque Nacional Cotopaxi

over Baños (visible from the town). The path then continues to the tiny settlement of **Runtún**, some two hours away. The views are great!

West of town, turn right by a religious shrine and walk down to Puente San Martín and visit the impressive falls of **Cascada Inés María**, a few hundred meters to the right of the bridge. You can also cross the bridge and continue to the village of **Lligua**, about three hours away. From this road, trails climb up the hills to your right.

Jungle Trips Many jungle trips from Baños are advertised, but not all guides are experienced. Guides should have licenses (see Travel Agencies & Guides, earlier). Much useful general information about jungle trips is given in the Northern Oriente chapter under Misahuallí.

Three- to seven-day jungle tours cost about US$30 to US$45 per person, depending on the destination (there is usually a three- or four-person minimum). Some focus more on Indian culture and plants; others focus more on wildlife. Don't expect to see many animals in the rainforest – it takes patience and luck. June to September is the busy season, and reservations are a good idea if you want to go on a specific date during that season – but if you just show up and don't mind waiting around, you can usually hook up with a tour. Baños is always full of travelers and is a good town in which to organize a group if you are not already with one.

Rain Forestur (☎/fax 740 743, rainfor@ interactive.net.ec), on Ambato near Maldonado, has received several recommendations for its tours to Reserva Producción Faunística Cuyabeno (see the Northern Oriente chapter for details on this reserve). These tours cost US$45 per person per day, plus the reserve's entry fee. There is a four-person minimum and a 12-person maximum. Other areas of both primary and secondary jungle can also be visited on different tours. Tours last three days to a week. Some of the agency's guides speak English, German or French (as well as Spanish). Rain Forestur also has a Quito

office (☎/fax 02-239 822), at Amazonas 420, near Roca.

Vasco Tours (☎ 740 017), on Alfaro near Martínez, is run by the Vasco brothers, and their guide Juan Medina is recommended. Jules Verne Expeditions (☎/fax 740 253, julver@interactive.net.ec), at Oriente 11-69, near Halflants, is another company that arranges good jungle trips.

Climbing & Backpacking Climbers are not able to ascend the currently erupting Volcán Tungurahua (5016m), and the refuge on that volcano has been destroyed. However, many local agencies arrange tours to good spots for watching the eruptions.

Climbs of Cotopaxi and Chimborazo can be arranged. A reputable climbing outfitter is Expediciones Amazónicas (☎ 740 506), Oriente 11-62, near Halflants, which has rental equipment and licensed guides. Willie Navarette is also recommended; contact him at Café Higuerón (see Places to Eat, later). Rain Forestur (see Jungle Trips, earlier) has rental equipment and licensed climbing guides and can tailor your itinerary to include acclimatization. Jules Verne Expeditions (see Jungle Trips, earlier) has good equipment and guides. The going rate for climbs with a minimum of two people is US$60 to US$80 per person per day, plus park fees. Beware of cheap but inexperienced guides.

The jagged, extinct Volcán El Altar (5319m) is hard to climb, but the wild páramo surrounding it is a good area for backpacking and camping. The active but remote Volcán Sangay (5230m) can also be explored on weeklong trekking expeditions.

Detailed information about these volcanoes is given later in this chapter under Parque Nacional Sangay.

Mountain Biking Several companies rent mountain bikes for rates starting at about US$4 per day. Check the equipment carefully, as maintenance is sometimes poor. Go to several companies to find the bike that's best for you. One popular ride is the dramatic descent to Puyo, which is about 70km east, on the edge of the Oriente. Parts of the road are unpaved. There is a passport control at Shell, so carry your documents. From Puyo (or earlier), you can simply take a bus back to Baños, putting your bike on the roof (see Getting There & Away, later in this section). This route into the Oriente is described in the Northern Oriente chapter, under the section From Baños to Puyo. Various other mountain-biking options are available, and the outfitters will be happy to tell you about them.

Horseback Riding Ángel Aldáz (☎ 740 175), at Montalvo and Mera, rents horses for about US$10 per half day, or more if you also want a guide. Christián, at Hostal Isla de Baños (see Places to Stay, later), arranges guided horseback-riding trips that last a half day, a full day, or two to nine days. Christián speaks English and German. There are other places that rent horses, but these two outfitters have received the best recommendations. Their horses are in good shape and are suitable for both beginners and experienced riders. Also, Caballos José (☎ 740 746), at Maldonado and Martínez, is reportedly quite good.

Horses can be rented by the hour, but by the time you saddle up and get out of town, it's hardly worth going for such a short period. Many half- or full-day trips start with a long jeep ride out of town, and the actual riding time is short – inquire carefully to get what you want.

White-Water Rafting GeoTours (☎ 740 673, fax 740 332), on Maldonado half a block south of the bus station, is run by an Ecuadorian/Swiss couple. Half-day trips to Río Patate are offered for US$30 and leave on demand. Trips last four hours (two hours on the river), and a snack is included. Also available is a full day to Río Pastaza for US$60, leaving at 8:30 am. This trip is 10 hours, with four hours on the river, and lunch is included. Transportation, a guide, raft, paddles, life jackets, wet suits and helmets are all provided. Experience is not necessary, although you should know how to swim. Jules Verne Expeditions (see Jungle Trips, earlier) also offers river trips.

Language Courses

One-on-one or small-group Spanish classes are offered at Spanish School for Foreigners (☎ 740 612), at 16 de Diciembre and Espejo, and at Si Centro de Español y Inglés (☎/fax 740 360), at the end of Páez.

Special Events

Baños became the seat of its canton on December 16, 1944, and an annual fiesta is celebrated on this and the preceding days. There are the usual processions, fireworks, music and a great deal of street dancing and drinking at night. Fun! Also, there are processions and fireworks during the entire month of October as the various barrios of Baños take turns to pay homage to the local icon, Nuestra Señora de Agua Santa.

Places to Stay

There are scores of hotels to choose from, so only a selection can be briefly described here. All of them closed when the town was evacuated in 1999, but over half reopened by mid-2000. Many hotels charge US$6 or less per person and are a good value, although rates may change due to dollarization and Tungarahua's activity.

The rooms of some of the cheap hotels vary in quality – check your room before accepting it. Other hotels charge double rates for one night but will drop their prices if you stay longer (negotiate this when you check in, not when you check out). Usually there are plenty of rooms available, but your choice may be limited and prices may be high if you arrive on a Friday night or if there is a fiesta under way.

Hotels in Baños can be noisy – it is a vacation town, after all. For some quieter places, see Around Baños, at the end of this section.

Budget One of the cheapest places is the well-known, family-run *Pensión Patty* (☎ 740 202, Alfaro 556), which has friendly management and information on trekking, climbing and horseback riding in the area. It is popular with budget travelers. Basic rooms go for under US$2 per person and vary in quality – some of the older ones are pretty funky, but the price is right. There is one hot and several cold showers, as well as a communal kitchen.

The friendly *Residencial Timara* (☎ 740 599), on Maldonado near Martínez, has rooms for about US$2 per person; there is hot water and kitchen facilities. *Hostal Santa Clara* (☎ 740 349), on 12 de Noviembre near Ibarra, is popular and has kitchen facilities, hot showers and a garden. Rooms in the old house cost US$2 per person, and singles/doubles with hot showers in the clean new cabins cost US$5/8. The friendly *Residencial Lucy* (☎ 740 466), on Rocafuerte near Alfaro, has rooms with private bath and hot water for US$2.50 per person. Rooms with shared bath are US$2.

There are many other simple hotels that charge about US$2 to US$3 per person. One of these is *Hostal Plaza Agoyán*, on Rocafuerte near 12 de Diciembre. It has a few rooms overlooking Parque de la Basílica. *Hostal El Oro* (☎ 740 736), on Ambato near Mera, is another. There are private hot showers in each room, and the staff is friendly and helpful. *Hostal El Rey* (☎ 740 332), on Oriente at Reyes, is around the same price. It has three rooms sharing a hot shower and a few rooms with private showers. *Hostal La Cascada* (☎ 740 946) is right next to the bus terminal – good for early departures. Rooms are about US$3 per person and have private hot showers.

Hostal Los Nevados (☎ 740 673), a block east of Parque de la Basílica, is an excellent value. Spacious rooms with private hot showers cost just US$2.50 per person. *Hostal Las Orquídeas* (☎ 740 911, fax 740 717), on the corner of Parque Central, has light, clean rooms (some have balconies) with private hot shower for US$3 to US$4 per person. The similarly priced *Hotel Casa Blanca* (☎ /fax 740 092), at Maldonado and Oriente, has rooms with private hot showers and cable TV. Also try *Hostal Montoya* (☎ 740 124), on Oriente between Maldonado and Halflants, for rooms with similar prices and facilities.

The very popular *Hostal Plantas y Blanco* (☎/fax 740 044, option3@hotmail .com), on Martínez at 12 de Noviembre, is attractively decorated with plants and has a pleasant rooftop terrace (for breakfast) and a steam bath. The rooms cost US$6 per person with private bath, or US$5 with shared bath. There are laundry and Internet facilities, and the place is often full. Around the corner, *Hospedaje Santa Cruz* (☎ 740 648), on 16 de Diciembre, is clean and a good value at US$6 per person with bath and hot water. *Residencial Rosita*, across the street, is similar. *Hostal El Castillo* (☎ 740 285, Martínez 255) is also good. The pleasant rooms cost US$4 per person and have showers with hot water (most of the time). Guests are provided with three meals for US$2.50.

Other accommodations in the range of US$3 to US$6 per person include the hotels on the busy and noisy pedestrian block of Ambato. Some of these are *Residencial Baños* (☎ 740 284), *Residencial Cordillera* (☎ 740 536) and *Hostal Bolívar* (☎ 740 497). Also in this price range are the modern but unremarkable *Hotel Alborada* (☎ 740 814) and *Hotel Achupallas* (☎ 740 422/389), both on Parque de la Basílica, and clean *Residencial Las Vegas* (☎ 740 426), at Alfaro and Rocafuerte. Other decent places with private hot showers in this price range include *Hostal Los Andes*, on Oriente near Alfaro, and *Residencial Charvic* (☎ 740 298/113), at Maldonado and Oriente. The good, clean, family-run *Hostal Magdalena* (☎ 740 233/364, Oriente 1037) has rooms with private bath and hot water, as well as a parking lot. It is secure and closes at 10 pm (but you can ring a bell to get in if you let them know you are going out). *Hostal Kattyfer* (☎ 740 856), on 16 de Diciembre near Montalvo, is another acceptable option.

The French-run *L'Auberge* (☎ 740 936), on 16 de Diciembre near Montalvo, charges US$6/9 for rooms with private hot showers – some rooms have a fireplace.

Mid-Range For US$6 to US$8 per person, *Hostal Flor de Oriente* (☎ 740 418, 09-801 117, fax 740 717), at Ambato and Maldonado, has very clean rooms with private bath, hot water and telephone. Some rooms have cable TV. There is a decent restaurant downstairs, and parking is available. American breakfast is included. Another good choice is the German-run *Hostal Isla de Baños* (☎/*fax 740 609, islab@ecuanex.net.ec, Halflants 1-31*), which has simple but spacious and clean rooms with private bath and hot water. Rates are US$7 to US$10 per person. The hotel is set in attractive gardens and has a good restaurant and bar.

The small but pretty *Café Cultura* (☎/*fax 740 083, ivonsol@uio.satnet.net*), near Museo Huillacuna, has seven comfortable rooms with private bath; two rooms have a fireplace. A terrace gives views of the waterfall, and a restaurant serves breakfast, lunch and afternoon tea. Rooms are US$9 per person.

Hostería Monte Selva (☎ *740 566, 820 068, fax 854 685*), near the south end of Halflants, has attractive wooden cabins set on a lush hillside just above Baños. The plant-filled gardens have a pool and a sauna. It is the nicest looking of the hotels in the center. Doubles cost US$20, including continental breakfast. There is a bar and restaurant. *Hostal Casa Real* (☎ *740 215*), on Montalvo near Santa Clara, has nice clean rooms for US$12/20 and larger rooms for up to US$40. Its restaurant/bar sometimes has live music. *Hotel Palace* (☎ *740 470, fax 740 291, Montalvo 20-03*), by the waterfall, is clean and pleasant and has an attached restaurant that's good. There is a garden, a small swimming pool, a sauna, a spa, a Turkish bath, a games room (darts & ping pong), children's swings, and a small museum of archaeology and numismatics (coins). Singles with private bath, TV and telephone are US$24, plus US$6 for each additional person (up to four) in the old-fashioned house, and about US$7 more for larger rooms in the new annex. The owners are friendly. Rates include use of the facilities, but nonguests can use them too for a few dollars.

Hotel Sangay (☎ *740 490/917, fax 740 056*) is just opposite the Piscina de La Virgen baths. There are squash and tennis courts, a swimming pool, a Jacuzzi and sauna, and a restaurant and bar. All rooms have private bath, hot water, telephone and cable TV. The hotel is popular with Ecuadorian tour groups, but it is gloomy when there aren't groups to fill up the 72 rooms. Rooms in the hotel building are US$20/30, and rooms in the cabins are US$35/45, including continental breakfast and use of the facilities. Nonguests can use the pool and other facilities for a small fee.

The much quieter, low-key *Villa Gertrudis* (☎ *740 441*), at Montalvo and Ibarra, is also set in pretty gardens and has a big pool. The rate is US$30 per person, including two meals, but the place is often full. Nonguests can use the pool for about US$2.

Around Baños About 2km from town by footpath or 4km by road is the Piscina El Salado, with four nearby hotels that are quieter than most of the places in Baños. There are two basic residenciales right by the baths that have good views of Tungurahua – *El Salado* and *Puerto del Salado*. Rates are about US$3.50 per person.

About 10 minutes away from the baths are *Cabañas Bascún* (☎/*fax 740 334*), which has both a hot and a cold pool, a water slide, a sauna, a tennis court and a restaurant. The pool facilities are open only on weekends and holidays, but the hotel rooms and restaurant are open all week. The rooms in the cabins are clean and cost about US$20/30. Family rooms are available on a sliding scale, with the largest sleeping nine people for about US$75. The place is popular as a family weekend getaway. Nonresidents can use the pool and sauna for about US$4.

Between the Bascún and the Piscina El Salado is a B&B called *Casa Nahuazo* (☎ *740 315*). It is run by the friendly Aniko Bahr, who arrived in 1981 with the Peace Corps and somehow never left. The hotel is very quiet and is a good place to get travel information. There is an English-language book exchange. The five clean and pleasant double rooms have private bath, hot water, fresh fruit and flowers. Rates are about US$15/24, including continental breakfast. The kitchen provides snacks or light meals (at a low extra cost) until 5 pm.

Finally, high above Baños is the town's most exclusive hotel, the Swiss-managed

Luna Runtún (☎ 740 882/3, fax 740 376, info@lunaruntun.com). By road, it's 6km beyond Baños; follow the signs east of town on the road to Puyo. Luna Runtún can be reached on foot by climbing up from Baños for about 3km along either of the main trails. Most guests do not carry their suitcases up a steep trail but prefer to drive in. The trails are there for a downhill hike back into Baños. Horseback riding and guided hiking can be arranged, and hikes range from a gentle botany walk or cultural excursion to more strenuous climbs. On the grounds are a volleyball court and children's playground. The views are gorgeous, including views of the volcanic explosions of Tungurahua. The 32 rooms and one suite are spacious and comfortable, all with large bathrooms and views. Rates include an American breakfast and a complete à la carte dinner. Standard rooms are US$100/150; superior rooms have a private terrace overlooking Baños and run US$192 per double; the presidential suite, which has a fireplace, costs US$234.

Places to Eat
Ecuadorian and European cuisine alike are available in Baños.

Donde Marcelo (☎ 740 427), on Ambato near 16 de Diciembre, has Ecuadorian food and a very popular bar upstairs. The service is friendly and efficient, and the food is quite good, but slightly pricey. This is the heart of Baños' busy pedestrian street. You can sit outside of Marcelo's and people-watch while having a beer. On the same block, *Restaurant Latino* and *Restaurant Los Alpes* are simpler but have decent, cheaper Ecuadorian food. A block away, *La Abuela Café* (☎ 740 507) is a recommended little place and is often full with people lingering over a sandwich, a dessert or a light meal.

Also in the pedestrian section of Ambato, *Mamá Inés* has a few Mexican dishes and other international food items; it is very popular. Opposite, *La Casa Vieja de Dusseldorf* (☎ 740 430) is also quite good and reasonably priced, although the menu is more local than German. On the next block

of Ambato, *Rico Pan* (☎ 740 387) is good for breakfast (including granola and yogurt), juices and snacks; it sells some of the best bread in town. There are several other cheap restaurants and bakeries on Ambato and around the market.

Restaurant Monica, on Alfaro near Espejo, continues to be a gringo hangout, despite its slow and inefficient service. Menus in 12 languages hang on the wall, but the menu prices may differ from what you are charged.

El Jardín, on Parque de la Basílica, is also a popular hangout and has a variety of meat and fish dishes that can be enjoyed on the outdoor patio. *Café Hood*, on 16 de Diciembre near Martínez, features international vegetarian food and has a book exchange, incense, art and music. It's open 8 to 11 am and 1:30 to 9 pm daily except Tuesday, and it is a current favorite among young travelers. One reader writes that it's like a student café in Berkeley, California. *Casa Hood*, on Martínez near Halflants, is an offshoot of Café Hood. It has similar food, and at 8 pm, movies are shown. It is closed Monday. *Café Higuerón* (☎ 740 910, 12 de Noviembre 2-70) has a good variety of meat and vegetarian plates, teas and yummy desserts. It is open 8 am to 10 pm daily except Wednesday. Even though this is one of the town's better restaurants, the prices aren't very high.

The popular *La Closerie de Lilas* (Alfaro 6-20) has good French-influenced meals at very reasonable prices. *Le Petit Restaurant* (☎ 740 936), at L'Auberge (see Places to Stay), also has food with a French twist, but it is not as cheap as La Closerie de Lilas. Nevertheless it's popular with travelers, and the food is good, but – as is the way of most French restaurants – portions are modest. The service is leisurely, and it's a place to hang out. Videos are shown on some days, and there are sometimes live *música folklórica* performances in the evenings. *Café Mariane*, on Halflants near Rocafuerte, has Mediterranean cuisine with a French influence.

Several places serve well-priced Italian food; the small but friendly *La Bella Italia*

(☎ 740 072), on Rocafuerte near Alfaro, is especially tasty. The food is freshly made, so don't come expecting super-fast service. The young Ecuadorian owner lived in New York for several years, speaks English and has a good feel for what North Americans like in their Italian food. Some travelers prefer *Paolo's Pizzería* (☎ 740 944), near Café Hood, which has pasta as well as pizza, and still others recommend *Scaligeri*, on Alfaro, which is run by Italians.

Regine Café Alemán (☎ 740 641), on Rocafuerte near 16 de Diciembre, has a German menu; it's good for breakfast starting at 8 am, as well as hearty lunches and dinners, coffee and other drinks. Among other things, there are tasty potato pancakes and innovative concoctions of tea, coffee and hot chocolate laced with various alcoholic beverages. German newspapers are available. It's closed on Tuesday. *Café Cultura* (☎ 740 083), in the hotel of the same name, features homemade breads, quiches, fruit pies, fresh fish, pastries, fruit juices and various other delectable items.

La Casa Mía (☎ 740 609/090, Halflants 131), adjoining Hostal Isla de Baños, is an elegant restaurant specializing in a variety of Ecuadorian food. There is a live música folklórica and dance show at 8:30 pm. The service is good and friendly; prices range from US$3.50 for the meal of the day to US$6 for special orders. *Posada El Marqués* (☎ 740 187) has live music some nights and good food. Go there early and see what's happening.

Sol de Los Andes (☎ 740 514), adjoining Hostal El Castillo, serves Ecuadorian food and will prepare cuy with advance notice. It has a *peña* (bar with music) weekend evenings.

On certain days (particularly during fiestas), you can buy cuy at some of the market restaurants. They are normally roasted whole, and some people find the sight of their little roasted feet sticking up and their tiny teeth poking out a bit disconcerting. Surprisingly, they taste quite good – a little like a cross between chicken and rabbit. In fact, the local nickname for them in some areas is *conejo,* which means 'rabbit.'

Another local food popular in Baños is toffee. You can see people swinging it onto wooden pegs in the doorways of many of the town's shops – the swinging blends and softens the toffee. You can try a fresh, soft piece or buy a box of hardened toffees as a souvenir.

Artwork of indigenous artist Pablo Sanaguano

Entertainment

Nightlife in Baños consists mainly of chatting with new friends in the restaurants after a strenuous day of soaking in the pools.

There are several bars that are frequented by travelers, but their popularity tends to wax and wane from year to year – new ones open and close frequently. Try the copycat *Hard Rock Café*, on Alfaro, for inexpensive drinks and old rock classics. The somewhat-pricier *bar* above Donde Marcelo is also popular and has rock music and a dance floor that can get lively on weekends.

The friendly and hip *Bamboo Bar*, at 16 de Diciembre and Martínez, has Latin and rock music with dancing. This is one of the most popular bars in town. *Peña Ananitay*, on 16 de Diciembre near Espejo, has live folklórica late on weekend nights. It is very popular and gets very crowded, but it's one of the best places in town to hear Andean music. Posada El Marqués and Sol de Los Andes (see Places to Eat, earlier) have weekend peñas with varied music.

La Burbuja (☎ 740 520) is a disco on an alley off the east end of Ambato. It is open Wednesday to Saturday nights, but there's rarely much happening, except perhaps on weekends after 10 pm (bring all your friends and make it happen). There's a US$2 cover on weekends.

Travelers hang out in the European restaurants mentioned earlier – they tend to stay open later than most. All of these are suitable for solo women travelers (less suitable are the many small pool halls, especially on the back streets, which are frequented mainly by men).

Getting There & Away

Buses from Ambato's bus terminal leave about every half hour for Baños. The fare is under US$1, and the ride is about an hour. From Quito and many other towns, it's sometimes quicker to catch a bus to Ambato and change rather than wait for the less-frequent direct buses.

The Baños bus terminal is within walking distance of most hotels – it's a small town. Buses for Quito (US$2.80, 3½ hours) leave almost every hour, or you can take more frequent buses to Ambato and change for other destinations. The road to Riobamba is currently closed.

Ticket offices in the bus terminal sell tickets for buses to the Oriente (Puyo or Tena) but usually won't guarantee you a seat or give you a refund if the bus has standing room only. You can, however, buy a ticket from the driver, so you could wait for a bus to pass by and then board if there's room. The two-hour ride to Puyo costs about US$1.50, and the five-hour trip to Tena costs US$3.50.

Getting Around

Westbound buses leave from Rocafuerte, behind the market. They are marked 'El Salado' and go to the baths of that name. The fare is about US$0.10. A taxi to these baths costs about US$0.80. Eastbound buses that go as far as the dam at Agoyán leave from Alfaro at Martínez.

PARQUE NACIONAL SANGAY

Stretching for about 70km south and southeast of Baños, the 517,765-hectare Parque Nacional Sangay contains some of the remotest and most inaccessible areas in Ecuador. The park was established in 1979 and became a World Heritage Site in 1983, protecting an incredible variety of terrain. Its western boundary is marked by the Cordillera Oriental, and three of Ecuador's highest volcanoes are within the park. The northernmost, Tungurahua, used to be accessed easily from Baños (although it is currently not accessible because of eruptions), while the more southerly volcanoes, El Altar and Sangay, require a much greater effort. The area around the park's namesake Volcán Sangay in particular is very rugged and remote, and relatively few people have penetrated it. Nevertheless, the routes to the three volcanoes provide the most frequently used ways to access the park.

From the park's western areas, which climb to over 5000m around each of the three volcanoes, the terrain plunges from the high páramos down the eastern slopes of the Andes to elevations barely above 1000m at the park's eastern boundaries. In between is terrain so steep, rugged and wet (over 400cm of rain annually in some eastern areas) that it remains a wilderness in the truest sense. A few small and remote Andean communities (not large enough to be graced by the title of 'village') dot the páramos, but the thickly vegetated slopes east of the mountains are the haunts of very rarely seen mammals, such Andean spectacled bears, mountain tapirs, pumas, ocelots, jaguarundis and porcupines. Nobody lives there.

Only one road of any importance enters this national park, going from Riobamba to Alao (the main access point to Volcán Sangay) and petering out in the páramos to the east. Another road is still under construction. When this dirt road is completed, it will link Guamote (in the highlands) with Macas (in the southern Oriente), passing through the southern extremities of the park. This road has been under construction since 1992 and is scheduled for completion in 2001. Since construction began, Unesco has placed Parque Nacional Sangay on its 'National Parks in Peril' list, because 8km of the road will pass through the park, and a much longer section will form the park's southern boundary. Local authorities say that the road's construction has destroyed 20 lakes and has contributed to erosion, deforestation, loss of habitat, damage to water drainage basins and the cutting of wildlife corridors. Colonization, which is sure to follow in the wake of this road, is the greatest future threat to the park.

Volcán Tungurahua

With a (pre-eruption) elevation of 5016m, Tungurahua is Ecuador's 10th-highest peak. It was a beautiful, cone-shaped volcano with a small cap of snow perched jauntily atop its lush green slopes. Since the many eruptions beginning in late 1999, much of the snow has melted, and the cone and crater have changed in shape. Tungurahua is just within the northern boundaries of Parque Nacional Sangay.

Until 1999, many travelers liked to walk part of the way up the volcano, perhaps as far as the village of Pondoa, or to the (now destroyed) refuge, at 3800m. Beyond the refuge, it gets steep, but the mountain was considered one of Ecuador's easier 5000m peaks to climb. It will probably be many months before it becomes stable enough to climb again. Ask in Baños about the current situation.

Volcán El Altar

At 5319m, this jagged and long-extinct volcano is the fifth-highest mountain in Ecuador. It is considered the most technically difficult of Ecuador's peaks and was not climbed until 1963. The wild páramo surrounding the mountain and the greenish lake (Laguna Amarilla, or 'Yellow Lagoon') within the blown-away crater are targets for adventurous backpackers with complete camping gear. Although the area looks almost uninhabited, do not leave any gear unattended, or it may disappear.

To get to El Altar, take a bus from Riobamba to Penipe, a village halfway between Riobamba and Baños. Penipe was evacuated in 1999, and the road between Penipe and Baños, considered to be in the most dangerous zone, is closed. However, buses from Riobamba may go as far as Penipe. From Penipe, go to Candelaria, about 15km to the southeast. There is supposedly a daily bus between Penipe and Candelaria; trucks go there occasionally, or you can hire a pickup truck in Penipe. From Candelaria (which has a very simple store), it is about 2km to Hacienda Releche (not a place to stay), near which there is a Parque Nacional Sangay station. You pay the park fee (US$10) there and can stay the night for another US$2. The station has cooking and washing facilities; to see if the station is open, check with the climbing guides in Baños, Ambato or Riobamba.

From Candelaria, it is a full-day hike to the crater. Guides and mules can be hired in Candelaria. There are many trails in the area, and it is worth having a guide to show you the beginning of the main trail to El Altar, which is less than an hour away from the station. Once you're on the main trail, the going is fairly obvious.

The best times to go are December to March. The wettest months in the Oriente are July and August, which means that El Altar frequently clouded in at that time. El Altar is far enough south of Tungurahua that even a massive explosion should not affect hikers in the area.

Volcán Sangay

This 5230m volcano is one of the most active in the Andes – it is constantly spewing out rocks, smoke and ash. The volcanological situation changes from hour to hour and year to year. The mountain is not technically difficult to climb, but people attempting it run the risk of being killed by explosions, so climbing attempts are rare. You can hike to the base if you wish, although the approach is long and tedious, and the best views are from afar.

To get there, take a bus southeast from Riobamba to the villages of Licto or Pungalá, which are next to one another (you can ask in Riobamba's bus terminal about these buses). From there, occasional trucks (which leave early in the morning on most days) go another 20km (one hour) to the village of Alao, where there is a national-park ranger station. There, you pay the park fee, get information and are allowed to sleep for a nominal fee. There are a couple of simple stores in Alao, and guides are available there for the three- or four-day hike to base camp – you'll probably get hopelessly lost without a guide. Rates are about US$15 to US$25 per day plus food and shelter. Most guides will watch you climb the mountain from the base camp – very few will go up with you! One that does is Carlos Caz, and he charges the higher rate for climbing up there.

Another approach is to take the incomplete highway from Guamote to Macas. The road goes southeast as far as the village of Atillo and then becomes a mule trail dropping down through the eastern Andes to the village of San Vicente, about two or three days away. En route, you pass through the southernmost extremity of the national park (see the Southern Oriente chapter). This long and ambitious hike, as well as the approaches and climbs of Sangay and El Altar, are described in guidebooks mentioned in the Books section of the Facts for the Visitor chapter. The South American Explorers has some recent expedition reports on file.

GUARANDA
☎ 03

Guaranda is the capital of the agricultural province of Bolívar but is nevertheless is a small town with a population of about 20,500. Its name derives from that of the Indian chief Guarango. Guaranda is a quiet, dignified provincial town surrounded by pretty hills – there are supposedly several of these, which inspires locals to call their town 'the Rome of the Andes.' It certainly can't be described as exciting, and the main reason you'd want to go there is probably for the bus rides, which offer spectacular views.

Information

Banco de Pichincha, at Azuay near Convención de 1884, is open 9 am to 2 pm weekdays. Filanbanco, at Cañizares near Salinas, has a Visa ATM.

Andinatel is on Rocafuerte near Pichincha, and the post office is on Azuay near Pichincha.

Several clinics (including Clínica Bolívar, ☎ 981 278) and pharmacies are found near Plaza Roja, south of the hospital.

Things to See & Do

The main market day is Saturday, with a smaller market Wednesday. The best place for the market is Plaza 15 de Mayo, which is worth visiting even on ordinary days for its pleasantly quiet, forgotten colonial air (ignore the school on one side). The market at Mercado 10 de Noviembre is held in a modern, ugly, concrete building.

Walk the streets for a few hours; you'll end up in the last century. If you have nothing to do, go down to the Parque Montúfar and see if one of the statues there still has a bees' nest under its right armpit! It's been there for at least a decade. You can take the risk of going for some honey if you like.

A traditional local activity is the evening *paseo* (stroll) around Parque Simón Bolívar, from about 6 to 9 pm nightly.

Carnaval is very popular – people stream in from all over the province and beyond for

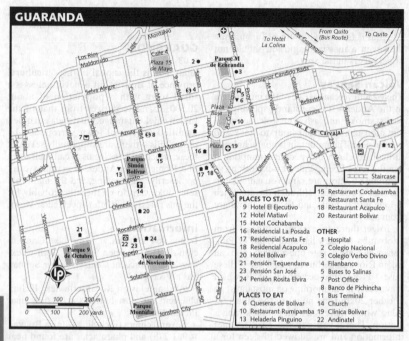

GUARANDA

PLACES TO STAY
9 Hotel El Ejecutivo
12 Hotel Matiaví
15 Hotel Cochabamba
16 Residencial La Posada
17 Residencial Santa Fe
18 Residencial Acapulco
20 Hotel Bolívar
21 Pensión Tequendama
23 Pensión San José
24 Pensión Rosita Elvira

PLACES TO EAT
6 Queseras de Bolívar
10 Restaurant Rumipamba
13 Heladería Pinguino

15 Restaurant Cochabamba
17 Restaurant Santa Fe
18 Restaurant Acapulco
20 Restaurant Bolívar

OTHER
1 Hospital
2 Colegio Nacional
3 Colegio Verbo Divino
4 Filanbanco
5 Buses to Salinas
7 Post Office
8 Banco de Pichincha
11 Bus Terminal
14 Church
19 Clínica Bolívar
22 Andinatel

such rural festivities as water fights, dances and parades. Groups of local amateur musicians stroll from house to house playing music and getting invited in for a drink or snack. The local drink of choice is 'Pájaro Azul' (Blue Bird), an aguardiente flavored with local herbs (one Guarandeño said chicken is used to flavor this drink!). Many consider this to be one of Ecuador's best Carnavales.

About 3km out of town is a hill with a 5m-high monument, *El Indio de Guarango*, from which you get a good view of Guaranda, Volcán Chimborazo and the surrounding countryside. There is a tiny museum near the monument. A taxi will take you for about US$1. The monument is clearly visible from the northwest end of town, and you can walk there – ask locals for directions.

Places to Stay

Most of the hotels in town are basic cold-water cheapies. The water supply is erratic

in most of them. They include *Pensión San José*, on Sucre between Rocafuerte and Espejo; the more basic *Pensión Rosita Elvira*, opposite Pensión San José; and *Residencial La Posada*, on Arregón near 10 de Agosto. *Pensión Tequendama*, on Rocafuerte near José García, is used by couples for stays of a few hours. These all charge US$2 or less per person.

The pleasant *Hotel Bolívar* (☎ 980 547, Sucre 7-04), near Olmedo, has simple but clean rooms around a flowery courtyard; the reception area shows off archaeological artifacts. This is the best budget choice; the rates are about US$3 per person with shared bath and about US$5 with private baths; hot water may be available. The similarly priced *Residencial Acapulco* (☎ 981 953), on 10 de Agosto near 9 de Abril, has hot showers but is otherwise basic, and next door, *Residencial Santa Fé* has an overly amorous manager according to one female reader, although other travelers have found the place acceptable. *Hotel El Ejecutivo* (☎/fax 982 044, García Moreno 8-03) has one hot-water bathroom shared between each of the two rooms. Rates are about US$5 per person, and rooms have TVs.

On the outskirts of town is *Hotel Matiaví* (☎ 980 295), near the bus terminal. It has cleanish basic rooms with private baths and hot water for about US$4 per person.

The best place in town, although it's not very good, is *Hotel Cochabamba* (☎ 981 958, 981 124, fax 982 125), on García Moreno near 7 de Mayo. Rates are US$5/8, or US$9/12 with private bath, TV and phone. Rooms vary widely in quality.

A 15-minute walk out of town on Avenida Guayaquil is a tourist complex called *Hotel La Colina* (☎/fax 980 666, 981 954); it is often empty midweek. Located on a hill, it features some rooms with good views, a restaurant, a bar, a small indoor swimming pool and Jacuzzi, and a garden with swings for children. The rates are about US$21/28 for comfortable rooms with private bath and hot water; there are also a couple of minisuites for US$10 more.

Places to Eat

There are few restaurants, and they close early – many by 7:30 pm. Several of the best places to eat are in hotels. The best in town is supposedly *Restaurant Cochabamba*, at the hotel of that name, but it has been criticized for serving only a few selections from the rather impressive-looking but overpriced menu. It is closed Monday.

Progressively cheaper are the restaurants *Bolívar*, *Acapulco* and *Santa Fé*, all in the hotels of the same name. Restaurant Bolívar has a reasonable selection of food and the walls are covered with antique musical instruments. A set lunch here is about US$1, compared to about US$3 at Restaurant Cochabamba. Restaurant Acapulco has cheap food, especially *chaulafan* (a rice dish) and is often full with locals.

There are several eateries around Plaza Roja, of which *Restaurant Rumipamba* is the best, though nothing special. *Queseras de Bolívar*, also on Plaza Roja, sells cheeses of the province, makes cheese sandwiches,

and has info about visiting the nearby village of Salinas, where cheese production is an important part of the economy. On the west side of Parque Simón Bolívar, you'll find ice cream at *Heladería Pingüino*.

Getting There & Away

Most buses leaving from the bus terminal head east on García Moreno and Avenida E de Carvajal – you can't miss it. Buses depart from about 4 am to 7 pm. Afternoon buses can get booked up in advance, so plan ahead.

The most frequent departures are for Ambato (US$1.60, two hours) and Quito (US$3, five hours), with buses for these destinations leaving about once an hour with various companies. Almost as frequently, there are buses for Babahoyo (US$2.25, four hours) and Guayaquil (US$3, five hours). There are five daily buses on the spectacular but poor road to Riobamba (US$2, three hours), and buses at 7:45 am and 2 pm via the less populated El Arenal route (two hours), which is best for reaching the turnoff to the Chimborazo mountain refuges.

There are also several buses a day to **Chillanes**, a small town some 50km (or three hours) south of Guaranda. There is reportedly a basic pensión there. It certainly would be getting off the beaten track if that's what you want. The Chillanes area produces coffee and aguardiente. En route to both Babahoyo and Chillanes, you pass through the old town of **San Miguel**, which still has wooden colonial buildings with carved balconies. Buses for San Jose de Chimbo and San Miguel leave several times an hour. There are also several buses a day to other villages, such as San Luis, Caluma and Echeandia, if you want to explore a remoter area.

Buses for Salinas leave from the north end of Plaza Roja at 6 am. Trucks for Salinas leave from near here Saturday (to coincide with Guaranda's market) and occasionally on other days as well. The fare is about US$1.

SALINAS
☎ 03

About 35km north of Guaranda, in wild and beautiful countryside, is the peaceful community of Salinas. It is known for its excellent cheeses, homemade salamis, dried mushrooms, chocolate and rough-spun sweaters, and you can visit the small cooperative factories that produce them. The people are very friendly and not much used to seeing travelers. It's an interesting destination for people who enjoy venturing off the beaten track and wish to see how people live in a remote rural Ecuadorian community. Market day is Tuesday. The countryside around offers pleasant walks. It is definitely very *tranquilo*.

There is a small store on the Salinas plaza that sells the naturally dyed, rough-spun sweaters for well under US$10. Prices are fixed, and other woolen goods are available. There is also a small restaurant, and you can buy cheese in 31kg balls!

Places to Stay

The clean and recommended *Hotel El Refuge* (☎ 758 778, fax 982 140), on the town's outskirts, offers beds at about US$3 per person; singles cost a little more. Simple dinners are US$1.50, and hot showers are available. The managers can arrange for local youths to guide you around the various cooperatives and give suggestions for hikes in the local countryside. Also ask at the store on the plaza about a cheap hostel run by the cheese-making cooperative.

Getting There & Away

Queseras de Bolívar cheese/sandwich shop in Guaranda (see that section, earlier) has information about getting to Salinas.

Otherwise, take a bus to Cuatro Esquinas, about 10km north of Guaranda on the road to Ambato. From here, it's about 25km to Salinas; wait for a passing truck to give you a ride (expect to pay).

To get back to Guaranda, hang out in Salinas' main plaza and flag down any vehicle. Most vehicles leaving town are going to Guaranda. The drive is a spectacular one.

RIOBAMBA

☎ 03

'All roads lead to Riobamba,' proclaims a road sign as you enter this city, and it is indeed true that Riobamba is at the heart of an extensive and scenic road network.

Whichever way you arrive or leave, try to plan your journey for daylight hours so as not to miss the great views.

The usual way to arrive is on the Panamericana from Ambato, which is 52km to the north. The road climbs over a 3600m pass that affords great views of Volcanes Chimborazo (6310m) and Carihuairazo (5020m) before dropping to Riobamba, at 2750m.

An even more spectacular route is the dirt road arriving from Guaranda. There is also a lower road from Baños that follows the Río Chambo valley and passes through numerous small villages. (One of these villages, Penipe, is where you'll find the dirt road that climbs toward the rugged peak of Volcán El Altar, which rises to 5319m. Looking back along this road will also give you views of Volcán Tungurahua.)

Riobamba, the capital of Chimborazo Province, has a fast-growing population of over 126,000. It is more or less the geographical center of Ecuador and has long been an agriculturally important area. Riobamba was a Puruhá Indian center before becoming part of the Inca Empire during the late 15th century.

The first Spanish colonialists built a city near present-day Cajabamba, about 17 miles farther south along the Panamericana. This was destroyed in a 1797 earthquake, and the survivors moved to the present site, which is on a large plain surrounded by several snow-capped peaks. The flat terrain of Riobamba enabled it to be built in a regular chessboard pattern, with wide avenues and imposing stone buildings. It has a rather sedate air, and Ecuadorians call it the 'Sultan of the Andes.' One of the main streets through town is called Primera Constituyente, in commemoration of the fact that Ecuador's first constitution was written and signed here in 1830.

Information

Tourist Office The helpful and friendly tourist information office (☎ 941 213), 10 de Agosto 20-72, is open 8:30 am to 5 pm weekdays.

Money Casa de Cambio MM Jaramilla Arteaga, on 10 de Agosto at Pichincha, is a

RIOBAMBA

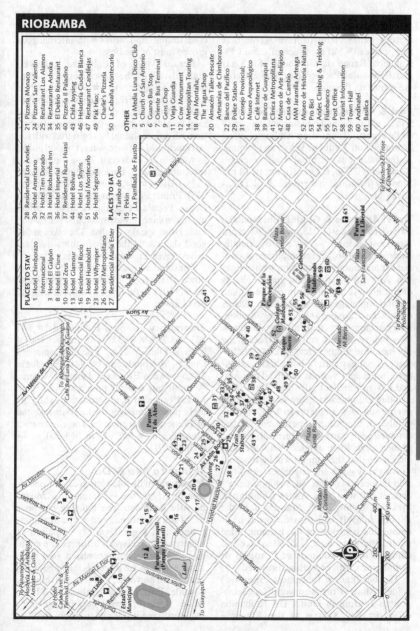

PLACES TO STAY
1 Hotel Chimborazo Internacional
3 Hotel El Galpón
8 Hotel El Cisne
10 Hotel Zeus
13 Hotel Glamour
16 Residencial Rocio
19 Hotel Humboldt
23 Hotel Whymper
26 Hotel Metropolitano
27 Residencial María Ester
28 Residencial Los Andes
30 Hotel Americano
32 Hotel Tren Dorado
33 Hotel Riobamba Inn
36 Hotel Imperial
37 Residencial Nuca Huasi
44 Hotel Bolívar
45 Hotel Los Shyris
51 Hostal Montecarlo
56 Hotel Segovia

PLACES TO EAT
4 Tambo de Oro
15 Pekin
17 La Parrillada de Fausto
21 Pizzería Mónaco
24 Pizzería San Valentín
25 Restaurant Los Alamos
34 Restaurante Ashoka
35 El Delirio Restaurant
40 Pizzería Il Paladino
43 Chifa Joysing
46 Heladería Ciudad Blanca
47 Restaurant Candilejas
49 Pak Hao;
Charlie's Pizzería
50 La Cabaña Montecarlo

OTHER
2 La Media Luna Disco Club
5 Church of San Antonio
6 Guano Bus Stop
7 Oriente Bus Terminal
9 Gens Chop
11 Vieja Guardia
12 Cow Monument
14 Metropolitan Touring
18 Alta Montaña;
20 Almacén Taller Rescate
Artesanías de Chimborazo
The Tagua Shop
22 Banco del Pacífico
29 Police Station
31 Consejo Provincial;
Museo Arqueológico
38 Café Internet
39 Banco de Guayaquil
41 Clínica Metropolitana
42 Museo de Arte Religioso
48 Casa de Cambio
52 MM Jaramilla Arteaga
Museo de Historia Natural
53 Pro Bici
54 Andes Climbing & Trekking
55 Filanbanco
57 Post Office
58 Tourist Information
59 Town Hall
60 Andinatel
61 Basílica

reliable place to change money, as is the casa de cambio in Hostal Montecarlo. Numerous banks claim to have ATMs that accept all cards, but many actually don't. Filanbanco, Banco de Guayaquil (for Visa) and Banco del Pacifico (for MasterCard) are shown on the map.

Post & Communications The post office is in an old-fashioned building at Espejo and 10 de Agosto. There is an Andinatel office downtown on Tarqui at Veloz, and another at the main bus terminal. Café Internet, Rocafuerte 22-30, is open 10 am to 10 pm Monday to Saturday; there are shorter Sunday hours.

Travel Agencies & Guides Alta Montaña (☎ 963 694, fax 942 215, aventura@ch.pro.ec), León Borja 35-17, is run by friendly Rodrigo Donoso, an accomplished mountaineer and photographer who speaks English. Apart from arranging guided climbs of the highest mountains in Ecuador, Alta Montaña manages three mountain refuges on Volcán Chimborazo (see that section, later); arranges acclimatization and training days before ascents; organizes treks along the Inca Trail to Ingapirca, around Chimborazo, to Sangay; offers horseback and bicycle tours and various other adventures; and has an excellent gift shop. Rates for a two-day Chimborazo ascent start at US$145 per person (six climbers) to US$200 (two climbers), including experienced guides, climbing gear, transportation, meals and use of the refuge. Keep in mind that there is no guarantee that the summit will be reached.

Also very good and experienced is Marcelo Puruncajas (☎/fax 940 964, ppurunca@ecu.net.ec), who runs Andes Climbing & Trekking, Colón 22-25. Marcelo does the guiding himself and provides gear; he is among the cheapest of the recommended guides, charging about US$300 to take two climbers to the summits of Cotopaxi or Chimborazo, with everything provided.

The best-known (and most expensive) guide is Marco Cruz, who works for Metropolitan Touring in Quito. His Riobamba office (☎ 940 818) is at the Albergue Abraspungo (see Places to Stay, later). He runs his own very comfortable hostal for acclimatization and works with international groups most of the time.

Enrique Veloz, of Riobamba, is the veteran advisor of the Asociación de Andinismo de Chimborazo (☎ 960 916), Chile 33-21, at Francia. He has climbed Chimborazo and the other peaks many times and may be able to guide you or give information. All guides should be registered with the Asociación. Make sure you get a good guide, as your life depends on it. These trips are not recommended for beginning mountaineers.

Pro Bici (☎ 942 468, 961 877, fax 961 923), Primera Constituyente 23-51 (next to Banco Popular; ring the doorbell), offers mountain-bike rentals and tours. The owner, Galo Brito, speaks English. The bikes are in good shape, and the guided tours have received several recommendations.

For standard tour arrangements, the local office of Metropolitan Touring (☎ 969 600, fax 969 601), León Borja 37-64, is among the best known.

Emergency Hospital Policlínico (☎ 961 705, 965 725, 968 232) is at the east end of town, at Olmedo 11-01. Locals recommend Clínica Metropolitana (☎ 941 930), Junín 25-28 between España and García Moreno. A small but central police station is on León Borja near the train station, while the main police station is at the southeast end of Primera Constituyente. You can contact the police at ☎ 961 913 or 969 300, or by dialing ☎ 911.

Things to See & Do
Museums In the old church of La Concepción, on Argentinos, is the renowned **Museo de Arte Religioso**. The building has been beautifully restored, and there are many rooms with a good variety of paintings, sculptures and religious artifacts. The major piece is a huge, gem-encrusted gold monstrance said to be priceless. Signage is not very good, however, and it is worth hiring a guide. Entrance costs about US$2; the guides work for tips. Hours change often but were recently 9 am to noon and 2 to

5 pm Tuesday to Saturday. On Sunday and on holidays, the museum may be open in the mornings only; it's closed Monday.

At Primera Constituyente and Carabobo is the Consejo Provincial (Provincial Counsel Office), which has a **Museo Archaeológico** that is open only occasionally. Colegio Maldonado, at Primera Constituyente and Larrea, has a small, unremarkable **Museo de Historia Natural** that is occasionally open (US$0.30).

Parks There is an observation platform at **Parque 21 de Abril** from which the city and surrounding countryside can be appreciated. There is also a tile-work representation of the history of Ecuador. The view of (currently erupting) Volcán Tungurahua rising behind the church of San Antonio is especially impressive.

Parque La Libertad is another quiet plaza. Its basilica is famous as the only round church in Ecuador. Begun in 1883, it took over 30 years to complete and was designed, built and decorated mainly by locals – a source of civic pride. It's often closed; try Sundays and evenings after 6 pm.

Parque Maldonado is a pleasant park alive with trees, flowers and (at sunset) birds. Riobamba's cathedral is on the northeastern side. In the park is a statue of the Ecuadorian geographer Pedro Maldonado (see Parque La Alameda, under Quito, in the Quito & Around chapter).

Also known as Parque Infantil, **Parque Guayaquil** boasts swings and slides for the kids, as well as a small lake, where rowboats can be rented. It's popular for family weekend picnics. The tiled cow monument at the north end, sculpted by Endara Crow, is one of the more unusual statues that you'll see in an Ecuadorian town.

One of the only places to buy crafts during the Saturday market is around **Parque de la Concepción** (see The Market, next).

The Market Saturday is market day, and there is much street activity then – especially around 5 de Junio and Argentinos, although almost every plaza and park in the city seems to be busy. The market is a colorful affair, with thousands of people from surrounding villages flocking to barter, buy and sell. It's rather incongruous to see a barefoot Indian woman leading a squealing piglet on a string through the streets of a major town.

New market buildings detract somewhat from the *ambiente*, and many market areas sell mainly food items and plastic consumer goods. Nevertheless, it is the shoppers, rather than the shopping, that are of interest to travelers. One plaza, however, has plenty of crafts for sale – this is Parque de la Concepción, at Orozco and Colón, the only part of the market oriented toward tourists (though other plazas are worth visiting).

An interesting Riobambeño handicraft is **tagua-nut carving**. These 'nuts' are actually seeds from a type of rainforest palm that grows in many lowland areas (see the 'Riches from the Rainforest' boxed text, in the North Coast chapter), but highland Riobamba has traditionally been a carving center.

Another interesting handicraft from the Riobamba area is the **shigra**, a tough woven bag made from *cabuya* (agave, or century plant) fibers. Their durability and practicality make shigras very popular souvenirs for many travelers, who often use them as day bags. Cabuya is also used to make rope and rope sandals.

There are also baskets and mats that have been woven by the Colta Indians from the reeds lining the shores of Laguna de Colta, a few kilometers south of Riobamba. Many clothing items, such as woven belts, fine ponchos and embroidered shawls, are also sold.

Note that Sunday, the day after market day, is dead in Riobamba, and most restaurants are closed. It definitely is a day of rest!

Special Events

Riobamba's annual fiesta celebrates the Independence Battle of Tapi on April 21, 1822. On and around that date, there is a large agricultural fair with the usual highland events – street parades, dancing and plenty of traditional food and drink. The city and hotels can be particularly crowded then.

Places to Stay

Budget Most hotels are in the town center, a couple of kilometers away from the bus terminal. The cheapest hotels near the terminal often lack water and are not recommended, although there are some better but slightly pricier ones there.

Most of the cheap hotels are near the train station, but many of them are very run down. *Residencial Ñuca Huasi* (☎ 966 669, *10 de Agosto 10-24*) is a very basic place that was once popular with backpackers. Rooms are grimy, and women have complained that the shared shower has a broken window through which a staff member spies. Rates are under US$2 per person, or under US$3 with a private bath and hot water between 7 and 9 am or 7 and 9 pm. Now popular is the clean and friendly (albeit noisy) *Hotel Imperial* (☎ 960 429, *Rocafuerte 22-15*). Rooms are US$3 per person, or US$3.50 with bath and hot water. The manager will arrange trips to Chimborazo.

Other basic hotels in the range of US$2 to US$3 per person include *Hotel Bolívar* (☎ 968 294), at the corner of Carabobo and Guayaquil, which has hot water. If that place is full, travelers watching their pennies can try the more basic *Hotel Americano*, *Residencial María Ester* or *Residencial Los Andes* (see the Riobamba map for locations).

Hotel Metropolitano (☎ 961 714), at León Borja and Lavalle, and *Hotel Segovia* (☎ 961 269, *Primera Constituyente 22-26*) both charge about US$4 or US$5 per person for adequate rooms with bath and hot water. Also at this price is little *Residencial Rocío* (*Brasil 21-68*), which is quiet and clean and has hot water in the morning and evening only.

For about US$6 per person, the friendly and recommended *Hotel Los Shyris* (☎ 960 323), at Rocafuerte and 10 de Agosto, has clean rooms with TV and cramped hot showers. The similarly priced *Hotel Whymper* (☎ 964 575, fax 968 575, *Ángel León 23-10*), has received mixed reviews from readers. Certainly, rooms vary considerably with regard to the views, but more readers seem satisfied than not. Breakfast is available at

an extra cost, and tours and transportation to Chimborazo can be arranged there.

Hotel Riobamba Inn (☎ 961 696, 941 311, fax 940 974, *Carabobo 23-20*) is run by the folks who run Hotel Imperial; rooms are a reasonable US$7 per person. It has good-sized rooms with private bath, hot water, TV and telephone, and there is a restaurant with limited hours. Others around this price include *Hotel Humboldt* (☎ 961 788, 940 814, *León Borja 35-48*), for which renovations (and price increases?) are planned, and *Hotel Canada Inn* (☎/fax 946 677, *Avenida de la Prensa 23-31*), catercorner from the terminal terrestre. Rooms have private hot baths and TV, and a restaurant is available. Also try the new *Hotel Tren Dorado* (☎/fax 964 890, *Carabobo 22-35*), which is convenient to the train station and has decent rooms with private hot bath and TV.

Mid-Range Half a kilometer from the bus terminal, the clean *Hotel Zeus* (☎ 968 036/7/8, fax 962 292, hotelzeus@laserinter .net, *León Borja 41-29*) has 50 good rooms with private bath, hot water and cable TV for US$12/18. The hotel has four floors, and there is no elevator, but otherwise, this is a good deal, and there is a decent restaurant and bar (room service is available). Also at about this price, try *Hotel Glamour* (☎ 944 406, fax 944 407, *Primera Constituyente 37-85*), which has similar services.

The best hotel in the center is the similarly priced *Hostal Montecarlo* (☎ 960 557, fax 961 577, *10 de Agosto 25-41*). Inside an attractively restored, turn-of-the-century house, the Montecarlo has 18 comfortable rooms with TV (but no phone), a restaurant and a café.

Two other mid-range hotels are on Argentinos, about a kilometer west of the center, in a quiet area. *Hotel Chimborazo Internacional* (☎ 963 474/5, fax 963 473) is at Argentinos and Los Nogales and has a restaurant, pool, Jacuzzi and sauna. There are 36 decent rooms with TV and phone for about US$12/21. (Note that Argentinos stops short of Los Nogales, and you need to climb stairs to get there, or take an alternate route by taxi.) The similarly priced *Hotel El*

Galpón (☎/fax 960 981/2/3, galpon@ch.pro .ec) is at Argentinos and Zambrano (called Coronel Morales on some maps) and also has a restaurant and pool, but the 44 rooms are rather worn.

The modern and pleasant *Hotel El Cisne* (☎ 964 573, 941 980, fax 941 982, elcisne@ ch.pro.ec), at León Borja not far from Duchicela, has rooms with bath and TV for US$14/22. A restaurant and sauna are on the premises.

Hostería El Troje (☎/fax 964 572) is 4.5km southeast of town on the minor road to Chambo. It has a pool, tennis court, restaurant (which has received mixed reviews) and bar; the rate is around US$20 for a double room. Many of the rooms have fireplaces. The similarly priced *Albergue Abraspungo* (☎ 940 820, fax 940 819) is 3.5km northeast of town on the road to Guano. Although it's new as a hotel, it is quite attractive and is built around a traditional hacienda. Spacious rooms, a restaurant and bar, and horseback riding are all available here, and climbing expeditions can be arranged.

About 15km north of Riobamba on the Panamericana is *Hostería La Andaluza* (☎ 904 223, 904 248, fax 904 234, 904 277, francarenas@yahoo.com). This colonial hacienda has been attractively restored and is now perhaps the best hotel in Chimborazo Province. There are a pair of restaurants, a small exercise room and sauna, and a bar with a fireplace. Nearly all the antique-furnished rooms have fireplaces, as well as cable TV and telephones. Rates are about US$30/50, but if you take a chance and just arrive, much lower rates can be negotiated. It is not often full, except possibly on weekends.

Places to Eat

Riobamba's many restaurants are fairly basic and cheap. Budget travelers can try *Restaurant Los Alamos*, on Lavalle and León Borja, or several other inexpensive places near the train station. Nearby, a favorite place in the evenings for both young locals and tourists is the lively *Pizzería San Valentin* (☎ 963 137), at León Borja and

Torres, where you have to order pizza at the counter, and where Mexican food is also available. It's closed Sunday and sometimes Monday. *Pizzería Il Paladino* (García Moreno 24-42) is more of a traditional pizza place and is open Monday to Saturday evenings. Some people call it the best in town; others vote for *Pizzería Mónaco* (☎ 947 342, Ibarra 22-46). This one is open Sunday, as is *Charlie's Pizzería*, at García Moreno and 10 de Agosto. Both have good vegetarian and meat pizzas and lasagnas.

Decent chifas include *Pak Hao*, next to Charlie's Pizzería, and the cheaper *Joysing* (☎ 961 285, Unidad Nacional 29-23), by the train station. Joysing is open until 10:30 pm daily and is the best bet for late-night dining. Also good is *Chifa Pekin*, on León Borja near Brasil. For vegetarian food, try *Restaurante Ashoka*, on Carabobo near Primera Constituyente.

Restaurant Candilejas (☎ 960 220, 10 de Agosto 27-33) looks nice and serves decent Ecuadorian food. If your Spanish is hopeless, look at the photo menu. Nearby, *La Cabaña Montecarlo* (☎ 968 609, García Moreno 24-10) is associated with and next to Hostal Montecarlo. Both service and food are satisfactory but pricey by Riobamba standards (meals are around US$4). It is closed Monday and on Sunday evenings, but a good café in the hotel serves food every day.

Tambo de Oro (☎ 962 668, Zambrano 27-20) is a lunchtime favorite for locals. It's in a private house, and the food is very good and reasonably priced. Hours are noon to 4 pm daily.

Riobamba's most atmospheric eatery, *El Delirio Restaurant* (☎ 960 029, 967 502, Primera Constituyente 28-16), is in a historic house where Simón Bolívar stayed and, on July 5, 1822, wrote his epic poem *El Delirio* about his attempted ascent of Chimborazo (he reached the snowline). Part of the restaurant is in an outdoor patio, and good meals start at about US$3 or US$4. It is closed Monday and on Sunday evenings. *La Parrillada de Fausto*, on Uruguay, is good for steaks and other meat dishes; it is closed Sunday.

For dessert, try **Heladería Ciudad Blanca** *(Rocafuerte 2-40)*, which does fruit salads in addition to ice cream.

If you're staying out at the Hostería La Andaluza (see Places to Stay, earlier in this section), you'll find its restaurant is as good as any in Riobamba itself. It is very popular on weekends for lunch, when the wealthier citizens of Riobamba descend upon the hotel, bringing the whole family. The restaurant in Albergue Abraspungo is also a popular destination for weekending locals.

Entertainment

Nightlife is limited. There are a few places on León Borja or just north of it and west of the center. Pizzería San Valentin (see Places to Eat, earlier) is a popular gathering spot. **Gens Chop** *(☎ 964 325, León Borja 42-17)* is a popular bar with dancing on weekends. **Vieja Guardia** *(Flor 40-43)* is another.

La Media Luna Disco Club, on Argentinos opposite the Hotel El Galpón, is open weekends. **Café Bar Luna Negra** *(☎ 09-560 391)*, 5.5km away on the road to Guano, advertises weekend dancing to blues, rock 'n' roll and música folklórica.

Shopping

The Tagua Shop, León Borja 35-17, has an excellent selection of tagua carvings, as well as the best selection of maps and travel books in town. Several other places nearby sell tagua carvings too. A block away on León Borja is Almacén Taller Rescate Artesanías de Chimborazo ('Workshop to Rescue the Crafts of Chimborazo'), where tagua and various local products are sold.

Getting There & Away

Bus Riobamba has two bus terminals. The main terminal, terminal terrestre, is almost 2km northwest of the center along León Borja. Buses bound for Quito (US$3, four hours) and intermediate points are frequent, as are the buses for Guayaquil (US$3.50, 4½ hours). Transportes Patria has a Machala bus at 9:45 am (US$5, eight hours), and there are overnight buses. There are several buses a day for Cuenca (US$5, 6½ hours) on a bad road. Buses for Alausí leave

20 times a day from 5 am to 8 pm with CTA (US$1.20, two hours). Buses for local towns leave from a smaller terminal to the south (see Getting Around, later). Flota Bolívar has seven daily buses to Guaranda (US$1.50, two hours); some continue to Babahoyo. Most go via the rougher southern route; the 8:45 am and 2 pm buses go via El Arenal for access to Chimborazo.

For buses to Baños and the Oriente, you have to go to the Oriente bus terminal, on Avenidas Espejo and Luz Elisa Borja. However, the road to Baños from Riobamba may be closed because of falling ash from Tungurahua – the road from Ambato may be open.

Train Train schedules from Riobamba have been changing a great deal in recent years, and you should inquire locally for the latest information (but don't assume that is accurate, either).

Recently, service from Quito to Riobamba (US$16, nine hours) left at 8 am Saturday, returning from Riobamba at 9 am Friday. Service for the famous Nariz del Diablo leaves Riobamba at 7 am Wednesday, Friday and Sunday (US$16). It picks up more passengers in Alausí and goes only as far as Sibambe, immediately below El Nariz del Diablo, where there are no services. From Sibambe, the train ascends El Nariz del Diablo and returns to Alausí, where passengers can spend the night, continue on to Cuenca by bus or return to Riobamba by bus. Riding on the roof is allowed. Inquire at the train station (☎ 961 909).

Getting Around

North of the terminal terrestre, behind the church of Santa Faz (with a blue dome), is a local bus stop for the city center, nearly 2km away. These buses run along León Borja, which turns into 10 de Agosto near the train station. Here you'll find a good selection of hotels. To return to the terminal terrestre, take any bus marked 'Terminal' on Primera Constituyente; the fare is US$0.10.

Three long blocks south of the terminal terrestre (turn left out of the front entrance), off Unidad Nacional, is a smaller terminal with frequent local buses for Caja-bamba, Laguna de Colta and the Chapel of Balbanera; the fare is US$0.25. Buses for Guamote also leave from there.

To visit the villages of Guano and Santa Teresita, take a US$0.20 local bus ride from the stop at Avenidas Pichincha and New York.

SOUTHWEST OF RIOBAMBA
☎ 03

The southbound Panamericana actually heads west out of Riobamba until it reaches a cement factory 10km away. There the road forks; the right branch continues on to Guaranda, and the main highway heads southwest to **Cajabamba**, about 7km farther.

Founded in 1534, Cajabamba was historically important until it was devastated by the 1797 earthquake, which killed several thousand inhabitants. Most of the survivors founded nearby Riobamba, but a few remained, and their descendants still live there. As you arrive, look up to your right and you'll see a huge scar on the hillside. This is the only sign of the landslide that caused much of the damage over two centuries ago.

Right around Cajabamba, the Panamericana splits – the easternmost branch is the Ecuadorian Panamericana and becomes a regular road when it hits the border with Peru, and the westernmost branch is the international Panamericana and is still referred to as such once it hits the Peruvian border. Throughout the rest of this chapter, references to the Panamericana should be understood as the Ecuadorian, not international, Panamericana.

Most of the buses from Riobamba continue down the Panamericana beyond Cajabamba; if you want to see some of the old town, get off at the junction of the main highway and Avenida 2 de Agosto on the right. Most bus drivers stop here. If you head down 2 de Agosto, you'll soon come to a history museum (on your right), which contains about a dozen fragments of carved rock dating from before the earthquake. It's not worth seeing, but maybe in the future, the museum will have a proper exhibit. Continuing down the road, you come to the earthquake-damaged town church on your left. There are no hotels, and there's little else to see.

Returning to the Panamericana, you'll see a few food stalls and very basic restaurants. Heading south on the main highway, you soon pass open fields that are the site of the interesting Sunday market. There are no permanent buildings; the Indians just lay out their wares in neat rows. Every Sunday morning, the bare fields are transformed by a bustling but surprisingly orderly throng of people who buy, sell and barter produce. Quichua, rather than Spanish, is spoken, and there are no tourist items; this is one of the more traditional markets in the Ecuadorian highlands. Amazingly, it takes place right by the side of the Panamericana – a measure of just how rural this part of Ecuador is.

Most buses from Riobamba continue about 4km beyond Cajabamba to Laguna de Colta. On the way, the road gently climbs to a notch in the hill to the south and the little chapel of **La Balbanera**. It is built on the site of the earliest church in Ecuador, which dates from August 15, 1534, although only a few stones at the front survived the devastating earthquake of 1797. The church has been almost completely rebuilt, and the curious traveler can enter to inspect its simple interior and look at the usual disaster paintings.

In La Balbanera, one painting carries the explanation: 'On the 17th of May, 1959, the train derailed, setting the whole convoy on fire. Señor Juan Peñafiel, the brakeman, prayed to the Divine Lady of La Balbanera, and her miracle saved the train near Alausí.'

Looking almost due north of the chapel, you can see Chimborazo looming up from 30km away. Next to the chapel are a few simple restaurants where you can sample local dishes. A little to the south of the chapel, there is a fork in the road. You can either continue south on the Panamericana or take the 100km detour to the right, via the junction of El Triunfo, and then return to the Panamericana at Cañar. Occasional road closures caused by landslides might make the detour impossible to avoid.

Opposite the fork in the road is **Laguna de Colta**. Its blue expanse is often choked up by reeds, which form an important crop for the local Colta Indians. Sometimes you can see the Coltas' rafts on the lake; the Indians cut the reeds for use as cattle fodder or to make the reed mats and baskets for which they are famous.

Some of the more traditional Colta Indian women can be easily identified, as they dye the fringes of their hair a startling golden color. If you have the time or inclination, you could walk around the lake in a couple of hours.

You can visit this area on a day excursion from Riobamba by taking local buses or by hiring a taxi. The views of the volcanoes, especially Chimborazo, are particularly good as you return from Laguna de Colta to Riobamba along the Panamericana – try to sit near the front of the bus.

VOLCÁN CHIMBORAZO

Not only is the extinct Volcán Chimborazo the highest mountain in Ecuador, but its peak (6310m) is also the farthest point from the center of the earth (due to the earth's equatorial bulge). For insatiable trivia buffs, it is higher than any mountain in the Americas north of it. Nearby is the ninth-highest mountain in Ecuador, the 5020m Carihuairazo. Climbing either mountain is an adventure only for experienced mountaineers with snow- and ice-climbing gear (contact the guides listed under Riobamba and Ambato or in the Quito & Around chapter), but reaching the refuge on Chimborazo is as simple as hiring a car.

Chimborazo and Carihuairazo are both within La Reserva de Producción Faunística Chimborazo, which is currently run by the Ministerio de Ambiente. It's called a 'fauna-production reserve' because hundreds of vicuñas live and breed here. Sharp-eyed travelers can even catch sight of them on the bus from Guaranda to Riobamba (via El Arenal), or sometimes on other routes. Hikers are likely to see these lovely animals, which are a wild relative of the llama.

The ministry recently announced a US$10 fee to enter the reserve. This is locally un-popular, because locals feel it will drive away the casual visitor. This fact, combined with the current lack of an information center and staffed entrance stations, means that no fee is currently being charged, but this may change.

Climbing

Most climbers acclimatize at a lower elevation (Riobamba or Quito are just adequate; higher lodges are a better choice) and arrive at Chimborazo's climbing refuges ready to climb. After a short sleep (more like a restless nap), climbers set out around midnight, when the snow is hard. There are several routes, but most parties now take the Normal Route, which takes eight to 10 hours to the summit and two to four to return (although fit, acclimatized climbers will be faster, one group took 20 hours for the roundtrip!).

The previously popular Whymper Route is currently unsafe. Just below the summit is a large bowl of snow that must be crossed; this gets notoriously soft during the day and is the main reason climbers leave the refuge at midnight. Because many parties climb this route, wands marking the way are often found. The sunrise high up on the mountain is unforgettable.

There are no proper refuges on Carihuairazo (although there is a dilapidated hut that could collapse any year now), so climbers usually set up a base camp on the south side of the mountain. When climbing, do not leave anything unattended, as it

could get stolen – there are shepherds in the area who are not dangerous but will sneak off with unattended gear. The climb is fairly straightforward for experienced climbers, but the usual ice-climbing gear is needed. Skiers and snowboarders have made some descents on this mountain. Quebrada Sachahaicu, a river valley on the southeast side of the mountain, has one of the biggest stands of undisturbed Polylepis forests in the country.

Hiking

The area around these mountains is also suitable for backpacking trips – the walk from Mocha (on the Panamericana north of Riobamba) or Urbina (see Places to Stay, later) over the pass between the two mountains and emerging at the Ambato-Guaranda road is as good a choice as any. Allow three days for this hike, and bring plenty of warm clothes. June to September is the dry season in this region. Maps are available at the IGM (see the Quito & Around chapter), or from the Tagua Shop, in Riobamba (see Shopping, under Riobamba, earlier).

Places to Stay

There are three small lodges on the lower slopes of Chimborazo, which are suitable for acclimatization, and two high climbing refuges, suitable as bases for climbing the volcano. Note that all of these places are very cold at night, so bring appropriate clothing. Blankets are provided in the lower lodges, but many people use their sleeping bags as well.

The cheapest place to stay is *La Casa del Condor* (named after the shape of the building) in the small indigenous community of **Pulingue San Pablo**, on the left, just after crossing over the boundary into the reserve on the Riobamba-El Arenal road. The community, although within the reserve, owns the surrounding land, and the Condor Project (see www.interconnection.org/condor) will enable them to improve their livelihoods in this harsh environment. Families still live in the small, rounded, thatched-roof huts typical of the area, but

The Chimborazo Area by Bus

The 99km road from Ambato to Guaranda is paved and climbs to bleak páramo at well over 4000m before dropping down to Guaranda, at 2650m, making it the highest paved road in the country.

The road passes within 10km of Volcanes Chimborazo (6310m) and Carihuairazo (5020m). If going to Guaranda, you should get seats on the left side of the bus for the best views of these giants, but the road twists and turns so you do get occasional views from the right side as well. In addition to the mountains, you get a good look at the harsh and inhospitable Andean páramo. Keep your eyes open for carunculated caracara, flocks of llamas and the little straw-covered domes that serve as homes to the local Indians.

When you leave Guaranda, you can take other equally exciting rides. You can continue on down the western slopes of the Andes to Babahoyo and the coast – a spectacular route that was once the most important connection between Quito and Guayaquil, though it is now infrequently used. Or you can head due east to Riobamba on a dizzying 61km dirt road that skirts the southern flanks of Chimborazo and provides fantastic views that are not for the faint of heart (sit on the left side of the bus). Finally, a new road to Riobamba via El Arenal gets you even closer to Chimborazo and avoids the steep dropoffs of the older route. This new road is partly paved and is used by climbers from Riobamba to reach the Chimborazo mountain refuge. Vicuñas are often seen from this road.

La Casa del Condor is a stone building with rooms for a weaving cooperative and accompanying sales, education and basic health care; and two rooms each with two bunk beds for travelers. Electricity reached the village in late 1999, and there is a gas-heated shower for guests. Basic kitchen facilities are available. The altitude here is over 3900m – perfect for acclimatization.

Locals are being trained to provide basic guiding services, and there are fine hikes in the area, which is a few kilometers south of Chimborazo. Beds are about US$1.50 per night. This is ecotourism at its most grass-roots level, and the money goes directly to the *campesino* villagers. Be patient when you arrive; it can take a while for the locals to find the person who has the key to the rooms. Information can be obtained from Riobamba resident Tom Walsh (☎ 03-941 481, fax 940 955, twalsh@ch.pro.ec), who has been instrumental in helping the villagers set up the project.

A few hundred meters beyond Pulingue San Pablo, to the right of the road, is *La Posada*, which is where Marco Cruz (see Travel Agencies & Guides under Riobamba, earlier) brings his groups for acclimatization. This is a fairly comfortable but much more expensive lodge, and it may not be available if a group has booked it.

Just outside the reserve's boundary, southeast of Chimborazo, is **Urbina**, which at 3618m consists of nothing more than a train station that was built in 1905. This historic building has been turned into *Posada La Estación*, a simple but comfortable hostal operated by Alta Montaña (see Travel Agencies & Guides under Riobamba, earlier). There are eight rooms that can sleep a total of 20 people, a hot shower, a fully equipped kitchen and meals. Rates are US$4 per bed. Good acclimatization, or simply scenic hikes, can be achieved from here as well.

Alta Montaña also operates the two climbers' refuges. The lower one is *Refugio Hermanos Carrel*, at 4860m, and the upper one is *Refugio Whymper*, at 5000m. The latter was named after Edward Whymper, the British climber who in 1880 made the first ascent of Chimborazo with the Swiss Carrels as guides. The lower refuge has 14 beds, while the upper one has 70 and is the best suited for a summit attempt. Both have caretakers, equipped kitchens, storage facilities and limited food supplies (soups and sandwiches). Beds are US$7 per night. At 5000m, Refugio Whymper is Ecuador's highest, and altitude sickness is a very real

danger. It is essential to spend several days acclimatizing at the elevation of Riobamba or even higher before going on to the refuge.

Getting There & Away

At least two buses a day go from Riobamba to Guaranda via El Arenal (ensure the bus goes via El Arenal). This road is paved up to a short distance beyond Pulingue San Pablo (see Places to Stay, earlier), which is reached in less than an hour. Another 7km on this road (now unpaved, although paving is planned) brings you to the signed turnoff for the Chimborazo refuges. The elevation here is 4370m. This is the cheapest access route. From the turnoff, it is 8km by road to the parking lot at Refugio Hermanos Carrel; you have to walk this road (or hitchhike if you are lucky). Because of the altitude, allow several hours for this walk. Refugio Whymper is almost 1km farther, and you have to walk (allow another hour if you are carrying a heavy pack).

Most hotels in Riobamba can arrange taxi service to Refugio Hermanos Carrel via this route. You'll probably need a pickup or similar vehicle to negotiate the final 8km from the road. Rates have been falling as the road to El Arenal becomes paved, but expect to pay about US$25 for a taxi to take you there, wait while you look around and take you back to Riobamba.

Another approach, for mountaineers prepared to go cross-country, is to take the same Riobamba-Guaranda road via El Arenal and continue about 5km beyond the refuge-bound road to a hairpin bend, from where you climb a gully east to the lower refuge, about 5km away. The hairpin bend is about 5km south of the Ambato-Guaranda road if you are arriving from the opposite direction.

To reach Posada La Estación (see Places to Stay, earlier), you can simply get off the weekly Quito-Riobamba train. Any other time, take a bus along the Panamericana and ask the driver for the Urbina road, almost 30km north of Riobamba. It's about 1km from the Panamericana by road to Urbina.

GUANO & SANTA TERESITA
☎ 03

These small villages are a few kilometers north of Riobamba and easily reached by bus. Guano is an important carpet-making center, and although most travelers won't have room in their luggage for a couple of souvenir carpets, it's interesting to see this cottage industry. To see some carpet stores, get off the bus in Guano's central plaza, and then walk down Avenida García Moreno. There are no hotels and only a few restaurants – one place to eat near the plaza is reportedly OK. Look for the topiary garden with El Altar rising in the background – a pretty sight.

From the main plaza, you can continue by bus to Santa Teresita, a few kilometers away. At the end of the bus ride, turn right and head down the hill for about 20 minutes to the *balneario* (spa), where swimming pools are fed by natural springs. The water is quite cool (22°C), but the views of Tungurahua and El Altar are marvelous. There is a basic cafeteria, and camping is permitted.

GUAMOTE
☎ 03

From Riobamba, the southbound Panamericana roughly follows the train tracks and crosses them quite often. Some 47km beyond Riobamba, you reach the village of Guamote, which has an interesting and unspoiled Thursday market – one of the largest rural markets in Ecuador. There is a basic pensión near the train tracks.

Guamote is at the beginning of a new road being built to the southeast, over the Atillo Pass in the Cordillera Oriental, down the eastern slopes of the Andes, past the southern edge of Parque Nacional Sangay and on to Macas, in the southern Oriente (see the Parque Nacional Sangay section, earlier, for more details). A bus leaves Riobamba at 2pm and goes through Guamote and on to Atillo, about 69km away.

Note that Guamote is located in a valley almost 1km off the Panamericana. Unless your bus is actually going to Guamote (usually only Thursday), you will be dropped off on the Panamericana and will have to walk in.

ALAUSÍ
☎ 03

Almost 50km south of Guamote, you reach Alausí, near the head of the Río Chanchán valley, down which the train tracks run to the coast. Just below Alausí begins the famous Nariz del Diablo (see the boxed text 'El Nariz del Diablo'). There is a busy Sunday market.

Orientation & Information

The main street is Avenida 5 de Junio, which is about six blocks long. Buses arrive and depart from this street, and most of the hotels are located along it. The train station

---

El Nariz del Diablo

The most exciting part of the train ride south of Riobamba is the hair-raising descent from Alausí to Sibambe through the area know as El Nariz del Diablo (the Devil's Nose). This is where the landslides caused by the torrential rains of the 1982–83 El Niño did the most damage. These tracks were repaired in the late 1980s, and now the spectacular ride attracts many travelers. Alausí is at 2607m above sea level according to one tourist brochure; another guidebook puts it at 2356m; and a sign at the Alausí train station attests to a third altitude: 2347m. Whatever the height, the first few kilometers of track are very steep, with almost 1000m of elevation lost in the short descent to Sibambe.

The steep descent is accomplished by a series of switchbacks down the steep mountainside. Occasional rickety-looking bridges cross steep ravines. Daredevils ride on the flat roof of the train, with nothing but empty space between them and the valleys far below. The local machos stand up on the roof, especially when going through tunnels, where there is barely enough clearance for the sombrero jammed jauntily on their heads. Actually, the greatest hazard is probably the train's emission of steam, soot and cinders during the ride – wear clothes you don't mind getting dirty.

SOUTH OF QUITO

is at the north end of 5 de Junio. There is an Andinatel office one block to the west of 5 de Junio, behind the fire station and near the train station. From the train station, head east and wander around to find a plaza, church, cobbled streets and balconied buildings – *tranquilísimo*.

Apart from the Sunday market, there is a smaller one Thursday. The feast of Sts Peter and Paul (June 28) is one of Alausí's major fiestas, and the town is very crowded then.

Places to Stay & Eat

Hotels are often full Saturday night for the Sunday market and Ecuadorian weekend visitors. There are no 1st-class hotels, and most accommodations are along 5 de Junio. The clean, family-run *Hotel Tequendama* (☎ 930 123) has hot water and charges US$3 per person. Breakfast is available. Other possibilities are the friendly *Hotel Panamericano* (☎ 930 156), which has electric showers and a basic restaurant and charges US$6 for a double; *Hotel Europa*, which also has a restaurant; and *Residencial Alausí* (☎ 930 361), on Esteban Orozco, just off the south end of 5 de Junio, which is new and has nice rooms.

Hotel Gampala (☎ 930 138) has erratic hot water and may try to charge inflated rates. Bargain – US$6 a double is the most you should pay. Its restaurant overcharges, too. Your best bet is *Hotel Americano* (☎ 930 159, García Moreno 159), a block east of 5 de Junio, near the train station. Good, clean doubles with private hot bath are about US$7.

Apart from the hotel restaurants, there are a couple of basic restaurants along the main street, mostly serving *meriendas* (set dinners). There's really not much choice, but the food is quite adequate.

Getting There & Away

Bus The buses from Riobamba (US$1.20, 1½ hours) arrive every hour or so. Buses turn off the Panamericana and drop down into town, where they normally stop near Hotel Panamericano. Buses for Cuenca (US$3, five hours) also leave from here several times a day, but less often Sunday.

Buses between Riobamba and Cuenca don't normally enter town, but they leave passengers on the Panamericana, from which it is almost a 1km walk down into town.

Old buses (or pickup trucks acting as buses) leave from 5 de Junio for nearby destinations. Some of the rides can be quite spectacular, especially the one to Achupallas (see that section, later), about 23km by road to the southeast. Make sure that any sightseeing ride you take is coming back to Alausí, as there are few if any places to stay in these villages.

There are also buses and trucks to the village of Chunchi, about 25km farther south on the Panamericana. Here you'll find a local Sunday market and a few basic places to stay.

Train Alausí used to be a major railroad junction, but services are now limited to the Riobamba-Sibambe run (see Getting There & Away under Riobamba, earlier, for a description) and are subject to occasional cancellation. The train leaves Alausí daily at 9:30 am, and tickets go on sale at 8 am. This train usually arrives from Riobamba and is often quite full, but ticket sales are orderly. The fare is US$12 for foreigners. Ecuadorians are charged a fraction of that price, but if foreign travelers don't subsidize the train service, it will be shut down. It takes about two hours to go over the famous Nariz del Diablo (see the boxed text). Roofriding is allowed, but the roof is often full with riders from Riobamba or tour groups who pile on while their guide stands in line to buy tickets.

ACHUPALLAS
☎ 03

This village is the starting point for a three-day hike south along the old Inca road to Ingapirca, the most important Inca ruin in Ecuador (see the Cuenca & the Southern Highlands chapter). Occasional trucks leave Alausí for Achupallas, or you can hire a taxi (pickup) for about US$7 one way. Alternately, there is transportation from Alausí to Guasuntos (also known as La Moya), from where you can wait for trucks to

Achupallas. It is about 10km from Alausí to La Moya and another 15km to Achupallas. There is nowhere to stay at either place.

The hike from Achupallas to Ingapirca is a good one (see the hiking guides that are recommended in the Books section of the Facts for the Visitor chapter). The Inca road is faint in places, but you could probably find your way to Ingapirca with a compass and map, asking the locals for directions if you don't have a hiking book. Head south, and pack some extra food in case you get temporarily lost. The area is remote but inhabited, so don't leave your stuff lying around outside your tent, and be prepared for persistent begging from children. The area is covered by three 1:50,000 topographical maps available from the IGM in Quito. These are the Alausí CT-ÑV-A3, Juncal CT-ÑV-C1 and Cañar CT-ÑV-C3 sheets.

Cuenca & the Southern Highlands

The three southern Sierra provinces – Cañar, Azuay and Loja – are noticeably different from the seven highland provinces to the north. Geographically, they are lower, with few peaks reaching 4000m. The topography is rugged nevertheless, and communication with the rest of Ecuador has been developed only relatively recently.

Cuenca, the major city of the region and Ecuador's third largest (population 280,000), didn't have paved highway connections with Guayaquil and Quito until the 1960s, and even today, these highways are not in particularly good shape. Due to its isolation until recent times, the area is rich in history, and the region has a strong flavor of the colonial past.

Highlights

- Indulging in a shopping spree for panama hats and filigreed jewelry in Cuenca

- Hiking and camping in the newly declared Parque Nacional Cajas

- Visiting Ecuador's best Inca ruins at Ingapirca

- Exploring the unique cloud forests of Parque Nacional Podocarpus

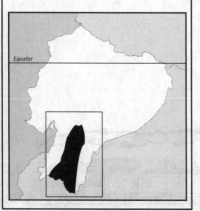

Equator

The southern highlands had a colorful history even before the Spanish conquest. These were the lands of the Cañari Indians, an independent culture with exceptional skill in producing ceramics, fine weavings, and gold jewelry and other metalwork.

In the late 15th century, the Cañaris were conquered by the Incas, who built several major centers. These included the city of Tomebamba, near present-day Cuenca, and the fortress of Ingapirca, the best-preserved pre-colonial ruin found in Ecuador today. The Inca influence was short lived, however, and the Spanish conquistadors under Pizarro took control by the 1530s. Cuenca was (re)founded relatively late, in 1557. Several other important towns of the region were founded earlier, such as Loja in 1548.

Cuenca and Loja are the only towns with a population of more than 100,000, and the rest have fewer than 30,000 people, except for Azogues. Many villages have cobbled streets and old houses with balconies, and the tradition of handicrafts, ranging from jewelry-making to weaving, is strong. A journey through the provinces of the southern highlands is a journey into the past.

Cuenca

☎ 07

Barely half a century before the arrival of the Spaniards, the powerful Inca Tupac- (or Topa-) Yupanqui was undertaking the difficult conquest of the Cañari Indians, who struggled bravely to stem the expansion of the Inca Empire. After several years of bitter fighting, Tupac Yupanqui's forces prevailed.

The Inca began construction of a major city whose splendor and importance were to rival that of the imperial capital of Cuzco. The Indians told of sun temples covered with gold sheets and palaces built using the finest skill of Cuzqueño stonemasons, but what happened to Tomebamba, as the city was called, is shrouded in mystery.

CUENCA & S HIGHLANDS

CUENCA & THE SOUTHERN HIGHLANDS

GUAYAQUIL
San Jacinto de Yaguachi
Durán
Milagro
Guayas
Cumandá
Bucay
Sibambe
Huigra
Chunchi
To Quito
Pallatanga
Alausí
Guasuntos
Achupallas
Chimborazo
Volcán Sangay 5230m
To Puyo
Rio Sangay
Atillo
9 de Octubre
Parque Nacional Sangay
MACAS
Sevilla
El Triunfo
La Troncal
Suscal
Zhud
El Tambo
Ingapirca
Cañar
Biblián
AZOGUES
Paute
Gualaceo
Chordeleg
Sucúa
Logroño
Morona-Santiago
Rio Paute
Rio Upano
Vieja Cordillera de Cutucú
Reserva Ecológica de Manglares-Churute
Jesús María
Naranjal
Cañar
Laguna Toreadora Ranger Station
Migüir
Parque Nacional Cajas
Angas
San Joaquín
Soldados
Baños
Sayausí
CUENCA
San Bartolomé
Sígsig
Limón
Indanza
San Juan Bosco
Rio Zamora
Rio Coangos
Isla Puná
Canal de Jambelí
Panamericana (International)
Azuay
Girón
Santa Isabel
Oña
Cordillera
Chigüinda
Nueva Tarqui
Gualaquiza
Bomboiza
Andes (Ecuadorian) de los
Puerto Bolívar
MACHALA
El Guabo
Pasaje
El Oro
Panamericana (Ecuadorian)
Cordillera del Cóndor
Rio Cenepa
Santa Rosa
To Huaquillas
Arenillas
Torata
Saracay
Paccha
Piñas
Zaruma
Portovelo
Saraguro
Rio Yacuambi
28 de Mayo
La Paz
El Pangui
Rio Cumaina
Represa de Tahuín
Rio Puyango
Balsas
Chaguarpamba
El Cisne
San Pedro de la Bendita
Rio Zamora
Guadalupe
Yantzaza
Zumbi
Namírez
Nambija
PERU
Puyango
Alamor
Celica
Olmedo
Catamayo
LOJA
Cajanuma Ranger Station
ZAMORA
Romerillos
Rio Nangaritza
Rio Nangaritza
Rio Catamayo
Catacocha
El Empalme
Gonzanamá
Malacatos
Vilcabamba
Bombuscara Ranger Station
Parque Nacional Podocarpus
Sozoranga
Macará
Cariamanga
Loja
Valladolid
Zamora-Chinchipe
Rio Nampataki
Rio Nampatakai
106
To Piura
Zumba
Rio Mayo
Rio Marañón

0   20   40 km
0   10   20 miles

2°S
3°S
4°S
5°S
80°W   79°W   78°W

By the time Spanish chronicler Cieza de León passed through in 1547, Tomebamba lay largely in ruins, although well-stocked storehouses indicated how great it had recently been. Today it is difficult to imagine Tomebamba's splendor, for all that remains are a few recently excavated Inca walls by the river that bears the town's name.

Río Tomebamba divides Cuenca in half. South of the river are fairly recent suburbs, the stadium and the modern university. To the north is the heart of the colonial city, which lies at about 2530m above sea level.

Although Cuenca has expanded to become Ecuador's third-largest city, it still retains a pleasantly provincial air, although the people are more conservative than in Quito. (An African-American traveler reported that he was stared at constantly in Cuenca; black people are a rarity.)

The old colonial center has churches dating from the 16th and 17th centuries and is a delight to stroll around. The earliest building is the original cathedral, the construction of which began in 1557 (the year Cuenca was founded by the Spanish conquistador Gil Ramírez Dávalos). In 1999, this history was honored by UNESCO, which declared Cuenca's center to be a World Cultural Heritage Site.

There are cobbled streets and red-tiled roofs, art galleries and flower markets, shady plazas and museums. The majority of the hotels, too, are near the center, so the traveler can conveniently enjoy a relaxing few days in this colonial city.

Cuenca also makes a good base from which to visit Parque Nacional Cajas, as well as local thermal baths, villages and markets (described in the Cuenca Area section, later in this chapter). The ruins of Ingapirca are described in the North of Cuenca section, later.

For a good view of the area, take a taxi south of town along Avenida Fray Vicente Solano to the church at Turi, a southern suburb about 4km away from the center. The white church is perched on a hill, and Cuenca stretches out below you.

INFORMATION
Tourist Offices
The tourist information office (☎ 882 058, fax 831 414) is at Hermano Miguel 6-86. The staff is friendly and tries to help with city maps and information. Hours are 8 am to 4 pm weekdays, but the office is usually closed around 1 pm for lunch.

The Parque Nacional Cajas office is at Bolívar 5-33, 3rd floor. It has limited information; most travelers just go directly to Cajas and get information when they arrive. Good maps are hard to find.

Money
The several branches of Filanbanco and Banco de Guayaquil have Visa ATMs; branches of Banco del Pacífico have Master-Card ATMs. Banks are shown on the map.

Post & Communications
The post office is on the corner of Gran Colombia and Borrero. Pacifictel is at Malo 726.

Several email cafés have opened, and new ones open every month. Try the following: Café Oficina, at Luís Cordero and Jaramillo; Zon@net, at Hermano Miguel 4-46; CyberCom Café, at Presidente Córdova and Borrero; Abrahám Lincoln Cultural Center, at Honorato Vásquez and Borrero.

Travel Agencies & Guides
Several local agencies and guides have been recommended for tours to Ingapirca, Parque Nacional Cajas, nearby villages and markets, and other various local attractions. There are also numerous travel agencies that can arrange standard tours or sell airline tickets. Note that entrance fees, which are not included in many tours, can add a substantial amount to the total cost – check first.

English- and Italian-speaking Eduardo Quito is a good local guide who has received several recommendations. He works with Ecuaturis (☎ 843 647, fax 829 524, equito@az.pro.ec), Hermano Miguel 9-56, and charges about US$35 per person (two minimum) to take a group to Ingapirca or Cajas and a host of other local destinations. After hours, call him at home (☎ 823 018). Expediciones Apullacta (☎ 837 681), Gran

Colombia 11-02, also offers day tours to Ingapirca, Cajas and other places starting at US$35 per person. These tours are competitively priced and popular.

Ecotrek (☎ 841 927, 834 677, fax 835 387, ecotrek@az.pro.ec), Calle Larga 7-108, near Luís Cordero, is run by well-known local adventurer Juan Gabriel Carrasco, who speaks English and is recommended for trekking, mountaineering (rock and ice) and Amazon travel – especially to the Miazal area, in the southern Oriente. The latter costs about US$120 per person per day, including a flight in. Ecotrek also arranges tours to Kapawi Ecolodge & Reserve (see the boxed text in the Southern Oriente chapter).

Juan Diego Dominguez is another well-known English-speaking adventure guide. He owns Nomada's Adventures (☎ 820 158, 09-882 338, pdelsol@impsat.net.ec), Hermano Miguel 6-91, as well as the Posada del Sol hotel. Nomada's will arrange similar adventure tours to Ecotrek, as well as mountain-biking trips. Juan Diego is quite a good birder.

English-speaking naturalist guide Edgar 'Negro' Aguirre, at Aventuras Río Arriba (☎ 830 116, fax 840 031, negro@az.pro.ec), Hermano Miguel 7-14, is another good choice for a variety of tours.

English-speaking Humberto Chica, at Cabañas Yanuncay (see Places to Stay, Mid-Range, later in this section), organizes overnight tours to Cajas (three days; US$100 per person), the southern Oriente (five days; US$250 per person) and other areas. Tours are small and personal and include food, accommodations and transportation.

Monta Runa (☎ 005 937, 846 395, fax 834 387), Hermano Miguel 8-54, has been recommended for horseback riding.

Camping Equipment
A store at the corner of Presidente Córdova and Malo, signed *Artículos Deportivos*, sells Camping Gaz and other supplies.

Laundry
Lavahora (☎ 823 042), Vasquez 7-72, charges about US$2 for washing and drying a load. La Química, on Borrero near Córdova, is another choice.

Medical Services
Of the several hospitals and clinics, Clínica Santa Inés (☎ 817 888), at Daniel Córdova 2-113, has had several recommendations. Clínica Hospital Monte Sinai (☎ 885 595), Miguel Cordero 6-111, is also well recommended. These clinics have some English-speaking staff.

Emergency
In an emergency, dial ☎ 911. The police station (☎ 101 or 810 068) is at Luís Cordero and Presidente Córdova. *Migraciones* (immigration) is also here.

Dangers & Annoyances
Although Cuenca is generally a safe city, the riverside at night is considered a bit dangerous, except in well-lit areas.

THINGS TO SEE & DO
Río Tomebamba is attractively lined with old colonial buildings, and washerwomen still lay out clothes to dry on its grassy banks. Avenida 3 de Noviembre follows the river's northern bank and makes for a pleasant walk.

Most of the sites described below are closed on weekends or, in the case of churches, are open irregular hours.

Casa de Cultura
At the southwest corner of Parque Calderón is the Casa de Cultura. There is a good art gallery there with frequently changing exhibits. Most paintings are by local artists and are for sale, but there is absolutely no pressure to buy. In fact, it's hard to find a salesperson if you happen to see a work that you're seriously interested in. There's also a bookstore of art-oriented books in Spanish and a coffee shop.

Churches
Four blocks east of Museo de las Conceptas is where colonial Cuenca's boundary used to be, marked by the **church and plaza of San Blas**. Originally built in the late 16th century, the small colonial church has since been replaced by an early-20th-century building. The modern church is one of the

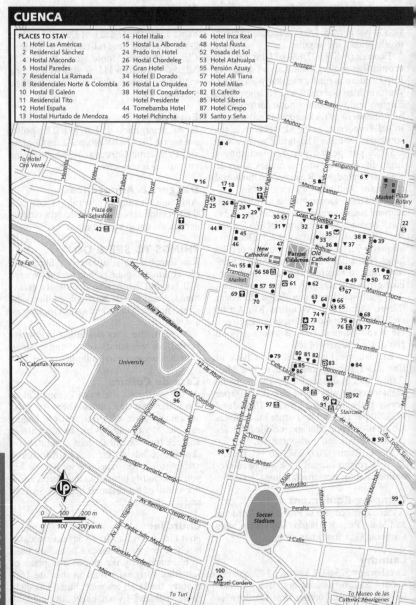

CUENCA

PLACES TO STAY
1 Hotel Las Américas
2 Residencial Sánchez
4 Hostal Macondo
5 Hostal Paredes
7 Residencial La Ramada
8 Residenciales Norte & Colombia
10 Hostal El Galeón
11 Residencial Tito
12 Hotel España
13 Hostal Hurtado de Mendoza
14 Hotel Italia
15 Hostal La Alborada
24 Prado Inn Hotel
26 Hostal Chordeleg
27 Gran Hotel
34 Hotel El Dorado
36 Hostal La Orquídea
38 Hotel El Conquistador;
    Hotel Presidente
44 Tomebamba Hotel
45 Hotel Pichincha
46 Hotel Inca Real
48 Hostal Ñusta
52 Posada del Sol
53 Hotel Atahualpa
55 Pensión Azuay
57 Hotel Alli Tiana
70 Hotel Milan
82 El Cafecito
85 Hotel Siberia
87 Hotel Crespo
93 Santo y Seña

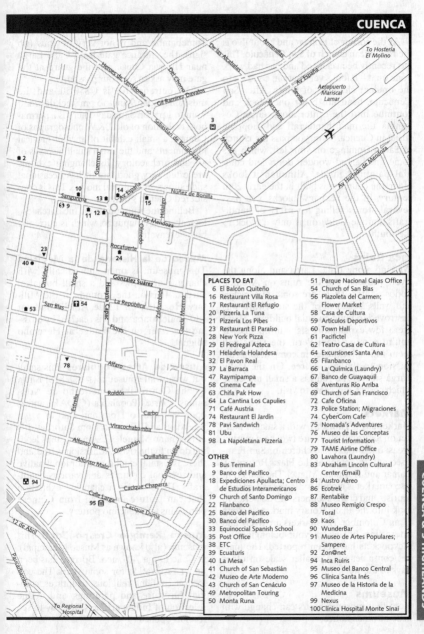

CUENCA

PLACES TO EAT
6 El Balcón Quiteño
16 Restaurant Villa Rosa
17 Restaurant El Refugio
20 Pizzería La Tuna
21 Pizzería Los Pibes
23 Restaurant El Paraíso
28 New York Pizza
29 El Pedregal Azteca
31 Heladería Holandesa
32 El Pavon Real
37 La Barraca
47 Raymipampa
58 Cinema Cafe
63 Chifa Pak How
64 La Cantina Los Capulíes
71 Café Austria
74 Restaurant El Jardín
78 Pavi Sandwich
81 Ubu
98 La Napoletana Pizzería

OTHER
3 Bus Terminal
9 Banco del Pacífico
18 Expediciones Apullacta; Centro
   de Estudios Interamericanos
19 Church of Santo Domingo
22 Filanbanco
25 Banco del Pacífico
30 Banco del Pacífico
33 Equinoccial Spanish School
35 Post Office
38 ETC
39 Ecuaturis
40 La Mesa
41 Church of San Sebastián
42 Museo de Arte Moderno
43 Church of San Cenáculo
49 Metropolitan Touring
50 Monta Runa

51 Parque Nacional Cajas Office
54 Church of San Blas
56 Plazoleta del Carmen;
   Flower Market
58 Casa de Cultura
59 Artículos Deportivos
60 Town Hall
61 Pacifictel
62 Teatro Casa de Cultura
64 Excursiones Santa Ana
65 Filanbanco
66 La Química (Laundry)
67 Banco de Guayaquil
68 Aventuras Río Arriba
69 Church of San Francisco
72 Cafe Oficina
73 Police Station; Migraciones
74 CyberCom Cafe
75 Nomada's Adventures
76 Museo de las Conceptas
77 Tourist Information
79 TAME Airline Office
80 Lavahora (Laundry)
83 Abrahám Lincoln Cultural
   Center (Email)
84 Austro Aéreo
86 Ecotrek
87 Rentabike
88 Museo Remigio Crespo
   Toral
89 Kaos
90 WunderBar
91 Museo de Artes Populares;
   Sampere
92 Zon@net
94 Inca Ruins
95 Museo del Banco Central
96 Clínica Santa Inés
97 Museo de la Historia de la
   Medicina
99 Nexus
100 Clínica Hospital Monte Sinai

city's largest and is the only one in Cuenca built in the form of a Latin cross.

At the corner of Bolívar and Montalvo is the republican **church of San Cenáculo**. This has recently been cleaned and has had work done on it – it looks very bare in contrast to the opulent churches of Quito. After San Cenáculo, head north for one block and continue into the center along Gran Colombia, the main handicraft and shopping street in Cuenca. Soon, you pass the **church of Santo Domingo** on your left, which has some fine carved wooden doors and colonial paintings inside. Although it looks older, the church was built in the early 20th century. In the next few blocks, you pass several stores selling a variety of handicrafts. Parque Calderón is only a block to the south.

Inca Ruins

Walking along Calle Larga and along the river, you come to the ruins on Avenida Todos Santos. There are some fine niches and walls, but most of the stonework was destroyed to build colonial buildings. There are a few explanatory signs in Spanish. If you're coming from Peru, the ruins will seem rather lackluster in comparison. Admission to the site is free. On the Calle Larga side of the ruins is a small museum, which costs a few cents to visit.

Markets

Market day is Thursday, with a smaller market on Saturday. There are two main market areas: one around the church of San Francisco and the other at the Plaza Rotary, by Lamar and Hermano Miguel. The San Francisco market is mainly for locals rather than tourists, and crafts shoppers will do better to look into the Plaza Rotary market or along Gran Colombia. The markets are lively and interesting, but watch your belongings, as pickpockets have been reported. The market continues on a smaller scale on other days of the week.

Museums

Note that museum hours can change with little advance notice.

Museo del Banco Central This museum is in the southeast part of town near Río Tomebamba and is not very obvious (no sign). The entrance gate is on Calle Larga near Huayna Capac, and the guard at the gate may ask to see your passport.

The entrance fee is US$0.50, and the museum is open 9 am to 5 pm weekdays and 9 am to 1 pm on Saturday. There is a permanent collection of old B&W photographs of Cuenca, a small exhibit of ancient musical instruments and the usual small displays of art and archaeology. Its changing exhibits are often very good, and it has occasional slide shows and cultural movies. This is considered Cuenca's best museum.

Behind the museum is an Inca archaeological site, Pumapungo, which is currently being excavated.

Museo de la Historia de la Medicina This museum is open sporadically, with changing art shows and a small botanical garden. It is on the grounds of the Military Hospital, on 12 de Abril, south of Río Tomebamba, and it is reached by crossing the river on the bridge at Hermano Miguel.

Museo de Artes Populares This small but worthwhile museum (☎ 828 878) is run by the Centro Interamericano de Artesanías y Artes Populares (CIDAP) and is open 9:30 am to 1 pm and 2:30 to 5 pm weekdays and 10 am to 1 pm Saturday. It's at Hermano Miguel 3-23, on the steps leading down to the river. Admission is free, and there is a small exhibit of traditional native and regional costumes and various handicrafts. There is also a changing exhibition that can feature anything from Chinese porcelains to Cuencano pottery.

Museo Remigio Crespo Toral This museum (also known as Museo Municipal), at Calle Larga 7-07, near Borrero, has been under restoration for some years. The collection contains religious sculptures, colonial furniture and paintings, and a fine selection of Indian artifacts. Stop by to see if it has opened.

Local showing how to pan for gold, near Baños

Wildflowers, Parque Nacional Cotopaxi

The volcanic crater lake of Quilotoa, west of Latacunga

ROB RACHOWIECKI

Cuenca's Río Tomebamba, lined with colonial buildings and drying laundry

DAVID PEEVERS

Panama-hat factory near Cuenca

DAVID PEEVERS

Cuencano spending a restful day in the plaza

ROB RACHOWIECKI

The facade and blue domes of Cuenca's new cathedral

Museo de las Conceptas Considered Cuenca's best religious museum, Museo de las Conceptas (☎ 830 625) is housed in the Convent of the Immaculate Conception, at Hermano Miguel 6-33, three blocks up from the river and opposite the tourist office. The museum is in what used to be the old infirmary of the convent, which was founded in 1599. Parts of the building date to the 17th century. The chapel of the infirmary has a display of crucifixes by the noted 19th-century local sculptor Gaspar Sangurima.

Other parts of the building display a variety of religious art: paintings, carvings, statuettes, nativity scenes etc. There is also a display of photographs showing the austere daily life of the nuns and an audiovisual presentation at 11 am and 3 pm. Museum hours are 9 am to 5 pm Tuesday to Friday and 10 am to 1 pm Saturday; check for possible Monday hours. Admission is US$1.

Museo de Arte Moderno On Mariscal Sucre and Talbot, this museum (☎ 831 027) is open 9 am to 1 pm and 3 to 6 pm weekdays – sometimes on weekends. Admission is free (donations requested). There is a small permanent collection and changing shows of (mainly) local artists and sculptors.

Museo de las Culturas Aborígenes This museum (☎ 811 706, 880 010) is at the southeast end of town, at 10 de Agosto 4-70, near Sánchez. You can walk there from the center in well under an hour, or take a taxi for about US$1. The museum houses a private collection of about 5000 archaeological pieces representative of some 20 pre-Columbian cultures of Ecuador. This collection rivals that of the Banco Central and is well labeled. Hours are 8:30 am to noon and 2:30 to 6 pm weekdays plus Saturday mornings, and admission is US$1.

Parque Calderón

The main plaza, or Parque Calderón, is dominated by the **new cathedral**, with its huge blue domes. It is particularly attractive when illuminated, although the lighting hours are unpredictable. The marbled interior is rather stark. Construction began in

1885, and the cathedral was supposed to be much taller than it is – an error in design meant that the tall bell towers could not be supported by the building.

Almost unnoticed on the other side of the park is the squat **old cathedral** (also known as El Sagrario), which was renovated for the 1985 visit of Pope John Paul II to Ecuador. Construction of this building began in 1557, the year that Cuenca was founded. In 1739, it was used as a triangulation point by La Condamine's expedition to measure the shape of the earth. It is currently being restored and reportedly will be used for cultural events rather than religious services.

Plaza de San Sebastián

Continuing west along Sucre brings you to this plaza, also known as the Parque Miguel León. This is a quiet and pleasant park with the interesting 17th-century **church of San Sebastián** at the north end and the Museo

CUENCA & S HIGHLANDS

de Arte Moderno at the south end. In 1739, the Frenchman Juan Seniergues, a member of La Condamine's geodesic expedition, was killed in this plaza during a fiesta, apparently because of an affair with a local woman.

Plazoleta del Carmen

A block from Parque Calderón, at the corner of Sucre and Aguirre, is this small plaza and the **church of El Carmen de la Asunción**, founded in 1682. Although the church itself is open infrequently, there is a colorful and attractive daily **flower market** in front of the church – a pretty sight. Turning left down Aguirre brings you to the 19th-century San Francisco church and market, a block away.

SPECIAL EVENTS

Cuenca's Independence Day is November 3, which combines with November 1 and 2 (All Saints' Day and All Souls' Day) to form an important holiday period for the city. The markets are in full swing, and there is music, dancing, parades and drinking. Hotel rooms are difficult to find at this time, and prices rise. April 12 is the anniversary of the foundation of Cuenca and is similarly celebrated for several days around that date.

Carnaval, as in other parts of Ecuador, is celebrated with boisterous water fights. No one is spared – I saw a whole bucket of water poured from a balcony over an old nun's head! Cuenca seems to be more enamored of these soggy celebrations than the rest of the country; Easter and New Year's are also popular with water-throwers. Protect your camera gear.

There is a colorful parade on Christmas Eve, starting in the suburbs in late morning and emerging, finally, near the cathedral in the afternoon. It may be held on the Saturday before Christmas. Corpus Christi (usually the ninth Thursday after Easter) is also colorfully celebrated for several days.

COURSES & WORK

The Centro de Estudios Interamericanos (☎ 839 003, 823 452, info@cedei.org), Gran Colombia 11-02, offers courses including Spanish, Quichua, Portuguese, Latin American literature and indigenous culture.

Students who already speak Spanish can take internships in areas ranging from ethnomusicology to export. These courses are offered for full semesters and for college credit three times a year, although students wishing to learn Spanish on a 'drop-in' basis can also be accommodated.

The center also offers English classes, which are taught by native English speakers with a college degree. This is an opportunity to work in Ecuador, particularly if you have training in teaching English as a second language, although tutors with a degree in other fields can also find work.

Other schools that may offer Spanish or other courses, or that may need English-speaking teachers, include Sampere (☎ 823 960, fax 841 986, samperec@samberecen .com.ec), Hermano Miguel 3-43; Equinoccial (☎/fax 834 758), Luís Cordero 9-32, which also offers salsa-dancing lessons; and Nexus (☎ 884 016, fax 888 221, nexus@cue .satnet.net), Peralta 1-19, near 12 de Abril.

PLACES TO STAY

Hotels seem pricey in Cuenca, partly because they will try to charge as much as they think they can get. Try bargaining. The top-end hotels have two prices (the one for gringos is about twice what locals pay). This system is trickling down into the mid-priced hotels as well. Use the following prices as a rough guideline only. Speaking Spanish and traveling by local transportation will probably get you better rates than if you don't speak Spanish and arrive at a hotel in a rented car. Not fair? Maybe, but that's how it is.

Note that the first week in November and mid-April are holiday periods, during which hotel rooms are more difficult to find.

Most hotels (except a few of the most desperately cheap, which are not listed here) have hot or at least tepid water. There are, however, occasional problems with water supply, so make sure the water is running before you pay extra for a room with private bath.

There are several hotels within a kilometer of the bus terminal, but most are a bit farther away, in the downtown area.

Budget

The cheapest hotels are in the center. A good number of them are in the market area near Mariscal Lamar and Cueva, which one reader suggests is a poor area after dark, although it seemed OK to me. All these have warm or hot showers.

The basic but reasonably clean *Residencial Colombia* (☎ 827 851, Cueva 11-61) is among the best of the super-cheapies at about US$1.50 per person with shared showers. Next door, a decent basic place is *Residencial Norte* (☎ 827 881, Cueva 11-63), at US$2.50 per person, or US$3 with private bath. Rooms are large, and there's plenty of hot water. These two places get hectic on market days.

Pensión Azuay (☎ 824 119, Padre Aguirre 7-61) is basic but adequate at US$1.75 per person with shared showers. *Residencial La Ramada* (☎ 833 862, Sangurima 5-51) is friendly has rates starting at US$2 (shared bath); a few rooms with private bath go for a little more.

Residencial Sánchez (☎ 831 519, Muñoz 4-28) is a fair value at US$2.50 per person for rooms with private bath; rooms with shared bath are a hair cheaper. There is a courtyard with a café. The hospitable *Hotel Pichincha* (☎ 823 868, 832 405, Torres 8-82) has large, clean rooms for US$3 per person with towels and shared bathrooms.

The friendly *Hostal Paredes* (☎ 835 674, fax 834 910, Luís Cordero 11-29) is in an early-20th-century building and is reputedly one of Cuenca's oldest hotels. The spacious rooms are furnished with colonial-style furniture, and there are many flowers. Rates are US$3.50/6 for singles/doubles with shared bath and US$12 for doubles that have a private shower, although hot water may be erratic. *Hotel Milan* (☎/fax 831 104, 835 351, Presidente Córdova 9-89) has friendly staff, is popular and charges US$4.50/8 for rooms with private shower, telephone and cable TV. Some rooms have balconies, and there is a simple restaurant. The comfortable *Hotel Siberia* (☎ 840 672, Luís Cordero 4-22) has a cheery 2nd-floor restaurant and rooms with private bath and TV for US$4.50 per person.

A few minutes' walk toward town from the bus terminal is the clean *Hostal La Alborada* (☎ 831 062, Olmedo 13-92), at US$3/4 for rooms with shared bath or US$6 for doubles with private bath. All rooms have a TV. Nearby, the modern, clean *Hostal El Galeón* (☎ 831 827, Sangurima 2-36) has spacious rooms with bath and TV for US$4 per person. Between these two are several other decent places, such as *Residencial Tito* (☎ 829 734, fax 843 577, Sangurima 1-49), which also costs US$4 per person for rooms with bath, TV and phone, although many rooms lack windows. The clean and friendly *Hotel España* (☎ 831 351, Sangurima 1-17) has rooms with bath and cable TV for US$7/11, including breakfast. The modern *Hostal Hurtado de Mendoza* (☎ 831 909), at Huayna Capac and Sangurima, has helpful staff and good-sized doubles with cable TV for US$12. A decent restaurant is downstairs.

Young international travelers favor *El Cafecito* (☎ 832 337, elcafec@cue.satnet.net, Honorato Vásquez 7-36), which has an overflowingly popular restaurant and bar. Behind, with a garden, are rooms with shared showers for US$4 per person and rooms with private showers for US$6, but there are few singles. This hotel may be a useful source of travel information, and live music and happy hours (5 to 7 pm) are other attractions. Another favorite with backpackers is *Hostal Ñusta* (☎ 830 862, Borrero 8-44), which has about eight oversized rooms sleeping one to six people at US$6 per person, including breakfast. Private baths and a TV lounge are featured. The friendly *Gran Hotel* (☎ 831 934, 835 154, fax 833 819, Torres 9-70) charges US$6/10 for rooms with bath and TV. There is a restaurant and an attractive courtyard, although rooms near it can be noisy.

Hostal La Orquídea (☎ 824 511, fax 835 844, Borrero 9-31) is clean and comfortable for US$8/10 (with bath and TV). It has a restaurant. *Prado Inn Hotel* (☎ 807 164, fax 804 812, Rocafuerte 3-45) has large rooms with TV and shower for US$10/12. Some staff speak English, and a bar and restaurant are on the premises.

Hostal Macondo (☎ 840 697, fax 833 593, macondo@cedei.org, Tarqui 11-64) is quiet and friendly and has kitchen privileges and a nice courtyard. This place is affiliated with Hostelling International. Good-sized rooms cost US$9/13 (shared bath), and a few have private bath for US$13/18. Reservations are recommended for the high season.

Mid-Range

For an excellent value, try *Hotel Alli Tiana* (☎ 831 844, 821 955, fax 821 788), at Presidente Córdova and Padre Aguirre. It has modern rooms – some of which have balconies, TV and telephone – for about US$11/16. The 6th-floor restaurant has excellent views. Also good is the friendly and clean *Hotel Atahualpa* (☎ 831 841, fax 842 345, Sucre 3-50), which includes breakfast in its rates of US$15/19. Also at this price is the more modern *Tomebamba Hotel* (☎ 823 797, 831 589, Bolívar 11-19), with pleasant, clean rooms with telephone, TV and minifridge. Near the bus terminal and airport, *Hotel Italia* (☎ 840 060, 842 884, fax 864 475), Avenida España at Huayna Capac, is similar and boasts cable TV and room service. Both of these hotels have restaurants.

Just under 3km southwest of the center, you'll find *Cabañas Yanuncay* (☎ 883 716, ☎/fax 819 681, yanuncay@etapa.com.ec, Calle Canton Gualaceo 2-149). Take a taxi or bus (they run frequently) out along Avenida Loja and take the first right after 'Arco de la Luz,' 200m along the river. Rooms are in a private house or in two cabins in the garden. Rates are US$12 per person for rooms with private bath, including breakfast, kitchen privileges and the use of a sauna and whirlpool. Dinners cost US$6 and are made with organic products from the owner's farm. The owner, Humberto, speaks English and German and arranges local tours. He is friendly; a female reader found him overly so.

Back in town, the attractive *Hostal Chordeleg* (☎ 824 611, fax 822 536, Gran Colombia 11-15) has a decent restaurant and rooms with TV and telephone for about US$10/18 in a refurbished older building with a nice patio. The similarly priced *Hotel Las Américas* (☎ 831 160, 835 753, fax 833 850, Cueva 13-59) is a modern hotel with attentive service and a good, reasonably priced restaurant. The back rooms are quieter, but the ones in front have large windows. Both hotels include breakfast.

Hostal Santo y Seña (☎ 841 981, 3 de Noviembre 4-71) features a lovely garden and nine comfortable rooms for US$12 per person, including breakfast. The Cuencano owners are knowledgeable about the arts scene in town and host occasional live musical evenings.

Posada del Sol (☎ 838 695, fax 838 995, pdelsol@impsat.net.ec, Bolívar 5-03) is a small hotel in an attractive 18th-century house with local artwork. Comfortable rooms with telephone and plenty of hot water are US$18/24, including continental breakfast; there's a vegetarian restaurant as well. Some rooms have balconies. The owner also runs Nomada's Aventures, so all local tours and transfers can be arranged conveniently.

At about US$25/30 including breakfast (with cheaper walk-in rates), *Hotel Inca Real* (☎ 823 636, 825 571, fax 840 699, incareal@cue.satnet.net, Torres 8-40) has been charmingly renovated and has cozy carpeted rooms with TV and telephone. There is a nice restaurant and bar.

Hotel Presidente (☎ 831 979/066/341, fax 824 704, Gran Colombia 6-59) is a well-run, modern hotel with good-sized, very clean rooms for about US$21/30, which seems like a fair value. Apart from all the usual amenities, it has a 9th-floor bar with a great view of the city. Next door, the modern *Hotel El Conquistador* (☎ 831 788, 841 703, fax 831 291, hconquitsa@etapa.com.ec, Gran Colombia 6-65) has a coffee shop, restaurant and bar, and room service is provided. It has a disco on weekends. Rates are about US$34/40, but there are discounts for residents.

Top End

The most worthwhile of the top-end hotels is *Hotel Crespo* (☎ 842 571, fax 839 473, Calle Larga 7-93). It is in an attractive, century-old building overlooking Río Tomebamba. Of the 31 rooms, 12 have lovely river views. The rooms are spacious and have high, molded ceilings, wood-paneled walls and classical furnishings, although the bathrooms are on the small side. There is an elegant restaurant (service can be too leisurely for some people) and room service. Rooms with view of the river are US$54/65; others are US$8 less.

The fanciest hotel downtown is the modern **Hotel El Dorado** (☎ 831 390, fax 831 663, eldorado@cue.satnet.net, Gran Colombia 7-87), which has a good restaurant and piano bar with views from the 7th floor. It also has a coffee shop and lobby bar downstairs, a disco and a sauna/exercise room. The 92 rooms are modern and spacious and cost about US$97/116, including breakfast and a welcome cocktail. An airport shuttle is available.

Finally, if you want to stay out of town, try **Hostería El Molino** (☎ 875 367/59, fax 875 358), which is 7.5km out of town on the Panamericana Norte (leave town on Avenida España). There is a good pool, restaurant and bar, and rooms are spacious and attractive. Doubles cost about US$60.

If you want the most expensive place, try the Swiss-run **Hotel Oro Verde** (☎ 831 200, fax 832 849, ecovc@gye.satnet.net), on Avenida Ordóñez Lazo at the northwestern edge of Cuenca, just over 3km from the city center. The hotel is popular with North Americans (US embassy staff stay here on their jaunts down to Cuenca) and is set in pleasant gardens with a small pool, a little lake with boats and a playground. There's an expensive restaurant with room service, as well as a sauna and exercise room. Rates are US$115/135, and suites cost US$185.

For a few other choices, see Baños, later in the chapter.

PLACES TO EAT

Many restaurants are closed on Sunday, and some on Saturday, too. New restaurants open regularly – a few are aimed at travelers.

The best hotels in town have good restaurants that are open to the public. These are often among the first to open, and their breakfasts are usually the cheapest meals available – you can relax with coffee and croissants in pleasant surroundings. Set

lunches at the cheaper hotels' restaurants are also a good deal.

The coffee shop at Hotel El Conquistador has decent coffee, and the one at El Dorado serves breakfast at 6:30 am. Both Hotel Presidente and El Dorado have top-floor restaurant/bars with good city views – go for a snack if you are economizing, but El Dorado is a good value for a tasty meal. (See Places to Stay, earlier.)

El Cafecito, in the hotel of that name, is usually crowded, noisy and fun for young travelers. The food is reasonably priced and tends toward pizza and hamburgers.

Restaurant El Refugio (Gran Colombia 11-24) is quite elegant and a good value for lunch. It serves Ecuadorian food. Also inexpensive is the vegetarian **Restaurant El Paraíso** (Ordóñez 10-19), where a tasty set lunch is just US$1.

Slightly pricier choices – US$2 or US$3 for a meal – are the locally popular **El Balcón Quiteño** (☎ 824 281, Sangurima 6-49), where tasty Ecuadorian food is served in a bright, plastic environment; and **Chifa Pak How** (☎ 844 295, Presidente Córdova 7-72), which is among the best of the several chifas in town. **El Pavon Real** (☎ 846 678, Gran Colombia 8-33) serves huge, American-style breakfasts, inexpensive but filling lunch specials, and Ecuadorian meat and rice dinners. Locals recommend the family-run **Pavi Sandwich** (11-11 Jaramillo) for good, freshly made sandwiches; wash one down with some coconut milk!

Heladería Holandesa (☎ 831 449, Malo 9-55) serves up excellent ice cream, cakes, coffee, yogurt and fruit salads, and it is a very popular hangout for international travelers. Prices are not low, but the food is delectable. Also popular is **Café Austria** (Malo 5-45), which has delicious Austrian-style cakes and coffee. **Raymipampa** (☎ 834 159), under the colonnade in front of the new cathedral, is full of character and is a good place to hang out. It's very popular with both locals and travelers, who enjoy the large portions, although the service and food gets mixed reviews.

Upstairs in the Casa de Cultura, on the corner of Parque Calderón, **Cinema Café**

(☎ 822 446) is named for the movie posters it displays; it doesn't show films. It's a quiet place for sandwiches, desserts and coffee. **Ubu** (*Honorato Vásquez 7-56*) is super popular and has a variety of reasonably priced international dishes. Torrential rains in late 1999 caused the colonial roof to cave in, but it will mostly likely reopen.

Lovers of Italian food will find plenty to choose from. Two pizzerias on Gran Colombia, on either side of Luís Cordero, are **Los Pibes** and **La Tuna**. Both have pasta, pizza and other dishes. Farther up Gran Colombia is **New York Pizza** (☎ 842 792, 825 674, *Gran Colombia 10-43*), which readers have also recommended and which delivers pizza to your room. Also good for Italian food is **La Napoletana Pizzería** (☎ 823 172, *Avenida Fray Vicente Solano 3-04*), which will also deliver pizza. It is popular with locals and is often full.

El Pedregal Azteca (☎ 823 652, *Gran Colombia 10-33*) is in an attractive old building. It is Mexican-run and serves good Mexican dinners Monday to Saturday and lunches Tuesday to Saturday. There is live music some evenings. Although the restaurant is popular with travelers, its portions aren't big but cost US$4 or US$5, so this is not for the starving student on a budget.

Another pleasant building with a nice atmosphere is **La Barraca** (☎ 842 967, 825 094, *Borrero 9-68*), which serves good and reasonably priced local dishes and rather more expensive international food. It's popular with locals and travelers alike, and board games are provided for entertainment while you have a coffee or beer and wait for a meal.

La Cantina Los Capulies (☎ 832 339, 831 120), Presidente Córdova and Borrero, has a pleasant, elegant patio; good but pricey Ecuadorian meals; and live entertainment on weekends. One traveler reported that it is 'full of US tour groups.' Opposite, and also popular with tourists, is **Restaurant El Jardín** (☎ 831 120, 838 508, *Presidente Córdova 7-23*), reputed to be one of the best in town. A full meal with tax, tip and a modest wine will cost about US$30 to US$40 for two – not bad. The subdued light-

ing is either romantic or too dark to read the menu, depending on your mood. The menu tends toward continental and French.

Giving the El Jardín competition for 'best in town' is **Restaurant Villa Rosa** (☎ 837 944, *Gran Colombia 12-22*). It's in a pretty, covered courtyard within a colonial house and serves both local and international dishes, with an emphasis on elegant Ecuadorian dining. It is closed on weekends.

If you're leaving town – or arriving, for that matter – you can eat at the bus terminal, where 24-hour snack bars and daytime restaurants serve adequate food.

On Gran Colombia, about 1km west off the map, is an area of mid-priced restaurants and bars that are popular with more affluent young locals and any travelers who find their way there. There are several places around the 20 and 21 block of Gran Colombia. A few hundred meters farther west, Gran Colombia becomes Ordóñez Lazo, where there are other bars and Hotel Oro Verde.

ENTERTAINMENT

Though Cuenca is Ecuador's third-largest city, entertainment is quite limited. *El Mercurio* is the Cuenca newspaper for cinema listings. Note that **Teatro Casa de Cultura** is not the same place as the Casa de Cultura, which occasionally also has movies or lectures – both are shown on the map.

A good place to start is one of the restaurants favored by young travelers – El Cafecito, Raymipampa or Heladería Holandesa (see Places to Eat, earlier), where you'll find notices advertising currently popular nightclubs.

Apart from the area of restaurants and bars on Gran Colombia, other popular bars for young people include the trendy **WunderBar**, on Hermano Miguel at Calle Larga, and the laid-back **Kaos** (*Honorato Vásquez 6-11*), with couches, pool tables and snacks.

For dancing, check out **La Mesa** (*Gran Colombia 3-35*), with an energetic salsa scene; **Ego**, at 12 de Abril and Unidad Nacional (taxis know it), which mixes salsa, merengue and Latin rock; or **ETC**, under Hotel El Conquistador, which has similar music but an older crowd.

SHOPPING

Cuenca, the center of the panama hat industry, is one of the best places to buy these hats. Most hotels can tell you of a favorite choice, and hatmakers may leave their advertising in hotel lobbies. Note that these panama hats are of the highest export quality and are not cheap, but they are a good value.

Other crafts of the Cuenca area include *ikat* textiles, which are made with threads that have been tie-dyed before weaving; this method dates to pre-Columbian times. Traditional colors are indigo (a deep reddish blue), but red and black have appeared recently. Handmade ceramic tiles, plates, cups and bowls are also popular, as are baskets. Typical Cuencano baskets are huge and come with lids – few people can manage to take one of them home. Gold and silver filigreed jewelry from the nearby village of Chordeleg is for sale, as are the usual weavings, carvings and leatherwork of Ecuador.

Wandering down Gran Colombia and the blocks just north of the Parque Calderón will bring you to several good craft stores.

The Thursday market, at Lamar and Hermano Miguel, is mainly for locals (which means pigs and polyester, fruit and furniture – just about anything except used cars). There are a few stalls with crafts for sale. Visitors should watch for pickpockets and purse/camera snatchers – I wouldn't bring a camera to this market unless I were with friends to watch my back.

GETTING THERE & AWAY
Air

The passenger terminal of Aeropuerto Mariscal Lamar is conveniently only 2km from the heart of town, on Avenida España. TAME has an airport desk (☎ 862 400) for inbound/outbound flights and another office downtown (☎ 843 222), at Malo 5-08. Flight schedules to and from Cuenca change several times a year, so the information provided here may not be the most current. You should inquire locally.

TAME has one flight a day to and from Guayaquil Monday to Saturday mornings.

On weekdays, it flies twice a day to and from Quito; once a day on weekends.

For flights to Loja, Machala and some coastal cities, fly into Guayaquil and change; for most other cities, change in Quito. Austro Aéreo (☎ 832 677, 848 659), Hermano Miguel 5-42, has three or four flights a week to Macas and Guayaquil.

Bus

The well-organized bus terminal is on Avenida España on the way to the airport, about 1.5km from the town center.

There are dozens of different bus companies with offices in the terminal. Some run two or three buses every hour, while others run two or three every week. Buses vary widely in size, speed and comfort.

Buses leave for Guayaquil (five hours) many times daily. A new road via the north side of Parque Nacional Cajas and Molleturo is being built, which will cut the journey time to under four hours; this road has yet to open. Buses leave for Machala (3½ hours) about every hour; a few continue to Huaquillas, or you can go to Machala and change.

Buses for Azogues (45 minutes) leave at least every hour, many continuing to Cañar (1½ hours) and Alausí (US$3, four hours). Buses for El Tambo (7km beyond Cañar) leave every 30 minutes and get you within 8km of Ingapirca. Direct buses to Ingapirca (2¼ hours) run at 9 am and 1 pm daily.

For Quito (eight to 11 hours), there are buses about every hour; driving time depends on route and road conditions. For destinations between Alausí and Quito, there are several departures daily; it takes six hours to reach Riobamba.

There are buses every hour 6 am to 10 pm via Saraguro continuing to Loja (six hours). For destinations south of Loja, it is best to change in Loja.

If you want to go into the southern Oriente, 11 buses a day go to Macas (10 to 12 hours) and several others to Gualaquiza (eight hours).

Buses to the Gualaceo Sunday market depart from the corner of Avenidas España and Benalcázar, about 100m southwest of the bus terminal. They leave every few minutes on market day and less frequently on weekdays for the ride, which lasts almost an hour. Some buses go from the terminal through Gualaceo to Sígsig.

There is an information desk at the terminal where you can ask about other destinations. Fares are usually almost US$1 per hour of travel.

GETTING AROUND

Taxis cost about US$1.25 between downtown and the airport. City buses (US$0.10) pass the terminal frequently, although they tend to be rather full just after a plane arrives. Downtown, buses depart from the stop by the flower market on Padre Aguirre – not all are marked, so ask the drivers.

City buses leave from the front of the bus terminal for the center (US$0.10), and buses for the terminal leave from the bus stop on Padre Aguirre by the flower market. Most (but not all) buses are marked 'Terminal;' ask the driver to be sure.

Local buses (US$0.10) for Baños leave from Avenida Torres by the San Francisco market. Local buses for Turi, 4km south of the center, travel along Avenida Fray Vicente Solano.

Localiza rents cars and has two offices. One (☎ 803 198/3) is at the airport; the other (☎ 863 902, ☎/fax 860 174) is at España 1485, near Granada (400m northeast of the airport). IRC Inter Rentacar (☎ 801 892, 863 195, fax 806 688) is at the airport.

Bikes can be rented for US$15 a day, helmets included, from Rentabike (☎ 831 295), adjoining Hotel Crespo. A guide costs an extra US$10.

The Cuenca Area

☎ 07

Several local attractions draw both Cuencanos and foreign visitors to the area surrounding Cuenca. The region offers plenty

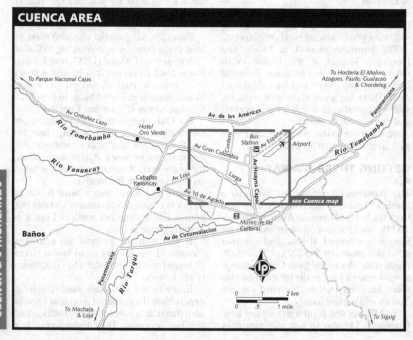

of outdoor activities – you can store up your energy by lounging in the hot springs or expend it by taking a strenuous backpacking trip into the mountains.

BAÑOS

This is a much smaller version of the Baños described in the South of Quito chapter. Here you'll find sulfurous hot springs with public pools and restaurants – a popular getaway for Cuencanos.

The village is about 5km southwest of Cuenca. Take a local bus there, or take a taxi for US$2. Use of the thermal pools costs about US$0.40; twice that for a private bath.

There are a couple of *basic residenciales* by the baths, charging about US$4 per person for rooms with hot water. A short distance away is the comfortable *Hostería Durán* (☎ 892 485/6, fax 892 488, bduran@az .tro.ec), which has a private thermal swimming pool, sauna, pleasant gardens, and the best restaurant in the area. A spacious double room is about US$25. Apart from the Durán, there are several simple restaurants in the area serving inexpensive Ecuadorian food.

PARQUE NACIONAL CAJAS

This 28,800-hectare park lies about 30km west of Cuenca and is famous for its many beautiful lakes – well over 200 have been named, and there are countless smaller ponds, pools and puddles. There are trout in the lakes, and fishing is permitted. The terrain is bleak and rough, and the lakes shine like jewels against the harsh countryside. It is rugged hiking and camping country, much of it *páramo* at around 4000m above sea level. None of the area is above 4500m, so it doesn't normally snow, although the winds and rains can make it very cold. Hikers and campers should be well prepared with warm, windproof gear and plenty of energy. Several readers have written to say that they underestimated the cold weather and had a very cold trip – bring protective clothing!

The Laguna Toreadora ranger station is on the northern side of Cajas, a few hundred meters from the park entrance. Just a few kilometers before the entrance, on the left, is a park information booth that is supposed to collect the entrance fee of US$10, although it has no maps and little information. Many guides will just drive past this booth. You can obtain better information at the ranger station, but it lacks maps as well.

In sheltered hollows and natural depressions of the terrain, small forests of the quinua *(polylepis)* tree are seen. This tree grows at the highest altitudes of any tree in the world, and the quinua thickets provide welcome protection from the elements for all kinds of unusual plants and animals. Everything is on a small, tightly packed scale, and forcing your way into one of these dense dwarf forests is like entering a scene from a Grimm fairy tale.

Bird watchers will have a great time looking for the many different species found on the lakes, in the quinua forests and in the surrounding páramo. These are the habitats of such evocatively named birds as the giant conebill, titlike dacnis and gray-breasted mountain toucan. A variety of exotically named hummingbirds can also be seen: the rainbow-bearded thornbill, sapphire-vented puffleg and purple-throated sunangel, just to name a few. Even the LBBs (little brown birds) that hop unobtrusively through the thickets have interesting names, such as mouse-colored thistletail. Bring binoculars if you have them.

There are a number of signed trails in the most popular area (around Laguna Toreadora) that are suitable for hikes of a few hours. Also near the lake is a trail signed for Mirador Ajahuaico, which goes to the top of a nearby mountain and offers impressive views. Multiday treks are possible all the way across the park – the two most popular trails are shown on the map but are poorly signed, so compass skills are important. Hikers may want to buy topographical maps from the IGM (see Orientation under Quito, in the Quito & Around chapter). Four 1:50,000 maps cover the area: Cuenca CT-NV-F4, Chaucha CT-NV-F3, San Felipe de Molleturo CT-NV-F1 and Chiquintad CT-NV-F2.

CUENCA & S HIGHLANDS

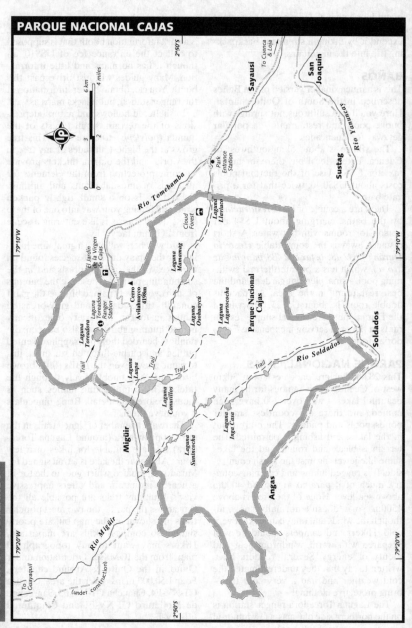

PARQUE NACIONAL CAJAS

The driest months are August to January, but it can rain anytime – those hundreds of beautiful lakes need to be kept full! During the dry season, daytime temperatures can go into the high teens Celsius (up to 70°F); night temperatures can go well below freezing. Wet-season temperatures are less extreme. Annual rainfall is about 1200m. Water temperatures are usually about or below 5°C (40°F) – you can leave your swimming suit at home.

Places to Stay

You can usually sleep for a small fee at the ranger station (but don't rely on it – there are only eight beds), which has a kitchen. Beds have mattresses only, so bring a sleeping bag. Camping is allowed anywhere in the recreation area for US$2 per night. The bus passes within a few hundred meters of the ranger station. At Km 25, shortly before the ranger station, there are some cabins that are sometimes closed.

Getting There & Away

Buses from Cuenca leave at 6 or 6:30 am (except Thursday) from the church of San Sebastián for the cramped, two-hour ride to the Laguna Toreadora ranger station on the northern side of Cajas, 34km from Cuenca. There is a return bus in the afternoon at about 3 pm (check with the driver). About 10km before the park, on the right, is El Jardín de la Virgen de Cajas, where the Virgin Mary appeared to a young girl in 1989. There is now a shrine there, and it is a popular picnicking spot with Cuencanos on weekends. The bus is often crowded and has been known to leave early – get to the bus stop well before 6 am. Sometimes a second bus runs. It is particularly crowded with local fishing enthusiasts on weekends. Make sure the driver knows to drop you off at the park entrance – the bus continues 12km beyond it to the village of Migüir.

A new road is being built beyond Migüir to Guayaquil, but the route is plagued with landslide problems. If the road does open, it will be the fastest route from Cuenca to Guayaquil and will make access to Cajas easier.

A southern road passes the park at the villages of Soldados and Angas. This road is in very poor shape, but there are buses on Monday, Wednesday, Friday and Saturday leaving from Del Vado and Loja in Cuenca at 6 am.

It is 34km to Soldados and 56km to Angas; the trip takes about four hours. There are small ranger stations but almost no facilities at either of these tiny and remote villages; Cajas lies to the north of you. Buses return to Cuenca in the afternoon.

Apart from the bus, you can take a taxi (about US$25) or go on a day trip with one of the tour agencies in Cuenca.

GUALACEO, CHORDELEG & SÍGSIG

These villages are all famous for their Sunday markets. If you started from Cuenca early in the morning, you could visit all three markets and be back in Cuenca in the afternoon. Buses leave Cuenca from the southwest corner of the bus terminal. The best-known markets are at Gualaceo and Chordeleg, which are within a few kilometers of one another.

Gualaceo has the biggest market (mainly produce, animals and household goods) and the best hotel selection. Chordeleg's market is smaller but important for textiles and jewelry. Sígsig's market is farther away from Cuenca and is less visited by tourists. All three villages are good examples of colonial towns.

Gualaceo

In addition to being an important market town, Gualaceo has some importance as a tourist resort and is a pretty location by Río Gualaceo. It is 25km due west of Cuenca, at about 2370m above sea level. There are several restaurants by the river, and a stroll along the banks is a nice way to spend an afternoon. The town is quite progressive, and its spacious, modern church has nice stained-glass windows. There are several restaurants and places to stay, as well as a Pacifictel office.

Market Note that the Sunday market is several blocks from the bus terminal in Gualaceo, although there are some souvenir stands near the bus plaza that may fool you into thinking that is the market. There is also an animal market across the covered bridge, on the east bank of the river. The market is not geared toward tourists (there are very few crafts for sale) but is colorful and fun to visit. Heavy knitted sweaters are a good buy.

Despite the paucity of crafts at the Gualaceo market, many of the surrounding villages are known for the manufacture of a variety of handmade goods, ranging from musical instruments to textiles to hats. It is possible to arrange crafts tours with guides in Cuenca if this interests you. There is a small display of crafts from the area in Parador Turístico Gualaceo (see Places to Stay & Eat, next).

Places to Stay & Eat There are several places to stay in the town center for about US$3 per person. The friendly *Residencial Gualaceo* (☎ 255 006, Gran Colombia 3-02) sometimes has hot water and is a basic, reasonably clean, family-run place – you have to walk through their kitchen to reach the rooms. Half a block north on Gran Colombia, *Residencial Carlos Andrade* (☎ 255 379) is fairly basic and friendly and has reasonably large rooms with hot water.

The best place in the area is the pleasant *Parador Turístico Gualaceo* (☎ 255 110/126), about 1km south of town along Gran Colombia. It is set in attractive gardens with flowers and birds and has a swimming pool and Turkish bath. Horseback riding can be arranged. It has a decent restaurant and bar that serves meals to both guests and visitors. There is a disco that opens on demand (10 people paying a cover charge, usually on weekends). Clean, flower-filled rooms with private bath and hot water cost about US$16/22.

Gualaceo has several cheap, basic restaurants near the bus plaza and around the main market plaza. The best of these is *Restaurant Don Q*, just off the northwest corner of the market.

The stalls on market day serve a variety of local dishes, such as whole roast pigs (you don't have to eat it all).

Chordeleg

Chordeleg is 4km or 5km south of Gualaceo and has many stores selling crafts – it is known as a jewelry center throughout Ecuador. It's especially popular with Guayaquileños looking for highland bargains. Some people complain that it is too 'touristy' and that the quality of the jewelry is lower than in the past. If you're shopping for souvenirs or gifts, you can choose from gold and silver filigree jewelry (by far the most interesting items), as well as a small selection (look hard) of woodcarvings, pottery, textiles, panama hats and embroidered clothing. A reader who is a goldsmith wrote that the walk to Chordeleg is pleasant, but the gold work there is nothing special.

There is a pleasant central plaza with a small, modern church containing simple but attractive stained-glass windows. Also on the plaza is a small village museum that manages to pack more into it than some bigger city museums. It's open 8 am to 5 pm daily except Monday and is free. There are displays about the history and techniques of many of the local handicrafts, such as filigreed metalwork, panama hat making and ikat weaving. Some of the locally made work is for sale, and I'm told the money goes directly to the artisans. Guides are available. It helps if you understand Spanish. There is one basic residencial and several simple restaurants.

The tiny village of **San Bartolomé** is between Chordeleg and Sígsig and is famed for its guitar makers and other artisans. Guided tours from Cuenca often stop here and take you in to visit the craftspeople in their houses.

Sígsig

Sígsig is a pleasant colonial village where little happens apart from the Sunday market. It is about 25km south of Gualaceo and is the center of a hat-making region. On the outskirts, Asociación de María Auxiliadora, in the old hospital, is a hat-making cooperative that sells hats more cheaply than in Cuenca and provides more income for the hat makers. A women's weaving cooperative is also in town. There are a couple of restaurants on the main market plaza, and there is a basic pensión, *Toral T*. A few blocks from the plaza is a bus office. The ride out here from Cuenca is nice.

Getting There & Away
Buses from Cuenca with Cooperativa de Transportes Gualaceo take under an hour to reach Gualaceo. The buses leave every 15 minutes on market day and at least every hour on weekdays. You can continue the 4km or 5km to Chordeleg on foot or take a local bus. Buses pass the Chordeleg plaza for Sígsig at least once an hour and charge US$0.50 for the 40-minute ride. Sit on the right-hand side of the bus for good views of the river canyon on the way to Sígsig. Buses return from Sígsig to Cuenca about every hour for US$1.

A new road to Gualaquiza via **Chigüinda** (600 inhabitants; 1750m) was completed in 1998. Buses from Sígsig to Chigüinda leave daily at 9 am (three hours). In Chigüinda, you can stay with Doña Mercedes Orellana, who rents rooms near the bus stop, and hike in the pretty hills around town. From here, open-sided *ranchera* trucks go to Gualaquiza via the remote villages of Aguacate and Río Negro daily. Rancheras also go to other remote villages, if you want to get off the beaten track.

North of Cuenca

☎ 07

Of the various sites of interest north of Cuenca, the most important is undoubtedly the Inca site of Ingapirca.

AZOGUES
About 35km north of Cuenca on the Ecuadorian Panamericana lies Azogues, a bustling town of over 33,000 inhabitants and the capital of Cañar province. The town produces panama hats, though these are finished in and sold from Cuenca. Saturday is market day.

The Pacifictel and post office are on the main plaza. Filanbanco, on Bolívar two blocks south of the plaza, changes traveler's checks and has a Visa ATM.

Things to See
The **church of San Francisco** dominates the town from a hill to the southeast, reached by a 30-minute climb or a short taxi ride. The original church dates from colonial times, but it was completely rebuilt in the 1940s, and only parts of the altar retain the colonial style. Outside, sweeping views of the town and surrounding countryside make the climb worthwhile. The building is sometimes illuminated at night – sitting on the dark hill, it looks almost as if it were floating in midair. Part of the Saturday market is held below the church.

Biblian, a village 9km north of Azogues on the Ecuadorian Panamericana, is the home of **Santuario de la Virgen del Rocío** (Sanctuary of the Virgin of the Dew). This church is highly visible to the east of the main highway on a steep hill dominating Biblian and looks more like a fairytale princess's palace than it does a church.

It was originally a small colonial shrine built into a cliff, but in the 1940s, it was enlarged into a church with the altar built into the rock where the shrine was. There is a huge pilgrimage here on September 8 (see Special Events under Loja, later in this chapter) and a lesser one on Good Friday.

Places to Stay & Eat
The reasonably clean *Hotel Charles II* (☎ 241 883), at the corner of Serrano and Emilio Abad, near the main plaza, charges about US$4 per person for rooms with private hot showers. The cheaper *Hotel Charles I* is reportedly dirty. *Hotel Chicago* (☎ 241 040), at 3 de Noviembre and 24 de Mayo, also is about US$4 per person and is OK. Its restaurant has good, cheap set lunches and is one of the best in town. The best hotel is *Hostal Rivera* (☎ 248 113, fax 244 275), at 24 de Mayo and 10 de Agosto. It has a restaurant and 24 clean rooms with TV, telephone and private hot shower for US$8/12.

Several other inexpensive places to eat are found in town.

Getting There & Away

The main bus plaza is just off the Ecuadorian Panamericana, which is renamed 24 de Mayo as it goes through Azogues. There are many daily departures for Quito, Guayaquil and Machala; for other destinations, it is best to go to Cuenca and change buses.

For buses to Cañar, it may be best to stand on the highway outside the bus plaza and wait for one to come by – often, Cuenca-Cañar buses don't pull into the bus plaza – see what the locals are doing.

For Cuenca, there is a local bus terminal on Rivera about three blocks south of the main market. Buses for Cuenca leave as soon as they are full – several times an hour from dawn until about 7 pm. Later on, you can catch buses to Cuenca by waiting on the Panamericana outside the main bus plaza. The fare to either Cuenca or Cañar should be about US$0.50.

CAÑAR

The small town of Cañar, on the Ecuadorian Panamericana, is 66km north of Cuenca and 3104m above sea level. The colorful local market on Sunday is visited by Cañari Indians coming down from the remote villages in the surrounding mountains.

Cañari men wear distinctive belts made by an unusual weaving method that gives rise to designs and motifs appearing on both sides of the belt. These may be available in the market – they are also woven by the local prisoners, and if you head down to the jail, you will be allowed in to make purchases.

Hostal Ingapirca (☎ 235 201), Calle Sucre at 5 de Junio, charges US$3/5 for rooms with private hot shower. *Residencial Monica* is on the corner of the main plaza and charges a little less. If these are all full, you can find accommodations in unsigned private houses – ask around.

There are adequate simple restaurants; none are noteworthy.

The Ingapirca Ruins

Ingapirca (3230m) is the major Inca site in Ecuador, but opinions are mixed about the significance of the ruins. They have never been 'lost,' as were the Inca ruins at Machu Picchu in Peru. The Frenchman Charles-Marie de La Condamine drew accurate plans of Ingapirca as far back as 1739. The ruins are referred to as a fortress, but its garrison – if there was one – must have been quite small.

Archaeologists think that the main structure, an *usnu* (elliptical platform)

ROB RACHOWIECKI

known as the Temple of the Sun, had religious and ceremonial purposes. This building boasts some of the Inca's finest mortarless stonework, including several of the trapezoidal niches and doorways that are hallmarks of Inca construction. The less-preserved buildings were probably storehouses, and the complex may have been used as a *tambo* (stopping place) for runners carrying imperial messages from Quito to Tomebamba.

Unfortunately, the ruins were well known and lacked protection, so many of the dressed stones that were used for the buildings were stolen over the centuries for use in colonial and modern building projects. Ingapirca's importance is now recognized, and the ruins are officially protected.

Frequent buses from Cuenca's bus terminal charge under US$1 and take 90 minutes.

INGAPIRCA

This is Ecuador's most important site and is about 1km away from the bus stop in village of Ingapirca. The weekly market is on Friday.

The archaeological site is open daily 8 am to 6 pm. A small, on-site museum is near the entrance. A few signs in English and French help explain the site, and local guides are available for a nominal charge. Admission is US$5.

For more information on Ingapirca, see the boxed text 'The Ingapirca Ruins.'

Places to Stay & Eat

There is a *shelter* near the site entrance with toilet facilities and benches. You can sleep there if you have a sleeping bag and mat (there are no beds), and camping is reportedly allowed. This is included in the US$5 admission fee.

Inti Huasi (☎ 290 767) is a small, clean hotel and restaurant at the entrance to the village, by the bus stop. It charges about US$5 for a double with bath and hot water. Rooms with shared bath are cheaper. The owner is Mama Julia, a friendly Cañari woman.

Posada Ingapirca, a steep 500m drive above the archaeological site, is the restaurant of choice for some tour groups; it's a little pricey but OK. The building is a converted old hacienda with views of the site. Rooms with private hot showers, minibar and heater are mid-range in price. Information and reservations can be made in Cuenca with Grupo Santa Ana (☎ 831 120, 838 508, fax 832 340, santaana@aracno.net), Cordóva at Borrero.

Getting There & Away

Agencies in Cuenca organize day trips, or you can rent a taxi for the day, which should cost about US$35 – bargain for the best rate. Tours start at about US$35 per person – see Travel Agencies & Guides under Cuenca, earlier in this chapter, for details.

For an economical visit, catch a direct bus from Cuenca at 9 am or 1 pm. If you take the morning bus, you can spend a few hours at the ruins and return in the afternoon.

South of Cuenca

☎ 07

About 20km south of Cuenca, the road forks. The Ecuadorian Panamericana heads south to Loja via the towns of Oña and Saraguro. The right fork heads southwest to Machala.

FROM CUENCA TO MACHALA

This paved road goes through impressive mountain scenery and is well worth doing in daylight. Some 23km from the fork in the Panamericana, you'll pass the small town of **Girón**. As you look down on it from the road, you'll see a neat-looking town of red-tiled roofs interspersed with brightly colored red, blue and green tin roofs. There is a cheap hostal here.

At **Santa Isabel**, 37km beyond Girón, buses may stop for a meal break. There are several restaurants and a basic pensión in this bustling little community. The town is an agricultural center for tropical fruits grown in the area, which is about 1600m above sea level. Banana and papaya plantations are seen interspersed among the cornfields.

Just below Santa Isabel, the scenery changes suddenly and dramatically as the road winds through completely barren mountains with no signs of life. Just as suddenly, a forest of columnar cacti appears, which soon gives way to cloud forest mixed with tropical agriculture.

About 45km beyond Santa Isabel is the town of Pasaje, and 25km farther is Machala. Both are described in the South Coast chapter.

OÑA (SAN FELIPE DE OÑA)

The Ecuadorian Panamericana climbs steadily from Cuenca and has good views of the páramo in the southern Ecuadorian Andes. Oña, 105km south of Cuenca, is reached after almost three hours. It's a small town with a couple of simple restaurants and a basic pensión.

SARAGURO

Just beyond Oña, the road crosses the provincial line into Loja and continues rising and falling through the eerie páramo scenery until it reaches Saraguro, almost four hours and 165km south of Cuenca. This small town is named after the Saraguro Indians (see the boxed text). Their interesting market day is Sunday, when local Indians show up in their traditional black clothing.

There are a few very basic places to stay, none with private bathrooms. *Residencial Armigos* and *Pensión Saraguro* are both near the church and are the best places. Both are cheap, and the latter has hot water. Local stores or businesses may rent a room – ask around.

There are two or three basic restaurants; the best are *Mama Cuchara*, on the plaza, and *Salón Cristal*, behind the church, which serves only lunch.

Loja is 62km to the south, and buses leave Saraguro hourly during the day for the 1½-hour ride. The bus office is a block from the main plaza. Buses also leave for various small villages in the area. For Cuenca, it is best to wait in the plaza for a northbound bus from Loja to pass by.

LOJA

From Saraguro, the road continues to drop steadily to Loja, at 2100m – a pleasant elevation that leads to a temperate climate. The proximity of the Oriente influences Loja's climate. June and July are the wettest months, when roads into the Oriente may be closed by landslides caused by torrential rains. October through December are considered the most pleasant months.

Loja was founded by the Spanish captain Alonso de Mercadillo on December 8, 1548, and so it is one of the oldest towns in Ecuador. None of the earliest buildings has survived, although houses from the 18th century can be found.

With about 130,000 inhabitants, Loja is both an important provincial capital and a college town, with two universities, a music conservatory and a law school. A small hydroelectric project became operational in 1897, at the base of Pedestal Hill, a short distance west of the town center. The project generated 34 kilowatts and gave Loja the distinction of being the first city in Ecuador to have electric energy.

Although the town itself is not particularly exciting, it is attractive, and travelers on their way to Peru via the border town of Macará find this a convenient place to stop. The highland route to Peru through Loja and Macará is slower and rougher but much more scenic than the more traveled route through the coastal towns of Machala and Huaquillas. Loja is also the departure point for visiting Vilcabamba (see that section, later in this chapter) and Zamora, in the southern Oriente (see the next chapter). The road between Cuenca and Loja is being improved, and the one between Loja and Machala is also very scenic.

Information

Tourist Offices The tourist information office (☎/fax 572 964) is at Bernardo Valdivieso 08-22. The Ministero del Medio Ambiente (☎ 563 131, 577 125), which is responsible for administering Parque Nacional Podocarpus, is at Sucre 4-35.

Peruvian Consulate The consulate (☎ 571 668, 579 068) is at Sucre 10-64. Hours are 8:30 am to 5 pm weekdays.

Money Banks change money only until 1 or 2 pm. Filanbanco takes traveler's checks and has a Visa ATM, and Banco de Guayaquil has a MasterCard ATM. If you are arriving from Peru, get rid of Peruvian currency at the border, as rates are poor in Loja.

Post & Communications The post office is at the corner of Colón and Sucre. The Pacifictel office is a block east of Parque Central, on Eguiguren. Internet connections are available at Faisanet, Colón 14-84, or Cybercafe, on Plaza Santo Domingo.

Travel Agencies Franklin Hidalgo's Hidaltur (☎ 571 031, fax 562 554, fhidalgo@loja.telconet.net), 10 de Agosto 11-67, is recommended for international travel services

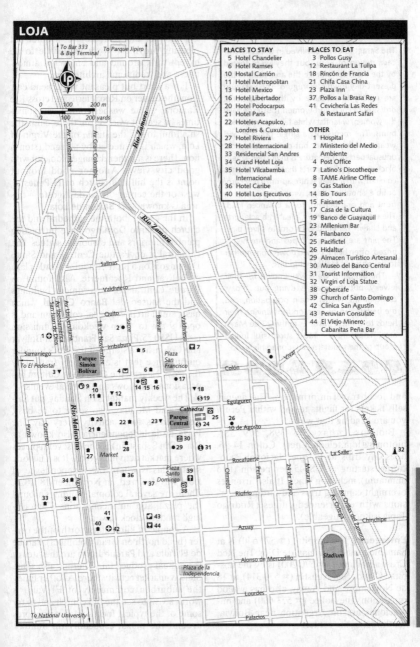

LOJA

To Bar 333 & Bus Terminal
To Parque Jipiro

0   100   200 m
0   100   200 yards

PLACES TO STAY
5 Hotel Chandelier
6 Hotel Ramses
10 Hostal Carrión
11 Hotel Metropolitan
13 Hotel Mexico
16 Hotel Libertador
20 Hotel Podocarpus
21 Hotel Paris
22 Hoteles Acapulco,
    Londres & Cuxubamba
27 Hotel Riviera
28 Hotel Internacional
33 Residencial San Andres
34 Grand Hotel Loja
35 Hotel Vilcabamba
    Internacional
36 Hotel Caribe
40 Hotel Los Ejecutivos

PLACES TO EAT
3 Pollos Gusy
12 Restaurant La Tullpa
18 Rincón de Francia
21 Chifa Casa China
23 Plaza Inn
37 Pollos a la Brasa Rey
41 Cevichería Las Redes
    & Restaurant Safari

OTHER
1 Hospital
2 Ministerio del Medio
   Ambiente
4 Post Office
7 Latino's Discotheque
8 TAME Airline Office
9 Gas Station
14 Bio Tours
15 Faisanet
17 Casa de la Cultura
19 Banco de Guayaquil
23 Millenium Bar
24 Filanbanco
25 Pacifictel
26 Hidaltur
29 Almacen Turístico Artesanal
30 Museo del Banco Central
31 Tourist Information
32 Virgin of Loja Statue
38 Cybercafe
39 Church of Santo Domingo
42 Clínica San Agustín
43 Peruvian Consulate
44 El Viejo Minero;
    Cabanitas Peña Bar

Av Cuxibamba
Av Gran Colombia
Río Zamora
Río Zamora

Salinas
Valdivieso
Quito
Sucre
Bolívar
Valdivieso
18 de Noviembre
Imbabura
Av Universitaria
Av Iberoamerica
San Juan de Dios
Samaniego
To El Pedestal

Parque Simón Bolívar

Plaza San Francisco

Colón
Vivar

Eguiguren

Cathedral
Parque Central

10 de Agosto

Rocafuerte
La Salle

Plaza Santo Domingo

Riofrío

Av Pío Jaramillo

Olmedo
Peña
24 de Mayo
Macará
Av Orillas del Zamora
Chinchipe

Azuay

Alonso de Mercadillo

Stadium

Plaza de la Independencia

Lourdes

To National University

Palacios

Río Malacatos
Guerrero
Pinta
Aguirre

Market

CUENCA & S HIGHLANDS

The Saraguro Indians

The Saraguro originally lived in the Lake Titicaca region of Peru, but they were forced by the Incas to colonize the area around the present-day town of Saraguro. The Saraguro are readily identifiable by their traditional dress. Both men and women (but especially the women) wear flat white felt hats with wide brims. The men sport a single ponytail and wear a black poncho, but perhaps the most unusual part of their attire is their knee-length black or navy-blue shorts that are sometimes covered with a small white apron. They carry double shoulder bags, with one pouch in front and one behind, for a balanced load. The women wear heavy, pleated black skirts and shawls fastened with ornate silver pins. The pins are known as *tupus* and are highly prized, often being passed down from mother to daughter as family heirlooms.

The Saraguro were well known for their jewelry, but this craft is dying out. Today, cattle-raising is their main occupation, and the people can be seen on foot driving their herds to tropical pastures in the 28 de Mayo area. They are the most successful Indian group of the southern Ecuadorian highlands.

and local travel information. The agency sells tickets for flights to and within Peru if you are heading that way.

Biotours (☎/fax 578 398, 579 387, biotours@loja.telconet.net), Colón 14-96, does day trips to Parque Nacional Podocarpus starting at US$45 per person (two minimum), including lunch. It also arranges overnight camping trips and birding excursions with experienced guides (Rodrigo Tapia is knowledgeable).

Emergency The hospital (☎ 570 540) is at Samaniego and San Juan de Diós. The Red Cross ambulance (☎ 570 200) is by the hospital. Clínica San Agustín (☎ 570 314), at 18 de Noviembre and Azuay, also has a good reputation. The police (☎ 573 600) and migraciones are on Argentina near Bolivia, southwest of the center.

Things to See & Do

For most of the year, Loja is a quiet but pleasing provincial town with little to do except walk around and enjoy the atmosphere and traditional architecture.

For a short but pleasant walk, head east from the center on Rocafuerte and cross Río Zamora, where washerwomen can sometimes be seen at work. From there, climb the small hill to see the statue of the **Virgin of Loja**, which is protected by a caged (stone) lion. There is a rather damaged **lookout** with good city views. Another good lookout point is the hill and **church of El Pedestal**, west of the center off 10 de Agosto – this area is known as **El Balcón de Loja**.

In the center, both the **cathedral** and the **church of Santo Domingo** have interesting painted interiors and elaborate statues. The cathedral is on Parque Central, and Santo Domingo is on a pretty, traditional little plaza at Bolívar and Rocafuerte. Also found on Parque Central are government buildings and the **Museo del Banco Central**, which has a small archaeological collection and is open 9 am to 4 pm weekdays. Admission costs US$0.25. **Plaza San Francisco**, at Bolívar and Colón, has a statue of the city's founder on his horse that is attractively framed by the trees. Nearby, the **Casa de la Cultura** has occasional art shows and cultural events.

The weekly **market** is on Sunday, but Saturday and Monday also seem to be busy, and there is some activity every day. The **Plaza de la Independencia** (also known as Plaza San Sebastián) is one of several places where market activities go on. It is a historic spot – this is where the independence of Loja was declared on November 18, 1820. There are several colonial buildings around the plaza, and an incongruous 32-meter-high modern clock tower.

A couple of kilometers north of the center (head north on Gran Colombia), **Parque de El Valle** and **Parque Jipiro** are the sites of the annual produce fair. There is also some Sunday-market activity there. At other times, the suburban community of El Valle is worth a visit to see the old church and to try some of the typical food sold in comedores around the plaza, especially on Sunday, when families go to eat *cuy* (whole roasted guinea pig). The nearby Parque de Jipiro has a small lake with a miniature island adorned by a white statue of a larger-than-life Venus. This island is sometimes the scene of symphony performances. The musicians cluster around the statue, and the audience must content itself with listening from the shores of the lake – the orchestra takes up the entire island. Boats can be rented.

At the south end of town is the national university (☎ 571 841, 570 252), set in a large park containing a **botanical garden** that can be visited 9 am to 4 pm weekdays and 1 to 5 pm weekends. Admission is US$0.50.

Northeast of town is the UTPL (☎ 570 275), which sometimes has demonstrations of how ceramics are made and has items for sale. Ask locally for directions. Their ceramics are also sold at the Almacen Turístico Artesanal, itself in an interesting older balconied building on Bolívar near Rocafuerte.

Special Events
From late August to the beginning of November, the cathedral is home to La Virgen del Cisne (the Virgin of the Swan), carved in the late 16th century by Diego de Robles. Throughout the rest of the year, the statue is kept some 70km away, in the village of El Cisne (see the boxed text 'La Virgen del Cisne,' later in this chapter). El Día de La Virgen del Cisne is celebrated in Loja on September 8 with huge processions; an annual international produce fair is held for about four or five days on either side of the 8th (it's called 'international' because Peruvians attend it).

An important fiesta celebrating the independence of Loja takes place on November 18. Festivities may go on for a week, featuring parades and cultural events. The feast of San Sebastián, which coincides with the foundation of Loja, is celebrated on December 8.

Places to Stay
Loja appears to have an excess of accommodations. They often fill up for the annual fiestas but may temporarily close due to lack of guests at other times. Owners of places that are still open may be willing to bargain, especially for two or more people sharing a room. The hotels are close together, so wander around until you find one that appeals to you.

Budget Loja's cheapest hotels are generally more acceptable than the cheapest hotels in many towns. The basic but clean and friendly *Hostal Carrión* (☎ 568 548, fax 575 429, Colón 16-36) is a good value at US$2 per person for rooms sharing hot showers (there are 18), or US$4 per person for rooms with private showers and TV (there are 16). The clean and decent *Hotel Caribe* (☎ 572 902, Rocafuerte 15-52) is another reasonable shoestring choice; rooms with shared hot shower cost US$2 per person.

Other OK places with shared bath and hot water at about US$2 per person include the clean *Hotel Mexico* (☎ 570 581), at 18 de Noviembre and Eguiguren, and the popular but spartan *Hotel Londres* (☎ 561 936, Sucre 07-41), with plenty of hot water but flimsy

Loja: The Garden of Ecuador

Loja is very close to the Oriente, and the surrounding countryside is green and pleasant. The people are proud of the great variety of plant species found in the region.

They tell the story of the beautiful Countess of Cinchón, the wife of an early-17th-century Peruvian viceroy, who was dying of malaria. A Franciscan monk cured her with quinine extracted from the bark of a tree found in the Loja area. After her recovery, fame of the 'miraculous' properties of the tree spread throughout the Spanish Empire and the world. Today, the scientific name of the tree is *Cinchona succirubra*, after the countess.

German scientist and explorer Alexander von Humboldt visited the area in 1802 and called it 'the garden of Ecuador.' British botanist Richard Spruce also mounted an expedition here in the mid-19th century. In recent times, the area has been recognized for its biological value, and in 1982, Parque Nacional Podocarpus (see that section) was established in the nearby mountains.

locks (bring your own padlock). Next door, at US$2.50 per person, *Hotel Cuxubamba* (☎ 560 865) has dark and basic rooms with private hot showers. *Hotel Chandelier* (☎ 563 061, Imbabura 14-84) boasts a TV in every room and charges US$2 per person for rooms with shared shower (rooms with private shower are a dollar more). *Residencial San Andres* (☎ 547 017, Miguel Riofrío 18-21) lacks hot water but may be the cheapest at US$3 for a double.

The popular *Hotel Los Ejecutivos* (☎ 560 004, Universitaria 10-96) has 14 rooms with private bath and TV at US$3 per person and is often full. The friendly *Hotel Paris* (☎ 561 639, fax 570 146, 10 de Agosto 16-49) charges about US$4.50 per person for OK carpeted rooms with private hot bath and cable TV. *Hotel Internacional* (☎ 570 433, 10 de Agosto 15-28) is friendly and has a restaurant. Rooms with shared bath cost about US$2.50 per person or US$4.50 with private bath and TV. Readers report that there is plenty of hot water.

Hotel Metropolitan (☎ 570 007/244, 18 de Noviembre 6-41) has friendly and chatty management and decent wood-floored rooms with private hot shower and TV at US$4.50 per person.

Rooms with hot water, color TV and telephone are found at *Hotel Riviera* (☎ 572 863), Universitaria and 10 de Agosto, which charges US$9 for a double.

Mid-Range The aging *Hotel Vilcabamba International* (☎ 573 393/645, fax 561 483), on Aguirre and Riofrío, overlooks Río Malacatus (the river is not very scenic here). Rooms have TV and telephone and are clean and comfortable but rather worn. Rates are a reasonable US$15 for a double. *Hotel Acapulco* (☎ 570 651, fax 571 103, Sucre 07-49) has been upgraded and is clean and popular. Smallish but attractive rooms with TV, private bath and hot water go for US$8.50/15 including breakfast; there is a restaurant, and there maybe a telephone in your room.

The following hotels all have restaurants. *Hotel Podocarpus* (☎/fax 581 428, 579 776, 584 912, hotelpod@hotmail.com, Eguiguren 16-50) has comfortable, light, spacious (arm-chairs surrounding a coffee table) but rather stark-looking rooms with cable TV and telephone. Avoid Room 204, which is right over the night-entrance bell. The staff is friendly, and breakfast is included in the US$10/18 charge – a good deal. The helpful and friendly *Grand Hotel Loja* (☎ 575 200/201, 586 600/1, fax 575 202), Aguirre and Rocafuerte, has nice doubles for US$24, but a drawback is the noisy street outside. *Hotel Ramses* (☎ 571 402, 579 868, fax 581 832, Colón 14-31) has nice big carpeted rooms with huge writing desks and lamps, as well as the usual cable TV and telephone. Rates are a good value at US$16/21, including breakfast. Across the street, *Hotel Libertador* (☎ 560 779, 578 278, 570 344, fax 572 119, Colón 14-30) is the most upscale hotel at this time. Rooms with the usual amenities cost about US$25/33.

Places to Eat
The locally popular *Restaurant La Tullpa* (☎ 570 210, 18 de Noviembre 06-36) is good for inexpensive Chinese and Ecuadorian food from 7:45 am to 9:30 pm daily. A local speciality is *cecina* (a salty fried pork – like thick lean bacon – served with yucca). *Chifa Casa China*, by Hotel Paris, is also good. *Pollos Gusy* is a chicken restaurant popular with local youngsters. *Pollos a la Brasa Rey* is also OK for chicken. *Cevichería Las Redes* (18 de Noviembre 10-41) has seafood and other dishes in pleasant surroundings for under US$3 – good food at a good price. Nearby, *Restaurant Safari* (10-65 Azuay) is cheap and popular with locals; there are several other cheap places on Azuay. *Plaza Inn*, on Parque Central, is a popular fast-food joint for local students.

The fanciest restaurant outside the hotels is *Rincón de Francia* (☎ 578 686, Valdivieso 06-50), which has a small outdoor courtyard, a romantically dark interior, art displays and meals that are international rather than French. Prices are very reasonable – most full meals are under US$5.

The best hotels are also good for meals. *La Castellana*, in Hotel Libertador, is one of Loja's best restaurants, and the restaurants in other better hotels, especially Hotel Ramses, serve decent food.

Entertainment

Although Lojanos are known as good singers and guitar players, nightlife is fairly low key. My favorite bar is *El Viejo Minero (Sucre 10-76),* which serves drinks and snacks in a rustic but quiet and friendly environment. For a livelier atmosphere, try the nearby and somewhat raunchier *Cabanitas Peña Bar (Sucre 10-92),* which has dancing as well. For dancing with pool tables (OK, dance with a person if you must), try *Latino's Discotheque (Imbabura 12-76). Bar 333*, in front of the bus terminal, is another dance club. *Millenium Bar*, on Parque Central, looks good for late-night weekend action.

A military band often plays in Parque Central on Sunday evenings – the young population of the town comes to watch the band and each other. Plaza de la Independencia sometimes has 'Cultural Thursdays' – free outdoor performances of dance or music.

Getting There & Away

Loja is served by La Toma airport, in Catamayo (this village is described later in the chapter), some 30km to the west. TAME has a 6 am flight from Quito from Monday to Saturday, returning from Loja at 7:25 am. On Monday, Thursday and Friday, a dawn flight leaves Guayaquil and returns at 7 am. Check with TAME (☎ 585 224) at its office on the east side of town. Note that flights in late August and early September are often booked well ahead of time for the fiestas.

A thrice-weekly flight to Piura, Peru was recently announced – ask local travel agencies about it.

Taxi drivers hang out in front of the TAME office and will arrange to pick you up from your hotel to take you to the airport. They charge about US$3 per person in a shared cab (four passengers). Alternately, you can arrange transportation with the better hotels or take a bus into Catamayo.

Almost all buses leave from the bus terminal. An information booth near the entrance will direct you to where you want to go. Transportes Loja has the most buses, but there are many other companies.

There are several buses a day to Quito (14 to 16 hours) and points in between, such

Highland village street scene

as Riobamba and Ambato. There are also several buses a day to Macará, on the Peruvian border (six hours); Guayaquil (nine hours); Machala (seven hours); Zamora, for access to the southern Oriente (two hours); Cuenca (six hours); and other towns en route to these final destinations. Huaquillas, on the main route to Peru, can also be reached by a night bus in about seven or eight hours, thus avoiding having to backtrack to Machala. Buses also go to small, remote towns in the southern Sierra and southern Oriente where tourists don't go. Ask at the terminal.

Transportes Sur-Oriente has buses to Vilcabamba once an hour, and Vilcabambaturis runs faster (one hour) minibuses every 30 minutes from 6:15 am to 9:15 pm. Shared taxis to Vilcabamba are faster and leave from Aguirre, 10 blocks south of Mercadillo. Buses for Catamayo, which is near the airport (45 minutes), leave the bus terminal frequently 6 am to 9 pm. Catch the first bus to be sure of making the flight out.

PARQUE NACIONAL PODOCARPUS

Created in 1982, this is Ecuador's southernmost national park. Its 146,280 hectares cover a wide range of habitats, with altitudes ranging from over 3600m, in the páramo and lake-covered mountains southeast of Loja, to about 900m, in the rainforests south of Zamora in the southern Oriente. In between, the countryside is wild and rugged, and home to many rare animal and plant species.

Podocarpus receives a lot of rainfall, so be prepared for it. October through December are the driest months on the west side of the park. See the Vilcabamba section, later in this chapter, for information on obtaining tours of the park's area.

For information on the eastern part of the park, see Zamora, in the southern Oriente chapter. For the western and central parts of the park, information might be available at the Ministerio del Medio Ambiente in Loja. Admission to the park is US$5, and verbal information, and perhaps a basic map, are available at the park. Note that the entrance fee is valid for five days, and you can use the ticket to visit the Oriente side.

If you are in Quito, you can get topographical maps at the IGM (see Orientation under Quito, in the Quito & Around chapter). The western side of the park is covered by two 1:50,000 maps: Río Sabanilla CT-ÑVII-B2 and Vilcabamba CT-NVII-B4. Alternately, the 1:100,000 Gonzanamá CT-ÑVII-B map covers the area in less detail. The eastern (Oriente) side of the park is covered by the 1:50,000 maps of Zamora CT-ÑVII-A1 and Cordillera de Tzunantza CT-ÑVII-A3.

Flora & Fauna

The biological diversity of the area has been remarked upon by a succession of travelers and explorers through the centuries. Scientists have found a high degree of endemism (species found nowhere else), apparently because the complex topography combines with the junction of Andean and Amazonian weather patterns to cause unique microclimates throughout the park. These areas give rise to many habitats within the park. Up to 90 different tree species have been recorded in a single hectare – apparently a world record.

Some of the most important plants here include three species of the park's namesake genus, *Podocarpus,* Ecuador's only native gymnosperm (a division of plants

that includes all conifers and a few smaller classes of tree). Also of interest is *Cinchona succirubra,* locally called *cascarilla,* from which quinine, the drug that cures malaria, is extracted (see the boxed text 'Loja: The Garden of Ecuador,' in the Loja section, earlier). Demand for this product has left few cascarillas outside of the park.

Animals include the Andean spectacled bear, mountain tapirs, puma, two species of deer and the Andean fox (locally called a wolf). All of these animals are hard to see but are prized by local poachers, who sometimes burn habitat in an attempt to flush out animals for their 'sport.' Birds are also of great interest and are more abundant and easier to see. Scores of species are known to be present, including the usual string of exotic-sounding ones, such as lachrymose mountain-tanager, streaked tuftedcheek, superciliaried hemispingus and pearled treerunner. (I promise, I am not making these names up!)

Ecology & Conservation

Despite being a national park, Podocarpus faces huge problems in protecting the varied habitats within its boundaries. Not least of these is that the legal boundaries are not respected by local colonists – logging often occurs within park limits. Cattle and horses are permitted within the park. Hunting is not permitted, but poaching is an ever-present problem.

The Nature Conservancy's Latin American Program reports that over 99% of the park has been granted in mining concessions, with gold being the mineral of interest. Mining companies and their armed guards work within the park; meanwhile, the park's handful of employees try to protect the park, carry out local environmental education programs, maintain trails and shelters, collect park fees and provide visitor information.

In 1990, Parque Nacional Podocarpus was named one of Ecuador's four most biologically significant and yet imperiled conservation areas. The Nature Conservancy sponsors the Parks in Peril program, providing financial support and ongoing management and training programs for Ecuadorians wishing to work in the parks – an essential project that is well worth supporting. The Peace Corps is also involved in park projects.

Getting There & Around
To get there, take a Vilcabamba-bound bus from Loja and get off at the Cajanuma park entrance, about 10km south of the city. There is a large sign on the left-hand side of the road. From the entrance – which may not be staffed – a trail (which you can take by car or on foot) leads 8.5km uphill to the Cajanuma ranger station. There is no public transportation there, although you could hire a taxi from Loja to the station (about US$10) and arrange to be picked up at a later time. Make sure the driver understands whether you want to go to the Cajanuma park entrance or the ranger station.

The ranger station has bunk beds and a camping area (the overnight fee is US$2). From the station, foot trails head up into the lake and páramo region – a full day of hiking is required to reach the lakes, where you can camp. Bird life is varied and interesting, both on the dirt road up to the ranger station and around the station, where there are shorter trails. How far you go depends on your equipment and how much food and energy you have. There are few facilities, so you should be entirely self-sufficient.

MALACATOS
The minor road from Loja passing Podocarpus continues due south and drops steadily through green, mountainous scenery to Vilcabamba, some 45km from Loja. En route, you pass through the village of Malacatos, distinguished by a large church with three blue domes that are visible from a great distance. Malacatos has a Sunday market, and there is a basic hotel and restaurant behind the main plaza.

Two kilometers from the village, on the main road, is *La Vieja Molina* (☎ 673 239), which has comfortable cabañas with private hot shower for US$16 (one or two people). The place has attractive gardens, a pool, lawn, sauna, whirlpool, children's slide and restaurant in an old farmhouse – a popular place for locals to relax on weekend day

trips. Reservations can be made at Loja's Hotel Libertador.

VILCABAMBA & AROUND
Vilcabamba has for many years been famous as 'the valley of longevity.' Inhabitants supposedly live to be 100 or more, and some claim to be 120 years old. This has been attributed to their simple, hardworking lifestyle, their diet of nonfatty foods and the excellent climate. Scientific investigation has been unable to substantiate these beliefs, but the legend persists; some folks believe in it, and it gives rise to tourism. The town offers access to some of the most biodiverse sections of Podocarpus and is one of Ecuador's most relaxing small towns, which also attracts travelers. The climate certainly is very pleasant, and the surrounding countryside offers lovely walks.

About 1.5km east of town is a small zoo of local animals, including an excellent collection of orchids. Admission is US$0.25.

Orientation & Information
Most of the town surrounds the main square, where there is a *Coordinación Turística* (tourist information office), travel agency, church, Pacifictel office, a few simple stores and some basic accommodations. A block away, Vilc@net has Internet connections, but telephone service is unreliable. There is a police station (☎ 580 896) and hospital (☎ 673 188) in town. There is a post office by the police and in the Primavera Arts store.

Things to Do
Orlando Falco, a trained, English-speaking naturalist guide, can be contacted in his craft shop, Primavera, on the plaza, or at the Rumi-Wilco Ecolodge or Pole House (see Places to Stay, later). He is passionate, interesting and experienced, and he leads walking tours to Podocarpus and other areas for about US$20 to US$30 per person (plus the US$10 park fee). Costs depend on the number of people in the group and area visited.

The folks at Cabañas Río Yambala (see Places to Stay) have a private reserve, camping gear, horse rental and plenty of hiking

VILCABAMBA & AROUND

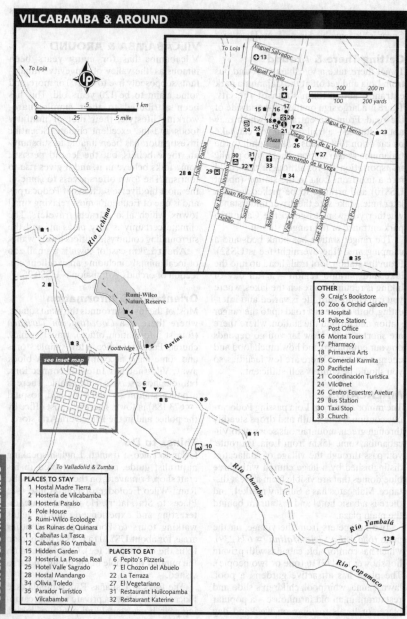

To Loja

To Loja

Miguel Salvador

Miguel Carpio

Rumi-Wilco
Nature Reserve

Río Uchima

Ravine

Footbridge

see inset map

To Valladolid & Zumba

Río Chamba

Río Yambalá

Río Capamaco

Agua de Hierro

Diego Vaca de la Vega

Fernando de la Vega

Jaramillo

Huilo Pamba

Av Eterna Juventud

Juan Montalvo

Hatillo

Sucre

Bolívar

Valle Sagrado

José David Toledo

La Paz

Plaza

OTHER
9   Craig's Bookstore
10   Zoo & Orchid Garden
13   Hospital
14   Police Station;
     Post Office
16   Monta Tours
17   Pharmacy
18   Primavera Arts
19   Comercial Karmita
20   Pacifictel
21   Coordinación Turística
24   Vilc@net
26   Centro Ecuestre; Avetur
29   Bus Station
30   Taxi Stop
33   Church

PLACES TO STAY
1   Hostal Madre Tierra
2   Hostería de Vilcabamba
3   Hostería Paraíso
4   Pole House
5   Rumi-Wilco Ecolodge
8   Las Ruinas de Quinara
11   Cabañas La Tasca
12   Cabañas Río Yambala
15   Hidden Garden
23   Hostería La Posada Real
25   Hotel Valle Sagrado
28   Hostal Mandango
34   Olivia Toledo
35   Parador Turístico
     Vilcabamba

PLACES TO EAT
6   Pepito's Pizzeria
7   El Chozon del Abuelo
22   La Terraza
27   El Vegetariano
31   Restaurant Huilcopamba
32   Restaurant Katerine

and riding opportunities with or without guides. This is an excellent option.

Caballos Gavilan, run by Gavin, a New Zealander who has lived here for years (☎ 571 025, or ask at the tourist office) rents horses for three-day treks at about US$75 per person (depending on group size). Several readers have enjoyed his trips.

Across from the tourist office, Avetur (☎ 673 151), also known as Centro Ecuestre, is a new cooperative of several local horse and mule owners that offers tours lasting from two hours to three days. The members work together to allow all horse and mule owners to get a fair chance at making money and to keep their horses rotated and in good condition. Most speak only Spanish. This is a good way of helping the local economy.

Monta Tours (☎ 673 147, fax 673 186) is run by a Frenchman who speaks some English and Spanish – he also has been recommended for horseback riding treks into the mountains with overnights in a simple lodge. Generally speaking, two- or three-day tours are recommended to see the area. Tours lasting less than a day just go around the village.

Places to Stay

Central Many people looking for peaceful settings stay in one of the recommended hotels outside of town; others prefer a more central location.

Vilcabamba's oldest and cheapest hotel is the simple *Hotel Valle Sagrado* (☎ 580 686), on the plaza. The rate for one of the 11 basic rooms with shared hot shower is US$2 per person, and the rate for one of the two rooms with private shower is US$3 per person. This place is often full. Highlights include a garden with hammocks and a volleyball area, laundry, kitchen privileges and a vegetarian restaurant. Behind the bus station, the similarly priced *Hostal Mandango* is also popular with budget travelers. Its Mirador Bar is a good place for a drink with views. For a family stay, call *Señora Olivia Toledo* (☎ 673 130), a block from the plaza. She charges US$2 per person for rooms with shared hot bath and kitchen privileges. Also ask at Comercial Karmita about renting a house for month-long stays. The clean and tranquil *La Posada Real* (☎ 580 904), in quiet grassy grounds on the northeastern outskirts, charges US$5 per person for one of seven large rooms with bath; breakfast is available.

The nicest place in the center is *Hidden Garden* (☎/fax 580 281, hiddengarden@ latinmail.com), which really does have a garden hidden within its doors. A small swimming pool and a super-hot shower nestle within the vegetation – a great place to relax or hang out with guests or the helpful and friendly staff, some of whom speak English. Rooms are rustically comfortable and all different (some with private shower), and there are kitchen privileges. Rates are US$6/10.50/14.25 for singles/doubles/triples.

On Vilcabamba's southeastern edge, *Parador Turístico Vilcabamba* (☎ 673 122, fax 673 167, parador99@hotmail.com) has a restaurant and 27 clean rooms with balconies and private bath for about US$6 per person. A garden and swimming pool are on the premises.

Surroundings Budget travelers will love *Rumi-Wilco Ecolodge* and *Pole House* (ofalcoecolodge@yahoo.com). Both are within the private Rumi-Wilco Nature Reserve, which is owned by naturalist guides Orlando and Alicia Falco, who have many years of local experience and have also guided professionally in the Galápagos and Amazon. They can be contacted at Primavera Arts or by mail at Correos Central, Vilcabamba, Loja. The ecolodge, near the reserve entrance and a few hundred meters from the Falcos' house, has natural adobe and tile rooms. Three rooms share one bath and a kitchen, another has a private kitchen, and four more up on a hill with nice views also share a bathroom and kitchen. The water is sun-warmed during the day. Most rooms cost US$3 per person.

Beyond the Falcos' house is the Pole House, so called because it is a cabin built on stilts and overlooking the river – the sounds of water and birds everywhere are very relaxing. The cabin comfortably sleeps four people and has a fully equipped kitchen with a fridge, a deck with a hammock, and a cold-water outdoor shower. The Falcos allow you to use their warm shower on request. A barbecue pit and pure drinking water from a private well complete the picture; it's a great place to relax for a week or more. Rates are US$14/15/16 for two/three/four people. It's about a 30-minute walk out of town.

About 4km southeast of town, the rustic **Cabañas Río Yambala** (*charlie@loja.telconet .net*) is run by Charlie and Sarah, who are very friendly. You can walk there or hire a taxi or pickup for US$2. They have six charming cabins of varying sizes, all with private hot showers and views, and limited self-catering facilities are available. Rates vary, depending on the room, but range from about US$6 for a single to US$17 for a quad. There are plans to build more over the next few years. A restaurant serving a small menu of tasty dishes, including vegetarian food and beer, is open to the public all day.

The owners arrange two- and three-day hiking and horseback riding trips into their private **Las Palmas** nature reserve on the edge of Podocarpus, where they have a simple lodge (bunk beds, toilet, shower, kitchen facilities). Camping trips into the park itself can also be arranged. Hiking trips are US$35/60 per person for two/three days, and riding trips are US$50/80, with a three-person minimum. Guides are locals, and they have limited English skills but are knowledgeable and friendly. A list of over 150 birds in Las Palmas is available (the number of birds is growing). Reservations and inquiries can be left at Comercial Karmita, a store on the plaza.

About halfway to Yambala, **Cabañas La Tasca** (☎ 673 186) has eight spartan but spacious cabins sharing four hot showers. The views are good (be prepared to climb 100m or so to the rooms), and kitchen facilities and balconies with hammocks are available. Rates are US$3 per person. It also has a recommended restaurant, open to the public until about 7:30 pm, with a small but well-prepared menu ranging from US$1 sandwiches to US$3 French dishes (its speciality). Horseback riding excursions are routinely arranged.

Closer in to town, **Las Ruinas de Quinara** (☎/fax 580 314) has a pool, a sauna, a game area, cable TV, tour information, a restaurant,

massage services and free purified water. Rooms have shared hot showers and are aimed at a young-traveler crowd looking for cheap fun. The owner has a local reputation for coercive, aggressive marketing, such as giving free accommodations to pretty Euro-girls who will meet travelers at the bus station and tell them how great his place is.

Heading about 1km north of town on the road to Loja, **Hostería Paraíso** (☎ 580 266) has a charming outdoor pool area, a pyramid-shaped bioenergetic room (remember that this is the Valley of Longevity), friendly owners, a restaurant/bar and six rooms with warm showers for about US$6 per person, including breakfast. A sauna and steam room are available for another US$2 (open to the public).

Farther out on this road is the well-run **Hostería de Vilcabamba** (☎ 580 271/2, fax 580 273, *raulcortes36@hotmail.com*), with a good restaurant, bar, massage, sauna, Jacuzzi and steam room. The 4.5-hectare grounds feature shaded hammocks, flower gardens and a playground for small children. Twenty-one rooms with private hot showers are a great value at US$11/15/18/22 for one/two/three/four people. Three bungalows sleeping up to seven people in three bedrooms sharing a bath are US$31. Nonguests pay about US$1 to use the pool and spa facilities, and the place is popular with locals on weekends.

The famous and popular **Hostal Madre Tierra Ranch & Spa** (☎/fax 580 269, *hmtierra@ecua.net.ec*), 2km north of town, is a rustic, laid-back hostal run by an Ecuadorian/Canadian couple since 1982. Bus drivers drop you off at the entrance; the hostal is about a five- or 10-minute walk down the lane. Many improvements have been added over recent years. Rooms are in the main lodge or in cabins spread over a steep hillside, some reached by long paths (bring a flashlight). Lodging includes breakfast and dinner (less without dinner). Meals are organic and/or vegetarian, and complimentary mineral water and juice is available all day. Much of the food is grown on the spacious ranch around the hostal.

The basic rooms (US$7 to US$10 per person) are small, old and have shared hot showers. The better, newer rooms (US$15 to US$25 per person) are spacious and well appointed. All have hot showers, and some have a coffeemaker and a balcony with a view. There are also two private cabins that cost US$36 a double. One is bamboo and has a balcony and a private outdoor hot shower; the other is stone and has a private shower and patio. A private cottage sleeping six in two bedrooms features a kitchen, two bathrooms, a fireplace and a balcony and is US$20 per person (US$80 minimum). Local hiking and riding information, a swimming pool with a café/bar, a book exchange, a video room and table games are available at no additional charge.

The full-service spa features clay baths (the clay is changed after every bath), hydromassage, Jacuzzi, contrast steam baths, facials, skin exfoliants, skin-glow treatments, colonic therapy and various massages. Most treatments are about US$5 to US$7, except for massages, which are US$20 for 75 minutes.

Places to Eat
The hotel eateries described above are all good. In addition, *La Terraza*, on the corner of the plaza, sells a small international menu (Italian, Mexican, Thai) and is arguably the town's best. *Huilcopamba* and *Restaurant Katerine*, near the plaza, are good, small Ecuadorian places. Huilcopamba is nice at breakfast, when the morning sun streams in. There's also *El Vegetariano*, near the center, which has creative and varied vegetarian fare.

Away from town, *El Chozon del Abuelo* is a bar with a pool table and good pizza; *Pepito's Pizzería* is also a good choice.

Shopping
The Primavera store, on the plaza, has lovely T-shirts that were hand-painted by a local artist, as well as a good selection of crafts and souvenirs. Nearby, Comercial Karmita is the best-stocked general store, and a pharmacy is around the corner.

One and a half kilometers east of town is Craig's bookstore, run by a colorful, friendly but somewhat eccentric American expat; he has a big book exchange with books written in several languages, as well

as chocolate-chip cookies, local gemstones, homemade jewelry, curios and interesting stories about them.

Getting There & Around
Buses all leave from the corner shown on the map. Frequent departures to Loja are by shared taxi (US$1, less than an hour), Vilcabambaturis minibuses or regular bus (two hours). Several buses a day continue south to Zumba.

Transportes Mixtos is a cooperative of 15 trucks, which have a standard fee of US$1 for getting to nearby places (as far as Hostal Madre Tierra) and US$2 for Cabañas Río Tambala. You can find them around the plaza.

ZUMBA
The all-weather road continues south of Vilcabamba through the village of Valladolid (where there's one basic pensión) to the small town of Zumba, about 115km south of Vilcabamba. The drive is through attractive countryside. Zumba is about 10km north of the border with Peru. Taxis can take you to the border, but border-crossing facilities are limited, because there is almost no infrastructure on the Peruvian side for continuing. However, a road has been planned since the recent border treaty with Peru. There is a basic pensión in Zumba and several buses a day from Loja.

CATAMAYO
The Panamericana continues west of Loja through Catamayo, Catacocha and on to the Peruvian border at Macará.

Loja was founded twice. The first time was in 1546, on what is now Catamayo; the second time was on its present site, two years later. Despite its long history, Catamayo is a totally unremarkable town except for its airport, La Toma, which serves Loja 30km away.

Places to Stay & Eat
The basic *Hotel San Marcos*, on the plaza, is quite popular; reasonably clean, large rooms go for about US$3 per person. The nearby *Hotel Turista* (☎ *677 126*) is similarly priced and has some cheaper rooms

without a shower. A few other basic places can be found.

Two or three kilometers outside Catamayo to the west is **Hostería Bellavista** (☎ 962 450). It has a pool, restaurant and bar and can arrange airport transfers or local tours. Rooms with private bath are about US$10/15. On Sunday, there is a popular buffet lunch featuring local dishes. A taxi from town costs about US$1.

There are several simple restaurants on or near the plaza. Dinner on the plaza while watching the center's leisurely activities is usually the best entertainment in town. The Chinese restaurant opposite Hotel Turista is recommended.

Getting There & Away
The local La Toma airport is about 2km south of town – a taxi will cost almost US$1. Services are described in Getting There & Away under Loja, earlier in this chapter.

Transportes Catamayo, just northeast of the plaza, has frequent buses to and from Loja. Transportes Loja, half a block west of the plaza, has numerous buses a day to Machala (six hours), a night bus to Huaquillas, many buses to Guayaquil (nine hours), five a day to Macará and six a day to Quito. Local buses from here can take you to the small villages to the north and south of Catamayo. The long-distance buses rarely originate in Catamayo but are just passing through; they usually have limited seating availability. Better services are available from Loja. Transportes Santa, on the plaza, has a few buses to Quito.

About 25km west of Catamayo, the road forks. The northwest fork goes to Machala, and the southwest fork goes through Catacocha to the border town of Macará.

EL CISNE & GONZANAMÁ
About 15km west of Catamayo, the Panamericana passes through the village of San Pedro de la Bendita. From here, a road runs north for another 22km to the village of El Cisne, home to the famous Virgin del Cisne (see the boxed text).

About 40km south of Catamayo, Gonzanamá is noted for its weavers and for the production of *alforjas* (saddlebags). You can stay in **Residencial Jiménez**, which has no hot water. From Gonzanamá, the road continues to the villages of Cariamanga and Sozoranga, which have basic pensiones, before ending in Macará at the border. This road goes through a remote area that is seldom visited by gringos.

CATACOCHA
It's a scenic but bumpy seven-hour ride from Loja to Macará. Catacocha is the halfway point on the more frequently used route and is the only place after Catamayo where you can break the journey.

Catacocha is the capital of the canton of Paltas and is only 1800m above sea level. From here, the Panamericana drops toward Macará and the Peruvian coast. It's a rural village, and on market day (Sunday), it seems as if there are almost as many horses as vehicles in town. There is reportedly a small local museum.

There are a few basic hotels, all a couple of blocks from the main plaza but in different directions. They charge between US$2 and US$4 per person – one traveler reports that *Guayaquil* is friendly. There are a few basic restaurants.

MACARÁ
From Catacocha, the road continues to drop steadily to Macará at a hot and dusty 450m above sea level. Macará is a small, unimportant town on the Peruvian border. The faster and more convenient coastal route carries almost 100% of the international traffic. The main advantage to the Macará route is the scenic descent from Loja. There may be police checkpoints on this road, which are no problem if your passport is in order.

Information
The bank in Macará does not have foreign exchange facilities. Because of the low volume of border traffic, few people change money. If you ask around, however, you will invariably find someone. There are usually moneychangers hanging out around the market. There is a Pacifictel office here.

Places to Stay & Eat

Cheap and basic hotels in the town center may have only cold water, but the weather is warm enough that it isn't a great hardship. Afternoon water shortages are common, so plan on a morning wash. The cheapest hotel is the poor **Hotel Guayaquil**, which is over a store on Bolívar between Rengel and Calderón – ask the store owners for rooms. **Hotel Amazonas** (*Rengel 418*) charges about US$2 to US$3 per person and is basic but clean and friendly.

Hotel Paraíso (*Veintimilla 553*) and **Hotel Espiga de Oro** (☎ 694 405), by the market, are both better. They charge about US$5 per person for clean rooms with private bath – still cold water, though. The Paraíso also has cheaper rooms without private bath, while Espiga de Oro has rooms with TV and a reasonable restaurant.

Hotel Turístico (☎ 694 099), on the outskirts of Macará on the way to the border, has simple, clean rooms with private bath and hot water for about US$12 a double. There is a restaurant, which is not always open. There is also a swimming pool – again, not always functioning.

There are a few simple restaurants around the intersection of Bolívar and Rengel, most of which are open only at meal times and have limited menus.

Getting There & Away

Transportes Loja is the main bus company. Buses to Loja (six hours) leave six times a day, with the last leaving at 3 pm. There are morning buses to Guayaquil and to Quito (20 hours). Transportes Cariamanga also has two morning buses to Loja.

To/From Peru Macará is about 3km from the border at Río Macará. Ecuadorian immigration offices are by the market plaza, and you need to get your exit stamp here before heading to Peru (arriving travelers come here to get entry stamps). Pickup trucks leave the market plaza once or twice an hour and charge about US$0.40 (or the Peruvian equivalent). You can take a taxi for US$1. Vehicles wait at the border to pick up passengers from Peru.

La Virgen del Cisne

This statue, famous throughout Ecuador, is housed in an enormous church in Gothic style surrounded by unpretentious houses of traditional *campesinos* (peasants or farmers). The church is locally referred to as El Santuario.

According to local lore, it was the ancestors of these campesinos who made the long and difficult journey to Quito in the late 16th century in search of a fitting religious statue. They returned in 1594 with the carving of La Virgen del Cisne and installed it in a small shrine. Since that time, this icon has been the 'Queen' of the campesinos.

The major religious festivals in El Cisne are on May 30 and August 15. After the August festival, thousands of pilgrims from Ecuador and northern Peru carry the statue on their shoulders to Loja (70km away), with many of the pilgrims walking the entire way. The Virgin finally arrives in Loja on August 20, where she is ceremoniously installed in the cathedral. On November 1, the process is repeated in reverse, and the Virgin rests in El Cisne until the following August.

For most of the year, tours and buses make day trips to the village from Loja and Catamayo to see the sanctuary and statue. But on procession days, forget it! You walk like everybody else – the road is so full of pilgrims that vehicles can't get through. This is a very moving religious festival for those who are so inclined.

Facilities for accommodations, transportation and food are inferior on the Peruvian side; it is best to stay in Macará, if possible. Peruvian buses and shared taxis leave the border for the Peruvian town of Sullana (two hours) on a paved road. Sullana has hotels and connections to nearby Piura, a major city. It is difficult to get transportation into Peru later in the afternoon and evening; therefore, crossing the border in the morning is advisable.

Lonely Planet publishes *Peru* for travelers continuing to that country.

The Southern Oriente

El Oriente is the term used by Ecuadorians for all of the Amazon Basin lowlands east of the Andes. Although the Amazon River itself does not flow through Ecuador, every one of Ecuador's rivers east of the Andes runs into the Amazon, and hence, all of the Oriente is part of the upper Amazon Basin. This area is all rainforest, merging into cloud forest in the eastern Andean foothills.

The Oriente can be conveniently divided into north and south by Río Pastaza. The main southern Oriente road begins at Loja and goes through Zamora north to Macas. Beyond Macas, the road was pushed through to Puyo (north of Río Pastaza) in the late 1980s, and though still unpaved, it is in fairly good shape – except after heavy rain. A combination of ramshackle buses,

Highlights

- Visiting historic Macas – Ecuador's most attractive jungle town
- Rafting on the Grade III and Grade IV rapids of Río Upano
- Visiting a Shuar Indian community in the jungles around Macas
- Staying in the heart of Achuar country at the upscale Kapawi Ecolodge

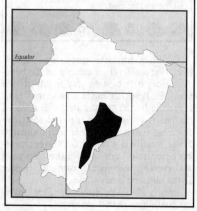

Equator

footbridges and possible foot slogs can get you from Macas to Puyo in a day – if a torrential rainstorm hasn't rendered the road impassable on the day you choose.

Most travelers to the Oriente visit the northern region, which admittedly has much more to offer the tourist. Indeed, the southern Oriente is the least-visited part of Ecuador and gives visitors a real sense of remoteness.

There are two surface routes into the southern Oriente. The most frequently used route is from Cuenca through Limón (officially named on most maps as General Leonidas Plaza Gutiérrez) to Macas. The other route runs from Loja through Zamora and continues north to Limón, where it joins the first route. Almost all the roads in this region are unpaved and subject to landslides and delays during the rainy season, so don't plan a very tight schedule in this area. June to August are the worst months.

ZAMORA
☎ 07

Although Zamora is only 64km by road from Loja, the journey takes over two hours. The road climbs from Loja, goes over a 2500m pass and then drops tortuously along the Río Zamora valley to the town of Zamora, at 970m above sea level. The scenery soon becomes tropical and the vegetation thicker, and you begin seeing strange plants, such as the giant tree fern. There are good views from both sides of the bus.

Zamora was first founded by the Spanish in 1549, but the colony soon died out because of Indian attacks. It was refounded in 1800 but remained very small. A local old-timer recalls that when he arrived in Zamora in the 1930s, there were only half a dozen buildings. In 1953, it became the provincial capital when the province of Zamora-Chinchipe was created, although it was still extremely small and isolated. The first vehicle did not arrive in town until 1962.

Saraguro Indians, wearing their trademark black shorts, are sometimes seen in

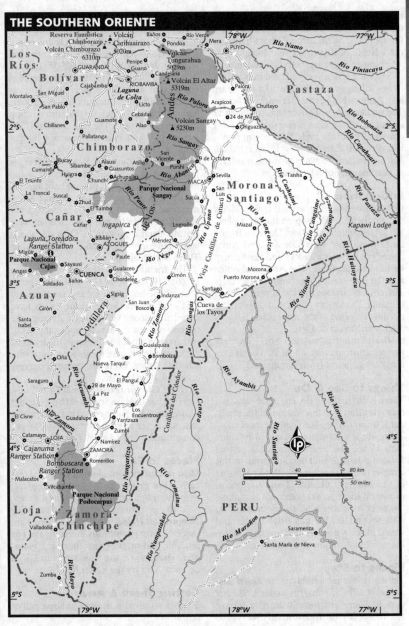

THE SOUTHERN ORIENTE

the Zamora area. They arrive there on foot, driving their cattle on the trail from Saraguro, through 28 de Mayo, to the Zamora-Yantzaza road. North of Zamora, Shuar Indians may also be seen, as well as colonists and miners.

Since the rediscovery of gold in Nambija (a few kilometers to the north) a few years ago, Zamora has been experiencing a boom. The sudden influx of miners has strained the resources of the area somewhat, and food costs are relatively high. The present population of the Zamora area is over 16,000, and although the town is growing, it still retains somewhat of a frontier feel.

Information

Central streets are signed, but few buildings use numbers. A gift shop on the main plaza has some local information. There's a Banco de Loja on José Luís Tamayo near Amazonas, but traveler's checks and plastic may be hard to negotiate. The Andinatel office and the post offices are shown on the map. The covered indoor market is near the bus terminal. The town's police station is on the northwest corner of the main plaza; the hospital is on Sevilla de Oro.

The weather is not too hot – daytime temperatures average about 20°C, and evenings are pleasant (with few insects).

Things to See & Do

There is not much to do. The main plaza is a concrete affair with few trees and little shade, but it is improving slowly as the trees grow. There are few foreign travelers. Most come here to see the nearby Parque Nacional Podocarpus (see that section, later in this chapter) or to continue north to see some of the southern Oriente. From the bridge shown on the map, you can walk east along the river on a dirt road to another bridge. This second bridge has little traffic and would make a good choice for early morning or late-afternoon bird watching.

Places to Stay

The basic but reasonably clean *Hotel Zamora* (☎ 605 253) charges under US$2 per person. There are some balconied rooms; ask to see them. *Residencial Venecia* is

similarly priced but not as good. Neither has private bathrooms or hot water, but you have to get used to that in the Oriente. Anyway, cold showers are refreshing in the hot weather. *Hostal Seyma* (☎ 605 583), on 24 de Mayo a block northeast of the plaza, has rooms that are a little nicer. The hotel is clean and friendly but quite noisy – rooms facing the road are quieter than those facing the inner courtyard. The rate is about US$3 per person, and it is the best low-budget value in town.

Brisas del Zamora, near the river, is being expanded and remodeled, but it should have clean rooms with private bath and TV for about US$6 per person. *Hostal Internacional Torres* (☎ 605 195) is modern but already getting a bit run down. Rooms have private electric showers, a TV, a telephone and a fan for about US$6/10 single/double. There is a restaurant.

The friendly and helpful *Hotel Maguna* (☎ 605 219, fax 605 113) has 14 basic rooms with private hot baths, TV and fan for about US$7 per person. Some of the rooms have excellent balcony views of Río Zamora; the others are not especially appealing. Staff will arrange guides and taxis to the national park and can prepare meals for groups with advance notice. There is a guarded parking area and a garden bar.

Hotel Gimifa Internacional (☎ 605 024, 606 103) has modern rooms with private hot showers and TV. Some rooms have city views, and others are interior. Rates are US$9 per person, and there's a small restaurant.

Places to Eat

Most restaurants are closed by 8 pm, so eat early. *Don Pepe's*, just off the main plaza, is locally popular and has a varied menu. Next to one another on the plaza are *King Burguer* and *Heladería Pingüino*. There are several *cheap restaurants* in and by the bus terminal and market, and there is a *panadería* (bakery) on the main street of Diego de Vaca. Also try the better hotels.

Getting There & Away

The bus terminal is at the southeast end of downtown.

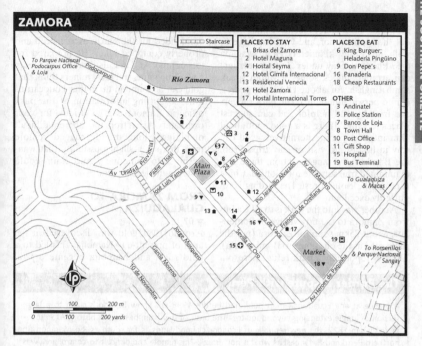

ZAMORA

⊏⊐⊏⊐⊏ Staircase

PLACES TO STAY
1 Brisas del Zamora
2 Hotel Maguna
4 Hostal Seyma
12 Hotel Gimifa Internacional
13 Residencial Venecia
14 Hotel Zamora
17 Hostal Internacional Torres

PLACES TO EAT
6 King Burguer;
   Heladería Pingüino
9 Don Pepe's
16 Panadería
18 Cheap Restaurants

OTHER
3 Andinatel
5 Police Station
7 Banco de Loja
8 Town Hall
10 Post Office
11 Gift Shop
15 Hospital
19 Bus Terminal

0   100   200 m
0   100   200 yards

With three companies, there are buses almost hourly to Loja (US$2, two hours) from 3 am to 8 pm. Pullman Viajeros continues through Loja to Cuenca (US$6, 10 hours) at 9:45 am, 6:15 and 10:30 pm. Transportes Loja has a bus to Quito at 3 pm, to Guayaquil at 5 pm, and to Machala at 8 pm.

Five daily buses north to Gualaquiza (five hours) usually originate in Loja and stop at the bus terminal in Zamora. Enough passengers normally get off at Zamora so that it's not very difficult to get a seat to continue north.

Zamora-Chinchipe buses are often open-sided trucks with tiny, uncomfortable bench seats. They provide frequent services to nearby villages as far north as Yantzaza. To visit the wild gold-mining town of Nambija, take Transportes Nambija.

For Parque Nacional Podocarpus, there are daily buses to Romerillos (two hours) leaving at 6:30 am and 2 pm.

Buses also go up Río Yacuambi valley as far as the mission town of Guadalupe and (if the rains haven't made the road impassable) on to La Paz. Trucks sometimes continue to the remote village of 28 de Mayo.

PARQUE NACIONAL PODOCARPUS

This national park, more fully described in the Cuenca chapter, has an information center in Zamora and ranger stations nearby. There are also less-frequently used entrances to the national park.

The park information office is on the right-hand side of the main road as you enter Zamora from Loja. There is a sign. At the information office, you can obtain basic maps and verbal information, and you can pay the US$5 national-park entrance fee, valid for up to five days. Camping is an extra US$2 per person per night.

The **Bombuscara** ranger station is at the park entrance about 8km south of Zamora by a rough road. The easiest way to get there is by taxi – it shouldn't cost more than US$3, but the road is poor, and you may have to walk the last few kilometers. Hotel Maguna (see Places to Stay under Zamora, earlier) can arrange guides, some of whom speak some English, for about US$3 per person (three-person minimum). The park rangers are friendly and helpful and can suggest places to camp. There is a good spot about 1km into the park. Alternatively, you can stay in hotels and visit on day trips. From the Bombuscara ranger station, there is a maintained trail suitable for a long day hike through the cloud forest. The birding is reportedly excellent.

Another way into the park is to take a bus from Zamora to the tiny village of **Romerillos**, about 25km south of Zamora (not the same road as the one going to Bombuscara). There is reportedly a park refuge here, but no ranger station. A rugged three-day loop trek leaves Romerillos, but is only recommended for the hardy, experienced and properly equipped hiker. Be prepared for lots of mud. At San Luís, there is reportedly a working mine, and local miners think that gold can be found in them thar Podocarpus hills, so getting information at the park office in Zamora is a good idea, for your own safety. Apart from the inherent difficult of hiking a long, muddy, rugged, remote trail, there is a slight possibility that wandering into someone's gold claim could result in unpleasantness.

FROM ZAMORA TO GUALAQUIZA
☎ 07

Around 1980, gold was discovered in the area of present-day **Nambija**. This led to a gold rush, and Nambija became a wild

---

The Border Dispute with Peru

A glance at any Ecuadorian map published before 1998 will show Ecuador's claim to a large section of jungle extending beyond Iquitos. The basis of this claim has a long history. After independence in 1822, the new republic of Ecuador claimed lands as far south as Río Marañon (in northern Peru) and as far east as what is now Brazil. This remote and difficult-to-control area was slowly settled by increasing numbers of Peruvians (as well as by a few Colombians and Brazilians). Ecuador gradually lost lands to these countries. In 1941, matters came to a head, and war with Peru broke out. Each country accused the other of beginning the aggression. The following year, a treaty signed at Río de Janeiro ended the war, and Peru was allotted a huge section of what had been Ecuador.

The Ecuadorians never officially accepted the full terms of this treaty, claiming that it was bulldozed through when most of the world was occupied with WWII; that Peru invaded the country; that the limits of the treaty were geographically invalid because a small section in the Cordillera del Cóndor, in the southeast, was ambiguously defined; and that the land was theirs anyway. However, the border as drawn up by the 1942 treaty was internationally accepted.

This dispute resulted in armed skirmishes every few years. The last major battles were in early 1981, when several soldiers were killed and aircraft shot down, and in early 1995, when several dozen soldiers were killed on both sides. These brief wars tended to be in January and February, coinciding with the anniversary of the signing of the contested treaty. Some political observers suggest that the wars serve politicians by increasing their popularity with citizens of both Ecuador and Peru during either periods of internal crisis or election years.

Finally, leaders of both countries agreed to a compromise, whereby Ecuador gained a square kilometer of land that was previously Peru's. President Mahuad, of Ecuador, and President Fujimori, of Peru, signed a binding peace treaty in 1998, and the countries have not only improved their diplomatic relationships, they have also improved their economic relationship with more trade.

mining town, with lots of heavy drinking, prostitution, gunfights, open sewers, muddy streets and constant frenzied mining action. A landslide in the late 1980s killed many people, and the town has calmed down somewhat in recent years.

Soldiers at the entrance of town now reportedly frisk people to make sure they aren't carrying weapons. A very small number of interested travelers trickle through this boomtown; visitors should bring no valuables and have a friendly and open disposition. The miners are a hard-bitten bunch, but a pack of cigarettes will help in making friends. Although Nambija itself is a new town, the area has been a source of gold for centuries. The Incas used to mine nearby, although few of the modern-day prospectors realize the historical significance of the area. There is a noisy and basic hotel, or you could come on a day trip from Zamora if you leave first thing in the morning. All the locals wear rubber boots – this is the best footwear for the very muddy streets.

From Nambija, the road follows the left bank of Río Zamora, so the best views are on the right side of the bus. There are beautiful vistas of open stretches of the river and heavily forested hills on either side, often with tropical trees flowering in bright reds, yellows and purples. The bus goes through many little Indian hamlets and *fincas* (farms) growing tropical produce such as coffee, sugarcane and citrus fruit. The road also goes near the mining area, so the journey is enlivened by the various interesting characters getting on and off the bus.

Yantzaza is the first village of any size on the road north of Zamora, 1½ hours away. In 1970, it consisted of only a couple of shacks, but since the Nambija gold boom, it has become one of the fastest-growing towns in the province. Its population is now several thousand, and there are restaurants and a couple of basic places to stay near the main square. These are likely to be full of miners, so it's probably best to continue to Gualaquiza.

North of Yantzaza, the population thins, and houses are seen infrequently. The road continues to follow the left bank of the gently dropping Río Zamora, and there are

fine tropical views – sit on the right-hand side of the bus. The road continues through the tiny village of Los Encuentros and on to El Panguí, where there is a basic hotel on the one main street. Just north of this village the road drops suddenly, and a lovely jungle panorama stretches out below. Soon, the road crosses the provincial line into Morona-Santiago Province.

Several kilometers before reaching Gualaquiza, a turnoff to the right leads to Bomboiza, where a **Salesian mission** can be visited.

GUALAQUIZA
☎ 07

Gualaquiza is a pretty little village of about 4000 inhabitants. It is set at an altitude of about 950m and surrounded by forested hills. Pleasant walks lead into the surrounding countryside. A rough road heads west out of town for about 15km to the village of Nueva Tarquí, where caves can be explored (it is essential to carry spare flashlights and batteries – who wants to die in a pitch-black cave with a broken flashlight?). There are reportedly some poorly explored Inca ruins in the Gualaquiza area – ask the locals for guidance.

The church on the main plaza looks like a toy building. There are cobbled streets and houses with attractive balconies, giving the town a Spanish colonial air. Gualaquiza closes down early and is definitely *tranquilo*. The Pacifictel office closes for lunch, and weekend hours are limited.

Places to Stay
Accommodations are limited, as this town is rarely visited. On the main plaza is the simple *Residencial Amazonas* (☎ 780 183, 780 715), and *Pensión Oriental* is on the main street, Calle Gonzalo Pezantes Lefebre.

Also on this street is the clean *Hotel Turismo* (☎ 780 113), which charges about US$3 per person. One reader reports that it is favored by couples for hourly stays and suggests that the new *Hotel Wakiz* (Orellana 08-52) is the best in town, at US$4.50 per person; the manager is friendly and helps with arranging cave tours. *Hotel Gualaquiza* (☎ 780 138) is another possibility.

Getting There & Away

There are several bus companies on the main street that each have two or three departures a day for various destinations. You can go south (Zamora and Loja), north (Limón, Sucúa and Macas) or west (Cuenca). The next significant town to the north is Limón (four hours). Buses to Cuenca go via Indanza (about 10km before Limón; it's also known as Plan de Milagro) and take about eight hours, but a new, more direct road via Sígsig is slated to open in 2001. To Macas, it's about 10 hours and costs US$4.50.

LIMÓN
☎ 07

From Gualaquiza, the road passes through pretty but sparsely populated countryside until it reaches the missions of San Juan Bosco and Indanza (also known as Plan de Milagro), about an hour before Limón.

Also known as General Leonidas Plaza Gutiérrez, Limón has a population of about 3000 and is a small, totally unprepossessing jungle town. Its primary importance is that it lies near the junction of the roads to Cuenca, Macas and Zamora. There is one main street with a few hotels, several simple restaurants and some bus offices.

Places to Stay

Both **Residencial Domínguez** and **Santo Domingo** are basic but clean, and each charges about US$2 per person. **Residencial Limón** (☎ 770 114) has large, clean rooms for about US$7 a double, but only one bathroom for all the guests. Avoid getting rooms on the street, as bus drivers park their buses with the engines running while they have a midnight snack or early morning breakfast. Reader Jörn Griesse recommends the clean **Hotel Dream House** (☎ 770 166), which has modern shared bathrooms, a decent restaurant and rates of US$2 per person.

Getting There & Away

Several times a day, various bus companies along the main street have bus service from Limón to the north, south and west. Few buses originate in Limón, however, so departure times are at best approximate. The road up to Cuenca climbs steeply from Limón (at 1400m) to a pass over 4000m in elevation – the ride is spectacular and should be done in daylight.

If you are going to Macas, sit on the right-hand side of the bus, as there are good views of Río Upano.

FROM MÉNDEZ TO MORONA
☎ 07

You pass through the quiet little village of Méndez (population 2000) on the way to Sucúa. Its official name is Santiago de Méndez, and it is less than two hours from Limón; the fare is about US$1. The houses have red-tiled roofs and flowery gardens. Half a block from the corner of its shady plaza are three very simple pensiones – **Anita, Miranda** and **Amazonas** – all charging about US$2 per person. Nearby, **Hotel Los Ceibos** looks a little better. There are only a couple of restaurants there.

About halfway on the road between Méndez and Morona lies the settlement of **Santiago**, on Río Santiago. There, you can hire dugout canoes to go upriver to Río Coangos for about US$30. From the Coangos, there is a trail to **La Cueva de los Tayos** (The Cave of the Oilbirds – see the boxed text on Oilbirds). The trail is in poor condition, and you should hire a guide – it is about a two- or three-hour hike. You will need to be self-sufficient, with sleeping gear and food, for this expedition.

The remote settlement of Morona is on Río Morona, near where it crosses the border with Peru. The border crossing here should be open by 2001, following the recent peace treaty. Readers trying this remote route are encouraged to write in with their information for the next edition of this book.

Until the late 1980s, the only way to reach Morona was by plane, but a newly constructed road now links the village with Méndez. The trip takes about 10 hours – ask around in Méndez for trucks going to Morona, or take a bus from Macas. There is only one place to stay, and it's extremely basic. This is a remote and poorly explored area.

Oilbirds

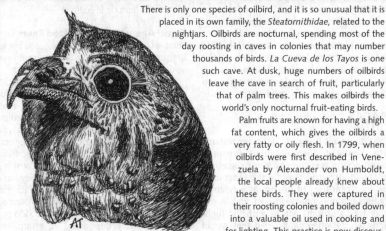

There is only one species of oilbird, and it is so unusual that it is placed in its own family, the *Steatornithidae*, related to the nightjars. Oilbirds are nocturnal, spending most of the day roosting in caves in colonies that may number thousands of birds. *La Cueva de los Tayos* is one such cave. At dusk, huge numbers of oilbirds leave the cave in search of fruit, particularly that of palm trees. This makes oilbirds the world's only nocturnal fruit-eating birds.

Palm fruits are known for having a high fat content, which gives the oilbirds a very fatty or oily flesh. In 1799, when oilbirds were first described in Venezuela by Alexander von Humboldt, the local people already knew about these birds. They were captured in their roosting colonies and boiled down into a valuable oil used in cooking and for lighting. This practice is now discouraged, although it still occurs occasionally.

Oilbirds feed on the wing, and their feet are poorly developed. They require caves with ledges upon which to build their cone-shaped nests, which are constructed of regurgitated fruit and are enlarged regularly. Two to four eggs are laid, and incubation is a relatively long 32 to 35 days. After hatching, the young are fed regurgitated fruit for up to four months, and during this time a nestling can reach a weight of 1½ times that of an adult. It was these fat chicks that were most highly prized as a source of oil. Once the chicks leave the nest, they lose their accumulated baby fat. Adults weigh about 400g and reach a length of about 45cm.

Because of their dark environment, oilbirds have well-developed eyes and exceptional night vision. They also have a sensitive sense of smell, which may help them detect the palm fruits' distinctive fragrance. The caves they roost in are often pitch black. To avoid crashing into the cave walls (and into other birds), oilbirds emit audible, frequently repeated clicks used for echolocation, much as bats do. In addition, they have a loud screaming call, which they use for communication. The combination of screams and clicks made by thousands of birds within the confines of a cave can be deafening.

SUCÚA
☎ 07

Sucúa, which has a population of 6000, is a Shuar Indian center. The Shuar were formerly called the Jivaro and were infamous for shrinking the heads of their defeated enemies. This practice still occurred as recently as two generations ago, and the *tsantsas* (shrunken heads) can be seen in various museums, notably Museo Municipal in Guayaquil. Most of today's Shuar have become missionized and look very Ecuadorian in their jeans and T-shirts, but you still might see older Indians, especially women, with elaborate facial or body tattoos.

There is a small plaza with shady trees, tropical flowers, cicadas and birds. From the plaza, walk down the main street and you'll come to the Shuar Cultural Center on your left, about a kilometer away. It's of little interest to casual visitors, but useful to people working with the Shuar. Market day is Sunday.

There are a few basic hotels, but most travelers stay in nearby Macas. Frequent buses or pickups leave for Macas (US$0.50, one hour) from dawn until dusk at the corner of the main plaza. The airport has charter planes into jungle communities and missions, but it is rarely used by travelers.

MACAS
☎ 07

This important town of 30,000 inhabitants is the capital of Morona-Santiago Province. It could very well be the most dignified, quiet and attractive town in the Oriente. It has four centuries of history as a Spanish trading and missionary outpost, and an old mule trail still joins Macas with the highlands near Riobamba. A road that would follow this trail is planned, and large segments of it have now been completed – it should be finished sometime in late 2000. A road north to Puyo has recently been completed but requires crossing Río Pastaza on two bridges (there's an island between them); the bridges can take cars but not large vehicles. Buses meet travelers at either end.

Despite its history, Macas is essentially a modern and developing town. The bus terminal and airport are both relatively new, and the main plaza was completed only in 1983.

Information
Money Banco del Austro, 24 de Mayo and 10 de Agosto, might be able to change traveler's checks. Delgado Travel, near the southwest corner of the main plaza, and Orientravel (☎ 700 731, fax 700 380, ortravel@cue.satnet.net), 10 de Agosto and Soasti, may change traveler's checks as well. Using credit cards is iffy.

Post & Communications There are is a Pacifictel and a post office (see the Macas map). World-Cyber (☎ 701 730), Soasti near Cuenca, has Internet access. Transfast is a courier service at Soasti and Tarqui.

Laundry Have your jungle-soiled clothes washed and dried at the laundry at 24 de Mayo and Juan de la Salinas.

Travel Agencies & Organized Tours Orientravel (see Money, earlier) has good booking services for national and international airlines, as well as local tour information.

Tsunki Tour Agency (☎ 700 464, tsunki@cue.satnet.net), on the 2nd floor of a building on Comin near 24 de Mayo, is a small operation run by friendly and knowledgeable Sarah Massie and Daniel Castro, who speak English and are trained in ecology and anthropology. They run trips lasting from one day to four days/three nights, visiting local Shuar families (with whom they have excellent relationships), Parque Nacional Sangay, the deep Amazon and protected private land. Rates are US$40 to US$55 per person per day, depending on group size (with a maximum of eight) and include a local guide, an English translator and good food. With advance notice, Tsunki can also arrange speleological expeditions with an accomplished caver; there are reportedly many caves in the area.

Tuntiak Expediciones de la Selva (☎ 700 185, ☎/fax 700 082), in the bus terminal, is run by Carlos Arcos, who is part Shuar and doesn't speak English. His father has a simple lodge (warm showers, kitchen facilities) in the village of Miazal, in the jungle about 50km southeast of Macas as the vulture flies. There is an airstrip in Miazal for chartered flights. Shuar villages, waterfalls, natural hot springs and an oilbird cave (see the boxed text 'Oilbirds') are in the vicinity. Tours often fly in and then depart by canoes down Río Mangosiza to Puerto Morona (six to eight hours), from where it's a 10-hour bus ride back to Macas. Tours of about five days cost about US$300 per person for two people, less for small groups.

IKIAAM Shuar Travel (☎ 700 497), near Hotel Peñon del Oriente, is another Shuar outfitter to try. The company's address has changed frequently in the past, but this is one of the few that's been around a while.

Yacu Amu Rafting (see the Quito & Around chapter) also arranges five- and eight-day trips on the Upano, which has Grade III and IV rapids and many waterfalls; it is also suitable for kayaking expeditions if you have the requisite experience.

Things to See & Do

The new **cathedral** was built on a small hill above the main plaza and replaced a quaint and simple old wooden church. The cathedral is dedicated to the 400th anniversary of the miraculous changes that happened to a painting of La Virgen de Macas in 1592. The story is told in a series of huge stained-glass windows, and the painting itself can be viewed on the altar. On the night of August 4, a **procession** in honor of the Virgin goes the 23km from Sucúa.

Behind the cathedral is a **view** of the wide Río Upano valley. From the cathedral's hill, there's a view of the town and – on a clear day – the often smoking Volcán Sangay, some 40km to the northwest. At 5230m, it is the seventh-highest mountain in Ecuador and is one of the most active volcanoes in the world.

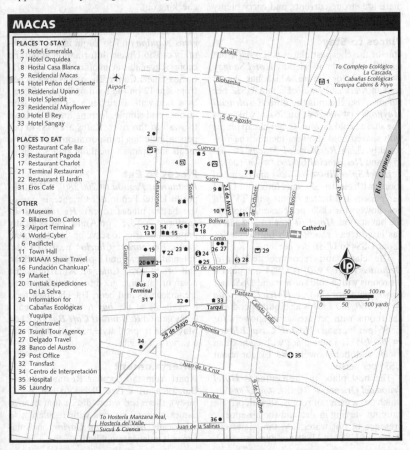

MACAS

PLACES TO STAY
5 Hotel Esmeralda
7 Hotel Orquidea
8 Hostal Casa Blanca
9 Residencial Macas
14 Hotel Peñon del Oriente
15 Residencial Upano
18 Hotel Splendit
23 Residencial Mayflower
30 Hotel El Rey
33 Hotel Sangay

PLACES TO EAT
10 Restaurant Cafe Bar
13 Restaurant Pagoda
17 Restaurant Charlot
21 Terminal Restaurant
22 Restaurant El Jardín
31 Eros Café

OTHER
1 Museum
2 Billares Don Carlos
3 Airport Terminal
4 World–Cyber
6 Pacifictel
7 Town Hall
12 IKIAAM Shuar Travel
16 Fundación Chankuap'
19 Market
20 Tuntiak Expediciones De La Selva
24 Information for Cabañas Ecológicas Yuquipa
25 Orientravel
26 Tsunki Tour Agency
27 Delgado Travel
28 Banco del Austro
29 Post Office
32 Transfast
34 Centro de Interpretación
35 Hospital
36 Laundry

A few blocks northeast of the center, at Don Bosco and Zabala, is a small children's park with a library and tiny **museum**. Ask the librarian to open it for you. It has a few archaeological artifacts dating to 2700 BC, a handful of ethnographic exhibits and some old photos of Macas.

The **Centro de Interpretación**, at the west end of Juan de la Cruz, has a small exhibit about Parque Nacional Sangay.

Complejo Ecológico La Cascada is a locally popular picnic area and pool on the road to Puyo, about a 90-minute walk from the center. Don't swim in the river here, as there are strong currents, and carry plenty of drinking water.

Places to Stay

One of the cheapest places is the basic but recently painted and friendly *Hotel Sangay* (☎ 700 457), on Tarqui, which has shared cold showers and rates of about US$2 per person. Also cheap is the little *Residencial Mayflower* (☎ 700 704), on Soasti, which has one shared cold shower. Other cheap places with shared cold showers include the reasonably clean *Residencial Macas* (☎ 700 254) and *Residencial Upano* (☎ 700 057).

Hotel Splendit (☎ 700 120) has basic old rooms with electric showers for about US$3 per person and better rooms with TV and hot showers for US$6 per person. Opposite the bus station, *Hotel El Rey* (☎ 700 528/9) has large clean rooms with hot water for about US$4 to US$6 per person.

The clean and recommended *Hotel Orquidea* (☎ 700 970) is US$4 per person for rooms with a cold shower and US$5 per person with hot shower. *Hotel Esmeralda* (☎ 700 160, 700 130) is also quite good and has rooms with private warm showers for US$5 per person. *Hostal Casa Blanca* (☎ 700 195) is a new place with eight clean rooms with hot showers and TV for about US$5 per person.

The best place in the center is *Hotel Peñon del Oriente* (☎ 700 124, ☎/fax 700 450), which has a menu of rooms, all with private bath but varying in size and the absence or presence of hot water, TV, fan, views etc. Rates are US$3 to US$8 per person.

About 2km south of town on the road to Sucúa is *Hostería del Valle* (☎ 700 226, 701 143, fax 700 302), which has clean, bungalow-style accommodations at US$8/14/18 for singles/doubles/triples with private hot bath, TV and breakfast. Other meals can be prepared on request. If you speak Spanish and get to know the owners, they will regale you with stories of what life was like here a few decades ago, before the current modernization. Nice folks.

Between the center and Hostería del Valle is the new *Hostería Manzana Real*. It plans on being the best in town, so it's worth checking out.

Finally, to experience some of the jungle near Macas, try the simple *Cabañas Ecológicas Yuquipa* on Río Yuquipa, a small tributary of Río Upano. Information about the cabins is available at an office (☎/fax 700 071) on Soasti near Comin. The cabins are reached from Km 12 on the road to Puyo, followed by a 4km walk. Facilities are minimal, with latrines and simple sleeping huts. You have to wash in the river. Rates are US$40 per person, including transportation from Macas, meals and Spanish-speaking guides.

Places to Eat

Restaurant Pagoda (☎ 700 280), a chifa opposite Hotel Peñon del Oriente, is one of the better places to eat. *Restaurant El Jardín* (☎ 700 573), on Amazonas, is locally popular and tries to serve an 'international' menu. *Restaurant Charlot*, next to Hotel Splendit, is cheap and looks clean. The clean and bright *Eros Café*, on Amazonas just north of Tarqui, is good for hamburgers, ice cream, snacks and beer. The cheapest food is available at the *bus terminal*. The curiously named *Restaurant Café Bar*, on 24 de Mayo, is a tropical-style bar with music and a variety of snacks.

Entertainment

Apart from the popular Restaurant Café Bar for a drink (see Places to Eat, previously), there are a few discos that change names and/or locations with regularity, so ask locally. *Billares Don Carlos*, on Amazonas, is a decent pool hall.

Shopping

Fundación Chankuap' is an indigenous-run shop selling local crafts and foods.

Getting There & Away

Air TAME (☎/fax 701 162), at the airport, has flights from and to Quito on Monday, Wednesday and Friday afternoons, leaving Quito at 11 am and leaving Macas at 12:10 pm; this is all subject to change. Tickets cost US$53 (less for Ecuadorians) one way. If flying from Macas to Quito, the left-hand side of the plane offers the best mountain views, including Sangay and Cotopaxi if the weather is clear.

Austro Aéreo (☎ 700 939), at the airport, has flights from Cuenca (US$35) at 10:20 am Monday, Wednesday and Friday, returning from Macas at noon.

The air force has cheap flights on most weekdays to various jungle airstrips and to Shell (in the northern Oriente). Seating is limited, and flights are often booked up several days in advance. Ecuadorians get preference on flights run by the military, and it is hard to get on these.

Aéreo Misional (☎ 700 142) has flights to the jungle, but these are primarily for locals and missionaries and are rarely available for the public.

Small aircraft can be chartered. This is best done by asking the tour agencies and guides.

Bus All departures are from the bus terminal. Various bus companies offer several departures a day for Cuenca (US$5, 10 hours) and Gualaquiza (US$4, nine to 10 hours). Buses to Sucúa (US$0.50, one hour) run every 30 minutes from 6 am to 7 pm.

Buses north to Puyo (US$3.50, five hours) leave several times a day. About halfway to Puyo, Río Pastaza must be crossed at the settlement of Chuitayo. Cars can cross a small bridge, but buses are too heavy, so passengers have to cross on foot and continue by a second bus waiting on the other side, a distance of almost a kilometer. A small restaurant at the bridge provides drinks and snacks. Some buses continue on to Tena (US$5.50, eight hours).

Transportes Macas runs small buses and pickup trucks to various remote parts of the province, including 9 de Octubre (for Parque Nacional Sangay) and Morona.

PARQUE NACIONAL SANGAY

This national park is more fully described in the South of Quito chapter. Most access to the park is from the north and west; access from the south and east is very difficult.

You can get buses from Macas to **9 de Octubre**, where you can stay in the schoolhouse or camp. The people are friendly and can tell you where the dirt road continues to San Vicente and then on to Purshi by footpath. Allow about eight hours to hike from 9 de Octubre to Purshi (though this section should be passable to vehicles by 2001). This small settlement is the official entrance to Parque Nacional Sangay. There is usually a ranger here, but the local people are also helpful. The entrance fee to the park is US$10. Trails lead a short distance into the park, but they peter out fairly quickly, and continuing requires a machete and a lot of perseverance – recommended for very experienced explorers only. The rainfall is high, the vegetation thick, and the terrain steep and broken.

It is possible to continue on foot beyond Purshi to Atillo in the highlands, from where a dirt road eventually connects with the Panamericana. A road is under construction and will eventually link Macas with Cebadas and Guamote in the highlands. Make local inquiries about the status of this road. In 1999, parts of the road were built but about 11km hadn't been begun yet. It could be open by 2001, but with the current economic crisis, who knows?

There is a park information center in Macas.

THE JUNGLE FROM MACAS

There are various ways to see more of the Oriente from Macas. It should be mentioned, however, that the best-known centers for tourism in the jungle are in the northern Oriente.

Many Ecuadorian maps show tracks or trails leading from Macas into the interior.

Kapawi Ecolodge & Reserve

Built on Achuar Indian land in the remotest part of the Ecuadorian Amazon, Kapawi is a culturally sensitive and unique ecotourism project. The Achuar people had very little contact with the Western world until the arrival of missionaries in the late 1960s. Since then, contact has remained relatively minimal, without the destructive influences of the oil and logging industries, which have hopelessly disrupted the lives of most other Oriente tribes. By the 1990s, however, the Achuar were aware enough of the outside world and found themselves at a crossroads – how could they continue following their traditional culture while slowly and successfully integrating positive aspects of the modern world into their lives?

The development of the Kapawi Ecolodge, in a pristine area of Achuar land, appears to have provided a solution to that problem. The most important aspect of the project is the carefully built partnership between Canodros, the lodge developers, and the Achuar community. At every step, the community was consulted and was freely provided important advice – both cultural and technical. The lodge buildings were constructed following traditional ideas of Achuar architecture and used no nails at all. The land for the buildings remains Achuar, and after the lodge opened in 1996, Canodros began paying a monthly rent of US$2000 for use of the land (and the rent increases 7% annually). Achuar workers were used in construction and are now used as lodge employees. Eventually, after 15 years, it is planned to turn the entire project over to Achuar hands.

Kapawi uses low-impact technology – such as solar power, trash management and recycling, and biodegradable soaps. The lodge has 20 individual double cabins built around a lake, and each has a private bath and a balcony with lake views. The food served is a mixture of locally provided produce, with some international food flown in. Local fruits are a highlight. A bar provides a relaxing area with a library and games section. Locally made handicrafts are for sale.

Guests visit the rainforest in small groups accompanied by two guides – an Achuar and a bilingual naturalist. The two work in tandem to explain the intricacies of the rainforest, both from an ecological and a cultural point of view. Visits to an Achuar family can be arranged, but photography is not allowed. Instead, the Achuar provide bowls of the traditional welcoming *nijiamanch* (manioc beer) and ask guests questions about their lives in addition to explaining some aspects of their own lifestyle – it's a great cultural interchange. In 1998, the project received a British Airways 'Tourism for Tomorrow' award for culturally sensitive ecotourism.

The lodge is just off Río Pastaza, on an oxbow lake on Río Capahuari. The only way to practically reach Kapawi is by light aircraft, which usually goes to the Achuar village of Wayusentsa (called Guayusentza on some maps) and is followed by a boat ride. Flights may leave and return from Quito via Macas or Shell-Mera; they cost US$150 roundtrip. Stays at the lodge cost US$600 per person for three nights/four days, US$720 for four nights/five days, and US$1100 per person for seven nights/eight days; these rates are based on double occupancy and include all meals and guided tours. In addition, there is a tax of US$10 per person levied by the Achuar community. These rates are subject to change.

Reservations can be made at the main Canodros office (in Guayaquil ☎ 04-285 711, 280 173, fax 287 651, eco-tourism1@canodros.com.ec) or at the branch office (in Quito ☎ 02-222 203, 220 947, 09-801 424, fax 02-454 586). The Web site is at www.kapawi.com. Major travel agencies can also make reservations. More information is available in an article called 'Kapawi,' by Arnaldo Rodríguez, published in *Cultural Survival Magazine*, Summer 1999.

These often lead to Shuar Indian villages and missions farther into the Oriente. The trails are usually overgrown, however, because transportation is mainly by light aircraft these days. It is difficult, but not impossible, to visit some of these villages.

You can hire an *expreso* light aircraft to take you to some of the better-known centers, such as **Taisha**, 70km due east of Macas by air. There is a basic place to stay there. With luck or the right contacts, flights can be arranged with the Salesian mission aircraft, but flights are often full, and inclement weather may cause days of delay. Hiring your own aircraft is subject to the availability of planes, and it costs about US$60 per person/per hour for a five-seater. Flights between Macas and Shell (in the northern Oriente) sometimes stop in Taisha. A Shuar guide, Carlos Arcos of Tuntiak Expediciones de la Selva (see Travel Agencies & Guides under Information in the Macas section, earlier), is a good contact.

Visiting nearby Shuar centers on foot or by bus is fairly straightforward. There are frequent buses to the mission of **Sevilla** (Don Bosco), about an hour's walk away on the other side of Río Upano.

From Sevilla, you can head south on foot along a broad track to the village of San Luís, about a four-hour walk. This makes a good day trip, and en route, you'll pass cultivated areas and Indian huts, where you may be invited to try some *chicha de yuca*. This traditional Shuar drink is made by the women, who grind up the yucca by chewing it and then spit it into a bowl, where it is left to ferment. If this doesn't appeal to you, bring a bottle of water. There are no facilities of any kind beyond Sevilla.

Most travelers now go to Puyo by road, crossing Río Pastaza at Chuitayo. Here, the bus drops travelers who cross the bridge on foot – it can handle cars and pickups, but not buses. Another bus meets travelers on the other side, and tickets are valid for both. There are basic snack bars by the bridge. South of Chuitayo, the bus passes through Shuar territory, and you can see a few of their oval-shaped, bamboo-caned, thatched huts on the sides of the road. Most of the Indians riding the bus look unremarkably Western, but occasionally a beautifully beaded bracelet or tattooed face is seen.

The Northern Oriente

North of Río Pastaza, which flanks Parque Nacional Sangay on the east, are the provinces of Pastaza, Napo, Orellana and Sucumbíos – these provinces form the northern Oriente. Unlike the southern Oriente, the northern Oriente is well connected with the capital – there are two roads to Quito and six times as many scheduled flights from Quito. Hence, this is the most visited part of Ecuador's jungle. In one long day of bus riding, you can go from Quito to the oil boomtown of Lago Agrio, in the far northeastern jungle, or to the tourist center of Tena, in the central Oriente. From either of these towns, travelers can continue to Coca and make a roundtrip for a brief look at Ecuador's Oriente.

These areas have been colonized by farmers, ranchers, loggers and oil workers. Therefore, transportation is relatively straightforward on these routes, but one shouldn't expect to see much in the way of wildlife. For that, tours into the interior are recommended; Tena, Misahuallí (just east of Tena) and Coca are among the better places from which to begin a more nature-oriented trip. Río Napo is Ecuador's major tributary into the Amazon – at the point it meets Peru's Río Marañón, the Amazon continues as a single river.

You should note that during the rainiest months (June to August), roads may be washed out, airports may be closed and travel delays are common. At all times, allow a leeway of a day or two if you need to return and make important connections in Quito.

Highlights

- Experiencing ecotourism at its finest at the Yachana Lodge
- Spotting exotic Amazonian wildlife at the Cuyabeno reserve
- Unwinding in the hot springs of Papallacta, perched on the edge of the Andes and the jungle
- Immersing yourself in Indian cultures through one of several community-based ecotourism projects in the area

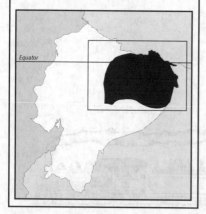

FROM BAÑOS TO PUYO
☎ 03

When it comes to incredible views of the upper Amazon Basin, it just doesn't get much better than the stretch of road from Baños to Puyo.

The road follows the Río Pastaza canyon as it drops steadily from Baños, at 1800m, to Puyo, at 950m. This road has recently been rebuilt, and buses now regularly make the journey (if Baños isn't closed because of Volcán Tungurahua). Just beyond the Agoyán hydroelectric project, the road passes through a tunnel. A few kilometers farther, a waterfall splashes from the overhanging cliff onto the road – quite a surprise if you're in the back of a pickup truck.

One of the most impressive sights along the way is the **Río Verde waterfalls**, which are near the eponymous village about 20km east of Baños. You have to walk down a short trail to a suspension bridge to appreciate the waterfall properly. There is a sign at the beginning of the trail that

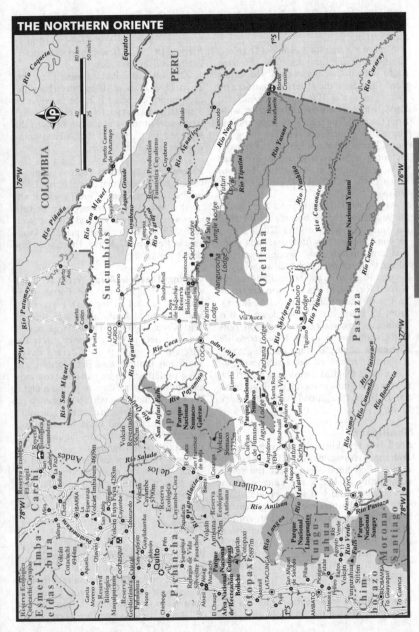

reads 'Pailón del Diablo.' If you have trouble finding the trail, ask at the village for directions.

Next to the sign for Pailón del Diablo is another sign for the guest farm *El Otro Lado*, which literally means 'the other side.' The trail to the waterfall continues by footbridge across Río Pastaza to El Otro Lado, which is about a 20-minute walk from the road. The place is tranquil and has bungalows, private hot showers and good views. Rates are about US$25 per person, including breakfast and dinner. You can make reservations at the Cultura Reservation Center (see Travel Agencies under Quito).

As the road drops beyond Río Verde, the vegetation rapidly becomes more tropical, and the walls of the Río Pastaza canyon are covered with bromeliads, giant tree ferns, orchids and flowering trees. The village of Río Negro is passed some 15km beyond Río Verde, and several kilometers beyond Río Negro is a bus stop known as La Penal (a few kilometers before Mera). From La Penal, a trail goes down to Río Pastaza and crosses it on a suspension footbridge, continuing to *El Monasterio de Cumandá*, almost an hour from the road. It's not a monastery but a simple guesthouse with tropical forest and waterfalls nearby; more information is available from Safari Tours (see Travel Agencies under Quito).

Shell-Mera

Shell is a few kilometers beyond Mera, and the two communities together are often called Shell-Mera. Near the small community of Mera, the canyon walls spread apart, and you see a breathtaking view of Río Pastaza meandering away to the southeast through the vast, rolling plains of the Amazon Basin. The right side of the bus is best for views. At about 1200m, there is no higher land between here and the Atlantic, which is almost 4000km to the east.

Orientation & Information Shell is a US missionary center with schools, churches and hospitals. The missions have flights into the Oriente and may provide emergency services. There is a Voz Andes missionary hospital (☎ 795 172), which provides emergency medical assistance.

At Shell is the Pastaza airstrip, serving Puyo, which is about 10km away. This is the most important airstrip in the province of Pastaza. You won't get lost in this place – it's a one-street town, and the airport is at the west end, on the way to Baños. Everything else lies east of the airport.

Places to Stay & Eat There a couple of basic hotels in Shell that charge about US$2 or US$3 a night. *Hostal Cordillera* seems to be the best, because rooms have private showers, but equally good rooms with shared showers at a cheaper price are available at *Residencial Azuay*. There are a few simple restaurants.

Getting There & Away Weekday flights with the Ecuadorian Air Force, FAE (Fuerza Aerea Ecuatoriana), leave from Shell and go to Quito and towns such as Tena, Coca, Lago Agrio and Macas, as well as to a variety of jungle villages (there are different destinations on different days). Seating is limited, and Ecuadorians are given preference, so be patient – you may have to wait several days to get on a flight. For towns with bus service, it's faster to go by bus. Bus fares are cheap (around US$0.20 to Puyo and US$1.50 to Baños). Aircraft can be chartered – inquire at the airport (it's closed Sunday).

There is no bus terminal in Shell or Mera; wait on the main road in Shell and flag down a bus that's heading to Puyo or Baños. Ask locals for the best corners on which to do this.

PUYO
☎ 03

With a growing population of over 25,000, Puyo is the provincial capital of Pastaza. Until the early 1970s, it had a real frontier atmosphere and was the most important town in the Oriente. Since the discovery of oil, however, the frontier has been pushed

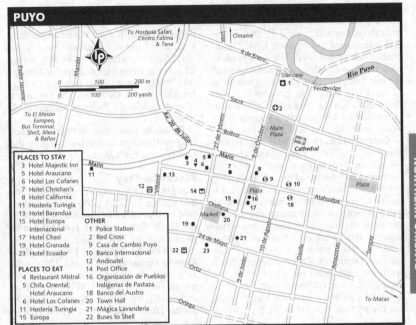

PUYO

To Hostería Safari,
Centro Fatima
& Tena

Omaere

4 de Enero

Río Puyo

Staircase

Footbridge

Sucre

Av. 20 de Julio

27 de Febrero

Bolívar

Main
Plaza

9 de Octubre

Cathedral

To El Mesón
Europeo,
Bus Terminal,
Shell, Mera
& Baños

Plaza

Marín

Marín

Atahualpa

Villamil

Orellana

Market

Davila

Amazonas

Sangay

24 de Mayo

10 de Agosto

Ortiz

Ortega

5 de Junio

To Macas

PLACES TO STAY
3   Hotel Majestic Inn
5   Hotel Araucano
6   Hotel Los Cofanes
7   Hotel Christian's
8   Hotel California
11 Hostería Turingia
13 Hotel Barandua
15 Hotel Europa
    Internacional
17 Hotel Chasi
19 Hotel Granada
23 Hotel Ecuador

PLACES TO EAT
4   Restaurant Mistral
5   Chifa Oriental;
    Hotel Araucano
6   Hotel Los Cofanes
11 Hostería Turingia
15 Europa

OTHER
1   Police Station
2   Red Cross
9   Casa de Cambio Puyo
10 Banco Internacional
12 Andinatel
14 Post Office
16 Organización de Pueblos
    Indígenas de Pastaza
18 Banco del Austro
20 Town Hall
21 Mágica Lavandería
22 Buses to Shell

deep into the jungle, although Puyo remains an important, if not especially attractive, Oriente town.

Information

Street signs are not much in evidence in Puyo.

The banks shown on the map may change traveler's checks, but usually only from 9 am to 1 pm weekdays. The Casa de Cambio Puyo has longer hours but poor rates. ATMs and credit-card advances are unreliable. The post office and Andinatel are shown on the map.

The Voz Andes mission hospital (☎ 795 172) in Shell is the best bet for medical emergencies. The Red Cross in Puyo (☎ 885 214) is on the north side of the main plaza. The police station is marked on the map.

Clothes left at Mágica Lavandería (see the map) in the morning will be ready to pick up by the evening. Market day is Sun-

day. Many of the town's businesses are open Sunday and closed Monday.

Things to See & Do

Early risers may see a spectacular view of jagged snowy peaks rising up over a jungle covered with rolling morning mist. Later in the morning, the mountains usually disappear into the clouds. The jagged peaks belong to **El Altar** (5319m), the fifth-highest mountain in Ecuador and about 50km southeast of Puyo. Occasionally, you can also catch a glimpse of **Sangay** (5230m). A good view can be had from the main plaza on a clear day (and sometimes from the road to Shell-Mera).

Less than 1km north of the center, by Río Puyo, is **Omaere** (☎ 883 001), which calls itself a pedagogical ethnobotanical park and is open 8:30 am to 6 pm daily. The park offers tours guided by local natives who explain the importance of the many plants of the rainforest. Life-sized replicas of the houses of several Oriente tribes are in the park, and the guides show off the utensils and products used by the inhabitants. Entrance costs about US$2.50, including the guided tours. The park plans to offer rustic overnight accommodations; call for information. There may be possibilities to work at Omaere as a volunteer. Get there by following Loja north of town for about half a kilometer, until you reach the bridge over the river, and follow the sign.

Centro Fatima (☎ 884 105) is 9km from Puyo on the Tena road. This wildlife-rescue and research center covers 28 hectares and is involved in such projects as reproducing endangered species and domesticating and raising rainforest animals as livestock for local communities. The center is staffed by biologists, conservationists and volunteers (who pay about US$10 a week for a bed and use of the kitchen facilities). The volunteers come from various countries, and most are biology or conservation students. Visitors can take a guided tour of the facilities and see the animals that are being bred, which include tapirs, capybaras and other rodents, various monkeys, parrots and reptiles. The center is open 9 am to 4 pm daily, and a 45-minute guided tour costs US$2.50, after which you can stay longer. You can get there from Puyo by taking a taxi or any bus to Tena. You can also ask for directions at OPIP (see the boxed text 'Organización de Pueblos Indígenas de Pastaza').

Fiestas de Fundación de Puyo, the week-long celebrations of Puyo's founding day, take place in early May.

Places to Stay

Budget Two basic, reasonably clean places that charge US$2 to US$3 for rooms with cold bath are **Hotel Granada** (☎ 885 578), on 27 de Febrero, and **Hotel Ecuador** (☎ 883 089), on 24 de Mayo.

A better cheap hotel to try is **Hotel Europa Internacional** (☎ 885 220, fax 885 120), on 9 de Octubre. Large rooms with private bath cost about US$3.50 per person, and there is a good view from the roof. Opposite, **Hotel Chasi** (☎ 883 059) charges

Organización de Pueblos Indígenas de Pastaza

This organization (OPIP; ☎/fax 883 875), on 9 de Octubre between Atahualpa and Orellana, represents about 130 small indigenous communities totaling about 20,000 people. OPIP can provide information about local indigenous issues; it works with Papangu Tours (same address) to provide travelers with the opportunity to visit villages, stay with local families and learn about their lifestyles. Guided tours with small groups (two-person minimum) cost about US$35 per person per day. Popular options include day tours in the Puyo area and three-day/two-night excursions to local villages using both river and on-foot travel. There are also more expensive options (up to US$70 per person per day) that last for several days and include light-aircraft flights to remote villages. The philosophy of Papangu Tours is to provide communities with the opportunity to develop and benefit from their own forms of cultural ecotourism. Also, ask here about possibilities to work in volunteer projects in the area.

Also at OPIP is Yana Puma (Quichua for 'black jaguar'), an art gallery/store/restaurant with a small but good selection of books about the Oriente (mainly in Spanish, but there are a few in English), as well as crafts made in the area. You can see balsa-wood animals being made before you buy them. Other crafts include ceramics, woven bags, hammocks, jewelry and various other jungle oddities and treasures. The restaurant has a small menu of local specialities, such as *maito de pescado* (fish wrapped in banana leaves and baked over an open fire). Hours are 8 am to 9 pm daily at Yana Puma, although the restaurant tends to just do lunch.

US$4 per person for rooms with private bath, but it also has rooms with shared bath for US$2.25 per person. A block away, the similarly priced *Hotel California* (☎ 885 189) is also acceptable, although the street-side rooms are noisy.

Hotel Araucano (☎ 883 834, 885 686, fax 885 227, Marín 575) is clean, friendly and helpful. All rooms have a private hot bath and a fan, and some have a TV and fridge. There is a restaurant on the premises and a tour office next door. Top-floor rooms have views of Sangay. Rates are US$4 to US$6 per person, including breakfast.

Hotel Barandua (☎ 885 604), on Villamil at Atahualpa, is clean and charges US$5 per person for rooms with bath. Also good is *Hotel Majestic Inn* (☎ 885 111/238), on Marín at 29 de Junio, which charges about US$6 per person for rooms with hot water and cable TV. *Hotel Christian's* (☎ /fax 883 081), on Atahualpa, has similar rooms for about US$7.50 per person and advertises car rental.

Mid-Range The new *Hotel Los Cofanes* (☎/fax 885 560, 883 772, loscofanes@yahoo .com, 27 de Febrero 629) has 30 spacious, tiled, modern rooms with a telephone, fan and local cable TV, as well as a restaurant with room service. Rates are US$10/17 for singles/doubles, and group discounts are offered.

Hostería Turingia (☎ 885 180, fax 885 384, Marín 294) has been a Puyo institution for years. The accommodations are rather cramped bungalows with fans, TVs, telephones and hot water. Each of the 24 older wooden rooms cost about US$14/18, and each of the 22 newer rooms cost about US$18/23. The bungalows are set in a tropical garden with many plants and a tiny plunge pool. The restaurant here is quite good but overpriced.

Another reasonable choice is *Hostería Safari* (☎ 885 465/6, fax 851 424), about 5km away on the road to Tena. It has a nice garden with a pool, Jacuzzi and sauna; a games area; a gift shop and a restaurant and bar. Rooms with private bath and hot water

cost US$26 per person, including breakfast and dinner.

Places to Eat

A few restaurants in the center are adequate, if not memorable. The clean *Restaurant Mistral* is good for snacks and light meals. *Chifa Oriental*, next to Hotel Araucano, is also OK. The pleasant *El Mesón Europeo* (☎ 883 919, 823 920), about 200m east of the bus terminal, is Puyo's best and is quite inexpensive, with a good variety of meat, chicken and fish dishes.

The better hotels have decent, inexpensive restaurants. *Europa*, under the hotel of that name, is pretty good and has outside tables for watching the busy downtown street. The restaurants in Hotel Araucano and Hotel Los Cofanes are also good. Hostería Turingia has a good restaurant, but the set lunches are overpriced.

Getting There & Away

Air The provincial airstrip is in Shell (see Shell-Mera, earlier).

Bus The terminal is about 1km southwest of town. There are buses via Baños to Ambato (US$2.50, three hours), but be sure to check the current situation, as this road may be closed due to volcanic activity near Baños. Buses to Quito leave about every hour and go either via Baños or Baeza, depending on which roads are open. Buses to Tena (US$2.50, three hours) leave about every hour. Several companies serve these routes.

Buses to Macas (US$3.75, five hours) leave five or six times a day with Transportes San Francisco. The bus goes as far as Río Pastaza, where you have to transfer (see Macas, in the Southern Oriente chapter). Flota Pelileo has a 6:30 am departure to Coca (US$7, eight hours).

Centinela del Oriente runs ancient buses to various small villages in the surrounding jungle. The most important of these villages is Palora (three hours), which has a basic pensión. Palora is served several times a day. Various other nearby jungle villages can also be explored with various buses. Although the buses leave from the terminal, they'll stop at the street market at Atahualpa and Amazonas.

Getting Around
Small local buses providing service to Shell (US$0.20) leave every 30 minutes or so from south of the market along 27 de Febrero. A taxi ride from downtown to the bus terminal costs about US$0.80. You can rent a car at Hotel Christian's (see Places to Stay, earlier).

TENA
☎ 06
Now the capital of Napo Province and home to over 20,000 people, Tena was once the most easterly of Ecuador's early colonial missionary and trading outposts. It was founded in 1560, and there were several Indian uprisings in the early days, notably in 1578, when Jumandy, chief of the Quijos, led an unsuccessful revolt against the Spaniards. Tena survived the uprising, although many early colonial Oriente towns were completely wiped out by other Indian attacks. Today, the area is largely agricultural – cattle ranches and coffee and banana plantations abound. Situated at the junction of Ríos Tena and Pano, Tena is a becoming more and more a center for Ecuadorian tourism. The rivers have a moderating effect on the climate – the average year-round temperature is 24°C.

Information
The Andinatel and post offices are shown on the map. Internet facilities are available at the friendly Piraña.net (☎ 886 718/254), 9 de Octubre 238. It's open 10 am to 10 pm daily except Sunday, when it is open 4 to 9 pm. English is spoken, drinks are served, and there are a few books to exchange – it's a good place to hang out.

The banks shown on the map will change traveler's checks 9 am to 1 pm weekdays. ATM and credit-card facilities are unreliable.

Clínica Amazonas (☎ 886 495) is on Santa Rosa between Tena and Narvaez; it's open 24 hours and has the best reputation. The hospital (☎ 886 302/304) is south of town on the road to Puerto Napo. The police (☎ 886 101) are on the main plaza. *Migraciones* (☎ 887 691) is just north of the main plaza.

Organized Tours
Jungle Tours Amarongachi Tours (☎/fax 886 372), 15 de Noviembre 438, is a tour company that has been recommended by numerous readers. The friendly staff arrange various jungle excursions and book bus tickets for you after the trip. Amarongachi is a source of local information, and the owner also owns Hostal Travellers Lodging and Cositas Ricas (see Places to Stay and Places to Eat, respectively). Its tours are about US$35 per person per day, but it's cheaper if you go for several days and with a group. While on the excursion, you can stay with a family in the jungle, eat good local food, go for nature hikes, pan for gold, swim in the rivers and get a look at the rainforest. Although much of the land around Tena has been colonized, there are some nearby sections of uncut primary forest that can still be visited. Amarongachi also operates the Shangri La cabins, which are on a bluff 100m above Río Anzu (a tributary of Río Napo) and feature great views of the river and forest. The cabins are simple doubles, and food and services are provided by local families. Many family members speak Quichua as a first language and Spanish as a second; few speak English.

Also recommended are the local guides listed with Red Indígena de Communidades del Alto Napo para la Convivencia Intercultural y Ecoturismo (RICANCIE – Indigenous Network of Upper Napo Communities for Cultural Coexistence and Ecotourism; ☎ 887 072, ricancie@ecuanex.net.ec), 15 de Noviembre 774 (around the back). Tarquino Tapuy is a good contact at RICANCIE. Almost all of the guides speak Quichua and/or Spanish, but few speak English. The staff can arrange stays in local villages, as well as the usual jungle trips; they also know the locations of the numerous caves and petroglyphs found in the Tena region. About nine villages are represented, and

TENA

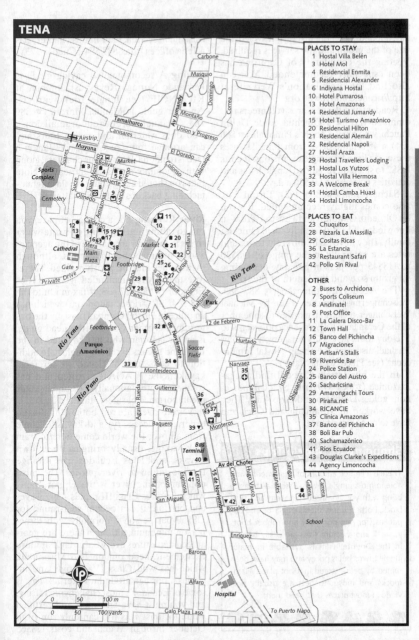

PLACES TO STAY
1 Hostal Villa Belén
3 Hotel Mol
4 Residencial Enmita
5 Residencial Alexander
6 Indiyana Hostal
10 Hotel Pumarosa
13 Hotel Amazonas
14 Residencial Jumandy
15 Hotel Turismo Amazónico
20 Residencial Hilton
21 Residencial Alemán
22 Residencial Napoli
27 Hostal Araza
29 Hostal Travellers Lodging
31 Hostal Los Yutzos
32 Hostal Villa Hermosa
33 A Welcome Break
41 Hostal Camba Huasi
44 Hostal Limoncocha

PLACES TO EAT
23 Chuquitos
28 Pizzaría La Massilia
32 Cositas Ricas
36 La Estancia
39 Restaurant Safari
42 Pollo Sin Rival

OTHER
2 Buses to Archidona
7 Sports Coliseum
8 Andinatel
9 Post Office
11 La Galera Disco-Bar
12 Town Hall
16 Banco del Pichincha
17 Migraciones
18 Artisan's Stalls
19 Riverside Bar
24 Police Station
25 Banco del Austro
26 Sacharicsina
30 Amarongachi Tours
30 Piraña.net
34 RICANCIE
35 Clínica Amazonas
37 Banco del Pichincha
38 Boli Bar Pub
40 Sachamazónico
41 Rios Ecuador
43 Douglas Clarke's Expeditions
44 Agency Limoncocha

NORTHERN ORIENTE

stays cost US$35 to US$60 per person per day, depending on the distance traveled, the size of the group and the services required. Visiting the community of Capirona has been especially recommended. You can also find the organization's Web site at http://ricancie.nativeweb.org.

Readers and Peace Corps volunteers recommend the local Quichua guide Delfín Pauchi, who owns Cabañas Pimpilala (☎ 886 434), a 45-minute drive from Tena. He uses these as a base for jungle excursions. It costs US$2 to sleep there; guided jungle hikes and activities cost about US$30 a day.

Sacharicsina (☎ 886 962), Tarqui 246, also comes highly recommended. It's run by Olmedo, Oswaldo and Fausto Cerda – a knowledgeable and friendly local Quichua family. They have eight different tours, and rates are generally in the range of US$30 to US$45 per person per day, depending on group size and the length of the trip.

The Agency Limoncocha (☎ 887 583, welschingerm@yahoo.de) is run by Michael Welschinger, a German married to a member of the Cerda family. This agency offers one- to five-day tours at US$25 per person per day. Michael also runs the cheap Hostal Limoncocha (see Places to Stay, later).

In the bus terminal, you'll find Sachamazónico (☎ 887 979), run by local indigenous guides Domingo and Lirio Andy. They have worked in Misahuallí and Coca and have a lot of experience.

Shopping for Jungle Trips

There is a limited amount of equipment available in most jungle towns. Essential items to bring with you are insect repellent and sunblock. Bottled water, sheets of plastic and tarpaulins (for rain ponchos) and rubber boots in small and medium sizes are easily bought in the Oriente. Film is available in major jungle towns but is pricey and may have been ruined by being stored in a hot place. Hammocks and mosquito nets are usually provided in most places that need them.

Douglas Clarke's Expeditions (see the Misahuallí section, later in this chapter) has a Tena office (☎/fax 887 584), Cuenca 173.

Caving A recommended caving guide is Fernando Noriega Reyes; ask for him at RICANCIE (see Jungle Tours, earlier). Another guide is Manuel Moreta (☎ 889 185, manuel.moreta@eudoramail.com), who does waterfall and caving tours and can arrange tours of Cuevas de Jumandí (see Archidona, later in this chapter), along with accommodations by the caves. Note that you should carry your own flashlights – including backups and extra batteries.

River Running For a change of pace, you can go rafting and kayaking on white-water rivers in the Tena area. Some of the agencies above offer river-rafting trips, although their guides may be poorly trained. Therefore, the only recommended agency is Ríos Ecuador (☎/fax 887 438, ☎/fax in Quito 02-558 264, info@riosecuador.com), which has an office in Hostal Camba Huasi, by the bus terminal. Gynner Coronel, the head guide, is an Ecuadorian who has kayaked in the USA and speaks excellent English. In addition to being one of Ecuador's foremost kayakers, he is AGAR-certified and has competed internationally. He understands the importance of safety standards.

Various rivers are run, both with rafts (no experience necessary) and kayaks. People from all over the world come here to train in kayaking, usually bringing their own kayaks, and Ríos Ecuador can arrange transportation to river put-ins. The most popular rafting river is the Upper Napo, which features Class III rapids – big waves and big fun. It can be run year-round for US$50 per person – normally with three-person minimum, although there are guaranteed departures every Saturday. For more excitement, head out on Río Misahuallí, which has wild Class IV+ rapids and includes a portage around a waterfall. This is some of Ecuador's most challenging rafting, and you must have an expert and certified guide for this! This trip can only run from October through March and costs US$65 per person. Transportation and lunch is included. Ask about other rivers and multiday trips.

A four-day white-water kayaking school (suitable for beginners) is offered for US$250 (a bargain, compared to rates in the US or Europe). Rental kayaks (US$15 per day, or US$30 with helmet, skirt, jacket and paddles) are available for experienced kayakers.

Things to See & Do

On a clear day, visitors to Tena are sometimes puzzled by the sight of a volcano looming up out of the jungle some 50km away to the north-northeast – this is Volcán Sumaco (see that section, later).

Parque Amazónico, across a gated covered bridge over Río Pano is a 27-hectare island with a self-guided trail passing labeled local plants and animal enclosures. Picnic areas, a swimming beach and a bathroom are available. The park is open 9 am to 5 pm; admission is about US$1.

The anniversary of Tena's foundation is celebrated on November 15. Market days are Friday and Saturday. Although there is nothing specifically aimed at tourists, the market is an interesting, bustling affair.

Places to Stay

Budget The cheapest hotels have suffered from water shortages, so check that there is running water. The following are about US$2 per person.

The basic but central *Hotel Amazonas*, on the corner of the plaza, is fine if you can get an outside room. *Residencial Jumandy*, a block north of the main plaza, is also acceptable. *Hostal Limoncocha* (see Agency Limoncocha, under Organized Tours, earlier in this section) is a white house up on a hill to your right as you arrive from the south; it has six rooms sharing two baths with hot water. Breakfast is available on request.

Barely a block south of the bus station, *Hostal Camba Huasi* (☎ 887 429) charges less than US$3 per person for large, clean, but bare rooms with private cold showers. This place is often full with river runners and kayakers, especially from October to

March. *A Welcome Break* (☎ 886 301, Agusto Rueda 331) is a five-room house with an equipped kitchen and a garden. Four rooms are doubles, and one is a quad; the owners are friendly. The rate is about US$4 per person.

The clean and popular *Hostal Travellers Lodging* (see Amarongachi Tours, under Jungle Tours, earlier) has comfortable rooms with private hot shower for US$3 to US$5 per person. There is a variety of rooms; some have several beds. Because it is popular with international travelers, it's a good place to get information and assemble a tour group.

The clean and friendly *Residencial Alemán* (☎ 886 409, 15 de Noviembre 210) charges US$3.25/5 for rooms with cold bath and fans, or US$8.50 for doubles with cable TV and hot showers. There is a parking area.

Other places to try in this price range include the friendly *Residencial Enmita* (☎ 886 253), on Bolívar, or the simpler *Residencial Alexander* (☎ 886 230), nearby. Some rooms have private showers. Across the Río Tena bridge, *Residencial Hilton* (☎ 886 329), at the north end of 15 de Noviembre, and the nearby *Residencial Napoli* (☎ 886 194) are clean and cheap. The new and clean *Hostal Villa Hermosa* (☎ 886 521, 887 258, 15 de Noviembre 622) has rooms with fan, TV and private bath for about US$5 per person.

Indiyana Hostal (☎ 886 334, Bolívar 349) is a small, family-run hotel with a garden and spotless rooms with fans (some rooms have air-conditioning), cable TV and private hot shower for about US$6 per person – a good value. The small but clean and friendly *Hostal Araza* (☎ 886 447, 9 de Octubre 277) has simple air-conditioned rooms with TV and hot shower for US$7/12. *Hostal Villa Belén* (☎ 886 228), north of town, charges about US$8 per person for very clean rooms with hot showers. There is a garden and a good, slightly pricey restaurant. All three of these places have secure parking.

Near the town center, *Hotel Turismo Amazónico* (☎ 886 487), at Amazonas and Calderón, charges about US$6 per person

NORTHERN ORIENTE

for older rooms with private cold bath, fan, cable TV, telephone and minifridge.

Hotel Pumarosa (*☎*/*fax 886 320, in Quito ☎ 02-443 023*), on Orellana, has a restaurant and 22 rooms with cable TV and telephone. Rooms with fans are about US$9/16, and rooms with air-conditioning are about US$10/17.

Mid-Range The clean and modern *Hotel Mol* (*☎ 886 808, fax 886 215, Sucre 432*) charges US$16/24 for rooms with private bath and hot water. The 11 pleasant, air-conditioned rooms have TV, telephone, fan and bath. Many have a balcony and are quite spacious. There is a small pool and a restaurant.

In a quiet riverside location, *Hostal Los Yutzos* (*☎ 886 717/769/458, Agusto Rueda 190*) has comfortable, clean, modern rooms with fans for US$12 per person, or US$15 with air-conditioning. Rooms have cable TV, hot shower and telephone; some have river views.

Places to Eat

There are a number of small and inexpensive restaurants. *Cositas Ricas*, next to Amarongachi Tours, is a favorite of travelers and serves vegetarian and Ecuadorian plates (about US$2) and good juices made with boiled water. The employees do a good job with clean food preparation for travelers' finicky stomachs. Hours are 7 am to 10 pm daily.

Chuquitos, just off the plaza, is recommended by locals and has a balcony with river views, a small menu of local food (especially fish) and the best lemonade in town. It is open for breakfast, lunch and dinner weekdays; on Saturday, it is open for breakfast and lunch only.

Pizzaría Le Massilia, on Orellana at Pano, serves some of the best and most innovative pizzas in the Oriente and is open noon to 10 pm daily. *La Estancia*, on 15 de Noviembre, has a nice thatched-roof jungle ambience and Ecuadorian food. Hours are 6 am to 9 pm daily. Near the bus terminal, *Restaurant Safari* is a plain, bright and very cheap Ecuadorian restaurant that is

popular with locals. For the best chicken in town, everyone goes to *Pollo Sin Rival*, two blocks south of the bus terminal. It's closed on Sunday.

Entertainment

On weekends, *La Galera Disco-Bar*, near Hotel Pumarosa, is the most happening place – although discos do come and go. *Boli Bar Pub*, on 15 de Noviembre across from the bus terminal, is the second choice of night owls. The little *riverside bar*, near the footbridge, is a nice place to watch the river flow while drinking an ice-cold beer and listening to the owner's salsa CD selection.

Getting There & Away

Air There is an airstrip at the north end of town. The Ecuadorian Air Force (FAE) has flights to Shell and Coca on Wednesday, but seats are booked well in advance and preference is given to Ecuadorians, so it's hard to get on – inquire at the airstrip.

Bus The terminal is on 15 de Noviembre, in the south end of town. There are 11 departures a day for Quito (six hours) via Baeza and 11 a day to Coca (seven hours). Jumandy has a night bus to Lago Agrio (10 hours) at 6:30 pm. These journey times are approximate, as bad roads, old buses and inclement weather all make trip lengths in the Oriente notoriously unreliable.

Getting Around

The local buses for Archidona (US$0.20, 15 minutes) leave about every half hour during daylight hours from the west side of the market. Buses for Misahuallí (US$0.50, one hour) leave about every hour from the bus terminal. There are about nine buses a day from the terminal to La Punta (US$0.60, 1½ hours), from where boats cross the river to Ahuano. About five buses a day go to Santa Rosa (US$0.70, two hours). Other local destinations are also served.

ARCHIDONA
☎ 06

Archidona is a small mission village that was founded in 1560 – the same as Tena, which is 10km to the south. Although it can be found on the earliest maps of Ecuador, Archidona has grown little in the intervening centuries.

The main plaza is a small, attractive and well-laid-out forest of tropical palms, vines, ferns, flowers and trees. Such a pretty plaza is a surprise in so small a village; it is probably the work of missionaries. Their carefully but strangely painted concrete-block church is also very colorful. A good day to visit Archidona is Sunday, when the local Quijo Indians come to their weekly market and to hear mass.

From the plaza, you can take a bus to Cotundo and ask to be dropped at the entrance to the **Cuevas de Jumandí**, about 4km north of Archidona. There are three main branches in the cave system, which apparently has not yet been fully explored. There is a snack bar and small amusement park (not always open), as well as a place to stay, by the caves. The entrance to the cave is lighted, but you must bring your own lights and equipment to see the stalagmites and other formations farther in. The cave is muddy, and rubber boots and old clothes are recommended. If you plan on going deep into the cave, you should have a local guide and equipment; entry costs US$0.50. Guides in Tena arrange expeditions into the caves with an overnight by the cave entrance.

These are by far the best known of the many caves in the area, and there are guides available in Tena to show you others. Some of the caves can be visited fairly casually, but many require crawling, wading or even swimming and require technical spelunking gear.

The next town of any importance to the north is Baeza, about 100km away. Baeza is at the junction with the Lago Agrio-Quito road and is described later in this chapter, under West of Lago Agrio.

Places to Stay & Eat

There are a couple of cheap and basic hotels near the plaza. *Residencial Regina* (☎ 889 144) has rooms with private bath and a friendly staff. The cheaper *Residencial Car-*

olina is also OK. There are a few simple and inexpensive places to eat.

VOLCÁN SUMACO

The 3732m cone of Sumaco is surrounded by rainforest and plagued by wet weather, and it is the remotest and least studied of Ecuador's volcanoes. It is dormant at this time, although volcanologists believe it is potentially active. It lies about 27km north of the new Tena-Coca road, from which it can be climbed in about five or six days roundtrip. The road to Coca leaves the Tena-Baeza road to the east about 24km north of Archidona. About 20km along the Coca road after turning off from the Tena-Baeza road, a short dirt road leads to the village of Huamaní.

In Huamaní, guides can be hired for the climb to the summit, which involves poorly marked trails and chopping through the jungle with a machete. It is easy to get lost, and therefore, guides are strongly recommended. Francisco Chimbo and Benjamin Shiguango (ask for them in the village) are experienced. The going rate is about US$12 per day for a guide – plus you have to provide food and shelter for the guide, as well as for yourself. In addition, a US$12 fee per climber is charged; it goes to the community of Huamaní.

Facilities in Huamaní are minimal, so bring food and equipment from Tena. The rainiest months (May to August) turn the trail into a mud bath, and the mountain views are clouded over. The driest months are reportedly October to December – this is the best time to go.

The volcano is within Parque Nacional Sumaco-Galeras, one of the remotest of Ecuador's national parks.

MISAHUALLÍ
☎ 06

This small village (also called Puerto Misahuallí) is at the end of the road running from Puerto Napo along the north bank of Río Napo. Along with Tena, it is a popular place from which to see some of the Oriente, because you can easily get here by bus from Quito in a day, so it is suitable for the traveler with a limited amount of time.

However, before you grab your hammock and pith helmet and jump on the next bus, you should realize that this isn't virgin jungle. The area has been colonized for decades, and most mammals have been either hunted out or had their habitats encroached upon to the point where they cannot survive.

What you will see, if you keep your eyes open – or better still, if you hire a local guide – is a variety of jungle birds, tropical flowers, army ants, dazzling butterflies and other insects.

In addition, you will see the people living in the jungle – colonists, gold-panners, oil workers, farmers, ranchers, military personnel, people in the tourism industry and entrepreneurs. The remaining Indian tribes live deeper into the jungle and, for the most part, prefer to be left alone. Most of the Indians in the area are either transplanted highlanders or acculturated locals.

The physical geography of this area remains rolling and rather rugged. The elevation is about 400m (with hills twice that high within a few kilometers), and there are many more ridges and valleys around here than what you'll see by the time you get to the flatlands of Coca, which is barely 100m above sea level. The more complex geography means that there are still some small areas that haven't been disturbed by colonists because they are hard to get to.

Buses can usually reach Misahuallí in any weather, but roads can be in poor shape during the wettest period (June to August).

If you want an excursion deep into the jungle, it can be arranged in Misahuallí. This

Anteaters are one of several mammals that one may spot in the jungle.

will require time, patience, flexibility and money – but it is still less expensive than jungle expeditions in other countries. Excursions can also be arranged in Coca, Baños, Dureno, Tena and Quito.

Information

There is no bank, nor any post office or Internet facilities (go to Tena for all that). You need to carry your passport on buses, boats and tours in the region.

Organized Tours

Travelers are encouraged to send recommendations and criticisms of guides for the next edition of this book. Tours booked out of Misahuallí cost US$20 to US$50 per person per day. Trips lasting several days need at least four (in some cases, six or eight) participants. Shop around carefully.

Jungle Tours The various restaurants in Misahuallí are good places to meet potential traveling companions for excursions, or to pick the brains of travelers returning from a trip. Any one of the several small restaurants on the plaza is a good place to start. Other places include the restaurant at Hostal Marena International, just off the plaza, and Hotel Albergue Español, just beyond Hostal Marena International. El Paisano restaurant is also popular with travelers. It's a small village, so you'll be able to cruise the likely places in a few minutes. If you want to see some of the river without taking a tour, you can take a trip on a passenger boat as far as Coca. These boats go several times a week.

Even if you don't usually enjoy organized tours, you should consider joining one if you want to see some of the jungle – particularly if this is your first visit. There are several guides available in Misahuallí (and more in nearby Tena) offering various tours ranging from one to 10 days in duration. Usually, you have to get a group together to make it economical. There are often other travelers looking to form a group.

Make sure that whomever you choose to work with gives you a good deal – not just the cheapest, but the best value for your money. Work the details out carefully beforehand to avoid confusion or disappointment. Common sense dictates that you make sure costs, food, equipment, itinerary and group size are all discussed thoroughly before the tour.

The most important matter to settle is the guide; a good guide will be able to show you a lot of things you would have missed on your own – particularly if you convey your enthusiasm and interest by asking questions. An inadequate guide will spoil the trip. Guides should be able to produce a Tourist Guide license on request.

Try to meet with your guide before you leave. Can you communicate adequately? Has he or she done this before? Can she or he show you the *achiote* plant (the red berries of which are crushed to make decorative body paints)? Can he or she find the vine that, when cut, provides water fit to drink? Can you go for a swim by a waterfall, go fishing from a dugout canoe, go bird watching or do whatever it is you want to do? What will be cooked for dinner and breakfast? Will game be hunted for the pot? (The area is overhunted, and a no-hunting policy is encouraged.) A few questions such as these will soon tell you if you and the guide are going to have a good trip together. Make sure that the guide you talk with will be the guide you go with; sometimes, inferior guides are substituted at the last minute. Most people have a great time, especially if they plan their excursion carefully.

One tour provider that has been around for many years is Douglas Clarke's Expeditions (in Tena ☎ 887 584), a block from the plaza; its costs are a bit higher than other outfitters', but the staff can arrange tours in advance, and it has received generally favorable reports. Several of the guides speak some English (despite his name, Douglas is Ecuadorian, and his English is limited). You can take a simple one-day walk as an introduction to the jungle; various plant and insect species are pointed out, and a swim under a hidden waterfall can be included. You can also take four- to eight-day trips, which include camping in a

No Keys in the Jungle

Many of the remoter lodges in the Oriente have a 'no key' policy. This means that none of the rooms has a lock and key. The idea is that you are so far away from civilization that there is no reason to worry about theft. The lodge employees are completely trustworthy (and even if they weren't, they'd have keys to your room, anyway). Generally speaking, this relaxed policy works just fine, but once in a while, something valuable disappears. It is easy to get lulled into a sense of false security by the laid-back attitude in these lodges. Even if you can't lock the room, don't leave your valuables lying around in plain sight – it is simply tempting fate.

jungle camp; all the necessary equipment is provided. Some canoeing in dugouts and hiking is involved. Other trips go to the Coca region, where there is a greater chance of seeing wildlife. These trips can all be organized to leave from Quito. Finally, you can opt for a 10-day trip that takes you far down Río Napo and back up Río Aguarico, with a chance of seeing macaws, parrots, toucans and rarer bird species. Caimans, various monkeys, wild pigs, anteaters or even a jungle cat are also sometimes seen. This trip must be arranged ahead of time. It is a rugged expedition, and there is little comfort. It is not for the fainthearted.

Note that similar expeditions are offered by some of the outfitters listed here, and they are often just as good.

Fluvial River Tours
Héctor Fiallos (☎ 886 189, in Quito 02-239 044) runs this company, which is also called Sacha Tours – it has also been around for years. The office is on the corner of the plaza. Fiallos himself is a good guide, but he has used inferior guides in the past, mixed in with some good ones. This situation seems to be improving according to recent reports, but check guides' licenses.

Misahuallí Tours
On the corner of the plaza, this agency is run by the cheerful and knowledgeable Carlos Lastra Lasso, who speaks some English. He uses good guides who get along well with travelers.

Ecoselva
This outfit is run by English-speaking Pepe Tapia González, who has a biology background. He is on the plaza.

Aventuras Amazónicas
Based in Residencial La Posada, on the plaza, this is run by Carlos and María del Carmen Santander. The staff does a good job.

Expediciones El Albergue Español
This outfit is based at the hotel of the same name, and several of its guides have been recommended.

Waterfall Walk This is a short trip offered by some guides as a one-day look at the local jungle, but it is one you can do yourself quite easily. First, take a Misahuallí-Puerto Napo bus and ask the driver to drop you off at Río Latas, about 15 or 20 minutes away from Misahuallí. All the drivers know *el camino a las cascadas* ('the trail to the falls'). Follow the river upstream to the falls, passing several swimming holes en route. Be prepared to wade. It takes about an hour to reach the falls, depending on how fast you walk. It's a nice place to swim and have a picnic.

Places to Stay & Eat
None of the accommodations in Misahuallí are expensive or particularly luxurious. Water and electricity failures are frequent. Although the cheapest places may look pretty run down, don't let their appearances make you think they are dangerous. They aren't – they are just cheap, beat-up jungle hotels.

On the plaza, you'll find *Residencial El Balcón de Napo*, which has small, concrete-block rooms – some of which look like jail cells. The rooms with windows are OK. The residencial is fairly clean by jungle standards, although the showers are a bit grungy. Rates are just under US$2 per person, making it the area's cheapest place to stay. Nearby, the rambling old *Residencial La Posada* charges about US$2.50 per person and has been renovated; some rooms have private baths.

El Paisano hotel and restaurant is popular with travelers. It is 100m from the plaza on the road past the military post and is well known. Clean, basic doubles with private bath are US$10. There is a pleasant garden with hammocks, and the open-air restaurant provides vegetarian dishes if requested in advance.

Half a block from the plaza is *Hostal Marena Internacional* (☎ 887 584), which has a rooftop restaurant with a view. Rates are about US$6 per person for large rooms with private bath. This hotel was formerly called the Dayuma and is part of Douglas Clarke's Expeditions.

The Spanish-run *Hotel Albergue Español* (☎ 09-558 360, in Quito ☎/fax 02-221 626) charges about US$6 per person with private bath – water is heated by solar energy. Group discounts are offered. Rooms are clean and have fans; some have river views. There is a restaurant, and the management is helpful. It is about 200m off the plaza, past Hostal Marena Internacional. The owners also have a lodge about 90 minutes away by boat; cabins with private bath sleep up to six people and cost US$35 per person, including transportation and meals. Also a few minutes from the plaza, *France Amazonia* (☎/fax 887 570) has six attractive stone cabins with thatched roof and private hot bath. Four are doubles, and two are triples. Rates are US$10 per person, and local tours can be arranged. The French owner provides decent meals.

Misahuallí Jungle Lodge is across Río Misahuallí, on the north side of Río Napo. Reservations can be arranged through its office in Quito (☎ 02-520 043, 504 872, fax 255 354, miltour@accessinter.net, Ramírez Dávalos 251). It's a comfortable lodge, with a pool, nice cabins, electricity, private baths, hot water and a number of trails. Guides are available. Rates are about US$60 a day in Quito, but if you just show up, you can get rooms with meals for much less if it's not busy.

There are various other lodges downriver from Misahuallí; they are described in the following sections of this chapter.

Getting There & Away

Bus Buses leave from the plaza about every hour during daylight hours; the last bus is at 6 pm. The main destination is Tena (US$0.50, one hour), where you can make connections to other places. Transportes Jumandy has a direct bus from Quito at 11 am, returning from Misahuallí at 8:30 am (US$3.50, seven hours).

Boat Motorized dugout canoes leave from the port for various destinations downriver. The port is a block away from the plaza. Since the opening of the Tena-Coca road and the construction of roads east along Río Napo, river traffic has dwindled, and most locals go by bus, because it is cheaper and more reliable.

It is still possible, however, to travel downriver by taking the occasional public canoe or by arranging a private charter. You are required to register with the *capitanía* (port captain) if heading downriver.

A passenger boat leaves every morning at 10:30 am for Coca, but it will go only with a minimum of six passengers for Coca. It may be several days between departures if there aren't enough people. The boat drops people off in the villages or settlements of (in geographical order) Ahuano, Anaconda Island, Hotel Jaguar, Santa Rosa, Mondaña (for Yachana Lodge) and Bellavista. This last village is about halfway to Coca. The fare to Coca is about US$20. If there are fewer people, the fare is about US$160 divided among the passengers, and you can leave any day. The journey to Coca takes about six hours if the river is running normally.

You won't see much wildlife, as the area is heavily colonized. Little houses on stilts huddle on the bank, prospectors pan for gold by the river's edge, and colonists wave and whistle for a ride. Impossibly tiny dugout canoes, loaded to the gunwales with an Indian family perched on a pile of

bananas, are steadily and gracefully poled upriver. Sudden rain showers force passengers to hurriedly dig out sheets of plastic but can enhance the beauty of the river. The jungle glows green in the late-afternoon sun, and a few pure white clouds suspended in a perfectly blue sky contrast dramatically with the muddy flowing river. The scenery is worth the discomfort.

Read the Dugout Canoe section in the Getting Around chapter for more information on traveling in this way.

JATUN SACHA
☎ 06

Jatun Sacha means 'big forest' in the Quichua language. This is a biological station and rainforest reserve on the south side of Río Napo, 23km east of Puerto Napo. It is run by Fundación Jatun Sacha (in Quito ☎ 02-432 240/173/246, fax 453 583, jatsacha@jsacha.ecuanex.net.ec), Pasaje Eugenio de Santillán N34-248 and Maurián, Urbanización Rumipamba, Quito; there is a Web site at www.jatunsacha.org. This nonprofit Ecuadorian organization was founded in 1985 with the goal of promoting rainforest research, conservation and education. The foundation also operates the Reserva Biológica Bilsa (see the Western Lowlands chapter) and the Reserva Biológica Guandera (see the North of Quito chapter).

At Jatun Sacha, scientists are currently carrying out surveys of what species are present. This may appear to be a simple task, but it is complicated by the fact that the area is one of the most species-rich regions on earth. Some of the plants and animals found here are unknown to science – exciting stuff! Herpetologists (scientists who study reptiles) claim that there are more species of 'herps' here than almost anywhere on the globe. Botanists echo this with regards to flowering plants. The reserve has expanded in size from an original 300 hectares in 1985 to 2000 hectares in 2000 – and a final total of about 4500 hectares is hoped for. Much of it is primary forest, although it is broken up by cleared sections. There are a few kilometers of trails and a small botanical garden.

Entrance is US$6, and a local guide can be hired for a few dollars more.

Unfortunately, neighboring areas are being rapidly cleared for logging and agriculture, and it is not known how long the incredible biodiversity of Jatun Sacha will remain. One of the goals of the foundation, however, is the furthering of rural development projects, which will help residents engage in economically viable and sustainable activities as an alternative to deforestation. Volunteers are welcome to apply for a variety of projects – the minimum stay is usually a month.

Jatun Sacha is one of the longest-standing and best local conservation and environmental projects in Ecuador. Tax-deductible (for US citizens) donations can be made to Rainforest Action Network (☎ 415-398-4404), 221 Pine St, Suite 500, San Francisco, CA 94104 USA.

Places to Stay & Eat

At the *research station* itself, there are four unscreened buildings that sleep about 30 people. Accommodations are primitive – bunk beds, mosquito nets and outdoor showers and latrines. A dining room and meals are available. Researchers and students can stay here for US$20 a day, including meals and access to the reserve trail system. Tourists (on a space-available basis) pay US$30 a day, including meals. Volunteers stay here at a very modest cost – about US$6 a day, including food.

Most tourists stay at *Cabañas Aliñahui* (also called 'the Butterfly Lodge'), which is partly owned and operated by Fundación Jatun Sacha. Aliñahui is about 3km east of the research station. There are about eight simple but comfortable screened cabins with electricity (solar panels); most cabins have two to four double rooms sharing one bathroom with a solar-heated shower. Each cabin has a shady patio with a hammock. There is an open-sided restaurant, bar and gift shop. The site is on a bluff above the river, and there are several thatched shelters with excellent views of the river and (on clear days) four of the Andean volcanoes – hence the name Aliñahui, which means 'good view'

in Quichua. These shelters are great places to relax.

Both jungle hikes and boat trips can be arranged to Jatun Sacha, to visit local villages that have ecotourism programs, or to pan for gold. Some of the staff and guides speak English, German or French. The food is plentiful, homemade and good. Several readers have recommended this place as one of Ecuador's best environmentally conscious lodges. Rates are US$60 per person per day, including three meals, or US$75 per day with guided tours. Multiday packages can also be arranged. Reservations can be made at Fundación Jatun Sacha (see the contact information provided earlier in this section) for both the research station and Aliñahui, or at the Quito office of Aliñahui (☎ 02-253 267, fax 02-253 266, alinahui@interactive.net.ec), Los Shyris 760 and República de El Salvador, office 204.

Getting There & Away

Motor canoes can be hired from Misahuallí for the approximately 10km downriver trip to Aliñahui or the reserve. Most visitors come by land. Jatun Sacha can help arrange transportation from Quito if your group takes one of its multiday tours. Otherwise, the best way is to go to Tena and take the Tena-Ahuano bus.

AHUANO
☎ 06

This small mission village is about one hour downriver from Misahuallí and can also be reached by bus from Tena to La Punta, followed by a river crossing. This is the end of the road – beyond Ahuano, you must travel by boat on Río Napo as far as Coca, where you can rejoin the road again. There is not much to do in Ahuano itself, although there are some nearby jungle lodges. There are a couple of basic stores but little other infrastructure in this village.

Places to Stay

Ask in the village about basic pensiones. The cheapest is *Hostal Samantha*, which charges about US$2 for a bed. *Casa de Stefan* has four rooms with private bath and four with shared bath. Curiously, rates are the same in both – US$10 per person, including breakfast, plus US$5 for lunch or dinner.

The comfortable *Casa del Suizo* is a jungle lodge that can accommodate up to 150 guests – it will be able to handle 170 by the end of 2000. The spacious cabins and rooms are very pleasant, with balconies or terraces, views, private showers, hot water, electricity and ceiling fans. Air-conditioning is being added to some rooms in 2000. International phone connections can be made at the front desk. There is a large, freeform pool and a good restaurant and bar – all in a scenic location by the river, which can be appreciated from a tower above the restaurant. On a clear day, you can see Andean volcanoes from there. The restaurant serves international and Ecuadorian buffets, with plenty to choose from – including vegetarian choices. The lodge has been recommended by travelers who want a taste of the rainforest without discomfort. There is a variety of tours available, including river trips (one involves returning to the lodge on small homemade balsa rafts – fun for families), jungle hikes, visits to missions and local communities, and wildlife walks, after which you can return to the comfort of the lodge.

Casa del Suizo is run by the same folks that run Sacha Lodge (see Along Río Napo from Coca, later in this chapter). The Quito office (☎ 02-566 090, 509 504/115, fax 236 521, sachalod@pi.pro.ec), Zaldumbide 375 and Toledo, takes reservations, although drop-in travelers can often be accepted because the large lodge is rarely full (except for holidays). You can visit the Web site at www.sachalodge.com. Rates for a four-day/three-night visit are US$210 per person for doubles/triples and US$273 for singles (although the single rate is only charged when the hotel is full). This rate includes meals and tours with bilingual guides. For an extra US$88 per person, private roundtrip transportation from Quito is available, including a stop in Papallacta for a dip in the hot springs and lunch (see Papallacta, under West of Lago Agrio, later in this chapter). These trips leave Quito every Wednesday, or any other day when there is at least four people. Rates for one night (or extra nights) are US$70 per person, including meals. Family rates include a 30% hotel discount for children under 12 and free bed and transportation for children under five. Longer stays can be arranged, including combination stays with Sacha Lodge.

Cabañas Anaconda (in Quito ☎/fax 02-545 426), on Anaconda Island, a few minutes from Ahuano, is a jungle-style lodge – it has bamboo walls and thatched roofs. Rooms have comfortable beds, mosquito screens and private bath but no electricity or hot water. Rates are about US$45 per person per day, including good meals; transportation from Quito is available (but pricey). Canoe trips and jungle excursions from the island are available at an extra cost; English-speaking guides are available with advance request. You'll see pet animals such as monkeys and peccaries; some of the caged exhibits have been criticized as being too small.

Getting There & Away

Bus Buses from Tena run eight times a day to La Punta, about 28km east of Puerto Napo on the south side of Río Misahuallí. (This bus can drop you off at Jatun Sacha and at the entrance to Cabañas Aliñahui, which leaves you with a 1km walk to the cabins themselves.) Even though the bus doesn't actually go to Ahuano, it's still called the Ahuano bus locally, because there isn't much happening at La Punta. There is no problem crossing Río Napo from La Punta to Ahuano.

Boat Dugout canoes wait at La Punta to take you across to Ahuano. The fare is about US$1 per person, and there are frequent boats, particularly after a bus arrives. Chartering your own boat costs more. These boats can drop you off at Casa del Suizo or Cabañas Anaconda (the latter costs several dollars.)

You can also get to Ahuano or any of the lodges by boat from Misahuallí. For more information, see the Misahuallí section, earlier. Most people go via bus to La Punta because it's a more frequent and less expensive service.

SELVA VIVA
☎ 06

This is a newly protected preserve of about 1000 hectares of primary forest surrounding the well-known AmaZOOnico animal-rehabilitation center. It's on a tributary of Río Napo about 3km east of Ahuano. The center was founded in 1994 by Angelika Raimann and Remigio Canelos (a Swiss/Quichua couple) to care for rainforest animals that have been confiscated from illegal traffickers or otherwise injured. Healthy animals are released back into the rainforest.

There are dozens of animals on the premises at any time, ranging from toucans to tapirs. The center is run on a bare-bones budget, and donations and volunteers (with veterinary skills) are welcomed. Admission to the center is about US$1.

Since the center opened, the owners have bought the surrounding rainforest and opened *Liana Lodge* to help fund both the rehab center and the new preserve. The lodge has six cabins, each with two double rooms with private hot shower and a view of the river. Rates are US$39 per person, including meals, taxes and local tours.

Selva Viva can be reached from La Punta (see Ahuano, earlier) by boat for about US$10. For cheaper access, take one of several daily buses from Tena to Santa Rosa, which is reached by a road branching off from the Tena-La Punta road. Ask the driver to stop at the Selva Viva entrance, and hike almost 2km downstream to the lodge. Call the lodge with your arrival time, and they can send someone to meet you with a canoe for US$1.50 (or for free if you are staying at the lodge).

For information and reservations, contact Selva Viva (☎/fax 887 304, amazoon@ na.pro.ec). English, Spanish, German, French and Quichua are spoken.

JAGUAR LODGE
This lodge is about 1½ hours from Misahuallí. Most visitors arrive by boat from Misahuallí, where there are more boats than in Ahuano.

This is a comfortable, modern hotel on the banks of Río Napo. It has about a dozen rooms with private bath (hot water and electricity are available when the generator is running), a swimming pool, an attractive main lodge with good views, a decent restaurant and bar, and a cable TV lounge. Spanish-speaking guides are available for a variety of guided tours. Rates start at US$28/39 for singles/doubles, and various overnight packages with meals and tours can be arranged at the Quito office (in Quito ☎ 02-523 577, fax 02-226 391), Leonidas Plaza Gutiérrez 180, near 18 de Septiembre.

YACHANA LODGE
This ecotourism lodge is part of an impressive project called FUNEDESIN (Foundation for Integrated Education and Development), an NGO whose mission statement is finding workable solutions in the struggle between the ideals of rainforest preservation and the realities of life in the Ecuadorian Amazon. The lodge not only uses local labor to provide visitors with a rainforest experience, it also is the center of a complex of other projects, such as organic agriculture, beekeeping, agricultural training, food processing, a clinic and associated health education, a canoe ambulance, emergency radio communication with remote villages and local empowerment through community organization. Visitors are encouraged to tour the various facilities.

It is important to note that the community is strongly involved in the projects – locals don't just accept them as handouts. The medical facilities are not free, for example. Villagers needing health care but unable to make a financial contribution can pay with a sack of fruit (which is then used in the food-processing plant to make jam, chutney, dried fruit etc), or they can contribute labor to the ongoing needs of the project.

The Yachana Lodge complex is in the tiny community of Mondaña, almost halfway between Misahuallí and Coca on

Río Napo. The lodge itself has 11 rooms (each sleeping two or three people) and three family cabins with a double and a triple room. Each room has a private shower and a balcony. Water is heated by a unique method, whereby about 90m of coiled copper tubing is covered by waste coffee husks from a local coffee-peeling machine. The waste acts as a compost pile and generates its own heat, and water emerging from the pipes is too hot to touch! Lighting is by solar power. There is a small conference center and library, a deck with a view and a restaurant serving tasty meals that are locally influenced and lean toward the vegetarian, chicken and fish end of the culinary spectrum.

Visitors typically stay for three or four nights, with set departures from Quito on Wednesdays and Saturdays (although other departure days or longer stays can be arranged with advance notice). The four-day/three-night option is US$320, and the five-day/four-night option is US$400. Children 12 and under are charged half those prices. Costs include everything except alcohol, soft drinks, personal expenses and (optional) air transportation from Quito to Coca (US$110 roundtrip). The lodge staff have jointly decided not to ask for gratuities. From Coca, it is a two-hour motorized canoe ride to the lodge, arriving by lunch on the first day. On the last day, guests are back in Coca in time to catch the late-morning flight back to Quito.

During the stay at the lodge, you can take part in a traditional healing ceremony, go on guided hikes along 20km of trails, take day or night rides in a canoe, take a class in basket weaving from a local expert, visit the projects in the area or just relax in a hammock. Local guides and Yachana's naturalists are treasure troves of information and speak excellent English. (For guides that speak other languages, make an advance request, and expect to pay more.)

Reservations should be made in Quito at FUNEDESIN/Yachana Lodge (in Quito ☎ 02-237 133/278, fax 02-220 362, info@yachana.com), Andrade Marín 1888. You can visit the Web site at www.yachana.com.

COCA
☎ 06
With 17,000 inhabitants, this is the capital of the new (in 1999) Orellana Province, which used to be the eastern part of Napo Province. Ecuadorian maps show the town's official name, Puerto Francisco de Orellana, but everyone calls it Coca. Located at the junction of Ríos Napo and Coca (hence its popular name), its official name derives from the fact that Francisco de Orellana came through here on his way to 'discover' the Amazon in 1542.

The Coca of today is a sprawling oil town with little to recommend about it, although it has a strange appeal for some travelers. There are few street signs, and every street except the main street, Napo, is unpaved and hence covered with dust, puddles or mud, depending on the season. Many of the buildings are just shacks, and the place has a real shantytown appearance – there isn't even a town plaza. However, with its new provincial capital status, the town may improve. A local tourist industry has developed because Coca is closer to primary rainforest than Misahuallí. Coca itself may not be especially attractive, but it is the haunt of oil workers and tourists looking for jungle expeditions.

Information
A tourist-information office is intermittently open at the dock on Río Napo. Information about nearby national parks may still be available from the old INEFAN office (☎ 880 171), on Amazonas at Bolívar. The Andinatel office is open 8 to 12:30 pm, 1:30 am to 4 pm and 6 to 9 pm weekdays and 8 to 11 am and 5 to 8 pm weekends. There is a post office, but service is very slow.

Don't plan on using traveler's checks or credit cards. Medical services are limited; Clínica Sinai, at Napo and García Moreno, is better than the hospital.

Travelers arriving and departing by river must register their passport at the capitanía, by the landing dock.

Organized Tours
Read the section on Jungle Tours under Misahuallí, earlier, for general information that is also useful for tours out of Coca.

Coca is closer to the Huaorani (Auca) Indian villages than other any major town in the Oriente, and tours are available to visit these villages. Some tours may have a negative impact on the Indians, who prefer to be left alone in some areas – don't take any tour that involves visits to the Huaorani unless the guides have been approved by the tribe (see the boxed text 'Visiting the Huaorani').

Guides charge around US$35 per person per day, and group sizes are usually four to six people. Smaller groups have to pay more per person. It is easier to find people to make up a group in Quito or Misahuallí than it is in Coca, but prices may be higher if the trip is booked in Quito. Trips usually last three to 10 days. You may have to bargain to get the best rate, but make sure everything you expect is included. Note that some outfits may charge as little as US$20 or as much as US$70 a day. The cheapest outfitters have unreliable boats, poor food, and guides that don't speak English. If you go with a cheap one, don't be surprised if you have to spend the night on the side of the river because your boat's engine breaks down!

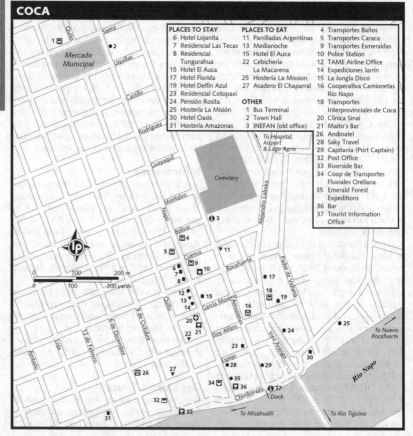

COCA

PLACES TO STAY
6 Hotel Lojanita
7 Residencial Las Tecas
8 Residencial Tungurahua
15 Hotel El Auca
17 Hotel Florida
19 Hotel Delfín Azul
23 Residencial Cotopaxi
24 Pensión Rosita
25 Hostería La Misión
30 Hotel Oasis
31 Hostería Amazonas

PLACES TO EAT
11 Parrilladas Argentinas
13 Medianoche
15 Hotel El Auca
22 Cebichería La Macarena
25 Hostería La Mission
27 Asadero El Chaparral

OTHER
1 Bus Terminal
2 Town Hall
3 INEFAN (old office)
4 Transportes Baños
5 Transportes Caraca
9 Transportes Esmeraldas
10 Police Station
12 TAME Airline Office
14 Expediciones Jarrín
15 La Jungla Disco
16 Cooperativa Camionetas Río Napo
18 Transportes Interprovinciales de Coca
20 Clínica Sinai
21 Maito's Bar
26 Andinatel
28 Saky Travel
29 Capitanía (Port Captain)
32 Post Office
33 Riverside Bar
34 Coop de Transportes Fluviales Orellana
35 Emerald Forest Expeditions
36 Bar
37 Tourist Information Office

Tour agencies and guides change often; as Misahuallí becomes less central, guides move from there to Coca or Tena. As Baños experiences its volcanic problems, guides from there move to other places looking for work. Coca's new provincial-capital status attracts new guides. Every year yields a new crop of guides, ranging from experienced but expensive to cheap but disorganized.

Hotel El Auca doesn't arrange tours but is probably one of the best places in town to meet guides looking for work, as well as to meet other travelers who can tell you of their experiences or help form a group. Ask here about guides to the rarely visited Parque Nacional Sumaco-Galeras. Opposite this hotel, Expediciones Jarrín is one of the cheapest outfits in town, but there have been negative reports about the services it provides (poor equipment and poor guides who speak no English) – but shoestringers looking for adventure might take this all in stride.

Among the best-established guides is Luís García, who runs Emerald Forest Expeditions (☎ 881 155, in Quito ☎/fax 02-541 543, emerald@ecuanex.net.ec), on Napo near the waterfront. This place has some English-speaking guides. Standard trips last from four days/three nights to seven days/six nights, at US$220 to US$385 per person; there is a two-person minimum and a 10-person maximum. Accommodations consist of camping or rustic lodges. Other trips can be arranged, starting at US$35 a day, depending on group size and the services required.

A good source of information about the Huaorani is Randy Smith (☎ 880 489, 881 563, in Quito 02-540 346, panacocha@hotmail.com, Casilla 17-21-841), a Canadian who has more than a decade of experience living and working with and for the Huaorani. You can visit his Web site at www.aamazon-green-magician.com. Randy lives in Coca, but he is sometimes in the jungle for weeks, so allow time to arrange a tour with him. Anybody in Coca knows where he lives, and sometimes, his Quichua partner, Ramiro Viteri, can help you out – he speaks some English. Randy is knowledgeable and opinionated (see the Books section of the Facts for the Visitor chapter), and he leads a somewhat alternative lifestyle, partly because of living like a Huaorani for years – if you can deal with it, you can have a rewarding experience.

Tropic Ecological Adventures (see Travel Agencies under Quito) also does tours to Huaorani territory. Kem Pery Tours (see Travel Agencies under Quito) does tours to Bataboro Lodge, on the edge of Huaorani territory (see Vía Auca, later in this chapter).

The folks at Hotel Oasis (see Places to Stay, later) own Yarina Lodge, an hour downriver from Coca, and the Yuturi Lodge, several hours from Coca (see Along Río Napo from Coca, later, for descriptions of both lodges). Saky Travel, on Espejo near Napo, also organizes jungle tours.

Guides who have been recommended for travel outside of Huarani territory include Whymper Torres of Selva Tour (☎ 880 336). He is entertaining, but he allegedly hunts for tourists' meals and catches animals for photo opportunities – activities that should not be encouraged. Ernesto and Patricio Juanka have received several warm recommendations, but apparently they are trying to start up an office in Quito. Hostal El Auca (see Places to Stay, later) should be able to let you know how to contact them.

Places to Stay

Hotels in Coca sometimes suffer from water shortages in the showers and lavatories.

Budget The best of the super-cheapies is *Hotel Lojanita* (☎ 880 032), on Napo at Cuenca – it has clean rooms and shared cold baths at about US$2 per person, or US$3 with private bath and fan. On the same block, *Residencial Las Tecas* and *Residencial Tungurahua* are very basic and not recommended for solo women travelers. The similarly priced *Pensión Rosita* (☎ 880 167) is one of the hotels nearest to the port, and it is often crowded and noisy. It has variously been described by travelers as musty, dirty and barely habitable – it's also a poor

Visiting the Huaorani

Trips are sometimes offered in Misahuallí, Tena or Coca to visit the villages of 'primitive' Huaorani (Auca) Indians – getting to these villages usually requires a two- or three-day walk into the jungle.

If going on one of these tours, go with a guide who is a Huaorani or who has had a long and understanding relationship with the tribe. Some non-Huaorani guides are insensitive to the needs of this Indian group, which is undergoing the painful process of integration into 21st-century life. A few guides are just inexperienced local youngsters trying to make a living, and through simple ignorance or sheer bravado, the Indians are treated in a degrading or abusive manner.

During the 1980s, poorly led groups of tourists were regularly taken to gawk at 'real' Indians in the 'real' jungle. The Indians stared miserably and with little interest at the frequent hordes of tourists and the parade of goods that to travelers seemed basic: backpacks, a change of clothing, sleeping bags, rain gear, sunglasses, cameras, penknives, cigarette lighters, plastic water bottles, canned food and so on.

The tourists expected and demanded the basic necessities of water and a place to sleep, while the tribe's thoughts were ignored and little was given in return. Finally, in 1990, Moi Vicente Enomenga, the coordinator of the first Huaorani National Assembly, wrote that this exploitation had to stop, that tours were banned in Huaorani territory, and that this would be enforced by spears and arrows if necessary. These efforts led to a marked decrease in tourism in the area for a few years.

Although some remote Huaorani villages still don't want to see outsiders, in the last few years, other villages have made arrangements with trusted guides. Some of the best are listed under Coca in this chapter. Moi himself is also now working at allowing non-exploitative tourism in the area (read *Savages*, by Joe Kane, for more on this story).

choice for single women. The **Residencial Cotopaxi**, at Amazonas and Espejo, is slightly better at US$3 per person with bath.

The friendly **Hotel Oasis** (☎ 880 206) costs US$3 per person for basic rooms with cold bath and fan. The staff can arrange trips to the Yuturi and Yarina Lodges farther down Río Napo (See Along Río Napo from Coca, later in this chapter). **Hotel Florida** (☎ 880 177) is dark and dismal but otherwise OK. Rooms have a bath and TV, and rates are US$4/7. Another bearable choice at this price is **Hotel Delfín Azul**.

Hotel El Auca (☎ 880 127, 880 600) is popular and often full by mid-afternoon. Most rooms now have fans and private hot showers for about US$5 or US$6 per person. It has the nicest garden in Coca and an acceptable restaurant. This is the best budget choice.

Hostería Amazonas (☎ 880 444) charges US$6 to US$8 per person for plain but clean rooms with electric hot shower, TV and fan. Some rooms have river views or refrigerators.

Mid-Range On the riverfront, **Hostería La Misión** (☎ 880 260/544, fax 880 263, in Quito ☎/fax 02-564 675) is the best hotel, at US$14/19 for rooms with fan or US$18/25 for rooms with air-conditioning. All rooms have hot water and cable TV; some have a minifridge. The air-conditioned rooms are in high demand and are often booked ahead. There is a good, slightly pricey restaurant and bar. There is also a pool with a waterslide and river views.

Places to Eat

The restaurants at Hostería La Misión and Hotel El Auca are considered among the best in town. **Medianoche**, opposite Hotel El Auca, stays open late and is good – especially for chicken. The locally popular **Parrilladas Argentinas**, upstairs at Amazonas and Cuenca, is the best place for a steak, but not much else is on the menu. The airy windows are a plus. **Asadero El Chaparral**, on Espejo near 9 de Octubre, is another place to eat meat – and it's cheaper and more down home than Parrilladas Argentinas. For fish, try *Cebichería La Macarena*, on Eloy Alfaro near Quito.

Entertainment

La Jungla Disco, over the restaurant of Hotel El Auca, is the place to dance on weekends. *Bar*, at the south end of Napo (formerly the well-known Papa Dan's), has a tropical feel and an outdoor garden, as does the *riverside bar* at the southwest end of Chimborazo, which may have dancing on weekends. Another popular place is *Maito's Bar*, on Napo. As is true of all bars in Coca, unaccompanied females may receive unwanted attention.

Getting There & Around

Air Aerogal (☎ 881 452/3), at the Coca airport, offers regular service from and to Quito (US$53). Flights return to Quito at 11:30 am Monday to Saturday, with additional 4:45 pm flights on Monday and Friday. These times change often. The TAME office, on Napo at Rocafuerte, will sell tickets for these flights, but it does not operate them at this time. Flights are often overbooked, and reconfirming is essential; however, you can sometimes get a seat on the day of the flight.

The airport terminal is almost 2km north of town on the left-hand side of the road to Lago Agrio. A taxi ride there costs about US$1.

Bus A bus terminal is at the north end of town, but a few buses still leave from offices in the town center (see the Coca map). The situation is changeable, so make careful inquiries about the departure point of your bus.

Transportes Baños has several daily buses to Quito (US$9, nine to 13 hours, depending on the route). Transportes Jumandy, in the bus terminal, has several buses a day on the new road to Tena (US$6, seven hours). Transportes Esmeraldas has a night bus to Quito. All three companies have buses to Lago Agrio (US$2, three hours). Transportes Caraca has a 3 pm bus that goes to Guayaquil. Transportes Loja, at the terminal, has various buses with

frequently changing schedules. Transportes Interprovinciales de Coca has ramshackle buses that go south to Río Tiguino at 7 am, 11 am and 1 pm.

Open-sided trucks called *rancheras* leave from the terminal for various destinations between Coca and Lago Agrio, and to Río Tiputini to the south. Pickup trucks and taxis at Cooperativa Camionetas Río Napo provide service to just about anywhere you want to pay to go.

Boat Since the completion of the new Tena-Coca road, it is difficult to get boats to Misahuallí. Usually, at least 10 passengers are required, and the trip takes about 14 hours, so you are advised to take the trip in the opposite direction, from Misahuallí to Coca, which takes only six hours. The boat fare is about US$20, so the bus (to Tena and then change) is much cheaper and quicker.

The capitanía may be able to give you information about getting a boat farther downriver. Alternatively, you can just go down to the boat dock and ask around.

Destinations of interest downriver include the Pompeya and Limoncocha area, Sacha Lodge, La Selva Jungle Lodge, Pañacocha, Yuturi Lodge and Nuevo Rocafuerte (all these places are described later in this chapter). Boat services to these destinations are irregular, infrequent and comparatively expensive. Coop de Transportes Fluviales Orellana has a weekly passenger boat for Nuevo Rocafuerte (nine to 15 hours) at 8 am Monday morning, returning Friday. The fare is about US$20. Otherwise, you have to hire your own boat, which is expensive.

VÍA AUCA
☎ 06

This road from Coca crosses Río Napo and continues south across Río Tiputini and Río Shiripuno, ending near the small community of Tiguino, on Río Tiguino. There are daily rancheras that go as far as Tiguino. This used to be Huaorani territory and virgin jungle. Vía Auca is an oil-exploitation road that was built in the 1980s. The Huaorani have been pushed eastward (some groups went westward) into their new reserve. The jungle is being colonized, and cattle ranches and oil rigs are replacing the jungle. This is what happens when an oil-exploitation road goes in. Conservationists are trying to prevent this from happening along the road built by Maxus in Parque Nacional Yasuní (see that section, later in this chapter).

The rivers crossed by the road provide access to remote parts of both the Huaorani Reserve and Yasuní, but you should seek the local advice of authorized guides about the advisability of taking trips down these rivers. Some tours may be possible, but others enter the territories of Huaoranis, who either are strongly opposed to tourism or want to manage it on their own terms. Taking the road to Tiguino in the morning and returning to Coca is no problem if you are interested in seeing what it looks like. The trip takes about three or four hours and costs about US$3. If you leave first thing in the morning, you will have no problem doing the roundtrip.

Three to four hours downriver on Río Tiguino is the remote and simple *Bataboro Lodge*, which is sometimes inaccessible during very high or low water levels. There is only river transportation Monday and Friday. The lodge charges US$55 per person for rooms with shared bath, and there are two rooms with private bath for US$75, including meals and transportation from Coca. It's in a remote area, and upkeep of the trails is erratic. Safari Tours and Kem Pery Tours (see Travel Agencies under Quito) have information about this lodge.

ALONG RÍO NAPO FROM COCA
☎ 06

Several jungle lodges can be reached by boat from Coca.

Yarina Lodge

Just an hour downstream from Coca, this lodge has 20 rustic cabins with private baths. The surroundings offer river views, some short trails and the opportunity to watch birds and paddle canoes. Spanish-speaking local guides offer tours. Rates are a reason-

able US$30 per person, including meals and some tours; bilingual naturalist guides are available at an extra cost. Multinight tours are available. This place is a reasonable choice for budget travelers seeking a comfortable introductory jungle experience. Information and reservations can be obtained at Hotel Oasis (see Places to Stay under Coca, earlier).

Pompeya and Limoncocha Area

Pompeya is a Catholic mission about two hours downriver from Coca on Río Napo. There is a school and a small archaeology museum there, and *basic food and lodging* can be arranged. The museum has a fine collection of indigenous artifacts from the Río Napo area and pre-Columbian ceramics. A small admission fee is charged. Some archaeologists believe that before the arrival of Europeans, the indigenous population of Río Napo (and other parts of the Amazon Basin) was many times greater than it is today.

From Pompeya, you can walk 8km north on a new road to the ex-North American mission of Limoncocha, where there is a *basic place to stay and eat* (US$2 per person). Nearby, the locally run Limoncocha Biological Reserve has a lake that recommended for bird watching at dawn and dusk. Oil-company operations jeopardized the lake and the birds in the 1980s and early 1990s. However, the creation of the reserve led to an improvement of the oil-company operations, and the birds are recovering. The reserve has a *rustic lodge* with about a dozen rooms – each with a cold shower and four beds. Food is available, and local guides can take you around the lake, although they do not speak English. Overnight stays cost less than US$20 per person, including meals, but it is not easy to make reservations – ask around in Coca, or just show up.

To get to Pompeya, take a boat from Coca – ask at the docks. Limoncocha can also be reached by bus (several a day) from the oil town of **Shushufindi**, a two- or three-hour trip from either Coca or Lago Agrio. In Shushufindi, there are several basic places to stay; *Hotel Shushufundi* is better than most. A local guide charmingly describes the town as having 40 prostitutes and no doctors. The police in this area are said to be particularly corrupt and have been known to steal valuables at a passport checkpoint on this road. Keep alert. Two daily buses from Shushufindi to Limoncocha continue to Pompeya.

Sacha Lodge

Opened in 1992, this Swiss-run lodge provides comfortable accommodations in the deep jungle. Sacha Lodge is built on the banks of Laguna El Pilche, a lake about 1km north of Río Napo. Getting there is half the fun – a three-hour ride in a fast motor-canoe from Coca is followed by a walk through the forest on an elevated boardwalk and then a 15-minute paddle in a dugout canoe to the lodge.

The main building – which has a restaurant, bar and small library – is three stories high and has a little observation deck at the top. It is linked by boardwalks to 10 cabins, each with two rooms. Each room has a private bath and hot water (a rarity in this neck of the woods), as well as a deck and hammock with fine forest views. All rooms are screened (although mosquitoes don't seem to be a problem) and have electric lights and ceiling fans. Buffet-style meals are plentiful and delicious, and both vegetarians and meat-eaters are catered to well.

Possible activities include hiking, canoeing and swimming. Hikes and canoe trips are made in small groups, typically consisting of about five tourists and two guides. One guide is a local, and the other is usually a bilingual naturalist guide – their experience and interests vary, so ask if you have particular interests. A network of trails ensures that you get to explore different places every day. Trails vary in length, and destinations include flat rainforest; hilly rainforest; and various lakes, rivers and swamps – each have different types of flora and fauna. A 43-meter-high observation deck atop a huge ceiba tree (reached by stairs built around the tree's trunk) is a few minutes' walk away from the main lodge. A

canopy walkway is under construction. A butterfly farm provides educational and photographic possibilities. Special interests, such as bird watching, photography, plants or fishing, can be catered to with advance request (each guide has different specialities), and a birding list is available. Tours to Indian villages are not arranged.

Most guests come either on a four-day/three-night or a five-day/four-night package – the first option is Friday-to-Monday, and the second is Monday-to-Friday. Once you arrive, you won't be disturbed by a new influx of guests until it's time to leave. On your arrival day, you arrive early enough for a short afternoon hike, but on your departure day, you leave before dawn. Rates are US$577 per person for the three-night trip and US$720 for the four-night trip, and singles cost US$695/870, although you won't be forced to pay this rate unless the lodge is full. Airfare is an additional US$120 roundtrip from Quito to Coca, but you can meet the tour at Coca and travel overland.

Reservations should be made at the Quito office (☎ 02-566 090, 509 504/115, fax 236 521, sachalod@pi.pro.ec), Zaldumbide 375. You can visit the Web site at www.sachalodge.com.

Añangucocha Lodge

This is a new and rustic lodge on Laguna Añangucocha, which is reached by paddling for about two hours up a narrow blackwater tributary of Río Napo. Facilities are still being developed but consist of simple palm-thatch huts and separate latrines. The manager, Jiovanny Rivadeneyra, is well known in Ecuadorian birding circles as an excellent guide. Wildlife viewing and bird watching in this remote area is excellent, and Jiovanny works hard to make you feel as welcome and as comfortable as possible.

Currently, the rate is US$25 per person, including meals and transportation, but this price will rise once the lodge's facilities improve. In addition, there is a US$10 fee, because the lodge is within Parque Nacional Yasuní. Volunteers to help build the lodge and teach English to locals are accepted.

Reservations and information are available from Coca guide Oscar Tapuy (☎ 881 486) or from the author of *Common Birds of Amazonian Ecuador*, Chris Canaday (canaday@accessinter.net).

La Selva Jungle Lodge

This North American-run lodge provides a high-quality, responsible tourism experience. Many local people are employed, and the staff offers excursions into the rainforest with informed and interested guides. It also incorporates local food into the cuisine and avoids annoying visits to the unacculturated Indians living in the vicinity. In 1992, the lodge won the World Congress on Tourism and the Environment award.

Accommodations are in 16 double cabins and one family cabin (three rooms), each with private cold bath and mosquito screens. Kerosene lanterns light the rooms. Meals are excellent by any standards and absolutely outstanding for Oriente standards.

There is also a small research facility, where scientists and students can work on their projects. Discounted accommodations are available for researchers if arranged well in advance – often, researchers pay off part of their expenses by giving guided jungle excursions to interested visitors. One project that has been successful is the breeding of butterflies near the lodge. Visitors are able to see this operation, which affords excellent opportunities to photograph rainforest butterflies and learn about their life cycles.

Excursions are accomplished both by dugout canoe and on foot along several kilometers of trails. There is a 35-meter-high canopy platform located about 20 minutes away from the lodge on foot. Bird watching is a highlight – over 500 species have been recorded in the La Selva area, including the rare zigzag heron, which bird watchers from all over the world come to see. About half of Ecuador's 44 species of parrots have been recorded near here, as well as a host of other exotic tropical birds – including toucans, trogons, jacamars, tanagers, antbirds and fruitcrows. Monkeys and other mammals are frequently seen. Of course, there are tens of thousands of plant and insect species.

Small groups of tourists are accompanied by a local indigenous guide and an English-speaking guide (often North American or European). Although the indigenous guides speak no English, my guide had a remarkable 500-word English vocabulary consisting of 'OK' and the names, in English, of all the birds that are seen near the lodge. Our conversations were never very long – 'Zigzag heron, OK?' 'OK!!' was about the extent of one – but I certainly got a lot out of the experience.

The lodge is five to six hours downriver from Coca by regular passenger canoe, but visitors usually pay for a complete package from Quito. This includes air transportation to Coca and river transportation in La Selva's private launches, which go twice as fast as the ordinary passenger boats. The lodge is on Laguna Garzacocha, which is reached by taking a 1km boardwalk through the forest on the north shore of Río Napo. Then, a half-hour paddle in a dugout canoe takes you to the lodge – this part of the journey is wonderful – Garzacocha, with its several tributaries and varying vegetation, must surely be one of the prettiest small jungle lakes anywhere.

The lodge has a four-day/three-night minimum. Prices include river travel from Coca, accommodations, all meals and all guide services. The bar tab, laundry, gratuities and airfare (US$120 roundtrip) is extra.

The three-night package (Wednesday to Saturday) costs about US$550 per person; the four-night package (Saturday to Wednesday) costs US$685 per person. You can combine any number of three- and four-day packages to make seven-, 10-, 11- or 14-day stays – these are discounted. They also arrange a one-week 'Light Brigade' tour, which involves camping in the jungle – but in style! Rates are US$1324 per person.

Information and reservations are available from the Quito office of La Selva (in Quito ☎ 02-554 686, 550 995, fax 02-567 297), 6 de Diciembre 2816. You can visit the Web site at www.laselvajunglelodge.com.

Pañacocha

Pañacocha is Quichua for 'Lake of Piranhas.' There is a small community near the lake where you can stay. Pañacocha is approximately five hours downstream from Coca, or about halfway to Nuevo Rocafuerte.

Cheap accommodations are available at a variety of small local places and private houses, where rates start as low as US$5 for a double. *Cabañas Pañacocha* is used by Randy Smith (see Organized Tours under Coca, earlier) and charges about US$20 per person. The more expensive *Pañacocha Lodge* (in Quito ☎ 541 972/977, Robles 610), near Mera, is another possibility. The very rustic (you have to bathe in the river) *Cabañas Jarrín* can be reserved through Expediciones Jarrín (see Organized Tours under Coca, earlier in this chapter).

A popular activity is to go piranha fishing – the fish are fairly easy to catch and make for good eating, but don't let them get their razor-sharp jaws around your finger, or you might lose it.

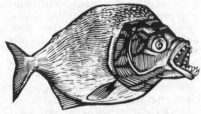

Piranhas are tasty and easy to catch.

Yuturi Lodge

This lodge is built on Río Yuturi, a southern tributary of Río Napo about 20 minutes beyond Pañacocha. There are 15 rustic cabins with private cold showers, mosquito nets and good views. All the guides here are indigenous, so you have to speak Spanish. The usual foot and canoe trips are available. Reservations can be made at Hotel Oasis (see Places to Stay under Coca, earlier) or in Quito at Yuturi Jungle Adventure (in Quito ☎/fax 504 037, 503 225, 544 166, yuturi@yuturi.com.ec), Amazonas 1324 and Colón. Rates are about US$400 for five days/four nights,

from Coca with regular Monday departures, or US$240 for three nights, with regular Friday departures.

Nuevo Rocafuerte

This small river town is on the Peruvian border about 12 hours from Coca along Río Napo. Since the 1998 peace treaty with Peru, this is officially a legal border crossing, although basic infrastructure such as regular boats and simple hotels are still lacking. Guides are available in Nuevo Rocafuerte for trips into Parque Nacional Yasuní.

Places to Stay & Eat A basic inexpensive *pensión* in Nuevo Rocafuerte provides beds, and a small store has basic supplies, but you should bring everything you need with you. There is no restaurant, but by asking around, you can find someone to cook simple and inexpensive meals for you.

Getting There & Away The weekly canoe from Coca departs early Monday morning. The 12-hour trip is usually broken at Pañacocha for a meal.

The return canoe leaves Nuevo Rocafuerte early Thursday morning. Because travel is against the flow of the river, the return trip may require an overnight stop. The fare is about US$10 each way.

PARQUE NACIONAL YASUNÍ

Yasuní lies south of Río Napo and includes most of the watersheds of Ríos Yasuní and Nashiño, as well as substantial parts of Río Tiputini. This 962,000-hectare national park is by far the largest in mainland Ecuador and was established in 1979 (and expanded in 1990 and 1992) to conserve a wide variety of different rainforest habitats.

These habitats can be divided into three major groups: 'terra firme,' or forested hills, which are never inundated even by the highest floods; 'varzea,' or lowlands, which are periodically inundated by flooding rivers; and 'igapó,' which are lowlands that are semipermanently inundated. Thus, Parque Nacional Yasuní has wetlands, marshes, swamps, lakes, rivers and rainforest.

NORTHERN ORIENTE

The biodiversity of this varied and remote tropical landscape is staggeringly high. Not many scientists have had the opportunity to visit the park, but those that have report much higher species counts than they had expected – including many new species. The animals there include some of the rarer and more difficult to see jungle wildlife, such as the jaguar, harpy eagle, puma and tapir.

Because of the importance of the park's incredible biodiversity, UNESCO (United Nations Educational, Scientific and Cultural Organization) has declared Yasuní an international biosphere reserve.

Except for about 20 Huaorani families, the national park is almost uninhabited. Most Huaorani live outside the park's boundaries – especially in the Reserva Huaorani, which acts as an ecological buffer zone for the national park. This was created in 1991, encompassing much of what used to be the western part of Yasuní and providing the Huaorani with a suitable area of rainforest in which to live in a traditional manner. Meanwhile, the eastern and southern borders of Parque Nacional Yasuní

were extended to Río Cururay, so that the size of the park remains about the same.

On the face of it, this huge, remote national park surrounded by a buffer zone is a modern conservation success story. Unfortunately, this is not entirely the case. Oil has been discovered within the boundaries of the park. In 1991, despite Yasuní's protected status, the Ecuadorian government gave the US-based oil company Conoco the right to begin oil exploitation. Conoco was soon replaced by the Maxus Oil Consortium, a subsidiary of Du Pont. It is understandable that the Ecuadorian government wants to make money from its oil reserves, but much of the profit will benefit foreign interests rather than Ecuador's.

Where drilling begins, a road soon follows, thus opening up pristine rainforest to colonization, deforestation and degradation. It is the roads and the subsequent colonization that cause greater long-term damage than the oil drilling itself. A 110km road has been built into the park, but in an attempt to avoid the problems associated with colonization, the road is open only to oil-company workers, local indigenous people and a few scientists with permits.

Degradation caused by the oil-drilling process itself does occur. This includes contamination of soil and drainage systems by oil and the waste products associated with oil exploitation, as well as the noise pollution and destruction of vegetation causing the exodus of wildlife from the region. Nevertheless, this degradation has so far been reasonably well contained, and wildlife is reportedly very abundant – but you can't go there to see it unless you're a researcher or an oil worker.

Various international organizations – such as the Nature Conservancy, Conservation International and the Natural Resources Defense Council – in coalition with Ecuadorian groups such as Fundación Natura and local grassroots conservation groups, have worked hard to minimize the oil company's impact in Yasuní. Although Parque Nacional Yasuní remains threatened by oil exploitation, hope remains that the threat will not develop into as destructive a pattern, as has occurred in other parts of the Amazon.

In common with the majority of Ecuador's preserved areas, Yasuní is woefully understaffed. In 1990, there was only one ranger, and since then, a few more have been trained and hired. At present, the only permanently staffed ranger station is at Nuevo Rocafuerte, with some other seasonal stations on the southern boundaries of the park. Some of the guides in Coca can take you on trips into the park.

The annual rainfall is about 3500mm, depending on which part of the park you are in. May to July are the wettest months; January to March are the driest. This is one of the few remaining true wildernesses in Ecuador. The beauty of this area is its remoteness and inaccessibility, which allows the wildlife to remain in the region relatively undisturbed.

NORTH FROM COCA
☎ 06

The bus ride from Coca to Lago Agrio shows how the discovery of oil has changed the Oriente. In the early 1970s, this was all virgin jungle, and communications were limited to mission airstrips and river travel. Today, there are roads and buses, and there are always signs of the oil industry – the pipelines, oil wells or trucks.

A short way north of Coca, the bus heads east and passes the belching wells of the Sacha oil works. It continues through the small oil town of **La Joya de las Sachas**, where *Hotel America* is the best of a few poor hotels. The road is narrow but in good condition and almost entirely paved. It follows the oil pipeline for most of the way, and there are several stretches with vistas of the jungle in the distance.

You'll frequently see tropical birds that have learned to coexist with people; one of the most common is the all-black ani, with a long, drooping tail and extremely thick bill. The bus passes occasional small communities and crosses Río Aguarico, the region's main river. Lago Agrio is a few kilometers beyond.

LAGO AGRIO
☎ 06

Lago Agrio's official name is 'Nueva Loja,' because many of the early Ecuadorians who colonized the area came from Loja. But US oil workers working for Texaco nicknamed the town 'Lago Agrio' after a small oil town in Texas called Sour Lake, and the nickname has stuck. Locals simply call the town 'Lago.' It became the capital of the new province of Sucumbíos in 1989.

Since the discovery of oil, Lago Agrio has changed from virgin jungle to Ecuador's most important oil town. Although once a boomtown, the town's growth has leveled off somewhat, and it now has a population of about 24,000.

Although it's the oldest and biggest of Ecuador's oil towns, Lago Agrio is still just an oil town, and an oil town is an oil town is an oil town. It's got its full quota of seedy bars, prostitutes, drunks and questionable characters, but it's also a bustling provincial capital, and the well-lit hotel area is safe. However, most travelers spend as little time here as possible; it's simply an overnight stop. The drive from the jungle up into the Andes is beautiful, and it's worth doing in daylight. Lago Agrio is a base for excursions into the jungle on the road that is being pushed ever deeper into the Oriente.

Information

There are few street signs and almost no building numbers.

The Colombian consulate (☎ 830 084) is upstairs on Avenida Quito. Look for its sign on the 2nd floor. Migraciones, the police station, the post office and Andinatel are shown on the map. The Frente de Defensa de la Amazonía (FDA), Eloy Alfaro 352, can send and receive email.

Banks don't change money. The many casas de cambio on Avenida Quito near Avenida Colombia change Colombian pesos. Hotel El Cofan changes traveler's checks at poor rates.

LAGO AGRIO

PLACES TO STAY
9   Araza Hotel
11 Hotel El Cofan
14 Residencial Chimborazo
15 Hostal Secoya
16 Residencial Marsella
17 Hotel Paris
18 Hotel Oro Negro
19 Residencial Ecuador
21 Hotel Casablanca
22 Hotel Americano
24 Hotel Machala 2
25 Hotel Lago Imperial
28 Hotel La Cabaña
30 Hotel Willigram
31 Hotel D'Mario
32 Hotel Gran Colombia
34 Hotel Guacamayo

PLACES TO EAT
10 Pingüino
29 Cafetería Jackeline
33 Restaurant Machala

OTHER
1   Town Hall
2   Sionatour
3   Artesanías Wuarmi Wuankurina
4   TAME Airline Office
5   Andinatel
6   Migraciones
7   Frente de Defensa de la Amazonía
8   Taxis/Trucks to La Punta
12 Police Station
13 Casa de Cultura
20 Colombian Consulate
23 Casas de Cambio
26 Banco Internacional
27 Clínica González
35 Post Office
36 Transportes Putumayo

The best medical attention is at Clínica González (☎ 830 728, 831 691), at Avenida Quito and 12 de Febrero.

Organized Tours

Most travelers have already booked a tour in Quito or elsewhere by the time they arrive in Lago. Finding a guide in Lago is harder than in most other jungle towns.

Sionatour (☎ 830 232), 12 de Febrero 267, was founded to promote direct community-based ecotourism in three local Siona indigenous communities – Orahuëayá, Biaña and Puerto Bolívar. These communities are several hours from Lago by road and canoe, and they provide basic lodging with shared cold showers and toilets. Tours are guided by Spanish-speaking Siona natives, and there are opportunities to interact with, learn about and photograph villagers, as well as to explore the rainforest. Tours costs US$40 to US$60 per person per day, depending on the number of people and the services desired.

La Frente de Defensa de la Amazonía (FDA; ☎ 831 930, admin@fda.ecuanex .net.ec), Eloy Alfaro 352, is a good place to contact guides in local villages, including the

Crossing the Colombian Border

It's certainly possible to enter Colombia from Lago Agrio; the border is less than 20km to the north, and there are always numerous Colombians in town. However, the area is notorious for smugglers, and in early 2000, FARC (Revolutionary Armed Forces of Colombia) rebels crossed the border and kidnapped a group of tourists and local oil workers, who were then released over a period of weeks. Another FARC incursion later that year resulted in a deadly firefight with Ecuadorian soldiers. The Colombian border area is dangerous, and although travelers have written about crossing the border (in both directions) without any problems in the late 1990s, you should avoid this area unless local information indicates that relative safety has returned. If you must go this way, expect numerous passport and baggage checks by the Ecuadorian and Colombian military. Check with immigration authorities in Lago Agrio about where to get an exit stamp in your passport, as border-crossing posts may not be functioning.

The most frequently used route from Lago Agrio is to La Punta (about 1½ hours away), on Río San Miguel. Then take a motorized canoe for the short river crossing (about 30 minutes) to Puerto Colón, on the Colombian side of the river. In Puerto Colón, there are several daily buses that leave for Puerto Asís (about six hours by unpaved road), where there are places to stay and transportation by road, air and river to other parts of Colombia. Puerto Asís is on Río Putumayo, and you can take a boat from here to Leticia, at the tri-border of Colombia, Peru and Brazil. Boats aren't frequent, however, and the trip takes several days. If you leave Lago Agrio at dawn, you should be in Puerto Asís by mid-afternoon. A larger town with more facilities is Mocoa, which is three hours north of Puerto Asís by paved road. Mocoa has the Colombian *migraciones,* where you should get a passport stamp whether arriving or leaving Colombia.

There are other routes from Lago Agrio into Colombia, but they are rarely used.

Cofan village of Dureno (see Along Río Aguarico, later in this chapter). FDA maintains daily radio contact.

Another good and knowledgeable contact for local indigenous and environmental affairs is Manuel Silva. You can find him at the Casa de Cultura library (☎ 830 624), at Manabí and Quito, 2nd floor. He can arrange tours with notice of a day or two. In Quito, all the companies visiting Cuyabeno go through Lago, and Tropic Ecological Adventures (see Travel Agencies under Quito) can arrange visits to local villages.

Things to See
The Sunday morning market can be quite interesting when the local Cofan Indians (see Dureno, under Along Río Aguarico, later in this chapter) come into town to buy staples and sell their handicrafts, such as necklaces made of seeds and iridescent beetle wings.

Places to Stay
Budget Most hotels are on Avenida Quito. Mosquitoes can be a problem, especially in the rainy months (June to August), so look for fans or mosquito nets in the rooms. None of these hotels have hot showers, but some are air-conditioned.

Hotel Willigram (☎ 830 163) charges US$2/3 for singles/doubles, or US$2.50/4 with private bath. Rooms are basic but not too bad – as long as you bring your own padlock for the doors. The basic but well-run *Hotel Oro Negro* (☎ 830 174) is one of the town's oldest hotels and charges US$2.50 per person for rooms with shared baths. Other basic cheapies to try are *Residencial Ecuador, Residencial Marsella,* or *Residencial Chimborazo.*

Hostal Secoya (☎ 830 451) looks decent and has clean, basic rooms with fans for US$2.75 per person, or US$4.50 with private bath. *Hotel La Cabaña* (☎ 830 608) also looks OK at US$2.75 per person, or US$4 with private bath. *Hotel Machala 2* (☎ *830 073*) has basic but clean rooms with private bath and TV at US$4 per person; free bottled water is provided. Next door, *Hotel Lago Imperial* (☎ *830 452/3*) has clean rooms with private bath for US$5/9. The new, clean *Hotel Casablanca* (☎ *830 181*) charges about US$6/10 for rooms with private bath, TV and fan; next door, *Hotel Americano* looks similar. *Hotel Paris* is also in this price range.

Hotel Gran Colombia (☎ *830 601, 831 032, fax 831 031*) has air-conditioned rooms with TV and telephone for US$10/15 and a few rooms with fans at US$4 per person. The owners also run the nearby *Hotel Guacamayo* (☎ *830 601, 831 032, fax 831 031*), where rooms are about US$4 or US$5 per person; some rooms have air-conditioning.

In the middle of the town's hotel row, *Hotel D'Mario* (☎ *830 172, fax 830 456*) is clean and popular. Rooms range from about US$6/7 for singles/doubles with private bath and fan to US$12/18 for air-conditioned rooms with TV, telephone and minifridge.

Mid-Range There are two better hotels. *Hotel El Cofan* (☎ *830 527, 832 409, fax 830 526*) charges about US$18/24 for clean but plain air-conditioned rooms with private bath, hot water, TV, telephone and minifridge. American breakfast is included. The hotel is often full, so get there early or call ahead. It was recently under renovation, so prices may go up.

The newest and best is *Araza Hotel* (☎ *830 223, 831 247, fax 831 287*), with 38 very clean, modern rooms with the same amenities as Hotel El Cofan. Rates are US$27/42, including American breakfast.

Places to Eat
Restaurant Machala, on Avenida Quito, is just one of several outdoor restaurants strung along the south side of the street. Others are part of the accompanying hotels and are similar but slightly pricier. The ones mentioned here are considered among the best in town (although the restaurants at Hotel El Cofan and Araza Hotel are also

good). These places are mid-priced and serve reliable meaty dishes – vegetables are hard to come by. *Cafetería Jackeline* is good for breakfasts and snacks and has good fruit salads and hamburgers. *Pingüino* is the best ice-cream place. There are many other eateries along Quito, and if you walk a block or two north, you'll find plenty of cheaper places.

Shopping
Artesanías Wuarmi Wuankurina, next to and loosely affiliated with Sionatour, sells local Siona, Secoya and Cofan art and crafts, with profits going to the artisans.

Getting There & Away
Air TAME has a daily flight (except Sunday) from Quito at 10:30 am, returning to Quito at 11:30 am. Additional flights are at 3:45 pm Monday and Friday, returning at 4:45 pm. The one-way fare is US$53 for foreigners. Flights are often full, but it's always worth getting on the waiting list and going to the airport in the hope of cancellations. Tour companies sometimes book up more seats than they can use. The TAME office (☎ 830 113) is on Orellana near 9 de Octubre. It is usually open weekdays, but its hours are quite erratic. Often everyone packs up and goes to the airport.

The airport is about 3km east of town, and taxis (which are usually yellow or white pickup trucks) cost about US$1.50, depending on how well you bargain.

If you are arriving in Lago Agrio by air, you'll see buses waiting, but these are usually private oil-company buses and won't give you a ride. There are usually taxis hanging around – see if you can share a ride with someone to avoid the muggy 3km walk.

Bus The bus terminal is about 2km northwest of the center. Several companies have buses to Quito (US$6 to US$8, eight hours). Each company has a variety of buses – they range from slow, noisy old monsters to smaller and faster buses. They all seem to break down periodically. There are one or two daily departures, mainly overnight, to Tena, Cuenca, Guayaquil and Machala. The best way to get to Tena is to take a Quito bus to Baeza and change there.

Buses to Coca aren't usually found in the bus terminal; you have to catch one at Avenida Quito in the center – ask locally for where to wait.

To get to the Colombian border, taxis/trucks leave from the corner of Alfaro and Colombia and go to La Punta during the day. Buses with Transportes Putumayo go to Tetetes or Puerto Carmen de Putumayo several times a day; they leave from south of the market. They also go through the jungle towns of Dureno and Tarapoa and have access to Reserva Producción Faunística Cuyabeno. Ask at Transportes Putumayo for information about getting to the jungle east of Lago.

ALONG RÍO AGUARICO
☎ 06
Dureno

There are two Durenos. The Cofan village of Dureno (described in this section) lies on the southern banks of Río Aguarico, about an hour east of Lago Agrio by bus or dugout canoe. The Cofan village is 23km east of Lago Agrio; if you miss the turnoff for it, you will end up at the colonists' village of Dureno, 27km east of Lago Agrio. There are basic *comedores* in the colonists' village, and you could find *floor space* to sleep on if you asked around.

River transportation is infrequent, but Transportes Putumayo has several buses a day to Tarapoa or Tipishca, which pass the Dureno (Cofan village) turnoff, 23km from Lago Agrio. It is marked with a small sign that is not very obvious; it's best to ask the driver for Comuna Cofan Dureno. From the turnoff, follow the path until you reach Río Aguarico, about 100m away. It's best to call ahead by radio (see Organized Tours, under Lago Agrio, earlier) to arrange for transportation across the river. Otherwise, you can yell and whistle to attract the attention of the villagers on the other side – this might not always work.

In the village, you'll be given a roof over your head in an Indian-style hut – bring a hammock or sleeping mat, as there are no beds. Bring your own food and stove, as supplies are not available in Dureno. There is a modest fee for the river crossing and a place to sleep.

NORTHERN ORIENTE

Cofan dwelling

ROB RACHOWIECKI

The Cofans are excellent wilderness guides and know much about medicinal and practical uses of jungle plants. You can hire a guide with a dugout canoe for about US$35 per day. Up to six people can be accommodated in a dugout, so it's cheaper in a group. The guides Delfín Criollo and Lauriano Quenama have been recommended by readers and have a cabin that sleeps eight people. They speak Cofan, with Spanish as their second language, but they do not understand English. Hector Quenama and Lino Mandua also work as guides. This is off-the-beaten-path tourism and is not for those expecting any comfort. They have one- to four-day trips within the area, but they don't go to Cuyabeno. Although you won't see much wildlife, jungle plants will be shown and explained to you. These trips are more for the cultural experience than for wildlife watching. Ask questions!

An American missionary family works in the village – although they don't arrange trips or provide services for travelers, they can be of assistance in an emergency.

You can look for Cofan people in Lago Agrio on weekends. They come to sell their handicrafts and to do some shopping during the Sunday morning market, so look for them around the market area. They often wear their distinctive traditional clothing and are easy to spot. The Cofan men wear a one-piece, knee-length smock called a *kushma,* along with a headband (sometimes made of porcupine quills) around their short hair. The women wear very brightly patterned flounced skirts, short blouses that expose an inch of midriff and bright-red lipstick and have beautiful, long, dark hair. Ask to join them after the Sunday morning market, when they return to Dureno – they will then be able to show you where to get off the bus, and you can cross the river with them.

The Cofan Indians are related to the Secoya people, and there used to be tens of thousands of them before early contact with whites decimated them (mainly by disease). This, unfortunately, is the history of most Amazonian Indian groups. Before the discovery of oil, most Cofans' exposure to non-Indian people was limited to the occasional missionary, and they still remain quite shy, as opposed to the Otavaleño Indians, for example.

Flotel Orellana

This large, flat-bottomed riverboat has three decks, 20 double cabins and two quadruples – each with private bath and hot water. Cabins have an upper and lower bunk. The *Flotel* cruises Río Aguarico in the sections close to the Peruvian border and provides a comfortable base from which to tour the region. These tours are operated by Metropolitan Touring (see Travel Agencies under Quito), Ecuador's biggest travel agency, and the prices and quality are commensurate. Bilingual naturalist guides accompany the boat to explain the wildlife and surroundings. Day trips to shore are taken in dugout canoes, and short nature hikes (often on boardwalks) and canoe rides on a lake are part of the adventure. Nights are spent in relative luxury aboard the *Flotel,* which provides good food, a bar and lectures about the jungle. Metropolitan Touring is taking an increasingly active role in promoting responsible ecotourism by using local guides, trying to minimize impact on the culture and environment of the region, and educating clients about the rainforest.

Voyages on the *Flotel* are for three or four nights and are all inclusive from Lago Agrio (you can arrive and leave by air via Lago Agrio for an extra US$106 roundtrip or make your own way overland). The three-night trip is Friday to Monday, and the four-night trip is Monday to Friday. Rates are US$521/621 for three/four nights (per person for double occupancy – including transfers from Lago Agrio, all meals and guiding services). There are discounts of about US$120 in the low season (April to early June, and September to November).

Zabalo

This is a small Cofan community on Río Aguarico near the confluence with the smaller Río Zabalo.

Randy Borman, born and raised in the Oriente as the son of American missionaries, lives at Zabalo with his Cofan wife and family, along with a handful of other Cofan families. He speaks and lives as a Cofan, and he guides occasional groups on excursions into the jungle. Metropolitan Touring's *Flotel* sometimes makes a stop near here, and you can visit an area across the river from the village, where they have an interpretive center with a Cofan guide. Souvenirs are sold, and a rainforest walk to see medicinal and other plants, accompanied by the Cofan guide, are part of the program, but entering and visiting the village itself and taking photographs are not allowed.

For an in-depth visit with the Cofan people, you can stay in one of four cabins, each with two double rooms, mosquito nets and a shared outhouse with showers and toilets. Also possible is a six-day trekking/canoeing expedition into the jungle, with stays in rustic shelters. Rates are US$65 to US$100 per person per day, depending on group size and trip requirements (English-speaking guides cost more than Spanish-speaking ones).

Contact Randy Borman (in Quito ☎ 02-470 946, cofan@attglobal.net) for information and reservations, or check out the informative Cofan Web site (yes, a traditional culture with a Web site!) at www.cofan.org.

RESERVA PRODUCCIÓN FAUNÍSTICA CUYABENO

This reserve covers 603,380 hectares of rainforest around Río Cuyabeno in northeastern Ecuador. The boundaries of Cuyabeno have been changed several times, and it is now substantially larger than it originally was.

The reserve was created in 1979 with the goals of protecting this area of rainforest, conserving its wildlife and providing a sanctuary in which the traditional inhabitants of the area – the Siona, Secoya and Cofan Indians – could lead their customary way of life. There are several lakes and swamps in Cuyabeno, and some of the most interesting animals found here are

Faux Dugout Canoes

Transportation for Amazonian indigenous people has always been the traditional dugout canoe, painstakingly crafted from a single tree trunk. Building a large canoe requires a 200-year-old tree – in contrast, the useful life of a dugout canoe rarely exceeds 10 years. Dugouts were formerly used for communal and family purposes, with minimal impact on the rainforest, but as colonists, ecotourists and others demanded an ever-increasing number of these sturdy craft, the building of dugout canoes has contributed to the depletion of the oldest trees in the rainforest.

This year, Ecuador's Cofan Indians began developing a less-damaging way to build dugout canoes. In a project aptly name *Eco-canoa* and funded by an unusual combination of the European Union, an oil company and a Cofan support group, the Cofans began experimenting in using their wooden dugouts for molds to make similarly shaped canoes out of fiberglass. Three expert fiberglass boatbuilders from Ecuador's Manabí coast were hired to teach the Cofans how to use the material. The Indians learning this new form of dugout-canoe construction were handpicked by Randy Borman, an American Cofan born and raised in Ecuador's rainforest and now married to a Cofan woman. He is the chief of the most traditional remaining group (in the Zábalo community) and is savvy to both international concerns and the needs of his Cofan people.

The Cofans hope not only to save ancient rainforest trees by using fiberglass canoes, but also to start a tribal cottage industry supplying these boats to tourism companies and other villages and tribes. The Zábalo community has already received several international awards for conservation initiatives – it looks like it may be heading toward another one.

aquatic species, such as freshwater dolphins, manatees, caiman and anaconda. Monkeys abound, and tapirs, peccaries, agoutis and several cat species have been recorded. The bird life is prolific.

336   The Northern Oriente – Reserva Producción Faunística Cuyabeno

Its protected status notwithstanding, Cuyabeno was opened to oil exploitation almost immediately after its creation. The new oil towns of Tarapoa and Cuyabeno were built on tributaries of Río Cuyabeno, and both of these towns and parts of the trans-Ecuadorian oil pipeline were within the reserve's boundaries. Roads were built, colonists followed, and tens of thousands of hectares of the reserve were logged or degraded by spills of oil and toxic waste.

At least six oil spills were recorded between 1984 and 1989, and others occurred unnoticed. Many of the spills found their way into Río Cuyabeno itself, which is precisely the river basin that the reserve was supposed to protect.

It was interesting to see how MAG, the government body originally charged with overseeing the reserve, managed to remain apparently oblivious to oil development in the midst of the protected area. An informative leaflet published in 1991 by MAG's Division of Natural Areas and Wildlife urged the visitor: 'We must contribute to a national ecological conscience!' Ten rules for visiting Cuyabeno were listed. The No 1 rule was 'Put litter in its place.' Other rules include: avoid getting lost, do not molest the wildlife, do not make unnecessary noise, do not damage the trees, and inform the authorities of any 'irregularities.' Yet the leaflet made no mention whatsoever of oil exploitation and colonization within the reserve!

Various international and local agencies set to work to try to protect the area, which, although legally protected, was in reality open to development. Conservation International funded projects to establish more guard stations in Cuyabeno; train local Siona and Secoya Indians to work in wildlife management; and support CORDAVI, an Ecuadorian environmental-law group that challenged the legality of allowing oil exploitation in protected areas.

Finally, in late 1991, the government shifted the borders of the reserve farther east and south and enlarged the area it covered. The new reserve is both remoter and better protected. Vocal local indigenous groups (which are supported by Ecuadorian and international NGOs, tourists, travel agencies and conservation groups) are doing a better job of protecting the area than the government did in the original reserve. Although the threat of oil development and subsequent colonization is always present, there is now a solid infrastructure in place to prevent uncontrolled development from ruining the reserve. This is due in part to the hard work of the local people, but also to the positive economic impact of tourism.

The Cuyabeno Reserve has now become a tourist destination. It is quite easy to visit the reserve without being aware of the problems it has faced, and many large areas of the reserve remain quite pristine.

Several agencies in Quito offer tours of Cuyabeno. These tours go far beyond the colonized areas, and there is a good chance of seeing some of the wildlife. Travel is mainly by canoes and on foot – except from December to February, when low water levels may limit the areas accessible by canoe.

One company is Nuevo Mundo Expeditions (see Travel Agencies under Quito). Its tours are among the best – they are marked by a conservationist attitude and led by well-informed, bilingual guides. The tours use the *Cuyabeno River Lodge* as a base for further exploration. The lodge has comfortable cabins built in native style but feature private (cold-water) bathrooms. You can arrange trips farther into the jungle and you stay at a *camp* near Laguna Grande. 'Ecofishing' trips with a biologist guide are also available. The rate for five days/four nights is US$700, including flights from Quito and all food and guiding services.

Neotropic Turis (☎ 02-521 212, 09-930 778, fax 02-554 902, info@neotropicturis.com), Amazonas N24-03, near Wilson, in Quito, runs the comfortable and recommended *Cuyabeno Lodge* (different from the Cuyabeno River Lodge, mentioned previously). The place is staffed by Siona natives and is the only lodge on Laguna Grande. The lodge has seven cabins with two double rooms each. Two cabins have private bathrooms, and the rest have shared bathrooms with hot water. Lighting is by gas and kerosene lamps, and a solar panel provides power for warming water and running a radio. Tours are four days/three nights and five days/four nights (or longer if desired) and include transfers from Lago Agrio, native and bilingual naturalist guides, trips by canoe and foot, accommodations, meals, drinking water, coffee and tea. Canoes and kayaks are available to paddle on the lake. Rates are US$250 to US$380 for the three-night option and US$320 to US$480 for the four-night option, depending on the number of clients. Neotropic Turis can also arrange any other tours in Ecuador to go with your jungle trip; you can visit the Web site at www.neotropicturis.com.

Metropolitan Touring (see Flotel Orellana, earlier) also operates the *Iripari Camp* and the *Imuya Camp* – both located on the shores of lakes of the same name as the camps. Iripari is south of Río Aguarico, about halfway between Zabalo and the Peruvian border, and Imuya is north of the Aguarico off Río Lagartococha, which forms the border of Peru. Both are in remote areas. Both camps are quite small and rustic, with private, screened double rooms and shared bathrooms. Good food and experienced naturalist guides are part of the programs to these lodges, which can be combined with a Flotel excursion for a longer stay in the jungle. Metropolitan Touring also has a couple of more primitive camps at which you sleep on hammocks or floor mats. Costs are similar to that of the Flotel program.

Several other companies in Quito and Baños offer cheaper tours to the Cuyabeno Reserve, but check carefully that they offer you the type of experience that you are after. Some companies include a day of travel to and from Quito in their itineraries – others don't. Note that while these companies can make arrangements for you in advance, the best rates can usually be obtained by going to their offices and seeing when their next trip is leaving and if there is room on it. This is particularly true of single travelers or couples who want to join a larger group to save money.

You can visit Cuyabeno independently, but ever since the increase in local indigenous control over tourism in the area, this is no longer a recommended or inexpensive option. Most visitors go with an organized group, which is the best way to go to get the most out of your visit.

Entry to the reserve costs US$20 per person from July to September and US$15 during other months (less for Ecuadorian residents). This is usually added to the cost of any tour – ask in advance if you are on a tight budget. In Tarapoa, there is a guard post where you can pay the fee and ask for information. There are a few other guard posts within the reserve.

Most visitors come during the wetter months of March to September. In the less rainy months, river levels may be too low to allow easy navigation. Annual rainfall is between 2000mm and 4000mm, depending on location, and humidity is often between 90% and 100%. Bring sun protection, rain gear, insect repellent, water-purification tablets and food.

WEST OF LAGO AGRIO
☎ 06

The road west of Lago Agrio roughly follows Río Aguarico for about 50km before turning southwest and beginning the long climb up into the Andes. There are two major landmarks on this ascent: On the left of the road, some 95km from Lago Agrio, are the San Rafael Falls (also called the Coca Falls). At about 145m high, they are the biggest falls in Ecuador. To the right of the road is the 3485m Volcán Reventador, which means 'the exploder' and which had a period of major activity in the late 1970s. Unfortunately, it's obscured by cloud cover more often than not.

Volcán Reventador

Just north of the bridge crossing Río Reventador, there are a couple of houses, and just north of those, on the northwest side of the road, there is a trail that climbs up Volcán Reventador. It is hard to find the beginning of the trail, and there are various confusing little paths, so you should ask anyone you see (note that there are very few people around here). After a few minutes, the trail crosses the river, and about half an hour later, the trail goes through a grove of palm trees. Beyond that, there is only one trail to the summit, but it is steep and slippery in places. There is almost no water, and the climb takes two days – it's only for experienced hikers who have plenty of extra water bottles and camping gear. Technical climbing is not involved, but it's easy to get lost in the lower slopes, so hiring a guide is a good idea. Try Guillermo Vásquez in the community of Pampas, about 3km west of the San Rafael Falls; Edgar Ortiz at Hotel Amazonas in El Reventador; or Lucho Viteri in Baeza.

This area is within the eastern boundaries of Reserva Ecológica Cayambe-Coca, which includes Volcán Cayambe, mentioned in the North of Quito chapter. There are no signs or entrance stations. There is reportedly a guard station located in the village of **El Chaco**, about 20km beyond the Río Reventador bridge on the way to Baeza. In El Chaco, there are a couple of very basic *residenciales*.

Bus drivers on the Lago Agrio-Quito run usually know the San Rafael Falls, but few of them know about the Río Reventador bridge or climbing the volcano. So ask about the falls, even if you plan on climbing Reventador.

San Rafael Falls

You can glimpse the San Rafael Falls briefly from the road. To see them properly, get off the bus just beyond the bridge crossing Río Reventador, at a concrete-block hut on the left side of the road. Make sure you get off the bus at Río Reventador and not at the bigger community of **El Reventador**, which is about 15km away in the direction of Lago Agrio (and has a *cheap hotel*). Most bus drivers know the entrance; ask for *la entrada para la cascada de San Rafael*.

From the hut, it's about 2.5km down a steep trail to the falls. Near the top of the trail is the *San Rafael Lodge*, and beyond the lodge is the trail to the falls, which may or may not be passable to vehicles for some

or all of its length. The lodge is currently for sale, so ask travel agencies in Quito if they know anything about it, or just show up – it is rarely full, but there may not be much food available if there isn't a group staying there. I'm told you can *camp* within sight of the falls for US$1.50 per person. The rooms at the lodge have shared bathrooms, and hot water is available when it's turned on. Once back on the road, flag a bus down when you want to go on, but be prepared to wait, as buses are sometimes full.

The falls are quite impressive, but the best thing about them, at least from some people's point of view, is the great bird watching in the area. The Andean cock-of-the-rock is one of the more spectacular species regularly seen here.

Baeza & Around

Beyond Río Reventador, the road continues climbing, following the trans-Ecuadorian oil pipeline and Río Quijos all the way. There are enchanting views of beautiful cloud forest full of strange species of birds and plants. You pass several small communities, and in six hours, you reach Baeza, 170km from Lago Agrio.

Baeza is on the junction with the road to Tena and is the most important village between Lago Agrio and Quito. It was an old Spanish missionary and trading outpost. It was first founded in 1548 and was refounded three more times since. The pass from Baeza via Papallacta to the Quito valley was known well before the conquest, but the road from Baeza to Lago Agrio has been opened only by the oil boom, so Baeza is both a historical and a geographical junction. It is also recommended as a good, quiet and inexpensive spot to stay for walks in the surrounding hills. The plants of the Andean foothills and the bird life are outstanding.

Places to Stay & Eat Facilities are very limited. There is a gas station, a basic hotel and a restaurant in the *Oro Negro* complex, at the junction of the road going to Tena. Rooms with shared bath are about US$2 per person.

About 2km away from the junction, heading toward Tena, you reach the village of Baeza proper. There you'll find the basic but clean *Hotel Samay* in the center, which charges about US$4 a night. *Hostería El Nogal de Jumandy* is at the west end (the end nearest the road junction) and also is cheap but is used by truck drivers and prostitutes. At the east end (the end toward Tena) is the newer *Hostal San Rafael*, which has good, clean rooms for US$6 per person. *El Viejo* is one of the better of the simple restaurants.

About 10km away on the road to Lago Agrio, at the village of **San Francisco de Borja**, is *Cabañas Tres Ríos*, about .75km east of and across Río Quijos from the village. There are eight cabins, each with private hot showers and patios. It caters mainly to kayakers and is often full with kayaking groups from November to February. Contact Small World Adventures (☎ 1-800-585-2925, info@smallworldadventures .com), PO Box 262, Howard, CO 81233, USA for more information.

About 17km south of Baeza on the road to Tena is the village of **Cosanga**, on the outskirts of which is *Cabañas San Isidro Labrador* (in Quito ☎ 02-465 578, 547 403, fax 02-228 902, Carrión 555, Quito). It is an Ecuadorian-owned cattle ranch on the eastern slopes of the Andes at about 2000m. Some of the land has been left undisturbed, and the birding here is 1st class. You can stay here by advance reservation for only about US$80 per person, including meals served by the friendly family who owns the place. Rooms have private baths and hot water.

Getting There & Away There are no bus stations in these villages. You must flag down passing buses and hope that they have room. Buses to and from Lago Agrio, Tena and Quito pass through regularly. If coming from one of these towns, you may find that bus companies will only sell you a ticket for the whole journey (eg, Lago Agrio-Quito). If you don't want to pay full price, you have to jump on the bus just after it leaves the terminal, hope you can get a seat and pay the driver a prorated fare.

Papallacta

The westbound road from Baeza continues climbing steadily for some 40km until the village of Papallacta. About 1.5km beyond the village, on the right as you head to Quito, are the **Termas de Papallacta**. A 2km road brings you to this hot-spring complex.

The setting is grand: on a clear day, you can see the snowcapped Antisana (5753m) about 15km to the south. The hottest spring is very hot, and there's a refreshing, cold plunge pool, as well as other pools at various temperatures. The complex has been developed as a comfortable hotel and spa that is popular with upper-class Quiteños on weekends. There are many different pools – some hot, some warm, one cold, some suitable for swimming, some just for soaking, some private, some public. There are two sets of pools: Fuentes de Juventud and Jambiyacu. They are opposite one another, and the Fuentes is a little more expensive and extensive. The entry fee is about US$1 to US$2 for day visitors, and nice changing rooms and toilet facilities are provided. The area is beautiful, the pools are clean, and there aren't too many visitors midweek, although it's busy on weekends. (There is also a slightly cheaper and more easily accessible set of baths on the outskirts of the village, although if you are here for the hot springs, you are better off getting to Termas de Papallacta, which isn't prohibitively expensive and has more services.) Papallacta is a nice place to relax and soak away the aches and pains of a jungle expedition.

Quito is only 67km away, and the drive is spectacular. The road climbs over the Eastern Cordillera via a sometimes snow-covered pass nearly 4100m high. This pass is literally the rim of the Amazon Basin. If you're driving up from the Oriente, be prepared for the cold. Beyond the pass is the valley of Quito.

Places to Stay & Eat In the village of Papallacta, *Residencial Viajero* has simple rooms for about US$2 per person. The shared showers are heated (naturally), the rooms have good views, and the simple *Restaurant Alicia* is below. The similarly priced **Hotel Quito** is decent and also serves food. On weekends, the restaurant moves the tables to allow for dancing. Rooms have a private toilet, but the showers are shared.

At the Baños Termales, west of town, the **Termas de Papallacta** (in Quito ☎/fax 02-557 850, 09-701 621, papallac@ecnet.ec) is the only complete hotel/hot-springs complex in the area. (The Quito office is at Foch E6-12 and Reina Victoria, room 4A; and the Web site is at www.papallacta.com.ec). There are a camping area for US$4 per person, rooms with shared bathrooms for US$22/36, rooms with private bathrooms

for US$47/72/97 for one/two/three people, and cabins that sleep up to six for US$106.

Getting There & Away Any of the buses from Quito heading toward Baeza, Tena or Lago Agrio can drop you off in Papallacta. If you want to go to the Termas de Papallacta complex, make sure that the driver lets you off on the road to the baths, 1.5km before the village. Also ask in the bus terminal about buses to Papallacta that don't continue to other destinations.

To leave Papallacta, wait for a bus to Quito, Tena or Lago Agrio and flag it down. Ask locals about the best place to wait.

The Western Lowlands

A physical map of Ecuador shows the country neatly divided by the massive range of the Andes. To the east lie the jungles of the upper Amazon Basin, and to the west are the coastal lowlands. The western drop of the Andes is dramatic and steeper than the eastern side. Lowlands at below 300m are soon reached; from Ecuador's highest peak (Chimborazo at 6310m), it is only 50km due west to the 300m contour, a gradient of about 12%. It does not stay low all the way to the coast, however. After dropping to almost sea level, the land rises again in a barren, scrubby and almost uninhabited range of 700-meter-high hills before dropping to the coast. Therefore, the coastal lowlands are subdivided into the coast itself, west of the coastal hills, and the flat lowlands lying east of the hills and west of the Andes. The latter is described here, in addition to the descent down the steep western slopes of the Andes.

The western lowlands were once forest, but well over 90% of these forests have now been cleared to develop banana plantations and other forms of agriculture, predominantly cacao and African oil palm. The forests that used to exist here were very different from those found in the Oriente – indeed, botanists estimate that about half the plant species that once grew in these western Andean slopes and lowlands were found nowhere else! Almost no forest is left in the flat lowlands, but in the more difficult-to-reach areas of the steep western slopes of the Andes, a few áreas have become belatedly protected, thus preserving small parts of a unique ecosystem that is on the verge of disappearing from the globe. The small Reserva Biológica Maquipucuna, the Río Palenque Science Center, areas around Mindo and a couple of other private reserves are included in this chapter. The larger Reserva Ecológica Cotacachi-Cayapas protects some of the northern parts of the western lowlands, but access to the reserve is very difficult from

the western lowlands – it is easier to access from the area north of Quito and from the north coast, and so the reserve is described in those chapters.

Some travelers think of Ecuador as a 'banana republic' – one of those tropical countries that produces bananas and little else. Indeed, until the export of oil began in 1972, bananas were Ecuador's most important product, and they remain the country's major agricultural export.

Fortunately for agriculturalists and the Ecuadorian economy, the western lowlands are fertile, and huge banana and palm tree plantations can be seen through this area. It has not been developed much for tourists, and many people rush through it on their way to the coast or highlands. If

Highlights

- Touring around Mindo – one of the best areas in Ecuador for bird watching
- Staying in an affordable ecolodge on the western slopes of the Andes
- Paying a visit to a Tsachila medicine man near Quevedo
- Straying from 'the gringo trail' and discovering untraveled towns and villages

Equator

341

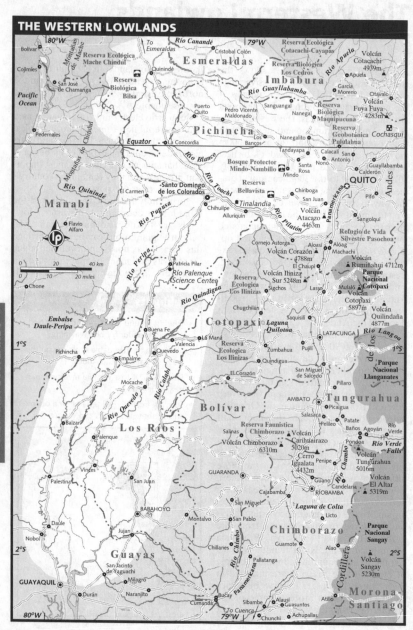

THE WESTERN LOWLANDS

you're interested in seeing some of the tropical, banana-republic Ecuador – that is, the kind of countryside that was typically Ecuadorian before the recent oil boom – then it is worth taking a couple of days to travel slowly through this area.

NANEGALITO
☎ 02

This village, a couple of hours northwest of Quito, marks the road junction with a choice of heading southwest to Bosque Protector Mindo-Nambillo or Reserva Bellavista, or north to Reserva Biológica Maquipucuna, all of which are described in this chapter. Buses to these places pass through Nanegalito. There is an Andinatel office in the village.

Places to Stay & Eat

In Nanegalito, stay at *Pensión Don Fabara* (☎ *865 187*), which has six basic rooms sharing a hot shower. It's just US$1 per person.

About 1km past Nanegalito toward Mindo is a sign for *La Sigcha*, a small, rustic cloud-forest lodge owned by Patricio Ruales, who can be contacted in *Restaurant Sabrozon* in Nanegalito (the best restaurant in town). From La Sigcha's sign, it's a steep 1.5km downhill (4WD is essential) to the lodge, where there is a cabin sleeping six and another sleeping 16. (The last 400m is down a muddy trail and over a suspension footbridge; it must be hiked.) Cold showers, home cooking, solitude, a tiny pool, bird life, views, cloud-forest foot and horse trails (horses available) that lead to waterfalls and no electricity are the attractions here. The entrance fee is US$2 for day use (including a short horse ride); beds cost US$4, and meals cost US$2.

At Km 32, about 4km before Nanegalito, is *Café Tiepolo*, which has received recommendations but is open only on weekends.

TANDAYAPA
☎ 02

From Km 32, 400m past the Café Tiepolo (see Nanegalito, earlier) a road branches south (left) to Tandayapa, a village 6km away. Here you'll find the new *Tandayapa Bird Lodge* (☎ *529 589, 09-735 536, iainc@ tandayapa.com)*, which advertises multilingual birding guides and rooms ranging from beds in dorms (US$30 per person, including meals) to rooms with private bath (US$55/85, including meals). Packages can be arranged. The lodge's Web site is at www .tandayapa.com.

RESERVA BIOLÓGICA MAQUIPUCUNA

This reserve, which covers over 3000 hectares, is only about 30km northwest of Quito as the condor flies, but because of the topography of the land, Maquipucuna lies on the western slopes of the Andes. It protects a variety of premontane and montane cloud forests in the headwaters of Río Guayllabamba at elevations ranging from about 1200m to 2800m. In 1987, the reserve was purchased by The Nature Conservancy and is administered by Fundación Maquipucuna, a nonprofit conservation organization.

About 80% of the reserve is undisturbed primary forest – the remainder is secondary growth and includes a research station and ecotourism lodge. The reserve and research station were established to investigate, among other things, the sustainable use of the tropical forests, as well as to provide conservation education to Ecuadorians. The biggest problem facing the reserve is uncontrolled colonization, which is often condoned or actively supported by the government. Colonists are deforesting the areas bounding the reserve, and this, combined with indiscriminate hunting, has severely reduced the plant and animal life in the area around Maquipucuna, as well as the western lowlands in general. Nevertheless, the story would be much worse if it were not for the efforts of Fundación Maquipucuna, which is doing an admirable job in the face of these difficulties. In the reserve, almost 350 species of bird (a bird list is available), 240 species of butterfly, 45 species of mammal and thousands of plants have been documented, and more are being inventoried.

Information

The rustic lodge has a capacity of 18 in four quadruple rooms with double bunks and one room with a double bed. There are shared bathrooms with hot showers, restful decks and balconies with forest views, and a simple restaurant serving nourishing meals. Accommodations are US$50 per person, including three meals. Day guests pay a US$5 entry fee and can hire a guide for US$10. There are seven trails, ranging from an easy 1km walk to a demanding 5.5km hike.

More information is available from Fundación Maquipucuna (☎ 02-507 200, fax 507 201, root@maqui.ecx.ec), Baquerizo 238 y Tamayo, La Floresta, Quito. Several conservation workshops have been held, some in collaboration with US organizations and aimed particularly at the local people. This education, inventory and research work is urgently in need of financial support – contributions are welcomed at the address above. In the UK, the contact is Rainforest Concern (☎ 020-7229 2093, fax 7221 4094, rainforest@gn.apc.org); in the USA, write to The Choco-Andean Rainforest Corridor, Institute of Ecology, University of Georgia, GA 30602-2202.

Getting There & Away

A Transportes San José de Minas bus from Anteparra and Plaza San Blas (near El Ejido) in Quito leaves at 1 pm, and a Transportes Alóag bus from Quito's Terminal Terrestre leaves at 2 pm daily for Nanegal, with return buses leaving at 4 am and 9 am (there may be another bus Sunday). About 12km beyond Nanegalito (or shortly before Nanegal), at a place that is locally called La Delicia, you get off the bus and walk on the road to your right for about 7km to the reserve. At La Delicia, there is a country store and a sign that reads 'Departamento Forestal.' Fundación Maquipucuna can provide updated bus information or arrange a private vehicle from Quito (US$75 total for one to four visitors).

If you are driving, 4WD is recommended from La Delicia to the reserve, although high-clearance 2WD can make it in the dry season.

Hitchhiking is possible, but there's little traffic out here.

RESERVA BIOLÓGICA LOS CEDROS

This remote area covers 6400 hectares of cloud forest to the north of Maquipucuna. Several new species of insects, frogs and orchids have been discovered here. A canopy walkway is under construction.

Transportes San José de Minas (see Getting There & Away under Reserva Biológica Maquipucuna, earlier) has a daily 8 am bus from Quito to Sanguangal (six hours), where there are a couple of pensiones, or ask for Gringo Pepe's Hacienda. From Sanguangal, it's a six-hour hike. The reserve is recommended by the South American Explorers, and rates are US$30 a day, including meals – this might be just the adventure for you. Volunteer positions may be arranged (there is a charge of US$250 a month), and most visitors are either researchers (who must have their projects planned and approved in advance) or birders.

For more information, contact Los Cedros (☎ 02-540 346), Alemania and Eloy Alfaro, 4th floor, Quito. Safari Tours (see Information under Quito) also has information on getting there and can arrange transportation.

RESERVA BELLAVISTA

This small 110-hectare reserve is in the same western Andean slopes as Maquipucuna (see that section, earlier), at about 2000m above sea level. About 25% is primary forest, and the rest has been selectively or completely logged but is being reforested. Various conservation projects are under way. There is a well-marked trail system, and the area is highly recommended by birders.

The main lodge is a wooden geodesic dome with a library/restaurant/bar on the ground floor, over which are five small rooms with private baths, topped by a two-story dormitory sleeping area (reached by a ladder) with a shared bath, a restaurant and a 360° balcony – a fine place to wake up, surrounded by cloud-forest views. These are wonderful sleeping spots if you like to share with others, but they are not suitable for people needing privacy or for those unable to climb narrow ladders. A couple of more spacious two-bedroom cabins with bath are being built, and camping is permitted. About a kilometer from the main lodge is a research station with a kitchen and hostal-type accommodations.

Rates per person are US$5 (camping), US$10 (hostal) and US$17 (dorm). Private rooms are US$39/66/91 for singles/doubles/triples. Three meals a day cost US$24 daily (or individual meals can be purchased), and the rate for children 12 and under is discounted by 50%. Variously priced (depending on accommodations) packages including transportation from Quito, and guided hikes are offered. For more information, contact Richard/Gloria Parsons (☎/fax 02-232 313, 224 469, at Bellavista 09-490 891, aecie3@ ecnet.ec), Jorge Washington E7-23 and Reina Victoria, Quito. It may be hard to get through on the phone; if so, leave a message and they'll call you back.

Reaching the lodge is not easy. Take a bus to Nanegalito, then hire a pickup truck (ask at the restaurant or at a store for Señor Bermúdez, who knows the route well – but there are other drivers) for about 16km. Otherwise, get off the bus at Km 32 (about 4km before Nanegalito) and hike up a steep 12km dirt road. If driving, you can also reach Bellavista using unpaved 12km roads from Km 42 or from Km 58. The last one is in the best condition for cars.

MINDO
☎ 02

This small village, about a three- or four-hour drive west of Quito, is a popular destination for bird watchers and fans of natural history who want to see some of Ecuador's western forests at a reasonable cost. Mindo is at about 1300m elevation and has an area of premontane forest nearby called the **Bosque Protector Mindo-Nambillo**. A local private group is preserving the area, which is very beautiful and excellent for bird watching.

Beyond Mindo, the poor road drops to **Los Bancos** (also known as San Miguel de los Bancos), shortly beyond which the road improves and continues through Puerto Quito (see North of Santo Domingo, later) and on to intersect with the main road between Santo Domingo de los Colorados and the north-coast port of Esmeraldas. This is an infrequently used route from Quito to the western lowlands.

Information

Amigos de la Naturaleza-Mindo (amigos-mindo@hotmail.com) is a local conservation organization and has an office in Mindo. It has information about the area and can give you directions and guides to Bosque Protector Mindo-Nambillo, which is about 4km away. There is a charge of US$10 per person for a guided day hike, or US$5 per person just to enter the reserve and hike the trails on your own. There is also a lodge. Ask in central Mindo for the location of the office (there is no street address or phone number).

A highly recommended birding guide is Vinicio Perez (he speaks a little English, but his wife is fluent), who runs the Bird-watcher's House (a hostal; also see the listing under Places to Stay, later). His Quito contact is (☎ 612 955, 451 035), or just ask for him in Mindo – he's often available, although expensive. International tour groups use him, and he reportedly has found 100 different species in one day! Other local guides who know birds are Efraín Toapanta (who speaks some German) and Hugolina Oñate. Tom Quesenberry, at El Monte Sustainable Lodge (see Places to Stay, later), is also a trained naturalist guide.

British birder Simon Allen has written *A Birder's Guide to Mindo*. You can contact him by writing to h_t_allen@msn.com or to 63 Goldstone Crescent, Hove, BN3 6LR, UK.

Mindo Orchid Garden, on the outskirts, costs US$1 to visit and includes a 30-minute guided tour. Caligo Butterfly Garden, which is about 3km from town, is also worth a visit and is inexpensive. Inner-tubing on Río Mindo is also popular; ask at your hotel.

WESTERN LOWLANDS

Places to Stay & Eat

There are some basic but friendly places to stay and eat in the village and more comfortable and expensive places in the surroundings.

Budget At the edge of Mindo, as you are arriving, is the clean and friendly *Hostal Bijao (in Quito ☎ 02-525 730),* which has six rooms with private bath and three more sharing a bath. There is hot water and an excellent, family-run *restaurant* that is also open to nonguests. Rates are about US$3 to US$4 per person.

Next to the central park (which is basically a soccer field), the British/Ecuadorian-run *Gypsy Hostal (☎ 351 061, 352 805, gypsyhostal@yahoo.com)* has seven screened rooms sharing two bathrooms with hot water, a balcony with hammocks, and a *restaurant/bar* serving all meals and beer – accompanied by chats with the British landlord, Keith. He has Mindo's only public cable TV (but only turns it on by request or if something important is happening, such as an international soccer match). Beds cost US$3 per person.

Vinicio Perez's *Birdwatchers House* (see Information, earlier in this section) is a good choice for dedicated birders looking for cheap sleeps. Beds cost about US$6 per person, and Vinicio is building another, larger hotel next door.

Another budget hotel in the center (all charging around US$3) is *Arco Iris*, which has about 30 simple rooms, some with private bath. *Hotel Armonía (☎ 224 713, 546 013),* across the soccer field from Gypsy Hostal, is reportedly OK.

There is a new *pizzería*, or you can ask to eat at *Margarita Mora's*, who reportedly prepares good homemade food. By the soccer field, *Restaurant del Falero* is a new local recommendation; it has both national and international food.

Mid-Range *El Monte Sustainable Lodge* (☎ /fax 02-558 889, info@ecuadortravel.com) is about 4km south of Mindo along a winding dirt road. Run by a warmhearted and knowledgeable young US/Ecuadorian

couple, this place is a real find. From a tiny parking area, it's reached by a *tarabita* (handpowered cable car) over Río Mindo. Alternatively, you can cross a footbridge at Mindo Gardens Lodge (see the next paragraph) and then hike for about a kilometer. El Monte has three lovely private cabins, as well as a communal lodge. The two-story, A-frame, riverside cabins all sleep up to four people and have a hot shower and sitting room. The lodge has a restaurant with a library, bar and games. Rates are US$55 per person, including all meals (vegetarian, fish, poultry; no red meat) and guided activities (birding, hiking, tubing, horseback riding); a two-night minimum is suggested. Reservations are recommended to ensure that the owners can guide you (they'll meet you in Mindo) and that you have a cabin to yourself (sharing is unnecessary). You can visit the lodge's Web site at www.ecuadorexplorer.com/elmonte.

Mindo Gardens Lodge (in Quito ☎ 02-252 488/89/90, fax 253 452, casablan@uio.satnet.net) is about a kilometer north of El Monte Sustainable Lodge and is reached by car. Set in nicely landscaped gardens, the lodge has four main buildings. The central building has an elegant *dining room* with an international menu (open to the public), as well as a games room (with a pool table and cable TV) and bar. Outside, there is a barbecue and pizza oven, which is used as needed. The three cabins all have three bedrooms, each with a private hot bath and all sharing a sitting room. The rooms sleep two to four people. Two cabins are riverside, and the third is surrounded by forest. The lodge can arrange local tours and is run well. Rates are US$62 per person, including all meals; children under 12 get discounts.

Centro de Educación Ambiental is run by Amigos de la Naturaleza (see Information, earlier) and is between the two lodges listed previously, but it is reached by foot – the road doesn't go there. Ask how to get there in Mindo. Accommodations are rustic but well constructed and attractive. A dorm with 15 mattresses (bring a sleeping bag) plus four private double rooms share bathroom facilities (cold water only). Rates are about US$16 to US$22 per person, including meals.

Hostería El Carmelo de Mindo (☎/fax 408 355) is almost a kilometer out of town and offers a variety of rooms with and without private bath. This place was being remodeled recently; call for rates.

Getting There & Away

Bus From Quito, Cooperativa Flor de Valle (☎ 527 495) goes to Mindo daily at 3:20 pm and also at 8 am Friday, Saturday and Sunday. The bus leaves from M Larrea just west of Ascunción, near Parque El Ejido. Get there early, as the bus fills up. The bus returns from Mindo to Quito daily at 6:30 am and at 2 pm Friday, Saturday and Sunday. The journey costs US$2 and takes 2½ hours.

There is also a Mindo bus from the Santo Domingo de los Colorados bus terminal at 2 pm daily with Cooperativa Kennedy (five hours). There are buses from Mindo to Santo Domingo at 7 am and 1 pm.

Car If you rent a vehicle, you could then continue on through Los Bancos down into the lowlands – an interesting and beautiful drive. There is a paved road from Mitad del Mundo via Calacalí, Nanegalito, Santa Rosa and on to Mindo. This route takes about two hours. An unpaved and more scenic road goes from Quito via Nono and joins the paved road near Santa Rosa. This road is in poor condition, and 4WD is advised in the wet months (the driest months are June to September). Allow about four hours for this route.

QUITO TO SANTO DOMINGO
☎ 02

The most common route from the highlands to the western lowlands is the main road from Quito to Santo Domingo de los Colorados. From Santo Domingo, you can head south through Quevedo and Babahoyo, in the lowland province of Los Ríos (described later), and on to Guayaquil, on the south coast; or you can go northwest toward Esmeraldas, on the north coast.

From Quito, the bus heads south through the 'Avenue of the Volcanoes' to **Alóag**,

where the road to Santo Domingo branches off from the Panamericana. Since the bus often refuels here, a common sight is the hordes of snack sellers lustily hawking their delicacies.

The descent into the lowlands is a spectacular and sometimes terrifying one. It is best to make the journey in the morning, as in the afternoon, both the passengers' and the driver's views are often obscured by fog. Despite almost nonexistent visibility, the drivers hurtle down the western slopes of the Andes at breakneck speeds. Amazingly, accidents are very rare, but near misses are somewhat more common.

The road to Santo Domingo begins in high páramo, with views of the extinct **Volcanes Atacazo** (4463m) and **Corazón** (4788m) to the north and south, respectively. The tortuous descent follows the left bank of Río Pilatón, and occasionally, waterfalls cascade into the narrow gorge. The road passes the village of **Cornejo Astorga** (also known as Tandapi) and follows Río Toachi valley. The vegetation becomes increasingly tropical, and if you're lucky, you may see orchids growing on the roadside. Higher temperatures are noticeable by the time you pull into the village of **Alluriquín**.

Shortly before reaching Santo Domingo, you pass an oil pressure station. The road follows the trans-Ecuadorian oil pipeline for the last third of its distance. If your bus is continuing beyond Santo Domingo, it may avoid the town altogether, because there are a couple of bypasses; normally, however, even long-distance buses pull into Santo Domingo for a break.

About 16km outside of Santo Domingo, *Tinalandia (in Quito ☎/fax 449 028, info@ tinalandia.com)* is a hotel known for its extensive grounds, which include (rarely used) nine-hole golf course and nature trails; the place is also excellent for birding. The vegetation is premontane wet forest at an elevation of about 600m. Accommodations consist of bungalows or cabins with private baths and hot showers. Rates are US$80/105 for singles/doubles, including three meals. The hotel is sometimes booked by bird-watching groups, so you have to take your chances if you don't have a reservation. (Major travel agencies in Ecuador can make reservations for you, or you can contact the place yourself.) The driest months (May and June) are particularly popular with birders. You can make day visits to the grounds for US$10. Tinalandia is about 86km after the turnoff from the Panamericana in Alóag. There is a small stone sign on the right side of the road as you drive from Quito, and the hotel itself is about half a kilometer up a track on the left side of the road. If you are on a bus to Santo Domingo, ask the driver to let you off at Tinalandia – all the drivers know it.

SANTO DOMINGO DE LOS COLORADOS
☎ 02
Better known as Santo Domingo, this is one of the fastest-growing cities in Ecuador and has a population close to 200,000. It is important as a transportation hub, with major roads heading north, south, east and west. Just 500m above sea level and only 130km from Quito, Santo Domingo is the nearest lowland tropical town that is easily accessible from the capital, so it is a popular weekend destination for Quiteños – but it's of limited interest to travelers.

Information
Because Sunday is Santo Domingo's main market day, the town closes down Monday. There are the usual Andinatel and post offices (see the map), and the Filanbanco (which has a Visa ATM) will exchange US dollars and traveler's checks at rates close to Quito's; it's on the corner of Los Tsachilas and Avenida Quito. Banco de Guayaquil, on Avenida Quito east of town, has a Mastercard ATM. The two Bancos del Pichincha change US cash. Megacentro, near the intersection of Avenida 29 de Mayo and Esmeraldas, is the only supermarket in town.

SANTO DOMINGO DE LOS COLORADOS

WESTERN LOWLANDS

PLACES TO STAY
2 Hotel El Colorado
5 Hotel Diana Real
6 Hotel Puerta del Sol
7 Hotel Ejecutivo
8 Hotel Unicornio
9 Hotel Amambay
10 Hotel Genova
11 Hostal Jennefer
12 Hotel Caleta
15 Residencial San Martín
19 Hostal Las Brisas

PLACES TO EAT
12 Cebichería Caleta
13 Chifa Tay Happy
18 Elite Restaurant
20 Chicken Restaurant
21 Chicken Restaurant

OTHER
1 Banco de Pichincha
3 Megacentro Supermarket
4 Local Buses
14 Town Hall
16 Banco del Pichincha
17 Filanbanco
22 Andinatel

Things to See & Do

The town's greatest fame is for the Tsachila Indians (see the boxed text), who are not much in evidence here.

Santo Domingo is a convenient city in which to make bus connections or break a long journey. There are lively street markets and a busy Sunday market, when activities spill out onto surrounding streets, but watch your belongings carefully in these areas. These markets are for locals, and mainly mundane things – such as clothing, produce and kitchen utensils – are sold there.

Río Toachi is nearby, and city buses go there. Just across the river is a modest resort with a few restaurants, a swimming pool (you may prefer to swim in the river) and some games courts.

Santo Domingo is the capital of its canton and celebrates its cantonization day on July 3, when there are fairs and agricultural festivals – the town and the hotels are quite crowded then.

Places to Stay

The town is crowded during the July 3 celebrations and on weekends (due to the Sunday market and weekend visitors from Quito); prices may be higher then. You will have a better choice of hotels midweek. Most of the cheapest hotels are in the center, near the market area, which is not very safe at night. Some new cheap hotels have opened near the bus terminal, 3km from the center. The better hotels are away from the center.

Note that many hotels offer TV – four or five local channels with poor reception. Make sure it is cable and has 20 or 30 channels before paying extra. The cheapest hotels lack fans; ask for a table fan.

Budget Opposite the bus terminal, try *Hostal Patricia* (☎ 761 906), which has rates of US$2 to US$3 per person for rooms with a private cold shower. Some rooms have TV. Others nearby are *Hotel España* and *Hotel Sheraton* (☎ 751 988) (hot water is advertised), both with similar prices.

In the center, there are many cheap hotels, of which the following is just a selection of the better places. *Hotel Ejecutivo* (☎ 752 893, 763 305), by the market, has rooms for US$2 to US$4 per person, depending on the size of the rooms and whether you want TV. All have private bath, and there is a café. The friendly *Hotel Caleta* (☎ 750 530, Ibarra 137) is US$3/5 for singles/doubles in clean rooms with cold showers. Cheaper options include the clean and helpful *Residencial San Martín* (☎ 750 813), at 29 de Mayo and Tulcán, with a rate of US$2 per person; *Hotel Unicornio* (☎ 760 147), at 29 de Mayo and Ambato; and others along 29 de Mayo toward the market.

A good budget choice is the clean *Hostal Jennefer* (☎ 750 577), at 29 de Mayo between Latacunga and Ibarra, which has rates of US$4.50/8 for large singles/doubles with a warm electric shower and fans. *Hotel Genova* (☎ 759 694), at 29 de Mayo and Ibarra, is a clean choice with large rooms with private bath (electric showers) and TV for US$5/8.

Other cheapies include *Hostal Las Brisas* (☎ 750 560), on Avenida Quito near Iturralde, and *Hotel Amambay* (☎ 750 696), on 29 de Mayo between Ambato and Latacunga. *Hotel El Colorado* (☎ 750 226, 754 299), at 29 de Mayo and Esmeraldas, has many cheap rooms and is clean enough but is run down.

For something a bit more upscale, *Hotel Diana Real* (☎ 751 380, 751 384, fax 754 091), on 29 de Mayo at Loja, has clean rooms with fan, cable TV, hot shower and telephone for US$8/12. There is also a restaurant. For a dollar more, the new *Hotel Puerta del Sol* (☎ 750 370, ☎/fax 751 437), on 29 de Mayo near Cuenca, is about the same.

Better hotels are out along Avenida Quito. The first is *Hotel La Siesta* (☎ 751 013, 751 860, Avenida Quito 606), which charges US$9/12 for rooms with fan, cable TV, hot shower and phone. It has a decent restaurant. *Hotel del Toachi* (☎ 754 688/9), almost a kilometer out of town, charges US$8/12 for characterless but clean rooms with private shower, hot water, fan, TV and telephone. There is a swimming pool and a good pizzería next door.

Mid-Range About 1.5km east of town on Avenida Quito is the well-known *Hotel Zaracay* (☎ 750 316, 750 429, 751 023, 754 873, fax 754 535), which charges US$33/43 for spacious, air-conditioned rooms with bath, TV, telephone and balcony – or almost half that for rooms with fans. The food is pricey but good, and the rooms are in jungle-style cabins with thatched roofs. The pleasant gardens have a swimming pool, and there is a tennis court and casino. This hotel is popular, and reservations are a good idea (but not always necessary). Nearly opposite Hotel Zaracay is *Hotel Tropical Inn* (☎ 761 771/2/3/4, fax 761 775), which is of more modern construction and has a pool and restaurant. Both air-conditioned and ventilated rooms are about 20% cheaper than those at Hotel Zaracay, but they lack that thatched-roof character.

Places to Eat

Fried chicken – everywhere. A couple of good places are on Avenida Quito at 29 de Mayo, and more are found out along Avenida Quito.

On opposite corners of the main plaza, *Chifa Tay Happy*, which serves Chinese food, and the slightly upscale *Elite Restaurant*, which serves Ecuadorian food, are both OK.

Parrilladas Argentinas, on the traffic circle on Avenida Quito, has good grills but not much else. They are also on Km 5 on Vía a Quevedo – this one has more choices but closes by 8:30 pm; take a taxi.

Next to Hotel Toachi is *Ch' Farina* (☎ 750 295), which has the best pizza in town; it does take-out and delivery. A few other restaurants are nearby. Cebichería Caleta is open for lunch under the hotel of the same name and is locally popular for ceviche.

Entertainment

Head out along Avenida Quito. *Salsateca The Jungle*, just beyond Hotel La Siesta, is OK for dancing. *Colorados Pool Bar*, a few blocks farther, has good recorded music and pool and is suitable for women and men alike. A few other bars and cafés are found along this street.

Getting There & Away

The bus terminal is almost 2km north of town and has frequent buses to many major towns. Quito (2½ hours) and Guayaquil (five hours) are the most frequent destinations, and buses of several companies leave to those cities at least once an hour. The smaller *busetas* tend to be faster than the larger buses. It's easy to catch buses to intermediate points such as Quevedo or Daule, but you'll find fewer buses to Babahoyo, as most southbound buses take the Daule road after passing through Quevedo.

If you're heading south toward Peru and don't want to change at Guayaquil, try Transportes Occidentales, which has several departures a day to Machala (US$5 to US$6, eight hours); the buses are fairly slow, but they are large and reasonably comfortable.

There are buses about every hour to the north-coast town of Esmeraldas (US$2.50, 3½ hours), stopping at La Concordia and Quinindé. After going through Esmeraldas, some of these buses may continue to Atacames or Muisne.

Buses also go to the central coast, but not as frequently as to Esmeraldas. Bahía de Caráquez (US$3.50, six hours) and Manta (US$4.30, seven hours) are both served by several companies.

Express Sucre has buses to Cuenca (US$5, 10 hours). There are also buses to Latacunga, Ambato and Riobamba (US$3.50, five hours).

There is a local bus plaza at the west end of 3 de Julio, where you can find beat-up old bone-shakers to take you to nearby villages. It can be interesting to take one of these buses just to see the countryside, but make sure that there is a return bus, as these villages often don't have restaurants – let alone a place to stay. You can also find buses here returning to Quito via La Concordia and (San Miguel de) Los Bancos – an uncomfortable eight-hour ride, but there is beautiful scenery. Buses to Mindo may leave from this plaza or the bus terminal; ask locally.

Getting Around

Bus The most useful city bus is signed 'Centro' and runs past the bus terminal, through the center and out along Avenida Quito, past Hotel Toachi and Hotel Zaracay on the way to the Río Toachi swimming area. The fare is US$0.10. The return bus, signed 'Terminal Terrestre,' heads west along 29 de Mayo, picking up passengers for the terminal.

Taxi A taxi from the bus terminal to the center should cost just under US$1.

NORTH OF SANTO DOMINGO
☎ 02

The main road goes to the port of Esmeraldas (see the North Coast chapter), almost 200km away.

The **Bosque Protectora La Perla** (☎ 02-725 344, 02-759 115) is about 42km northwest of Santo Domingo. This 250-hectare reserve is a good spot for birding and nature walks; guided hikes and camping are also possible. Visits are US$5 per person (including a guide), and a maximum of 10 visitors are allowed on any given day. Advance reservations are requested, and exact directions can be obtained at the time of reservation.

A few kilometers beyond is the village of **La Concordia**, which has a basic hostal. About 50km northwest of Santo Domingo (just past La Concordia), a new paved road leads eastward to Puerto Quito and Pedro Vicente Maldonado and eventually reaches Mitad del Mundo.

About 87km northwest of Santo Domingo, is the small town of **Quinindé** (also known as Rosa Zárate; the area code is 06). There are a couple of basic hotels in this town, of which *Paraíso* has been suggested. Approximately 40km west of Quinindé is the Reserva Biológica Bilsa.

Puerto Quito

About 2km east of Puerto Quito, at Km 140, a sign points to *Aldea Salamandra (in Quito ☎ 02-449 881, 253 967, fax 254 709, aldeasalamandra@yahoo.com),* about 500m away on the banks of Río Caoni. This is a very tranquil, rustic hideaway where you can swim and canoe in the river; it's also an excellent place to go bird watching or to just relax. There are no showers (you can wash in the river) or flushing toilets. Beds cost US$7 per person, and packages that include three meals and guided excursions are US$17 a day or US$100 a week. The place is gaining popularity among young budget travelers, but it is far from 'discovered.'

Rooms with private showers are available at *Cabañas del Río (☎ 02-238 712, 09-491 154),* which is also on Río Caoni. They sleep two to eight, and rates are US$40 per person, including meals and guided walks.

Although Puerto Quito is only 300m above sea level, there is no malaria reported in this area.

Puerto Quito is reached by frequent buses from Quito's Terminal Terrestre (use Transportes Kennedy, San Pedrito or Alóag) and by less frequent buses from Santo Domingo.

Pedro Vicente Maldonado

This small village is the home of the new *Arashá Rainforest Resort & Spa (☎ 02-265 757, 449 881, 253 937/8, fax 260 992, arasha@ porta.net).* This is the most luxurious hotel in the biodiverse forests of Ecuador's western slopes. In addition to birding, hiking and wildlife-watching excursions, the resort offers a pool, a whirlpool, waterfalls, a kid's swimming area, rafting, two international restaurants, a bar, a games and video room, a conference room and beautiful grounds. There are 26 cottages with a total of 47 rooms, all with private bath. Rates are still in flux but are expected to be around US$100.

The hotel lies 3km outside the village at Km 120 and about 200m off the main road to Puerto Quito. It has a Web site at www.arasha1spa.com.

Reserva Biológica Bilsa

This 3000-hectare reserve lies in the Montañas de Mache (a small range of coastal mountains) at an elevation between 300m and 750m. It preserves some of the last remaining stands of premontane tropical wet forests. The biodiversity here is exceptionally high – it is rated as one of the world's megadiversity hot spots. Howler monkeys are common, jaguars and pumas have been recently recorded, isolated populations of endangered birds have been found, and new species of plants have been discovered. Clearly, the area holds a lot of potential for conservation, research and education – the primary goals of Fundación Jatun Sacha, which founded the reserve in 1994. Jatun Sacha is one of Ecuador's primary research and conservation organizations.

Bilsa was founded in memory of US ornithologist Ted Parker, botanist Al Gentry, and Ecuadorian conservationist Eduardo Aspiazu – three noted scientists who died nearby in 1993 in an aircraft accident while carrying out research to inventory the flora and fauna of the area.

During the wet months of January to June, access is only on foot or mule via a 25km muddy trail, but vehicular access may be possible in the dry months. This difficulty of access is what has contributed to the preservation of the area in the first place, so don't feel bad about it! There is a rustic field station that accommodates up to 45 visiting researchers and natural-history visitors for US$20 a day, including food. Bedding and mosquito nets are provided, and five trails offer hiking and exploring opportunities. Various research and volunteer programs are under way (volunteers pay US$75 a week for room and board). Reservations should be made with the reserve

Even if you don't get to see a howler monkey in the wild, there's a good chance you'll hear its eerie call.

manager Michael McColm through Jatun Sacha (☎ 250 976, ☎/fax 441 592, mccolm@jsacha.ecuanex.net.ec).

RÍO PALENQUE SCIENCE CENTER

Río Palenque Science Center is just off the main Santo Domingo-Quevedo road, about 46km south of Santo Domingo and 56km north of Quevedo. Renowned orchid expert Dr Calaway Dodson owns this small private preserve of 180 hectares, which contain about 100 hectares of primary rainforest. Although this is not a very large area, it is one of the largest tracts of western-lowlands forest left in the area. It forms a habitat island and is surrounded by agricultural land. There are about 70 hectares of African oil-palm plantation within the science center, and more palm, banana, cacao and other crops are grown for many kilometers around the center. The elevation is about 200m, and it is hot and humid for much of the year, particularly from December to July. It is drier during the rest of the year.

There are facilities for researchers, including a small laboratory and a small library of books and papers relevant to the area. A flora checklist published in 1978 mentions 1100 plants at the center, and of these, about 100 species were new to science. This gives an indication of how important it is to preserve what little there is left of this unique habitat. Bird lists include over 360 species from the area, and insect lists are equally impressive. Because of the small size of the preserve, however, there are no large and few small mammals present. Slowly, the pressure of the surrounding agricultural lands is lowering the species counts for the science center – if a species dies out or leaves, it is unlikely to come back again.

There are about 3km of trails at the center, and the bird watching is excellent. A day-use fee of US$5 is charged.

Places to Stay & Eat

The *field station* has six quadruple rooms, shower and toilet facilities, and an equipped kitchen. Accommodations are adequate but not luxurious. Rates are US$15 per person per night if you bring your own food, or US$30 if you have the caretaker prepare meals for you. The nearest *store* is in the village of Patricia Pilar, about 2km north of the entrance to the science center.

Reservations and information are available from Fundación Wong (in Guayaquil ☎ 04-208 670/80, fundacion@grupowong .com). If the place is not full of researchers (it usually isn't), you can just show up.

Getting There & Away
From Santo Domingo, you pass through the village of Patricia Pilar about 2km before reaching the sign on the left reading 'Centro Científico Río Palenque.' From there, a dirt road leads about 1.5km to the field station. The road is usually locked with a chain, but the caretaker has the key.

Any bus between Santo Domingo and Quevedo can drop you off or pick you up at the entrance road to the center.

QUEVEDO
☎ 05
It's just over 100km from Santo Domingo to Quevedo on a gently descending paved road. During the first 15km, you see frequent signs on the side of the road advertising the homes of Colorado Indian *curanderos* (medicine men). This is where you can visit them, but expect to pay for both cures and photography.

There are villages about every 20km along this road. The most important is the small market town of **Buena Fe**, about 15km before Quevedo. Buena Fe has a couple of basic hotels on the main street. The land is agricultural, with many banana plantations, and as you get closer to Quevedo, there are African palm and papaya groves.

Quevedo, which has about 100,000 inhabitants, is an important road hub and market town; tamarind and many other products pass through here. At only 145m above sea level, the town is depressingly hot, but the mountains, which feature cooler temperatures, are not far away. The Ecuadorian Chinese community has settled in this bustling and progressive town, so there are many chifas and Chinese-run businesses.

Information
Money Banco del Pichincha, on the corner of the main plaza, changes US cash and traveler's checks. Banco Internacional, at 7 de Octubre and Quarta, will change US cash only. Filanbanco, at Bolívar and Quarta, has a Visa ATM.

Post & Communications The post office is poorly marked, and you can't really tell it's there when it's not open. Its entrance is through an alley in a business block near Bolívar. Pacifictel is on 7 de Octubre near Decimatercera.

Things to See & Do
The daily early-morning produce market on Malecón E Alfaro by the river is quite colorful, and you can walk along the river before it gets hot. The market at Séptima and Avenida Progreso has plenty of plastic junk but also has hammocks if you need one.

Quevedo celebrates its cantonization on October 7 with street parades and with a fair on the days preceding the 7th. (The road 7 de Octubre is the main drag.) Hotels are liable to be quite full then.

For most people, the main attraction is the drive from Latacunga, which is gorgeous.

Places to Stay
Budget There are many cheap hotels in Quevedo, but they are often depressingly similar – peeling walls, a lumpy bed and a

Pumas can be found in Reserva Biológica Bilsa.

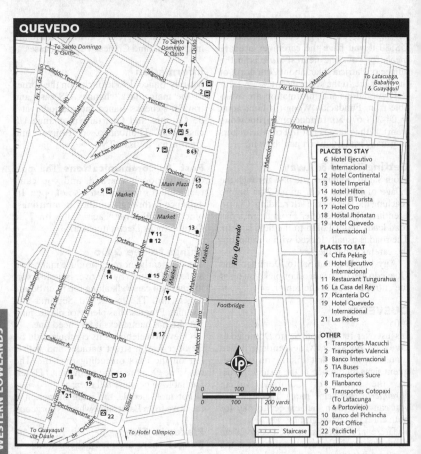

QUEVEDO

PLACES TO STAY
6 Hotel Ejecutivo
   Internacional
12 Hotel Continental
13 Hotel Imperial
14 Hotel Hilton
15 Hotel El Turista
17 Hotel Oro
18 Hostal Jhonatan
19 Hotel Quevedo
   Internacional

PLACES TO EAT
4 Chifa Peking
6 Hotel Ejecutivo
   Internacional
11 Restaurant Tungurahua
16 La Casa del Rey
19 Picantería DG
19 Hotel Quevedo
   Internacional
21 Las Redes

OTHER
1 Transportes Macuchi
2 Transportes Valencia
3 Banco Internacional
4 TIA Buses
7 Transportes Sucre
8 Filanbanco
9 Transportes Cotopaxi
   (To Latacunga
   & Portoviejo)
10 Banco del Pichincha
20 Post Office
22 Pacifictel

0   100   200 m
0   100   200 yards

▭▭▭▭ Staircase

broken window or no window at all. Some of the rooms in one place are marginally better than others, so it is worth asking to see another room if you don't like the first one you see. Many of the cheaper hotels suffer from water shortages, so check that the water's running if you want to shower immediately. Some hotels will turn the water pump off to save water but will turn it on when requested. People often swim in the river.

There are hotels with fans and air-conditioning that have basic rooms, but it's not worth paying for them unless you really want the air-conditioning.

The basic *Hotel El Turista (Novena 318)* has reasonably clean rooms for about US$3 per person, or rooms with private bath and TV for US$6 per person. The water is cold and only available during certain hours. The shabby but secure *Hotel Imperial (☎ 751 654, Séptima 104),* by the river, has basic rooms with cold-water private bathrooms and fans. Many of the rooms have river views (although some windows are reportedly broken), which is why the windows lack curtains – there are no buildings opposite. The market nearby may preclude sleep early in the morning, but the views of the goings-on are interesting. Other places for about US$3 can be found within a few blocks, but they are definitely worse.

For about US$4 per person, the following are acceptable. *Hotel Hilton* (☎ 751 359, Novena 429), looks pretty bad from the outside, but the rooms inside are OK – particularly the ones on the 2nd floor, some of which have private baths. The cheapest place with air-conditioning is the otherwise very basic *Hotel Continental*, at 7 de Octubre near Octava. Some rooms without air-conditioning are US$3 per person, and the hotel is sometimes used by short-stay clients.

Mid-Range The clean but dark *Hostal Jhonatan* (☎ 750 483, 752 296/8, June Guzman 705) has rooms with bath, TV, fan and phone for US$7/11; rooms with air-conditioning are US$11/14. *Hotel Ejecutivo Internacional* (☎ 751 780/1, fax 750 596), at 7 de Octubre and Quarta, has reasonably sized air-conditioned rooms that vary somewhat in quality – the interior rooms are nicer and quieter. Rates are about US$7/11. *Hotel Oro* (☎ 757 450, Bolívar 1043) charges US$10 per person for clean air-conditioned rooms with private cold shower, TV and telephone, and it has a popular restaurant downstairs (see Places to Eat, later).

Hotel Quevedo Internacional (☎ 751 875/6, Decimasegunda 207) has fair rooms with air-conditioning, TV, telephone and private hot showers for about US$17/23. The restaurant is quite good.

Finally, the best place to stay is on the eastern edge of town – *Hotel Olímpico* (☎ 750 455, 750 210, fax 751 314), on Decimanovena at Bolívar. This is a tourist complex, complete with an Olympic-sized swimming pool, waterslides, tennis courts, a casino, a good restaurant and a bar. Rooms are around US$30/45. It is popular and often full, so call ahead.

Places to Eat

With its large Chinese community, Quevedo has plenty of chifas. There are several along 7 de Octubre, of which *Chifa*

Peking is popular with locals. *La Casa del Rey*, at Bolívar and Novena, is another inexpensive, locally popular place. *Restaurant Tungurahua*, on 7 de Octubre near Séptima, is always packed for its cheap set lunches. *Las Redes* (June Guzman 801) is good for seafood. *Picantería DG*, under Hotel Oro, is popular for a variety of Ecuadorian food. The *restaurant in Hotel Olímpico* has been recommended as the best in town. The *hotel restaurants* of Quevedo Internacional and Ejecutivo Internacional are also acceptable.

Getting There & Away

Bus There is no central bus terminal, so you have to roam the streets looking for the various terminals; the main ones are on the map. Quevedo is 180km from Guayaquil by flat road and 235km from Quito by mountainous road, so it's not surprising that the bus situation heavily favors Guayaquil. In fact, there are only two companies with direct buses to Quito (US$3.25, four hours). Transportes Macuchi has the most buses to Quito; one leaves about every hour from 3 am to 4 pm. Or you can take one of the frequent Transportes Sucre buses to Santo Domingo, where you can change to equally frequent buses to Quito. Transportes Sucre also has buses to Portoviejo.

Buses to Guayaquil (US$2.25) are very frequent and take 2½ to four hours, depending on the bus. Ask at Transportes Sucre or TIA, which normally go via Daule. If you want to go via Babahoyo (US$1.30, 1½ to two hours), you should go with Transportes Valencia, which has buses every 20 minutes from 3:15 am to 7:45 pm.

Transportes Cotopaxi has hourly departures 3 am to 5 pm to Latacunga (US$3, 5½ hours), as well as an 8 am and a 1 pm bus to Portoviejo (US$3.50, four hours). This route, from Latacunga via Quevedo to Portoviejo, is one of the least-frequently traveled and also one of the prettiest highland-to-coast routes. The buses are old, crowded and uncomfortable, but the journey is more interesting than the standard routes.

Tsachila (Colorado) Indians

Santo Domingo de los Colorados used to be famous for its resident Tsachila Indians (better known as Colorado Indians, after whom the town is named), who painted their faces with black stripes and dyed their bowl-shaped haircuts a brilliant red using a natural dye from the *achiote* plant. You can buy postcards of them all over Ecuador, but the Indians are now fairly westernized, and you are unlikely to see them in their traditional finery unless you go to one of their nearby villages and pay them to dress up. Photographers are expected to give 'tips,' but the Tsachilas are becoming increasingly unhappy with their role as models for foreign photographers. Please be sensitive to this.

The best-known Colorado village is **Chihuilpe**, about 7km south of Santo Domingo on the road to Quevedo and then about 3km east on a dirt road. Some of the older Indians, notably the *gobernador* (headman) Abraham Calazacon (who died in the 1980s) and his brother Gabriel, earned reputations as *curanderos* (medicine men), and people still come from all over Ecuador to be cured. The present gobernador is Abraham's son, Nicanor Calazacon, who continues the traditional work of a curandero. Nearby, the house of Agosto Calazacon is a tourist center, and there is now a small museum here that describes Tsachila history and culture.

There are other Colorado villages in the area south of Santo Domingo, but for the most part, the villagers prefer to be left alone. Apart from going to the tourist center in Chihuilpe, you can also visit one of the curanderos who advertise their trade in the first 15km of the route to Quevedo. They mainly sell curative herbs, but some may offer other healing treatments. A taxi from Santo Domingo to Chihuilpe will cost US$10 to US$15 for a two- to three-hour trip.

FROM QUEVEDO TO GUAYAQUIL
☎ 04

If your southbound bus crosses Río Quevedo, then you are going to Babahoyo; if it doesn't, then you are heading to Daule, which is the most frequent route to Guayaquil.

About 20km away from Quevedo on the road toward Daule, you reach **Empalme** – or Velasco Ibarra, as it's officially called. Here the road forks; the westbound route is an unpaved road to Portoviejo, and the southbound route is a paved road to Guayaquil. Empalme is a busy little junction town with several basic restaurants and pensiones. You're in the heart of banana country here, and it continues that way to **Balzar**, another small market town with a basic hotel.

Near **Palestina**, the banana plantations give way to rice paddies, and *piladoras* are frequently seen along the road. Piladoras are husking-and-drying factories, with tons of rice spread out on huge concrete slabs to dry in the sun (assuming you're traveling in the dry season). Not everyone can afford the commercial piladoras, and often you see a poor campesino spreading out his few bushels of rice to dry on the tarmac at the side of the road. In other areas, similar piladoras are used to dry crops such as coffee, corn and cacao.

About three quarters of the way to Guayaquil, you'll reach **Daule**. This is another small commercial and agricultural center with basic hotels. Three hours after leaving Quevedo, the bus reaches Guayaquil, which is Ecuador's major port and largest city and is described in the South Coast chapter.

BABAHOYO
☎ 05

With about 80,000 inhabitants, Babahoyo is the capital of the flat agricultural province of Los Ríos. North of it lie banana and palm plantations, south of it are rice paddies and some cattle. Huge flocks of white cattle egrets can make the ride from Babahoyo to Guayaquil very pretty.

Babahoyo was once an important town on the route between Guayaquil and Quito. In the 19th century, passenger and cargo

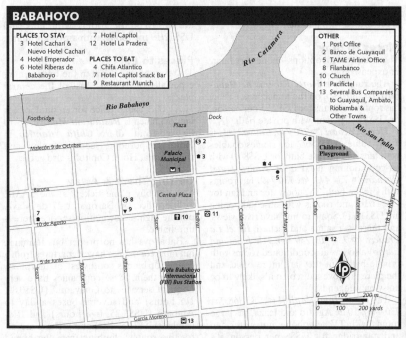

BABAHOYO

PLACES TO STAY
3 Hotel Cachari &
    Nuevo Hotel Cachari
4 Hotel Emperador
6 Hotel Riberas de
    Babahoyo

7 Hotel Capitol
12 Hotel La Pradera

PLACES TO EAT
4 Chifa Atlantico
7 Hotel Capitol Snack Bar
9 Restaurant Munich

OTHER
1 Post Office
2 Banco de Guayaquil
5 TAME Airline Office
8 Filanbanco
10 Church
11 Pacifictel
13 Several Bus Companies
    to Guayaquil, Ambato,
    Riobamba &
    Other Towns

Río Catamara

Río Babahoyo

Footbridge   Dock

Plaza

Malecón 9 de Octubre   Río San Pablo

Palacio
Municipal

Children's
Playground

Barona

Central Plaza

10 de Agosto

5 de Junio

Flota Babahoyo
Internacional
(FBI) Bus Station

García Moreno

0   100   200 m
0   100   200 yards

boats regularly steamed up Río Babahoyo as far as this town and then transferred to mules for the ride up to Quito. Perhaps because of its low elevation and propensity for flooding, the area was called Babahoyo, which translates as 'slimepit.'

Although it's not exactly exciting, Babahoyo is a bustling and energetic town with much commercial activity. The central streets are very busy, and gringos are an uncommon sight.

Information

Filanbanco has a Visa ATM, and Banco de Guayaquil has a MasterCard ATM; see the map for their locations. The post office is in the government buildings on the central plaza, and the Pacifictel office is on 10 de Agosto between Bolívar and Calderón.

Things to See & Do

Babahoyo, only 7m above sea level and on the banks of Río Babahoyo, was badly

flooded during the 1982–83 El Niño. To get some idea of what the flood was like, go to the plaza at the edge of the river. The flood-retaining walls, some 6m high in the dry season, were completely washed away in places. The water flooded the surrounding streets for several weeks, and inhabitants waded knee-deep or used canoes to get around.

Before the floods, there were floating houses on the river; they just rose and fell with the waters. A few drifted loose, but most remained undamaged. You can cross the river by canoe for a nominal fee; there are frequent departures from the dock.

The church on the central plaza has a large, modern mural of the Virgin and Child decorating the entire front. The otherwise pleasing effect is marred somewhat by the massive iron doors, which look more like the doors of a maximum security prison than the entrance to a place of worship.

Babahoyo foundation day, May 27, 1869, is celebrated with parades.

Places to Stay

There are several options – none very fancy or expensive.

The run-down *Hotel Riberas de Babahoyo* (☎ 730 082), on the Malecón at Carbo, has rooms with fans for US$2.25 per person, or US$3 per person with private bath.

Hotel Cachari (☎ 730 749, Bolívar 111) is a fair value at US$6/7 for singles/doubles with fans and private bath, or US$8/10 with air-conditioning. Next door, *Nuevo Hotel Cachari* (☎ 734 443, fax 730 749) has rooms with private bath, TV, hot water and fan for US$11/16, and rooms with air-conditioning are US$14/19. Some rooms have river views, and there is a sauna and Jacuzzi. *Hotel La Pradera* (☎ 730 413, 730 564, 5 de Junio and Carbo) also has air-conditioned rooms with private bath, but they are more basic, and the place is above a disco, so it's likely to be noisy on weekends.

The clean *Hotel Capitol* (☎ 733 368, fax 730 446), 10 de Agosto and Icaza, has large rooms with TV, telephone, hot water, fan and minifridge for US$8 per person; it's US$12 per person for a room with air-conditioning. *Hotel Emperador* (☎ 730 535, 731 373, fax 732 518), at Barona near 27 de Mayo, has 32 modern rooms with TV, telephone and private hot shower. Rates are US$9/14 for rooms with fans and US$12/19 for rooms with air-conditioning.

Places to Eat

There are many *chifas* in the town center, especially on Barona east of the central plaza.

A good, cheap place for an outdoor (or indoor) lunch is *Restaurant Munich*, on 10 de Agosto at Alfaro. *Chifa Atlantico*, in Hotel Emperador, seems popular, and *snack bar* at Hotel Capitol is also good.

Getting There & Away

You can buy plane tickets at the TAME airline office, on Barona at 27 de Mayo, but the flight-confirmation service there is unreliable.

Babahoya has no proper bus terminal, but most companies have departures from a couple of blocks southwest of the plaza. Among them, these companies have very frequent services to Guayaquil (US$0.80, 1½ hours) and several buses a day to Ambato (US$3.25, five hours) and Riobamba (US$3.25, 4½ hours). These are attractive routes, climbing from the humid lowlands to the scenic flanks of Chimborazo. You can also get buses to most towns in the province. Flota Babahoya Internacional has the most frequent service to Guayaquil.

The North Coast

This chapter covers the two northern coastal provinces – Esmeraldas and Manabí. See the boxed text 'Ecuador's Coast,' in the Fact about Ecuador chapter, for an overview of the entire coast.

SAN LORENZO
☎ 06

Until the mid-1990s, San Lorenzo was accessible only by boat or train and had an isolated feel. Now, roads from highland Ibarra and coastal Esmeraldas have made San Lorenzo easily accessible, and the town is growing. Until recently, most travelers arrived by an exciting train ride down from Ibarra; now, the train doesn't run, because the bus is quicker and cheaper, and San Lorenzo – although it's prospering with its newfound road connections – is no longer on a popular tourist route.

San Lorenzo is not very well laid out, but it is small and most everyone knows where everything is. The main reason to be here is to travel along the coast. You can head north into Colombia or south toward Reserva Ecológica Cotacachi-Cayapas. Boat travel is still possible, despite the road.

Information

Buses into town arrive passing the train station and continue to a central park. On the road between the station and the park are the better hotels. The boat port is a couple of blocks beyond the park.

The police station on the park or the *capitanía* (captaincy) at the boat dock take care of passport formalities if traveling into or out of Colombia.

There are no banks yet, although some stores will change small amounts of Colombian currency or US dollars. The telephone office is near the train station.

The Catholic hospital that is in San Lorenzo is reputedly the best in the area north of Esmeraldas.

Places to Stay & Eat

Rooms should have a bed with a mosquito net and a fan; the mosquitoes can be bad, especially in the wet months. Bring insect repellent or mosquito coils. The town suffers from occasional water shortages, so take showers when you can. New hotels are being built as the town grows. The following all have mosquito nets.

As you arrive in town, the first obvious place is *Gran Hotel San Carlos* (☎/fax 780 284), two or three blocks after the train station on the left (the telephone office is on the right). It is clean and safe (a locked gate lets you in) and has 35 rooms at US$3 per person with shared bath and US$4 with private bath and fan. Across the street is

Highlights

- Discoing the night away with young party animals from all over the world in Atacames

- Visiting the 'ecocity' of Bahía de Caráquez and taking advantage of various alternative tour opportunities.

- Sampling the coast, culture, archaeology and ornithology of Parque Nacional Machalilla

- Watching whales from June to early October near Puerto López

Equator

NORTH COAST

the cheaper and basic **Residencial Vilma**. Two blocks farther, on a side street to the left, the friendly **Hotel Pampa de Oro** (☎ 780 214, 780 263) is similarly priced and has rooms with TV for an extra US$0.50, although San Lorenzo has poor reception of about eight local channels. Next door is the restaurant **La Estación**, which is the most upscale in town (white tablecloths and wine glasses!) and has meals for about US$3 or US$4.

Another long block into town brings you to **Hotel Continental** (☎ 780 125, 780 304, in Ibarra ☎ 06-958 526), which has rooms with TV and warm showers. Rates are US$5/8 for singles/doubles with fan and US$8/12 with air-conditioning; this is currently the 'best' in town. Just beyond, across the street on the right, **Hotel Imperial** (☎ 780 242) charges US$2.50/3 with shared bath and US$3.50/6 with private bath, but a nearby dancehall might make it noisy at night. In fact, most hotels suffer from noise, especially on Friday and Saturday nights. Behind the Imperial is the very cheap and basic **Hostal San Lorenzo**. Continuing on into the park, you'll find the friendly **Hotel Carondolet** (☎ 780 202), which has clean rooms with bath for US$3 or US$4 per person. Note that per person rates are usually negotiable for couples using one bed.

Apart from La Estación, there are simple, hole-in-the-wall restaurants, although some produce pretty good food. **La Red** has a great shrimp dish; it's to the right just before Hotel Imperial. There is no sign; look for a fishing net hanging over the door (la red means 'fishing net'). **La Conchita** is recommended as well. Both places are quite cheap. Note that it's hard to find breakfast before 8 am.

Getting There & Away
Bus La Costeñita and Transportes del Pacífico take turns with hourly departures from 5 am to 4 pm for Borbón (US$1.75, two hours) and Esmeraldas (US$4.50, six hours). The road is mostly paved but has some badly potholed or unpaved sections. These buses leave from the central plaza, in front of Hotel Carondolet.

Buses for Ibarra leave after they arrive from Ibarra – around 11 am. They pass the train station, continue into the park, and return.

Train Trains to and from Ibarra stopped running in 1998. It used to be a great ride (especially sitting on the roof), and there is talk of reopening the line on a private basis for tourists. However, you'll probably have to take the bus from/to Ibarra (see Ibarra, in the North of Quito chapter, about taking a train halfway).

Boat Ask at the dock, two blocks from the central plaza, about boat departures. Since the opening of the road to Borbón and Esmeraldas, boat traffic has declined.

La Tola (US$4.25, 2½ hours) is the most common destination for travelers leaving San Lorenzo by boat, and it is served by two companies: La Costeñita and Transportes del Pacífico. They take turns and between the two of them have several departures from 5:30 am to 2 pm daily. Most boats to La Tola stop at Limones (see that section, next) en route, but few travelers stop there. If you take an early-morning boat to La Tola, you can connect with a bus on to Esmeraldas. Tickets are sold in San Lorenzo for the complete journey, or you can buy the bus portion when you get to La Tola. The bus takes about four or five hours from La Tola to Esmeraldas, so the whole trip from San Lorenzo to Esmeraldas can be done in one day and costs about US$8.

There may be a boat to Borbón, although this kind of transportation has largely been superceded by buses.

The motorized dugout journey via Limones to La Tola is interesting. The dugouts are small enough to travel through the coastal mangrove swamps, and you'll see black scissor-tailed frigatebirds circling overhead, squadrons of pelicans gliding by and schools of jellyfish floating past the boat. Don't forget to bring protection against sun, wind, rain and spray.

There are boats at 7 am and 11 am to La Frontera (US$2.50, two hours), in Colom-

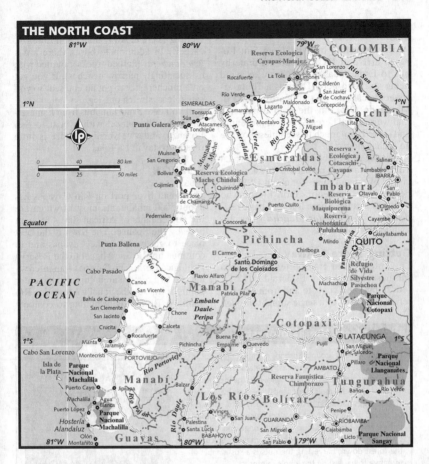

THE NORTH COAST

bia, from where bus connections via La Palma take you farther into Colombia. If you need a Colombian visa, you can get one in Esmeraldas or Quito. Passport formalities for exiting/arriving in Ecuador can be handled either at the capitanía, on the dock, or at the police station, two blocks away. Few foreigners take this route; the journey is done in motorized dugouts.

LIMONES
☎ 06

Limones is a small town at the mouth of the deltas of Río Santiago and Río Cayapas. It

has a population of about 7000 and is economically important: timber is logged in this area and floated down the river to Limones, where there is a sawmill. There are few amenities in town, and the two hotels are pretty crude.

Limones is basically an island and is reached only by boat, which is why the San Lorenzo-Limones-La Tola boat service keeps running despite the new road. You can sometimes see Chachi Indians (formerly known as the Cayapas) here, although more can be seen at Borbón and farther up Río Cayapas.

LA TOLA

☎ 06

People traveling by boat from San Lorenzo arrive at La Tola and continue by bus to Esmeraldas. Arrive early to avoid being stranded here. There is a Tolita archaeological site on the nearby island of **Manta de Oro**, but the gold ornaments that were found here are now in museums, and there is not much to see unless you are an archaeologist.

Reader Sayo Aoki writes that near La Tola, the Majagual mangrove forest can be visited by dugout canoe for about US$5 per person. Ask for Señora Orin Flores, who works as a guide. There is a very basic *residencial*, and **Comedor Maurita** is recommended for local food.

Getting There & Away

La Costeñita and Transportes del Pacífico run buses to and from Esmeraldas (US$3, four hours) and boats to and from San Lorenzo. (You can buy a single straight-through ticket from San Lorenzo to Esmeraldas; see Getting There & Away under San Lorenzo, earlier.) In addition to buses, there are a few *rancheras* (flatbed trucks mounted with excruciatingly narrow benches). If you get on a ranchera, try to get an end seat so you can at least stretch one leg.

If you take a morning bus from Esmeraldas, you will connect with a boat to San Lorenzo, and vice versa, so there is little reason to stay in La Tola.

BORBÓN

☎ 06

This small river port on Río Cayapas has about 5000 inhabitants, most of whom are the descendants of African slaves brought here by the Spanish. The town is the best place to get boats up the Cayapas and to continue up Río San Miguel to the Reserva Ecológica Cotacachi-Cayapas – an interesting trip to a remote area. It is also the entry point for trips up the equally interesting Río Santiago. Borbón is beginning to compete

Riches from the Rainforest

In the rainforests around Borbón, a small tagua-nut industry has developed. Known as 'vegetable ivory,' tagua nuts come from a palm tree that grows in the local forest. The nuts (which are actually seeds) are the size of small chicken eggs and soon become extremely hard. They can be carved into a variety of novelties, such as animal statuettes, miniature cups, chess pieces, rings and buttons. By providing economically viable alternatives to cutting the forest down, harvesting the nuts is a sustainable alternative to harvesting the whole rainforest.

Apart from in the Borbón market, you will find tagua-nut products for sale in other areas along the coast, in Riobamba and in Quito gift shops. The ornaments are reminiscent of ivory and make good and inexpensive souvenirs of the rainforest – and buying them helps to preserve that forest. Local carvers are becoming increasingly proficient, but quality varies, so look carefully for the best pieces.

Tagua-nut carver at work

Some tagua buttons have found their way into the North American clothing market, where you may find clothes labeled with a 'Tagua Initiative' tag, which explains to consumers how the buttons help make tropical forests worth more standing up than cut down.

in importance with Limones. Market day is Sunday.

Information

Angel Ceron is the principal (headmaster) of the local school, Colegio Luz y Libertad. He also runs the hotel La Tolita Pampa de Oro. Ceron is a good source of information about the area; he can tell you how to get to some of the local archaeological sites that pertain to the Tolita culture, which existed here around 2000 years ago. There is not much to be seen – these sites are mainly of interest to professional archaeologists.

A local NGO called SUBIR (Sustainable Uses of Biological Resources) has an office in Borbón. It's developing local ecotourism projects on Río Santiago and in San Miguel (see Excursions, later in this section).

The US-run mission in Borbón can be of assistance to travelers. If you are driving, they may let you park your vehicle in their parking lot while you take river trips or whatever. Ask for directions in town – most people know where it is.

Places to Stay & Eat

All of the hotels are very basic. The best place is the friendly *La Tolita Pampa de Oro*, which charges about US$2.50 per person – it's also a good source of visitor information. Above the *ferretería* (hardware shop) and opposite the mission, new rooms are being built and should be open by the time this goes to print. These will be the best in town. *Residencial Capri* charges US$2 per person for basic rooms with mosquito nets – toilet facilities are primitive. *Hotel Panama City* is another cheap place to stay.

There is a comfortable jungle lodge some distance away by the river (see Excursions, later).

Most restaurants are basic comedores that don't bother with a menu – ask them what they have. Some can get raucous with checker or domino playing and beer drinking in the evening.

Getting There & Away

Bus La Costeñita and Transportes del Pacífico between them run buses to Esmeraldas

(US$3, four hours) or San Lorenzo (US$2, two hours) about every hour from 7 am to 6 pm. Most of the roads are paved. However, some sections are badly potholed, and unpaved stretches exist.

Boat A daily passenger boat leaves at 11 am for San Miguel (US$8, five hours). This boat can drop you at any location on Ríos Cayapas or San Miguel (see Excursions, later in this section). Other boats run irregularly to other destinations – ask around at the docks.

Fletes, or private boats, can be hired any time to take you anywhere if you have the money. These are not cheap – expect to pay about 15 times the fare that you would be charged in a passenger boat. Of course, this is not a problem if you're with a group.

Excursions

Farther up Río Santiago (about five hours by boat from Borbón), near the border of Reserva Ecológica Cotacachi-Cayapas, is the remote community of **Playa de Oro**, so named because gold has been panned in the region for centuries. Here, SUBIR has a lodge that has eight clean rooms with comfortable beds and mosquito nets; bathroom facilities are shared. SUBIR organizes biocultural tours based at the lodge and visits to see the nearby rainforest and people. The guides are knowledgeable locals but don't necessarily speak English. Tours from Borbón cost about US$50 per person per night, including meals, guided hikes, boat rides and village visits.

The most reliable boat service from Borbón is the daily passenger boat to San Miguel (see that section, later), which is used more often by travelers – although you certainly won't find hordes of tourists. There are several stopping places along the way.

The first is *Steve's Lodge*, at the mouth of Río Onzole, about an hour from Borbón. Run by a friendly Hungarian named Steve Tarjanyi, the lodge has six comfortable double rooms with great river views.

Rates are US$45 per person, including meals, or US$280 per person for a three-night stay, including meals and a guided boat tour up Río Cayapas to the Reserva

Ecológica Cotacachi-Cayapas (camping in the reserve is also an option). There are discounts for groups of four or more. Guides speak English.

Beyond Steve's Lodge, the boat to San Miguel stops at a number of communities and missions. River travel is made interesting by passengers ranging from Catholic nuns to Chachi (Cayapas) Indians embarking or disembarking in the various tiny ports – usually no more than a few planks at the water's edge.

The first mission is the Catholic **Santa María**. Here, there is a clean dormitory that sleeps six people; ask for Señora Pastora, who will show you where to sleep and cook meals. There is also a basic **residencial**, or you can **camp**. The next mission is the Protestant **Zapallo Grande**; you can find a basic place to sleep here, too. Chachi crafts are often for sale. Both missions have medical clinics, and local people will offer to take you on tours. There are also a number of other communities, such as Pichiyacu, Playa Grande, Atahualpa and Telembi, that are the homes of mainly Chachi Indians or Afro-Ecuadorians.

Finally, you'll reach San Miguel.

SAN MIGUEL
☎ 06

This small, friendly village is the main base from which to visit the lowland sections of the Reserva Ecológica Cotacachi-Cayapas. There is a ranger station on a small hill overlooking the village – the view of the rainforest and river from here is quite spectacular. There are about 30 houses in the village, one of which is a small store selling soft drinks, crackers, sardines, candy, oatmeal and little else. The inhabitants of the village are Afro-Ecuadorians. Chachi Indians' houses are scattered along the shores of the river nearby.

Someone has taken a machete to the grass in front of the ranger station, making it into a rough lawn – but it is a haven for chiggers. Put on repellent, especially around your ankles, before you disembark at San Miguel.

Places to Stay & Eat
The *guardaparque* (park ranger) will let you stay in the ranger station for US$5 per person

per night. There are four beds but no running water or mosquito nets. Larger groups can sleep on the floor or camp outside. The station has a cold shower, a toilet and kitchen facilities. A shop sells a few very simple food supplies, or you can buy basic meals (rice and fried bananas with a little soup) for about US$5. The people are friendly.

Ask at the SUBIR office in Borbón about its lodge in the area. It's not always open but is more comfortable than the ranger station.

Getting There & Away
The driver of the daily passenger canoe from Borbón spends the night about 15 minutes downriver from San Miguel. He will not come back to San Miguel unless he knows for sure that he has a passenger. It is essential to make arrangements with the boatman about the day you want to be picked up. The canoe leaves San Miguel around 4 am, when it is still dark. Dawn on the river makes this a nice trip.

RESERVA ECOLÓGICA COTACACHI-CAYAPAS
This 204,420-hectare reserve is by far the largest protected area of western Andean habitats in Ecuador. It covers an altitudinal range from about 200m above sea level in the San Miguel area to 4939m above sea level at the summit of Cotacachi. Thus, the type of habitat changes rapidly from lowland tropical wet forest to premontane and montane cloud forest to páramo, with many intermediate habitat types. This rapid change of habitat produces the so-called 'edge effect' that gives rise to an incredible diversity of flora and fauna.

These are the haunts of such rarely seen mammals as the giant anteater, Baird's tapir, jaguar and, in the upper reaches of the reserve, the spectacled bear. The chances of seeing these are remote, however. You may see monkeys, squirrels, sloths, the nine-banded armadillo, bats and a huge variety of bird species. It is certainly a great area for birding.

There are two principal ways to visit the reserve. You can go in from the highlands (as described in the North of Quito chapter), or you can go in from San Miguel, as described later in this section. Whichever way you elect to go, you will find it extremely difficult to descend from the highlands to the lowlands or climb up in the opposite direction. The areas near the reserve boundaries can be visited in both the lowlands and the highlands; the steep and thickly vegetated western slopes of the Andes in between are largely trackless and almost impenetrable. This is bad news if you want to visit the interior of the reserve but good news for the species existing there – they will probably be left alone for a little while longer.

Both the lower reaches of the reserve and the rivers leading into this area are the home of Chachi (Cayapas) Indians, of which about 5000 remain. The Chachi Indians are famous for their basketwork, and there are stores in Borbón, Limones, Esmeraldas and Quito selling their crafts. You can buy them far more cheaply directly from the Indians on the river – however, be warned that the baskets tend to be very large, so getting them home may be a minor problem. Many of the Chachis live in traditional style in breezy, open-sided, thatched-roof houses built on stilts near the river. Fishing and subsistence agriculture are their main sources of food, and many of the Indians speak only the Chachi tongue. Some groups now live on or close to missions; others are largely beyond missionary influence. In these groups, both men and women go bare breasted.

Over the last few decades, the Chachi Indians have been swept by a form of river blindness that is supposedly carried by a blackfly, which is particularly prevalent in April and May. Some 80% of the Indians have the disease to a greater or lesser extent. Insect repellent works to keep the insects off you, and taking chloroquine as a malarial prophylactic also works to prevent the disease.

The area is very rainy. Up to 5000mm of rain has been reported in some of the more inland areas, although it is somewhat less wet around San Miguel. The rainy season is December to May, and the river levels are high then, which makes the local people consider it to be the best time to travel. It is also the season with the highest concentrations of mosquitoes, blackflies and other insects, but they tend to be really bad only at dawn and dusk, so cover up then. Even during the rainy months, mornings are often clear. The drier months of September to December are usually less buggy, and there is a better chance of seeing wildlife, although river navigation may be limited.

Entrance into the reserve costs US$5, which is payable at the ranger station in San Miguel. The rangers will act as guides. They charge about US$10 per day plus food, and two guides are needed for many trips – one for each end of the dugout canoe. These canoes are paddled and poled – they don't have outboard engines; not many people have engines out here. Alternately, you can visit on a guided tour with one of the lodges. Note that the SUBIR lodge in Playa de Oro is also an access point for the reserve.

It is about two or three hours by canoe from San Miguel to the park boundaries. Another one or two hours brings the visitor to a small but pretty waterfall in the jungle. There are a few poorly marked trails, for which a guide is almost essential. There are places to camp if you have tents and all the necessary gear. There are plans to build a

Armadillo

hut by the waterfall and another somewhere within the reserve – ask the guides about whether these plans have materialized. When they have, a small fee will be charged.

THE ROAD TO ESMERALDAS
☎ 06

The bus journey to Esmeraldas from San Lorenzo via Borbón is bumpy and uncomfortable. It is very dusty in the dry season and muddy in the wet season. The section between San Lorenzo and Borbón starts along the Ibarra road and then turns inland through the forest, which, because the road is new, has not been colonized – yet. A short side road stops at the village of **Maldonado**. Around Borbón, signs for the nearby national reserves discourage wood cutting.

Beyond Borbón, there are a number of villages, most with a basic residencial if you get stuck. One of these villages is **Lagarto**, where Río Lagarto is crossed. Soon after crossing Río Lagarto, the routes from Borbón and La Tola unite. Beyond, the road passes through the village of **Montalvo** (no hotel) and on to the coastal village of **Rocafuerte**, which has very basic residenciales and simple restaurants selling tasty fresh seafood. People from Esmeraldas drive out here on weekends for a good meal in a rural setting. Rocafuerte has a medical clinic and celebrates its annual fiesta on August 31.

A few kilometers farther, the road passes through the two **coastal villages of Río Verde**: Palestina de Río Verde, just beyond the river, and then Río Verde, a few kilometers farther. Río Verde was the setting of Moritz Thomsen's *Living Poor*. At the river crossing, look for a large frigatebird colony visible in the trees along the banks. Palestina de Río Verde has a couple of residenciales. Between the two villages is the recommended *Hostería y Restaurante Pura Vida* (☎ 744 204, 09-455 337, pura_vida_verde@yahoo.com), the best place to stay between San Lorenzo and Esmeraldas. This quiet and remote Swiss/Ecuadorian-run hostal charges about US$10 per person, and arranges rental bikes, fishing, excursions and volunteering

in local schools. Some rooms have private baths, and a restaurant and small children's pool is on the premises.

Almost 20km beyond Río Verde is the village of **Camarones**, which, as its name implies, sells delicious shrimp lunches in the simple beachfront restaurants during weekends and holidays. Ask around about cabins for rent if you want to stay by the beach; *Cabañas Fragatas* is one such place. A few kilometers beyond Camarones, the road passes the Esmeraldas airport on the east side of Río Esmeraldas. The city is on the west side, but there is no bridge until San Mateo, about 10km upriver. It is a half-hour drive from the airport to Esmeraldas.

ESMERALDAS
☎ 06

This important city of 126,000 inhabitants is the capital of the province of Esmeraldas. It was near here that the Spanish conquistadors made their first landfall in Ecuador. Esmeraldas has been an influential port town throughout Ecuador's history, and it is now the largest port in northern Ecuador. Although fishing and shipping are important, the oil refinery near the terminal of the trans-Andean oil pipeline has given Esmeraldas another source of income and employment, as well as its share of noise and pollution. This, combined with the fact that Esmeraldas is considered Ecuador's most dangerous major city, makes it an unattractive destination.

Most tourists just spend the night (if they have to) and continue southwest to the towns of Atacames, Súa and Muisne, where the best beaches are to be found. Esmeraldas also has beaches in the northern suburb of Las Palmas, but they are not as good and are reportedly dirty.

Information

There is no tourist office. The immigration office (☎ 710 156) is at the Policía Civil Nacional, 3km out of town (take a cab). You should have your passport stamped here if you are leaving or entering Ecuador via the rarely used coastal route to Colombia. The Colombian consul is in Las Palmas, one

ESMERALDAS

PLACES TO STAY
1 Apart Hotel Esmeraldas
2 Hotel Janbirs
3 Hostal Residencial Sandri
4 Hotel Turismo
11 Hostal Miraflores
12 Hotel Asia
15 Hotel Costa Esmeraldas
16 Nuevo Hotel
20 Hotel El Galeón
26 Residencial Zulema
27 Hostal Americano
28 Hotel Diana

PLACES TO EAT
10 Fuente de Soda
    Estrecho de Bering;
    Las Redes Restaurant
13 Parrilladas El Toro
29 Restaurant Las Vegas
30 Chifa Asiática
32 Fuente de Soda Porteñito

OTHER
5 Post Office; Andinatel
6 Aerotaxi
7 Transportes Esmeraldas
8 Transportes La Costeñita
9 Church
14 Transportes Occidentales
17 TAME Airline Office
18 Banco del Pichincha
19 Transportes Panamericana
21 Transportes Gilberto
    Zambrano
22 Reina del Camino
23 Banco Popular
24 Filanbanco
25 Transportes del Pacífico
31 Police Station

block from Hotel Cayapas (see Places to Stay, Mid-Range, later).

Money Banco del Pichincha, Banco Popular (which has a MasterCard ATM) and Filanbanco (which has a Visa ATM) change US cash and traveler's checks; see the map for their locations.

Post & Communications The post office is at the corner of Montalvo and the Malecón. Andinatel is upstairs, from where there's a good view of Río Esmeraldas and the riverside market.

Medical Services The hospital (☎ 710 012) is on Avenida Libertad between Esmeraldas and Las Palmas, on the north end of town. Several private clinics are in the center and provide better services; ask your hotel for a recommendation.

Emergency There is a police station at the corner of Bolívar and Cañizares.

Dangers & Annoyances Be careful in the market areas (especially the south end of the Malecón) and anywhere away from the main streets. There are drug problems and thieves. Avoid arriving in Esmeraldas after dark, and stick to well-lit streets to avoid these problems. Don't carry cameras, and keep your money well hidden. Electricity and water supply are erratic. The incidence of malaria is high during the wet months. Single women have reported that they get hassled more often in Esmeraldas than elsewhere.

Things to See & Do

The market across from the Andinatel office is open daily and sells Chachi (Cayapas) basketry among other things. Watch for thieves.

Simón Bolívar's birthday, July 24, is one of the more vigorously celebrated holidays in Esmeraldas.

Places to Stay

There are many hotels, but the cheapest ones are poor. Mosquitoes are a problem, particularly during the wet months, and you should have either a fan or a mosquito net in your room to keep the insects off you. Some hotels lack these.

There are quite a few Ecuadorian vacationers and businesspeople in Esmeraldas, and hotels are sometimes full. Single rooms can be especially hard to find. You could stay in the nicer and pricier suburb of Las Palmas, 3km north of the center, or go directly to a coastal resort such as Atacames.

Budget Many of the cheapest hotels are close to bus terminals, noisy and not well kept. Many places suffer from water problems and turn on water on request only. For under US$2 per person, try *Hostal Miraflores* or *Hotel Turismo* (☎ 712 700), which are just OK. *Nuevo Hotel* (☎ 711 327) is US$2 per person, or US$3 for a room with a poor private bath.

Residencial Zulema (☎ 711 789, 710 910, 712 424), on Olmedo near Cañizares, is a step up at US$3 per person with bath. The clean *Hotel Asia* (☎ 714 594, 710 648, 711 852, 9 de Octubre 116) is OK for US$3 per person with bath (some rooms have a TV). Also about US$3 per person, the friendly

and helpful *Hotel Diana* (☎ 710 333, Cañizares 224) has decent small rooms with private bath and fan.

The clean *Hostal Residencial Sandri* (☎ 713 547), on Libertad near Montalvo, has rooms with private bath, fan and TV for US$4 per person; rates are US$5 with air-conditioning. The hotel is secure, but the market area isn't, so be careful. *Hostal Americano* (☎ 713 978, Sucre 709) is OK and similarly priced.

The good-value *Hotel Costa Esmeraldas* (☎ 723 912, 720 640, Sucre 813) charges US$4 per person for rooms with bath, hot water, TV and fan, or US$6.50 for rooms with air-conditioning. Also decent is *Hotel Janbirs* (☎ 721 791), on Libertad between Espejo and Pichincha; it has air-conditioned rooms with TV and warm showers at US$5/8 for singles/doubles.

Hotel El Galeón (☎ 713 116, 723 820, fax 714 839), near the corner of Olmedo and Piedrahita, is run down and charges US$7 per person for rooms with fan and private bath.

Three kilometers north, in the quieter suburb of Las Palmas, *Hotel Ambato* (☎ 721 142, 721 144), at Kennedy and A Guerra, is reasonable at US$5/8 for rooms with bath, fan and TV.

Mid-Range The best hotel close to the town center is *Apart Hotel Esmeraldas* (☎ 728 700/1/2/3, fax 728 704, Libertad 407), but it's aimed at businesspeople rather than tourists. Singles/doubles are US$19/25, and the air-conditioned rooms have minifridges, telephone, TV and room service. There is a casino, a guarded parking lot and a restaurant/bar. Locals come to the Sunday buffet brunch.

In Las Palmas, almost all of the hotels are on Avenida Kennedy, which is the main street and parallels the beach. Reach it by heading north on Libertad. *Hotel Cayapas* (☎ 721 318, 721 319, 721 320, Kennedy 401) is one block from the budget Hotel Ambato. It has a pleasant garden. Simple but clean air-conditioned rooms with telephone, TV and hot water are US$15/20, and there is a restaurant that offers room service.

Places to Eat

The better hotels in Esmeraldas and Las Palmas have decent restaurants; the one in Hotel Cayapas (mentioned earlier) is above average. The food in the many small and cheap pavement cafés and comedores is often good – try the places along Olmedo between Mejía and Piedrahita. On the east side of the central plaza, *Las Redes Restaurant* is good for seafood, and the nearby *Fuente de Soda Estrecho de Bering* is a good place for snacks and ice cream, as well as for watching the busy goings-on in the plaza. *Chifa Asiática*, on Cañizares near Sucre, is the best place for Chinese food. *Parrilladas El Toro*, on 9 de Octubre near Olmedo, is OK for those seeking meat dishes. *Restaurant Las Vegas (Cañizares 214)* has also been recommended by travelers for good food at reasonable prices. *Fuente de Soda Porteñito*, at Sucre and Mejía, is locally popular and has good coffee.

Entertainment

The coast is known for its lively African-influenced music. There are no particular places where you can go to listen to shows; impromptu gatherings are the norm. The best way is to make friends with the locals and ask them. There are several discos – most are in Las Palmas. Note: Women should not go to any of these places unescorted by a man.

Getting There & Away

Air TAME has flights from Quito to Esmeraldas every morning from Monday to Thursday and on Friday and Sunday afternoons. The fare is about US$20. TAME may have flights to Cali, Colombia, twice a week, but only during the beach high season (December to April). Ask locally. Also ask locally about light aircraft flying to coastal destinations south of Esmeraldas.

The TAME office (☎ 726 863, fax 726 862) is on Bolívar just off the corner of the central plaza. You can also buy a ticket at the airport (☎ 727 058) if the flight is not full. Make sure you get a seat assignment at the airport, or you won't get on – there are different windows for buying tickets and getting seat assignments, so you have to wait in line twice. It's not very organized.

Bus There is no central bus terminal. There is a direct road to Quito via Santo Domingo de los Colorados. The fastest service to Quito is with Aerotaxi (US$6, five hours), on Sucre between Rocafuerte and 10 de Agosto, but the drivers go frighteningly fast. Transportes Occidentales and Transportes Esmeraldas, both near the central plaza, are slower and a little cheaper. The latter has the most departures and also has buses to Machala (see the South Coast chapter). Transportes Panamericana, on Piedrahita between Colón and Olmedo, has the most luxurious buses to Quito, but the fare is a couple of dollars more expensive, and the trip takes seven to eight hours. The buses leave at 11:45 am and 11:15 pm.

Transportes Occidentales and Transportes Esmeraldas also have frequent buses to Guayaquil (US$5.50 to US$7, eight hours). Transportes Occidentales has buses to Guayaquil, as well as an early-morning and an early-evening bus to Machala (US$8, 11 hours) if you want to go to Peru the next day. Reina del Camino has five buses a day to Manta (US$6.20, nine hours) and one goes to Bahía de Caráquez (US$6.20, eight hours). Transportes Gilberto Zambrano has buses to Santo Domingo.

Transportes La Costeñita and Transportes del Pacífico buses for Atacames and Súa (US$0.60, less than an hour) leave frequently from 6:30 am to 8 pm. There are several buses a day to Muisne (US$1.40, 2½ hours). These companies also go to Borbón (four hours) and on to San Lorenzo (US$4.50, six hours). Buses also go to other small provincial villages.

Note that buses from Esmeraldas to Borbón pass the airport, and passengers arriving by air and continuing to towns on the way to Borbón by bus don't need to backtrack to Esmeraldas.

Taxi Taxis will take you from Esmeraldas to Atacames for US$12 or to Muisne for US$20; you can call ☎ 711 020 to have one pick you up at your hotel.

Getting Around

The airport is 25km away from town, across Río Esmeraldas. Passengers and cabdrivers gather in front of the TAME office a couple of hours before the flight, and four or five passengers are crammed into each taxi at a cost of about US$3 per person. Incoming passengers get together to do the same thing at the airport. At the airport, you can hire a taxi for about US$20 to take you directly to Atacames and can thus avoid Esmeraldas completely.

To get to the airport cheaply, take a La Costeña or Transportes del Pacífico bus to Borbón (it stops at the airport). They may not sell you a ticket at the office, so board without a ticket and pay the driver – it costs about US$0.50 to go to the airport.

Take a Selectivo bus signed 'Las Palmas No 1' northbound along Avenida Bolívar to get to the port of Esmeraldas and to the beaches of Las Palmas. The fare is US$0.15. A taxi charges US$0.75.

ATACAMES
☎ 06

This small resort town, almost 30km west of Esmeraldas, has built up a reputation among young international travelers as the place to go for a moderately priced beach vacation. Simple accommodations can be found right on the oceanfront, so you can walk straight out of your room onto the beach. Atacames is also popular

with visitors from Colombia and Quito and can get extremely crowded, particularly on weekends and national holidays. The wet-season weekends (especially Christmas, Carnaval and Easter) are very popular with locals, and the months of April to October are more popular with foreign visitors. However, many travelers are looking for quieter places.

There is little to do in Atacames apart from sunbathe and swim, eat and drink, and hang out in bars and discos with newfound friends. Some travelers love it and stay for days or weeks; others tire quickly of the homogenous discos and restaurants.

Orientation & Information

The main road from Esmeraldas goes through the center of town. The center and the beach area are separated by Río Atacames. The beach area is now a long strip of hotels, restaurants and bars. To get to the ocean and beach hotels, you have to walk a few blocks and cross Río Atacames. Buses do not go down to the beach.

There is little reason to go into the town center except to catch a bus, change cash or traveler's checks at the Banco del Pichincha or go to the Andinatel office.

Dangers & Annoyances

The beach has a powerful undertow and no lifeguards. People drown every year, so stay within your limits.

Fishermen at work in Atacames

ROB RACHOWIECKI

Thieves thrive wherever there is a conglomeration of travelers. This is certainly true of beach areas, and Atacames is no exception. Camping is definitely not recommended, because thieves cut through the tent material and rob you even while you're asleep inside. Stay in a beach cabin or hotel, and make sure that it has secure locks on the doors and shutters on the windows.

Assaults have been reported by people walking the beaches at night. Stay in front of the hotel area – women have been raped and travelers have been mugged just a short distance away from the hotel area. It is safe if you stay in well-lit areas in front of the hotels – it is definitely dangerous beyond these areas. Even during the day, you shouldn't walk the beaches alone or even as a couple.

Bring insect repellent or mosquito coils, especially in the wet season (although the insects aren't bad in the dry months). The cheapest hotels may have rats, so stay in a medium-priced hotel in order to minimize the chance of seeing them.

Although the chance of being bitten by a sea snake is remote, every once in a while, they get washed up on the beaches. Don't pick them up – they are venomous.

Places to Stay

Atacames gets very full on weekends, especially holiday weekends, when prices rise to what the market will bear and single rooms are unavailable unless you want to pay for a double. Therefore, the rates given below are an approximate guideline only. You are advised to arrive Sunday to Wednesday, when you can try bargaining, especially if you plan on staying a few days. Rooms are often geared toward families and have several beds, so go in a group if you'd like to economize more. Even in the low season, singles often cost the same as doubles, and cheap per person rates only apply to rooms sleeping four to six people.

New hotels, or old hotels under new management and name, open frequently. There are some 50 hotels to choose from within a few blocks of the beach. Addresses are not used, so you need to ask or walk around.

Before you agree to rent your room or cabin, always check it for security.

Most showers have brackish water (which is quite salty) – only the more expensive hotels have freshwater showers.

Budget Set back from the beach, *La Casa del Manglar* (☎ 731 464) is clean and friendly; rates are US$8 to US$16 for doubles, and the more expensive ones have a private bath. *Cabañas Los Bohios* (☎ /fax 731 089) has quite nice little double cabins with bath at US$10 and may have singles midweek in the low season. *Rincón Sage* (☎ 731 246) has decent rooms with bath for US$12 double, and there is a nice rooftop patio. *Hostal Jennifer* (☎ 710 482) has occasional singles and charges about US$8 per person with bath; less without. Rooms are a bit bigger than in many budget hotels.

The popular *Hotel Galerías Atacames* (☎ 731 149) has English-speaking owners, and doubles with bath for US$16 on weekends; rates are less at other times. There is also a good restaurant. Nearby, *Hotel El Tiburon* (☎ /fax 731 145) is clean and similarly priced; it costs much less per person for quad or sextuple rooms, all of which have a private bath. *Hotel Villa Hermosa* (☎ 731 547, 731 306) is clean, comfortable and has 18 rooms for two to eight people at US$4 to US$6 per person, depending on the season and the room. *Hotel Chavalito* (☎ 731 113) has rooms with private baths for US$12 to US$20, depending on the room. The two best rooms, at the front of the hotel, have balconies with ocean views.

Mid-Range European-owned *Cabañas Caida del Sol* (☎ /fax 731 479) has nice little cabins with fan and minifridge for US$20 to US$40 for two to four people. Away from the center, the quiet *Villas Arco Iris* (☎ 731 306, 731 547, fax 731 437) provides clean and comfortable cabins with private bath, kitchen facilities and a little porch with a hammock. Rates are US$25 to US$45 for one to four people, and readers report that the staff is friendly and accommodating.

Hotel Casa Blanca (☎ /fax 731 031/96, in Quito ☎ 02-569 029, fax 569 030) has clean, air-conditioned rooms with TV and telephone for US$60 on weekends and US$40 during the week. Rooms with fans are about US$10 cheaper. A pool and restaurant are on the premises. *Hotel Castel Nuevo* (☎ 731 046, in Quito ☎ 02-223 608, fax 223 452) has similarly priced rooms with fans but no air-conditioning; it also has the largest swimming pool in Atacames.

Places to Eat

There are many simple comedores close to the beach near the footbridge. They all tend to serve the same thing – whatever was caught that morning. Make sure you ask the price before you get served or else you may be overcharged. A whole fish dinner will start at around US$3. All the comedores seem to be alike, which is why they are not described individually. Wander around until you find one that suits your fancy. Many of them double as bars or dancing places in the evenings, and their popularity changes with the seasons. Keep your ears open, and you'll soon hear where it's happening.

Several readers have recommended *Pizzería No Name* for authentic, Italian-made pizzas.

Entertainment

There is no shortage of loud beach bars and discos.

Getting There & Away

All buses stop on the main road near the road to the footbridge; there is no bus terminal. If leaving Atacames, you normally pay for your ticket after you board the bus. Buses for Esmeraldas (US$0.60, 45 minutes) normally begin from Súa, and there are plenty of seats. Most buses from Esmeraldas to Atacames continue on to Súa, Same and Tonchigüe for about US$0.50. Buses for Muisne (US$1.20, 1½ hours) are often full when they come from Esmeraldas, and you may find it easier to return to Esmeraldas and then retrace your route. Otherwise, be prepared to ride on the roof or stand the whole way.

There are several daily direct buses to Quito (six to eight hours) for which you should buy tickets in advance. Ask your hotel about where to buy tickets.

SÚA
☎ 06

This small fishing village is more bustling than Atacames from a fishing point of view, but it is a much quieter place to stay if you'd rather watch the boats at work than just hang out on the beach. The fishing industry attracts its attendant frigatebirds, pelicans and other sea birds, and the general setting is attractive, although the beach is less clean because of fishing activities. Because it is quieter and less popular than Atacames, it is easier to find weekend prices that aren't inflated. There is an Andinatel office.

Súa is about a 6km walk by road from Atacames. It's said that you can walk along the beach at the lowest tides, but if you try this, be careful not to get cut off by the tide, and go with several friends to avoid getting robbed.

Places to Stay & Eat

There's much less to choose from than in Atacames, but prices are lower. The good-value *Hotel Chagra Ramos* (☎ 731 006, 731 070) has a little beach, nice views and charges US$5 or US$6 per person for pleasant rooms with bath. There is also a good, inexpensive restaurant there. *Hotel El Peñón de Súa* (☎ 731 013) is 300m away from the beach but has nice rooms with a private shower and a little patio for US$4 per person. *Hotel Buganvillas* (☎ 731 008) has also been recommended by readers and is about US$5 per person. There are a handful of other places.

Getting There & Away

Buses to and from Esmeraldas run about every 45 minutes. It takes 10 minutes to get to Atacames (US$0.30) and about an hour to get to Esmeraldas (US$0.60). You pay on the bus.

If you want to go farther along the coast to Muisne, you have to wait out of town along the main road for a bus passing from Esmeraldas (it's often full).

SAME

☎ 06

This small village (pronounced 'SAH-may') is a quiet beach resort about 6km southwest of Súa. Same lacks the crowds of Atacames and is slightly more expensive. The attractive gray-sand beach is palm-fringed and clean.

Places to Stay & Eat

La Terraza (in Quito ☎ 02-544 507), which is near the beach, charges US$7 per person and is the cheapest place to stay. It's a good value. La Terraza's restaurant and bar is popular, although the service is slow. Also reasonably priced is *Cabañas Seaflower* (☎ 945 038), which has a restaurant.

Cabañas Isla del Sol (☎/fax 731 151), at the end of the beach, has simple but adequate cabins sleeping four to six people for about US$12 per person. There is a restaurant and pool. Also on the beach is *Hostería El Rampiral* (in Quito ☎ 02-246 341, 435 003, fax 472 038), which has rooms for US$16 per person. There is a pool and restaurant, and rooms reportedly have TVs and minifridges.

El Acantilado (in Quito ☎ 02-235 034, 453 606) is on a cliff overlooking a small but private beach. There are cabins for four to eight people, and each has kitchen facilities and a daily maid service. Rates are about US$20 per person, and there is a decent restaurant.

Hotel Club Casablanca (in Quito ☎ 02-252 077, fax 253 452, casablan@uio.satnet .net) is a 1st-class resort with swimming pool and games facilities. Rates are about US$50 to US$70 for a double.

TONCHIGÜE

☎ 06

This beach is a continuation of the Same beach (mentioned earlier). *El Acantilado* is a hotel between Same and Tonchigüe. There is also the cheaper *Hotel Luz del Mar*, where rooms are around US$4 per person.

At Km 10, west of Tonchigüe on the road to Punta Galeras, is *Playa Escondida* (☎ 09-733 368), which allows camping at US$5 per person and has rooms for US$8 per person.

Run by a Canadian named Judy, this place is a quiet, private and safe area. There is a restaurant.

MUISNE & AROUND

☎ 05

This small port is on an island at the end of the road from Esmeraldas and has a minor banana-shipping industry. It is relatively remote and far fewer people come here compared to the more popular beaches, such as Atacames.

There are some mangroves remaining in the area, and this is one of the few places where the remains are, to some extent, protected (see the boxed text 'Maltreated Mangroves').

Orientation & Information

At the end of the road from Esmeraldas, motorized dugouts cross Río Muisne to the island (US$0.20). Boats leave every few minutes. When you disembark at Muisne, you'll see the main road heading southwest, directly away from the pier into the town 'center.' There is an Andinatel office. Although Muisne is in Esmeraldas Province (area code 06), for some reason, the local area code is the same as the more southerly Manabí Province (05).

It's best to continue on the main road, past the town square, and toward the ocean. The main road deteriorates into a grassy lane, and it's about 1.5km to the beach.

Dangers & Annoyances

There have been reports of theft from beach cabins, some of which are not very secure. Bring your own padlock, and check the windows. Single travelers, women especially, are advised not to wander along the beach away from the hotels and restaurants – rapes and muggings have been reported.

Note that water shortages occur frequently in Muisne.

Places to Stay & Eat

There are only budget hotels. Although there are a handful of hotels near the river and the bus stop, most travelers cross the river to the island and then continue to the beach. During the rainy months, mosquitoes can be bad, so look for mosquito nets over your bed.

About 400m before arriving at the beach and one block to the right of the 'main road,' you pass *Hotel Galápagos* (☎ 480 158). This is the most expensive hotel in Muisne, at US$6 per person for rooms with private bathroom. The rooms on the left-hand side of the hotel (as you face it) are quieter. The Galápagos is the best and most secure place to stay (but take the usual precautions against theft). However, the concrete rooms are not very attractive.

Maltreated Mangroves

Ecuador's coastal mangroves are an important habitat. In addition to helping to control the erosion of the coast, they provide homes, protection and nutrients for numerous species of fish, birds, mollusks and crustaceans (see Flora & Fauna in the Facts about Ecuador chapter). Unfortunately, mangroves have been in a no-man's-land, and it has been difficult to say who owns these coastal tropical forests that are semipermanently inundated. Squatters took over areas of mangroves as their own, but this was not in itself a problem, because they were able to use the mangroves sustainably. Only small sections were cut for charcoal production or building materials. The mangroves also supported cottage industries – such as fishing, shrimping and crabbing – as well as some sport fishing. Thousands of families along the coast were gainfully employed in these industries without impacting the mangroves.

This all changed in the 1980s with the arrival of shrimp farms, which produced shrimp in artificial conditions in numbers many times greater than could be caught by ordinary shrimping methods in the wild. To build these shrimp farms, it was necessary to cut down the mangroves. The prospective owner of a shrimp farm simply took over an area of mangroves, paid off anyone who was living there with what seemed like a sizable sum, cut down the mangroves, and began the shrimp-farming process. The net profits of the shrimp farms were very high, and the idea soon caught on and spread rapidly along the coast, resulting in the complete destruction of 80% to 90% of Ecuador's mangroves during the 1980s and early 1990s.

Although there are now laws controlling this destruction, it has continued, because the laws are difficult to enforce in the remote coastal areas. The short- and long-term effects of the shrimp farms have been negative in many ways. Where previously many families could find a sustainable livelihood in the mangroves, now there are shrimp farms employing only a handful of seasonal workers. Where before there were mangroves protecting a large diversity of species, now there are just commercial shrimp. Where before there were mangroves controlling coastal erosion, now there is erosion – plus pollution from the wastes of the shrimp farms. It is another case of a handful of entrepreneurs getting very rich at the expense of thousands of families' livelihoods and the environment.

In 1999, the shrimp industry suffered dramatically when diseases such as white spot wiped out entire shrimp farms in a matter of days. Estimates on the economic losses vary, but certainly Ecuador's shrimp exports were only a small fraction of the previous year's. Meanwhile, desperate efforts are being made in Muisne, Bahía de Caráquez and a few other coastal towns to start replanting mangroves.

On the beach itself, the friendly *Hotel Calade* (☎ *480 279*) charges US$3 to US$4 per person for clean but basic rooms with mosquito nets; some have baths. This hotel has recently been popular with gringos and has a restaurant. Equally good is the similarly priced *Hotel Playa Paraíso* (☎ *480 192*), which has shared baths, mosquito nets, and Byron – the friendly English-speaking owner who plans on expanding all services. There is also a restaurant.

A couple of other cheap places to stay and several inexpensive restaurants and bars are found along the beach. Everything is within a five-minute walk; look around for what looks best for you.

Getting There & Away

Bus La Costeñita and Transportes del Pacífico have buses about every 30 minutes from Muisne to Esmeraldas (US$1.40, 2½ hours), passing Same, Súa and Atacames en route. There are five buses a day to Santo Domingo de los Colorados (where connections to Quito or Guayaquil are made). Buses or pickups (depending on road conditions) go south to **Daule** about every hour, from where boats go to Cojimíes. Alternatively, take an Esmeraldas bus to El Salto (a road junction with a basic comedor) and wait for southbound traffic there to get to Daule.

Boat There are one or two boats a day from Muisne to Cojimíes (US$6, two hours). They leave from the dock at the end of the road from Esmeraldas. However, now that the road to Daule is open, fewer people are taking this route, and it might disappear altogether.

Excursions

You can take a boat trip up Río Muisne to see the mangrove forests (see the boxed text 'Maltreated Mangroves'). Passenger canoes go once or twice a day to San Gregorio (1½ hours). You can get information about the area from *Antojitos Bar & Cafe*, about three blocks from the boat landing in Muisne – ask for the Cotera brothers, who know a lot about the area. To get back to

Muisne, stand by the river and flag down any boat heading downriver.

COJIMÍES
☎ 05
Cojimíes, a small port with road connections to the south, is the northernmost point of the Manabí Province. It is sometimes cut off by heavy rains in the wet season (January to May). Because it is so isolated, food prices in Cojimíes tend to be expensive. The locals party late on Saturday night.

The village is on a headland that is constantly being washed away into the ocean. Consequently, the village has to keep moving inland, and the houses closest to the sea get washed away every few years. The locals say that the cemetery, now near the shoreline, was once way at the back of the town. There is a Pacifictel office.

Places to Stay & Eat

There are a few very basic (wash in a bucket) places to stay on or just off the one main street in Cojimíes. The best place is *Hotel Costa Azul*, which has rooms for US$4 per person.

Hotel Coco Solo (☎ *09-586 952, in Quito 02-240 404, 461 677, cocosolo25@hotmail .com*) is 14km south of Cojimíes – it's a hotel lost in the coconut groves that's great for lovers of deserted beaches and the noise of the wind clattering through the palm leaves. Rates are about US$8 per person in the cabins; there is a restaurant with a limited menu and a pool table. Horseback riding can be arranged. Apart from making reservations using the contact information provided earlier, you can reserve through Guacamayo Bahíatours (see Travel Agencies under Bahía de Caráquez, later in this chapter).

There are a few basic restaurants with pricey meals. Ask around for small comedores in people's houses – the meals are cheaper and often better.

Getting There & Away

Air About 1km from the center, there is a small airstrip with occasional flights in light aircraft to other coastal towns.

NORTH COAST

Bus The Costa del Norte bus office is on the main street and can give transportation information. Trucks to the next village of Pedernales (see that section, next) cost US$2 and take about an hour – they simply run along the beach for much of the way. Departures depend on the tide – if the tide is rising, you could be in town for 12 hours or more before the next vehicle can make it out. Buses sometimes go farther, depending on the state of the 'road.'

Boat At a shack by the beach, you can buy tickets for the boat to Muisne (US$6, two hours). Although a posted schedule lists daily departures, boats don't stick to the schedule. It's easier to take a boat to Daule and continue by road from there.

PEDERNALES
☎ 05

Pedernales is about 40km south of Cojimíes and, with some 12,000 inhabitants, it is the most important market town between Muisne and Bahía de Caráquez. With the recent opening of a decent road to Santo Domingo, Pedernales has become still more important. In the 1980s, fishing and agriculture (bananas, cacao and coffee) were the main industries. In the 1990s, the shrimp industry expanded from the south and became more important; there are many shrimp ponds and hatcheries in the area. This new industry gave Pedernales a freewheeling boomtown atmosphere, but that has been somewhat curtailed by recent outbreaks of shrimp diseases.

Pedernales is about 8km north of the equator. Despite its location on the coast, the beaches are poor.

Places to Stay
The best budget hotel in town is *Hotel Playas* (☎ 681 092), which is clean and friendly, but you have to bargain hard. Rooms with private bath and TV rent for US$4 per person for Ecuadorians – but gringos are often charged twice that! Being friendly and speaking Spanish is the best approach to avoid being overcharged.

There are several cheaper places that aren't as good but are OK for most budget travelers. Try the basic *Hostal Rosita* or *Hostal Playas* (☎ 681 125).

Among the best in town is the newer *La Catedral del Mar* (☎ 681 136), which has rooms for about US$10 per person.

Getting There & Away
Air AECA (in Guayaquil ☎ 04-288 110, 290 849) has flights to Pedernales in small aircraft from Guayaquil; the frequency of flights is subject to passenger demand.

Bus A Costa del Norte bus office on the main street sells tickets for Cojimíes (northbound) or San Vicente (southbound; US$3.50, four hours). Southbound departures are on the hour from 5 am to 5 pm. The buses (which are sometimes trucks or rancheras) usually follow the beach, and the ride is very fast on the hard-packed sand, especially between Pedernales and Cojimíes. There are some rougher stretches south of Pedernales. Bus travel to Cojimíes depends on tides and road conditions, and delays are frequent during the wet months of January to May. A new road via Chamango to Daule avoids Cojimíes; if you take a bus in the morning you can easily connect in Daule for buses to Muisne and farther north.

A recently paved road heads inland to El Carmen and on to Santo Domingo. Opposite the Costa del Norte office is Transportes Santo Domingo, which has six buses a day (US$3, three hours) to Santo Domingo.

JAMA
☎ 05

This village is a small market town midway between Pedernales and San Vicente. Several shrimp hatcheries are in the area. There are a couple of basic places to stay. *Hotel Jamaica* has showers and is as good as any.

Buses (trucks) between Pedernales and San Vicente pass through Jama in either direction but may be full when they come through. If so, you can ride on the roof.

CANOA

☎ 05

This village is about 18km north of San Vicente and has a wide quiet beach that is considered one of the best in the area. At the north end of the beach are some caves where hundreds of bats roost. The caves are easiest to visit during low tides.

There are no banks, but there is a phone. Buses between Pedernales and San Vicente come through about every hour.

Places to Stay & Eat

The beachfront **Hotel Bambu** (*☎ 09-753 696, in Quito ☎/fax 02-226 738*) is a great place to stay. There is a volleyball area and places to rent boogie boards and land sails, and horseback-riding and boat trips can be arranged. There are six rooms with shared bath for US$5 per person; four small rooms with bath for US$10/14/20/25 for one to four people; and four larger rooms with bath for US$15/18/25/30 for one to four people. Some bathrooms have hot water. Backpackers with tents can camp for US$1. Low-season discounts are available, and there is a decent bar and restaurant. English and Dutch are spoken.

A few blocks inland is the friendly **La Posada de Daniel** (*☎ 09-785 353*), which

---

Río Muchacho Organic Farm

This working organic farm offers much more than just organic tropical produce. It also practices sustainable permaculture and has built a primary school, where apart from learning their ABCs, children are taught sustainable farming practices, reforestation and waste management. The family who lives on the farm welcomes visitors, who are encouraged to participate in the daily activities of Río Muchacho.

The farm lies along the river of the same name and is reached by a rough 8km track branching inland from the road north of Canoa. Although trucks can make it there during dry months, transportation is normally on horseback, just as the local *montubios* (coastal farmers) do. After touring the farm, inspecting the crops and learning about permaculture and organic farming, visitors are free to choose from a variety of activities. They can help milk the cows and make a local cheese; harvest and prepare whatever crops are ripe; roast and grind their own coffee; go fishing for river shrimp; make ornaments from tagua nuts or kitchen utensils from gourds; relax with a mud facial mask and aloe-vera shampoo treatment; or go hiking, riding or bird watching (there are many species to keep the birder busy).

Visitors also get to stop by the school and maybe give an impromptu English lesson; eat homemade (mainly vegetarian) montubio meals with the family; enjoy a campfire cookout; and, of course, practice their Spanish (the family doesn't speak English). Volunteers are welcome to stay longer and work in the school or on the farm, depending on their interests and abilities; they are charged $200 a month for food and lodging. This is an excellent ecocultural experience for travelers who want to learn about real montubio life.

Accommodations are very rustic and are not for everyone. Many guests love the tree house built in a fig tree over the Río Muchacho. This is a simple platform with a mattress on the floor – no luxury here. On the river bank, another basic cabin with river views sleeps four, and a couple of rooms with small balconies over the tackle shed sleep two each. Showers and clean composting toilets are shared. Thus, guest groups are kept small, and reservations are a good idea.

The farm is owned and managed by Guacamayo Bahíatours (see the Bahía de Caráquez section, later). Rates are US$90 per person for three days and two nights; that includes guided ferry/bus/horseback transportation from Bahía de Caráquez, activities, meals and accommodations. Longer and shorter visits can be arranged, and the company earmarks 10% of tour fees to support the school and other conservation work.

has a restaurant, a swimming pool (not always usable) and 16 clean and rustic-looking small wooden rooms (watch your head!) with cold shower for US$4.50 per person. Rooms sleep two to seven people. *Hostal Shelmar* is smaller; there is another basic pensión in town.

The best food is at the charcoal-fired kitchen of *Restaurant Torbellino*, presided over by Doña Sofía Hernandez. Her *biche* (a local soup of several tropical vegetables flavored with peanuts) can't be beat; you can get it vegetarian or add fish or shrimp. She does excellent ceviches and other seafood as well.

The wide beaches of the area are slowly being developed. About 2km south of town, on a deserted beach (reached by the road to San Vicente), is *Hotel Sol y Luna (in Quito ☎ 02-562 096)*, which has eight large units – each with two bedrooms and a private bath – at US$6 per person. There is a small restaurant and a boat. There is also a swimming pool that functions during busy holiday weekends. A kilometer farther south, *Cabinas Pacific Fun* has 10 simple cabins with bath for US$4 per person. Almost next door, *Sun Down Inn* has a bedroom with bath (more planned) and a restaurant selling Mexican snacks. Rates are US$5 per person. Neither place has a phone.

SAN VICENTE
☎ 05

A short ferry ride across Río Chone from the more important town of Bahía de Caráquez, San Vicente has a beachside church with interesting murals and stained-glass work, bus transportation north, the regional airport and a few hotels. However, most travelers stay in Bahía de Caráquez.

Places to Stay & Eat
Near the center, the basic *Hostal San Vicente (☎ 674 182, 674 160)* charges US$3 per person for rooms with shared bath and US$4.50 for rooms with private bath. This is the best of the basic places. The quite good *Hotel Vacaciones (☎ 674 116)* charges US$9 per person or more during busy weekends for air-conditioned rooms. There is a pool

and a decent restaurant. On the northern outskirts of town, on the way to Canoa, there are several hotels, such as *Hotel Monte Mar (☎ 674 197)*, which has the best views of Bahía de Caráquez across the bay, a pool, a good restaurant, and rooms with and without air-conditioning in the US$20s and US$30s. Other places in this price range (all with restaurant and pool) include *Cabañas Alcatraz (☎ /fax 674 179)* and the cheaper *Hotel Las Hamacas (☎ 674 134)*.

Getting There & Away
Air The airport building here is impressive; unfortunately, there are no scheduled flights, although charters can be arranged. It's at the south end of town; you can either walk or take a cab (it's a short ride).

Bus Costa del Norte, Transportes Pedernales and other companies leave hourly from near the market (by the passenger-ferry dock) to Pedernales (three hours), and some continue to Cojimíes. Reina del Camino has several buses a day to Chone (see Inland from Portoviejo, later in this chapter), Santo Domingo and Guayaquil, as well as morning and evening buses to Quito.

Boat Passenger launches take 10 minutes to reach Bahía de Caráquez and leave several times an hour from 6 am. The fare is US$0.20 until 6 pm and US$0.30 after dark until midnight. A car ferry leaves about every half hour – foot passengers can cross at no charge. You can hire boats for trips anywhere you want for US$6 an hour.

BAHÍA DE CARÁQUEZ
☎ 05

This small coastal town (20,000 inhabitants) looks bigger than it is; the numerous high-rises north of the center are condos and holiday homes that remain empty for much of the year. In the first half of the 20th century, this was Ecuador's most important port, but problems with sandbanks led to the development of the ports in Guayaquil and Manta, and Bahía (as locals call it)

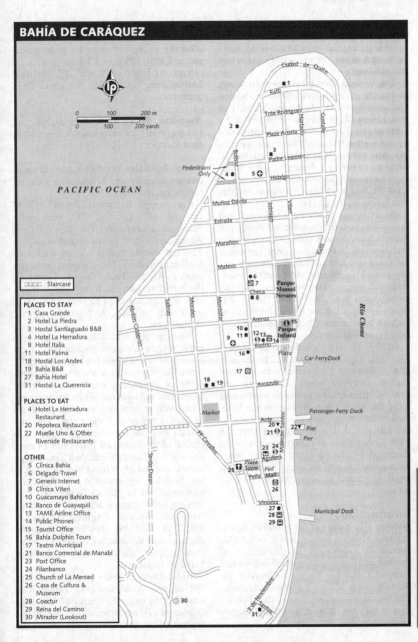

BAHÍA DE CARÁQUEZ

PACIFIC OCEAN

Río Chone

Ciudad de Quito

Ratti
Tnte Rodríguez
Plaza Acosta
Padre Leannen
Hidalgo
Muñoz Dávila
Estrada
Marañón
Mateus
Checa
Arenas
Riofrío
Plaza
Ascazubi
Ante
Aguilera
Plaza Sucre
Peña
Vinueza
Gonzále
Hurtado
Bolívar
Intriago
Viteri
Ratti
Malecón Santos
FF Cevallos
Sexto Durán
3 de Noviembre
3 de Santos

Pedestrians Only

Parque Manuel Nevares
Parque Infantil
Car-Ferry Dock
Passenger-Ferry Dock
Pier
Pier
Municipal Dock
Market
Ped Mall

▭▭▭ Staircase

0   100   200 m
0   100   200 yards

PLACES TO STAY
1 Casa Grande
2 Hotel La Piedra
3 Hostal Santiaguado B&B
4 Hotel La Herradura
8 Hotel Italia
11 Hotel Palma
18 Hostal Los Andes
19 Bahía B&B
27 Bahía Hotel
31 Hostal La Querencia

PLACES TO EAT
4 Hotel La Herradura Restaurant
20 Pepoteca Restaurant
22 Muelle Uno & Other Riverside Restaurants

OTHER
5 Clínica Bahía
6 Delgado Travel
7 Genesis Internet
9 Clínica Viteri
10 Guacamayo Bahíatours
12 Banco de Guayaquil
13 TAME Airline Office
14 Public Phones
15 Tourist Office
16 Bahía Dolphin Tours
17 Teatro Municipal
21 Banco Comercial de Manabí
23 Post Office
24 Filanbanco
25 Church of La Merced
26 Casa de Cultura & Museum
28 Coactur
29 Reina del Camino
30 Mirador (Lookout)

NORTH COAST

became a backwater. It regained fame during the early 1990s, when President Sixto Durán (1992–96) had a holiday home here, and many upper-class Ecuadorians followed suit.

The 1998 El Niño hit Bahía particularly badly; the city was cut off by landslides, and streets turned into rivers of mud. This was followed, in August 1998, by a 7.2 earthquake. Fortunately, it was preceded by numerous tremors, allowing people to get into streets. When the big quake hit, toppling or severely damaging some buildings, only one person was killed, but at least 20 died in the horrendous mudslides that followed the quake.

By mid-1999, roads were reopened and hotels and restaurants were operating, but tourists were almost nonexistent after the bad press of 1998. In late 1999, numerous buildings still had earthquake damage, but the town's economic and touristic infrastructure was working well. Several interesting local tours are worth taking, but beach-lovers will have to go elsewhere, as Bahía's beaches have been eroded and can only be used at low tide.

In 1999, Bahía declared itself an 'ecocity.' The town market may very well be the only one in Ecuador that recycles rather than throws away its waste. There are two organic farms nearby, as well as what is said to be the world's first organic shrimp farm. Reforestation projects are aimed both at the hillsides that were damaged after the 1998 El Niño and at mangroves that were damaged by shrimp farms. Various other agroecological and recycling ventures are being promoted by a handful of visionary locals.

Information

Money Filanbanco, at the corner of Aguilera and Malecón Santos, has a Visa ATM. Banco de Guayaquil, at the corner of Bolívar and Riofrío, changes US dollars and traveler's checks. Banco Comercial de Manabí is on Malecón Santos near Ante. The tourist office at Arenas and the Malecón may or may not be open, depending on government funding.

Post & Communications The post office is on the map. The telephone office closed after the quake, but there are phones next to the TAME office, on Riofrío.

Genesis Internet (☎ 692 263, vladirv@ hotmail.com, Bolívar 713), charges US$0.15 a minute.

Medical Services Clínica Bahía and Clínica Viteri are recommended by locals; their locations are shown on the map.

Travel Agencies Two recommended agencies are friendly and helpful with local information and tours.

Guacamayo Bahíatours (☎ 690 597, ☎/ fax 691 412, fax 691 280, ecopapel@ ecuadorexplorer.com), at Bolívar and Arenas, is owned by an Ecuadorian/New Zealand couple and is a good source of local information. The company arranges tours to Río Muchacho Organic Farm (see the boxed text on this farm). The staff can also arrange day trips to visit other agroecological projects, such as an organic shrimp farm.

You can also take a tour through mangrove forests in a canoe paddled by a local fisherman to see coastal wildlife, especially birds. Trips to local islands with seabird colonies (including one of the biggest frigatebird colonies on this coast) are combined with an explanation of the problems facing the mangrove habitat and a visit to a private zoo that has Ecuador's largest collection of domesticated fowl from all over the world. Other trips include hikes through coastal tropical dry forest and whale watching (from late September to early October – otherwise, go to Puerto López; see that section, under Parque Nacional Machalilla Area, later in this chapter). The cost is US$12 to US$30 per person, depending on the tour and the number of people. Information about volunteer work is also provided on request.

Bahía Dolphin Tours (☎ 692 097/86, fax 692 088, archtour@telconet.net), on Bolívar near Riofrio, owns the Chirije archaeological site (see Things to See & Do, later in this section). Day and overnight tours to the site can be arranged; the cost is about US$100 for a day tour, which can be split among two or three people. Ask about the price for larger groups. The company has English-, French- and German-speaking guides. The staff can arrange packages with overnights at Chirije and in Bahía, combined with visits to panama-hat workshops, shrimp farms, frigatebird islands and other local places.

Delgado Travel, on Bolívar north of Checa, does standard airline ticketing.

Work & Volunteering Ask at Genesis Internet (see Post & Communications, earlier) about teaching small children for two hours in the morning in exchange for a bed with a local family; there is a two-week minimum for this. Guacamayo Bahíatours (see Travel Agencies, next) can provide information on obtaining various kinds of volunteer work.

Things to See & Do
A small **archaeology museum** in the century-old Casa de Cultura is open 10 am to 6 pm Tuesday to Friday. **Teatro Municipal** has occasional live performances. The **mirador** (lookout) gives good views of the area and can be reached on foot or by a short cab ride.

Chirije archaeological site, 15km south of Bahía and 3km north of San Clemente, is an earthen hill riddled with artifacts – such as ceramics, burials, cooking areas, garbage dumps and jewelry – dating mainly from the Bahía culture (500 BC–AD 500). The site is owned by Bahía Dolphin Tours (see Travel Agencies, earlier in this section). The sheer number of remains leads archaeologists to think this was an important ancient port. Only small sections of the site have been professionally excavated, and some pieces are exhibited in the tiny onsite museum, but visitors will find shards of pottery all over the place. Unfortunately, a lack of funds has halted archaeological excavation, but the sites that have been studied thus far have been roofed to preserve them; these sites can be inspected.

To visit the site, it is essential to go with a guide (see Bahía Dolphin Tours under

Travel Agencies, earlier); otherwise, it's difficult to gain an appreciation for the place. Jacob Santos is recommended – he speaks perfect English and gives an enjoyable and enthusiastic tour. Chirije is cut off by high tides, so visits have to be planned with this in mind. You can spend the night and take advantage of trails into the coastal tropical dry forest. Five large cabins sleep up to eight (a squeeze) and have porch, private bath and kitchen if you want to spend a few days and cook for yourself. Rates are US$50 per cabin, including breakfast for two, and there is a restaurant on request. Because you are cut off by high tides, this really is 'getting away from it all.' You can take a day tour and then add a night if you like the place.

Places to Stay
Budget Most cheap places have water-supply problems. A good low-budget choice is *Bahía B&B* (☎ 690 146, Ascazubi 322), which has friendly, helpful staff and an English- and French-speaking owner (he'll tell you which wall of the 100-year-old building fell down in the quake). Rooms are small and rather musty but have fans and clean beds. Rates are US$3.25 per person for rooms with shared bath or US$4.25 per person with private bath, and a full breakfast is included. Next door is the cheaper and more basic *Hostal Los Andes* (☎ 690 587). *Hotel Palma* (☎ 690 467, Bolívar 910) is also very cheap but only OK.

Bahía Hotel (☎ 690 509, ☎/fax 693 833), on the Malecón at Vinueza, has 40 older rooms with private bath, fan and TV for US$4.75 per person. *Hostal La Querencia* (☎ 690 009, Santos 1800) has similarly priced rooms, some with private bath. The best budget choice is *Hostal Santiaguado B&B* (☎ 692 391, Padre Leannen 406), which has eight large rooms with reliable water at US$4.50 per person with shared bath or US$5.50 with private bath. Breakfast is included; Guacamayo Bahíatours (see Travel Agencies, earlier) makes reservations.

Mid-Range At Bolívar and Checa, *Hotel Italia* (☎ 691 137, fax 691 092) has small but very clean rooms with private hot showers, cable TV, telephone and either air-conditioning or a fan. There is a decent little restaurant with some local specialties. Rates are US$12/15 for singles/doubles with fan or US$19/25 with air-conditioning.

Hotel La Herradura (☎ 690 446, fax 690 265), at Bolívar and Hidalgo, has friendly staff, one of the town's better restaurants and pleasant decorations. Air-conditioned rooms with telephone, TV and private hot showers are about US$30, and some rooms have balconies with ocean views. Cheaper rooms with fans are available. *Hotel La Piedra* (☎ 690 780, 691 463, fax 690 154, apartec@uio.satnet.net), on Ratti near Bolívar, also has a decent restaurant and bar. Rooms with private bath, air-conditioning, telephone and cable TV cost US$22 to US$45. These prices may rise when the tourists return. The most upscale place is *Casa Grande*, on Ratti at Viteri, which has seven comfortable large rooms in a private house that is owned by Bahía Dolphin Tours, which makes reservations (see Travel Agencies, earlier). Rates are US$50 for doubles, including a full breakfast.

Places to Eat

Check out the reasonable and inexpensive restaurants overlooking the river. The best is *Muelle Uno*, and there are several others nearby. Opposite, *Pepoteca Restaurant*, at Ante and the Malecón, has set lunches for US$1.20 and good à la carte meals. The *Hotel La Herradura restaurant* (see Places to Stay, earlier) is good but a little pricey.

Getting There & Away

Air The regional airport is in San Vicente. Scheduled flights were once available, but they aren't now. Manta and Portoviejo have the nearest scheduled flights. Ask at the travel agencies or at the TAME office for current flight information.

Bus Two bus companies have offices next to one another on the south end of the Malecón. Coactur has buses to Portoviejo

(US$1, two hours) hourly 4 am to 8 pm; some continue to Manta or Guayaquil (US$4.50, six hours). Reina del Camino has buses at 6 am and 10 pm to Quito (US$5, eight hours). You can also ask the staff at these two companies about buses to Santo Domingo, Esmeraldas and other places. Buses to local towns such as Chone are often rancheras, and they leave from various places in town. Ask if you need them.

Arriving buses will go as far as the ferry if you ask the driver.

Boat See the San Vicente section, earlier in this chapter, for boat information. The passenger- and car-ferry docks are shown on the map.

PORTOVIEJO
☎ 05

This large city of over 180,000 inhabitants is the capital of Manabí Province and is important for coffee, cattle and fishing. Founded on March 12, 1535, it is one of the oldest cities in Ecuador and is the sixth largest. Portoviejo has a thriving agricultural-processing industry and is an important commercial center, with good road connections to Quito and Guayaquil. Although it's a bustling town, Portoviejo is not visited much by tourists, who prefer to head to the coast. However, it is friendly and is a reasonable overnight stop from Quito en route to the coast.

Information

Limited tourist information is available at Gual 234.

There are many banks. Filanbanco, at Pacheco and Gual, has a Visa ATM, and Banco del Pacífico, at 9 de Octubre and Rocafuerte, has a MasterCard ATM. Banco del Pichincha, on Parque Central, changes traveler's checks.

The post office and the Pacifictel office are shown on the map.

The public hospital (☎ 630 766, 630 555, 630 087) is at the southeast end of Rocafuerte, 1km from the center; take a taxi or call the Red Cross ambulance (☎ 652 555).

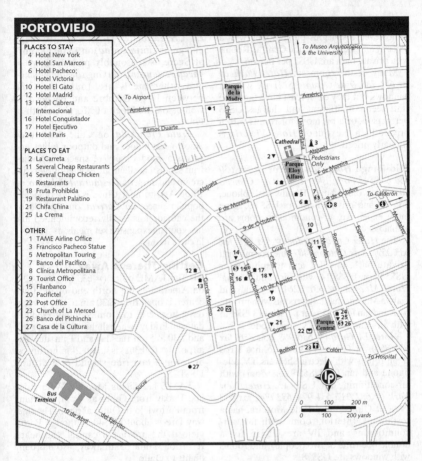

PORTOVIEJO

PLACES TO STAY
4   Hotel New York
5   Hotel San Marcos
6   Hotel Pacheco;
     Hotel Victoria
10 Hotel El Gato
12 Hotel Madrid
13 Hotel Cabrera
     Internacional
16 Hotel Conquistador
17 Hotel Ejecutivo
24 Hotel Paris

PLACES TO EAT
2   La Carreta
11 Several Cheap Restaurants
14 Several Cheap Chicken
     Restaurants
18 Fruta Prohibida
19 Restaurant Palatino
21 Chifa China
25 La Crema

OTHER
1   TAME Airline Office
3   Francisco Pacheco Statue
5   Metropolitan Touring
7   Banco del Pacifico
8   Clínica Metropolitana
9   Tourist Office
15 Filanbanco
20 Pacifictel
22 Post Office
23 Church of La Merced
26 Banco del Pichincha
27 Casa de la Cultura

Clínica Metropolitana, at 9 de Octubre and Rocafuerte, is another choice.

Metropolitan Touring (☎/fax 636 596, 651 070, 631 761, porturis@gye.satnet.net), Olmedo 706, does standard tours and airline ticketing.

Things to See
Despite the town's colonial history, there's little to see. Wander down to the pleasant **Parque Eloy Alfaro**, which has what may well be the starkest, barest modern **cathedral** in Ecuador. Next to the cathedral is a **statue** of Francisco Pacheco, the founder of Por-

toviejo. There is reportedly a small **Museo Arqueológico** in the university, out of the center, on Universitaria. The **Casa de Cultura**, on Sucre, has occasional shows, but opening hours are erratic and unpredictable.

Note that Chile is a street market between Duarte and Gual and is impassable to cars during the day.

Places to Stay
Budget The friendly *Hotel Paris* (☎ 657 272, Sucre 513) is one of Portoviejo's oldest hotels (check out the early-20th-century pressed-tin ceiling in the entry). It's simple, safe and

clean, but it looks rather dilapidated. There is, however, a spacious public lobby with a balcony and views of Parque Central. Rooms with private bath are US$2 per person.

Many of the rooms at *Hotel Pacheco* (☎ *651 788, 9 de Octubre 512*) are without windows, but they do at least have fans. The staff seems indifferent and charges US$3 per person, or a bit more for rooms with a private bath. Next door, *Hotel Victoria* is similarly priced.

Mid-Range *Hotel San Marcos* (☎/*fax 630 650, 636 596, porturis@gye.satnet.net, Olmedo 706*) is an older hotel. Rooms with phone, TV, fan and private bath are US$6/9; some more expensive, air-conditioned rooms are available.

The *Hotel Conquistador* (☎ *631 678, fax 633 259, 18 de Octubre 407*) has rooms with private bath, fan, TV and telephone for US$5/9, or US$8/14 with air-conditioning. *Hotel Madrid* (☎ *631 326*), at Gual and García Moreno, has large rooms with private bath and fan for US$5 per person or US$8/15 with air-conditioning, TV and phone.

Hotel El Gato (☎ *636 908, 632 856, fax 632 850*), at Gual and Olmedo, has large clean rooms with electric showers, TV, telephone and fan for US$5/9, or rooms with air-conditioning for US$9/13. *Hotel New York* (☎ *632 037, 631 998, 632 006, fax 632 044*), at Olmedo and F de Moreira, has a restaurant. Interior rooms with fan, air-conditioning, and TV are US$15 for a double bed (one or two people), and rooms with windows are US$18.

Hotel Cabrera Internacional (☎ *633 200/1, fax 633 199, García Moreno 102*) charges US$10/18 for air-conditioned rooms with TV and telephone, or US$12/22 for larger rooms with minifridge. All of these hotels are just OK.

The town's best is *Hotel Ejecutivo* (☎ *632 105, 630 840, fax 630 876*), on 18 de Octubre between Gual and 10 de Agosto. It provides car rental, has a good but pricey restaurant, and charges US$42/46 for carpeted rooms with window, minifridge, hot bath, cable TV and telephone (or US$10 less for interior rooms).

Places to Eat

La Crema, below Hotel Paris, is cheap and good. *Chifa China*, on 18 de Octubre at Sucre, is reasonably priced. Rows of *cheap restaurants* serving roasted chicken and other meals are found on Gual between 18 de Octubre and Pacheco, as well as on the block of Morales south of Gual.

Fruta Prohibida, on Chile near 10 de Agosto, has indoor and outdoor tables and serves a good variety of snacks, including fruit salads, excellent juices, hamburgers, ice cream and desserts. *Restaurant Palatino*, on 10 de Agosto near Chile, is a good, locally popular place. *La Carreta*, on Olmedo by the cathedral, is locally recommended and has good, inexpensive set meals, as well as à la carte items.

Getting There & Away

Air The TAME office (☎ 633 600, 632 429), on América at the north end of the town center, is open from 8:30 am to noon weekdays; from 2:30 to 3 pm Monday, Wednesday and Friday (when flights are coming in); and 2:30 to 5 pm Tuesday and Thursday. The airport (☎ 650 361) is about 2km northwest of town; a taxi ride should cost around US$1.25.

TAME has flights Monday, Wednesday and Friday from Quito at 4 pm, returning from Portoviejo to Quito at 5 pm. The one-way fare is about US$40. Although Portoviejo is the provincial capital, the beach resort of Manta, 35km away, also has daily flights to Quito.

AECA (☎ in Guayaquil 04-288 110, 290 849) has flights to and from Guayaquil on some days in light aircraft; ask at the airport.

Bus Most travelers arrive at the bus terminal 1km southwest of downtown. It's best to take a taxi (US$0.75) to/from the terminal for security.

Most companies don't have a ticket office; you pay US$0.02 to enter the terminal and ask for buses to your destination, which leave regularly, and you pay aboard the bus. A few long-distance bus companies

The Río Verde waterfalls, 20km east of Baños

Canoes on Río Napo, in the Oriente

Yes, butterflies are attracted to sweat!

Hiker and buttressed tree roots, in the Oriente

Sunset on the lagoons of Reserva Producción Faunística Cuyabeno, in the Oriente

Laundry day on Río Napo, in the Oriente

Illegal wildlife poaching is an ongoing problem.

Oriente landscape with Manta de Novia (Bridal Veil) Falls

in the terminal sell tickets in advance. These include Coactur, which has several buses an hour to Manta (US$0.80, one hour), Bahía de Caráquez (US$1, two hours) and Guayaquil (US$3.50, four hours). Reina del Camino has buses to Quito (US$5.50, or US$7 for better 'ejecutivo' buses) and other destinations, such as Santo Domingo (US$4, five hours).

Co-op 15 de Octubre and Co-op Jipijapa have buses to Jipijapa (US$0.90) about every 45 minutes. Change there for Puerto López. Other small nearby villages are served by small bus companies, and there are frequent departures.

INLAND FROM PORTOVIEJO
☎ 05

Manabí is an important agricultural province, and a relatively good road system links Portoviejo with a number of canton capitals. The towns, often quite large, act as market centers for coffee, cattle, citrus, corn, cotton, yucca and bananas. They are colorful and bustling, and the people are hardworking, tough, old-fashioned and friendly. Tourists rarely visit these towns, even though the region is easy to travel in using the small local buses, and you can find cheap and basic hotels in the bigger towns. This area provides a great glimpse of rural and provincial Ecuadorian life for those travelers who want to get off the beaten track.

Approximately 20km north of Portoviejo, **Rocafuerte** is known for its confectionery made of coconuts and caramel. **Calceta**, 43km northeast of Portoviejo, is known for sisal production. Sisal is the fiber gathered from the spiny-leaved agave plant that grows in the region. The sisal fibers are used for ropes and sandals, among other things.

From Calceta, a good road continues about 25km northeast to the sizable town of **Chone**, known for its macho cowboys and tough-guy attitudes. Local lore has it that the women are beautiful, but the men won't let outsiders get near them – this is not the feminism capital of the world. There are plenty of basic hotels and one good mid-range one – *Atahualpa the Oro* (☎ 696 627). From Chone, a paved road

continues northeast, linking the coastal lowlands with Santo Domingo de los Colorados. This road climbs to over 600m above sea level as it crosses the coastal mountains, then drops down on the eastern side of these mountains to the canton capitals and market towns of **Flavio Alfaro** and **El Carmen** before reaching Santo Domingo. From El Carmen, you can get buses back to Pedernales.

MANTA
☎ 05

Manta, with over 200,000 inhabitants, is the major port along the central Ecuadorian coast and an important local tourist resort and commercial center. Despite its popularity among Ecuadorian tourists, foreign travelers tend to pass through quickly to find quieter and cleaner beaches elsewhere.

Orientation
The town is divided into two by Río Manta. Manta, on the west side, and Tarqui, on the east side, are joined by road bridges. Avenidas and calles in Manta are named with single or double digits; avenidas and calles in Tarqui begin at 101. Manta has the main offices, shopping areas, 1st-class hotels and the bus terminal. Tarqui has more hotels, but they are older and more run down, and Tarqui beaches more prone to theft and similar problems. Streets with numbers over 110 are in a particularly insalubrious neighborhood. The main residential areas are to the southwest of Manta business district, while the best beaches are to the northwest of Manta.

Information
Tourist Offices Limited information is available at the tourist office in the town hall. There is also an information center at the entrance to Playa Murciélago. You can extend your tourist card at the police station on 4 de Noviembre (Malecón de Manta turns into 4 de Noviembre outside of the map's extents).

Money There are branches of Banco del Pacífico (which have MasterCard ATMs), and branches of Filanbanco (which have

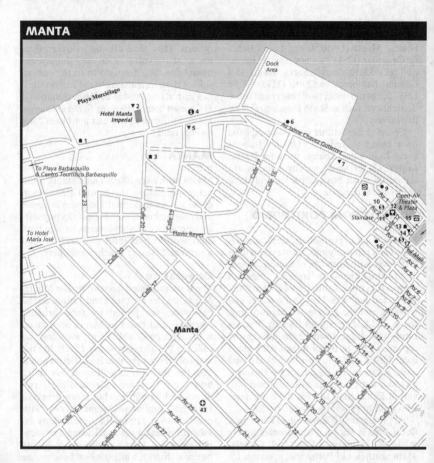

MANTA

Visa ATMs). Both banks, as well as Banco del Pichincha, change traveler's checks. See the map for their locations.

Post & Communications The post office is on Calle 8, and Pacifictel is on the Manta waterfront. You can send email from the Cyber Café, on Avenida 1 near Calle 14.

Travel Agencies Metropolitan Touring (☎ 623 090) is on Avenida 4 between Calles 12 and 13. Delgado Travel (☎ 622 813, fax 628 491), at Avenida 2 and Calle 13, arranges car rentals. Localiza Rent-a-Car is on

Avenida Jaime Chavez Gutierrez between Calles 16 and 17.

Medical Services The public hospital (☎ 611 849, 611 515) is on Avenida 24 and Calle 13. Clínica Manta (☎ 921 566) has doctors of various specialties, including Dr Oscar Pico Santos, who has been generally recommended. There are many pharmacies around town.

Emergency Contact the police by calling ☎ 101 or ☎ 920 900. There is a police station on 4 de Noviembre (Malecón de Manta

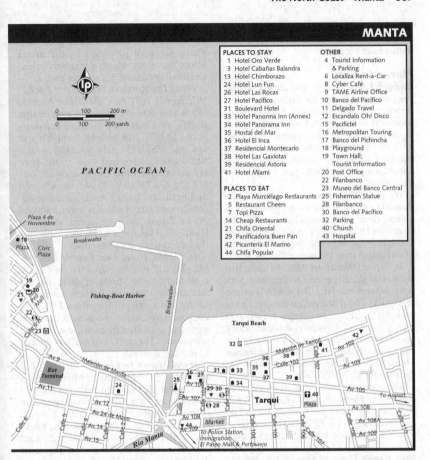

MANTA

PLACES TO STAY		OTHER	
1	Hotel Oro Verde	4	Tourist Information
3	Hotel Cabañas Balandra		& Parking
13	Hotel Chimborazo	6	Localiza Rent-a-Car
24	Hotel Lun Fun	8	Cyber Café
26	Hotel Las Rocas	9	TAME Airline Office
27	Hotel Pacífico	10	Banco del Pacífico
31	Boulevard Hotel	11	Delgado Travel
33	Hotel Panorama Inn (Annex)	12	Escandalo Oh! Disco
34	Hotel Panorama Inn	15	Pacifictel
35	Hostal del Mar	16	Metropolitan Touring
36	Hotel El Inca	17	Banco del Pichincha
37	Residencial Montecarlo	18	Playground
38	Hotel Las Gaviotas	19	Town Hall;
39	Residencial Astoria		Tourist Information
41	Hotel Miami	20	Post Office
		22	Filanbanco
PLACES TO EAT		23	Museo del Banco Central
2	Playa Murciélago Restaurants	25	Fisherman Statue
5	Restaurant Cheers	28	Filanbanco
7	Topi Pizza	30	Banco del Pacífico
14	Cheap Restaurants	32	Parking
21	Chifa Oriental	40	Church
29	Panificadora Buen Pan	43	Hospital
42	Picantería El Marino		
44	Chifa Popular		

turns into 4 de Noviembre outside of the map's extents).

Things to See & Do

The **Museo del Banco Central**, on Malecón de Manta, is worth a visit to understand more of the Manta culture. The exhibit is small, but it is well laid out and labeled in Spanish. Hours are 8:30 am to 4:30 pm weekdays; there is a nominal admission fee.

Manta's **fishing-boat harbor** is busy and picturesque at high tide and dead in the mud at low tide. In Tarqui, there is a huge **statue** of a Manabí fisherman, and beyond it is the protected sandy **Tarqui Beach**. At the end of the beach are more fishing boats – it's interesting to watch the fishermen unload their cargo in the early morning, but don't bring valuables. There is a **children's playground** in the plaza east of Plaza 4 de Noviembre.

Playa Murciélago, in Manta, is a less protected beach and has bigger waves (although they're still not very big). There is a powerful undertow that can sweep swimmers away even when the beach appears fairly calm. It is a couple of kilometers northwest of the town center and is the town's most popular beach, with plenty of snack bars and places to rent umbrellas. Farther northwest is **Playa Barbasquillo**, which is quieter still and has a tourist resort complex.

Places to Stay

Budget Prices tend to rise during holiday weekends and during the high seasons (December to March and June to August). Single rooms can be hard to find, so consider traveling here with a friend or partner to economize. At other times of the year, particularly midweek in the low season, hotels can be almost empty, and you can bargain for cheaper rates.

Hotel Chimborazo (☎ 612 290), on Avenida 1 north of Plaza 4 de Noviembre, is a noisy dive. Some rooms have bathrooms. Rates are about US$3/4 for singles/doubles, and this is the only cheap place in Manta. Most budget travelers stay in Tarqui.

In Tarqui, *Hostal del Mar*, on Calle 104, is OK at US$2.50 per person for rooms with cold showers and fans. The similarly priced and quirky *Hotel Miami*, on the east end of Malecón de Tarqui, has simple rooms with fans, private bathrooms and cockroaches. Some rooms have good ocean views. Other cheap but basic places are *Residencial Montecarlo* and *Residencial Astoria*; see the map for their locations.

The student- and youth-group-oriented *Boulevard Hotel* (☎ 625 333, 620 627, 621 836), on Calle 103 near Avenida 105, is OK and charges US$4 or US$7 per person (with fan or air-conditioning) in the high season.

Mid-Range *Hotel El Inca* (☎ 620 440, 610 986, fax 622 447), on Calle 105 near Malecón de Tarqui, charges US$12 for a double with fan and cold-water bath, or US$15 with air-conditioning, TV and phone. Some rooms have ocean views. There is an attached restaurant. The similarly priced *Hotel Pacífico* (☎ 623 584, 622 475), on Avenida 106 near Calle 102, has quite nice rooms with fans or air-conditioning.

Hotel Panorama Inn (☎ 611 552), on Calle 103 near Avenida 105, has rooms for US$7 to US$15 per person, depending on the amenities you choose. Rooms are rather worn but spacious; all have private bath-

rooms; many have air-conditioning; and some have a TV, telephone and good view. There are pool privileges at the *annex* across the street, which is similarly priced and has a restaurant but smaller rooms.

Hotel Las Rocas (☎ 612 856, 610 299, 620 607, fax 623 163), on Calle 101 at Avenida 105, is a favorite of Ecuadorian tour groups. Rooms are clean but a bit worn and overpriced at US$12/16 with hot bath, TV and fan, and US$16/22 with air-conditioning, and include coffee and toast in the poor restaurant. *Hotel Las Gaviotas* (☎ 620 140, 621 854, 624 738, fax 620 940), on Malecón de Tarqui near Calle 106, has adequate air-conditioned rooms with hot water, bath and phone (some have an ocean view) for US$22/24. There is a restaurant, although the café and bar are preferable.

In Manta, *Hotel Lun Fun* (☎ 622 966, 612 400, 622 976, fax 610 601), on Calle 2 near Malecón de Manta, is good, modern and comfortable and is the best hotel close to the bus terminal. Rates are US$35/45 for good-sized, clean rooms with bath, hot water, air-conditioning, minifridge, TV and telephone. There is a good but pricey Chinese restaurant.

Hotel Manta Imperial (☎ 621 955, 622 016, fax 623 016) is next to Manta's Playa Murciélago. Rooms are rather worn and have private bath, cable TV and either fan or air-conditioning; some have a beach view. A swimming pool, a disco on weekends and a somewhat mediocre restaurant complete the scene. Rates for singles or doubles are about US$18 to US$30, depending on the room.

On the next beach northwest of Murciélago is *Centro Turístico Barbasquillo* (☎ 620 718, 625 976, fax 622 456). There is private beach access and a beach bar, pool, sauna, gym, disco, kid's playground and a restaurant. Rates for air-conditioned rooms with TV and telephone are US$30/38, including breakfast.

Hotel Cabañas Balandra (☎ 620 316, 620 915, 625 550, 628 144, fax 620 545), north of downtown Manta on Calle 20, is two blocks away from Playa Murciélago. The very comfortable two-bedroom cabins have air-conditioning, minifridge, TV, bath, telephone and balconies with views of the ocean. The complex has a restaurant, a small pool and a guarded parking lot. Rooms start at US$50.

Top End At Calle 29 and Calle Flavio Reyes, to the northwest of downtown, is *Hotel María José* (☎ 612 294), an eight-room luxury hotel. The rooms are air-conditioned and have the usual facilities (including room service), and a pool is on the premises. Rates start at about US$60.

The new 60-room *Hotel Oro Verde* (☎ 629 200/209, fax 629 210), on Playa Murciélago at Calle 23, is a full-service hotel on the beach and has a pool, tennis court, gym and sauna. Rates are around US$90.

Places to Eat

Many cheap outdoor comedores on the east end of Tarqui Beach serve fresh seafood. Behind them are several restaurants, of which *Picantería El Marino*, at Malecón Tarqui and Calle 110, is one of the best, but it is only open 8 am to 5 pm. *Panificadora Buen Pan* is good for baked goods.

Near the bridge joining Tarqui with Manta is *Chifa Popular* (☎ 621 346). It's cheap and good. In Manta, there is the cheap *Chifa Oriental*, on Calle 8 at Avenida 4.

Near Playa Murciélago, *Topi Pizza* (☎ 621 180), on Malecón de Manta near Calle 15, is open late and has a good variety of pizza and other Italian dishes. Opposite Playa Murciélago at Calle 19, *Restaurant Cheers* (☎ 620 779) is a popular steak-and-seafood restaurant with an outdoor courtyard.

Along Playa Murciélago are numerous bars and restaurants, all of which serve similarly adequate, reasonably priced food. There are also many cheap restaurants at Calle 11 and Avenida 1, and many hotels have restaurants as well (see the Places to Stay section, earlier).

1500 Years of Seafaring

Manta has a long history. It was founded by Francisco Pacheco on March 2, 1535, 10 days before he founded Portoviejo. But even before its Spanish foundation, Manta (named Jocay by the local Indians) was an important port. The Manta culture thrived throughout the whole western peninsula from about AD 500 until the arrival of the conquistadors, and many artifacts made by these early inhabitants have been found.

The pottery of the Manta culture was well made and was decorated with pictures of daily life. Through these pictorial decorations, archaeologists have learned that the Manta people enhanced their appearance by skull deformation and tooth removal, thus increasing the backward slope of their foreheads and chins and emphasizing their large, rounded, hooked noses.

Also evident in their pottery was the Mantas' astonishing skill in navigation (this was also recorded in detail by the early conquistadors). They were able to navigate as far as Panama and Peru, and claims have been made that they reached the Galápagos. There are records claiming that the Manta seafarers sailed as far north as Mexico and as far south as Chile.

Not only were their navigational and ceramic skills well developed but the Mantas were also skilled stonemasons, weavers and metalworkers. People wishing to learn more about the Manta culture should visit the museum in town.

After the conquest, the town of Manta had a history of attack and destruction by pirates from various European countries. Attacks in 1543, 1607 and 1628 left the city ruined, and many survivors fled inland (to Montecristi in particular).

Today, the descendants of the seafaring Manta people continue to demonstrate their superb marine skills as fishermen, navigating their small open boats many kilometers out in the open ocean for days at a stretch.

Entertainment

During the high season, there are plenty of dancing places. *Escándalo Oh!* (☎ 623 653) is a Manta discotheque on Calle 12 between Avenidas 1 and 2. *El Paseo Mall*, on the road to Portoviejo, has a big cinema complex, as well as other American-style mall attractions.

Getting There & Away

Air The TAME office (☎ 622 006, 613 210) is on the Manta waterfront, past the open-air theater. TAME has flights to Manta from Quito every morning Monday to Saturday and every Sunday afternoon. Schedules often change, and the one-way fare is about US$25. During the coastal high season (December to April), there are three flights a week from Guayaquil; that service could be continued into other months. You can buy tickets at the airport on the morning of the flight, but the planes tend to be full on weekends and holidays.

AECA (☎ in Guayaquil 04-288 810, 290 849) has flights from Guayaquil in light aircraft when there is passenger demand.

The airport (☎ 621 580) is some 3km east of Tarqui, and a taxi costs about US$1.

Bus There is a large central bus terminal in front of the fishing-boat harbor in Manta, and almost all buses leave from there, which makes things easy. There are several companies with buses to most major Ecuadorian cities. Journey times and prices are similar to Portoviejo's (see that section, earlier). Some of the smaller companies running buses to nearby Manabí towns and villages don't have an office in the terminal, but their buses leave from there anyway, and you pay aboard the bus.

CRUCITA AREA

☎ 05

The fishing village of **Crucita** is reached by going north from Portoviejo. There, you'll find several good seafood restaurants, a very long beach (best at low tide) and hang gliders (there are competitions every few months). The hang gliding tends to attract affluent Ecuadorians. The beach in front of town is not very clean, but heading north or south brings you to much better ones. There are several places to stay, including *Hostal Hipocampo* (☎ 676 167), which has been there for years and offers adequate rooms with private bath for about US$6 per person, and the newer *Hostería Zucasa* (☎ 634 908), which is a bit more expensive and modern. There are a few other choices.

Northward, the next villages are **San Jacinto**, about 13km beyond Crucita and slightly inland, and **San Clemente**, about 3km beyond San Jacinto and on the coast. There are good, sandy beaches between these villages, both of which have restaurants and cheap or mid-range places to stay. In San Jacinto, *Hotel San Jacinto* is one of the best ones.

On the outskirts of San Clemente, there is *Hostería San Clemente*, which has a swimming pool, and *Cabañas Tío Gerardo*, which has cabins with enough sleeping space for two to six people. There are also a bunch of other places. Beyond San Clemente, a road continues northeast along the coast to Bahía de Caráquez, about 20km away.

Crucita, San Jacinto and San Clemente can be easily reached from Portoviejo. All have been developing a tourist industry since the 1990s, although they were hard-hit in the 1997–98 El Niño. Most visitors are Ecuadorians – the place has yet to be discovered by foreign travelers. Beware of walking barefoot in these places – a worm infection has been reported.

MONTECRISTI

☎ 05

This town, about 30km west of Portoviejo, is an important center for both the panama-hat industry and for wickerwork. There are many stores along the main road and along the road leading into the town center. If you go in toward the center and ask around, you can see the manufacturing of panama hats in various stages.

The town is an old colonial one; it was founded around 1628, when many of the inhabitants of Manta fled inland to avoid the frequent plundering by pirates. The many unrestored colonial houses give the village a rather tumbledown and ghostly atmosphere.

The main plaza has a beautiful church dating back to the early part of the last century. It contains a statue of the Virgin (to which miracles have been attributed) and is worth a visit. In the plaza is a statue of Eloy Alfaro, who was born in Montecristi and was president of Ecuador at the beginning of the century. His tomb is in the town hall by the plaza.

Montecristi can be reached during the day by frequent buses (US$0.20, 15 minutes) from the bus terminal in Manta.

PARQUE NACIONAL MACHALILLA AREA
☎ 05

Jipijapa

Pronounced 'Hipihapa,' this town is an important agricultural center. Sunday is market day and is busy – signs outside many merchants' stores in the center read 'Compro Café' (Coffee Bought Here), and panama hats are sold. Filanbanco has a Visa ATM and cashes traveler's checks; it is the only place to do this southbound along the coast until Santa Elena. A new bus terminal on the outskirts facilitates fast onward travel.

A few very basic hotels are available. The dirty *Pensión Mejía*, near the central plaza, is barely acceptable for US$2 per person. The best place is *Hostal Agua Blanca* (☎ 601 138), about a kilometer from the bus terminal on the road to Puerto Cayo; rates are US$4 per person.

From the terminal, buses to Portoviejo, Manta and Puérto López leave frequently; fares are about US$1. Buses to Guayaquil and Quito leave several times a day.

Puerto Cayo

About 30km west of Jipijapa, the road reaches the Pacific Ocean at the fishing village of Puerto Cayo, which has no banks or phones. Near the beach, a few kilometers north of town, *Hostería Luz de Luna* (in Quito ☎ 02-407 279, 400 563, fax 400 562) has over 20 clean cabins with bath, a pool, a restaurant (the best in the area) and tours to Isla de la Plata and Parque Nacional Machalilla. Rates are about US$14 for a double. *Hotel Puerto Cayo*, at the south end along the beach, is more expensive but no better. The more central *Hostería Los Frailes* (in Jipijapa ☎ 601 365) charges about US$12 for doubles, which are reasonable rooms with private baths; there is a restaurant. Also nearer the center, *Residencial Zavala's* and *Cabañas Alejandra* are cheaper.

Parque Nacional Machalilla

This is Ecuador's only coastal national park, and it is important in that it preserves a small part of the country's rapidly disappearing coastal habitats. The park was created in 1979 to protect about 50km of beach (less than 2% of Ecuador's coastline), some 40,000 hectares of tropical dry forest and cloud forest, and about 20,000 hectares of ocean (including offshore islands, of which Isla La Plata is the most important).

From December to May, it is sunny and uncomfortably hot, with frequent short rainstorms. From June to November, it is cooler and often overcast.

Most archaeological sites within and near the park mainly date from the Manta period, which began around AD 500 and lasted until the conquest. There are also remains of the much older Machalilla and Chorrera cultures, dating from about 1500 to 500 BC, and the Salango culture, which dates from 3000 BC. None of the sites are striking.

The tropical dry forest found in much of the inland sectors of the park forms a strange and wonderful landscape of characteristically bottle-shaped trees with small crowns and heavy spines – a protection against herbivores. In the upper reaches of the park, humid cloud forest is encountered. Some of the most common species include the leguminous algarrobo (*Prosopsis juliflora*), which has green bark and is able to photosynthesize even when it loses its leaves.

The kapok (or ceiba) tree (*Ceiba pentandra*), with its huge planklike buttresses surrounding the base of the gray trunk, has fruits that yield a fiber that floats and doesn't get waterlogged. The kapok fiber was used in life jackets before the advent of modern

NORTH COAST

PARQUE NACIONAL MACHALILLA AREA

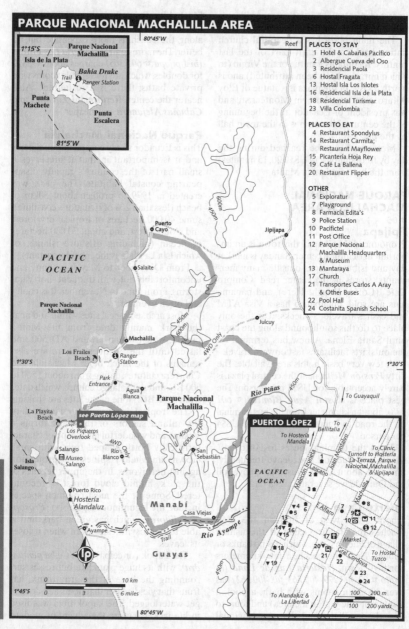

PLACES TO STAY
1 Hotel & Cabañas Pacífico
2 Albergue Cueva del Oso
3 Residencial Paola
6 Hostal Fragata
13 Hostal Isla Los Islotes
16 Residencial Isla de la Plata
18 Residencial Turismar
23 Villa Colombia

PLACES TO EAT
4 Restaurant Spondylus
14 Restaurant Carmita;
   Restaurant Mayflower
15 Picantería Hoja Rey
19 Café La Ballena
20 Restaurant Flipper

OTHER
5 Exploratur
7 Playground
8 Farmacía Edita's
9 Police Station
10 Pacifictel
11 Post Office
12 Parque Nacional
   Machalilla Headquarters
   & Museum
13 Mantaraya
17 Church
21 Transportes Carlos A Aray
   & Other Buses
22 Pool Hall
24 Costanita Spanish School

synthetics. Fig *(Ficus* species), laurel *(Cordia* species) and palo santo *(Pursera graveolens)* trees are also commonly seen. The tall spindly candelabra cactus that grows profusely on some hillsides belongs to the genus *Armatocereus.* Also common is the prickly pear, of the genus *Opuntia.*

Within this strange-looking forest, a variety of bird and animal life is found. Well over 200 species of birds have been recorded, including a variety of coastal parrots, parrotlets and parakeets, as well seabirds, such as frigatebirds, pelicans and boobies – some of which nest in the offshore islands. Other animals include deer, squirrels, howler monkeys, anteaters and a variety of lizards, snakes and iguanas.

This unique tropical dry forest once stretched along much of the Pacific coast of Central and South America, but it has suffered from human interference more than most other tropical forests. It has now almost entirely disappeared and is one of the most threatened tropical forests in the world. It is particularly vulnerable to fire and to grazing by goats, which eat young trees before they have developed their protective spines and the full complement of chemicals that make the mature trees less palatable to herbivores.

Many of the goats are illegally introduced by poor campesinos who don't have other land to graze their animals on. This is typical of the management problems facing the Ecuadorian national-park system as a whole.

Fortunately, Machalilla's uniqueness has led to its being better managed than some parks. It has a park superintendent and several rangers who work with the local people to establish better protection of the park. Locals are trained to work as guides and to maintain a museum and archaeological area.

Information The **park headquarters and museum** are in Puerto López. The small museum is open 8 am to 4 pm daily (no charge). Entrance fees to any or all sectors of the park are US$20 (valid for five days). Bona fide students with ID pay US$10, and

locals pay only US$1 – and there is the usual controversy about this difference. This fee is charged in all sectors of the park, so carry your ticket.

Isla de la Plata This island, which is part of Parque Nacional Machalilla, can be reached by hiring a boat in Puerto López. The name, which means 'silver island,' is derived from the local legend that Sir Francis Drake buried treasure there, although other stories suggest that the abundance of guano shining in the sun gives rise to the name. The island has nesting colonies of seabirds – blue-footed boobies are usually seen. Red-footed boobies, frigatebirds and pelicans have also been frequently recorded, as well as a variety of gulls, terns, petrels and other seabirds. Albatrosses may be seen from April to October. There are a few coral reefs as well, and you can snorkel if you bring gear or take a tour that features snorkeling. Dolphins are often seen on the trip over to the island, and from mid-June to early October (especially July to August), humpback whales are regularly sighted, and the boats stop for photography and observation.

The island has been locally and aptly dubbed as 'the poor person's Galápagos.' (Some scientists don't like this term, claiming there are biological differences.) There are no facilities except for some very grungy toilets by the ranger station at the landing beach, where there is also a sheltered picnic area and basic snacks for sale. From here, a steep climb up almost 200 steps takes you to the middle of the island, from where two loop trails, the 3.5km Sendero Machete and the 5km Sendero Punta Escaleras, can be hiked. Most guides choose the shorter one, saying there are better animal sightings. Either way, the trail is rough, and good footwear is advised.

Places to Stay You can camp in several places within the park, but check with park authorities about the availability of water – particularly during the May-to-December dry season.

People in Agua Blanca will put you up in their houses. Basic food is available on request, but it's best to bring some of your own if you have special requirements. Spending two nights with a family in Agua Blanca, including meals and a guide, should cost around US$30 for two people (plus the park-entrance fee). You can also camp near Agua Blanca (see Agua Blanca, later in this section). In San Sebastián, you can stay with locals, and camping is allowed, but there is no campground per se (see San Sebastián & Julcuy, later in this section).

Most people stay in hotels in Puerto López or at the nearby Alandaluz Ecological Tourist Center (see Hostería Alandaluz, later).

Getting There & Away At least every hour, buses run up and down the coast between Puerto López and Jipijapa. You should have no difficulty, therefore, in getting a bus to drop you off at the park entrance or in finding one to pick you up when you are ready to leave.

Trucks occasionally go from the main road to Agua Blanca and back; most likely, you'll have to walk or hire a taxi in Puerto López to get to Agua Blanca. This costs about US$8 (you can share the price among other riders).

You can arrange boat trips to Isla de la Plata through the tour agencies in Puerto López.

Agua Blanca
About 5.5km north of Puerto López, a park entrance is on the right side of the road. A dirt road goes through tropical dry forest to Agua Blanca, 6km from the entrance. This little village has an **archaeological museum** (8 am to 6 pm) explaining the excavation of the Manta site, which is about a half-hour walk away. The site can be visited, but a local guide is required. About US$3 per person will cover the entrance fee to the museum and a guided visit to the site. Only the bases of the buildings can be seen, but there are plans to restore some of the approximately 400 buildings excavated at the site, which is thought to have been an important political capital of the Manta people.

San Sebastián & Julcuy
From Agua Blanca, a four-hour hike to the southeast goes up through a transition zone to a remnant area of cloud forest at San Sebastián, about 600m above sea level and 10km away. Guides are required and are available in Agua Blanca to take you to either the archaeological site or San Sebastián. Horses can be hired if you don't want to hike. The hike up to San Sebastián gives you a good look at the transitional forests as you climb close to 800m in elevation; overnight trips are recommended. Camping or staying with local people are the only accommodations.

Instead of taking this hike, you can continue through Agua Blanca up the Río Julcuy valley to the northeast. From Agua Blanca, it is a six- to seven-hour hike up this road through the park, coming out at the village of Julcuy, just beyond the park boundary. From Julcuy, it's about another three hours to the main Jipijapa-Guayaquil road. This road may be passable to 4WD vehicles in good weather, but it is mainly a horse trail.

Machalilla
This village is a little over 10km north of Puerto López. There is a decent beach and you can stay at the budget- to mid-priced *Hotel Internacional Machalilla*.

Los Frailes
About 10km north of Puerto López, just before the town of Machalilla, a ranger station admits you to a dirt road going 3km to the coast at the pretty beach of Los Frailes, which is suitable for swimming. Hikers can take a 4km trail through the coastal forest; there are two lookouts. Seabirds such as blue-footed boobies can be seen, especially if you have binoculars.

Puerto López
This is a busy fishing village, with a population of about 15,000. You can watch the fishermen come in and unload their catch most mornings – the fish are gutted on the spot, and the air is full of wheeling frigatebirds and vultures trying to grab the scraps. If you

make friends with the local fishers, they may take you out on a fishing trip.

Buses running from La Libertad (on the south coast) to Jipijapa often stop here for about 10 minutes while passengers buy snacks. Sometimes, children get on the bus, yelling 'Corviche Caliente!' This snack, found only in this region, consists of a dough made of flour and banana paste; it's stuffed with salty fish. Served hot – maybe with a dash of salsa – it will give your taste buds something new to think about.

Puerto López is the nearest town of any size to Parque Nacional Machalilla, and it houses the park headquarters.

Information There is no bank. The Pacifictel office cannot make international calls. There is a post office and a police station; see the map for their locations. The biggest pharmacy is Farmacía Edita's. A small clinic is north of town. A small playground and a ramshackle pool hall keep the young and the not-so-young amused.

Organized Tours There are a dozen or more agencies offering tours to Isla de la Plata and/or the mainland part of the park. They can be roughly divided into about eight licensed companies and several unlicensed, 'pirate' companies.

From June through September, whale-watching tours combined with visits to Isla de la Plata are popular. During July and August, good whale sightings are pretty much guaranteed, and in June and September, sightings may be brief, distant or just of single animals. Once you reach the island, lunch is provided, a guided hike is taken, and there is a short time for snorkeling. Several readers have complained that the time allotted for snorkeling is too short (about 10 or 15 minutes) and that the masks are not very good. Whatever the agencies tell you, snorkeling is not a major part of the tour. The trip to the island takes well over an hour going flat out, and can be rough, so take medication if necessary, and bring a rain jacket for the wind and spray.

Licensed companies charge a standard price (recently, US$30) plus the park-entry fee. They all have boats with two outboard engines (both are used for speed, but the boat can return on one if the other breaks down), and are equipped with life jackets, radios (for communicating with other boats to figure out where the whales are, as well as with the shore) and basic toilet facilities. These agencies are found along General Cordova down to and along Malecón Julio Izurieta. They offer similar services and take turns, so just ask in any agency.

On the Malecón, you'll be approached by folks offering a much cheaper whale-watching expedition on fishing boats. Prices go as low as US$15 and no park fee (because the island is not visited). Beware of these trips. The boats are slow, they roll a lot, and people prone to seasickness are almost guaranteed to throw up. There are limited life jackets, no radio and only one engine, and rarely are there any toilet facilities.

Outside of the whale-watching season, similar tours to the island are offered to see the birds and sea lions, and dolphins may well be spotted.

Most of the operators will also arrange a variety of other local trips, such as camping and/or horseback riding in the Aguas Blancas/San Sebastián areas and visits to local beaches. It is usually cheaper to make your own way to Aguas Blancas and hire locals there, and the tours aren't any worse, but they may take longer to arrange.

Two companies on the Malecón offer scuba-diving trips to people with certification. Equipment is provided, but it looked rather worn and beat up. Exploratur (☎ 604 123) seemed to be slightly better than Mantaraya (☎ 604 233) next to the Restaurant Carmita, but check them both. Note that these companies are not recommended as better than others for nondiving trips.

Spanish Lessons Try Costanita Spanish School (fax 604 200), which charges about US$170 to US$250 per week for four hours a day of one-on-one tuition, board and lodging with a local family, as well as for local tours.

Places to Stay Puerto López has experienced a miniboom in hotels recently. They can be busy during the busy whale-watching season, and the local coastal January-to-April high season, but reservations are rarely necessary unless you want to stay in a specific place.

The cheapest is *Residencial Isla de la Plata* (☎ 604 114), on Cordova near the Malecón. It has basic rooms and questionable shared bathrooms, but the rate is only about US$1.50 per person. *Albergue Cueva del Oso* (☎ 604 124, fax 604 128, Lascano 116) is part of the IYH chain. Rooms are simple but clean; two have two beds and two are dorms with six beds. Hot showers, a TV lounge, an equipped kitchen and a local handicraft store are provided. Rates are officially US$3 per person (10% less for IYH members), although they were recently about US$2. *Residencial Turismar*, on the Malecón, has friendly owners and charges US$2.50 per person for basic rooms with private bath. A public balcony features ocean views. Friendly and popular with budget travelers, *Villa Colombia* (☎ 604 189, 604 105, hostalvc@uio.satnet.net) is several blocks from the coast but offers kitchen and laundry facilities and various rooms. Most are with bath, at US$3.50/6 for singles/doubles, but some dormitory rooms have beds for US$2.50. There is hot water.

Three blocks uphill from the market, *Hostal Tuzco* (☎ 604 120, 604 132) has 13 small, clean rooms with private hot showers and fans for US$3.50 per person; the owners are doctors, and a small pharmacy is next door. Other cheapies to try include *Hostal Fragata* (☎ 604 156, 604 187), which has some rooms with private bath, and the basic *Residencial Paola*.

Hostal Isla Los Islotes (☎/fax 604 128, 604 108), on the Malecón at Cordova, has seven clean but spartan rooms with private hot bath for about US$9 to US$25 for one to five people. The oldest good place is *Hotel & Cabañas Pacífico* (☎ 604 147, fax 604 133), on Alejo Lascano at the Malecón, which has modern but uninspiring rooms with private bath and hot water for about US$15/16 for singles/doubles (about half that in older

cabins, some of which have shared baths). Air-conditioning is advertised for a few rooms. There is a restaurant, a garden area, and parking, and tours are arranged.

About a 10-minute walk on the beach north of town brings you to the pleasant *Hostería Mandala* (☎/fax 604 181). You can't miss it – a huge sculpture of three whale flukes waving in the air marks the spot and can be seen from the main road as you arrive by bus. The place, which is run by an Italian/Swiss couple who have been in the Ecuadorian tourism industry for many years, is very clean and attractively decorated by the owners' art. Several languages (including English) are spoken, and a restaurant in the attractive main lodge serves Italian and local seafood. There is also a bar, a games room and a library there, and the owners live onsite. Surrounding the main building are about 10 small, thatched-roof cabins at US$7/10 for singles/doubles, as well as six larger cabins for US$10 (singles) to US$26 (quads). All have private hot showers and a porch, and all are by the ocean. Private parking is offered.

Hostería La Terraza (☎ 604 235) is about 1km northeast of town. There is a sign near the clinic on the north side, from where it is a steep climb, rewarded by sweeping views of the whole coastal area. Peter, the German owner (who speaks English as well), has been in the area for years and will drive down to pick you up if you call. The hostería offers six cabins; all have one double bed plus a bunk bed, a warm private shower, and a porch with a hammock and ocean views. There is guarded parking. Rates are US$12/22/30/38 for one/two/three/four people, and breakfasts with the best ocean view in the area are US$2 to US$3.50. You can arrange dinners in advance or eat in town and arrange to be picked up in the evening.

Places to Eat *Restaurant Carmita*, on the shorefront, is a good, reasonably priced restaurant that serves seafood and other dishes. It's been around for years and is everyone's favorite standby. Next door, *Restaurant Mayflower* is a locally popular restaurant with some Chinese dishes. There are several others along the Malecón, and *Picantería Hoja Rey* is another good choice. *Restaurant Spondylus* is popular and pushes its tables aside on weekend evenings to make a dance floor. Breakfast, lunch and dinner are served, and the food is adequate and reasonably priced. It's the best place for weekend entertainment. In the center, convenient to the bus stops, *Restaurant Flipper* is a good cheap choice.

Several new places have opened in the past few years. For a breakfast on a balcony with a view of the ocean, *Café La Ballena* is an excellent choice. The American owners have lived and worked on the coast for over two decades and have lots of information. Breakfasts are varied and are cooked to order – just ask, and Diane will do it the way you want it. During the day and into the evening, stop by for yummy pies, sweets, sandwiches, pizza or a cold beer. The owners also run a small B&B just south of Hostería Alandaluz (see that section, later).

Bellitalia is a few blocks north of the center; follow the signs. It's in a private house and serves only dinner (starting at 6 pm) in an enchanting candlelit garden environment. The Italian owners have a short menu of Italian and local specialties, all of which are cooked to order. This place has received rave reviews from local cognoscenti. Prices are not much more than anywhere else, and it's definitely worth it.

Getting There & Away Transportes Carlos A Aray, at Cordova and Machalilla, has direct buses to Quito (US$5, 11 hours) at 9:15 am and 6 pm. Several other companies between Jipijapa and La Libertad stop at the same corner at least every hour during daylight hours. These buses will drop you off at any point you want along the coast. There are also buses to and from Santa Elena (on the south coast) about every hour. Ask locals for precise advice. Note that these buses are also used as local transportation.

Salango

This fishing village is about 5km south of Puerto López. Isla Salango is less than 2km out to sea – you could hire a fishing boat to take you out and see the seabirds, but they are not as numerous as on Isla de la Plata.

The small, modern and well-laid-out **Museo Salango** (☎/fax 901 195, 901 208) has exhibits about the local archaeological sites – a worthwhile stop. Many signs are in English, and the accompanying gift shop sells work by local artisans. A research center is behind the museum. Admission is about US$1.40, and the hours are 9 am to 5 pm Wednesday to Sunday.

Places to Stay & Eat About 300m from the museum, *El Delfín* is an excellent seafood restaurant that locals rave about. Food preparation is slow: place your order, spend 45 minutes in the museum, and come back for lunch. The owner is building four rooms for travelers. A couple of blocks past El Delfín is the thatched-roof *El Pelicano*, which is also a recommended place to eat.

A couple of kilometers south of Salango, *Hostería Piqueros Patas Azules* (☎ 604 135) has a small archaeological museum and some tastelessly amusing features, such as statues in the showers where it appears that the water is falling from the legs. If you can live with that, the rooms and restaurant/bar are quite good, and there is a nice beach nearby, as well as a mud bath, all of which makes it popular with Guayquileños looking for a getaway. Readers have recommended this place. Rates start around US$15/25 for singles/doubles with bath, and some larger rooms and cabins are available.

A short way farther south *Hostería Río Chico* (☎ 604 199, fax 604 200) has four quadruple rooms and five quintuple rooms with a private hot bath. Two of the quads share a kitchen. There are also two dorms with 16 and 30 beds, each sharing five bathrooms. A restaurant is on the premises, as is a garden with a volleyball net. Obviously, the place caters to groups. Rates are around US$2.50 per person, depending on group size, and local tours can be arranged in advance.

Hostería Alandaluz

About 5km south of Salango, the road passes through the village of Puerto Rico.

Hostería Alandaluz (☎ 604 103) is about 1km farther south. This is an alternative, Ecuadorian-run hotel, built mainly of local fast-growing and easily replenishable materials, such as bamboo and palm thatch. The organic gardens on the grounds produce some of the spices, herbs, fruits and vegetables that are served at meal times. Some of the lavatories are also organic, and by using sawdust, it is possible to convert human waste to (more or less) odor-free fertilizers and conserve water. Everything that can be recycled is, and local communities are encouraged to follow suit. The idea is to create a self-sustaining hotel that has a minimal impact on the environment.

There is a bar and a dining room that serves good meals (with a predominantly seafood and vegetarian menu). The nightly set meals are usually a better bet than ordering à la carte. There is a volleyball area and a small games room. The beach is close by, and you can bathe undisturbed, although the waves are rather wild. Don't go out far unless you are a very confident swimmer.

The hotel has been a success, and most of the original rustic rooms have been replaced by more modern versions, although the original organic concepts have been retained to a great extent. However, prices have risen, and this is no longer a budget-traveler's hotel, but people who stay here continue to give good reports.

The management works with Pacarina Tours and will try to help travelers organize trips to Machalilla, the museums and the nearby islands (although this depends on how many people are staying there). The ambience is relaxed, and some people end up staying for days as they unwind from a fast-paced travel schedule. Others find the place too laid-back and move on quickly. It's definitely a unique place that most travelers have strong opinions about – usually positive.

A small camping area provides tents at US$3.50 per person (it costs US$3 to camp if you have a tent). The older cabins (which are being phased out or replaced) are US$7/12/15/18 for one/two/three/four people; bathrooms are shared. Larger cabins with private bath and sitting rooms are US$25/44/53/64, and cabins on the beach are US$35/50 for singles/doubles.

Reservations can be arranged in Quito (☎/fax 543 042, info@alandaluz.com), Baqueadano 330 and Reina Victoria, 2nd floor. Often, there are spaces available if you just show up at the hotel, and prices for walk-ins can be somewhat cheaper, although the place may be booked full for Friday and Saturday nights. Try to get there early in the day.

Any bus going up or down the coast can drop you off in front of the hotel (see Getting There & Away under Puerto López, earlier, for more details).

The South Coast

This chapter covers the southern coastal provinces of Guayas and El Oro. See the boxed text 'Ecuador's Coast,' in the Facts about Ecuador chapter, for an overview of the entire coast.

Guayaquil

☎ 04

The province of Guayas is named after the Puna Indian chief of the same name who fought bravely against the Incas and then later against the Spanish. The provincial capital, Guayaquil, is a combination of the names of the chief and his wife, Quill, whom he is said to have killed, before drowning himself, rather than allowing her to be captured by the conquistadors.

Guayaquil is by far the country's most important port, and with a population of approximately 2,118,000, it is also Ecuador's most populous city. More exports and imports pass through Guayaquil than all other Ecuadorian ports combined.

Travelers to Ecuador tend to avoid Guayaquil because of its reputation as a hot, humid and crowded port town with many dangerous areas. (The heat and humidity are especially oppressive from January to April.)

It does, however, have its attractions. There are shady plazas, colonial buildings, friendly people, interesting museums and a pleasant riverfront walk. Nearby are several parks and reserves with unique bird life; a local ornithologist claims that there are twice as many endemic species within 50km of Guayaquil as there are in the Galápagos. Most of these are small brown birds – not as spectacular as the Galápagos endemics – but they are of interest to dedicated birders. See Travel Agencies & Guides, under Orientation & Information, next, to find out about bird-watching guides.

ORIENTATION & INFORMATION

Most travelers stay in the center of town, which is organized in a gridlike fashion on the west bank of Río Guayas. The main east-west street is 9 de Octubre, terminating at the river by La Rotonda – the famous statue of liberators Bolívar and San Martín. Many downtown streets are one way. The Peruvian consulate is on the corner of Chile and 9 de Octubre; the US embassy is on José de Antepara, between Hurtado and 9 de Octubre. See the Facts for the Visitor chapter for contact information and business hours.

The airport is about 5km north of the center, and the bus terminal is about 2km

Highlights

- Taking in the good restaurants, fine museums and lively people of Guayaquil – Ecuador's largest city
- Sighing at 'the lovers' – two 8000-year-old embracing skeletons in Santa Elena
- Riding the waves in the simple village of Montañita – the surfing capital of Ecuador
- Wandering through the petrified forests of Puyango

Equator

THE SOUTH COAST

north of the airport. A suburb that is frequently visited for its good restaurants and nightlife is Urdesa, almost 4km northwest of the center. There are many other suburbs – most of them residential or industrial; some of them poor and dangerous for the average tourist. There are no tourist offices.

Immigration & Documents

To extend your tourist card, go to the immigration office in front of the bus terminal. Cabdrivers know it.

Money

There are dozens of banks. Branches of Banco del Pacífico have MasterCard ATMs, and branches of Banco de Guayaquil and Filanbanco have Visa ATMs. See the map for their locations.

Post & Communications

Pacifictel and the main post office share the same huge building bounded by Ballén and Carbo. The Internet café on the 3rd floor of the Museo Arqueológico del Banco del Pacífico is open to the public during museum hours (see Downtown Area, under Things to See & Do, later in this section). In Urdesa, Internet Cappucine, 424 Estrada, is open 10 am to midnight daily. Look for more to open by the time you read this.

Travel Agencies & Organized Tours

Anybody who has anything to do with travel will try to sell you a Galápagos trip. However, there are more agencies in Quito, and prices are no lower in Guayaquil.

Tours to the Galápagos are generally expensive. More information is given in the Galápagos section. Try Galasam Tours (☎ 312 447, 304 488, fax 311 485), 9 de Octubre 424 (at Córdova), office 1106; there is also an office in Quito (see Travel Agencies under Quito).

Canodros (☎ 285 711, 280 164, fax 287 651, eco-tourism1@canodros.com.ec), Manzana 5, Solar 10, Vía Terminal Terrestre, is the operator for *Galápagos Explorer,* the newest and most expensive cruise ship in the islands. Canodros is also the operator for the Kapawi

Lodge (see the Southern Oriente chapter); you can visit the Web site at www.kapawi.com.

Chasquitur (☎ 281 084/5, 292 155, fax 285 872), Urdaneta 1418, is good for local day tours, city tours and ecotourism. Ecuadorian Tours (☎ 287 111, fax 280 851, ectours@gye .satnet.net), 9 de Octubre 1900, is the American Express agent. There are several travel agencies on or near the southernmost block of Cordova.

Tours to nearby beaches are also available, but for small groups, taking a bus or hiring a taxi for the day is more economical.

There are a handful of local birding guides who can help you search for the more elusive local species, but be warned that they are in big demand with professional and academic tour groups and may be unavailable or too expensive for individual birders. Contact Nancy Hilgut (☎ 284 712) in the evening or Karl Berg (☎ 272 238, kberg@ ucsg.edu.ec) if you are a serious birder.

Bookstores

For English-language (and other) books, the best store is Librería Científica (☎ 328 569), Luque 225.

Libraries

The public library (☎ 533 134) is at Museo Municipal. Use the back entrance, on 10 de Agosto, for the library and the front entrance, on Sucre, for the museum.

Laundry

Most laundries in Guayaquil specialize in dry cleaning rather than washing, drying and folding. One that does both is Lava Express, which has a central location at Carbo 302, between Icaza and Rendón (☎ 567 284), as well as an Urdesa location, at Calle Sexta and Bálsamos (☎ 880 645).

Medical Services

The best hospital in Guayaquil (and the whole coastal region) is Clínica Kennedy (☎ 286 963, 289 666), on Avenida del Periodista (also known as San Jorge), by the Policentro shopping center in the Nueva Kennedy suburb, near Urdesa. The clinic has specialists for almost everything.

Reader-recommended physicians in Guayaquil include Dr Alfonso Guim León (☎ 532 179, 531 783), Boyacá 1320, and Dr Ángel Sáenz Serrano (☎ 561 785), Boyacá 821.

Patients should be prepared to pay at the time of treatment. To give you an idea of cost, an X-ray and treatment for a simple fracture (no hospitalization) might run US$30 to US$40.

Emergency

You can reach the Red Cross ambulance by calling ☎ 560 674/5, 561 077. The police are at ☎ 101, or ☎ 392 221/30.

Volunteering

Junto con los Niños works with street kids in the slum areas of Guayaquil. Volunteers can help with whatever they do best – administration, education, sports programs etc. A one-month minimum is preferred. Contact Sylvia Reyes (☎ 208 093, 208 095, fax 201 240) to help however you can. Ms Reyes speaks English.

Dangers & Annoyances

Guayaquil has a reputation for theft problems. Take the normal precautions of visiting any large city: Avoid walking in ill-lit areas at night. At all times, keep money and valuables well hidden. Avoid wearing expensive watches or jewelry, and dress in simple clothing in public. If arriving or departing from the bus terminal or airport with luggage, taxis are safer than public buses. Public buses are usually OK if you are with a couple of other travelers or if you just keep your hand luggage, which you can easily keep your eagle eye and firm handhold on.

Always be alert for pickpockets and bag snatchers, especially near hotel entrances. Well-dressed thieves may even enter hotel lobbies in search of poorly attended bags or bulging pockets. Taking a taxi to your hotel helps, but ask your cabdriver to help you take your luggage into the hotel.

Despite all this, visiting Guayaquil is not necessarily any more dangerous than visiting New York or Rome.

THINGS TO SEE & DO

The majority of interesting sights are on or within a few blocks of the waterfront road Malecón Simón Bolívar (also just called El Malecón). Keep your eyes open for plaques and signs. Guayaquil is full of them, and they provide interesting historic information (if you read Spanish).

Sunday is a good day to walk around, because there isn't much traffic (although some museums may be closed). On other days, start early in the day to avoid the heat. Keep your eyes open for possible thieves hanging around. There is an Olympic pool (see map) that is open to the public for two-hour sessions. There is a nominal fee; inquire at the gate for hours.

The Malecón

This is being extensively remodeled for the 21st century. Heading north along the Malecón, with Río Guayas to your right, you pass several **monuments**. One is to the UN, known in Spanish as the ONU (Organización de Naciones Unidas), and another is the famous Moorish-style **clock tower**, which dates originally from 1770 but has been replaced several times. Occasionally, the tower is open to visitors, who can climb the narrow spiral staircase inside.

Across the street from the clock tower is the **Palacio Municipal**, an ornate gray building that is separated from the simple and solid **Palacio de Gobierno** by a small but pleasant pedestrian mall. In the ped mall, there is a **statue** commemorating some of the victories of liberator General Sucre. Both buildings were built in the 1920s. The Palacio de Gobierno replaced the original wooden structure, which was destroyed in the great fire of 1917. In those times, Guayaquil was still a small city with under 100,000 inhabitants – a far cry from the city of today.

Continuing along the Malecón, you soon come to the famous statue of **La Rotonda** – one of Guayaquil's more impressive monuments, particularly when it is illuminated at night. It shows the historic but enigmatic meeting between Bolívar and San Martín that took place in 1822.

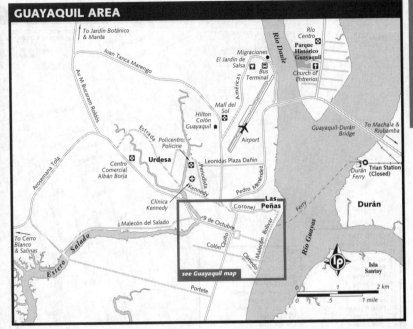

GUAYAQUIL AREA

Bolívar was the Venezuelan who liberated Venezuela, Colombia and Ecuador from Spanish colonial rule. San Martín was the Argentinian liberator who defeated the Spanish in Chile and Peru. After their secret meeting in Guayaquil, San Martín returned to Argentina before moving to France, while Bolívar continued his triumphs in Bolivia.

From La Rotonda, there are good views north, along the riverfront, of the colonial district of Las Peñas at the foot of Cerro Santa Ana and, far beyond, the impressive Guayaquil-Durán bridge – the biggest in the country.

Many people like to continue along the waterfront to the picturesque colonial district of Las Peñas. Several piers are passed en route – some are working docks, but others have restaurant boats. You can eat seafood and sip a beer while you watch the busy traffic of the Malecón on one side and Guayaquil's river traffic on the other.

Las Peñas

At the northern end of the Malecón, you'll see a short flight of stairs leading up to the small **Plaza Colón**, which has two cannons pointing out toward the river, commemorating a battle against Dutch pirates in 1624. The narrow, winding **Calle Numa Pompillo Llona**, named after the Guayaquileño (1832–1907) who wrote the national anthem, begins from the corner of the plaza. This historic street has several unobtrusive plaques set into the walls of some houses, indicating the simple residences of past presidents. The colonial architecture has not been restored per se, but it has been well looked after and is interesting to see. Several artists now live in the area, and there are a few art galleries.

Numa Pompillo Llona is a dead-end street, so retrace your footsteps to the Plaza Colón, and instead of continuing back along the Malecón, turn right and walk past a small plaza with a brightly painted **statue**

SOUTH COAST

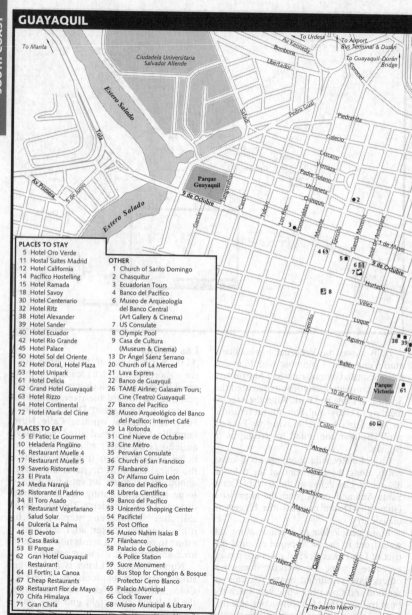

GUAYAQUIL

PLACES TO STAY
5 Hotel Oro Verde
11 Hostal Suites Madrid
12 Hotel California
14 Pacífico Hostelling
15 Hotel Ramada
18 Hotel Savoy
30 Hotel Centenario
32 Hotel Ritz
38 Hotel Alexander
39 Hotel Sander
40 Hotel Ecuador
42 Hotel Río Grande
45 Hotel Palace
50 Hotel Sol del Oriente
52 Hotel Doral, Hotel Plaza
53 Hotel Unipark
61 Hotel Delicia
62 Grand Hotel Guayaquil
63 Hotel Rizzo
64 Hotel Continental
72 Hotel María del Cisne

PLACES TO EAT
5 El Patio; Le Gourmet
10 Heladería Pingüino
16 Restaurant Muelle 4
17 Restaurant Muelle 5
19 Saverio Ristorante
23 El Pirata
24 Media Naranja
25 Ristorante Il Padrino
34 El Toro Asado
41 Restaurant Vegetariano
   Salud Solar
44 Dulcería La Palma
46 El Devoto
51 Casa Baska
53 El Parque
62 Gran Hotel Guayaquil
   Restaurant
64 El Fortín; La Canoa
67 Cheap Restaurants
69 Restaurant Flor de Mayo
70 Chifa Himalaya
71 Gran Chifa

OTHER
1 Church of Santo Domingo
2 Chasquitur
3 Ecuadorian Tours
4 Banco del Pacífico
6 Museo de Arqueología
   del Banco Central
   (Art Gallery & Cinema)
7 US Consulate
8 Olympic Pool
9 Casa de Cultura
   (Museum & Cinema)
13 Dr Ángel Sáenz Serrano
20 Church of La Merced
21 Lava Express
22 Banco de Guayquil
26 TAME Airline; Galasam Tours;
   Cine (Teatro) Guayaquil
27 Banco del Pacífico
28 Museo Arqueológico del Banco
   del Pacífico; Internet Café
29 La Rotonda
31 Cine Nueve de Octubre
33 Cine Metro
35 Peruvian Consulate
36 Church of San Francisco
37 Filanbanco
43 Dr Alfonso Guim León
47 Banco del Pacífico
48 Librería Científica
49 Banco del Pacífico
53 Unicentro Shopping Center
54 Pacifictel
55 Post Office
56 Museo Nahim Isaías B
57 Filanbanco
58 Palacio de Gobierno
   & Police Station
59 Sucre Monument
60 Bus Stop for Chongón & Bosque
   Protector Cerro Blanco
65 Palacio Municipal
66 Clock Tower
68 Museo Municipal & Library

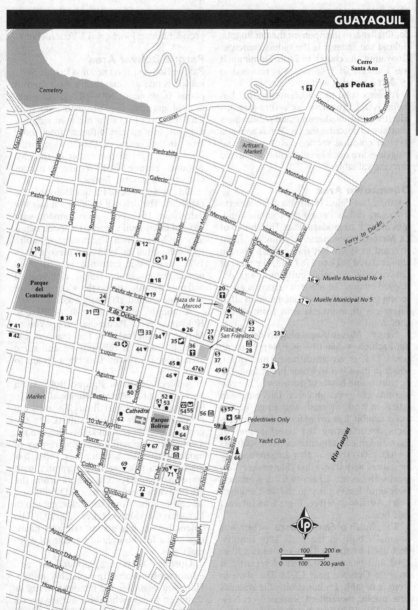

GUAYAQUIL

Cerro
Santa Ana

Las Peñas

Cemetery

Artisan's
Market

Ferry to Durán

Parque
del
Centenario

Muelle Municipal No 4

Muelle Municipal No 5

Plaza de la
Merced

Plaza de
San Francisco

Market

Cathedral

Parque
Bolívar

Pedestrians Only

Río Guayas

Yacht Club

0   100   200 m
0   100   200 yards

of a fireman (there are two fire stations nearby), and past a **statue of the conquistador Orellana**, to the **open-air theater Bogotá**. Behind the theater is the oldest church in Guayaquil, the **church of Santo Domingo**. It was founded in 1548 and was restored in 1938. It is worth a visit.

It's important to note, however, that Las Peñas is unfortunately not a very safe district, though Ecuadorian guide publications continue to describe the Las Peñas area as a 'typical colonial section.' Robberies and muggings are occasionally reported – avoid carrying valuables.

Downtown Area
South of Las Peñas (walk along Rocafuerte if you are in Las Peñas) the colonial buildings blend into modern ones. The **church of La Merced** is comparatively modern (constructed in 1938), but the original wooden church dated back to 1787 and, like most of Guayaquil's colonial buildings, was destroyed by fire. The modern version is worth seeing for its richly decorated golden altar. There's a pleasant plaza in front of the church.

Nearby, **Museo Arqueológico del Banco del Pacífico** (☎ 566 010, 563 744), Paula de Icaza 113, is air-conditioned and quiet, which in itself is a welcome break from the hot hustle and bustle of downtown. The collections are good and well laid out, with labels in both Spanish and English. The main exhibit has ceramics and other artifacts documenting the development of Ecuadorian coastal cultures from 3000 BC to AD 1500. There is also a contemporary art gallery with shows that change every few weeks. Hours are 10 am to 6 pm weekdays (weekend hours are limited and changeable). Admission is free. There is an Internet café here.

The **church of San Francisco** – which was originally built in the early 18th century, destroyed by fire in 1896, reconstructed in 1902 and beautifully restored recently, is on 9 de Octubre near Chile. The plaza in front is notable for containing Guayaquil's **first public monument**, unveiled on New Year's Day 1880. It is a statue of Ecuador's

first native president, Vicente Rocafuerte, who held office 1835–39. (Ecuador's first president, Juan Flores, was a Venezuelan.)

Parque Bolívar Area
Parque Bolívar (also known as Parque Seminario) is one of Guayaquil's most famous plazas. In its small but well-laid-out ornamental gardens live prehistoric-looking land iguanas of up to a meter in length – they are of a species different from those found in the Galápagos. They're a surprising sight here, right in the center of the city. Around Parque Bolívar are many of Guayaquil's 1st-class hotels.

On the west side of Parque Bolívar is the **cathedral**. The original building on this site dates from 1547, but – as is common with most of Guayaquil's original wooden buildings – it burnt down. The present structure was completed in 1948 and renovated in 1978. The front entrance is extremely ornate, but inside, it is simple, high-vaulted and modern. High up on the white walls are some fine stained-glass windows.

A couple of blocks east of Parque Bolívar, over to Pichincha, brings you to **Museo Nahim Isaías B**. This museum has a small display of religious art and some archaeological pieces. It is open 10 am to 5 pm daily.

A block south of Parque Bolívar, on Sucre, you find **Museo Municipal** (☎ 516 391) and the municipal library. The museum is small but has varied exhibits. On the ground floor, there is an archaeology room, a colonial room and a changing display of modern art. The archaeology room has mainly Inca and pre-Inca ceramics, with some particularly fine pieces from the Huancavilca period (circa AD 500) and several figurines from the oldest culture in Ecuador, the Valdivia (circa 3200 BC). The colonial room has mainly religious paintings and a few household items from colonial times.

Upstairs, there are modern art and ethnography rooms, inexplicably joined. Here you might see the famous *tsantsas,* or shrunken heads (which are not always on display). Other jungle artifacts include beadwork, feather work, tools and weapons, but unfortunately, there are very few labels. There are also regional costumes and handicrafts. Another room on this floor contains paintings of presidents and famous men, of which a favorite is a wild and eccentric-looking Theodor Wolf, the geologist after whom the highest active volcano in the Galápagos is named. All in all, there's a varied collection with which to pass the time. A new historical wing is planned for 2000, and occasional concerts and lectures are advertised.

Hours are 9 am to 5 pm Tuesday to Saturday, and there is a US$1 admission fee (except Saturday, when it's free). Hours and admission fees change often.

Parque del Centenario

This is Guayaquil's largest plaza, covering four city blocks and featuring several monuments. The most important monument is the great central column topped by Liberty and surrounded by the founding fathers of the country – a monument to patriotism. The safest way to get there is along 9 de Octubre.

Casa de Cultura

On the west side of Parque del Centenario is the archaeology museum of the Casa de Cultura (☎ 300 500). The main attractions are the gold collection and the prehistoric-art exhibit. Hours are 10 am to 5:30 pm Tuesday to Friday and 9 am to 3 pm Saturday. There is also a cinema on the premises that shows good movies. Recently, the cinema had a foreign film season, with different films showing at 7:30 pm Monday, Wednesday and Friday. Foreign films are very popular, and the cinema is small – get there early to buy a ticket (under US$1). Other cultural events, such as art shows and lectures, occur regularly.

Museo de Arqueología del Banco Central

This excellent archaeology museum (☎ 327 402), at 9 de Octubre and José de Antepara, is well laid out and has a varied and changing display of ceramics, textiles, metallurgy

and ceremonial masks. The collection of Valdivia figurines is superb. The descriptions are good but are mainly in Spanish, although some recently installed computers have information in English. There is also an art gallery with changing shows and a cinema. Hours are 10 am to 6 pm Tuesday to Friday and 10 am to 2 pm weekends. Admission is US$1.

Parque Histórico Guayaquil

This new 8.5-hectare park (not to be confused with Parque Guayaquil) is across the Guayaquil-Durán bridge, on the east side of Río Daule. It is a new, ambitious project, divided into three areas, and should be open by the time you read this.

The wildlife area has 45 species of birds and other animals in a seminatural habitat taking up over half the park's space. An interpretive trail/boardwalk introduces the visitor to coastal habitats and wildlife. The urban architectural area, which has a restaurant, showcases the development of early-20th-century architecture in Guayaquil, with reproductions of turn-of-the-century buildings and audio-visual displays. The third area focuses on local traditions, with an emphasis on rural customs, crafts and agriculture.

Wheelchair access, children's areas and a general information area are all part of the infrastructure. Call ☎ 835 356 for hours and fees.

City Cemetery

This dazzling white cemetery contains hundreds of tombs, monuments and huge mausoleums. A walk, lined with palm trees, leads to the impressive grave of President Vicente Rocafuerte. It's best reached with a short cab ride.

Jardín Botánico

About a half-hour drive north of town is a botanical garden (☎ 417 004), which has recently gained recognition for its fine orchid collection (as well as hundreds of other plants). Paths and trails lead you past plant exhibits, and there is a gift shop, a café, a butterfly garden and an auditorium.

Insect repellent is recommended in the rainy months. The garden is open 8 am to 4 pm daily, except January 1 and December 24, 25 and 31. Admission is about US$1.50. With three days' advance notice, a guided tour can be arranged.

Call the gardens for information about getting there (recently, the No 63 bus went there and the No 22 bus went to a place that is a 10-minute walk away), or take a taxi and ask for Urbanización de Los Orquídeas. Chasquitur travel agency (☎ 281 084/5, 292 155, fax 285 872), Urdaneta 1418, runs tours and has information.

SPECIAL EVENTS

All the national holidays are celebrated vigorously in Guayaquil, but one stands out as the major annual festival…it is, in fact, a combination of two holidays: Simón Bolívar's birthday, on July 24 (1783), and the Founding of Guayaquil, on July 25 (1538). The already lively city goes wild with parades, art shows, beauty pageants, fireworks and plenty of drinking and dancing – a carnival atmosphere. Hotels are booked well in advance – the evening of July 24 is not a good time to arrive in Guayaquil without a hotel reservation. The festivities often begin July 23 or even July 22, depending on which day of the week the holiday falls in any particular year. Banking and other services are usually disrupted.

Other important dates are Guayaquil's Independence Day, on October 9 (1820), which combines with Día de la Raza (October 12) to create another long holiday, but it's much less exciting than July's festivities. New Year's Eve is celebrated with bonfires. Life-sized puppets called *viejos* (the old ones) are made by stuffing old clothes – they represent the old year. The viejos are displayed on the main streets of the city, especially the Malecón, and they are burnt in midnight bonfires – fun for the whole family. Less fun is the annual carnival (a movable feast held on the days immediately preceding Ash Wednesday and Lent), which, in addition to the traditional throwing of water, is 'celebrated' by dousing

passersby with all manner of unpleasant liquids – no one is exempt.

Locals say that holidays, especially July 24 and 25, are a good time to visit areas such as Las Peñas because of the sheer number of visitors. Generally, the locals are very friendly to foreign visitors during the holidays. Pickpockets still abound, but they are looking for easy targets (such as drunks). Leave your camera in your room, and come out to enjoy yourself.

PLACES TO STAY

The Guayaquil Tourist Board controls hotel prices, and each hotel is required to post its approved prices near the entrance. Perhaps surprisingly, most hotels do have the price list prominently displayed. You may be charged up to 23% tax on the listed price, but most of the cheaper hotels don't bother.

During holiday periods, finding a room can be problematic, especially in the better hotels, and prices are usually higher than the listed price. Hotel prices change frequently.

For some reason, there are not many single rooms to be had. In the cheaper hotels, there could be two or more beds in your room. If it's not the holiday season, you can persuade many hotel owners to give you a double or triple at the price of a single. During fiesta time, travel with a friend or be prepared to pay for a double.

Unfortunately, water shortages occur frequently. Most top-end hotels have fairly reliable water supplies (although unfortunately, this is because they can afford to pay premium prices for water, which is supposedly destined for the poor areas of town). The cheaper hotels may lack water at times, so grab a shower when you can.

Guayaquil has a two-tiered pricing system in the better hotels, where foreign tourists are charged about twice as much as residents.

Budget

Cheap hotels in Guayaquil are generally of a higher price and lower standard than in other cities. *Hotel Delicia* (☎ 324 925, Ballén 1105) is secure and clean and charges about US$3 per person with shared baths but is often full. Some rooms with private bath are US$7.50, single or double. Unfortunately, the neighborhood is not too good, but the friendly manager will suggest the safest streets in the area.

Hotel Ecuador (☎ 321 460, *Moncayo 1117*) is a decent place at US$7 for a basic double with cramped bath, a fan and a TV; singles cost the same. Dark interior rooms are slightly quieter and cheaper than the lighter outside rooms. A few rooms are air-conditioned, and a small restaurant is attached. *Hotel Savoy* (☎ 308 296), at Rendón and Boyacá, has basic rooms at US$4 per person and is just OK. The reasonable *Hotel Sander* (☎ 320 030, 320 944, *Luque 1101*) has cold-water private baths at US$5/8 (with fan) or US$6/9 (with air-conditioning).

Hostal Suites Madrid (☎ 307 804, 314 992, *Quisquis 305*) has air-conditioned rooms with hot bath and TV for US$6/9. Some rooms are dark and cramped, but overall, this is a fair value. A few rooms with fans are cheaper. *Pacífico Hostelling* (☎ 568 093/4, fax 302 077, *Escobedo 811*) doesn't belong to a hostel chain but does provide good clean rooms with bath, TV and fan for US$5/9 – another good value.

Hotel María del Cisne (☎ 323 563, 532 586, fax 532 610, *Chiriboga 224*) has clean rooms with air-conditioning, hot water, TV and telephone for US$9 a double. Singles lack air-conditioning and are US$7. It's a decent-enough place, although the neighborhood is not very good. *Hotel Centenario* (☎ 524 467, 513 744, fax 328 772, *Garaycoa 931*) is about US$9 for one or two people. Rooms vary – some have fans and others have air-conditioning; most have TVs and telephones. All have cold baths, and some are nicer than others. *Hotel Río Grande* (☎ 513 702, 514 248, *Luque 1035*) has large clean rooms with air-conditioning, cable TV and bath for US$9/11 or US$12 with outside view.

Hotel California (☎ 302 538, fax 562 548, *Urdaneta 529*) has adequate rooms with private baths, hot water, fan and TV for US$10/14; add air-conditioning, cable TV and minfridge for US$18/20.

Mid-Range

Hostal Ecuahogar (☎ 248 357, fax 248 341, *Sauces 1, Manzana F31, Villa 20*) is near the airport, on Isidro Ayora in front of Banco Ecuatoriana de Vivienda. It is part of the Hostelling International chain and charges US$12 per person for rooms with private bath and US$10 for beds in dorms with shared bath; prices include continental breakfast. There is a discount for hostel members. Hot baths, kitchen privileges, a café, information and pick-up service from the airport or bus station is available. The No 22 city bus goes by from the bus terminal.

In the rest of the hotels listed in this section, expect private baths, hot water, air-conditioning, telephone, TV, restaurants on the premises and similar amenities. *Hotel Ritz* (☎ 530 120, 324 134, fax 322 151, *9 de Octubre 709*) is OK and charges about US$14/18. *Hotel Alexander* (☎ 532 000, 532 651, fax 328 474, *Luque 1107*) is a fair value at US$19/24. A sauna and a decent restaurant are on the premises, and the hotel is favored by Ecuadorian businesspeople.

Several decent mid-range (and top-end) places are found near Parque Bolívar. Approximate prices given can vary substantially; booking by email can be almost twice as expensive as walking in and seeing what is available. The modern *Hotel Plaza* (☎ 327 140, 327 545, fax 324 195, igafe@telconet.net, *Chile 414*) has rooms with minifridges for about US$20/24, and there are a few more-expensive junior suites. Another decent choice for rooms in the US$20s is *Hotel Rizzo* (☎ 325 210, fax 326 209, *Ballén 319*). Rooms are a bit worn but comfortable, and continental breakfast is included. A good mid-price choice is *Hotel Doral* (☎ 327 133/75, 328 002, fax 327 088, hdoral@gye.satnet.net, *Chile 402*); it's clean and secure and has a good restaurant. Above-average (for Guayaquil) rooms are about US$30 a double, including breakfast.

Out in the suburbs and fairly close to the airport is *Tangara Guest House* (☎ 284 445, fax 285 872, *Ciudadela Bolivariana, Manuela Sáenz and O'Leary, Block F, Casa 1*). This is a quiet, friendly, family-run guesthouse. The rooms have private bath and hot water and are simple but clean, bright and air-conditioned. There are kitchen privileges and a TV room. Rates are US$36/44, and discounts are available for longer stays. Breakfast is available for US$4. Take a taxi the first time, then the owners can help you figure out the bus system.

Hotel Palace (☎ 321 080, fax 322 887, Chile 216) is clean and secure, and with almost 200 rooms, it usually has space available. The hotel has business and fax services, as well as a travel agency. The street-side rooms suffer from road noise, but if you live in a big city, perhaps you're used to it! Rates are US$44/66 for foreigners, but walk-ins speaking Spanish get quoted US$36/40. Also good at about this price range is *Hotel Sol del Oriente* (☎ 325 500, 328 049, fax 329 352, Aguirre 603). Rooms are spacious and have a minifridge, and the hotel has a decent Chinese restaurant and a sauna.

Top End

There is to be a big jump in prices from mid-range to top-end hotels. This is artificially created by the top-end hotels themselves, who consider themselves luxury class and charge nonresident tourists twice the rate for residents.

If you have any kind of residency status, use it. The prices given below are for non-residents and include the obligatory 20% tax. All these hotels have good restaurants. If you don't have a reservation, discounts may be negotiated at reception.

Grand Hotel Guayaquil (☎ 329 690, fax 327 251, grandhot@gye.satnet.net), at Boyacá and 10 de Agosto, is behind the cathedral. This hotel features a pool, two squash courts, gym, two saunas and massage. They have outdoor barbecues by the pool, as well as good indoor restaurants. Rates are US$85/95 for standard rooms – more for junior suites. *Hotel Continental* (☎ 329 270, fax 325 454, Chile 510) is right on Parque Bolívar. It is the oldest of the city's luxury hotels and is known for its restaurants: One has won international gastronomy awards, another specializes in Ecuadorian cuisine, and a third is open 24 hours. Rooms are US$105, single or double.

Hotel Ramada (☎ 565 555, fax 563 036, hotelca@gye.satnet.net, Malecón 606) overlooks Río Guayas. There is an indoor pool, a sauna and a casino. Full rates are US$140/160, but residents pay much less. Ask about off-season discounts; US$80 rooms were recently being offered. Hairdryers, radio-alarm clocks, and Internet connections are offered in the rooms, and the hotel is favored by businesspeople. If you stay here, bear in mind that the Malecón north of the hotel is not a good place to wander around at night. Also in this price range, *Hotel Unipark* (☎ 327 100, fax 328 352, ecuni@gye.satnet.net, Ballén 406) is more centrally located. Facilities include a sauna and gym, a children's recreation area, many stores and a casino. One of the restaurants has delightful views of Parque Bolívar.

Hotel Oro Verde (☎ 327 999, fax 329 350, ecovg@gye.satnet.net), at 9 de Octubre and García Moreno, is slightly away from the center and out by the US embassy. It has over 250 rooms and suites and is considered the best place to stay downtown – although the rooms aren't really much better for the price – you are paying for the service and the facilities (which include a pool, gym, sauna, casino, shops and several restaurants). Rooms are US$240/265 for singles/doubles, and suites go up to US$420.

Near the airport, on Avenida Francisco de Orellana, the new *Hilton Colón Guayaquil* (☎ 689 000, fax 689 149, sales_guayaquil@hilton.com) is another luxury choice, with almost 300 rooms and suites starting at US$230. Two restaurants, a 24-hour café, two bars and a deli serve good meals, and a pool provides a place to relax.

PLACES TO EAT

There are plenty of places to eat in Guayaquil's downtown area, ranging from cheap fast food to expensive gourmet meals. But for the best dining experiences, venture out to the northwestern suburb of Urdesa.

Downtown

For breakfast, *Dulcería La Palma*, a pavement café at Escobedo and Vélez, has good coffee and warm croissants, and it's a good place to wake up and ease into the day. This is also a good venue for snacks and light meals throughout the day. Also good for pastries and sandwiches is *El Devoto* (*Chile 306*).

A chifa is often a reasonable choice for the hungry budget traveler, and there are several on and around Colón. One of the very best is *Gran Chifa* (☎ *530 784, Carbo 1016*) – it's ornate and expensive-looking but in fact very reasonably priced. Around the corner, the cheaper *Chifa Himalaya* (☎ *519 599, 329 593, Sucre 309*) is good and popular, as is the nearby *Restaurant Flor de Mayo*, on Colón near Chimborazo. *Hotel Sol del Oriente* has a chifa, and there are many other chifas to choose from in this area.

There are many modern cafeterias, restaurants and fast-food places on 9 de Octubre, but they are not super cheap. A popular Ecuadorian beer 'n' burger joint with outdoor tables is the crowded *Media Naranja*, at 9 de Octubre and Aviléz.

A funky and fun place is *Ristorante Il Padrino*, on 9 de Octubre near Boyacá. This Italian restaurant serves meat and seafood and has plenty of Godfather character. Nearby, *Saverio Ristorante* (*Boyacá 1007*) also has good Italian fare. *Heladería Pingüino*, on Parque del Centenario, is good for ice cream. *Restaurant Vegetariano Salud Solar*, at Luque and Moncayo, serves good, simple and cheap food. On Chimborazo south of Parque Bolívar, are a number of *cheap restaurants* with good set lunches; they're popular with downtown office workers. Just off 9 de Octubre is *El Toro Asado* (*Chimborazo 124*), which is a reasonably priced grill specializing in steak and chicken.

On Parque Bolívar itself, *Casa Baska* (☎ *534 599, 534 597, Ballén 422*), next to Hotel Unipark, is one of Guayaquil's most memorable eateries. It's a genuine Spanish restaurant with a smoky European atmosphere and great food that won a 'best of Guayaquil' award in 1997. Prices are higher than average but well worth it. You must ring the bell to get in, and be prepared to wait for a table.

A great place to eat or snack is on a boat moored on the riverbank. There are several piers along the Malecón where restaurant boats are moored, and it is fun to spend some time watching the busy river traffic. A medium-priced place is *El Pirata*, a couple of blocks from La Rotonda. There is an indoor section and an open deck with sunshades. North of El Pirata, there are restaurants at *Muelle 4* and *Muelle 5* (☎ *561 128*). These all serve adequate seafood.

Many of the city's best restaurants are in the better hotels (all open to the public). *Gran Hotel Guayaquil* has breakfast specials from US$3 and up. The coffee is excellent, and coffee addicts can get many refills. Most of the better hotels offer good breakfasts – even if you are on a budget, this might be the chance for a lovely breakfast in comfortable surroundings where you can relax, read the newspaper or catch up on your journal.

El Parque (on the 4th floor of the Unicentro building – enter through Hotel Unipark) overlooks Parque Bolívar. Dinner there is a good value, and there are good views – but it's not cheap. The place also has less-expensive buffet lunches – help yourself to seconds and thirds. In Hotel Continental, the expensive *El Fortín* has won international gastronomic awards, and the reasonably priced *La Canoa* serves Ecuadorian specialties in a casual setting. There is a branch of La Canoa in Mall del Sol (see Shopping, later). *El Patio*, in Hotel Oro Verde, serves delicious Ecuadorian dishes at upscale prices. Still, it's cheaper than the hotel's French restaurant, *Le Gourmet*. The restaurants in the other top-end hotels are also very good, if pricey by Ecuadorian standards.

Urdesa

If you are adventurous enough to explore beyond the hotels and restaurants of the downtown area, you'll be well rewarded. The suburb of Urdesa, 4km northwest of the city center, is one of the best restaurant areas and is worth the trip if you like to eat well. The main drag, Estrada, is where you'll find most of the restaurants and bars.

La Parrillada del Ñato (☎ 387 098, *Estrada 1219)*, at Laureles, serves huge and juicy steaks, grills and barbecues, as well as pizzas – prices are fairly high, as is quality. Cheaper pizza is found at *Pizza Hut* (☎ 886 077, *Estrada 472)*, at Ebanos. Other Italian restaurants include *Trattoría La Carbonara* (☎ 382 714, 482 474, *Bálsamos 108)* and *Trattoria da Enrico* (☎ 387 079, 388 924, *Bálsamos 504)*, which has an aquarium in the ceiling!

A recommended Cuban restaurant is *Mesón Cubano* (☎ 367 611, *Ebanos 134)*. *El Caribe* (☎ 882 885, 385 538, *Estrada 1017)* Jiguas has excellent Cuban and Ecuadorian food. You'll find Swiss and Bulgarian (!) restaurants on this same block.

La Balandra (☎ 883 147, *Calle Quinta 504)* is signed Juan de Dios Martinez Mera, although nobody calls it that. It is one of Urdesa's most highly recommended seafood restaurants. The Japanese restaurant *Tsuji* (☎ 881 183, 882 641, *Estrada 816)* is not cheap but serves excellent food.

For vegetarian meals, stop by *Restaurante Vegetariano* (*Guaycanes 208)*, near Estrada. It's open for lunch only. *Café Al-Sindibad*, at Guaycames and Estrada, is an Arabic restaurant complete with water pipes.

ENTERTAINMENT

Read the local newspapers *El Telégrafo* and *El Universo* to find out more about what's going on. They print listings for the many cinemas in Guayaquil, of which about half are downtown. If you're buying the newspaper for the cinema listings, make sure that the newspaper has them. Occasionally, even the best papers omit the listing if there's been no change. English-language movies with Spanish subtitles are often shown, as well as pornos and B movies with titles such as 'Cannibals of the Amazon.' The better theaters downtown avoid this and are the following:

Cine Casa de la Cultura (9 de Octubre and Parque del Centenario)
Cine (Teatro) Guayaquil (☎ 305 867, 9 de Octubre 424)
Cine Metro (☎ 322 301, Boyacá 1221, at Vélez)

Cine Nueve de Octubre (☎ 531 788, 9 de Octubre 823, at Avilés)
Policine 1 & 2 (☎ 288 312, CC Policentro Shopping Center, Ciudadela Kennedy)

The Mall del Sol shopping center has a nine-screen cinema with recent Hollywood movies; other shopping centers are following suit, building multiscreen cinemas.

Estrada in Urdesa used to be a good street to hang out Friday and Saturday nights – it got so good that local authorities shut down many of the bars and nightclubs because this upper-class residential neighborhood did not enjoy the loud, late-night partying. By law, only established venues (defined as those that were over five years old in 1999) remain. *El Manantial*, at Estrada and Monjosa, survived the cut and is popular and crowded and has outdoor tables. Nearby is *Chappu's Bar*, which has an outdoor patio, an upstairs balcony and a tiny dance floor. A few other places are within a couple of blocks.

With the current economic crisis, there has not been a rush to replace these nightclubs, and many locals prefer to dance and party at private functions anyway. One place that has become very popular is *El Jardín de Salsa* (☎ 396 083), on the road between the airport and the bus terminal – every cabdriver knows it. The dance floor here is the biggest in Ecuador, and it's salsa, salsa, salsa. You don't have to dance, as there's plenty of seating for a beer and people watching.

Gamblers will want to try their luck at the casinos found at the top-end hotels, which also have discos on weekends.

SHOPPING

Guayaquileños like to shop at the outdoor black market called La Bahía, on Carbo and Villamil between Olmedo and Colón. It's crowded, busy and colorful. Anything from blue jeans to video cameras can be found here – some of it at bargain prices, much of it counterfeit. There are pickpockets, naturally, but the area has a high police profile and is not especially dangerous.

If you prefer a more sedate shopping atmosphere, try one of the several indoor shopping centers styled as North American shopping malls. Unicentro, downtown by Parque Bolívar, is the smallest. Policentro, in the Kennedy suburb at the end of Avenida del Periodista (San Jorge), is bigger and has many modern stores, as well as restaurants and a movie theater. Centro Comercial Urdesa is similar. Also in Urdesa is Centro Comercial Albán Borja.

The biggest and newest mall in Guayaquil – maybe the whole country – is Mall del Sol, near the airport. Plenty of shops, restaurants and cinema screens are found there.

The shopping centers are mainly geared toward general shopping, but they usually have one or two souvenir shops. The better hotels have stores selling good-quality and higher-priced crafts.

El Mercado de Artesanía (the Artisans' Market) is in a building taking up a whole block at Loja and Moreno. It's on the edge of the district of Las Peñas, however, so go with a couple of friends for added security. This is the place for a huge variety of crafts from all over Ecuador.

GETTING THERE & AWAY
Air
Guayaquil's Simón Bolívar Airport is one of Ecuador's two major international airports and is about as busy as Quito's. There are three terminals. The international and main national terminals adjoin one another and are on the east side of Avenida de las Américas, about 5km north of the city center. The Terminal de Avionetas (small-aircraft terminal) is about 1km south of the main terminal and is reached by turning left out of the main terminal and walking south along the busy Avenida de las Américas.

The main national terminal deals with most internal flights. Passengers for the Galápagos may go through the international terminal – particularly if they are changing in Guayaquil on a Quito-Guayaquil-Galápagos flight. The main terminal has a casa de cambio, which pays about as much as the downtown rate. It is open for most incoming international flights. There are also the usual cafeterias,

car rental agencies, gift shops and international telephone facilities.

Domestic There are many internal flights to all parts of the country, but times, days and fares change constantly, so check the following information. The most frequent flights are to Quito with TAME, which charges about US$50 one way. There two or three flights a day. For the best views, sit on the right side when flying to Quito.

TAME also has flights from Guayaquil to Cuenca on Monday to Saturday afternoons; to Loja on Monday, Thursday and Friday mornings; to Machala on weekday mornings and to Manta on Monday, Thursday and Friday mornings. TAME may have flights to Salinas on holiday-season weekends, subject to aircraft availability and passenger demand. Flights have been known to leave early, so get to the airport early.

TAME operates the only scheduled flights to Baltra Airport in the Galápagos. They leave daily in the morning and cost US$334 for the roundtrip (US$290 in the low season – from mid-January to mid-June and September through November). Cheaper fares are available to Ecuadorian residents.

Austro Aéreo, at the airport, has flights to Cuenca three times a week.

All the aforementioned flights leave from the main national terminal. Several small airlines have flights leaving from the Terminal de Avionetas. These airlines use small aircraft to service various coastal towns, such as Portoviejo, Bahía de Caráquez, Pedernales and Esmeraldas. Flights are subject to passenger demand, but there is usually a flight daily (except Sunday) to most of these towns leaving early in the morning. Flights may be more frequent in the wet season. Fares are reasonably low. Flights to other destinations may be available if there is passenger demand. Charters are possible. Bear in mind that because some of these flights are in five-passenger aircraft, baggage is limited to a small 10kg bag, and passenger weight is limited to 100kg.

The following is a list of domestic and charter airline offices in Guayaquil.

AECA (☎ 393 662, 394 869, 280 177), Terminal de Avionetas

Aerolitoral, Terminal de Avionetas

Austro Aéreo (☎ 296 685, 296 686, 284 048), Main Airport

AvioPacífico (☎ 283 304/5), Terminal de Avionetas

Compañía Vías Aéreas Manabitas (☎ 399 355), Terminal de Avionetas

TAME (☎ 560 778), 9 de Octubre 424, Gran Pasaje; (☎ 282 062, 287 155), Main Airport

International If you are leaving on an international flight, there is a US$25 departure tax.

Many airlines have offices in Guayaquil. Their addresses and phone numbers change frequently; check with a travel agent. Some of the most important are listed below.

Aerolíneas Argentinas (☎ 562 141)

Air France (☎ 320 313)

American Airlines (☎ 564 111) Córdova 1021, at 9 de Octubre, 20th floor

Avensa (☎ 288 900)

British Airways (☎ 325 080, 323 834) Vélez 206, at Chile

Continental Airlines (☎ 567 241, 288 987) 9 de Octubre 100, at the Malecón, 29th floor

Copa (☎ 883 751/2/3) Circunvalación Sur 631-A, at Ficus, Urdesa

Iberia (☎ 320 664, 329 558) 9 de Octubre 101, at the Malecón

KLM (☎ 282 713, 692 876/7)

Lacsa (☎ 562 950, 293 880) Córdova 1040, at 9 de Octubre, 9th floor

Lufthansa (☎ 324 360, 522 502) Malecón 1400, at Illingworth

Bus

To get to Bosque Protector Cerro Blanco (see that section, later), you can take a bus marked 'Chongón' from a stop at Moncayo and Sucre. All the drivers know where to stop for the entrance to the reserve.

The bus terminal is just beyond the airport. It boasts many simple restaurants, a bank, a hairdresser etc. There are scores of bus company offices, and you can get just about anywhere from there. The following selection gives an idea of what's available –

there are many more options. Fares will almost certainly change, but not drastically.

For the Santa Elena Peninsula (see that section, later in this chapter), you can take Transportes Villamil or Transportes Posorja, which have frequent buses to Playas (US$1.75, 1¾ hours) and Posorja (US$2, two hours). Co-op Libertad Peninsular (which has air-conditioned buses) and CICA both have buses to Salinas (US$2.25, 2½ hours) every 15 minutes.

If you're headed southbound or to Peru, take CIFA, Transportes Rutas Orenses or Ecuatoriana Pullman to Machala (US$3, 3½ hours) and Huaquillas (US$4, five hours). CIFA and Rutas Orenses run frequent small buses; the others run larger coaches. Transportes Loja has one bus at 6:30 pm to the border at Macará (US$8, 12 hours) and seven buses to Loja (US$6, nine hours).

Several companies run buses to Cuenca (US$4, five to seven hours). Supertaxis Cuenca and Buses San Luis run faster small buses, while Transportes Oriental runs larger, slower and cheaper buses. All three companies run buses about every hour.

Babahoyo (US$1, 1½ hours) is served by Transportes Urdaneta. Flota Bolívar has many slow buses daily to Guaranda via Babahoyo.

For Riobamba and Ambato, there are many companies taking as little as 3½ hours to Riobamba if the road is OK. These include: Transportes Andino, Transportes Patria, CITA, Transportes Gran Colombia and Transportes Chimborazo. One of the fastest is probably Transportes Andino.

Santo Domingo de los Colorados and Quevedo are served by Transportes Sucre, Transportes Zaracay and others.

Quito (US$7.50, seven to nine hours) is served by frequent buses with Flota Imbabura, Transportes Ecuador and Transportes Panamericana. All three are close to one another, so check around for what's best for you.

Among Transportes Esmeraldas, Transportes Occidental and AeroTaxi, there are many buses a day to Esmeraldas (US$5.50, seven hours).

Rutas Ecuatorianas and Reina del Camino have many departures for Portoviejo or Manta (US$4, four to five hours) and Bahía de Caráquez (US$5, 5½ hours).

There are many other companies at the terminal; most sell tickets in advance with a guaranteed seat. Otherwise, just show up at the terminal, and you'll often find a bus to your destination leaving within an hour or two. Friday nights and holidays can get booked up, so plan in advance if traveling then.

Boat

Cruise lines occasionally call at Guayaquil, and passengers may make brief forays ashore. A few cargo boats will take passengers to and from North America or Europe (see the Getting There & Away chapter). Generally, sailing between Guayaquil and a foreign port is more expensive and less convenient than flying.

Cargo boats steam for the Galápagos about once or twice a month. The round-trip from Guayaquil takes about 12 to 20 days, of which about three to four days are spent crossing the ocean from Guayaquil to the islands and the rest is spent in the archipelago. The trips are designed to deliver and pick up cargo from various Galápagos ports and are not very comfortable. Passengers are accepted, however, and although this is not a recommended way of getting to the islands, it is possible. See Getting There & Away in the Galápagos chapter for more details.

GETTING AROUND
To/From the Airport

The airport is on Avenida de las Américas, about 5km north of the town center. A taxi from the airport to the center will cost about US$2. Taxi drivers may try to charge higher fares from the airport – bargain. If you cross the street in front of the airport, you can take a bus downtown, and from the center, the best bus to take to the airport is the No 2 Especial, which only costs US$0.20 and takes under an hour. It runs along the Malecón but is sometimes full, so you should leave yourself plenty of time or take

a taxi. Taxis at airports tend to overcharge gullible new arrivals.

To/From the Bus Terminal

From the airport to the bus terminal is about 2km. You can walk the distance if you want – turn right out of the airport terminal and head for the obvious huge terminal. Or you can take a bus or taxi.

Buses from the center to the Terminal Terrestre leave from Parque Victoria (near 10 de Agosto and Moncayo).

Several buses leave from the terminal for the center. The No 71 bus charges a few cents more and is a little less crowded than the others. A taxi to the center is about US$2.

Bus

City buses are cheap (about US$0.20) but are always crowded, and the system is complicated. They are mainly designed to get workers and commuters from the housing districts to downtown and back again, and they are not much use for riding around the city center. They never seem to go exactly where you want to go, and what with waiting for them and battling the traffic, you'd be better off walking. The downtown area is less than 2 sq km, so it's easy to walk anywhere.

Car

If you're feeling affluent, you can rent a car; if you're not, then forget it, because it's not cheap. There are several car rental agencies at the airport. Make sure that insurance, tax and mileage are included in your rate. If you find a cheap deal, make sure the car isn't about to break down. See the Getting Around chapter for approximate average rates and other details.

Taxi

If you really must get somewhere in a hurry, you won't get there much quicker on a city bus than on foot. Take a taxi, but agree on the fare beforehand, as Guayaquil taxi drivers have a bad reputation for overcharging. You should be able to get between any two points downtown for about US$1 and to the airport, the Terminal Terrestre or Urdesa for about US$2.

Boat

The Armada del Ecuador (☎ 446 248) has ferries across Río Guayas to Durán about every 90 minutes; the fares are a few cents. Durán is a Guayaquil suburb that used to be the city's train station; now that the train doesn't run, there's little point in coming here apart from taking the inexpensive ferry ride across the river.

West of Guayaquil

☎ 04

This region is a fairly dry, relatively barren and sparsely populated area, but contains Guayaquileños' favorite beach resorts. It's busy during the high season (Christmas to April; especially weekends) but is very quiet at other times. These beaches are infrequently visited by foreign travelers, who prefer the more northerly areas.

BOSQUE PROTECTOR CERRO BLANCO

About 15km west of Guayaquil is the Cemento Nacional factory, which owns over 3500 hectares of protected tropical dry forest on the Cerro Blanco, north of the main coastal highway. This is a private reserve administered by Fundación Pro-Bosque in cooperation with the cement works, and there are several trails that take you into this area of rolling coastal hills.

Although fairly small in area, the reserve contains over 210 species of bird (including the endangered great green macaw, which is the reserve's logo, seven other endangered species and many endemic species), as well as 33 species of mammal – such as howler monkeys, peccaries, kinkajous, tamanduas, ocelots and jaguars. There are stands of dry forest with huge ceiba trees and over 100 other tree species, as well as views of coastal mangrove forests in the distance. This is one of the most interesting places to visit close to Guayaquil if you are interested in natural history.

Other features include a wildlife rescue center, where endangered species – including the great green macaw, ocelots, pumas and monkeys – are being cared for and reared. Many of the center's animals have been recovered from illegal poaching and collection activities. There is also a plant nursery.

Information

Cerro Blanco has a visitors center and a campground with barbecue grills, bathrooms and running water (even showers). The visitors center sells a bird list and booklets and dispenses information and trail maps. Backcountry camping may be permitted. There are rangers who patrol the area.

The reserve is open daily 8:30 am to 4:30 pm, but earlier entry can be arranged in advance for avid birders. Admission is US$5 for day use (discounts for residents) plus US$4 for overnight stays. There is a US$2 admission fee to view the animals in the rescue center – staff are normally on hand to answer questions about this conservation project. Reservations are requested from the Guayaquil office for weekday visits (two days' advance warning), or you can just show up on weekends, which are normally busier.

Spanish-speaking guides are available, but it is best to arrange one in advance in Guayaquil through Fundación Pro-Bosque (☎ 416 975, 417 004), Office 16, Edificio Promocentro, Eloy Alfaro and Cuenca. The guides' training is general – they don't specialize in any one subject. They can take groups of up to eight people and charge a few dollars a day.

The reserve can be contacted directly through the English-speaking director, Eric Horstman (☎ 871 900, fax 872 236, vonhorst@gu.pro.ec).

During the wet season, there are lots of mosquitoes, so bring repellent. There are few insects in the dry season, and it is easier to see wildlife, as the animals concentrate in the remaining wet areas and the vegetation is less thick. Early morning and late afternoon are, as always, the best times to see wildlife.

Brine fishing along the southern coast, north of Salinas

JOHN MAIER JR

Jutting rocks, Galápagos Islands

DAVID PEEVERS

Ship under construction, Puerto Ayora, Galápagos Islands

ALFREDO MAIQUEZ

Basking sea lions on Sombrero Chino (Chinese Hat), Galápagos Islands

CHRIS BEALL

Opuntia cacti along the shore of South Plaza Island, Galápagos Islands

Crater on Daphne Minor, Galápagos Islands

A shady spot for water on Isla Santa María (often called 'Floreana' or 'Charles'), Galápagos Islands

Getting There & Away

Buses from Guayaquil's Terminal Terrestre heading west (to any of the towns mentioned later) can drop you off at the entrance at Km 16 on the north side. There is a sign, and the cement factory is also in evidence just beyond it (get off before the factory). Local buses marked 'Chongón' also pass the entrance. Chongón buses leave from Moncayo at Sucre in central Guayaquil and are often the quickest way to get to Cerro Blanco, avoiding the trip out to the Terminal Terrestre. All the drivers know the Cerro Blanco entrance. A taxi will charge about US$10, depending on your bargaining ability.

From the reserve entrance, it is about a 10-minute walk to the information center and camping area.

PUERTO HONDO

A little west of Cerro Blanco is the small community of Puerto Hondo, at Km 17 on the south side of the Guayaquil-Salinas highway. It can be reached the same way as Cerro Blanco. There are basic stores and supplies. Club Ecológico Puerto Hondo will take visitors on canoe rides (US$7) into the mangroves in the area, which can be arranged in advance through Fundación Pro-Bosque (see the previous section). This has to be arranged in advance, as tours can only happen at high tide.

PROGRESO

Progreso (officially, it's Gómez Rendón, but it's always called Progreso) is a village 70km southeast of Guayaquil. Here the road forks and you can head west to Salinas and the Santa Elena Peninsula or east of Guayaquil to the resort of Playas. The fork is Progreso's claim to fame; there's no reason to stop there except to change buses.

From Guayaquil to Progreso, the paved road passes through very dry scrubland. It is amazing how quickly the land changes from the wet rice-growing areas in the regions north and east of Guayaquil to the dry lands of the west. Despite the dryness, the scenery is quite attractive and interesting, with strange, bottle-shaped kapok trees and bright flowers dotting the hilly landscape.

PLAYAS

From Progreso, the paved road heads due south for 30km to Playas (called General Villamil on some maps). This town is the closest beach resort to Guayaquil, which makes it crowded and littered during the high season, but the municipal authorities are trying to combat the Latin American habit of littering.

Playas is also an important fishing village. A generation ago, many of the fishing craft were small balsa rafts with one sail, similar to boats that were used before the Spanish conquest. Now, more modern craft are mainly used, but a few of the old balsa rafts can be seen in action. These interesting vessels usually come in at the west end of the beach, depending on winds and tides. Large flocks of frigatebirds and pelicans hoping for scraps wheel dramatically around the fishing fleet as it comes in to unload the catch.

Because of its proximity to Guayaquil, there are many holiday homes in Playas. It is busy from December to April but quiet at other times. It can be depressing on an overcast midweek day in the low season. Weekends are much busier than midweek.

In the high season, all the hotels are open, and prices rise a little – especially on weekends. Holiday weekends see prices as high as the market will bear. In other months, some of the cheaper hotels may close down. Those that are open have few guests and will sometimes lower their prices to have you stay there – try bargaining.

Information

Banco de Guayaquil changes dollars and has a MasterCard ATM. Pacifictel is 1km west of town on Avenida Jaime Roldos Aguilera. The police station and post office are shown on the map.

Thieves take advantage of careless vacationers; do not leave anything unattended on the beach, and exercise normal safety precautions. Mosquitoes are encountered most of the year, though not usually in large numbers. Food, liquor and drug stores are especially found on 15 de Agosto on the block west of Paquisha.

Places to Stay

Budget The cheapest places may have water shortages and normally lack furniture beyond a bed. Decor consists of faded paint work embellished with squished mosquitoes, which can be a problem in Playas, so get a room with mosquito netting (few budget hotels have them) or a fan. Some hotels may spray your room with repellent on request. Hotels near the central plaza are close to loud dance music continuing into the wee hours on weekends. Approximate prices are given for the high season.

The cheapest places are about US$3 for a room with one bed; rates may be the same for one person or a couple. Rooms with two beds cost US$6. The clean *Hostal Jesús de Gran Poder* (☎ 760 589) has pictures of Christ and little signs on the doors saying 'For the love of God, close the door quietly.' They will sell you a cold beer, though, so they aren't overly evangelical. Rooms are reasonably big and have shared bathrooms on every floor. *Hotel La Terraza* (15 de Agosto 557) is entered through a small store that stays open until 3 am, after which (they told me, with a grin) you sleep on the street.

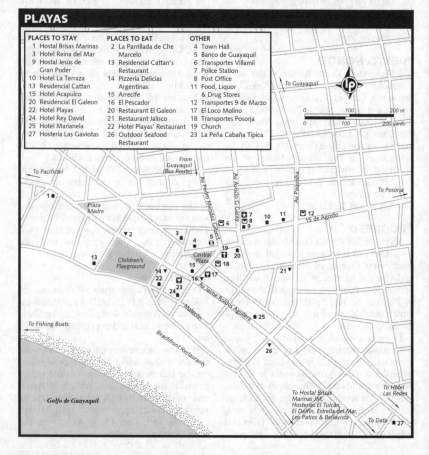

PLAYAS

PLACES TO STAY	PLACES TO EAT	OTHER
1 Hostal Brisas Marinas	2 La Parrillada de Che Marcelo	4 Town Hall
3 Hotel Reina del Mar	13 Residencial Cattan's Restaurant	5 Banco de Guayaquil
9 Hostal Jesús de Gran Poder	14 Pizzería Delicias Argentinas	6 Transportes Villamil
10 Hotel La Terraza	15 Arrecife	7 Police Station
13 Residencial Cattan	16 El Pescador	8 Post Office
15 Hotel Acapulco	20 Restaurant El Galeon	11 Food, Liquor & Drug Stores
20 Residencial El Galeon	21 Restaurant Jalisco	12 Transportes 9 de Marzo
22 Hotel Playas	22 Hotel Playas' Restaurant	17 El Loco Molino
24 Hotel Rey David	26 Outdoor Seafood Restaurant	18 Transportes Posorja
25 Hotel Marianela		19 Church
27 Hostería Las Gaviotas		23 La Peña Cabaña Típica

Rooms have private baths. ***Residencial El Galeon*** (☎ 760 270), which has a good, cheap restaurant, is clean and friendly. It's also one of the longest-established places. Rooms are old and come with and without bath; some have mosquito nets.

Other cheapies to try are ***Hotel Acapulco*** (☎ 760 343), which has a restaurant below; ***Hotel Reina del Mar*** (☎ 760 882), which can get loud on weekends with the attached disco and restaurant; and ***Hotel Marianela*** (☎ 760 058), which has basic rooms with and without private baths.

Hotel Playas (☎ 760 121) is near the beach and has varied rooms; some have air-conditioning, and others are run down with cramped private showers. Rates are US$8/12 and up for singles/doubles; there is a restaurant. ***Hostal Brisas Marinas*** (☎ 760 324), at the west end of town, is over a pharmacy and may be closed in the low season. Room are US$12 for a double with bath. At the east end of town, on the beach, the unrelated ***Hostal Brisas Marinas JM*** (☎ 761 730/1) has clean rooms with fans and hot electric showers for about US$10/16.

Hotel Rey David (☎ 760 024) is on the beach and has characterless rooms at US$12/16 for two/three people (no singles). ***Residencial Cattan*** (☎ 760 179), on the Malecón, provides a bed and three meals a day for US$15 per person, but the rooms themselves are basic with private shower. The restaurant isn't bad.

Southeast of the center, en route to Data and Posorja, are several quiet places which tend to fill up and overcharge on high-season weekends. Almost a kilometer southeast of the center, a block from the beach, ***Hostería Las Gaviotas*** (☎ 760 133) is friendly, quiet and has a decent restaurant, though the rooms are basic at US$7 with bath. Nearby, ***Hotel Las Redes*** (☎ 760 222) has rooms with fans and one double bed for US$9, or rooms with TV and air-conditioning for US$18; prices rise dramatically on holiday weekends. It has a restaurant.

Hostería El Delfín (☎ 760 125) is 1.5km southeast of the center and has decent rooms, some with a sea view, for US$18 a double with bath. They have a restaurant

and bar. Nearby are the similarly priced ***Hostería Estrella del Mar*** (☎ 760 430) and ***Hostería Los Patios*** (☎ 760 039). Both are decent places with double rooms with hot showers in the US$16 to US$20 range. Both have a restaurant, a bar and beach access.

Mid-Range Southeast of the center 1.3km is ***Hostería El Tucán*** (☎ 760 866, ☎/fax 760 127) which has a big swimming pool, a sauna, spa and a pricey restaurant. Large, clean, air-conditioned rooms with TV and hot showers are in the US$30s for single or double occupancy, depending on room size. Rooms sleeping up to five people are about US$50.

Finally, ***Hostería Bellavista*** (☎/fax 760 600) is about 2km southeast of town on the beachfront. The place is very popular with Swiss and German tourists. Ordinary rooms and three-bedroom villas are available, all with hot showers and fans, but no air-conditioning. Some have kitchenettes and dining areas, and discounts are offered for weekly stays. There's a restaurant and bar if you don't want to cook. Rates go from about US$20 for a single to US$70 for a villa that sleeps six. Reservations are suggested, and bikes, canoes and surfboards are available for rent.

Places to Eat

Seafood is the mainstay of local dining. The better hotels have decent restaurants. Cheaper good ones include ***Restaurant El Galeon***, below Residencial El Galeon, and ***Arrecife***, below Hotel Acapulco. Cheap food is also available at ***Restaurant Jalisco***. The most upscale place seems to be ***El Pescador***.

There are plenty of cheap, identical beachfront shacks with views of the ocean where you can eat a freshly caught fish or other seafood, washed down with a cold beer, for US$2 and up. There's a bunch more at the corner of Paquisha and Aguilera; some of these have some pretty wild-looking seafood, waving claws or snapping shells at passersby. ***Hotel Playas*** and ***Residencial Cattan*** also have restaurants.

For a change from seafood, head northwest on Aguilera for ***Pizzería Delicias***

Argentinas and *La Parrillada de Che Marcelo* (the latter has grilled meat). In between the two are some *Chilean empanada places*.

Entertainment

There are places to dance on most nights in the high season; in the low season, you can dance on weekends. Most discos are in the center and are loud, so you'll have no trouble finding them, but the action doesn't get under way until 10 or 11 pm. The outdoor *El Loco Molino* and the indoor *La Peña Cabaña Típica* are currently popular, but this changes every year.

Getting There & Away

Transportes Villamil (☎ 760 190) and Transportes Posorja have buses to Guayaquil (US$1.50, 1¾ hours). Buses leave every 20 minutes with either company from before dawn until about 7 pm.

Transportes 9 de Marzo have frequent buses to Posorja (US$0.50, 30 minutes) during the day – see the map for the locations of the buses.

The best way to get to Santa Elena is to go to Progreso and change, but buses from Guayaquil to Santa Elena are often full during the holidays.

On Sunday afternoons in the January-to-April high season, everybody is returning to Guayaquil, and the road becomes a one-way busfest, with few vehicles traveling south into Playas.

AROUND PLAYAS

There are two roads south of Playas – one follows the coast, and the other heads inland. The coastal road goes through the villages of Data de Villamil and Data de Posorja, which are often collectively called **Data**. These places are known for boat building. The inland road passes through the old village of **El Morro**, which is less important than it used to be. There is a huge old wooden church with dilapidated bamboo walls and three white wooden towers.

Both the inland and the coastal roads lead to **Posorja**, a fishing village with many working boats and hundreds of seabirds

wheeling overhead. The beach here is dirty and not good for swimming. Shrimping is becoming more and more important. Posorja is best visited on a day trip – it is about 20km southeast of Playas. Buses frequently go there from Playas with 9 de Marzo.

PUNTA PELADA

This is a long and fairly deserted beach stretching northwest from Playas. Salt flats, cliffs and cacti provide an interesting backdrop. There is reportedly good surfing here. The dirt road along the beach is a popular drive for those with their own vehicles – there is no public transportation here. Bring food and water, and don't leave anything unattended.

SANTA ELENA PENINSULA

The land west of Progreso becomes increasingly dry and scrubby, the ceiba (kapok) trees giving way to 5m-high candelabra cacti. Few people and animals are seen, although herds of tough, half-wild goats seem to thrive. Some of the few inhabitants scratch a living from burning the scrub to make charcoal, and once in a while, you see someone on the side of the road with bags of charcoal.

Just over halfway between Progreso and Santa Elena, a signed road to the left indicates the archaeology museum in the coastal village of **Chanduy**, 12km from the main road. Archaeological excavations nearby have led to the opening of the small Museo Real Alto (☎ 09-772 699, 09-758 353), on the outskirts of the village. The museum has displays on the 6000-year-old archaeology of the area and is open 9 am to 5 pm Tuesday to Saturday; admission costs under US$1. Chanduy is reached by bus or taxi from La Libertad (described later).

About 15km before reaching Santa Elena, a road to the right leads to the **Baños de San Vicente**, where there are thermal pools and mud baths. A government-operated tourist complex has been built here, and visitors can enjoy therapeutic and rejuvenating mud packs, hot tubs, massages or swims. Daily entrance to the complex, which is open 7 am to 7 pm, is about US$0.50; mud massages and other delights cost extra. There is one place to spend the night – **Hotel Florida** (☎ 282 195, 281 464), which is quite inexpensive, although the clientele is mostly Guayaqileños on day trips. On weekends, go early or late in the day to avoid the crowds.

Santa Elena

As you arrive in Santa Elena, the landscape changes. Not that it becomes any less dry; it is simply more built up. There are three towns near the end of the peninsula, and they all seem to run into one another, making the area almost one complete dusty urban zone with few open spaces.

Santa Elena itself has a nearby oil refinery and is the home of the peninsula's radio station. A new museum recently opened, **Los Amantes de Sumpa** (☎ 09-866 026). It has a fascinating display of in situ 8000-year-old skeletons shown in the positions that they were found, including two embracing as *amantes* (lovers). This is currently the oldest archaeological exhibit in the country, and it is well laid out and labeled in Spanish. Also here is a small botanical garden with labeled plants, a typical rural house of the 1930s, a balsa fishing boat and other items of interest. Hours are 9 am to 1:30 pm and 2:30 to 5 pm Monday, Tuesday, Thursday and Friday, and the US$1 admission includes a guided tour in Spanish. There is a small gift shop. The museum is a couple of blocks from the main road on the west side of town – ask any bus driver. The Web site is at http:/move.to/LosAmantes.

Hotels are limited. **Residencial El Cisne** (☎ 785 038, 940 038) is a clean, basic hotel on the main square. Most people stay in other towns on the peninsula.

La Libertad

La Libertad, the largest town on the peninsula, has about 50,000 inhabitants. It is an important fishing port, it has a nearby oil refinery, and it is the transportation hub for the area. It is a busy, noisy and dirty town with a reputation for theft. Few travelers like it, but it has an undeniably lively air. The beach here is mainly rubble, and the main reason to be here is to change buses.

The Banco del Pacífico near the plaza at the east end has a MasterCard ATM. Pacifictel is also on this plaza.

Places to Stay & Eat Cheap hotels are very poor and not too clean. *Hotel Viña del Mar* (☎ 785 979), at Avenida 3 and Guayaquil, has rates of US$6/10 for rooms with bath and fan; it is one of the more decent options. They have parking available. *Residencial Turis Palm* (☎ 785 159, 784 546, 9 de Octubre 626) is a bit cheaper and OK. Nearby, there are cheaper places.

The best places are away from the town center. *Hotel Samarina* (☎ 785 167, ☎/fax 784 100, fax 781 042), on 9 de Octubre at 10 de Agosto by the waterfront, about 1.5km northwest of the town, has an adequate restaurant, a swimming pool and air-conditioned rooms and bungalows starting at around US$30. The ocean is in front of the hotel, but there's not much of a beach.

About half a kilometer farther is the better *Hotel Valdivia* (☎/fax 775 144, 777 329), which has a swimming pool, a good restaurant and friendly staff. The rates are in the US$40s for clean air-conditioned rooms.

There are a couple of *Pingüinos*, which have good ice cream, and other cheap restaurants can be found on 9 de Octubre or Guayaquil. The better hotels have the best restaurants.

Getting There & Away

La Libertad is the center of bus services on the peninsula. For Guayaquil (US$2, 2½ hours), there are several choices. Cooperativa Libertad Peninsular (CLP), on the corner of 9 de Octubre and Guerro Barreiro, has buses about every hour all day long. Cooperativa Intercantonal Costa Azul (CICA), at 9 de Octubre and Diagonal 2, has the fastest and most frequent service. CICA buses often leave from opposite the Residencial Turis Palm, on 9 de Octubre; the ones from Guayaquil continue to Salinas and then return to Guayaquil from Salinas via La Libertad.

To get to Santa Elena, flag down one of the minibuses that run frequently along 9 de

Octubre. Frequent buses to Salinas run all day from Calle 8 and Avenida 2.

Transportes San Agustín is in a bus terminal near the market and has buses to Chanduy (described previously). Various small local coastal villages are served by transportation from the market area. For going north along the coast to the fishing villages of Palmar, Ayangue, Manglaralto (US$1, two hours) and Puerto López (US$2.80, three hours), take minibuses with Transportes Peninsulares Unidas, Cooperativa Manglaralto or CITM. The first company has departures about every half hour, but few of the vehicles make it as far as Manglaralto. Most go as far as Palmar, and some go to Ayangue. The other two companies have several buses a day that go through Puerto López and on to Jipijapa (US$3.50, five hours). Note that buses may be booked up in advance during weekends in the high season.

Punta Carnero

This is a point of land in the middle of a wild and largely deserted beach some 15km in length. There is a resort hotel on the point, **Punta Carnero Inn** (☎ 775 450, 779 041, fax 776 072), which overlooks the ocean from a cliff top. Comfortable, balconied rooms cost about US$70 (high season) for a double with bath and air-conditioning. There is a restaurant, a swimming pool and a play area for kids. Reservations can be made at Hotel Plaza in Guayaquil (see Places to Stay – Mid-Range, under Guayaquil, earlier). Nearby, **Hostería Vista del Mar** (☎ 775 370) has cheaper rooms and cabins with or without air-conditioning (but all have hot showers) at US$20 to US$50 for a double. There is a restaurant and a swimming pool, and there is also a tennis court.

The ocean in front of the hotels may be too wild for swimming, but the beach is good for walks. The sea abounds with fish, and sportfishing is a popular activity. Boats and equipment can be chartered from Salinas. The area has also been recommended for bird watching – some unusual arid land birds and shorebirds (such as the Chilean flamingo) have been reported in the area.

Salt lagoons are seen along this coast. Whales may be observed in July, August and September.

Buses from La Libertad will get you to Punta Carnero, but most visitors come with their own vehicle.

Salinas

This important resort town with a permanent population of over 20,000 inhabitants is on the tip of the Santa Elena Peninsula. About 150km west of Guayaquil, it is the most westerly town on the Ecuadorian mainland. The westernmost point is a hill called La Choclatera, which lies within a military base. Reportedly, you can visit it by taxi if you leave identification with the guards until you leave.

Salinas is called the best resort in Ecuador, and its modern hotels and high-rise condos make it the seasonal haunt of affluent Ecuadorians. It's relatively overpriced yet quite crowded during the high season and still fairly expensive and dead in the off season. The water is warmest for swimming from January to March. During Carnaval, the place is completely full with beachgoers playing volleyball, sailing and enjoying themselves. The beaches are not spectacular and are spoiled by the high-rise backdrop. In July and August, the place is overcast, dreary and really dead.

There is a Yacht Club, and the *capitanía* (captaincy), on the west end of the waterfront, is where you are supposed to register if arriving/leaving by yacht. During the January-to-April high season, international yachts come through and occasionally need a crew member.

The streets are haphazardly arranged and poorly signed. Most locals go by landmarks rather than street names. Salinas is a long town, and its streets parallel the beach for just a few blocks inland. Most businesses are found within two or three blocks of the coast.

Information Salinas lacks a tourism office. Banco del Pacífico, at Calle 18 and Gallo (one block from the beach), has a MasterCard ATM, and Filanbanco, at Calle

17 and Gallo, has a Visa ATM. Pacifictel, on Calle 20 at Gallo, can make international connections.

Pesca Tours (☎ 772 391, in Guayaquil ☎ 443 365, fax 443 142) offers fishing boats for US$350 a day (6 am to 4:30 pm). Boats take up to six anglers and include a captain, two crew members and all fishing gear. You have to provide your own lunch and drinks; they'll provide a cooler (and will fill it for you for a fee). Boats are 32 or 35 feet long; larger and more expensive boats are available. The best season is September to December for marlin, dorado and wahoo. Pesca Tours' Web site is at www .pescatours.com.ec.

Birders need to seek out the Oyster-catcher Bar (☎ 778 329, 782 201), on Calle 50 at the Malecón – but it's changed location a few times. The owner, Ben Haase (who speaks Spanish, English and Dutch) knows more about coastal birds than anyone in the area.

Places to Stay Locals stay at holiday homes rather than at hotels. There are no very cheap accommodations, and hotels may close down in the off season.

Budget Budget hotels are about US$4 to US$6 per person in the low season and up to US$10 in the high season. Try the family-run *Hotel Florida* (☎ 772 780), at the Malecón and Avenida 2, which is clean but out of town, near the naval base. Some rooms have sea views or private baths, and a restaurant is on the premises. *Hotel Albita* (☎ 773 211, 773 662), on Avenida 7 between Calle 22 and 23, is OK and has slightly musty rooms with fans and private baths. *Residencial Rachel* (☎ 772 501, 772 526), at Calle 17 and Avenida 5, has cheap rooms with shared baths and pricier rooms with private baths and TV. *Hotel Oro del Mar*, at Calle 22 and Enríquez, has clean rooms with cold-water shower and fan.

The friendly *Hotel Yulee* (☎ 772 028, 09-893 400), in an old, rambling building near the main plaza, charges US$15/25 for air-conditioned rooms with private bath, hot water and TV, or substantially less for rooms lacking air-conditioning and/or bath. There is a restaurant and a garden.

Mid-Range On Enríquez near Rumiñahui you'll find *Hotel Francisco 1* (☎ 774 106), with 11 air-conditioned rooms with hot showers, telephone and cable TV for about US$25/35 in the high season. There is also a pool and restaurant. The modern *Hotel Salinas Costa Azul* (☎ 774 268/9, fax 774 267), at the east end of Salinas at Enríquez and Calle 27, charges US$25 for decent air-conditioned doubles with bathrooms and TV. There is a small restaurant and a swimming pool. Farther east is *Hotel Tropikal Inn* (☎ 773 338), at Calle 38 and Avenida 3, which charges US$50 for a double with air-conditioning, TV, refrigerator and hot shower. Breakfast is included, and there is a pool and restaurant. The small *Hotel El Carruaje* (☎ 774 282, Malecón 517) has pleasant, modern rooms – most with an ocean view – at US$35/50. Its restaurant is very good, and this place is usually full in the high season.

Top End On the Malecón *Hotel Casino Calypsso* (☎ 772 425/35, fax 773 583, calypsso@

Sportfishing from Salinas

Beginning about 13km offshore from Salinas, the continental shelf drops from 400m to over 3000m (about 40km offshore), so a short, one-hour sail can take you out into really deep water. Swordfish, sailfish, tuna, dorados and marlin are some of the fish to go after – the black marlin occasionally weigh over 600kg. Black marlin are the world's third-biggest sport fish, after a couple of shark species. The world-record weight for black marlin is 707kg, which was set in 1953 in Peru. Locals claim that there is an 800kg black marlin on the Ecuadorian coast.

Salinas occasionally hosts world fishing competitions. The best fishing is from September to December, when boats may be booked up several days in advance.

gye.satnet.net) has spacious, tiled, comfortable and air-conditioned but characterless rooms with TV, telephone, fridge and (in some cases) good ocean views. Both one- and two-bedroom units are available. The hotel has a pool, Jacuzzi, sauna, restaurant, travel agency and – if you have any money left – a casino. Rates are US$65 to US$190; during the high season, don't expect any bargains!

Places to Eat The food is good at *Cevichelandia*, the local nickname for a series of cheap seafood stalls at Calle 17 and Enríquez, but they are mainly for lunch.

There are various restaurants, bars and discos along the waterfront east of the center, but they're mostly closed in the low season. *Pingüino*, at Calle 21 and the Malecón, has ice cream. The names, prices and quality of other places change from year to year, but a walk along the waterfront will yield a number of choices.

Entertainment During weekends in the high season, the place comes alive with discos and clubs, mainly near the Malecón. Also check the Oystercatcher Bar (see Information, earlier). Salinas is pretty dead otherwise.

Getting There & Away Buses enter town along the Malecón and continue to the naval base, where they turn around and head back to La Libertad along Enríquez. During the low season, most buses go only as far as La Libertad. Those that continue to Guayaquil usually stop at La Libertad for up to an hour to pick up more passengers. The CLP bus office is on Calle 7 by Avenida 5.

During the high season, there are direct buses to Guayaquil, and there may be flights to and from Guayaquil.

NORTH ALONG THE COAST

From La Libertad, many buses run north along the coast. Some go only a short way, but many make it as far as Puerto López and Jipijapa, in the province of Manabí (see the North Coast chapter). The beaches en route are often very good, and there are several

fishing villages where Guayaquileños have holiday homes – these places are becoming increasingly well known among foreign travelers. The season from Christmas to May is hot and sunny but wet – the scenery is lush and pretty between rain showers. The ocean is warmest January to March. The rest of the year is dry, cooler and cloudier. It can sometimes be gray and miserable during the dry months, especially July and August. The coast views are good, so sit on the ocean side of the bus.

The first place of interest is the village of **Ballenita**, just north of Santa Elena. On the outskirts of Ballenita is *Farallón Dillon* (☎ 786 643, 785 611, ddillon@gu.pro.ec), where there is a nautical museum and a lookout point from which migrating whales can be seen June to September. English is spoken, and food, tourist information and lodging can be arranged.

Valdivia, a village 50km north of La Libertad, has a small museum displaying artifacts from the Valdivia period (around 3000 BC), but the best pieces of antiquity are in Guayaquil museums. About 5km before reaching Valdivia, the fishing village of **Ayangue** is passed, and 5km before that (40km north of La Libertad), the village of **Palmar**. Both are close to pleasant beaches and have attracted Guayaquileños into buying holiday homes there. The area is fairly crowded with visitors during high-season weekends, but only Ayangue has a couple of small hotels, including the budget *Un Millón de Amigos* (☎ 916 014) and the mid-range *Cumbres de Ayangue* (☎ 916 040).

North of Valdivia, the dry landscape begins to get a little wetter. The cactus and scrub give way to stunted trees and the occasional banana plantation.

Manglaralto & Dos Mangas

Manglaralto is the main village on the coast of Guayas Province north of La Libertad. The nice beach has decent surf but little shade. **Fundación Pro-Pueblo** (see the boxed text) has its office here.

There are a few simple pensiones, particularly near the north end of the beach. A good choice is *Hostería Marakayá* (☎ 901

294), 100m from the beach, which has clean rooms with private hot bath for about US$5/7.50, or twice that for rooms with air-conditioning. Mosquito nets are provided. The owners are friendly, helpful and knowledgeable about the area. Another budget choice is *La Cueva de Freddy*, on the beach, about 2km south of Manglaralto.

Restaurant Las Pangas, on the beach, is a good place to eat.

A few kilometers inland from Manglaralto is the village of Dos Mangas. Here, the land begins to rise into the Cordillera de Colonche – coastal hills reaching an elevation of 834m. By asking around in Dos Mangas, you can find guides and horses for excursions into the hills, where you will discover waterfalls in the rainy season.

Montañita

Approximately 5km north of Manglaralto is the village of Montañita. Like other places along the coast, it's a fishing village with nice beaches. The surfing is reputedly the best in Ecuador, and new hotels have recently opened – most serving the budget market. Montañita is becoming increasingly popular on the budget-traveler circuit. There is a Pacifictel office.

Since 1987, there has been an annual international surfing competition here – usually around Carnaval, when waves of 2m to 3m are common. This attracts competitors from all over Latin America, as well as a sprinkle of surfers from other places. The best surfing is from December to May, with both left and right beach breaks, and a right break on the point at the north end of the beach. Some kind of action can be found in other months if you are patient. Surfboards can be rented, and locals are happy to show beginners the basics (which is recommended for novices).

Places to Stay & Eat There are two areas: one is in town and the other is at 'the point' – a 10- or 15-minute walk north along the unlit coastal highway. Carry a flashlight at night.

In Montañita, a good choice is *La Casa Blanca* (☎ *005 934, 901 340, lacasablanca@ hotmail.com*), run by Francisco, a friendly

Fundación Pro-Pueblo

This NGO (☎ 04-901 208, 901 195, 09-772 615, propueblo1@propueblo.org.ec) can provide travelers with information about visiting remote villages that are off the beaten track. Local families will provide simple accommodations, meals, guides and mules for a nominal fee. Ask about what would be best to bring with you to share with the families.

The villages involved are about an easy day's walk or horseback ride away from Manglaralto and from each other. Visiting them will give travelers a chance to experience some rural hospitality and lifestyle while putting tourist dollars into the pockets of villagers. Overnight tours into the coastal hills can be arranged for bird watching, visiting remote waterfalls or seeing orchids and other natural delights.

Apart from bring tourism to these small villages, Pro-Pueblo supports the sustainable economic development of the region by encouraging the production of arts and crafts – including tagua-nut jewelry, panama hats, sandstone and wood carvings, reproductions of ancient ceramics and products made from recycled paper. Apiculture and the farming of organic produce are also important projects.

guy who speaks English and some other European languages. He has a dorm for US$2 per person, rooms with shared bath for US$3 per person and rooms with private bath for US$5 per person. He'll give discounts for groups and longer stays, and hot water is provided. The highlight is Francisco's living room, where cable TV, Internet access, snacks, drinks, games and couches are available after a hard day of surfing. The living rooms is open to the general public.

Also in Montañita is the slightly cheaper *El Centro del Mundo*, which has an open-air dorm that sleeps 25 people on mattresses under mosquito nets, as well as a few rooms with shared and private baths. It is right next to the beach, and it has a café and a pool table. Other basic cheapies to try are

SOUTH COAST

Pre-Columbian Coastal Ceramics

Some of Ecuador's oldest archaeological sites (dating back to about 3000 BC) are found in the Valdivia-Manglaralto area. Although there is little to see for the traveler, villagers in the Valdivia area will offer genuine pre-Columbian artifacts for sale. Many of these are replicas, and those that are genuine are illegal to export out of Ecuador (or to import into most other countries).

Buy ceramics that are advertised as replicas. Many are very attractive and quite authentic-looking, and not only do they make good souvenirs, but purchasing them encourages and supports the work of local artisans and discourages the removal and exploitation of genuine archaeological artifacts.

Hostal D Lucho and *Hostal La Piraya*. There are several simple comedores as well.

Strung along the main highway to the north are a few other cheap accommodations, most of which are open only during the high season. Near 'the point' are several good year-round options. The attractively rustic *La Casa del Sol* (☎ 901 302, 09-892 896) is very popular and has rooms both with shared and private hot baths. Rates vary from US$4 to US$10 per person, but in the high season, triple or quad occupancy is expected, and people who want singles and doubles pay a surcharge. This hotel is 100 yards from the beach and often hosts barbecues and fires in the high season; it's Web site is at www.casasol.com. Across the street is *Hotel Las Tres Palmeras* (☎ 09-755 711), which has six modern rooms with cross-ventilation, mosquito nets and a hot-water shower for US$10 per person. *Tres Palmeras Restaurant* is run by a Texan who makes the best Tex-Mex food in Ecuador. There is also a full beachside bar.

Beyond these two, closer to 'the point' is *Hotel Montañita* (☎ 901 296, fax 901 299, in Guayaquil ☎ 281 996, 284 871), which has 36 rooms of varying sizes sleeping one to four people. All have mosquito nets, fans and private showers (some hot), and rates are about US$12 per person in the high season; less in the low. There is a restaurant, bar, laundry and a garden with hammocks.

Farther north is the upscale *Hotel Baja* (☎ /fax 901 218/9), which has about 35 air-conditioned rooms and cabins (some sleeping up to six) with hot showers, a swimming pool, a Jacuzzi, a games room and a restaurant (which is only open in the high season). Rates are US$15 to US$50, depending on occupancy and season.

North of Montañita

A few kilometers farther north is the coastal village of Olón, which has a decent beach and a couple of inexpensive hotels. Seven kilometers north of Olón, the provincial line between Guayas and Manabí is crossed – see the North Coast chapter for travel in places north of Olón.

South of Guayaquil

Places in Guayas Province south of Guayaquil are of little interest to Guayaquileño vacationers compared to the area west of the city. For the most part, this area is visited by travelers on their way to Peru.

RESERVA ECOLÓGICA DE MANGLARES CHURUTE
☎ 04

This 50,000-hectare national reserve protects an area of mangroves southeast of Guayaquil. Much of the coast used to be mangrove forest – an important and unique habitat (see Habitats, under Flora & Fauna, in the Facts about Ecuador chapter). This is one of the few remaining mangrove coastlands left – the rest have been destroyed by the shrimp industry. Inland is some tropical dry forest on hills reaching 700m above sea level.

This is a poorly researched region, but preliminary studies of the area within the reserve indicate that the changing habitat from coastal mangroves to hilly forest supports a wide biodiversity with a high degree of endemism. Manglares Churute is a rarely visited place, partly because there is still relatively little infrastructure for tourism and partly because it is not much publicized. Dolphins have frequently been reported on the coast, and many other animal and bird species are seen by wildlife watchers, who are the main visitors.

Information

The reserve entrance is on the left side of the main Guayaquil-Machala highway, about 46km south of Guayaquil. At the entrance is an information center (☎ 09-763 653) where you pay the US$10 entrance fee. The park rangers can arrange boats for you to visit the mangroves (a recent report said the fee is US$60 for the whole day, and the boat can take four or five people); there are also several kilometers of hiking trails. The best season for boats is January to May, when water levels are high (but there are more insects then). Maps may be available at the information center. There is room for a few people to sleep here.

Bordering the reserve is another area protected by Fundación Andrade. Nancy Hilgut is the contact here, and she can guide you. Chasquitur does tours to Manglares Churute (see Travel Agencies & Guides, under Guayaquil, earlier in this section).

Getting There & Away

Any bus between Guayaquil and Naranjal or Machala can drop you off at the information center. When you are ready to leave, you can flag buses down. There is a sign on the road, and drivers know it.

MACHALA
☎ 07

South of Guayaquil is the important city of Machala, with about 217,000 inhabitants. It is the capital of El Oro Province and lies in an important banana-growing area. During the 200km drive from Guayaquil, you see plantations of banana, coffee, pineapple and citrus fruit. About halfway to Machala, you pass through Naranjal, an important agricultural center with several hotels but otherwise of little interest.

Despite its economic importance, Machala is not of great tourist interest. Most travelers on their way to and from Peru pass through here, but few people stay more than a night.

It isn't totally devoid of interest, however, as the local international port of Puerto Bolívar, only 7km away, is worth visiting (see that section, later in this chapter). Machala has a highly touted International Banana & Agricultural Festival during the third week in September, when an international contest is held to elect *La Reina del Banano* (The Banana Queen).

On the main road to Machala, southeast of the city, stands the statue of **El Bananero** – a man carrying a large branch of bananas. This is Machala's most telling monument. Watch for it as you arrive in town.

Information

Tourist Office & Travel Agencies A tourist information office (☎ 932 106), upstairs at 9 de Mayo and Pichincha, is open erratically on weekdays. A block southwest of the Central Plaza are Delgado Travel and other travel agencies (see the map), which can help with travel arrangements and limited information.

Peruvian Consulate The consulate (☎ 930 680), at Bolívar and Colón, is open on weekday mornings.

Money Several banks near the Central Plaza change money. Filanbanco has a Visa ATM, and Banco de Guayaquil has a MasterCard ATM; see the map for their locations. There's a Banco del Pacífico at Junín and Rocafuerte.

Post & Communications The post office and Pacifictel office are shown on the map. Netcomsys, Ayacucho 1519, offers Internet access.

SOUTH COAST

MACHALA

PLACES TO STAY

1   Hotel Marsella
4   Hotel Mosquera Internacional
6   Hotel Montecarlo
7   Residencial La Internacional
    Residencial Machala
8   Araujo Hotel
11 Hotel Ejecutivo
12 Hotel Inés
15 Hotel Oro
21 Gran Hotel Machala
22 Hotel Suites Guayaquil
24 Hotel Perla del Pacífico
25 Hostal La Bahía
26 Hostal Mercy
27 Rizzo Hotel
34 Hotel Internacional
    San Francisco
41 Hotel Ecuatoriano Pullman
42 Residencial La Cueva
    de los Tayos

PLACES TO EAT

5   Hotel Montecarlo
10 Chesco Pizzería
11 Hotel Ejecutivo
15 Hotel Oro
20 Don Angelo's
32 Bar Restaurant El Bosque
33 Restaurant Chifa Central
34 Hotel Internacional
    San Francisco

OTHER

2   Pacifictel
3   Netcomsys (Internet)
9   Filanbanco
13 Church
14 Town Hall
16 CIFA Buses to Huaquillas
17 Banco de Guayaquil
18 Travel Agencies
19 Delgado Travel
26 Hospital
29 Post Office
30 Banco del Pacífico
31 Rutas Orenses
33 Cooperativa Pullman Azuay
35 Tourist Information
36 CEDTA (Charter Airline)
37 TAME Airline Office
38 Transportes El Oro
39 CIFA Buses to Guayaquil
40 Ciudad de Piñas
41 Ecuatoriana Pullman
43 Transportes Occidentales
44 Transportes Cooperativa Loja
45 Peruvian Consulate
46 Panamericana
47 Transportes TAC

Medical Services The hospital (☎ 930 420, 937 581) is shown on the map. There are numerous clinics and pharmacies nearby.

Market Area The blocks of Olmedo and Pasaje northeast of the market are full of street stalls, are noisy and impassable to cars during the day and are mildly unsafe at night.

Places to Stay
Machala has a far better range of hotels than does the border town of Huaquillas, so travelers are better off staying here (the border is closed from 6 pm to 8 am).

Prices may rise for September's Banana Festival and national holidays.

Budget Most cheap hotels have only cold water, but the weather is hot enough that it's not a great hardship. In fact, fans and air-conditioning are much more appealing than a hot shower!

The friendly *Residencial La Cueva de los Tayos* (☎ 935 600), on Sucre near Buenavista, is clean and charges US$2.50 for a basic room with private bath and one bed (single or double occupancy). Rooms with shared bath are about US$2. Also friendly is the similarly priced *Residencial La Internacional* (☎ 930 244), at Guayas near Olmedo, although bathrooms are shared. Around the corner, the basic *Residencial Machala*, at Sucre and Guayas, is cheaper. Also acceptable is *Hostal La Bahía* (☎ 920 581), at Olmedo and Junín. Other cheapies are north and east of the market area.

One of the best budget hotels, often full by lunch, is the very good and clean *Hostal Mercy* (☎ 920 116, Junín 609). Rates are US$3.50 per person for rooms with bath and air-conditioning; some cheaper rooms with fans are available, and there is parking. *Gran Hotel Machala* (☎ 930 530), at Montalvo and Rocafuerte, has basic but clean rooms with fans at US$2.50 per person with shared bath or US$3 with private bath. *Hotel Ecuatoriano Pullman* (☎ 930 197, 962 077, 9 de Octubre 912) is convenient for the adjoining bus terminal; it's not any noisier than elsewhere. Reasonably clean

but worn rooms with private bath are US$3.50 per person with fan, US$5 with air-conditioning. *Hotel Suites Guayaquil* (☎ 922 570, 937 557) is similarly priced.

The decent *Hotel Inés* (☎ 932 301, fax 931 473, Montalvo 1509) charges US$4/7 for singles/doubles with private bath and fan, US$7/11 with air-conditioning and US$12 with cable TV; there is parking. *Araujo Hotel* (☎ 935 257, 931 464), at 9 de Mayo and Boyacá, has parking and small but clean air-conditioned rooms with hot water and TV for US$6/8. Also OK is *Hotel Mosquera Internacional* (☎ 931 752, 931 140, 930 210, 930 392, fax 930 390), on Olmedo near Ayacucho, which charges US$6/9 for small, clean rooms with TV, cold shower and fan; rooms with air-conditioning cost US$8/11.

The clean *Hotel Internacional San Francisco* (☎ 922 395, 930 441, 930 457), on Tarqui near Sucre, charges US$10/12 for rooms with a fan and US$11/15 for rooms with air-conditioning, TV and phone. *Hotel Perla del Pacífico* (☎ 930 915, 931 474, fax 937 358, Sucre 826) charges US$11/15 for worn but clean, air-conditioned rooms with TV and telephone. Neither hotel has hot showers.

Hotel Marsella (☎ 935 577, 932 460, 937 705), at Las Palmeras and 9 de Octubre, has an unprepossessing, hole-in-the-wall entrance but also has decent air-conditioned rooms with hot showers, TV and telephone for US$12/15. A few cheaper rooms have fans.

Mid-Range All the hotels in this price range have clean rooms with private bathrooms, hot water, cable TV and air-conditioning; they all have cafés or restaurants too. *Hotel Ejecutivo* (☎ 923 162, 933 992, fax 933 987), at Sucre and 9 de Mayo, has rather worn rooms at US$15/17 for singles/doubles. *Hotel Montecarlo* (☎ 931 901, 933 462, fax 933 104), at Guayas and Olmedo, is a little nicer at US$18/23. *Hotel Oro* (☎ 937 569, 930 783, 932 408, fax 933 751), at Sucre and Montalvo, charges US$18/24 for pleasant, carpeted rooms with direct-dial phones, a minifridge and lots of hot water. Despite its location near the market, it is safe when entering from Sucre.

Traditionally the best hotel in the center – complete with a decent restaurant, a swimming pool, a sauna, a disco and a casino – is *Rizzo Hotel* (☎ 921 511, 921 906, fax 933 651, Guayas 2123). It's the oldest good hotel, and it has been renovated. Rates are US$20/26.

Top End In the suburbs outside of town, *Oro Verde* (☎ 933 140, fax 933 150) is Machala's only luxury hotel. Spacious double rooms are US$138 (much less for residents), and the hotel has all the expected amenities, including car rental, a travel office and a small shopping mall. It's a 10-minute cab ride from the center of town.

Places To Eat

There are many chifas, and the locally popular *Restaurant Chifa Central*, on Tarqui near 9 de Octubre, has a wide variety of good and reasonably priced meals. For a pleasanter outdoor ambience, try *Bar Restaurant El Bosque*, at 9 de Mayo near Bolívar. Its simple but decent meals are served 8 am to 3 pm. Either of these place will fill you up for under US$2.

Don Angelo's, on 9 de Mayo just south of the Central Plaza, is cheap and open 24 hours. *Chesco Pizzería* (☎ 936 418, 913 786), on Guayas between Sucre and 9 de Octubre, serves good pizzas and has takeout and delivery.

The best hotels (see Mid-Range and Top End under Places to Stay, earlier) have slightly more expensive restaurants, but the food is good.

If you have some spare time, consider heading over to Puerto Bolívar for a fresh seafood lunch.

Getting There & Away

Air TAME (☎ 930 139, 932 710), on Montalvo near Pichincha, has weekday morning flights to Guayaquil that continue to Quito. Afternoon flights are sometimes available. It's cheaper to fly from here to Quito (about US$55) than from Guayaquil if you aren't a resident. Opposite TAME is CEDTA (☎ 921 045, 930 609), which has 10-passenger planes for morning and afternoon flights to Guaya-

quil for about US$15. You can charter planes with them. There are no scheduled weekend services. There is also a new, thrice-weekly flight from Machala to Piura, Peru.

The airport is barely 1km from the town center, and a taxi ride there will cost about US$1. If you are on foot, walk southwest along Montalvo. Note that the airport closes when the weather is rainy or foggy, meaning flights may be delayed.

Bus CIFA goes to the Peruvian border at Huaquillas (US$1.30, 1½hours) every 30 minutes during daylight from the corner of Bolívar and Guayas. These buses go via Santa Rosa and Arenillas (see To/From the Peruvian Border, later in this chapter). Make sure your documents are handy, as there are passport checks en route. You may have to leave the bus to register, but the driver is used to this and will wait for you. Buses with Transportes El Oro, on Rocafuerte between Junín and Tarqui, go only to Santa Rosa.

CIFA buses also go to Guayaquil (US$3, 3½ hours) from its depot on 9 de Octubre near Tarqui. There are several other companies in the area. Rutas Orenses, on 9 de Octubre near Tarqui, has efficient and frequent services to Guayaquil. Ecuatoriana Pullman, 9 de Octubre near Colón, goes there in larger air-conditioned coaches.

Panamericana, at Colón and Bolívar, has large coaches that run daily to Quito (US$7, 11 hours) at 8 am, 8 pm and other times. It also has buses to Santo Domingo, as well as a 6 pm bus all the way to Tulcán. Transportes Occidentales, at Buenavista and Olmedo, has morning, afternoon and night buses to Quito, as well as a night bus to Esmeraldas (US$6.50, nine hours).

Ciudad de Piñas, at Colón and Rocafuerte, has hourly buses from 4:30 am to 7:30 pm to Piñas (US$1.40, two hours).

Cooperative Pullman Azuay, at Sucre at Tarqui, has many buses daily to Cuenca (US$3.50, four hours). A few direct buses take three hours.

Transportes Cooperativa Loja, on Tarqui near Rocafuerte, goes to Loja (US$4.50, six hours) several times a day; ask the driver to set you down at the Puente Nuevo de

Alamor to connect with buses to Puyango. Nearby, Transportes TAC goes to Zaruma (US$2, three hours) from 4 am to 7 pm hourly.

Getting Around
Bus The No 1 bus, which is usually crowded, goes northwest from the central plaza along 9 de Octubre to Puerto Bolívar (US$0.20, 15 minutes). The No 1 bus returns into town along Pichincha and goes southeast as far as the statue of El Bananero, almost 2km from the center.

Car Localiza (☎ 935 455), at the airport, rents cars. Hotel Oro Verde (see Places to Stay, Top End, earlier) also arranges car rental.

A taxi ride to Puerto Bolívar costs under US$2.

PUERTO BOLÍVAR
☎ 07
The international port Puerto Bolívar is 7km from Machala and is that city's maritime outlet for the south coast's banana and shrimp exports. There are some simple but decent seafood restaurants by the waterfront, where you can enjoy a freshly prepared lunch while watching seabirds wheeling overhead and ships sailing by. However, this place is best avoided at night.

The port is protected from the ocean by islands and mangroves. Motorized dugouts can be hired for cruising the mangroves to go bird watching or to go to the nearby island beach at Jambelí (see that section, later).

Getting There & Around
Bus The No 1 bus from Machala's central plaza runs to Puerto Bolívar frequently.

Boat Boats leave Puerto Bolívar for Jambelí at 7 and 9 am and 1 and 3 pm weekdays. Boats return from Jambelí about an hour later. There are many more departures (dependent on passenger demand) on weekends and holidays. The fare for the 20-minute trip is about US$1 per person; you can alternatively hire a boat carrying up to

20 passengers for US$9 to take you from Puerto Bolívar to Jambelí anytime.

Boats can also be hired to take you to other beaches, which offer little shade and, with the exception of Jambelí, are undeveloped (so carry food, drink, sunblock and insect repellent – the mosquitoes can be nasty in the wet season).

JAMBELÍ
☎ 07
This long though rather muddy beach is on the ocean side of the island sheltering Puerto Bolívar. This is the favorite resort of holidaymakers from Machala; it can be (relatively) busy on weekends and completely overcrowded during Carnaval and Semana Santa – but it is not very well developed. There is little shade and abundant mosquitoes in the wet months. If you are a birder, a good reason to visit is to see the wide variety of coastal and pelagic birds and to search for the rufous-necked wood-rail, a rarely seen bird of the mangroves. Boats can be hired. Note that most of the mangroves have been cleared for shrimp farms.

Places to Stay & Eat
There are a couple of cheap and basic places to stay, charging about US$3 per person or less. It's best to call their owners in Machala to make sure it is open. Places include *Las Cabañas del Pescador* (☎ in Machala 937 710) and *Hotel María Sol* (☎ in Machala 937 461). There are plenty of beach-side shacks serving seafood on weekends, but many are closed midweek.

Getting There & Away
See the information given for Puerto Bolívar (earlier). Note that arriving boats drop you off on a canal on the mainland side of the island, and you have to walk a few hundred meters to the beach.

PASAJE
☎ 07
This small town about 25km east of Machala is the capital of its canton and the center of a banana-growing region. It is the last town of any size before the attractive road from

Machala to Cuenca begins to rise into the mountains (see the Cuenca & the Southern Highlands chapter).

Places to Stay

At Bolívar and Olmedo, *Hotel San Martín* (☎ 912 275), has air-conditioned rooms with private bathrooms for about US$6/9. There are a few cheaper places.

ZARUMA
☎ 07

This old gold-mining town is in the mountains southeast of Machala. Now, the gold is almost all worked out, although visits to a mine can be arranged by asking for permission at the *municipalidad* (town hall). Some archaeological ruins have been discovered in the area; people have probably been mining gold here since pre-Columbian times.

The town is small, and the best reasons to visit are to see the century-old architecture (quaint wooden buildings with elaborate balconies) and admire the mountainous views. The nearby towns of Piñas (15km away) and Portovelo (7km away) are also known for gold-mining and can be visited as well.

Places to Stay

The best place in Zaruma is *Roland Hotel* (☎ 972 800), on the outskirts as you arrive from the coast by bus. Rates are US$7/10 for rooms with TV and hot shower.

There is an inexpensive country hotel, *Pedregal*, about 3km outside Zaruma. Roughly 12km north of Zaruma is a good country resort, *Los Rosales de Machay*, which boasts a pool, pretty gardens, a decent restaurant and comfortable doubles for US$20. Take a taxi or drive there.

Getting There & Away

Transportes TAC has frequent buses between Machala and Zaruma (see Getting There & Away under Machala, earlier).

PIÑAS
☎ 07

Piñas is known as a coffee-producing area. In 1980, a new bird species was discovered near here – El Oro parakeet. There are re-

The El Oro species of parakeet was discovered near Piñas in the 1980s.

portedly a couple of orchid collectors who will be happy to show you their plants. The area is hilly; a nearby hilltop with a cross and a good view can be reached on foot or by taxi. Few travelers come to this quiet but pleasant town; it is well off the beaten track.

Places to Stay

The best place in Piñas is the friendly *Residencial Dumari* (☎ 976 118), in the town center; the rooms are clean and cost about US$2 per person, or US$3.50 for rooms with TV and private warm shower. *Hotel Las Orquídeas* (☎ 976 355) is also OK and has a decent restaurant next door.

Getting There & Away

Ciudad de Piñas bus company has frequent buses between Machala and Piñas (see Getting There & Away under Machala, earlier).

EL BOSQUE PETRIFICADO PUYANGO
☎ 07

This small petrified forest became a reserve in 1988 to protect the fossil remains and wildlife of the area. Despite its small size (2659 hectares), Puyango is known for its birds, and over 130 species have been listed – there are undoubtedly more. A bird list should be available at the reserve. The flora and geology is also of great interest, and research is under way in the area. Fossilized Araucaria tree trunks – many of them millions of years old and up to 11m long and 1.6m in diameter – have been found. Various other fossilized trees, ferns and extinct plants are present. This is the largest petrified forest in Ecuador – perhaps in the whole continent.

Puyango is in a valley at about 360m above sea level, some 55km inland from the coast. The valley is separated from the ocean by the Cordillera Larga, which reaches over 900m above sea level. Despite the separation, the area experiences a coastal weather pattern, with warm temperatures and most of the annual 1000mm of rainfall occurring from January to May.

Camping is allowed for a small fee, and a lookout point and trails have been constructed. There is reportedly an information center.

The nearby village of Puyango is composed of some 20 families. There is no hotel as such, although the villagers will find you a bed or floor space if asked. The local people have been taught about the reserve, and some of the locals will act as guides. They'll show you where to see the fossilized trees and give you some ideas about where to look for the local wildlife. Even better, they will tell you about themselves, their interests and their families. The nearest village with basic hostales is Alamor, south of Puyango.

For more information, call the Machala office (☎ 930 012).

Getting There & Away
If you are driving, head from Machala to Arenillas, and from there, continue south through Palmales (22km from Arenillas) and on to Puyango (38km south of Palmales). This road is paved. Alternatively, a road heads west from the Loja-Macará (on the Peruvian border) highway, about halfway between Macará and Catacocha (see the Cuenca & the Southern Highlands chapter). This road goes via Celica and Alamor to Puyango and is less frequently used.

Buses with Transportes Cooperativa Loja leave from Machala and Loja and will enable you to go through Puyango. The service is irregular, but you should be able to get to Puyango from either city within a day if you start in the morning. Alternatively, take a CIFA bus to Arenillas, where you can catch an infrequent local bus to Puyango.

Because Puyango is close to the border, there may be passport checks.

TO/FROM THE PERUVIAN BORDER
☎ 07
It is about an 80km drive from Machala to the border town of Huaquillas – this is the route taken by most overland travelers to Peru. There are two or three passport checks en route, but these take only a minute (assuming your passport is in order). Foreign travelers may have to get off the bus and register their passports at a control booth – the drivers know the routine and will wait for you.

Santa Rosa & Arenillas
The bus to Huaquillas passes through banana and palm plantations, as well as through dusty market towns of Santa Rosa and Arenillas, of which Santa Rosa is the most important. Buses between Machala and Huaquillas pass by frequently.

Places to Stay The following accommodations are all in Santa Rosa. At Vega Dávila and Colón, *Hotel Santa Rosa* (☎ 943 677) charges US$8 for doubles with fan and bath or US$11 for doubles with air-conditioning. *Hotel América* (☎ 943 130), at Colón and El Oro, is slightly cheaper. *Residencial Dos Piños* (☎ 943 338), at Cuenca and Libertad, charges US$3 for a room but caters also to short-stay clients.

Huaquillas
☎ 07
This dusty town (population about 30,000) is of importance only because it is at Ecuador's border with Peru. There is a busy street market by the border, and the place is full of Peruvians shopping on day passes (Ecuador is much cheaper than Peru). It's a bustling but not particularly attractive introduction to Ecuador if you're arriving from Peru. Huaquillas continues across the border into Peru, where it becomes known as Aguas Verdes. The two sides are divided by Río Zarumilla.

Money Banks in Huaquillas or Aguas Verdes do not normally do exchange transactions, so you have to rely on street moneychangers, identified by their black briefcases. However, the new Filanbanco on República at Portovelo, about two blocks from the border crossing, may change money.

If leaving Peru, it's best to get rid of as much Peruvian currency as possible before arriving in Ecuador. If leaving Ecuador, your US currency is easily exchanged in Peru. Check with other travelers going the opposite way for up-to-date exchange rates and currency information.

Traveler's checks can also be exchanged, but with some difficulty – usually, cash is preferred and gets a better rate.

Places to Stay & Eat There are several basic hotels near the border, but most aren't particularly good. Hotels tend to be full by early afternoon with Peruvian shoppers, and you may have to take whatever is available or go to Machala. Most travelers continue on to Machala (or if heading to Peru, they go to Tumbes, which is less than an hour from the border and has plenty of hotels).

For about US$3.50 per person for rooms with bath, *Hotel Rodey* (☎ 907 736), at Teniente Cordovez and 10 de Agosto, is clean and reasonable. *Hotel Gabeli* (☎ 907 149, Teniente Cordovez 311) is just OK at US$1.50 per person for rooms with shared bath or US$2 for rooms with private bath. There are several other cheapies nearby, none salubrious and some catering to short-stay clients.

Hotel Lima (☎ 907 900, 907 794), at Machala and Portovelo and three blocks from the border, is OK at US$4/6 for singles/doubles with bath and fan or US$6/8 with air-conditioning. *Hotel Vanessa* (☎ 907 263, 1 de Mayo 323), about seven blocks from the border, is reasonably quiet and has clean, air-conditioned doubles for US$10.

Getting There & Away There is not a main bus office, but you will see buses on the main street a few blocks from the border. CIFA buses run frequently to Machala (US$1.30, 1½ hours). Panamericana, behind *migraciones* (immigration office), has sev-

eral buses a day to Quito (US$10, 12 hours), some via Santo Domingo and others via Ambato. Ecuatoriana Pullman has frequent buses to Guayaquil (US$4, five hours). A few buses go to Cuenca and Loja.

Crossing the Border
The border is Río Zarumilla, which is crossed by an international bridge. As you enter Ecuador from the bridge, you'll find yourself on the main road, which is crowded with market stalls and stretches out through Huaquillas.

The Ecuadorian migraciones, formerly two blocks from the border, is now inconveniently about 3km from the bridge and is reached by taxi (about US$1.25) – or a bus to Machala can drop you off. All entrance and exit formalities are carried out at this office, which is open 8 am to noon and 2 to 6 pm daily except Sunday, when it closes at 4 pm.

Arriving in Ecuador You first need an exit stamp in your passport from the Peruvian authorities. After walking across the international bridge, take a taxi or Machala-bound bus 3km to the Ecuadorian migraciones office. Entrance formalities are usually straightforward. All tourists need a T3 tourist card, which is available free at the office. If you're not entering as a tourist, you need a student, resident, worker or business visa, which must be obtained from an Ecuadorian embassy (usually the one that serves your home country).

Exit tickets from Ecuador and sufficient funds (US$20 per day) are legally required but are very rarely asked for. You will receive your T3 card (keep it for when you leave) and an identical stamp in your passport allowing you up to a 90-day stay. Instead of 90 days, 30 or 60 days are sometimes given, but it is easy to obtain a renewal in Quito or Guayaquil.

Leaving Ecuador If you are leaving Ecuador, stop at the Ecuadorian migraciones office, 3km from the border, and present your passport and T3 tourist card (the duplicate copy of the small document you filled out on arrival). You will receive an exit stamp in your passport, and the immigration authorities will keep your T3 card. You must have an exit stamp to legally leave (and later re-enter) Ecuador. There are no costs involved. If you have lost your T3 card, you should be able to get a free replacement at the border, assuming that the stamp in your passport has not expired.

Continue on to the border by taxi or take a Machala-Huaquillas bus (no local buses).

As you cross the international bridge, you will be asked to show the exit stamp in your passport to the Ecuadorian bridge guard. On the Peruvian side (called Aguas Verdes), you normally have to show your passport to the bridge guard, but full entrance formalities are carried out in the immigration building about 2km from the border. Taxis and mototaxis are available for about US$0.50 per person.

Most European nationalities, North Americans, Australians and New Zealanders don't need a visa to enter Peru. They and many other nationalities normally just need a tourist card, which is available at the Peruvian immigration office. If you do need a visa, you have to go back to the Peruvian consulate in Machala.

Although an exit ticket out of Peru is officially required, gringo travelers are rarely asked for this unless they look thoroughly disreputable. Other Latin American travelers are often asked for an exit ticket, however, so if you're a non-Peruvian Latin American (or traveling with one), be prepared for this eventuality. If necessary, there is a bus office in Aguas Verdes that sells (nonrefundable) bus tickets out of Peru. The immigration official will tell you where it is.

From the immigration building, shared colectivos (about US$1.50 per person) go to Tumbes – beware of overcharging. Tumbes has plenty of hotels, as well as transportation to take you farther into Peru – see Lonely Planet's *Peru*.

The Galápagos Islands

The Galápagos Archipelago is world famous for its incredibly fearless and unique wildlife. Here, you can swim with sea lions, float eye-to-eye with a penguin, stand next to a blue-footed booby feeding its young, watch a giant 200kg tortoise lumbering through a cactus forest, and try to avoid stepping on iguanas scurrying over the lava. The wildlife is truly phenomenal. The scenery is barren and volcanic and has a haunting beauty all its own – although some find it bare and ugly. A visit to the Galápagos is for the wilderness and wildlife enthusiast – not for the average sunseeker.

Compared to the rest of Ecuador, the Galápagos are very expensive to visit. Flying from Quito and spending a week cruising the islands during the high season will cost at least US$900, even for the most thrifty of budget travelers. You can pay over three times that for the most expensive of the top-end tours. Therefore, the trip is recommended only for those truly interested in wildlife and geology, as there isn't much else to see. However, if you are interested in natural history, visiting the Galápagos will be the highlight of your trip to Ecuador.

Highlights

- Hiking the cliff-top trail on South Plaza – a superb vantage point for watching seabirds
- Walking on uneroded, century-old lava flows on San Salvador
- Climbing to the summit of Bartolomé for a picture-perfect view of the islands
- Snorkeling among playful sea lions

Five of the islands are inhabited. The total population is officially 17,000 people but is certainly higher and growing, and it has at least tripled since the early 1980s. The inhabitants make a living mainly from tourism, fishing and farming. About half the residents live in Puerto Ayora, on Isla Santa Cruz.

Santa Cruz, in the middle of the archipelago, is the most important island from the travelers' point of view. On the south side of this island is Puerto Ayora, the largest town in the Galápagos and the place from which most tours are based. North of Santa Cruz, separated by a narrow strait, is Isla Baltra, which is home to the islands' major airport. A public bus and a ferry connect the Isla Baltra airport with Puerto Ayora (see Getting Around, later in this chapter).

Isla San Cristóbal, the easternmost island, has the provincial capital (Puerto Baquerizo Moreno), a few hotels and an airport. Despite its political status, more tours start from Isla Baltra and Puerto Ayora.

The other inhabited islands are Isla Isabela, with the small port of Puerto Villamil; and Isla Santa María (Floreana), with Puerto Velasco Ibarra – both have places to stay and eat. Infrequent public ferries or private boats provide interisland transportation (see Getting Around, later in this chapter).

The remaining islands are not inhabited by people but are visited on tours. The area code for the entire archipelago is ☎ 05. See the Facts for the Visitor chapter for information on planning your trip and for recommended books about the islands. The full-color Galápagos Wildlife Guide (pages 449–80) will help you to identify and learn something about the islands' animals.

HISTORY

The Galápagos Archipelago was discovered by accident in 1535, when Tomás de Berlanga, the Bishop of Panama, drifted off course while sailing from Panama to Peru. The bishop reported his discovery to King Charles V of Spain and included in his report a description of the giant *galápago* (tortoise), from which the islands received their name.

It is possible that the Indian inhabitants of South America were aware of the islands' existence before 1535, but we have no definite record of this. In 1953, Norwegian explorer Thor Heyerdahl discovered what he thought to be pre-Columbian pottery shards on the islands, but the evidence seems inconclusive.

For more than three centuries after their discovery, the Galápagos were used as a base by a succession of buccaneers, sealers and whalers. The islands provided sheltered anchorage, firewood, water and an abundance of fresh food in the form of the giant Galápagos tortoises, which were caught by the thousands and stacked, alive, in ships' holds. The tortoises could survive for a year or more and thus provided fresh meat for the sailors long after they had left the islands.

The first rough charts of the archipelago were made by buccaneers in the late 17th century, and scientific exploration began in the late 18th century. The Galápagos' most famous visitor was Charles Darwin, who arrived in 1835, exactly 300 years after the Bishop of Panama. Darwin stayed for five weeks, making notes and wildlife collections that provided important evidence for his theory of evolution, which he was just then beginning to develop.

Ecuador officially claimed the Galápagos Archipelago in 1832. For roughly one century thereafter, the islands were inhabited by a few settlers and were used as penal colonies, the last of which was closed in 1959.

Some islands were declared wildlife sanctuaries in 1934, and the archipelago officially became a national park in 1959. Organized tourism began in the late 1960s, and now, an estimated 50,000 to 60,000 people visit the islands each year.

GEOGRAPHY

The Galápagos are an isolated group of volcanic islands that lie in the Pacific Ocean on the equator about 90° west of Greenwich. The nearest mainland is Ecuador, some 1000km to the east, and Costa Rica, almost

HMS *Beagle*, on which Darwin sailed to the Galápagos Islands.

1100km to the northeast. The land mass of the archipelago covers 7882 sq km, of which well over half consists of Isla Isabela, the largest island within the archipelago and the 12th-largest in the South Pacific. There are 13 major islands (ranging in area from 14 sq km to 4588 sq km), six small islands (1 sq km to 5 sq km) and scores of islets, of which only some are named. The islands are spread over roughly 50,000 sq km of ocean. The highest point in the Galápagos is Volcán Wolf (1707m), on Isla Isabela.

Most of the islands have two – sometimes three – names. The earliest charts gave the islands both Spanish and English names, and the Ecuadorian government assigned official names in 1892. An island can thus have a Spanish name, an English name and an official name. The official names are used here in most cases; the few exceptions will be indicated.

GEOLOGY

The earliest of the islands visible today were formed roughly four to five million years ago by underwater volcanoes erupting and rising above the ocean's surface (the islands were never connected to the mainland). The Galápagos region is volcanically very active – over 50 eruptions have been recorded since their discovery in 1535. In 1991, the infrequently visited northern island of Marchena erupted, as did the westernmost large island of Fernandina in 1995, followed by Cerro Azul on Isabela in October 1998.

THE GALÁPAGOS ISLANDS

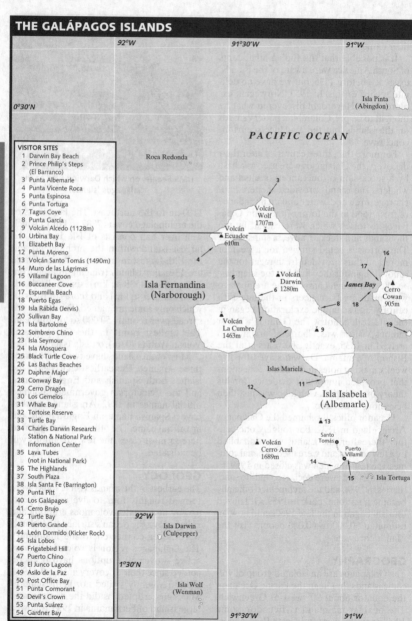

92°W   91°30'W   91°W

0°30'N

PACIFIC OCEAN

Isla Pinta
(Abingdon)

Roca Redonda

VISITOR SITES
1   Darwin Bay Beach
2   Prince Philip's Steps
    (El Barranco)
3   Punta Albemarle
4   Punta Vicente Roca
5   Punta Espinosa
6   Punta Tortuga
7   Tagus Cove
8   Punta García
9   Volcán Alcedo (1128m)
10 Urbina Bay
11 Elizabeth Bay
12 Punta Moreno
13 Volcán Santo Tomás (1490m)
14 Muro de las Lágrimas
15 Villamil Lagoon
16 Buccaneer Cove
17 Espumilla Beach
18 Puerto Egas
19 Isla Rábida (Jervis)
20 Sullivan Bay
21 Isla Bartolomé
22 Sombrero Chino
23 Isla Seymour
24 Isla Mosquera
25 Black Turtle Cove
26 Las Bachas Beaches
27 Daphne Major
28 Conway Bay
29 Cerro Dragón
30 Los Gemelos
31 Whale Bay
32 Tortoise Reserve
33 Turtle Bay
34 Charles Darwin Research
    Station & National Park
    Information Center
35 Lava Tubes
    (not in National Park)
36 The Highlands
37 South Plaza
38 Isla Santa Fe (Barrington)
39 Punta Pitt
40 Los Galápagos
41 Cerro Brujo
42 Turtle Bay
43 Puerto Grande
44 León Dormido (Kicker Rock)
45 Isla Lobos
46 Frigatebird Hill
47 Puerto Chino
48 El Junco Lagoon
49 Asilo de la Paz
50 Post Office Bay
51 Punta Cormorant
52 Devil's Crown
53 Punta Suárez
54 Gardner Bay

Volcán
Wolf
1707m

3

Volcán
Ecuador
610m

4

Isla Fernandina
(Narborough)

5

Volcán
Darwin
1280m

6

7

James Bay

16

17

Cerro
Cowan
905m

18

8

19

Volcán
La Cumbre
1463m

9

10

Islas Mariela

11

12

Isla Isabela
(Albemarle)

13

Santo
Tomás

Volcán
Cerro Azul
1689m

14

Puerto
Villamil

15   Isla Tortuga

92°W

Isla Darwin
(Culpepper)

1°30'N

Isla Wolf
(Wenman)

91°30'W   91°W

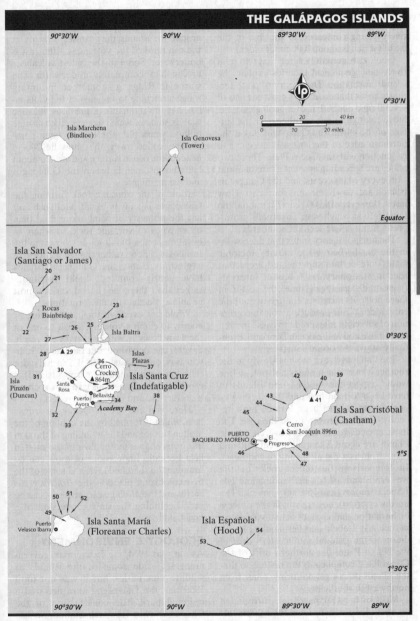

THE GALÁPAGOS ISLANDS

90°30'W   90°W   89°30'W   89°W

0°30'N

0   20   40 km
0   10   20 miles

Isla Marchena
(Bindloe)

Isla Genovesa
(Tower)

1
2

Equator

Isla San Salvador
(Santiago or James)

20
21

Rocas
Bainbridge

23
24

22
27   26   25
28   29   Isla Baltra

0°30'S

36   Islas
Plazas
37

30   Cerro
Crocker
864m

31   Santa
Rosa   35

Isla Pinzón
(Duncan)   Bellavista   34

32   Puerto
Ayora
33   Academy Bay

Isla Santa Cruz
(Indefatigable)

38

42   40   39
44   43   41
45
46   Cerro
San Joaquín 896m

PUERTO
BAQUERIZO MORENO
El
Progreso

Isla San Cristóbal
(Chatham)

48
47

1°S

50   51   52
49
Puerto
Velasco Ibarra

Isla Santa María
(Floreana or Charles)

Isla Española
(Hood)   54
53

1°30'S

90°30'W   90°W   89°30'W   89°W

THE GALÁPAGOS ISLANDS

Thus, the formation of the islands is an ongoing process; the archipelago is relatively young compared to the age of the earth (which is about 1000 times older).

Geologists generally agree that two relatively new geological theories explain the islands' formation. The theory of plate tectonics holds that the earth's crust consists of several rigid plates that, over geological time, move relative to one another over the surface of the earth. The Galápagos lie on the northern edge of the Nazca Plate, close to its junction with the Cocos Plate. These two plates are spreading apart at a rate of about 1km every 14,000 years, and the Galápagos Islands are slowly moving southeast. How fast is 1km every 14,000 years? It's about the same rate at which your fingernails grow – pretty fast by plate-tectonic standards.

The hotspot theory states that deep within the earth (below the moving tectonic plates) are certain superheated areas that remain stationary. At frequent intervals (measured in geological time), the heat from these hotspots increases enough to melt the earth's crust and produce a volcanic eruption of sufficient magnitude to cause molten lava to rise above the ocean floor and, eventually, above the ocean's surface.

The Galápagos are moving slowly to the southeast over a stationary hotspot, so one would expect the southeastern islands to have been formed first and the northwestern islands to have been formed most recently. This has proven to be the case. The most ancient rocks yet discovered on the islands are about 3.25 million years old and come from Isla Española, in the southeast. In comparison, the oldest rocks on the western islands of Isla Fernandina and Isla Isabela are less than 750,000 years old. The northwestern islands are still in the process of formation and contain active volcanoes, particularly Isabela and Fernandina. In addition to the gradual southeastern drift of the Nazca Plate, the northern drift of the Cocos Plate complicates the matter, so that the islands do not get uniformly older from northwest to southeast.

Most of the Galápagos are surrounded by very deep ocean. Less than 20km off the coasts of the western islands, the ocean is over 3000m deep. When visitors cruise around the islands, they can see only about the top third of the volcanoes – the rest is underwater. Some of the oldest volcanoes are, in fact, completely underwater. The Carnegie Ridge, a submerged mountain range stretching to the east of the Galápagos, has the remnants of previous volcanic islands, some of which were as much as nine million years old. These have been completely eroded away; they now lie 2000m beneath the ocean surface and stretch about half the distance between the Galápagos and the mainland.

Most of the volcanic rock forming the Galápagos Islands is basalt. Molten basalt has the property of being more fluid than other types of volcanic rock, so when an eruption occurs, basalt tends to erupt in the form of lava flows rather than in the form of explosions. Hence the Galápagos Islands have gently rounded shield volcanoes rather than the cone-shaped variety most people associate with the formations.

While not every visitor has the time or energy to climb a volcano, a visit to one of the lava flows is within everyone's reach. Several can be visited, but the one at Sullivan Bay, on the east end of San Salvador (also known as Santiago or James Island), is especially rewarding. This lava flow is about a century old and remains uneroded.

Here you can see *pahoehoe*, or 'ropy,' lava, which is formed by the cooling of the molten surface and the wrinkling of the skin into ropy shapes by the flow of the molten lava beneath. Impressions of trees can be found in the solidified lava, and some of the first colonizing plants – the *Brachycereus* cactus and the *Mollugo* carpetweed – can be seen beginning the slow conversion of a lava field to soil.

ECOLOGY & ENVIRONMENT

As early as 1934, the Ecuadorian government set aside some of the islands as wildlife sanctuaries, but it was not until 1959 that the Galápagos were declared a national park. The construction of the Charles Darwin Research Station, on Isla

Santa Cruz, began soon after, and the station began operating in 1964 as an international NGO. (The Galápagos National Park Service began operating in 1968 and is the key institution of the Ecuadorian government responsible for the park. The National Park Service and the Charles Darwin Research Station work together to manage the islands.) In 1986, the Ecuadorian government granted more protection to the islands by creating the Galápagos Marine Resources Reserve.

The national park covers approximately 97% of the total land mass – the rest is taken up by urban areas and farms that existed prior to the creation of the park. The Galápagos Marine Resources Reserve covers the 133,000 sq km of ocean and seabed within which the islands are located, plus a 20,000-sq-km buffer zone. A law that passed in 1998 enables the park and reserve to protect and conserve the islands and surrounding ocean; the law also encourages educational and scientific research while allowing sustainable development of the islands as an Ecuadorian Province.

Tourism

Few tourists had visited the islands before the station opened, but by the mid-1960s, organized tourism began, with a little over 1000 visitors a year. This figure soon increased dramatically. In 1970, an estimated 4500 tourists arrived, and by 1971, there were six small boats and one large cruise ship operating in the islands. In less than two decades, the number of visitors had increased tenfold; in the early 1990s, an estimated 60,000 visited annually. Figures for the late 1990s indicate that approximately 48,000 foreigners and 17,000 mainland Ecuadorians visit annually.

To cope with the increased demands of tourism, a second airport with regular flights to the mainland opened in the mid-1980s, and a third is being discussed. The number of hotels in Puerto Ayora and Puerto Baquerizo Moreno doubled from 15 in 1981 to about 30 a decade later. New hotel growth is now restricted. There are over 80 boats (with sleeping accommodations) carrying four to

Charles Darwin Foundation

Most tourists have the opportunity to visit the Charles Darwin Research Station. Visitors are encouraged to make donations to the organization, which carries out research and advises government and tourist agencies on minimizing the impact of tourism on the islands. (None of the US$100 park fee goes toward the research station.)

Outside of the islands, the research station is supported by contributions to the Charles Darwin Foundation. Donors contributing US$25 or more each year receive the English-language bulletin *La Carta* and the English-language scientific journal *Noticias de Galápagos*. These journals are great for keeping up with the latest happenings on the islands, including information about conservation issues, as well as interesting recent research and unusual wildlife observations.

Donations are tax deductible for citizens of the USA and several European countries. Addresses for donations are easily obtained in the research station and at most boats or hotels in the Galápagos. US citizens may contact the Charles Darwin Foundation at 100 N Washington St, Suite 232, Falls Church, VA 22046, USA. The best source of information about the Charles Darwin foundation and related organizations is at www.galapagos.org.

96 passengers; the majority carry fewer than 20 passengers. The resident population of the islands is growing at about 10% annually to provide labor for the booming tourism industry.

While this is good for the economy of Ecuador, inevitable problems have resulted. Among the more serious are entrepreneurial proposals of building luxurious high-rise hotels and introducing as many more cruise ships into the islands as possible. Fortunately, the Ecuadorian government has seen the sense of preventing these projects.

The wildlife of the Galápagos is unique. The islands have been called 'a laboratory of evolution' and are of immense importance to our understanding of the natural world. The incredible assemblage of wildlife is threatened not only by tourism, but also by the increased colonization that accompanies the booming tourist industry.

Overfishing

The introduction of domestic animals into the islands is only one of various difficulties the archipelago faces. Goats, pigs and rats can become feral and decimate (or cause the extinction of) native species in a few years.

Some islanders who recently arrived see the national park as a barrier to making a living; arson fires set by some newly arrived colonists burned about 10,000 hectares on Isla Isabela in 1994.

Overfishing has been a major problem in recent years. One of the most notorious examples was the taking of a reported seven million sea cucumbers in two months during 1994, after the Ecuadorian government

The Galápagos – Evolution in Action

When the Galápagos were formed, they were barren volcanic islands, devoid of all life. Because the islands were never connected to the mainland, all the species now present must have somehow crossed 1000km of open ocean. Those that could fly or swim long distances had the best chance of reaching the islands, but other methods of colonization were also possible (but more difficult).

Plant seeds or insect eggs and larvae may have been brought over in an animals' stomach contents or attached to the feathers or feet of birds. Small mammals, land birds and reptiles, as well as plants and insects, may have been ferried across on floating vegetation.

Galápagos wildlife is dominated by birds (especially seabirds), sea mammals and reptiles. There are no amphibians, because their moist skin is unable to withstand the dehydrating effect of salt water (although humans have recently introduced a couple of frog species). And, of course, there are plenty of tropical fish and marine invertebrates.

Compared to the mainland, there are few small land mammals and insects. The well-known fearlessness of the islands' animals probably comes from having no large predators to fear – there simply weren't any until pigs, goats, cats and other domesticated animals were introduced by human colonists. Domestic animals that escaped found little competition – now, their offspring is feral and has become a major problem for the islands' native species.

When the first migrating species arrived millions of years ago, they found the islands different from the mainland in two important ways: First, the islands were physically different, and second, there were few other species to compete with. Some colonizers were able to survive, breed and produce offspring. Obviously, the young were the same species as their parents, but some had subtle differences.

A classic Galápagos example of this situation is a bird that produces a chick with a bill that is very slightly different from those of its parents or siblings. In the different environment of the islands, some chicks with slightly different bills are better able to take advantage of the environment. These birds are said to be better adapted and are more likely to survive and raise a brood of their own.

These better-adapted survivors may pass on favorable genetic traits (in this case, a slightly better adapted bill) to their offspring, and thus, over many generations, certain favorable traits are selected for and other less favorable traits are selected against. Eventually, the difference between the original colonizers and their distant descendants is so great that the descendants can be considered a different species altogether. This is the essence of Darwin's theory of evolution by natural selection.

authorized a quota of 550,000. Although sea-cucumber fishing became illegal in December 1994, the Charles Darwin Foundation reports that close to one million sea cucumbers per month continued to be exported in 1995, chiefly for their purported aphrodisiac properties. Other illegal fishing activities include taking shark fins for shark-fin soup, killing sea lions for bait, and over-fishing lobster (the population of which has dropped far below normal numbers) to feed tourists and locals.

Fishermen hoping to make money fast have reacted in a hostile manner to the government ban on fishing for sea cucumbers and other animals. In January and September of 1995, armed fishermen urged on by two unscrupulous local government officials occupied the Charles Darwin Research Station and threatened to kill tortoises, beat up station personnel and burn portions of the park. Fortunately, the tense situation was defused with help from the Ecuadorian military and pressure from the US embassy.

The Galápagos – Evolution in Action

Because the earliest colonizers had little competition and a variety of different habitats to choose from, adaptive changes could occur in different ways to take advantage of different habitats or islands. Thus it wasn't only that a longer or broader or smaller bill would be better adapted – it could be that various types of bills could confer adaptive advantages to birds in different ecological niches. One ancestral species could therefore give rise to several modern species in this evolutionary process, which is called adaptive radiation. This explains the presence in the Galápagos of 13 similar, endemic species of finches – called 'Darwin's finches' in honor of the founder of evolutionary theory.

Charles Darwin, during his visit in 1835, noted the differences in bills in

Charles Darwin

these 13 species of finches; he also noted similar differences in other groups of animals. These observations, combined with many others, led to the 1859 publication of Darwin's On the Origin of Species, which is one of the most influential books ever published and which remains the mainstay of modern biological thought.

These evolutionary processes take thousands or millions of generations – new species don't normally appear over a single generation. For many years, evolutionary biologists were puzzled over how so many unique species could have evolved in the Galápagos over the relatively short period of about four million years (the age of the oldest islands). The answer has recently been provided by the geologists and oceanographers who found nine-million-year-old remnants of islands under the ocean to the east of the existing islands. Presumably, the ancestors of the present wildlife once lived on these lost islands, and therefore had at least nine million years to evolve – a figure that evolutionary biologists find acceptable.

Conservation Efforts

There are various solutions to the problems facing the Galápagos Islands. One extreme view is to prohibit all colonization and tourism – an option that appeals to few. Many colonists act responsibly and actively oppose the disruptive and dangerous tactics of the protesting fishermen. The tourist industry is important for Ecuador's economy, and the best solution is an combination of environmental education for both residents and visitors and a program of responsible tourism.

Management of tourism is an important part of the function of the park service. Various successful programs have been implemented to minimize the impact of tourism on the national park while increasing the tourists' enjoyment and learning. Most visitors understand that these regulations protect the islands as a unique living laboratory.

In 1998, a Special Law for the Galápagos was enacted. It enables 95% of the Visitor Entry Fee (US$100) to be retained by the Galápagos, with 40% going to the park, 40% to local authorities and the rest to other local interests. The 40% for the park is a significant amount – much more than what is collected for mainland parks. Also, the Galápagos Marine Resources Reserve was more than doubled in size.

By law, all tour boats must be accompanied by certified naturalist guides that have been trained by the National Park Service. On the better boats, these are 'Naturalist III Guides' – bilingual, university-educated biologists with a very real interest in preserving and explaining the wildlife. On the cheapest boats, 'Naturalist II Guides' are provided – they speak little English and may know less about the wildlife but will (at least in principle) keep visitors from littering or molesting the wildlife, and they may be able to identify species. Visits to the islands are restricted to the official visitor sites.

There are basically two types of tours around the islands: One goes from island to island, and visitors sleep aboard a boat. The other is hotel-based and goes out to visitor sites on day trips. The first system staggers excursions over different times of day (allowing dawn and dusk visits), and more outlying islands can be reached. The second system, on the other hand, tends to cram large numbers of tourists onto a few nearby destinations around the middle of the day.

Visitors are expected to obey park rules to protect wildlife and the environment; these are mostly a matter of courtesy and common sense. Don't feed or handle the animals; don't litter; don't remove any natural object (living or not); do not bring pets; and do not buy objects made of sea lion teeth, black coral, tortoise or turtle shells, or other artifacts made from plants or animals. You are not allowed to enter the visitor sites after dark or without a qualified guide, and a guide will accompany every boat. On all shore trips, the guide will be there to answer your questions and show you the best sites – and also to ensure that you stay on the trails and follow park rules.

With approximately 65,000 annual visitors, it is essential to have a system of protection for the islands. The rules are sensible and necessary and do not infringe upon your enjoyment of the Galápagos. The wildlife is so prolific that you'll see just as much on the trail as you would anywhere else, and staying on the trails helps ensure that other areas are properly protected.

GETTING THERE & AWAY

Air

TAME operates morning flights daily from Quito via Guayaquil to the Isla Baltra airport, less than two hours away from Puerto Ayora by public transportation (see Getting Around, later). It also has a daily flight from Quito via Guayaquil to San Cristóbal. One flight a week may be cut in the low season, and a second plane might be added in high season.

Flights from Guayaquil cost US$334 roundtrip and last 1½ hours. From Quito, flights cost US$378 roundtrip, and you have to check in again at Guayaquil and possibly board another aircraft. Flights are slightly discounted in the low season, and students with ID can get a discount of 15% with TAME.

Ecuadorian nationals can fly from Guayaquil for half the price foreigners pay, and Galápagos residents pay half that again. Some foreign residents of Ecuador or workers in the islands are also eligible, so if you have a residence visa you should make inquiries. Cheap flights to the islands are very difficult to get unless you are a resident. Nevertheless, rumors about such 'good deals' float around periodically – none are reliable or recommended.

There is a military logistic flight on every other Wednesday that occasionally has room for passengers. Ecuadorians are given priority, but they get cheap flights with TAME anyway, and so there are sometimes seats available for foreigners. Make inquiries at Avenida de la Prensa 3570, a few hundred meters from the Quito airport (ask for Departamento de Operaciones, Fuerza Aerea del Ecuador). Flights go from Quito via Guayaquil and stop at both San Cristóbal and Baltra. Foreigners pay US$284 round-trip for either destination.

Flights to the Galápagos are sometimes booked solid well in advance, but you'll often find that there are many no-shows. Travel agencies book blocks of seats for their all-inclusive Galápagos tours. First they sell them to people taking their tours; they will release the seats on the day of the flight when there is no longer any hope of selling their tour.

If you are tied into a definite itinerary, you should make a reservation; if you're flexible, you can buy your ticket at the airport when you want to fly. You have a better-than-even chance of getting a ticket, and it's unlikely that you'll be turned away two days in a row. During the high season, large cruise ships pick up passengers at Baltra on Monday, Wednesday, Thursday and Sunday – the busiest days. Tuesday is the quietest day to fly.

Some travel agencies will offer you a 'discount' on an airline ticket if you buy their tour of the Galápagos, which is OK if their tour happens to be what you want. Sometimes you can persuade an agency to sell you a discount ticket because they can't fill their tour space.

Fees & Taxes The US$100 Galápagos national-park fee must be paid at one of the airports after you arrive. You will not be allowed to leave the airport until you pay. Cash only is accepted in the islands. Children under 12 and students under 26 with a bona fide student ID card reportedly pay US$50.

Make sure you have your passport available when you pay your fees.

Boat

It's very hard to find boats to the Galápagos.

Cargo ships leave every few weeks and charge about US$150, one way. Conditions are tolerable. The journey to the islands takes about 3½ days, and you should be prepared to bring a sleeping bag or hammock, although a bunk in a cabin may well be available. These ships are mainly for cargo purposes, not for wildlife viewing. If you stay aboard while the boat spends about a week making deliveries around the islands, you are charged about US$50 a day, or you can get off and return later. The most reliable boat is the *Piquero*, which leaves Guayaquil around the 25th of every month. Contact Acotramar (☎ 04-401 004, 401 711, 402 371, 404 314, 404 316, 402 950, fax 444 852), Général Gómez 522 and Coronel, Guayaquil. Johnny Franco is reportedly the best contact there. Also try Transportes Maritimos y Fluviales (TRAMFSA, ☎ 04-566 449), Baquerizo Moreno 1119, office 602. Be prepared to wait weeks for a boat.

The cruise ships described later under Prearranged Boat Tours may put in to Guayaquil for annual maintenance. Occasionally, there is a possibility of taking one on its return to the islands – this is more expensive and more difficult to obtain than taking a cargo ship. September and October are the most likely months for it to happen.

You can travel to the Galápagos in your own boat, but the Ecuadorian authorities don't allow you to cruise the islands without a licensed guide, which must be arranged in advance – a time-consuming process. Most visiting boats will pay a US$35 mooring fee and a US$100 per person park fee; then they take a tour on a Galápagos boat.

GETTING AROUND
To/From Baltra Airport

Most visitors fly to Isla Baltra. Outside the airport, you will be met by a boat representative (if you are on a prearranged tour) and taken by bus on a five-minute drive to the boat dock.

If you are traveling independently, don't take these buses. Instead, take the public bus signed *Muelle* to the dock (a 10-minute ride) for the ferry to Isla Santa Cruz. A 10-minute ferry ride will take you across to Santa Cruz, where you will be met by a bus to take you to Puerto Ayora, about 45 minutes away. This drive (on a paved road) provides a good look at the interior and highlands of Santa Cruz – dry in the north and greener and wetter in the highlands and on the southern slopes. The ferry and second bus are scheduled to coincide with the departure of the first bus from the airport, so there isn't much waiting involved. You should be in Puerto Ayora about an hour after leaving the airport.

The combined bus/ferry/bus trip costs about US$2.50. A ticket booth at the airport sells combined tickets; get yours as soon as you can, as there is normally only one bus (although a second bus may run if there is enough of a demand). The journey is often crowded, and numbered seats are supposedly sold to combat this problem.

Buses from Puerto Ayora to Baltra (via the ferry) leave early every morning that there are flights from Baltra, and again later if there is a second flight. Tickets are sold at the CITTEG office (see the Puerto Ayora map). These same buses return from the airport after the plane from the mainland has landed. A second and third bus will run if there is enough demand.

To/From Puerto Baquerizo Moreno Airport

This airport is a short walk away from hotels and services.

Organized Tours

There are basically three kinds of tours in the Galápagos: day trips returning to the same hotel each night, hotel-based trips staying on different islands, and boat-based trips with nights spent aboard. Once you decide on what kind of tour you want, you can either fly to the islands and find a tour there, or make reservations in advance on the mainland or through a travel agent in your home country. Public transportation around the islands is very limited, so visiting the islands without taking a tour is a waste of time and money.

You can go to almost any island, but it takes time to reach the more outlying ones. It is best to visit a few central islands and inspect them closely rather than trying to cram as many ports of call as possible into your cruise. Interisland cruising takes up valuable time, and you don't see very much while at sea. Boats now have fixed itineraries, so you need to think far ahead if you want a tour that visits a specific island. Most fixed itineraries go to several of the most interesting visitor sites. Make sure you aren't stuck in Puerto Ayora for more than one night at the most.

One Hotel Although day trips are usually based in Puerto Ayora, a few operators now work out of Puerto Baquerizo Moreno, but their trips are more expensive and choices are limited. A typical day trip begins at dawn, with either a walk down to the dock or a bus ride across the island to meet a boat at the north side of Santa Cruz. Several hours are spent sailing to the day's visitor site(s), which you'll visit during the middle of the day with a large group. Only a few central islands are close enough to be visited on day trips.

Because a lot of time is spent going back and forth, the downside of this kind of tour is that there is no chance of visiting the islands early or late in the day. The cheapest boats may be slow and overcrowded; their island visits may be too brief; the guides may be poorly informed; and the crew may be lacking an adequate conservationist attitude. Therefore, the cheapest day trips are not recommended. Nevertheless, day trips are useful for people who cannot stand the idea of sleeping in a small rocking boat at night.

There are plenty of day-trip operators in Puerto Ayora who charge around US$40 per person per day. The one you choose will depend on which destinations they offer. Ask other travelers about the quality of the guides and boats of the local agencies.

Better and more expensive day trips – using fast boats with knowledgeable guides and staying in good hotels – can be arranged on the mainland. These trips are normally booked as a series of day trips lasting a week; they give a greater choice of islands to visit and are OK if you must take day trips. Prices range from US$700 to over US$1000 per week, including guided trips, hotel and meals, but not airfare or park fee. Book through Metropolitan Touring (see Travel Agencies in the Quito & Around chapter), which uses Hotel Delfín in Puerto Ayora, or through Hotel Galápagos and Red Mangrove Inn (both in Puerto Ayora, covered later in this chapter).

Multiple Hotels These tours go from island to island, and you sleep in hotels on three or four different islands (Santa Cruz, San Cristóbal, Floreana, Isabela). Tours typically last a week and cost US$700 to over US$1000 per person, plus airfare and park fee. However, few companies offer this kind of tour. Ask the agencies in Quito until you find one that does. This kind of tour may be possible to arrange more cheaply in Puerto Ayora, but again, only a few boats do this. Red Mangrove Inn (see Places to Stay under Puerto Ayora, later in this chapter) arranges trips, mixing both hotel nights on different islands with some nights aboard a boat.

Boat Tours Most visitors (non-Ecuadorians in particular) tour the Galápagos on boat tours, sleeping aboard the boat. Tours can last from three days to three weeks, although tours lasting from four to eight days are the most common. I don't think you can do the Galápagos justice on a tour lasting less than a week, but five days is just acceptable. If you want to visit the outlying islands of Isabela and Fernandina, a 10-day or two-week cruise is recommended. On the first day of a tour, you arrive from the mainland

---

Land Ho!

Almost all Galápagos visitor sites are reached by boat, and normally landings are made in a *panga* (small dinghy), which every boat carries for shore trips (the larger boats carry several). Most landing sites are sandy or rocky beaches – there are few docks. Landings are called 'wet' or 'dry.' During a wet landing, you will have to wade ashore in shallow water – sometimes up to your knees (occasionally deeper if you don't pay attention to your guide and what the waves are doing). Dry landings are made onto rocky outcrops or jetties – you probably won't get wet unless a rogue wave comes up and splashes you, or unless you slip on some seaweed and fall into the ocean (it happens).

---

by air at about lunchtime, so this is only half a day in the Galápagos, and on the last day, you have to be at the airport in the morning. Thus, a five-day tour gives only three full days in the islands. Shorter tours are advertised, but with the travel time at either end, they are not recommended.

Boats used for tours range from small yachts to large cruise ships. By far the most common type of boat is the motor sailer (a medium-sized motor boat), which carries eight to 20 passengers.

It is customary to tip the crew at the end of a trip. A tip may be anywhere between US$20 and US$50 per passenger per week, depending on the quality and cost of the tour. On an exceptionally good boat, you might tip more than US$50; on some of the cheapest boats, passengers tip less than US$20. The total tip is divided among the crew; the guide (if an experienced bilingual naturalist) may get as much as half (less for non-English-speaking guides who know little natural history). The cook and captain both get larger portions than the other crew members. Passengers should do the dividing – giving the money to one crew member and having that person deal with it is asking for complaints from other crew members.

Arranged Locally Most people arrive at the islands with a prearranged tour, although shoestringers come hoping to hook up with a tour when they get there. It's a bit cheaper to arrange a tour for yourself in Puerto Ayora than to pay for a prearranged tour from the mainland. Only the cheaper boats are available in the Galápagos; the better boats are almost always booked. Therefore, don't fly to the Galápagos hoping to get on a really good boat for less money – it rarely works that way.

Flying to the Galápagos and arranging a tour is not uncommon, but neither is it as straightforward as it sounds. It can take several days – sometimes a week or more. This is not an option for people with a limited amount of time, nor for people wanting a very comfortable boat. It is, however, a reasonable option for those with extra time and limited funds.

The best place to organize a tour for yourself is from Puerto Ayora. It is sometimes possible to do this in Puerto Baquerizo Moreno, but there are fewer boats available.

After arrival in Puerto Ayora, first find somewhere to sleep (especially during the high season, when the choice of rooms may

be limited), and then start looking for a boat. If you are alone or with a friend, you'll need to find more people, as even the smallest boats take no fewer than four passengers. There are usually people in Puerto Ayora looking for boats, and agencies (see Puerto Ayora, later) can help in putting travelers and boats together.

Finding boats in August and around Christmas and Easter is especially difficult. The less busy months have fewer travelers on the islands, but boats are often being repaired or overhauled at this time, particularly in October. Despite the caveats, travelers who arrive in Puerto Ayora looking for a boat can almost always find one within a week (often in just a few days) if they work at it. Some travelers have said that this method sucks – by the time they pay for hotels and meals in Puerto Ayora, they don't save anything. Others have said they enjoyed the adventure of hanging out in Puerto Ayora and waiting to see what happened.

The cheapest and most basic boats are available for about US$50 per person per day, which should include everything except park fees, alcohol and tips. The cheaper the boat, the more rice and fish you can expect to eat, and the more crowded the accommodations. A few boats even charge for bottled water. Check this before you leave.

Boats will not sail unless all passenger berths are taken or at least paid for – empty spots add to group space, and comfort doesn't come cheap. Bargaining over the price is acceptable and sometimes necessary.

Conditions on the cheapest boats can be cramped and primitive. Ask about washing facilities – they can vary from deck hoses on the cheapest boats to communal showers on the better boats and private showers in more expensive boats. Also inquire about water – on the cheaper boats, you may need to bring your own large containers of water. Bottled drinks are carried but cost extra – agree on the price before you leave, and make sure that enough beer and soda is loaded aboard. There's nothing to stop you from bringing your own supply.

Cruising aboard the *Albatros*

[Continued on page 481]

THE GALÁPAGOS ISLANDS

DAVID PEEVERS

Birds

There are 58 resident bird species on the Galápagos, of which 28 are endemic. An additional half-dozen regular migrants are frequently seen, and about 25 other migratory species are regularly, but not frequently, recorded. Several dozen other species are accidental and are rarely recorded.

Many people are confused about the difference between resident, migrant and endemic species. A resident species lives and breeds on the island year-round but may also be found in other parts of the world. A migrant is found on the island for only part of the year. An endemic species is a resident that does not normally breed anywhere else in the world (except in captivity or by accident).

Seabirds are the birds that make the strongest impression on most visitors. Amusing, spectacular and highly in evidence, the seabirds of the Galápagos will turn everyone into a bird watcher.

During a week of touring the islands, most careful observers will see about 40 species of birds. If two weeks are spent and some of the more outlying islands are visited, more than 50 birds can be recorded, particularly during the northern winter, when migrants are present. Even the most casual visitor will see 20 to 30 species. Enjoy your observations!

The birds described in this section are listed by family in standard taxonomic order. Colloquial Spanish names (sometimes there is more than one, and different names may be used in other Latin American countries) and scientific names are included. Uncommon migrants and accidentals are mentioned in passing but not described. A checklist for the 58 resident birds plus six common migrants is provided on page 508.

Bottom: The Galápagos penguin: shaky on shore but wicked in the water

Penguins (Spheniscidae)

The penguin family is found exclusively in the southern hemisphere. Most penguins are associated with the colder regions of the hemisphere, but the cool Humboldt current flowing from Antarctica along the South American coast enables the **Galápagos penguin** (pingüino de Galápagos; *Spheniscus mendiculus*) to live here. The Galápagos species is therefore the most northerly penguin in the world, and it is one of five endemic seabirds in the islands.

Although the Galápagos penguins normally breed in the western part of Islas Isabela and Fernandina, a small colony is often seen by visitors to Isla Bartolomé. They are occasionally present on Floreana or Santiago (across from the Sombrero Chino visitor site). Breeding can occur year-round, and two broods a year are possible under good conditions. Colonies are small and not tightly packed with nests.

ROB RACHOWIECKI

The clumsiness of penguins on land belies their skill and speed underwater. The best way to appreciate this is to snorkel with them – it is great fun, and you'll quickly realize how impossible it is to keep up with an underwater penguin!

Albatrosses (Diomedeidae)

Only one member of this family is a Galápagos resident, but a couple of other species have been recorded.

One of the world's most magnificently graceful flying birds is the **waved albatross** (albatros ondulado; *Diomedea irrorata*), which can spend years at sea without touching land. It is the largest bird in the islands – it averages 86cm in length, can weigh as much as 5kg and can have a wingspan as long as 240cm. Apart from a few pairs that have bred on Isla de la Plata (off the north coast of the mainland), the entire world population of some 12,000 pairs nests on Isla Española. Egg laying occurs mid-April to late June, and the colonies are active with parents feeding their single young through December. When the fledged bird finally leaves the nest, it does not return for four or five years. From January to March, all the birds are at sea.

Top: Waved albatrosses in a courtship display

Bottom, left to right: Audubon's shearwater, dark-rumped petrel

The waved albatross engages in one of the most spectacular ritualized courtship displays of any bird. Courtship tends to occur in the second half of the breeding season – especially during October. The display lasts up to 20 minutes and involves perfectly choreographed bowing, bill-clicking, bill-circling, swaying-and-freezing, honking and whistling – it is one of the most memorable sights of the Galápagos.

ROB RACHOWIECKI

True Petrels & Shearwaters (Procellariidae)

Eight members of this family have been recorded in the Galápagos. The **dark-rumped petrel** (petrel lomioscuro, pata pegada; *Pterodroma phaeopygia*) and the **Audubon's shearwater** (pardela de Audubon; *Puffinus lherminieri*) are the only residents and are frequently seen.

The dark-rumped petrel is also called the Hawaiian petrel – in Hawai'i, it is in danger of extinction because of introduced predators. It is also endangered in the Galápagos but is better protected here. The Audubon's shearwater is widespread in tropical waters around the globe. Both species breed in the Galápagos, but they are most frequently seen feeding at sea.

The birds are quite similar at first glance – both have black upperparts and white underparts. The dark-rumped petrel is 43cm long and has a wingspan of over 90cm – it is much larger than the more common shearwater, which has a length of 30cm and a wingspan of less than 70cm. Also, the petrel has a white cap, while the shearwater is entirely black on top.

These features are difficult to pick out when the birds fly by 100m from your boat.

The best way to tell these birds apart when you see them at sea is by their flight. The petrel characteristically glides over the ocean in a series of swoops and banks, displaying its contrasting black-and-white body surfaces. It is more likely to be seen far out at sea, where it feeds on fish and squid. Shearwaters skim the waves more directly, without the diagnostic swoops and banks of the petrel. The shearwaters are most likely to be seen closer to shore, feeding on small crustaceans and fish larvae.

Storm Petrels (Hydrobatidae)

The Galápagos has eight recorded and three commonly seen species of storm petrels, which are among the smallest of seabirds. The largest is only 20cm long and has a wingspan of 30cm – about the size of a swallow. Their diminutive size distinguishes storm petrels from true petrels and shearwaters. These birds, which are dark with a white rump, are locally called *golondrinas del mar,* which literally means 'swallows of the sea.'

The three commonly seen species are distinguished by the differences in the shape of the white area – a task for an experienced bird watcher or a good naturalist guide. They feed by grabbing scraps from the surface of the sea, which makes them look as if they are walking on water. The **white-vented (Elliot's) storm petrel** (paíño gracil; *Oceanites gracilis*), in particular, is often seen looking for food around anchored boats. Breeding colonies of the white-vented storm petrel have yet to be discovered.

The **wedge-rumped (Galápagos) storm petrel** (paíño de Galápagos; *Oceanodroma tethys*) and the **band-rumped (Madeiran) storm petrel** (paíño lomibandeado; *O. castro*) breed in huge colonies on Isla Genovesa. These colonies are estimated to number in the hundreds of thousands, but not much is known about them.

Tropicbirds (Phaethontidae)

The unmistakable **red-billed tropicbird** (rabijunco piquirrojo, piloto; *Phaethon aethereus*) is one of the most spectacular Galápagos seabirds. The most noticeable feature of this splendid white bird is its pair of tail streamers – these two feathers are often as long as the body. The birds are 76cm long (including tail feathers) and have a wingspan of just over 1m. They are extremely graceful in the air and often fly by in small groups, uttering a distinctive and piercing shriek. The coral-red bill and black eye stripe are noticeable at closer range. The birds nest in cliff crevices or

Top, clockwise from left: White-vented (Elliot's) storm petrel, tail of band-rumped (Madeiran) storm petrel, tail of wedge-rumped (Galápagos) storm petrel

Bottom: Nesting red-billed tropicbird

ROB RACHOWIECKI

rock piles on most of the islands, but they are most frequently seen from trails that follow cliff tops, such as on South Plaza, Genovesa and Española. They feed far out to sea, plunge diving for fish and squid.

Pelicans (Pelecanidae)

Pelicans have wide fingered wings and are good gliders. They are often seen flying in a squadronlike formation, flapping and gliding in unison to create an elegant aerial ballet.

The **brown pelican** (pelícano pardo; *Pelecanus occidentalis*) is instantly recognizable because of its huge pouched bill and large size (122cm long with a 2m wingspan), and it is often the first bird the visitor identifies. It feeds by shallow plunge diving and scoops up as much as 10L of water in its distensible pouch. The water rapidly drains out through the bill, and the trapped fish are swallowed. It sounds straightforward, but apparently, it isn't. Although parents raise frequent broods of two or three chicks, many of the fledged young are unable to learn the scoop-fishing technique quickly and thus starve to death.

Top: Nesting brown pelican

Bottom: Blue-footed boobies in a courtship display – note the larger pupil of the female, on the right

As the name suggests, these pelicans are generally brownish in color. During the breeding season, however, the adults acquire bright white and chestnut markings on their heads and necks. They nest year-round in most of the islands.

Boobies (Sulidae)

Four species of booby have been recorded, and three of them breed in the islands. Although not endemic, they are still among the most popular with visitors. It is easy to understand why – their appearance is amusing, and their colonies are among the most approachable. You can often get within a few feet of an active nest, which means great photographs. The boobies are in the same family as gannets and look very much like them; they are fast fliers and exceptional plunge divers. Punta Pitt, on San Cristóbal, is the only visitor site where all three species can be seen together.

The **blue-footed booby** (piquero patas azules; *Sula nebouxii*) is perhaps the most famous Galápagos bird and is often the first booby seen by visitors. Large active colonies on Seymour and Española are occupied throughout the year. The big, whitish-brown seabird (74cm to 89cm long with a wingspan of about 1.5m) really does have bright-blue feet, which it picks up in a slow, most-dignified fashion when performing a courtship display. Bowing, wing spreading and sky pointing (with the neck, head and bill stretched straight upward) are also features of courtship. Watching this clownish behavior is one of the highlights of any trip to the Galápagos. At first glance, the males and females

are almost identical, but you can tell them apart: the larger females have slightly bigger pupils and make honking noises, whereas the males whistle. Courtship, mating and nesting occur year-round – although the nest is actually just a scrape on the ground surrounded by a ring of guano. The young – of which there may be one, two or three – are covered with fluffy white down, which can make them look larger than their parents. In a good year, all three may survive – otherwise, the weakest will die of starvation.

The **masked booby** (piquero enmascarado, piquero blanco; *S. dactylatra*) is pure white with a black band at the edges of the wings and the end of the tail. The face mask that gives the bird its name is formed by a blackish area of bare skin surrounding the bill, which can be yellow or pinkish. It is the biggest of the Galápagos boobies (76cm to 89cm long with a wingspan of 152cm to 183cm). This booby is found on most of the islands. Males and females look the same, but their calls differ – the smaller males whistle, while the females utter a trumpeting quack. They often nest near cliff tops to give themselves an advantage when taking off, as they are large birds. Two eggs are laid, but the older sibling ejects the younger from the nest, and only one survives – even in a good year with plenty of food. Breeding is on an annual cycle (unlike the other boobies), but the cycle varies from island to island. On Isla Genovesa, the birds arrive in May; then courtship, mating and nest building ensue, and eggs are laid August to November. Most of the young have fledged by February, and then the colony is out at sea again until May. On Española, the colony is present September to May, and egg laying occurs November to February.

Top: Masked boobies in a courtship display

Bottom: Red-footed booby

The **red-footed booby** (piquero patas rojas; *S. sula*) is the smallest of the Galápagos boobies (74cm long with a wingspan of 137cm) and is readily distinguished by its red feet and its blue bill with a red base. Most adults are brown, but about 5% are white – this is a different color phase and does not represent a new, different or hybrid species. The red-footed booby is the most numerous of the Galápagos boobies, but it is also the least frequently seen; this is because it is found only on the more outlying islands, such as Genovesa, where there is a sizable colony estimated at 140,000 pairs. It feeds far out to sea and thus avoids competing with the blue-footed booby, which feeds close inshore, and with the masked booby, which feeds intermediately. The nesting behavior of this booby is quite different from the others. It builds rudimentary nests in trees (other boobies build guano-ringed scrapes on the ground) and lays only one egg. This can occur at any time of the year – usually when food is plentiful.

JEFF WILLIAMS

ROB RACHOWIECKI

Cormorants (Phalacrocoracidae)

Apart from the penguins, there is only one other flightless seabird found in the world – the **flightless**

cormorant (cormorán no volador; *Nannopterum harrisi*), which is endemic to the Galápagos. At about 90cm long, it is the tallest of the world's 29 species of cormorant and is the only one that has lost its ability to fly. It is found only on the coasts of Isabela and Fernandina.

To see this unique bird, you should plan on a two-week tour. If you think that is a long time, consider how long it must have taken for this cormorant to evolve into a flightless bird. Its ancestors were almost certainly able to fly, but when they reached the Galápagos, they found no predators in the rocky inshore shallows where they fed. Therefore, they didn't need wings to flee, and the cormorants that survived the best were the streamlined ones that could swim and dive strongly in the surf of the shallows. Thus, birds with small wings and strong legs had an advantage, and through natural selection, the flightless cormorant evolved.

Flightless cormorants nest in small colonies, and there are only about 700 to 800 pairs of birds in existence. That number dropped to 400 to 500 pairs after the disastrous El Niño year of 1982–83, although they have since recovered. Flightless cormorants are not endangered, but they could become so if predatory feral animals (especially wild dogs) are introduced into the islands where they breed.

The birds can breed year-round, although March to September is favored for egg laying. Unlike most seabirds, the adults do not mate for life – a female may leave a brood for the father to raise while she mates with another male, meaning a female may have two broods in a year.

Frigatebirds (Fregatidae)

These seabirds make an acrobatic living by aerial piracy, often harassing smaller birds into dropping or regurgitating their catch and then swooping to catch their stolen meal in midair. This occurs because frigatebirds have a very small preening gland and are not able to secrete enough oils to waterproof their feathers – therefore, they cannot dive underwater to catch prey. They are, however, able to catch fish on the surface by snatching them up with their hooked beaks. With their 230cm wingspan, the birds are magnificent fliers and have the largest wingspan-to-weight ratio of any bird.

As with many Galápagos seabirds, the frigatebird courtship display is quite spectacular. The males have flaps of bright-red skin hanging under their necks that are inflated into football-sized balloons to attract

Top: The endemic flightless cormorant is found only on Isabela and Fernandina.

females. It takes about 20 minutes for the pouch to inflate fully, and the male normally sits on a tree and displays himself skyward to passing females. Occasionally, a male is seen flying overhead with his pouch still distended – a strange sight.

There are two frigatebird species in the Galápagos: the **magnificent frigatebird** (fragata magna; *Fregata magnificens*) and the **great frigatebird** (fragata grande; *Fregata minor*). They are not easy to tell apart – both are large, elegant and streamlined black seabirds with long, forked tails.

North Seymour Island has a constantly active magnificent frigatebird colony and is the place where most people get a good look at these birds. There are also colonies on many of the other islands. Great frigatebirds tend to go farther out to sea and are found more often on the outer islands; recommended locations are Isla Genovesa and Punta Pitt (on Isla San Cristóbal). The males of both species are all black and are difficult to differentiate, but the magnificent frigatebird, at 107cm in length, is about 5cm longer than the great frigatebird. (This is almost impossible to discern in the field.) Also, the male magnificent has a metallic purplish sheen to its black plumage, while the great has a greenish sheen (this also takes an experienced eye to distinguish).

Females are easier to tell apart. Magnificent females have white underparts with a black throat and also have a thin blue eye ring. Great females have white underparts, including the throat, and have a reddish eye ring. Once you identify the females, you can assume that their mates are of the same species. Immature birds of both species, in addition to their white underparts, have white heads.

ROB RACHOWIECKI

Herons & Egrets (Ardeidae)

This family has five resident species in the islands, and three other species have been recorded. There is controversy among ornithologists about the naming and classification of some of these birds.

The **great blue heron** (garzón azulado, garza morena; *Ardea herodias*) is the largest heron in the Galápagos (138cm long with a wingspan of almost 2m) and will be familiar to visitors from North and Central America. Despite its name, it is a mostly gray bird. It is easily recognizable because of its long legs and great size. Like many members of this family, it often stands with its head hunched into its

ROB RACHOWIECKI

Facing page
Top: Male frigatebird with an inflated pouch

Middle: Female great frigatebird

Bottom: Adult male great frigatebird (left) with young

shoulders, and it always flies that way, with its legs trailing behind. Great blue herons are found along the rocky coasts of most of the islands, often standing motionless as they wait for a fish to swim by, although they will also eat lizards, young marine iguanas and birds. They tend to be solitary or in pairs, but they occasionally form a small colony of up to six nests. They breed year-round and often nest in mangroves.

The **common egret** (garceta grande, garza blanca; *Casmerodius albus*) is also known as the great egret or the American egret. The scientific name of *Egretta alba* has also been assigned to this bird. It is a large (102cm long with a wingspan of 137cm), all-white heron with a yellow bill and black legs and feet. It is less common than the great blue heron but is found in similar habitats and occasionally inland.

This page
Top left: Great blue heron

Top right: Common egret

Bottom: The lava heron, the only endemic heron in the Galápagos

The small, white **cattle egret** (garcilla bueyera; *Bubulcus ibis*) is distinguished from the common egret by its shorter neck, stockier appearance and yellow legs. It is 51cm long and has a wingspan of 91cm. This bird came originally from Africa and southern Eurasia and was unknown in the Americas until the 19th century. It was first recorded in the Galápagos in 1965 and is now common in pasturelands, especially in the highlands of Isla Santa Cruz.

The small **lava heron** (garcilla de lava, garza verde; *Butorides sundevalli*) is the only endemic heron in the Galápagos. It is 41cm long with a wingspan of 64cm, and its dark-green plumage camouflages it well against the lava shorelines, where it stealthily hunts for prey. It has

yellow-orange legs and breeds year-round, although September to March is the preferred time. Immature birds are brown and streaked. Lava heron nests are usually solitary (although there occasionally are groups in twos and threes) and are found under a lava outcrop or in mangrove trees. The herons are common on the rocky shores of all the islands, but because of their camouflage and solitary nature, they are a little difficult to see. Your naturalist guide should be able to show you one with no problem.

The **striated heron** *(B. striatus)* is about the same size but is paler than the lava heron. Ornithologists are uncertain whether the lava heron is simply a variety of the striated heron, a hybrid or a distinct species.

The common **yellow-crowned night heron** (garza nocturna, garcilla coroniamarilla; *Nyctanassa violacea*) tends to feed at night, but it can often be seen during the day in shaded areas along the coasts of all the islands. It is a stocky, gray heron with a black-and-white head and a yellow crown. It is 61cm long and has a wingspan of 117cm. Because of its nocturnal habits, its eyes are larger than the eyes of other herons. These herons breed in single pairs and build nests year-round in mangroves or under rocks.

Flamingos (Phoenicopteridae)

These large, long-necked, pink shorebirds are immediately recognizable. Only one species is found in the Galápagos. The wing feathers of the **greater flamingo** (flamenco; *Phoenicopterus ruber*) are black, and the birds look spectacular in flight with their long necks stretched out, their legs trailing. They are nervous birds, particularly when they are nesting, and visitors should act quietly when viewing flamingos, or the birds may desert their nests.

Greater flamingos, which are 122cm long with a wingspan of 152cm, breed in small colonies in salty lagoons. They build cone-shaped nests out of mud and lay a single egg in a depression at the top of the nest. They can breed year-round but prefer moist conditions, and so most breeding takes place in the wet season (January to May). There are commonly visited flamingo lagoons on Islas Floreana, Rábida and Santiago.

Flamingo feeding behavior is mildly bizarre – they feed by dangling their long necks into the water and swinging their upside-down heads from side to side. Water is sucked in through the front of their highly specialized bill and filtered through sieves before being expelled through the sides of the bill. Food consists of insects, small crabs, shrimp and other crustaceans – the pinkish color of the shrimp maintains the color of the birds' plumage.

Ducks & Geese (Anatidae)

Three species of ducks have been recorded in the Galápagos, but only one breeds there. If you see a

duck in the Galápagos, it is usually the **white-cheeked pintail** (patillo, anade cariblanco; *Anas bahamensis*), which breeds in small numbers on salt lagoons and ponds on most of the major islands. It can be seen year-round.

Hawks (Accipitridae)

The endemic **Galápagos hawk** (gavilán de Galápagos; *Buteo galapagoensis*) is the only raptor that breeds in the islands. It is 56cm long with a 122cm wingspan, and it has much broader wings than seabirds of a comparable size. The birds are dark brown with yellow legs, feet and ceres (the fleshy area at the base of the bill). Immature birds are lighter and heavily mottled.

These predatory birds have no natural enemies and are relatively fearless. This has led to their extinction by hunters on several islands, including Floreana, San Cristóbal, Seymour, Baltra, Genovesa and Daphne. They have been severely reduced on Santa Cruz, and just over a hundred pairs are estimated to remain in the Galápagos. Islas Santiago, Bartolomé, Española, Santa Fe, Fernandina and Isabela are the best islands on which to see them.

Breeding occurs year-round but is most frequent from May to July. The birds practice cooperative polyandry, in which a single female has two or more mates, and all the adults help in raising the young. It is not easy to separate the sexes, but the female is generally larger than the males.

Apart from the hawks, ospreys (Pandionidae) and peregrine falcons (Falconidae) visit occasionally.

Rails, Crakes & Gallinules (Rallidae)

The three Galápagos species of this family are common but are rarely seen because they are small and secretive. The tiny (15cm long) endemic **Galápagos rail** (pachay, polluela de Galápagos; *Laterallus spilonotus*) scurries around in the vegetation of the highlands, particularly on Santa Cruz and Santiago. It is dark with white spots on its wings. It rarely flies and escapes by running.

The slightly larger (20cm long) **paint-billed crake** (gallareta, polluela pinta; *Neocrex erythrops*) is similar to the rail but lacks white wing spots and has red legs and a red-and-yellow bill. The crake also dislikes flying. It is associated with farmlands, particularly on Santa Cruz and Floreana. It was first recorded in the islands in 1953.

The **common gallinule** (gallinula, gallareta común; *Gallinula chloropus*) is a 35cm-long chickenlike waterbird; it is also called the common moorhen. It is black with a red-and-yellow bill, yellow legs and a white patch under the tail. It lives on a few ponds and brackish areas of water in all the larger islands except Santiago. When swimming, it pumps its head back and forth.

Oystercatchers (Haematopodidae)

The **American oystercatcher** (ostrero americano, cangrejero; *Haematopus palliatus*) is an unmistakable 46cm-long black-and-white shorebird with a stout red 8cm-long bill, pink feet and yellow eyes. Although there are only between 100 and 200 pairs in the islands, they are spread out along the rocky coasts, and you are likely to see them on many of the islands. The first sign of their presence is often their repetitive, high-pitched call, described as 'kleep' in some birding books.

They nest mainly from October to March and are solitary nesters. One or two precocial young are hatched and join their parents within a few minutes.

Plovers (Charadriidae)

Plovers are small, compact wading shorebirds that tend to run in short bursts. Their bills are generally short and pigeonlike. Six or seven species have been recorded in the Galápagos; all are migrants. The two most common species sometimes remain year-round in small numbers.

The **semi-palmated plover** (chorlitejo semipalmado; *Charadrius semipalmatus*) is 18cm long and is mainly brown on top except for a white collar, forehead and stripe above the eye. Underneath it is white except for a brown chest band. Breeding birds may have a black band and head. The base of the bill is orange, and the legs are yellowish. It is most commonly seen on sandy beaches from August to April.

Bottom: American oystercatchers are often heard before they're seen.

ROB RACHOWIECKI

Whimbrel

Top: Semi-palmated plover

Middle: Groups of sanderlings are often seen flitting along the shoreline.

Bottom: Whimbrel

The 23cm-long **ruddy turnstone** (vuelve-piedras rojizo; *Arenaria interpres*) is found on rocky coasts, where it feeds, as its name suggests, by turning over small stones in search of prey. It is commonly found August to March. The ruddy turnstone has a brown back and a white chin and throat; underneath, it is white with a brownish breast patch. In breeding plumage (not often seen in the Galápagos), it has a black-and-white patterned head and chest and a bright-russet back. Its legs are orange. Some authorities suggest that the turnstones are sandpipers, not plovers.

Sandpipers (Scolopacidae)

Sandpipers are an extremely varied family of shorebirds. Most are waders, and they generally have longer necks and beaks and are slimmer than the plovers. Some 22 species have been recorded from the Galápagos – all of them are migrants that breed in the northern hemisphere. The four species described in this section are commonly seen August to April; a few individuals remain year-round.

The 25cm-long **wandering tattler** (correlimos vagabundo; *Heteroscelus incanus*) is the most frequently seen migrant but is rather nondescript. It is dark brownish-gray on top and on its breast, and it has a white belly and yellowish-green legs. It prefers rocky shores.

The common, 20cm-long **sanderling** (correlimos arenero; *Calidris alba*) is the palest of the small Galápagos waders. These birds prefer sandy beaches, where they run along the wave fronts like a flock of clockwork toys. They have light-gray backs, dark wingtips and white underparts. The legs and bill are dark. In breeding plumage, the head and upperparts are a rusty brown.

The **whimbrel** (zarapito trinador; *Numenius phaeopus*) is a common wader about 43cm long with a characteristic down-curved bill that is up to 10cm long. The dark legs are also long – 'long' is the operative word in identifying this shorebird. It has a mottled gray-brown plumage and light and dark stripes through the head. Unlike most other waders, it shows no wing patterns in flight.

The **northern phalarope** (falaropo picofino; *Phalaropus lobatus*), which is also called the red-necked phalarope, swims rather than wades and may be seen way out at sea in 'rafts' of hundreds of birds. These 18cm-long birds have white underparts and a blackish back with a pair of whitish longitudinal streaks. There is a conspicuous white wing bar in flight, and the bill is very thin.

Stilts (Recurvirostridae)

The **black-necked stilt** (tero real, cigüeñuela cuellinegra; *Himantopus himantopus*) is an elegant black-and-white wader and is also called the common stilt. It is slightly smaller (38cm long) than the oystercatcher, from which it is easily distinguished by its very slim shape, long red legs and slim black bill.

It is most frequently seen alone or in pairs, wading in lagoons. Stilts are solitary breeders and lay four eggs in a scrape at lagoon edges during the wet season. They are noisy, especially in flight.

Gulls, Terns & Skuas (Laridae)

There are two resident gull species (both endemic to the Galápagos) and two resident terns (neither of which are endemic). In addition, three other gull species, four other tern species and four skua species have been occasionally or rarely recorded.

The lovely **swallow-tailed gull** (gaviota blanca, gaviota tijereta; *Creagrus furcatus*) is gray and white with bright-red feet and legs and a crimson eye ring; it is 51cm long and has a wingspan of 114cm. This bird feeds at night and is the only nocturnal gull in the world (hence, its eyes are larger than those of most other gulls). It is frequently seen perched on cliff tops during the day. Although a few pairs nest on an island off Colombia, almost the entire world population nests in the Galápagos, and therefore the swallow-tailed gull is considered endemic.

Swallow-tailed gulls nest in colonies near small cliffs and beaches and can be seen on most major islands except the far western ones. Their breeding cycle lasts about nine or 10 months, so nesting can be seen at any time of the year. There are about 10,000 to 15,000 pairs in the islands.

The **lava gull** (gaviota morena, gaviota de lava; *Larus fuliginosus*) is the rarest gull in the world – it is estimated that only about 400 pairs exist. Despite this, you have a very good chance of seeing them, because they are widely distributed in the Galápagos. They are about 53cm long and are generally dark gray to black with white eyelids. They are solitary nesters and breed throughout the year.

The **brown noddy tern** (nodi, charraán pardo; *Anous stolidus*) is 38cm long and has a 76cm wingspan. It is generally dark brown with a whitish

Facing page
Top: Swallow-tailed gulls

Middle: Although the lava gull is the rarest gull in the world, you are likely to see one in the Galápagos

Lower middle: Brown noddy tern

Bottom: Galápagos dove

forehead, and is often seen feeding with pelicans. This tern may catch fish scraps from the water draining out of a pelican's bill, and it may even perch on the pelican's head in order to better reach the food. It nests at any time of year in small colonies on cliffs and in caves.

The black-and-white **sooty tern** (gaviotín sombrió; *Sterna fuscata*) also breeds in the Galápagos, but it is restricted to Isla Darwin, in the far north, and is therefore rarely seen.

Pigeons (Columbidae)

The pretty little **Galápagos dove** (paloma, tórtola de Galápagos; *Zenaida galapagoensis*) is 20cm long and has a reddish underneath, brownish upperparts, green neck patches, blue eye rings, and red legs and feet – a colorful bird.

Breeding occurs year-round. Two eggs are laid in a haphazard nest of grass and twigs under a rock, or in an abandoned nest of another species. When incubating, adults may walk away from a nest, feigning injury, to lure predators away from the nest. This behavior evolved long before doves arrived in the Galápagos and has been retained, even though it is of little advantage in the islands.

Cuckoos & Anis (Cuculidae)

Two species of cuckoos and two species of anis have been recorded; one of each is common.

About half of the 28cm-long **dark-billed cuckoo** (cuclillo piquioscuro, aguatero; *Coccyzus melacoryphus*) is tail – long tails are characteristic of this family. It is a dark-brown and gray bird. It has a light underside with a yellowish wash, white tail tips, a black beak and black legs. The cuckoo is reasonably common but secretive – therefore, its low, chuckling call is heard more often than the bird is seen. It is commonly found only on Islas Santa Cruz, San Cristóbal, Floreana, Isabela and Fernandina. The nesting season is January to May.

The **groove-billed ani** (garrapatero piquiestriado; *Crotophaga sulcirostris*) was introduced to the islands in the 1960s, and it is now seen regularly in the Santa Cruz highlands, where it now breeds. The similar **smooth-billed ani** (*C. ani*) was recorded in the same area during the 1980s. Both birds are all black and about 30cm long, and both have a distinctively long, floppy tail – distinguishing them is not easy.

Owls (Tytonidae & Strigidae)

The two families of owls are each represented by one species in the Galápagos.

This page
Bottom: Groove-billed ani

The small (25cm-long) **barn owl** (lechuza campanaria, lechuza blanca; *Tyto alba*) is found all over the world. The almost white, heart-shaped facial disk is the most striking feature of this pale owl, which, because of its nocturnal habits, is rarely seen. It is most common on Isla Fernandina but also has been recorded on Islas Santa Cruz, Isabela, Santiago and San Cristóbal.

The **short-eared owl** (lechuza de campo, bujo orejicorto; *Asio flammeus*) is much larger (36cm long with a wingspan of 94cm) and darker than the barn owl. Also, it is diurnal and is therefore seen much more often. It is found on all the main islands – but is least common on Fernandina and most common on Santa Cruz and Genovesa, where it is frequently seen hunting in the storm petrel colonies. Owls have specialized feathers that enable them to fly and glide soundlessly – a great advantage when hunting small birds, rodents and lizards. They can breed year-round but prefer the wet season. They nest on the ground in heavy vegetation and are territorial.

Tyrant Flycatchers (Tyrannidae)

The resident adult male **vermilion flycatcher** (mosquero bermellón, brujo; *Pyrocephalus rubinus*) is tiny (about 13cm long) but quite unmistakable with its bright-red crown and underparts. The upperparts, tail and eye stripe are almost black. Females are brown above and yellowish beneath, and the female's chest is almost white and lightly streaked. The vermilion flycatcher is widespread in the highlands of most islands, but you can occasionally see it by the coast. The trees and shrubs around the collapsed calderas of Los Gemelos, in the Santa Cruz highlands, is a good place to see this bird. They are territorial and like to breed during the rainy season. Their small nests are built in trees in the highlands.

The endemic **large-billed (Galápagos) flycatcher** (papa moscas, copetón piquigrande; *Myiarchus magnirostris*) is seen more frequently than the vermilion flycatcher. It is about 15cm long and is gray and brown with a yellowish belly – although its belly is less yellow than the female vermilion flycatcher. The large-billed flycatcher is widespread on all the main islands (except Genovesa) and is found in areas that are drier and lower than the areas where the vermilion flycatcher is found.

Swallows & Martins (Hirundinidae)

Five species of this family have been recorded, but only one is resident.

The **Galápagos (southern) martin** (martín sureño, golondrina; *Progne modesta*) is a 16cm-long, dark bird with a shallowly forked tail and pointed wings. The female is dark brown; the male is glossy black. It has

ROB RACHOWIECKI

ROB RACHOWIECKI

Top: Short-eared owl

Bottom: Male vermilion flycatcher

a characteristic flight of a few quick flaps followed by a glide. The dark plumage, small size, unique flight and pointed silhouette identify this martin. Martins are less common in the northern islands but are distributed throughout the Galápagos. They hunt for insects on the updrafts from cliffs and highlands.

Mockingbirds (Mimidae)

The fearless and endemic mockingbirds of the Galápagos are often seen on all the islands except Pinzón. These birds are a classic example of adaptive radiation – there are four species that descended from a common ancestor and that look very similar except for the bills, which differ in size and shape. The mockingbirds are 25cm to 30cm long and have gray-and-brown streaks; their tails are long and their bills are curved. You can tell these birds apart based on their geographic distribution. The mockingbirds lay two to four eggs from October to April – two broods may be raised during this period. The birds are territorial and build nests of twigs in trees, shrubs or cacti. Occasionally, they are cooperative breeders, with three or more adults raising a brood.

The **Galápagos mockingbird** (sinsonte de Galápagos; *Neosomimus parvulus*) is found on all the central and western islands except for Floreana, Española, San Cristóbal and Pinzón).

The **Charles mockingbird** (sinsonte de Floreana; *N. trifasciatus*) was originally found on the island of Floreana but is now extinct there. About 150 birds are left on the nearby islets of Champion and Gardner-near-Floreana.

The **Hood mockingbird** (sinsonte de Española; *N. macdonaldi*) is the largest of the four species and has a noticeably heavier bill than the others. It is easily found, but only on Española and on the nearby islet of Gardner-near-Hood.

The **Chatham mockingbird** (sinsonte de San Cristóbal; *N. melanotis*) is endemic to San Cristóbal, where it is common.

Top: Large-billed (Galápagos) flycatcher

Middle: Galápagos mockingbird

Bottom: Hood mockingbird

Wood Warblers, Tanagers, Blackbirds etc (Emberizidae)

There are at least four species of emberizids (which include wood warblers, tanagers and blackbirds) recorded from the Galápagos, of which only one is resident or commonly seen.

The tiny **yellow warbler** (canario, reinita amarillo; *Dendroica petechia*) is 13cm long and is the only bright-yellow bird in the Galápagos. It is yellow below and greenish olive above; the male has fine reddish streaks on the chest. The yellow warbler is found throughout the Galápagos, from the coasts to the highlands. Although they lay eggs only from December to April, they defend territories throughout the year.

Finches (Fringillidae)

The 13 Darwin's finches are the most famous and biologically important birds of the Galápagos. Some visitors find them disappointing; they certainly are not very spectacular to look at.

Darwin's finches are all endemic, and everyone will see some of them – although it takes an expert to be able to tell them apart. All 13 species are thought to have descended from a common ancestor, and their present differences in distribution, body size, plumage, beak size and shape, and feeding habits helped Darwin formulate his evolutionary theories.

The best island to separate three of the species is Española. There you'll find only the **warbler finch** (pinzón reinita; *Certhidea olivacea*), with its tiny, warblerlike bill; the **small ground finch** (pinzón terrestre chico; *Geospiza fuliginosa*), with its small, finchlike bill; and the **large cactus finch** (pinzón cactero grande; *G. conirostris*), which has a large bill. After that, the going gets more difficult. There are tree finches that are seen on the ground, ground finches that are seen in the trees, and cactus finches that may be seen in all sorts of places apart from cacti.

If you want to see all 13 species, you'll need to do some traveling. The **medium tree finch** (pinzón arbóreo mediano; *Camarhynchus pauper*) is found only in the highlands of Floreana. The **mangrove finch** (pinzón manglero; *Camarhynchus heliobates*) is found only on Isabela and Fernandina. Of the islands with visitor sites, the large cactus finch (mentioned previously) is found only on Islas Genovesa and Española. The other finches are more widely distributed.

The most famous of these birds is the **woodpecker finch** (pinzón artesano; *Camarhynchus pallidus*), which sometimes grasps a twig in its bill and pokes it into holes and cracks in dead trees or bark. With some perseverance, the bird may extract a grub or other prey that it would otherwise not have been able to reach. This remarkable example of tool use is very rare among birds. Mangrove finches also do this, although infrequently.

It is beyond the scope of this guide to describe individually all 13 finches adequately enough to enable you to identify them. (Note: The remaining

ROB RACHOWIECKI

ROB RACHOWIECKI

ROB RACHOWIECKI

Top: The yellow warbler is the only bright-yellow bird in the Galápagos.

Middle: Warbler finch

Bottom: Large cactus finch

seven species that are not highlighted in this text are listed below with their Spanish and scientific names.) If your tour guide is a very good naturalist, she or he will help you. Otherwise, consult one of the bird guides listed in the Facts for the Visitor chapter. One bird-guide author, Michael Harris, has about 25 pages on the finches alone and is often quoted as writing 'It is only a very wise man or a fool who thinks he is able to identify all the finches which he sees.'

Medium ground finch
Spanish name: pinzón terrestre mediano
Scientific name: *Geospiza fortis*

Large ground finch
Spanish name: pinzón terrestre grande
Scientific name: *Geospiza magnirostris*

Sharp-beaked ground finch
Spanish name: pinzón terrestre piquiagudo
Scientific name: *Geospiza difficilis*

Cactus finch
Spanish name: pinzón cactero chico
Scientific name: *Geospiza scandens*

Vegetarian finch
Spanish name: pinzón vegetariano
Scientific name: *Platyspiza crassirostris*

Small tree finch
Spanish name: pinzón arbóreo chico
Scientific name: *Camarhynchus parvulus*

Large tree finch
Spanish name: pinzón arbóreo grande
Scientific name: *Camarhynchus psittacula*

Top: Cactus finch on prickly pear cactus flower

Middle: Vegetarian finch

Lower left: Small tree finch

Bottom right: One of Darwin's finches – can you guess which?

Reptiles

The prehistoric-looking reptiles found all over the islands are easily approached and observed. Over two dozen species belonging to five families have been recorded, and most of them are endemic.

JEFF WILLIAMS

Tortoises (Testudinidae)

The most famous of the reptiles is, of course, the endemic **giant tortoise** (tortuga gigante, galápagos; *Geochelone elephantopus*), for which the islands are named. There is only one species, which has been divided into 14 subspecies; three of these are extinct. One of the best ways to distinguish them (apart from geographic distribution) is by differences in the shape of their carapaces (shells). These differences contributed to Darwin's thoughts while he was developing his theory of evolution.

Whalers and sealers killed many thousands of tortoises, particularly in the 18th and 19th centuries. Now only some 15,000 remain. A breeding project at the Charles Darwin Research Station appears successful, and the staff hopes to begin re-introducing animals into the wild. The easiest way to see both tiny yearlings and full-grown adults is at the research station. Although the tortoises are in enclosures, visitors are permitted to enter and get a close look at these giants, some of which can reach a weight of 250kg – or 3000 times more than newborn hatchlings, which weigh only about 80g. To see tortoises in the wild, you can go to the tortoise reserve (on Santa Cruz) or the Los Galápagos visitor site (on San Cristóbal), or you can climb Volcán Alcedo (on Isabela).

The tortoises are vegetarians and have slow digestive systems – a meal can take up to three weeks to pass through. Scientists guess that the tortoises' life span is about 150 years, but records have not been kept for long enough to know for certain. Sexual maturity is reached at about 40 years of age (now you know why they say 'Life begins at forty!'). Mating usually occurs toward the end of the rainy season. The males posture and shove other males in contests of dominance and then try to seek out a suitable mate – unsuccessful males have been known to attempt to mate with other males, or even with appropriately shaped boulders!

Once mated, the females look for dry and sandy areas in which to make a nest. They dig a hole about 30cm deep with their hind legs – this may take several days. Anywhere from two to 16 eggs are laid and are covered with a protective layer of mud made from soil mixed with urine. The eggs take about four to five months to develop, and hatchlings usually emerge between December and April.

Marine Turtles (Cheloniidae)

Leatherback and hawksbill turtles have been occasionally recorded in the Galápagos, but only the **pacific green sea turtle** (tortuga marina; *Chelonia mydas*) is a resident breeder. This marine turtle breeds and lays

Top: Giant tortoises may live to be 150 years old.

eggs in the Galápagos, but it is not endemic to the islands. Green sea turtles are quite promiscuous, and during the breeding season – especially November to January – much mating activity can be observed in the water.

Nesting occurs at night – mainly from December to June, with a peak around February – on many of the sandy beaches of the islands. The females dig a hole in the sand above the high-tide mark and deposit several dozen eggs – a process that takes about three hours. Once the eggs hatch, the hatchlings are very vulnerable to predation. If they reach the ocean, they swim off and stay away for years; almost nothing is known about this period of their lives. Turtles seem to have great navigational skills – they return to nest at the same beach where they were hatched. Tagged adults have been recovered as far away as Costa Rica.

The adult turtles are huge and may reach 150kg. Snorkelers sometimes see them swimming underwater, and it is an exciting sight to watch such a large animal serenely flap by.

Top: Pacific green sea turtle

Bottom: The endemic marine iguana is the only seagoing lizard in the world.

Iguanas & Lizards (Iguanidae)

The most frequently seen reptiles are the iguanas, of which there are three species (all endemic). There are seven endemic species of lizards.

The **marine iguana** (iguana marina; *Amblyrhynchus cristatus*) is the only seagoing lizard in the world and is found on the rocky shores of

most islands. This iguana has blackish skin, which in the males can change to startling blues and reds during the breeding season. Breeding occurs at different times on different islands; the males on Española are colorful year-round. Marine iguanas are colonial (often piling on top of one another), but when breeding, the larger males become territorial and aggressive, butting and pushing their rivals. Mated females lay two to four eggs in a sandy nest – these nests are guarded by the mothers, although the hatchlings, which emerge after three or four months, are not given much parental protection.

Marine iguanas feed mainly on intertidal seaweed, although mature males have been recorded offshore at depths up to 12m and can remain submerged for an hour or more. The row of spines along the entire length of their backs, their scaly skins, their habit of occasionally snorting little clouds of salt spray into the air, and their length – which can reach almost 1m – makes them look like veritable little dragons.

The two species of land iguanas look almost alike. They are yellowish in color and bigger than their marine relatives – adults weighing up to 6kg have been recorded. The **Galápagos land iguana** (iguana terrestre; *Conolophus subcristatus*) is found on Islas Isabela, Santa Cruz, Fernandina, Seymour and South Plaza, with South Plaza being the best place to see them. They were formerly found on most of the other islands, but hunting and competition with introduced animals (goats,

rats, pigs, dogs), which prey on the eggs, has caused their demise on many islands.

The similar **Santa Fe land iguana** (iguana terrestre de Santa Fe; *Conolophus pallidus*) is found only on that island. It is slightly bigger, on average, than the Galápagos land iguana and is somewhat yellower, with more pronounced spines. They can exceed 1m in length.

The preferred food of both species of land iguana is the prickly pear cactus, and the iguanas are sometimes seen standing on their rear legs in efforts to reach the succulent pads and yellow flowers. Their mouths are incredibly leathery, enabling them to eat the cactus pads whole without removing the spines.

Land iguanas are known to live for at least 60 years. They reach sexual maturity between six and 10 years of age. Mated females lay five to 15 eggs and, like the marine iguana, they defend their nests until hatching occurs. Land iguanas breed in different months on different islands.

Less spectacular than the iguanas, but also endemic, are the seven species of **lava lizard** (lagartija de Lava; *Tropidurus*) that are frequently

Top: Galápagos land iguana under prickly pear cactus

Bottom: Santa Fe land iguana

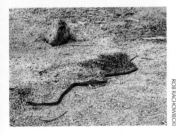

seen scurrying around. They can reach 30cm in length but are usually smaller. Their most distinctive behavioral patterns are rapid head bobbing and push-up stances to defend their territories and assert dominance. The male is larger and patterned with yellow, black and brown. The female is less strongly patterned but makes up for this with a flaming-red throat.

It is easy to separate the seven species of lava lizard by geographical distribution. Six islands have their own endemic species that are found nowhere else in the world. These are *T. bivittatus* on San Cristóbal, *T. grayi* on Floreana, *T. habellii* on Marchena, *T. delanonis* on Española, *T. pacificus* on Pinta and *T. duncanensis* on Pinzón. *T. albemarlensis* is found on most of the other islands except for Genovesa, Wolf and Darwin, which have no lava lizards.

Geckos (Gekkonidae)

These small, harmless nocturnal lizards, of which there are nine species (five endemic), are seen less often than the iguanas and lava lizards. They are often associated with human habitations and may be seen near houses at night. Geckos have adhesive pads on their digits and can climb vertical walls and even walk upside down on ceilings. Again, geographical distribution helps in separating the species. *Phyllodactylus bauri* is limited to Floreana and Española; *P. galapagoensis* is on several islands, including Santa Cruz, Isabela, Santiago, Daphne Major, Fernandina and Pinzón; *P. barringtonensis* is only on Santa Fe; and *P. gilberti* is only on Wolf. All four of those are endemic. There are three other species of gecko on San Cristóbal. These three are *P. tuberculosis, P. leei* and *Gonatodes caudiscutatus* – this last often lives in houses and has recently been introduced (*P. leei* is endemic). The most recently introduced are *P. reissi* and *Lepidodactylus lugubris*.

Snakes (Colubridae)

Finally, you may see the **Galápagos snake**, which is small, drab and nonpoisonous. There are three species of the genus *Alsophis* (formerly *Dromicus*) – all are endemic, all are of the constrictor type and all are difficult to tell apart. The adults reach a length of 1m and are not dangerous. A fourth species is *Philodrys biserialis*. Many visitors spend a week touring the islands without glimpsing even one snake.

Top: Male lava lizard

Bottom: The rarely seen Galápagos snake is not poisonous.

Mammals

In the Galápagos, the mammals are poorly represented because they had difficulty surviving a long ocean crossing. There are only six native mammals, of which two are seals, two are bats and two are rice rats.

Other land mammals are introduced species gone wild; they create a major nuisance to the native species by preying on them and by competing for food resources. They include feral goats, pigs, burros, cats, dogs, rats and mice.

Plainnose Bats (Vespertilionidae)

There are two bat species, which probably flew across or were blown over in a storm. The **hoary bat** *(Lasiurus cinereus)* is well known in North America, but not much is known about the endemic **Galápagos bat** *(L. brachyotis)*. Bats are occasionally seen flying around lampposts in the island towns. The Spanish word for bat is *murciélago*.

Mice & Rats (Cricetidae)

Two endemic species of **rice rat** are found in the Galápagos. *Nesoryzomys narboroughii* is on Fernandina, and *Oryzomys bauri* is on Santa Fe. Visitors occasionally catch a glimpse of these small rodents running around the trails of the appropriate island. These mammals probably floated across on vegetation rafts. It's thought that there were once seven species of rice rat, but five have become extinct since humans introduced the black rat.

Eared Seals (Otariidae)

Members of this family have external ears, use their front flippers for swimming, and can turn the hind flippers forward to enable them to 'walk' on land – true seals (Phocidae) can't do this. Both seal species found in the islands are members of the Otariidae.

Bottom: Female sea lion and pup

The native mammal you'll see the most of is the **Galápagos sea lion** (lobo marino; *Zalophus californianus*), which is a subspecies of the Californian sea lion and is found on most islands. There are an estimated 50,000 individuals in the Galápagos. The territorial bulls, which can reach 250kg, are quite aggressive and sometimes chase swimmers out of the water. They have been known to bite if harassed, so don't approach them too closely. The females and young, on the other hand, are extremely playful, and you can often watch them swimming around if you bring a mask and snorkel.

Sea lions live up to 20 years. Females are sexually mature at five years; males are capable of mating then too, but they don't do so until they are older. Dominant males patrol and guard particularly attractive beaches – these territories may contain up to 30 females. The dominant male has mating access to these females, but only for as long as he is able to keep other males away. Defending a territory is very demanding work, and males may go for days without getting much food or sleep.

ROB RACHOWIECKI

After several weeks of this, a fresh new male may challenge and beat a harem-master and take over his position.

Females become sexually receptive once a year. Gestation lasts nine months, and the pup (there is usually only one) is born around the beginning of the dry season. The mother nurses the pup for almost a week before returning to the water to feed; thereafter, she will continue to nurse the pup after fishing trips until the pup is five or six months old, when it will begin to learn to fish for itself. Even then, pups will continue to supplement their diet with milk, and some females may nurse two pups from different years.

The endemic **Galápagos fur seals** (foca peletera; *Arctocephalus galapagoensis*) are less commonly seen than the sea lions, which they superficially resemble. On close inspection, fur seals are quite different from sea lions. Fur seals are smaller and have a broader, shorter head that resembles a bear's (hence, the scientific name – 'arcto' means 'bear-like' and 'cephalus' means 'head' in Greek). Fur seals' ears are a little more prominent, and they have larger front flippers than sea lions.

Their fur is very dense and luxuriant and is made of two layers of hair. This attracted the attention of sealers, who decimated the population in the 19th century while hunting for the valuable skins. Because of their thick fur, the animals like to hide out in cool caves during the heat of the day and hunt at night. This secretive behavior helped the species survive the sealers' depredations. Today, fur seals are fully protected and have recovered – there are almost as many fur seals as sea lions, but the more secretive habits of the former explains why fur seals are less frequently seen by visitors.

The social and breeding behavior of fur seals is quite similar to that of sea lions – one difference is that male fur seals tend to defend territory from the land, while male sea lions defend from the water.

The best place to see fur seals is at Puerto Egas, on Santiago.

Whales & Dolphins (Order Cetacea)

Other marine mammals you may see when cruising between the islands are whales and dolphins. There are **seven whale species** regularly recorded in the archipelago, but they are difficult to tell apart because they are normally glimpsed only momentarily and from a distance. The seven species are the finback, sei, humpback, minke, sperm, killer and pilot whales.

Bottle-nosed dolphins *(Tursiops truncatus)* are often seen surfing the bow waves of the boats. If seen at night, the dolphins cause the ocean to glow with bioluminescence as they stir up thousands of tiny phosphorescent creatures that light up when disturbed. Less frequently seen are the common dolphin *(Delphinus delphis)* and the spinner dolphin *(Stenella caerulleoalba)*. The Spanish word for 'dolphin' is *delfín*.

Top: Galápagos fur seals

Fish

About 400 species of fish have been recorded in the Galápagos, and more are found quite frequently. About half of these fish are found in much of the tropical eastern Pacific, and about 50 are endemic. Merlen's *Field Guide to the Fishes of Galapagos* is available in Quito and is recommended for snorkelers. This guide describes and illustrates 107 of the most frequently seen species.

Snorkeling in the Galápagos is a rewarding experience, and schools containing thousands of tropical fish are routinely seen. It is interesting that many species of tropical fish change their color and shape as they age, and a few can even change their sex midway through life. This certainly makes identification confusing! Some of the naturalist guides working on the boats can help identify the more common species. To name but a few, these include blue-eyed damselfish, white-banded angelfish, yellow-tailed surgeonfish, moorish idols, blue parrotfish, concentric puffer fish, yellow-bellied triggerfish and hieroglyphic hawkfish.

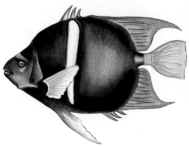

Sharks

The fish that often interest visitors most are the sharks *(tiburones)*. They are often seen by snorkelers, and their speed and grace underwater is almost otherworldly. In fact, one of the best reasons to snorkel in the Galápagos is the chance to see these magnificent animals in reasonable safety. For some reason, the sharks of the Galápagos have never been known to attack and injure a human swimmer. Despite this reassurance, you should leave the water if you cut or graze yourself.

There are several species found here, and the most common are the **white-tipped reef shark** *(Triaenodon obesus)* and the **Galápagos shark**

Top: Moorish idol

Middle: White-banded angelfish

Bottom: Galápagos shark

(Carcharhinus galapagensis). **Hammerheads** *(Sphyrna lewini)* are also occasionally seen.

Rays

Another kind of fish that provides the snorkeler with a real thrill is the ray (raya). Again, there are several species; all are harmless, with the exception of the **stingray** *(Urotrygon* spp.), which sometimes basks on the sandy bottoms of the shallows and can inflict an extremely painful wound to waders and paddlers. It is a good idea to enter the water by shuffling your feet along the sandy bottom – this gives stingrays the chance to swim away before you step on them.

Other rays are found in slightly deeper water and are often camouflaged on the sandy bottom. My first ray sighting was of the well-camouflaged **spotted eagle ray** *(Aetobatus narinari)* that lay on the bottom motionless and almost invisible. As I swam over it, the fish suddenly broke loose of the sand and flapped away, giving me a real shock. The sight of a meter-wide ray gently undulating through the water is quite mesmerizing. Sizable schools of beautiful golden **mustard rays** *(Rhinoptera steindachneri)* are also seen quite regularly.

Less frequently seen is the giant **manta ray** *(Manta hamiltoni)*, which is found in deeper offshore waters. You are most likely to catch sight of one as it leaps out of the water and falls back with a loud slap – with a maximum spread of 6m, these fish make a huge splash as they hit the water.

Invertebrates

The remaining animals encountered in the Galápagos do not possess a backbone and are hence collectively called invertebrates. The common phyla described in this section include Arthropoda (insects, spiders, barnacles, crabs and lobsters), Coelenterata or Cnidaria (jellyfish, sea anemones and corals) and Echinodermata (starfish, sea urchins and sea cucumbers). Also common (especially in tide pools), but not described here, are the phyla Mollusca (snails, chitons, shellfish and octopuses) and Porifera (sponges). There are other phyla that are less frequently encountered.

Arthropods

The first invertebrate that most visitors notice is the **Sally Lightfoot crab** *(Grapsus grapsus)*. This small crab is bright red above and blue below and is ubiquitous on almost every rock beach. Also present on rock beaches is a small black crab that blends well with the lava background. These are young Sally Lightfoots. The adults are far from camouflaged and rely on their alertness to escape predators. If you try to approach them, they will

Bottom: Sally Lightfoot crab on the lookout for a hungry heron

run away, and they are even capable of running across the surface of the water in tide pools. The crabs will, however, approach you if you sit as still as a rock. This is the strategy of the herons that prey on the Sally Lightfoots. Often you'll see a lava heron standing motionless on rocky beach. When a crab comes within reach, the bird will lunge forward and, if successful in capturing a crab, will then proceed to shake it and bang it against rocks until the legs fall off before devouring the animal.

Other crabs are found on sandy beaches. These are the pale **ghost crabs** (*Ocypode* spp.) that stare at you with unusual eyes at the end of long eyestalks. They leave the characteristic pattern of sand balls that are seen on most sandy beaches.

In tide pools, you may see the **hermit crab** (*Calcinus explorator*), which lives in an empty seashell that it carries around. As a young crab outgrows its protective shell, it finds a larger one to grow into. This 'moving house' occurs several times before the hermit crab reaches adult size. If you go farther into the water with mask and snorkel and poke around some of the rocky underwater crevices, you may find **lobsters**.

Insects are the most numerous animals in the world and literally millions of species are found in the tropics. A little over a thousand species are described from the Galápagos, and this comparatively small number reflects the difficulty that insects had in crossing almost 1000km of ocean to colonize the islands. There are not many colorful insect species. There are a few species of butterflies, ants, grasshoppers and wasps, and there are many more representatives of the beetle and moth groups. There is one species of bee, one preying mantis and two scorpions in the Galápagos. Mosquitoes, horse flies and midges are found and can sometimes make sunbathing on the beach unpleasant. Fortunately, these insects do not fly far, and nights spent aboard a boat anchored several hundred meters off shore will usually be insect-free.

Scorpions are rarely encountered, and although their sting can be painful, they are not normally dangerous.

Coelenterates

The phylum Coelenterata (or Cnidaria) is represented in part by **sea anemones**, which are stationary creatures that capture their food by waving stinging tentacles in the water. These tentacles do not create enough of a sting to hurt you if you brush against one in a tide pool or shallow area. Because of their appearance and the fact that they don't move from place to place, they are sometimes nicknamed 'sea flowers.'

Top: Sea urchin

Bottom: Sand dollar

Swimming coelenterates are represented in the islands by **jellyfish**, which also capture prey by using stinging tentacles. Contact with these can be quite painful, but fortunately, jellyfish aren't often seen in the main swimming spots. **Corals** are also coelenterates, but there are not many in the Galápagos. The Devil's Crown, off Isla Santa María, is one of the best places to see living coral. Dead coral is often found washed up ashore and sometimes forms a large part of a beach.

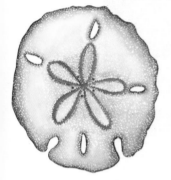

Echinoderms

While poking around underwater, be careful of the **sea urchin** (Diadema mexicana), which has beautiful, iridescent, black spines that are long, brittle and needle-sharp. Less painful encounters with sea urchins can be had with the **pencil-spined urchin** (Eucidaris thouarsii), which has blunt, pencil-like spines that often break off and are washed ashore, sometimes forming a large part of a beach. The endemic **green urchin** (Lytechnicus semituberculatus) is also common, and despite its prickly appearance, it can be held quite easily if you want to examine its tiny tube feet.

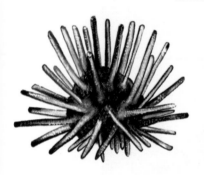

The prickly-ball appearance of urchins belies their taxonomic grouping. They are in fact radially symmetrical in five or more planes and are therefore members of the same phylum as the **starfish** and the **sand dollar**. The sand dollar looks like a flattened disc that has a starfish pattern on it. The starfish themselves are immediately recognizable but come in a fascinating array of sizes, colors, shapes and numbers of arms. The **sea cucumbers** are also echinoderms. They lie on the bottom and look unfortunately similar to turds.

Top: Marine iguanas frolicking on lava flow

Bottom: Giant tortoise at the Charles Darwin Research Station, Isla Santa Cruz

JASON EDWARDS

SALLY DILLON

Top: Puffy courtship display of the male magnificent frigatebird

Bottom: Blue-footed boobies in courtship display (male with wings raised), Isla Española

Overleaf: Sleepy sea lion pup

[Continued from page 448]

The most important thing to find is a crew with a good and enthusiastic naturalist guide who can point out and discuss the wildlife and other items of interest. It is worth paying more for a good guide. All guides must carry a license, which qualifies them as Naturalist I, II or III. Naturalist I guides have limited foreign-language and biology training, while Naturalist III guides are usually fluent in a foreign language and have a good academic background in natural sciences; Naturalist II lies in between.

Owners, captains, guides and cooks change frequently; in addition, many boats make changes and improvements from year to year. Generally speaking, a boat is only as good as its crew. You should be able to meet the naturalist guide and captain and to inspect the boat; always have an itinerary agreed upon with the boat owner or captain. You can deal with a crew member or boat representative during your search, but don't hand over any money until you have an agreed itinerary, and then pay only the captain.

You should get the itinerary in writing to avoid disagreements with other passengers and the crew during the cruise. Boats must register their itineraries with the National Park Service and with the port captain. Most itineraries are fixed in advance and cannot be changed. Still, you'll find that itineraries are generally good and include visits to some of the best visitor sites.

Prearranged Most visitors arrange tours before arriving at the islands. You can do this in your home country (expensive but efficient), or you can arrange something in Quito or Guayaquil (cheaper, but you sometimes have to wait several days or weeks during the high season).

If you are trying to economize, you may find that you can get a substantial discount by checking various agencies and seeing if they have any spaces to fill on departures leaving in the next day or two. This applies both to the cheaper tours and to some of the pricier ones. Particularly out of the high season, agencies may well let you travel cheaply at the last minute rather than leave berths unfilled. This depends on luck and your skill at bargaining.

Safari Tours (see Travel Agencies in the Quito & Around chapter) has a database of tours and can often get you on a boat quickly at a reasonable price. There is a US$25 flat fee to cover the expense of searching out the best tour for you. This seems like money well spent. Sangay Touring (see Quito) also has a good range of choices at fair prices. Galasam (Economic Galápagos Tours) has offices in Quito and Guayaquil (see those sections); this company's economy tours are suitable for budget travelers who don't want to organize their own tour once they get to the islands.

Seven-day economy tours use small boats with six to 12 bunks in double, triple and quadruple cabins. All bedding is provided, and accommodations are clean but spartan, with little privacy. Plenty of simple, fresh food and juice is served at all meals. Guides may speak English or may be educated in biology. There are toilets aboard, and fresh water is available for washing your face and drinking. Bathing facilities might consist of hosed sea water, but showers are available on some. Itineraries are preset and include visits to most of the central islands, allowing enough time to see the wildlife.

A one-week (eight-day) economy tour costs about US$500 to US$600 per person. There are weekly departures. Shorter, cheaper tours are available – four days or five days for under US$400. The US$100 park fee, airfare and bottled drinks are not included. There are weekly departures. Typically, for a one-week tour, you'll leave Quito on a specific morning (say Monday) and begin the boat tour Monday afternoon or evening. The tour may finish Sunday night or, possibly, Monday morning at the airport for your flight back. Shorter and cheaper tours are available. Sometimes, a one-week tour is a combination of two shorter tours; for example, a Monday-to-Thursday tour combined with a Thursday-to-Monday tour. People that paid for a full week on this kind of tour spend most of Thursday dropping off and picking up passengers, so try to avoid this.

If you add up the cost of the cheapest one-week tour plus airfare and park fees, you get almost no change out of US$1000. Sorry, budget travelers, that's the way it is. My feeling is that if you're going to spend this much, then seeing the Galápagos is probably important to you, and you will want to get as much out of it as possible. If economy class is all you can afford, and you really want to see the Galápagos, go! It'll probably be the adventure of a lifetime. But you might consider spending an extra few hundred dollars to go on a more comfortable, reliable boat and getting a decent guide (although the more expensive boats have their problems too).

For about US$700 to US$800 for eight days, you can take a more comfortable tourist-class tour – the usual extra costs (airfare, fees and taxes) apply. Many companies in Quito offer tours at about this price.

More luxurious boats are also available through agencies in Quito and Guayaquil. These typically are over US$1000 per person per week, plus the usual extras. The most expensive boats are reasonably comfortable and have superb food and excellent crews. Many of these boats run prearranged tours with foreign groups; you are not likely to find them available for budget or independent travel. If you want this kind of luxury, a good travel agent in Ecuador or at home will be able to help you with information.

There are a few large cruise ships carrying up to 80 passengers. These have the advantage of having comfortable double cabins with private showers, and they are spacious and more stable than the smaller boats. Each ship carries at least four experienced, multilingual naturalist guides, and passengers divide into four groups and land on the islands at half-hour intervals, thus avoiding the horrendous scene of 79 other people trooping around a visitor site all at once. Tours can be for three, four or seven nights. Rates start at over US$200 per person per night, depending on your cabin and whether or not you share it. Information and reservations are available from any major travel agent in Quito or Guayaquil.

Dangers & Annoyances Lonely Planet has received some letters criticizing the economy-class tours, and even people traveling on more expensive boats have reported problems – anything from sinking boats to sexual harassment. The more common complaints include last-minute changes of boat (which the contractual small print allows), a poor crew, a lack of bottled drinks, changes in the itinerary, mechanical breakdowns and overbooking. Passengers share cabins and are not guaranteed that their cabin mates will be of the same gender; if you are uncomfortable with sharing a cabin with a stranger of the opposite sex, make sure you are guaranteed in writing that you won't have to do this.

Because a boat is only as good as the crew running it, and because crews change relatively often, it is difficult to make blanket recommendations. Lonely Planet has not received consistently poor reports about any one boat, which suggests that problems are usually solved in the long run. Things go wrong from time to time, and when they do, a refund is difficult to obtain. If you have a problem, report it to the port captain at the *capitanía* in Puerto Ayora. If you are unable to do so while in the islands, reports can be mailed to El Capitán del Puerto, La Capitanía, Puerto Ayora, Galápagos, Ecuador. Reports are taken seriously, and repeat offenders do get their comeuppance – voice your complaints.

Bus

Isla Santa Cruz The CITTEG buses that leave from Puerto Ayora for the Baltra airport (see To/From Baltra Airport, earlier) will drop you off at the villages of Bellavista or Santa Rosa to explore some of the interior. Also, CITTEG buses from Puerto Ayora to Santa Rosa (under US$1) leave from the corner of Padre Julio Herrera and Charles Binford four or five times a day Monday to Saturday and less often on Sunday. Charters can be arranged for groups.

Note that neither of these villages has hotels at this time (although one is under construction near Santa Rosa). The most convenient way of seeing the interior and ensuring that you don't get stuck is to hire a bus or truck for the day with a group of other travelers.

Isla San Cristóbal There are a few buses that leave each day from Puerto Baquerizo Moreno and go to the farming center of El Progreso, 8km into the highlands. From here, you can rent jeeps for the final 10km ride to the visitor site of El Junco Lagoon. The road is being pushed eastward, and there are some buses that go farther than El Progreso.

Boat

INGALA (☎ in Puerto Ayora 05-526 151, 526 199) can give you up-to-date details of its interisland passenger-boat services. Unfortunately, its 24-passenger boat is old and is frequently being serviced. A new, larger vessel was introduced in 1995, but it isn't used any more. Perhaps another boat will be added, but you shouldn't rely on this service if your time is short. Priority is given to islanders and Ecuadorians, so it may take some days to be able to get on a boat.

Recently, boats left Puerto Ayora every Friday at 8 am to San Cristóbal, returning at 8 am on Tuesdays. Boats left Puerto Ayora every other Wednesday at 8 am to Floreana, returning at 8 am on Thursdays. Departure times change often and have decreased greatly since the last edition.

Fares are US$15 on any passage and should be bought a day in advance. Call INGALA to find out where tickets are sold. If you can't get on an INGALA boat, ask around for private trips, which are more expensive. The port captain knows which boats are scheduled to depart soon, as well as their destinations.

Air

A new airline, EMETEBE, flies a seven-passenger aircraft between the islands. It offers three flights a week between Baltra and Puerto Villamil (Isla Isabela), three flights a week between Baltra and San Cristóbal, and three flights a week between San Cristóbal and Puerto Villamil. Fares are about US$100 one way. This airline may buy

another plane and expand its services, or it may fold. You can contact EMETEBE at ☎ 526 177 in Puerto Ayora, ☎ 520 036 in San Cristóbal and ☎ 529 155 in Puerto Villamil.

ISLA SANTA CRUZ

With an area of 986 sq km, this is the second-largest island in the archipelago. A road crosses Santa Cruz from north to south and gives the visitor the easiest opportunity of seeing some of the highland interior of an island. The highest point is Cerro Crocker (864m).

This island has the highest population and the greatest number of tourist facilities. The main town is Puerto Ayora, where most visitors either stay while arranging a boat or anchor sometime during their cruise in the famous harbor of Academy Bay. In addition to the tourist facilities, there are about 10 national-park visitor sites and one privately owned visitor site on Santa Cruz.

Puerto Ayora

This town is on the central island of Santa Cruz, and it is where most visitors stay and visit. The population, currently about 12,000, is growing (too) fast and has doubled in less than a decade. This is because of immigration from mainland Ecuador, and new laws are attempting to control the growth – albeit not very effectively. There are the usual amenities: hotels, bars and restaurants, stores, a Pacifictel office, a post office, a TAME office, tourist agencies and information, a basic hospital, churches and a radio station. The airport is at Isla Baltra, about an hour away.

Information See the description of Isla Santa Cruz (under Visitor Sites, later in this section) for information on places to visit on the island.

Travel Information & Agencies There are several self-styled 'information centers' near the waterfront that will give you information about day trips and boat charters.

The Charles Darwin Research Station, about a kilometer east of town, has an exhibition hall, information kiosk, scientific

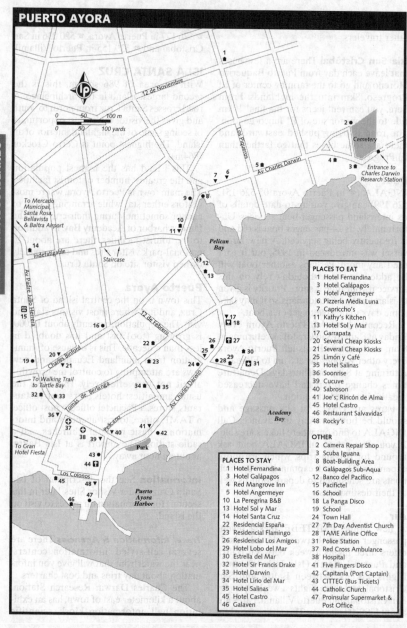

PUERTO AYORA

PLACES TO EAT
1 Hotel Fernandina
3 Hotel Galápagos
5 Hotel Angermeyer
6 Pizzería Media Luna
7 Capriccho's
11 Kathy's Kitchen
13 Hotel Sol y Mar
17 Garrapata
20 Several Cheap Kiosks
21 Several Cheap Kiosks
35 Limón y Café
35 Hotel Salinas
36 Soonrise
39 Cucuve
40 Sabroson
41 Joe's; Rincón de Alma
45 Hotel Castro
46 Restaurant Salvavidas
48 Rocky's

OTHER
2 Camera Repair Shop
3 Scuba Iguana
8 Boat-Building Area
9 Galápagos Sub-Aqua
12 Banco del Pacífico
15 Pacifictel
16 School
18 La Panga Disco
19 School
24 Town Hall
27 7th Day Adventist Church
28 TAME Airline Office
31 Police Station
37 Red Cross Ambulance
38 Hospital
41 Five Fingers Disco
42 Capitanía (Port Captain)
43 CITTEG (Bus Tickets)
44 Catholic Church
47 Proinsular Supermarket &
Post Office

PLACES TO STAY
1 Hotel Fernandina
3 Hotel Galápagos
4 Red Mangrove Inn
5 Hotel Angermeyer
10 La Peregrina B&B
13 Hotel Sol y Mar
14 Hotel Santa Cruz
22 Residencial España
23 Residencial Flamingo
26 Residencial Los Amigos
29 Hotel Lobo del Mar
30 Estrella del Mar
32 Hotel Sir Francis Drake
33 Hotel Darwin
34 Hotel Lirio del Mar
35 Hotel Salinas
45 Hotel Castro
46 Galaven

library and tortoise-raising pens. Walk the grounds at your own pace – tours are not organized.

The capitanía has information about (infrequent) boats to the mainland and has details of every boat sailing from Puerto Ayora. However, because boat captains don't have to file their routes until they are ready to depart, most information is useful only for departures within 24 hours.

The TAME office (☎ 526 165, 526 527) is open 7 am to noon Monday to Saturday and 1 to 4 pm weekdays. Reconfirming your departures is essential. Flights are often full, and there is sometimes difficulty in changing your reservation or buying a ticket.

Several travel agencies are found along the waterfront. Moonrise (☎ 526 403, 526 348, 526 589, sdevine@pa.ga.pro.ec) is run by the Devine family, who are well-established as Galápagos experts and guides. They can help with finding a tour boat or with confirming a flight, in addition to other things. Other places that might be able to help with cheap, last-minute tours are Galaven (☎ 526 359), Gala Travel (☎ 526 581) and Galasam (☎ 526 126). Reportedly, the cheapest is Galápagos Discovery, which also rents mountain bikes and other gear, but there have been several complaints about this one, so buyer beware.

Also, travelers can often book tours through their hotels.

Dive Centers Two professional dive centers in Puerto Ayora have been frequently recommended. Galápagos Sub-Aqua (☎/fax 526 350, sub_aqua@accessinter.net) is on Avenida Charles Darwin. It also has information offices in Guayaquil (☎/fax 04-304 132, 383 274), Dátiles 506 and Quinta, and in Quito (☎/fax 02-565 294), Pinto 439, office 101. Galápagos Sub-Aqua is a full-service dive center. If you have never dived before, they can supply you with all the equipment and teach you what you need to know (they can provide full-certification). Certified divers (who must have their PADI or NAUI cards) can take anything from a couple of dives to tours of various numbers of days. The head divemaster, Fernando

Zembrano, is very experienced, enthusiastic and friendly. He is also a licensed Galápagos guide and speaks English (as do most of the instructors).

Scuba Iguana (☎ 526 296, ☎/fax 526 497, 526 330, mathiase@pa.ga.pro.ec) is run by experienced divemaster Mathias Espinosa, who has guided Galápagos dives since the 1980s and is an underwater photographer, and by Hotel Galápagos owner, Jack Nelson, who has guided in the Galápagos for over 30 years. There is a nonsmoking policy on boats and in the hotel. Contact them at the hotel (see Places to Stay, later in this section).

Diving companies all over the world can also arrange diving tours on boats in the Galápagos. Rates vary from about US$78 to US$110 for two dives per day, depending on the destination.

Money Banco del Pacífico gives cash advances on MasterCards. Visa was not locally accepted recently, but this may change. US cash is the best currency.

Post & Communications The Pacifictel office is improving services, and mainland or international connections can be made.

The post office has slow and unreliable service. Making sure that your postcards are stamped and franked in the post office increases the chances of their arriving.

An Internet café will probably open by 2001.

Medical Services The hospital is not very sophisticated and is poorly supplied. Most sick people go back to the mainland.

Recycling Garbage disposal is a big problem in the islands. Residents have started a recycling system; look for and use garbage cans marked for recycling. Four-liter water jugs can be refilled with purified water at Residencial España (see Places to Stay, later in this section).

Places to Stay Hotels in Puerto Ayora range from cheap and basic to 1st class – by Galápagos standards, at least. There are no luxury hotels. Prices tend to rise during the heaviest tourism seasons (December to January and June to August).

It cannot be overemphasized that a cheap tour based at a single hotel and visiting other islands on day trips gives you only a superficial look at the Galápagos. Stay in Puerto Ayora by all means, but make every effort to visit the islands by taking a cruise of at least several days' duration – preferably a full week or more.

Street numbers aren't used in Puerto Ayora; refer to the map for locations.

Budget The eight-room *Residencial Los Amigos* (☎ 526 265) is a popular budget hotel that has rooms with shared cold showers for US$2.25/3.35/5.50 for singles/doubles/triples. It runs the *Symbol* yacht. Also popular is the friendly *La Peregrina B&B* (☎ 526 323), which has a garden and four simple rooms (all with private shower) sleeping two to four people at US$4.50 per person, including breakfast.

The 10-room *Residencial Flamingo* (☎ 526 556) is stuffy but cheap at US$2 per person with private cold shower. *Hotel Darwin* (☎ 526 493) is dingy and worn but OK at US$2 per person. *Hotel Santa Cruz* (☎ 526 573) is a friendly, six-room, family-run hotel charging US$2 per person for rooms with shared showers. *Hotel Sir Francis Drake* (☎ 526 222) has 13 OK rooms with cold showers and fans at US$3 per person. *Residencial España* (☎ 526 108) has seven rooms with private baths (cold water only) sleeping two to five people at US$3.50 per person; it also offers video rental. *Hotel Lirio del Mar* (☎ 526 212) is clean, similarly priced and similarly equipped. *Hotel Salinas* (☎/fax 526 107) has 22 clean modern rooms with private cold shower and fans for US$3/5/7. There is a restaurant, a TV room and a small garden as well.

Hotel Lobo del Mar (☎ 526 188, 526 569) has balconies with bay views. Rates are US$5/6/9 for rooms with cold bath. For about US$5 extra per person, three meals a day are included. The hotel has a lounge with cable TV and organizes day trips to various islands for about US$40 per passenger.

Estrella del Mar (☎ 526 427) also has sea views and has been recommended for its cleanliness and pleasant grounds. Rates are US$11 per person for rooms that have private hot showers; less for rooms lacking sea views. The similarly priced *Hotel Castro* (☎ 526 508, fax 526 113) is used for pre-arranged tour groups booked with Señor Miguel Castro, but it often has room for independent travelers. It is quiet and clean and has a private boat landing, a restaurant and a TV lounge. Rooms have private cold showers. Also at this price, *Gran Hotel Fiesta* (☎/fax 526 440) is on a quiet back street and has hot showers. Its garden has hammocks and access to a small lagoon.

Mid-Range & Top End Very pleasantly situated right on the waterfront, *Hotel Sol y Mar* (☎/fax 526 281) is a place where marine iguanas sunbathe with you on the deck and walk over your feet while you're having breakfast. The owner is Señor Jimmy Pérez, a rather colorful character who speaks English and runs Trans-Galápagos Tourism. He can also help you get a boat. Clean rooms with private hot bath and fan are US$18 to US$45 for doubles, depending on room (some are larger or have ocean views) and season. The bar and restaurant are recommended.

The family-run *Hotel Fernandina* (☎ 526 499, fax 526 122) is friendly and helpful. A pool and Jacuzzi are available to the public. Thirteen air-conditioned rooms with hot showers are US$50/80/108 for singles/doubles/triples. Its restaurant is open most days.

Hotel Angermeyer (☎/fax 526 277) is a modern hotel. It has 22 rooms with fans and private baths heated by solar panels. There is a small but pretty pool in a garden filled with coconut trees, as well as a good restaurant and bar with room service. Rates are US$56/78.

The small and intimate *Red Mangrove Inn* (☎/fax 526 564, redmangrove@ecuadorexplorer.com) has six rooms, all with private hot baths. Guests leave their shoes at the door. The inn is aimed at providing a relaxing place to stay; there is a Jacuzzi, bar and views of the bay. Rooms are US$61/98/134, but this is negotiable in the low season. Meals are available on request. The inn runs a variety of tours, including sea-kayaking, windsurfing, horseback riding, mountain biking and camping on a ranch in the highlands.

Hotel Galápagos (☎ *526 296, fax 526 330, hotelgps@pa.ga.pro.ec*) charges US$66/110/132 for 14 comfortable single/double/triple cabins with private bath, hot water, fans and ocean views. Its restaurant serves excellent meals (about US$8/16/20 for breakfast/lunch/dinner). A pleasant bar, a library of paperbacks and a scuba-diving center are on the premises. The hotel also provides hot showers to the public for US$1.25, including soap and towels.

Across the bay from Puerto Ayora is *Hotel Delfín* (☎ *526 297/8, fax 526 283, indefagi@ ayora.ecua.net.ec*), which has a semiprivate beach. All 21 rooms have both a beach view and private bathrooms (cold water only), and rates are less than those of the other good hotels. There is also a restaurant/bar and a pool. This is a very private location – you need a boat to get to this hotel from Puerto Ayora (call for a boat). The hotel is used as a base for day tours organized by Metropolitan Touring (see Travel Agencies in the Quito & Around chapter).

Places to Eat Puerto Ayora's restaurants and bars are good places to meet people. Some change owners or names quite often, as places frequented by seasonal influxes of people tend to do, so don't be surprised to find a differently named place at these locations. Service is leisurely. You can buy food and drinks in stores, but the choice is also limited and expensive compared to the mainland. Lobster is sold in some restaurants but has been dramatically overfished, and you are encouraged to forego lobster meals on the islands.

Down by the dock, *Restaurant Salvavidas* ('Lifejacket Restaurant') has, under various names, been the standard daytime dockside meeting place for years. You can grab a beer, snack or meal here while waiting for your panga. Nearby, *Rocky's* is another place to grab a drink before boarding your panga.

More places to eat are found out along Avenida Padre Julio Herrera. At the southeast end, you'll find *Cucuve*, which sells snacks varying from traditional *humitas* (like tamales) to ubiquitous *hamburguesas* (hamburgers). Opposite, *Sabroson* does open-air *parrilladas*. Up the street are several inexpensive, if unremarkable, places – look where locals are eating, especially at lunch. *Soonrise* is good for breakfasts of yogurt and fruit salad, as well as cheap set lunches. East from this street, along Charles Binford, are a number of *kiosks* selling cheap and well-prepared meals – mainly fish and meat dishes.

Walking north(ish) along the winding waterfront, *Joe's* and *Rincón de Alma*, on either side of Five Fingers disco, are popular for breakfasts, fast food and cheap set lunches. *Limón y Café* is a popular evening spot for light meals, snacks, a pool table and music. *Garrapata*, next to the La Panga disco, is considered the best restaurant in town – it has good food, friendly service and a decent bar. Prices are a bit higher than elsewhere, but far from prohibitive. *Kathy's Kitchen* has also been recommended, but it is open only during the high season. *Capriccho's* has organic food and vegetable salads, and the nearby *Pizzería Media Luna* has decent pizzas, as well as sandwiches and brownies – but it is open only in the afternoon and evening.

Most of the hotels have restaurants as well (see Places to Stay, earlier in this section).

Entertainment *Five Fingers* is a popular drinking and dancing spot on Avenida Charles Darwin. It has opened, closed and reopened in recent years. *La Panga* is a bar and disco, where local guides assure me 'the landings are always wet.' Limón y Café (see Places to Eat, earlier) is a popular place to hang, and other places open and close on an irregular basis.

Shopping You can purchase the famous Galápagos T-shirts in most souvenir shops, but the profits from those sold at the

Charles Darwin Research Station go to support that worthwhile institution. Please avoid buying objects made from black coral, turtle and tortoise shell. These threatened animals are protected, and it is illegal to use these animal products for the manufacture of novelties. The practice still continues, unfortunately. The most effective way of stopping it is by not buying such items. The sale of objects made from black coral is a particularly serious problem.

Many postcards are photographs or drawings by Tui de Roy, a resident famous for her beautifully illustrated books on Galápagos wildlife. Her mother, Jacqueline, and brother, Gil, make exquisite silver jewelry of the Galápagos animals. Their work is not cheap but is well worth the money. Reportedly, there is now an artisans' cooperative selling all these items.

You are advised to stock up on sunblock, insect repellent, toiletries, film and medications on the mainland. These have become increasingly available in recent years, but selection is still more expensive and not as wide as on the mainland.

Visitor Sites

About a 20-minute walk by road northeast of Puerto Ayora, the **Charles Darwin Research Station** can also be reached by dry landing from Academy Bay. It contains a national-park information center; an informative museum in the Van Straelen Exhibition Center (where a video in English or Spanish is presented several times a day); a baby-tortoise house with incubators, where you can see hatchlings and young tortoises; and a walk-in adult tortoise enclosure, where you can meet the Galápagos giants face to face. The tiny tortoises in the baby tortoise house are repatriated to their home islands when they weigh about 1.5kg (or are about four years old) – some 2000 have been repatriated so far. In the adult enclosures, you can get close enough to touch the tortoises, but touching the tortoises is not allowed. An elevated wooden boardwalk goes through the most interesting areas.

Several of the 11 remaining subspecies of tortoise can be seen here. Lonesome George,

the only surviving member of the Isla Pinta subspecies, is also here and can be viewed from the boardwalk. There is apparently a US$10,000 reward for finding a Pinta female, but before you go rushing off to find one, remember that Isla Pinta is off limits to visitors (except scientists and researchers). Although the chances of finding a Pinta female to breed with George are remote, attempts are being made to allow him to mate with a female from a closely related subspecies from Volcán Wolf. So far, he hasn't shown much interest, but things move slowly in the tortoise world, and something may happen any decade now.

Other attractions include paths through arid-zone vegetation, such as salt bush, mangroves and prickly pear and other cacti. A variety of land birds, including Darwin's finches, can be seen. T-shirts and other souvenirs are sold to support the research station.

A 3km trail takes you to **Turtle Bay**, southwest of Puerto Ayora, where you'll find a very fine white-sand beach and a spit of land providing protected swimming (there are strong currents on the exposed side of the spit). There are sharks, marine iguanas and a variety of waterbirds – including pelicans and the occasional flamingo. There are also mangroves. This is one of the few visitor sites where you can go without a guide, although there is no drinking water or other facilities. To get there, find the trail (see the Puerto Ayora map) and hike out for about half an hour.

Several sites of interest in the highlands of Santa Cruz can be reached from the trans-island road. Access to some sites is through colonized areas, so respect private property. From the village of Bellavista, 7km north of Puerto Ayora by road, one can turn either west on the main road continuing to Isla Baltra or east on a road leading in about 2km to the **lava tubes**. These underground tunnels are more than a kilometer in length and were formed by the solidifying of the outside skin of a molten lava flow. When the lava flow ceased, the molten lava inside the flow kept going, emptying out of the solidified skin and thus leaving tunnels. As they are on private property and are not administered by the national-park authorities, they can therefore be visited without an official guide. The owners of the land provide information, guides and flashlights (bring your own flashlight to be sure) for an entrance fee of about US$2. Tours to the lava tubes are offered in Puerto Ayora.

North of Bellavista is the national-park land known as **the highlands**. A footpath from Bellavista leads toward Cerro Crocker and other hills and extinct volcanoes. This is a good chance to see the vegetation of the Scalesia, Miconia and fern-sedge zones (see Habitats under Flora & Fauna, in the Facts about Ecuador chapter) and to look for birds such as the vermilion flycatcher or the elusive Galápagos rail and paint-billed crake. It is about 5km from Bellavista to the crescent-shaped hill of Media Luna and 3km farther to the base of Cerro Crocker. Because this is national-park land, a guide is required.

A part of the highlands that can be visited from the road is the twin craters called **Los Gemelos**. These are actually sinkholes, not volcanic craters, and they are surrounded by Scalesia forest. Vermilion flycatchers are often seen here, as well as short-eared owls on occasion. Los Gemelos are reached by taking the road to the village of Santa Rosa, about 12km west of Bellavista, and continuing about 2km beyond Santa Rosa on the trans-island road. Although the craters lie only 25m and 125m on either side of the road, they are hidden by vegetation, so ask your driver to stop at the short trailhead.

Near Santa Rosa, there is a **tortoise reserve**, where you can observe giant tortoises in the wild. The reserve is also a good place to look for short-eared owls, Darwin's finches, yellow warblers, Galápagos rails and paint-billed crakes (these last two are difficult to see in the long grass). A trail from Santa Rosa leads through private property to park land about 3km away. The trail is downhill and often quite muddy. Horses can be hired in Santa Rosa – ask at the store/bar on the main road for directions to the outfitter's house. The trail forks at the park boundary, with the right fork going up to the small hill of Cerro Chato (3km farther) and the left fork going to La Caseta (2km). The trails can be hard to follow, and you should carry drinking water. The reserve is part of the national park, and a guide is required. In 1991, a tourist entered the reserve without a guide, got hopelessly lost and died of thirst. Since then, another tourist almost suffered a similar fate but was rescued after nine days.

Next to the reserve is a private ranch owned by the Devine family. This place often has dozens of giant tortoises on it, and you can wander around at will and take photos for a US$2 fee. The entrance is beyond Santa Rosa, off the main road – ask locals for directions. Stay on the main tracks to avoid getting lost. Remember to close any gates that you go through. There is a café selling cold drinks and hot tea, which is welcome if the highland mist has soaked you.

The remaining Santa Cruz visitor sites are reached by boat and with guides. On the west coast are **Whale Bay** and **Conway Bay**, and on the north coast are **Black Turtle Cove** (Caleta Tortuga Negra) and **Las Bachas**. Between these two areas is the relatively new visitor site of **Cerro Dragón**. Conway Bay has a 1.5km trail passing a lagoon with flamingos; Whale Bay is visited less often. North of Conway Bay, Cerro Dragón has two small lagoons that may have flamingos and a 1.75km trail that leads through a forest of palo santo trees and opuntia cacti to a small hill with good views. There are some large repatriated land iguanas here.

There is no landing site in Black Turtle Cove, which is normally visited by panga ride. The cove has many little inlets and is surrounded by mangroves, where you can see lava herons and pelicans. The main attraction is in the water: marine turtles are sometimes seen mating, schools of golden mustard rays are often present, and white-tipped sharks may be seen basking in the shallows. It makes a very pleasant change to visit a marine site in a panga instead of walking. This site is occasionally visited by day boats from Puerto Ayora. The nearby Las Bachas beach, although popular for sunbathing and swimming, is often deserted.

ISLAS PLAZAS

These two small islands are just off the east coast of Santa Cruz and can be visited on a day trip from Puerto Ayora. Therefore visitors on a cruise should visit in the early morning or late afternoon to avoid the day groups. The heavy volume of visitors has led to some trail erosion.

The two islands were formed by uplift due to faulting. Boats anchor between them, and visitors can land on **South Plaza** (the larger of the islands), which is only about 13 hectares in area. A dry landing on a jetty brings you to an opuntia cactus forest, where there are many land iguanas. A 1km trail circuit leads visitors through sea lion colonies and along a cliff-top walk where swallow-tailed gulls and other species nest. The 25m-high cliffs are a superb vantage point to watch various seabirds, such as red-billed tropicbirds, frigatebirds, pelicans and Audubon's shearwaters. Snorkeling with the sea lions is a possibility, and out to sea, you may glimpse a manta ray 'flying.' Cactus forest, land iguanas, sea lions, seabirds galore – no wonder this is a favorite wildlife-watching site.

ISLA BALTRA

Most visitors to the Galápagos arrive by air to the Isla Baltra airport. Baltra is a small island (27 sq km) off the north coast of Santa Cruz. There are no visitor sites or accommodations here, but both public and private transportation from the airport to Puerto Ayora are available. People on a pre-arranged tour are often met at the airport and taken to their boats – a host of pelicans and noddies will greet you as you arrive at the harbor, and you can begin your wildlife watching within minutes of leaving the airport. Public transportation is described under Puerto Ayora (under Isla Santa Cruz, earlier in this chapter).

ISLAS SEYMOUR & MOSQUERA

Separated from Baltra by a channel, Isla Seymour is a 1.9-sq-km uplifted island with a dry landing. There is a circular trail (about 2.5km) leading through some of the largest and most active seabird breeding colonies in the islands. Magnificent frigatebirds and blue-footed boobies are the main attractions. Whatever time of year you come, there is always some kind of courtship, mating, nesting or chick rearing to observe. You can get close to the nests, as there is always at least one pair of boobies that chooses the middle of the trail as the best place to build their nest. Swallow-tailed gulls also nest here, and other birds are often seen as well. Sea lions and marine iguanas are common, and occasional fur seals, lava lizards and Galápagos snakes are seen as well. This is a small island, but it is well worth visiting for the wildlife.

Isla Mosquera is a tiny sandy island (about 120m by 600m) that lies in the channel between Islas Baltra and Seymour. There's no trail, but visitors land on the sandy beach to see the sea lion colony. Swimming and snorkeling with the sea lions is a popular activity.

ISLAS DAPHNE

These two islands of obviously volcanic origin are roughly 10km west of Seymour. Daphne Minor is the one that is very eroded, while **Daphne Major** retains most of its typically volcanic shape (called a tuff cone). A short but steep trail leads to the 120m-high summit of this tiny island.

There are two small craters at the top of the cone, and they contain hundreds of blue-footed booby nests. Masked boobies nest on the crater rims, and a few red-billed tropicbirds nest in rocky crevices in the steep sides of the islands.

The island is difficult to visit because of the acrobatic landing – visitors have to jump from a moving panga onto a vertical cliff and scramble their way up the rocks. The steep slopes are fragile and susceptible to erosion, which has led the national park authorities to limit visits to the island. Either you have to be lucky or you'll have arrange your visit well in advance.

ISLA SANTA FE

This 24-sq-km island, about 20km southeast of Santa Cruz, is a popular destination for day trips. There is a good anchorage in an attractive bay on the northeast coast, and a wet landing gives the visitor a choice of two trails. A 300m trail takes you to one of the tallest stands of opuntia cactus in the islands. Some of the cacti here are over 10m high. A somewhat more strenuous 1.5km rough trail goes into the highlands, where the Santa Fe land iguana may be seen if you are lucky. This species of iguana is found nowhere else in the world. The endemic rice rat is sometimes seen under bushes by the coast. Other attractions include a sea lion colony, excellent snorkeling, marine iguanas and, of course, birds.

ISLA SAN CRISTÓBAL

This 558-sq-km island is the fifth-largest in the archipelago and has the second-largest population. The provincial capital, Puerto Baquerizo Moreno, is on the southwest point. Despite being the capital, there is less tourist traffic here than in the larger and more traveler-friendly town of Puerto Ayora, on Isla Santa Cruz.

There are several visitor sites on or near San Cristóbal, but they are not frequently visited by boats from Santa Cruz. The Chatham mockingbird, a species found nowhere else, is common throughout the island.

Puerto Baquerizo Moreno

This is the capital of the Galápagos and is on Isla San Cristóbal. Although it is the second-largest town in the islands, with a population of about 5400, many of the inhabitants work in government-related jobs or fishing, and the town is still a long way behind Puerto Ayora for tourism. Facilities are improving, however, and this is an increasingly important tourist town.

Banco del Pacífico changes money. Phone service is poor, but this is being improved. Expensive Internet service is available next to Rosita's Restaurant. A small hospital and post office are in town.

Chalo's Tours (☎ 520 953) and a couple of other places offer local tours.

Things to See & Do Beside the cathedral (which has murals with Galápagos themes), a small museum with a statue of Darwin can be visited. An interpretation center on the north side of town has exhibits about the biology and history of the islands.

Frigatebird Hill is a short walk from town, and other local visitor sites are described in the Isla San Cristóbal section, under Visitor Sites, earlier in this chapter.

Places to Stay & Eat The cheapest hotels include *Hotel San Francisco* (☎ 520 304), which is clean and a good value for US$2.25 per person for rooms with private cold shower and fan. Also recommended is the friendly *Mar Azul* (☎ 520 139, fax 520 384), which has pleasant patios and rooms with private hot shower at US$3 per person. The recently remodeled *Hotel Chatham* (☎/fax 520 137) has comfortable beds and doubles with TV and hot shower for US$10. *Islas Galápagos* (☎ 520 203, fax 520 162) charges US$6/10 for singles/doubles and has air-conditioning in some rooms. *Los Cactus* (☎ 520 078) is clean, friendly and has private hot showers at US$8/11.50/17 for singles/doubles/triples.

Cabañas Don Jorge (☎ 520 208, fax 520 100, cabanasdonjorge@hotmail.com) charges US$12/20/24/28 for one/two/three/four people; rooms have private hot bath. Meals are available on request. *Hotel Orca* (☎/fax 520 233) is the largest hotel. Its 20 rooms have hot water and fans. There is a restaurant in the building, which is close to the beach. It works with Etnotur in Quito (see Travel Agencies in the Quito & Around chapter). Rates are US$34/45. The similarly priced *Hostal Galápagos* (☎/fax 520 157) is air-conditioned and clean but is not attended unless you call ahead. Casa Blanca restaurant (described later in this section) has information; it's in the center of town.

In the highlands at **El Progreso**, stay at *Casa del Ceibo* (☎ 520 248), which has two rooms at US$2 per person. Simple kitchen privileges are available, and a restaurant is open on weekends.

In Puerto Baquerizo Moreno, the best place to eat is *Rosita's Restaurant*, which serves tasty *bacalao* (a local fish). *Casa Blanca*, in the center of town, is also good, especially for drinks and snacks on the outdoor patio. *Miconia* is near the naval base and is popular with sailors; its spaghetti dinners are recommended. ***Sabor Latino*** is popular with locals for inexpensive set lunches. ***Cebichería Langostino*** is good for lunchtime ceviche. For dinner, try the pleasant ***Restaurant Genoa***, which has meals á la carte, or ***Albacora*** for seafood. There are several other places to eat.

Neptunus and ***Blue Star*** are bars that feature dancing on weekends.

Visitor Sites

About 1.5km southeast of Puerto Baquerizo Moreno is **Frigatebird Hill** *(Cerro de las Tijeretas)*. It can be reached without a guide via a foot trail. From the hill, there is a view of a bay below and the town behind. Both species of frigatebirds have nested here, but pressure from the nearby town appears to be driving them away.

A road leads from the capital to the village of El Progreso, about 8km to the east and at the base of the 896m-high Cerro San Joaquín, the highest point on San Cristóbal (buses go here several times a day from Puerto Baquerizo Moreno). Rent a jeep or walk east along a dirt road about 10km farther to **El Junco Lagoon** – a freshwater lake at about 700m above sea level. It's one of the few permanent freshwater bodies in the Galápagos. Here you can see white-cheeked pintails and common gallinules and observe the typical highland Miconia vegetation and endemic tree ferns. The weather is often misty or rainy.

Smaller than its name suggests, **Puerto Grande** is a well-protected little cove on San Cristóbal's northwestern coast. There is a good, sandy beach suitable for swimming. Various seabirds can be seen, but the site is not known for any special colonies.

About an hour northeast of Puerto Baquerizo Moreno by boat is the tiny, rocky **Isla Lobos**, the main sea lion and blue-footed booby colony for visitors to San Cristóbal. There is a 300m-long trail where lava lizards are often seen. Both the boat crossing and the trail tend to be rough, and there are better wildlife colonies elsewhere.

About a two-hour boat ride northeast of Puerto Baquerizo Moreno, is another little rocky island that, because of a resemblance to a sleeping lion, is named **León Dormido**. The English name is Kicker Rock. The island is a sheer-walled tuff cone that has been eroded in half; smaller boats can sail between the two rocks. Because the sheer walls provide no place to land, this site can only be seen from a passing boat.

At the north end of the island is **Los Galápagos**, where you can often see the giant Galápagos tortoises in the wild, though it takes some effort to get to the highland area where they live. One way to get there is to land in a bay at the north end of the island and hike up – it takes about two hours to reach the tortoise area by the trail. Some visitors report many tortoises, others see none. Good luck! The road from Puerto Baquerizo Moreno through El Progreso and on to El Junco Lagoon is slowly being pushed northeast. It may be possible to get to Los Galápagos by taking this road to the end and hiking in – ask in town.

The northeasternmost point of the island is **Punta Pitt**, where volcanic tuff formations are of interest to geologists (and attractive in their own right), but the unique feature of this site is that it is the only one on which you can see all three Galápagos booby species nesting. The walk is a little strenuous, but it is rewarding.

Other visitor sites on this island include **Cerro Brujo**, near the coast, and **Turtle Bay**. Both are at the northeast end and can be visited in association with Punta Pitt and Los Galápagos. Flamingos and turtles are among the attractions.

ISLA ESPAÑOLA

This 61-sq-km island (also known as Hood) is the most southerly in the archipelago and has two visitor sites. Because Española is somewhat outlying (about 90km southeast of Santa Cruz), reaching it requires a fairly long sea passage; captains of some of the smallest boats may be reluctant to go this far. The island is well worth visiting from late March to December, because it has the only colony of the waved albatross, one of the Galápagos' most spectacular seabirds.

The best visitor site on Española is **Punta Suárez**, at the western end of the island; a wet landing is necessary. A 2km trail takes visitors through masked and blue-footed booby colonies and past a beach full of marine iguanas before reaching the main attraction – the waved albatross colony.

Just beyond the colony is a blow hole through which the waves force water to spout about 20m into the air. If you sit on top of the cliffs between the waved albatrosses and the blow hole, you can watch seabirds performing their aerial ballet (and their less elegant attempts to land and take off).

Other birds to look out for are the Hood mockingbird, found nowhere else; swallow-tailed gulls; red-billed tropicbirds and oyster-catchers. The large cactus finch can also be seen and is found on few other islands. This is one of my favorite visitor sites in the Galápagos.

The beautiful white-sand beach of **Gardner Bay**, at the east end of Isla Española, is reached with a wet landing, and there is good swimming and a sea lion colony. An island a short distance offshore provides good snorkeling – there's one rock that often has white-tipped reef sharks basking under it.

ISLA SANTA MARÍA

Officially known as Santa María but often called Floreana or Charles, this is the sixth-largest of the islands, at 173 sq km.

Puerto Velasco Ibarra

This port is the only settlement on Isla Santa María (Floreana), which has only about 70 permanent inhabitants. There is not much to do in this tiny town, but a black beach nearby boasts a sea lion colony, and there's a flamingo lagoon within walking distance. A road goes into the highlands – there is very little traffic (a school bus goes up and back at 6 am and 3 pm) but it's easy walking. There is only one passenger boat every two weeks from Puerto Ayora, although others can be arranged.

Places to Stay & Eat The family of Margaret Wittmer (see the boxed text 'The Chronicles of Floreana') runs a small *hotel and restaurant* (☎ 520 250), where there is the island's only phone. They also have a small gift shop and post office. Rates are US$30/50/70 for beachfront rooms with hot water and fans, and three meals are US$20 a day. They are rarely full, and even if they were, you could ask them to show you somewhere to crash.

Visitor Sites

From the village of Puerto Velasco Ibarra, a road runs inland for a few kilometers to an area where you can see the endemic medium tree finch (this finch exists only on Floreana). Early settlers once lived in the nearby caves. This area, called **Asilo de la Paz**, is an official visitor site.

It is an all-day hike up there and back – you can hire a guide (local biologist/guide Felipe Cruz rented the town's dumptruck for my trip). There are no taxis.

There are three visitor sites on the north coast of Floreana. **Post Office Bay** used to have a barrel where whalers left mail. Any captain of a boat that was heading to where the mail was addressed would deliver it. The site continues to be used, but obviously, the barrel has been changed many times. About 300m behind the barrel is a lava cave that can be descended with the aid of a short piece of rope. Nearby is a pleasant swimming beach and the remains of a canning factory; a wet landing is necessary.

Also reached with a wet landing is **Punta Cormorant**. There is a greenish beach (green because it contains crystals of the mineral olivine) where sea lions play and the swimming and snorkeling are good.

A 400m trail leads across an isthmus to a white-sand beach where turtles sometimes lay their eggs. The beach is also good for swimming, but beware of stingrays – shuffle your feet when entering the water.

Between the two beaches is a flamingo lagoon, which is probably the main attraction of this visitor site. Several dozen flamingos are normally seen. This is also a good place to see other wading birds, such as the black-necked stilt, oystercatchers, willets and whimbrels. White-cheeked pintail ducks

The Chronicles of Floreana

DAVID PEEVERS

Margaret Wittmer, who died recently at age 95, was the last survivor of the original settlers of the Galápagos.

This island has had an interesting history. The first resident of the Galápagos was Patrick Watkins, an Irishman who was marooned on Floreana in 1807 and spent two years living there, growing vegetables and trading his produce for rum from passing boats. The story goes that he managed to remain drunk for most of his stay, then stole a ship's boat and set out for Guayaquil accompanied by five slaves. No one knows what happened to the slaves – only Watkins reached the mainland.

After Watkins' departure, the island was turned into an Ecuadorian penal colony for some years. In the 1930s, three groups of German settlers arrived on Floreana, and strange stories have been told about them ever since.

The most colorful of the settlers was a baroness who arrived with three lovers. Another settler, Dr Friedrich Ritter, an eccentric who had all of his teeth removed before arriving so as to avoid having dental problems, was accompanied by his mistress. The third group was a young couple from Cologne, the Wittmers.

Despite their common nationality, there was a great deal of friction among the groups, and mysteriously, one by one, the settlers died. The baroness and one of her lovers simply disappeared, while another lover died in a boating accident. The vegetarian Dr Ritter died of food poisoning after eating chicken. The only ones to survive were the Wittmers.

Margaret Wittmer, one of the original settlers, died in 2000 at the age of 95. Her children and grandchildren run a small hotel and restaurant in Puerto Velasco Ibarra. Although several books and articles have been written about the strange happenings on Floreana (including one by Wittmer herself), no one is really sure of the truth.

are often seen in the lagoon, and Galápagos hawks wheel overhead.

Another Floreana visitor site is the remains of a half-submerged volcanic cone poking up out of the ocean a few hundred meters from Punta Cormorant. Aptly named the **Devil's Crown**, this ragged semicircle of rocks is one of the most outstanding marine sites in the Galápagos.

A panga ride around the cone will give views of red-billed tropicbirds, pelicans, herons and lava gulls nesting on the rocks,

but the greater attraction is the snorkeling in and around the crater. There are thousands of bright tropical fish, a small coral formation, sea lions and (if you are lucky) sharks.

ISLA SAN SALVADOR
This official name is used less often than the old Spanish name (Santiago), or the English name (James). Santiago is the fourth-largest of the islands and has several excellent visitor sites within its 585 sq km.

The best site is **Puerto Egas**, on James Bay, on the west side of Santiago. Here, there is a long, flat, black lava shoreline where eroded shapes form lava pools, caves and inlets that house a great variety of wildlife. This is a great place to see colonies of marine iguanas basking in the sun. The tide pools contain hundreds of red Sally Lightfoot crabs, which attract hunting herons of all the commonly found species.

The inlets are favorite haunts of the Galápagos fur seal, and this site is one of the best places in the islands to see them. You can snorkel here with fur seals and many species of tropical fish. I have seen moray eels, sharks and octopuses during snorkeling trips here.

Behind the black lava shoreline is Sugar-loaf Volcano, which can be reached via a 2km footpath. Lava lizards, Darwin's finches and Galápagos doves are often seen on this path. It peters out near the top of the 395m summit, but from here, the views are stupendous. There is an extinct crater in which feral goats are often seen (the wild goats are a major problem on Santiago), and Galápagos hawks often hover a few meters above the top of the volcano. North of the volcano is a crater where a salt mine used to be; its remains can be visited by walking along a 3km trail from the coast.

Puerto Egas is one of the most popular sites in the islands – so popular that it was temporarily closed in late 1995 by the National Park Service because too many people were visiting it. It has since reopened.

At the north end of James Bay, about 5km from Puerto Egas, is the brown-sand **Espumilla Beach**, which can be reached with a wet landing. The swimming is good here, and by the small lagoon behind the beach you can see various wading birds – including, at times, flamingos. A 2km trail leads inland through transitional vegetation where there are various finches and the Galápagos flycatcher.

At the northwestern end of Santiago, another site that is normally visited by boat is **Buccaneer Cove**, so called because it was a popular place for 17th- and 18th-century buccaneers to careen their vessels. The beautiful cliffs and pinnacles, which are used as nesting areas by several species of seabirds, are the main attraction these days. This is best appreciated from the sea, but it is possible to land in the cove, where there are beaches.

Sullivan Bay is on Santiago's east coast. Here, a huge, black, century-old lava flow has solidified into a sheet that reaches to the edge of the sea. A dry landing enables visitors to step onto the flow and follow a trail of white posts in a 2km circuit on the lava. You can see uneroded volcanic formations, such as pahoehoe lava, lava bubbles and tree-trunk molds in the surface. A few pioneer colonizing plants, such as *Brachycereus* cactus and *Mollugo* carpetweed, can be seen. This site is of particular interest to those interested in volcanology or geology.

ISLA BARTOLOMÉ

Just off Sullivan Bay (see Isla San Salvador, earlier) is Isla Bartolomé, which has an area of 1.2 sq km. Here you can see the most frequently photographed and hence most famous vista in the islands. There are two visitor sites and footpaths. One begins from a jetty (dry landing), from where it is about 600m to the 114m summit of the island. This good but sandy trail leads through a wild and unearthly looking lava landscape; a wooden boardwalk and stairs have been built on the last (steepest) section, both to aid visitors and to protect the trail from erosion. There are a few pioneering plants on either side of the trail, but the main attraction is the view toward Santiago, which is just as dramatic as the photographs suggest.

The other visitor site is a small, sandy beach in a cove (wet landing). Here you have good snorkeling and swimming opportunities, including a chance to swim with the endemic Galápagos penguins that frequent this cove. Marine turtles and a gaudy variety of tropical fish are also frequently seen.

The best way to see and photograph the penguins is by taking a panga ride close to the rocks on either side of the cove – particularly around the aptly named Pinnacle Rock, to the right of the cove from the seaward side. You can often get within a few meters of these fascinating birds – the closest point to Puerto Ayora where you can do so. Other penguin colonies are on the western side of Isabela.

From the beach, a 100m trail leads across the narrowest part of Bartolomé to another sandy beach on the opposite side of the island. Marine turtles may nest here between January and March. Both beaches are clearly visible from the viewpoint described earlier in this section.

SOMBRERO CHINO

This tiny island just off the southeastern tip of Santiago is less than a quarter of 1 sq km in size. It is a fairly recent volcanic cone, which accounts for its descriptive name (it translates as 'Chinese Hat'). The hat shape is best appreciated from the north. There is a small sea lion cove on the north shore, where you can anchor and land at the visitor site. Opposite Sombrero Chino, on the rocky shoreline of nearby Isla Santiago, penguins are often seen.

A 400m trail goes around the cove and through a sea lion colony – marine iguanas scurry everywhere. The volcanic landscape is attractive, and there are good views of the cone. There are snorkeling and swimming opportunities in the cove.

ISLA RÁBIDA

This approximately 5-sq-km island, also known as Jervis, lies 5km south of Santiago. There is a wet landing onto a dark red beach where sea lions haul out and pelicans nest. This is one of the best places to see these birds nesting.

Behind the beach, there is a salt-water lagoon where flamingos and white-cheeked pintails are sometimes seen (although the flamingos have not been seen much during the 1990s). This lagoon is also the site of a sea lion bachelor colony where the *solteros,* deposed by the dominant bull, while away their days.

There is a .75km trail with good views of the island's 367m volcanic peak, which is covered with palo santo trees. At the end of the trail, there is a great snorkeling spot.

ISLA GENOVESA

This island is known more often by its English name of Tower. It covers 14 sq km and is the northeasternmost of the Galápagos Islands. As it is an outlying island, Tower is infrequently included on a one-week itinerary. If you have the time, however, and are interested in seabirds, this island is well worth the long trip. It is the best place to see a red-footed booby colony, and it provides visitors with the opportunity to visit colonies of masked boobies, great frigatebirds, red-billed tropicbirds, swallow-tailed gulls and many thousands of storm petrels. Other bird attractions include Galápagos doves and short-eared owls. Both sea lions and fur seals are present, and there are exciting snorkeling opportunities – hammerhead sharks are here.

The island is fairly flat and round, with a large, almost landlocked, cove named Darwin Bay on the south side. There are two visitor sites, both on Darwin Bay. **Prince Philip's Steps** (also called El Barranco) is on the eastern arm of the bay and can be reached with a dry landing. A steep and rocky path leads to the top of 25m-high cliffs, and nesting seabirds are sometimes found right on the narrow path.

At the top of the cliffs, the 1km-long trail leads inland, past dry-forest vegetation and various seabird colonies, to a cracked expanse of lava, where thousands of storm petrels make their nests and wheel overhead. Short-eared owls are often seen here, and it is an excellent hike for the bird enthusiast.

The second visitor site, **Darwin Bay beach**, is a coral beach reached by a wet landing. There is a .75km trail along the beach that passes through more seabird colonies.

You can take a pleasant panga ride along the cliffs. The panga is often followed by playful sea lions. This recommended excursion gives a good view from the seaward side of the cliffs and of the birds nesting on them.

Finally, this is the only regularly visited island that lies entirely north of the equator (the northernmost part of Isabela also pokes above the line). Cruises to Tower may well involve various ceremonies for passengers who have never crossed the equator at sea before.

ISLAS MARCHENA & PINTA

This island is also known as Bindloe. At 130 sq km, this is the seventh-largest island in the archipelago and the largest one to have no official visitor sites. There are some good scuba-diving sites, however, so you may get to see the island up close if you are on a dive trip.

The 343m-high volcano in the middle of the island was very active during 1991 – ask your guide about its current degree of activity. In the past, it was possible to see the eruptions from boats cruising in the northern part of the islands.

Isla Pinta is the original home of Lonesome George, the tortoise described earlier in the Isla Santa Cruz section. Pinta is the ninth-largest of the Galápagos Islands and is farther north than any of the bigger islands. Its English name is Abingdon. There are landing sites, but the island has no visitor sites, and researchers require a permit to visit.

ISLA ISABELA

The largest island in the archipelago is the 4588-sq-km Isabela (occasionally called Albemarle), which occupies over 58% of the entire land mass of the Galápagos. It is a relatively recent island and consists of a chain of five fairly young and intermittently active volcanoes, one of which, Volcán Wolf, is the highest point in the Galápagos at 1707m (some sources claim 1646m). There is also one small older volcano, Volcán Ecuador.

Although Isabela's volcanoes dominate the westward view during passages to the western part of Santa Cruz, the island itself is not frequently visited by smaller boats because most of the best visitor sites are on the west side of the island. The reverse 'C' shape of the island means that the visitor sites on the west side are reached only after a very long passage (over 200km) from Santa Cruz, and so either you have to make a two-week cruise or you visit Isabela without seeing many of the other islands.

Puerto Villamil

This is a small port on Isabela, the largest island, with about 1500 inhabitants (1200 are in Puerto Villamil). It is not much visited by travelers, although some tours do stop here. This island is a marvelous one. There are several active volcanoes and a large number of Galápagos tortoises, and it looks like Isabela is going to become more important in Galápagos tourism in the years to come.

From Puerto Villamil, an 18km road climbs to the village of Santo Tomás, where horses can be hired to go up Volcán Santo Tomás. There are several men in Puerto Villamil who work as guides – ask around.

There's nowhere to change traveler's checks; bring US cash. There is a Pacifictel office.

Places to Stay & Eat Clean and recommended, *San Vicente* (☎ 529 140) is also often full. It has six rooms at US$3/4 for singles/doubles with cold showers. Meals are provided upon request. Other cheapies are pretty rundown and basic; try *Hostal Loja* (☎ 529 174), which charges US$2 per person and has hot water, or *Los Delfines* (☎ 529 129), which also has hot water and charges US$3/4.

Tero Real (☎ 529 195) has clean rooms with private cold showers and a fridge for US$5/8. Meals are provided upon request. *Hotel Ballena Azul* (☎/fax 529 125, isabela@ga.pro.ec or isabela@hosteriaisabela.com.ec) is the best budget place in town. The singles have shared bathrooms, the doubles and triples have private bathrooms and solar hot water, and some rooms have beach views. Meals are available upon request. Rates are US$8 per person.

La Casa Marita (☎ 529 238, fax 529 201, hcmarita@ga.pro.ec) is attractive and has pleasant beachfront rooms sleeping up to four. All have hot showers and kitchenettes, and some have air-conditioning. Rates are US$35/50/65/80, including breakfast, and other meals are available upon request.

Restaurants tend to provide menus without prices, so always check on price (and taxes) before ordering. The best (and priciest) place to eat is *El Encanto de la Pepa*, which serves a good variety of dishes in a tropical setting.

Costa Azul is clean and cheaper, but has a more limited menu and lacks atmosphere. *Ballena Azul* has good food with many choices but very slow service – it's cooked to order, so order ahead of time. *La Iguana* has limited hours (weekends and holidays) and serves good pizzas and drinks under the palm trees. There are a few basic *comedores*.

Getting There & Away On Monday, Wednesday and Friday, EMETEBE has a Baltra-Isabela-Santa Cruz flight. On Tuesday, Thursday and Saturday, EMETEBE has a Santa Cruz-Isabela-Baltra flight. The Isabela stop may be canceled if there are no passengers who want to go there.

Buses to Santo Tomás and farther into the highlands leave at 7 am and noon, returning two hours later. Trucks can be rented at other times.

Visitor Sites

There are many visitor sites on Isabela. One of these is the summit of **Volcán Alcedo** (1128m), which is famous for its 7km-wide caldera and steaming fumaroles, where hundreds of giant tortoises can be seen, especially from June to December. The view is fantastic. Until 1998, it was possible to hike to and camp near the summit (two days were required). This long, steep, waterless and very strenuous trail has now been closed, but it may reopen in 2001 or 2002. If it does, advance permits will be required.

A few kilometers north of the landing for Alcedo is **Punta García**, which consists mainly of very rough *aa* lava; there are no proper trails, but you can land. Until recently, this was the only place where you could see the endemic flightless cormorant without having to take the long passage around to the west side. Recently, however, these birds have been present only intermittently, and visits to this site have declined.

At the northern tip of Isabela is **Punta Albemarle**, which used to be a US radar base during WWII. There are no trails, and the site is known for the flightless cormorants, which normally are not found farther to the

east. Farther west are several points where flightless cormorants, Galápagos penguins and other seabirds can be seen, but there are no visitor sites. You must view the birds from your boat.

At the west end of the northern arm of Isabela is the small, old Volcán Ecuador (610m), which comes down almost to the sea. **Punta Vicente Roca**, at the volcano's base, is a rocky point with a good snorkeling area, but there is no official landing site.

The first official visitor-landing site on the western side of Isabela is **Punta Tortuga**, a beach at the base of Volcán Darwin (1280m). Part of the land here was formed through a recent uplift. Locals report that one day in 1975, the uplift just appeared. One day there was nothing, and the next day there was an uplifted ledge – no one saw it happen.

Although there is no trail, you can land on the beach and explore the mangroves for the mangrove finch, which is present here but not always easy to see. This finch is found only on Islas Isabela and Fernandina.

Just south of the point is **Tagus Cove**, where early sailors frequently anchored. You can still see some of the names of the vessels scratched into the cliffs around the cove. A dry landing will bring you to a trail, which you follow for 2km past a saltwater lagoon and onto the lower lava slopes of Volcán Darwin, where various volcanic formations can be observed. There are some steep sections on this trail. A panga ride along the cliffs will enable you to see the historical graffiti and various seabirds, usually including the Galápagos penguin and flightless cormorant. There are snorkeling opportunities in the cove.

Urbina Bay lies around the middle of the western shore of Isabela and is a flat area formed by an uplift from the sea in 1954. Evidence of the uplift includes a coral reef on the land. Flightless cormorants, pelicans and marine iguanas can be observed on land, and rays and turtles can be seen in the bay. A wet landing onto a beach brings you to a 1km trail that leads to the corals. There is a good view of Volcán Alcedo.

Near where the western shoreline of Isabela bends sharply toward the lower arm of the island, there is a visitor site known for its marine life. **Elizabeth Bay** is best visited by a panga ride, as there are no landing sites. Islas Mariela are at the entrance of the bay and are frequented by penguins. The end of the bay itself is a long, narrow and convoluted arm of the sea surrounded by three species of mangroves. Marine turtles and rays are usually seen in the water, and various seabirds and shorebirds are present.

West of Elizabeth Bay is **Punta Moreno**. You can make a dry landing onto a lava flow, where there are some brackish pools. Flamingos, white-cheeked pintails and common gallinules are sometimes seen, and various pioneer plants and insects are found in the area. There is a rough trail.

On the southeastern corner of Isabela, there is the small village of Puerto Villamil. Behind and to the west of the village is the **Villamil Lagoon**. This visitor site is known for its migrant birds – especially waders, of which over 20 species have been reported here. The surrounding vegetation is dense and without trails, but the road to the highlands and the open beach do give reason-able access to the lagoons. Also west of Puerto Villamil is a new visitor site, **Muro de las Lágrimas** (Wall of Tears), which is the reportedly historical site of a wall built by convicts.

The massive **Volcán Santo Tomás** (1490m), which is also known as Volcán Sierra Negra, lies to the northwest. The tiny settlement of Santo Tomás is on the lower flanks of the volcano. Trucks or jeeps can be hired for the 18km ride from Puerto Villamil. From Santo Tomás, it is 9km farther up a steep trail to the rim of the volcano – horses can be rented in the village.

The caldera is roughly 10km in diameter and is a spectacular site with magnificent views. An 8km trail leads around the east side of the volcano to some active fumaroles. It is possible to walk all the way around the caldera, but the trail peters out. You should carry all your food and water or rent horses. Galápagos hawks, short-eared owls, finches and flycatchers are among the birds commonly seen on this trip. The summit is often foggy (especially during the June-to-December garúa season) and it is easy to

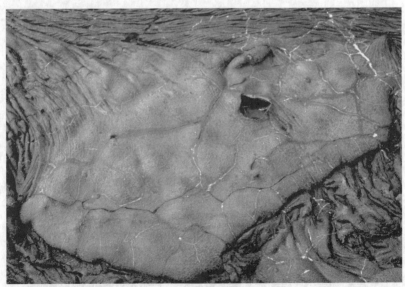

Lava formation

JASON EDWARDS

THE GALÁPAGOS ISLANDS

get lost – stay in a group. Nearby is Volcán Chico, a subcrater where you can see more fumaroles. These volcanoes are very infrequently visited.

ISLA FERNANDINA

At 642 sq km, Fernandina (infrequently called Narborough) is the third-largest island and the westernmost and youngest of the main islands. The recently formed volcanic landscapes are most impressive. Many eruptions have been recorded since 1813, the most recent being in 1995. This is the island on which you are most likely to see a volcanic eruption.

There is one visitor site at **Punta Espinosa**, just across from Tagus Cove on Isabela. The point is known for one of the greatest concentrations of the endemic marine iguanas, which are found by the thousands. Also, flightless cormorants, Galápagos penguins and sea lions are common here.

A dry landing brings you to two trails: a .25km trail to the point and a .75km trail to recently formed lava fields. Here you can see various pioneering plants, such as the *Brachycereus* cactus, as well as pahoehoe and aa lava formations.

OTHER ISLANDS

The one sizable island in the central part of the archipelago that has no visitor sites is **Isla Pinzón**, also called Duncan. It is a cliff-bound island, which makes landing difficult, and a permit is required to visit it (permits are usually reserved for scientists and researchers).

The northernmost islands are the two tiny islands of **Isla Wolf** (Wenman) and **Isla Darwin** (Culpepper). They are about 100km northwest of the rest of the archipelago and are very seldom visited, except occasionally on scuba-diving trips. Both have nearly vertical cliffs that make landing difficult; Isla Darwin was first visited in 1964, when a helicopter expedition landed on the summit. Various other rocks and islets are present in the archipelago, but all are extremely small.

Language

Although Spanish is the most widely spoken language in Ecuador, travelers to the region will encounter a mix of other European tongues, indigenous languages and colorful dialects. This chapter addresses such variations only briefly, mainly discussing the type of Spanish that is understood more or less throughout the region.

Every visitor to Ecuador should attempt to learn some Spanish, the basic elements of which are easily acquired (perhaps more so for speakers of English and Romance languages). A month-long language course taken before departure can go a long way toward facilitating communication and comfort on the road. Language courses are also available in Ecuador. Even if classes are impractical, you should make the effort to learn a few basic phrases and pleasantries. Do not hesitate to practice your new skills – in general, Latin Americans meet attempts to communicate in the vernacular, however halting, with enthusiasm and appreciation.

Latin American Spanish

The Spanish of the Americas comes in a bewildering array of varieties. Depending on the areas in which you travel, consonants may be glossed over, vowels squashed into each other, and syllables and even words dropped entirely. Slang and regional vocabulary, much of it derived from indigenous languages, can further add to your bewilderment.

Throughout Latin America, the Spanish language is referred to as *castellano* more often than *español*. Unlike in Spain, the plural of the familiar *tú* form is *ustedes* rather than *vosotros;* the latter term will sound quaint and archaic in the Americas. In addition, the letters 'c' and 'z' are never lisped in Latin America; attempts to do so could well provoke amusement or even contempt.

Phrasebooks & Dictionaries

Lonely Planet's *Latin American Spanish phrasebook*, by Anna Cody, is a good addition to your backpack. Another exceptionally useful resource is the *University of Chicago Spanish-English, English-Spanish Dictionary* – its small size, light weight and thorough entries make it ideal for travel. It also makes a great gift for any newfound friends upon your departure.

Pronunciation

The pronunciation of written Spanish is, in theory, consistently phonetic. Once you are aware of the basic rules, they should cause little difficulty. Speak slowly to avoid getting tongue-tied until you become confident of your ability. Of course, the best way to familiarize yourself with the pronunciation of the area you're traveling in is to chat with locals, keeping an ear out for regional variations.

Traditionally, there were three Spanish letters that did not exist in English: 'ch,' 'll' and 'ñ.' These followed 'c,' 'l,' and 'n' respectively in the alphabet, and had their own corresponding sections in the dictionary. However, in the mid-1990s, Spain's Academia Real de la Lengua Española abolished these as separate letters; hence, newer Spanish dictionaries list them in their English alphabetical order. The practice varies from region to region, so look for a 'ch' section in the phone book if you can't find 'Chávez' under 'c.'

Vowels Spanish vowels are generally consistent and have close English equivalents:

a is like the 'a' in 'father'
e is somewhere between the 'e' in 'met' and the 'ey' in 'hey'
i is like the 'ee' in 'feet'
o is like the 'o' in 'note'
u is like the 'oo' in 'boot'; it is silent after 'q' and in the pairings 'gue' and 'gui,' unless it's carrying a dieresis ('ü,' as in *güero*)

Consonants Spanish consonants generally resemble their English equivalents.

The following are the major differences in consonants:

b   resembles the English 'b,' but is a softer sound produced by holding the lips nearly together. When beginning a word or when preceded by 'm' or 'n,' it's pronounced like the 'b' in 'book' (*bomba, embajada*). The Spanish 'v' is pronounced almost identically; for clarification, Spanish speakers refer to 'b' as 'b larga' and to 'v' as 'b corta.'

c   is like the 's' in 'see' before 'e' and 'i'; otherwise, it's like the English 'k.'

d   is produced with the tongue up against the front teeth, almost like the 'th' in 'feather'; after 'l' and 'n,' it's pronounced like the English 'd' in 'dog.'

g   before 'e' and 'i' acts as a more guttural English 'h'; otherwise, it's like the 'g' in 'go.'

h   is invariably silent; if your name begins with this letter, listen carefully when immigration officials summon you to pick up your passport.

j   acts as a more guttural English 'h.'

ll   acts as a Spanish 'y,' although it is never a vowel; see Semiconsonant, below.

ñ   is like the 'ny' in 'canyon.'

r   is produced with the tongue touching the palate and flapping down, almost like the 'tt' of 'butter.' At the beginning of a word or following 'l,' 'n' or 's,' it is rolled strongly.

rr   is a very strongly rolled Spanish 'r.'

t   resembles the English 't,' but without the puff of air.

v   is pronounced like the Spanish 'b.'

x   is generally pronounced like the 'x' in 'taxi' except for a few words in which it acts as the Spanish 'j' (as in 'México').

z   is like the 's' in 'sun.'

Semiconsonant The Spanish **y** is a semiconsonant; it's pronounced as the Spanish 'i' when it stands alone or appears at the end of a word. Normally, 'y' is pronounced like the 'y' in 'yesterday'; however, in some regions of Latin America, it may be pronounced as the 's' in 'pleasure' or even the 'j' in 'jacket.' Hence, *yo me llamo* can sound like 'joe meh jahm-oh.'

Diphthongs Diphthongs are combinations of two vowels that form a single syllable. In Spanish, the formation of a diphthong depends on combinations of the two 'weak' vowels, 'i' and 'u,' or one weak and one of the three 'strong' vowels, 'a,' 'e' and 'o.' Two strong vowels form separate syllables.

An example of two weak vowels forming a diphthong is the word *viuda* (widow; pronounced **vyu**-tha). The initial syllable of 'Guatemala' is a combination of weak and strong vowels. In contrast, the verb *caer* (to fall) has two syllables (pronounced ca-**er**). Other examples include the following:

ai   as in 'hide'
au   as in 'how'
ei   as in 'hay'
ia   as in 'yard'
ie   as in 'yes'
oi   as in 'boy'
ua   as in 'wash'
ue   as in 'well' (unless preceded by 'q' or 'g')

Stress Stress is extremely important as it can change the meaning of words. In general, words ending in vowels or the letters 'n' or 's' have stress on the next-to-last syllable, while those with other endings have stress on the last syllable. Thus *vaca* (cow) and *caballos* (horses) are both stressed on their penultimate syllables, while *catedral* (cathedral) is stressed on its last syllable.

To indicate departures from these general rules, Spanish employs the acute accent, which can occur anywhere in a word. If there is an accented syllable, stress is always on that syllable. Thus *sótano* (basement), 'América' and 'Panamá' have the first, second and third syllable stressed, respectively. When words are written in capital letters, the accent is often omitted, but the stress still falls where the accent would be.

Basic Grammar

Although even colloquial Spanish comprises a multitude of tenses and moods, learning enough grammar to enable basic conversation is not particularly difficult. In general, Spanish word order in sentences resembles that of English.

Nouns & Pronouns Nouns in Spanish are masculine or feminine. In general, nouns ending in 'o,' 'e' or 'ma' are masculine, while those ending in 'a,' 'ión' or 'dad' are feminine. Of course, there are scores of exceptions to this rule: both *día* (day) and *mapa* (map) are masculine, while *mano* (hand) is feminine. To pluralize a noun, add 's' if it ends in an unaccented vowel – eg, *libro* (book) becomes *libros* – and 'es' if it ends in a consonant or accented vowel – eg, *rey* (king) becomes *reyes*. Fortunately for speakers of English, there is no declension of nouns as in Latin.

The personal pronouns are *yo* (I), *tú* or *vos* (you, informal), *usted* (you, formal; abbreviated Ud), *el/ella* (he/she), *nosotros/nosotras* (we), *ustedes* (you, plural; abbreviated Uds) and *ellos/ellas* (they). Note that to use the feminine plurals *nosotras* and *ellas,* the group referred to must be entirely composed of females; the presence of even one male calls for the masculine pronoun. In common speech, the personal pronoun may be omitted when it is the subject of a sentence if the subject's identity is made clear by the verb ending: *estoy aquí* rather than *yo estoy aquí* (both mean 'I am here').

The possessive pronouns are *mi* (my), *tu* (your, informal), *nuestro* (our) and *su* (his/her/their/your, formal; singular and plural). As in English, possessive pronouns precede the noun they modify; however, they must agree in number and gender with that noun – not with the possessor. Thus we get *nuestro hombre* (our man), *nuestra mujer* (our woman), *nuestros novios* (our boyfriends) and *nuestras novias* (our girlfriends). *Mi, tu* and *su* do not change with gender, but add an 's' for plural nouns: *mis libros* means 'my books.'

The demonstrative pronouns are *este* (this) and *ese* (that). Gender and number also affect demonstrative pronouns:

este libro	this book
estos cuadernos	these notebooks
esta carta	this letter
estas tijeras	these scissors
ese chico	that boy
esos muchachos	those guys
esa chica	that girl
esas muchachas	those gals

Articles, Adjectives & Adverbs The definite articles ('the' in English) are *el, la, los* and *las.* These four forms correspond to the four possible combinations of gender and number. Similarly, the indefinite articles ('a,' 'an' and 'some') are *un, una, unos* and *unas.* In Spanish, the definite article is used more extensively than in English, while the indefinite article is utilized less. As in English, the articles precede the nouns they modify, eg, *el papel* (the paper), *unas frutas* (some fruits).

In contrast, adjectives in Spanish usually follow the noun they modify. Those ending in 'o' agree with the noun in gender and number (thus *alto* means 'tall,' while *mujeres altas* means 'tall women'); those ending in other letters merely agree in number. To form a comparative, add *más* (more) or *menos* (less) before the adjective. For superlatives, add the *más* or *menos* as well as *lo, la, los* or *las* (depending on gender and number). For example, *pequeño* is 'small,' *más pequeño* 'smaller' and *lo más pequeño* 'the smallest.'

Adverbs can often be formed from adjectives by adding the suffix *-mente.* If the adjective ends in an 'o,' convert it to an 'a' before affixing the ending. Thus *actual* (current) becomes *actualmente* (currently) and *rápido* (rapid) becomes *rápidamente.*

Verbs Spanish has three main categories of verbs: those ending in 'ar,' such as *hablar* (to speak); those ending in 'er,' such as *comer* (to eat); and those ending in 'ir,' such as *reir* (to laugh). Verbs are conjugated by retaining the verb's stem and altering the ending depending on subject, tense and mood. While most verbs follow a complicated yet predictable pattern of conjugation, there are scores of 'irregular' verbs, often the most commonly used, that must be memorized. For a more detailed explanation of verb conjugation, refer to Lonely Planet's *Latin American Spanish phrasebook.*

LANGUAGE

Greetings & Civilities

In public behavior, Latin Americans are often cordial yet polite and expect others to reciprocate. Never, for example, address a stranger without extending a greeting such as *buenos días* or *buenas tardes*. The usage of the informal second-person singular *tú* and *vos* differs from country to country; when in doubt, use the more formal *usted*. You must *always* use *usted* when addressing the police or persons with considerable power.

Hello	*Hola*
Good morning/Good day	*Buenos días*
Good afternoon	*Buenas tardes*
Good evening/Good night	*Buenas noches*

(The above three are often shortened to *Buenos* or *Buenas*.)

Goodbye	*Adiós* or *Hasta luego*
Please	*Por favor*
Thank you	*Gracias*
Excuse me	*Discúlpeme* or *Perdón*
I'm sorry	*Lo siento*
My name is…	*Me llamo…*

What is your name?
¿Cómo se llama usted?
A pleasure (to meet you)
Mucho gusto
You're welcome/It's a pleasure
De nada/Con mucho gusto
Excuse me (when passing someone)
Permiso

Useful Words & Phrases

yes	*sí*
no	*no*
and	*y*
to/at	*a*
for	*por, para*
of/from	*de/desde*
in/on	*en*
with	*con*
without	*sin*
before	*antes*
after	*después de*
soon	*pronto*
already	*ya*
now	*ahora*

right away	*ahorita, en seguida*
here	*aquí*
there	*allí* or *allá*
I understand.	*Entiendo.*
I don't understand.	*No entiendo.*

I don't speak much Spanish.
No hablo mucho castellano.
I would like…
Me gustaría… or *Quisiera…*

Is/are there…?	*¿Hay …?*
Where?	*¿Dónde?*
Where is/are…?	*¿Dónde está/están…?*
When?	*¿Cuándo?*
What?	*¿Qué?*
Which (ones)?	*¿Cuál(es)?*
Who?	*¿Quién?*
Why?	*¿Por qué?*
How?	*¿Cómo?*
How much?	*¿Cuánto?*
How many?	*¿Cuántos?*

Use *¿Cómo?* to ask someone to repeat something.

Emergencies

Help!	*¡Socorro!* or *¡Auxilio!*
Help me!	*¡Ayúdenme!*
Thief!	*¡Ladrón!*
Fire!	*¡Fuego!*
police	*policía*
doctor	*doctor*
hospital	*hospital*
I've been robbed.	*Me han robado.*
They took my …	*Se me llevaron …*
money	*el dinero*
passport	*el pasaporte*
bag	*la bolsa*
Leave me alone!	*¡Déjeme!*
Go away!	*¡Váyase!*

Getting Around

plane	*avión*
train	*tren*
bus	*bus, camioneta, ómnibus*
small bus	*colectivo, micro*
ship	*barco, buque*
car	*auto* or *carro*
taxi	*taxi*
truck	*camión*

pickup	*camioneta*
bicycle	*bicicleta*
motorcycle	*motocicleta*
airport	*aeropuerto*
train station	*estación de ferrocarril*

hitchhike
    hacer dedo or *pedir un ride* ('ride' pronounced as in English)
bus terminal
    terminal de buses, terminal terrestre
I would like a ticket to…
    Quiero un boleto/pasaje a…
What's the fare to…?
    ¿Cuánto cuesta el pasaje a…?
When does the next plane/train/bus leave for…?
    ¿Cuándo sale el próximo avión/tren/bus para …?
Are there student discounts?
    ¿Hay descuentos estudiantiles? or *¿Hay rebajas para estudiantes?*

first/last/next	*primero/último/próximo*
first/second class	*primera/segunda clase*
one way/roundtrip	*ida/ida y vuelta*
left luggage	*guardería de equipaje*
tourist office	*oficina de turismo*

Traffic Signs Keep in mind that traffic signs will invariably be in Spanish and may not be accompanied by internationally recognized symbols. Pay especially close attention to signs reading *Peligro* (Danger), *Cede el Paso* (Yield, or Give Way; especially prevalent on one-lane bridges), and *Hundimiento* (Dip; often a euphemistic term for axle-breaking sinkhole). Disregarding these warnings could result in disaster.

Adelante	Ahead
Alto	Stop
Cede el Paso	Yield/Give Way
Curva Peligrosa	Dangerous Curve
Despacio	Slow
Derrumbes en la Vía	Falling Rock
Desvío	Detour
Hundimiento	Dip
Mantenga Su	
Derecha	Keep to the Right

No Adelantar	No Passing
No Rebase	No Passing
No Estacionar	No Parking
No Hay Paso	No Entrance
Peligro	Danger
Trabajos en la Vía	Roadwork
Tránsito Entrando	Entering Traffic

Accommodations

hotel
    hotel, pensión, residencial, hospedaje
single room
    habitación single/sencilla
double room
    habitación doble/matrimonial
Can you give me a deal?
    ¿Me puede hacer precio?/¿Me puede hacer promoción?/¿Me puede rebajar?

per night	*por noche*
full board	*pensión completa*
shared bath	*baño compartido*
private bath	*baño privado*
too expensive	*demasiado caro*
cheaper	*más económico/barato*
What does it cost?	*¿Cuánto cuesta?*
May I see it?	*¿Puedo verlo?*
I don't like it.	*No me gusta.*
the bill	*la cuenta*

Toilets

The most common word for 'toilet' is *baño*, but *servicios sanitarios* or just *servicios* (services) is a frequent alternative. Men's toilets will usually be signaled by *hombres, caballeros* or *varones*. Women's toilets will say *señoras* or *damas*.

Eating & Drinking

I (don't) eat/drink…	*(No) como/tomo…*
I'm a vegetarian.	*Soy vegetariano/a.*
water	*agua*
purified water	*agua purificada*
bread	*pan*
meat	*carne*
cheese	*queso*
eggs	*huevos*
milk	*leche*
juice	*jugo*
vegetables	*vegetales* or *legumbres*
fish	*pescado*

LANGUAGE

seafood	*mariscos*
coffee	*café*
tea	*té*
beer	*cerveza*
alcohol	*alcohol*

Post & Communications

post office	*correo*
letter	*carta*
parcel	*paquete*
postcard	*postal*
airmail	*correo aéreo*
registered mail	*correo certificado*
stamps	*estampillas*
public telephone	*teléfono público*
local call	*llamada local*
person to person	*persona a persona*
email	*correo electrónico*
phone call	*llamada (telefónica)*

collect call
   llamada a cobro revertido
long-distance call
   llamada de larga distancia

Geographical Expressions

The expressions below are among the most common you will encounter in Spanish-language maps and guides.

avenida	avenue
bahía	bay
calle	street
camino	road
campo, finca	farm
carretera, ruta	highway
cascada, salto	waterfall
cerro	hill
cerro	mount
cordillera	mountain range
estero	marsh, estuary
granja, rancho	ranch
lago	lake
montaña	mountain
parque nacional	national park
paso	pass
puente	bridge
río	river
seno	sound
valle	valley

Countries

The list below includes only countries whose names are spelled differently in English and Spanish.

Canada	*Canadá*
Denmark	*Dinamarca*
England	*Inglaterra*
France	*Francia*
Germany	*Alemania*
Great Britain	*Gran Bretaña*
Ireland	*Irlanda*
Italy	*Italia*
Japan	*Japón*
Netherlands	*Holanda*
New Zealand	*Nueva Zelandia*
Scotland	*Escocia*
Spain	*España*
Sweden	*Suecia*
Switzerland	*Suiza*
United States	*Estados Unidos*
Wales	*Gales*
I am from	*Soy de…*

Where do you live?
   ¿Dónde vive usted?
Where are you from?
   ¿De dónde viene usted?

Days of the Week

Monday	*lunes*
Tuesday	*martes*
Wednesday	*miércoles*
Thursday	*jueves*
Friday	*viernes*
Saturday	*sábado*
Sunday	*domingo*

Time

Eight o'clock is *las ocho*, while 8:30 is *las ocho y treinta* (eight and thirty) or *las ocho y media* (eight and a half). However, 7:45 is *las ocho menos quince* (eight minus fifteen) or *las ocho menos cuarto* (eight minus one quarter).

Times are modified by morning *(de la mañana)* or afternoon *(de la tarde)* instead of am or pm. Use of the 24-hour clock, or military time, is also common, especially with transportation schedules.

What time is it?	¿Qué hora es?
It's one o'clock.	Es la una.
At three o'clock…	A las tres…

It's two/three/etc o'clock.
Son las dos/tres/etc.

Numbers

1	uno
2	dos
3	tres
4	cuatro
5	cinco
6	seis
7	siete
8	ocho
9	nueve
10	diez
11	once
12	doce
13	trece
14	catorce
15	quince
16	dieciséis
17	diecisiete
18	dieciocho
19	diecinueve
20	veinte
21	veintiuno
22	veintidós
23	veintitrés
24	veinticuatro
30	treinta
31	treinta y uno
32	treinta y dos
33	treinta y tres
40	cuarenta
50	cincuenta
60	sesenta
70	setenta
80	ochenta
90	noventa
100	cien

101	ciento uno
102	ciento dos
110	ciento diez
200	doscientos
300	trescientos
400	cuatrocientos
500	quinientos
600	seiscientos
700	setecientos
800	ochocientos
900	novecientos
1000	mil
1100	mil cien
1200	mil doscientos
2000	dos mil
10,000	diez mil
50,000	cincuenta mil
100,000	cien mil
1,000,000	un millón
2,000,000	dos millones
1,000,000,000	un billón

Ordinal Numbers

As with other adjectives, ordinals must agree in gender and number with the noun they modify. Ordinal numbers are often abbreviated using a numeral and a superscript 'o' or 'a' in street names, addresses, and so forth: Calle 1a, 2o piso, (1st Street, 2nd floor).

1st	primero/a
2nd	segundo/a
3rd	tercero/a
4th	cuarto/a
5th	quinto/a
6th	sexto/a
7th	séptimo/a
8th	octavo/a
9th	noveno/a
10th	décimo/a
11th	undécimo/a
12th	duodécimo/a
20th	vigésimo/a

Galápagos Fauna Checklist

Keep track of your wildlife sightings with this handy list of all resident and endemic species of birds, reptiles and mammals found in the Galápagos. Additionally, six of the most common bird migrants are listed. The list is arranged in standard taxonomic order.

Key:
- •   Endemic
- R   Resident
- M   Migrant

BIRDS

Species	Sighted	Date	Notes
• Galápagos penguin	☐		
• Waved albatross	☐		
R Dark-rumped petrel	☐		
R Audubon's shearwater	☐		
R White-vented (Elliot's) storm petrel	☐		
R Wedge-rumped (Galápagos) storm petrel	☐		
R Band-rumped (Madeiran) storm petrel	☐		
R Red-billed tropicbird	☐		
R Brown pelican	☐		
R Blue-footed booby	☐		
R Masked booby	☐		
R Red-footed booby	☐		
• Flightless cormorant	☐		
R Magnificent frigatebird	☐		
R Great frigatebird	☐		
R Great blue heron	☐		
R Common egret	☐		
R Cattle egret	☐		
• Lava heron	☐		
R Yellow-crowned night heron	☐		
R Greater flamingo	☐		
R White-cheeked pintail	☐		
• Galápagos hawk	☐		
• Galápagos rail	☐		
R Paint-billed crake	☐		
R Common gallinule	☐		
R American oystercatcher	☐		
M Semi-palmated plover	☐		
M Ruddy turnstone	☐		
M Wandering tattler	☐		
M Sanderling	☐		
M Whimbrel	☐		
M Northern phalarope	☐		
R Black-necked stilt	☐		
• Swallow-tailed gull	☐		
• Lava gull	☐		

R	Brown noddy tern	☐		
R	Sooty tern	☐		
•	Galápagos dove	☐		
R	Dark-billed cuckoo	☐		
R	Groove-billed ani	☐		
R	Smooth-billed ani	☐		
R	Barn owl	☐		
R	Short-eared owl	☐		
R	Vermilion flycatcher	☐		
•	Large-billed (Galápagos) flycatcher	☐		
•	Galápagos (southern) martin	☐		
•	Galápagos mockingbird	☐		
•	Charles mockingbird	☐		
•	Hood mockingbird	☐		
•	Chatham mockingbird	☐		
R	Yellow warbler	☐		
•	Warbler finch	☐		
•	Small ground finch	☐		
•	Large cactus finch	☐		
•	Medium tree finch	☐		
•	Mangrove finch	☐		
•	Woodpecker finch	☐		
•	Medium ground finch	☐		
•	Large ground finch	☐		
•	Sharp-beaked ground finch	☐		
•	Cactus finch	☐		
•	Vegetarian finch	☐		
•	Small tree finch	☐		
•	Large tree finch	☐		

REPTILES

Species		Sighted	Date	Notes
•	Giant tortoise	☐		
R	Pacific green sea turtle	☐		
•	Marine iguana	☐		
•	Galápagos land iguana	☐		
•	Santa Fe land iguana	☐		
•	Lava lizard (7 species)	☐		
•	Gecko (5 species)	☐		
R	Gecko (4 species)	☐		
•	Galápagos snake (4 species)	☐		

MAMMALS

Species		Sighted	Date	Notes
R	Hoary bat	☐		
•	Galápagos bat	☐		
•	Rice rat (2 species)	☐		
R	Galápagos sea lion	☐		
•	Galápagos fur seal	☐		
R	Whales (7 species)	☐		
R	Dolphins (3 species)	☐		

Acknowledgments

A Ley, A Lukowsky, Aaron Gillette, Abraham A Leib, Adam & Samantha Stork, Adi Pieper, Adrian Hoskins, Agnes van Hulst, Alan Firth, Albert Cortés, Aldo Velez, Aler Grubbs, Alex Burckhardt, Alex Nash, Alexander Czarncbag, Alexander Stubb & Suzanne Innes-Stubb, Aleyt Hamerslag, Alfaris Lawalata & Marianne Koene, Alfred Persson & Frida Jarl, Ali Dale, Alice Archer, Alice Gilbey, Alison Van Horn & Tony Hall, Alistair Basendale, Alistair Bool, Allard & Flora Van Den Brink, Allison Blaue, Allison Wright & Alan Michell, Alyssa M Martin, Amber Hulls, Amy Brewster, Amy Denman, Amy Mackowski, Amy Tonn, Andrea Christ, Andrew & Karen Cockburn, Andrew & Wai Cheng, Andrew Holmes, Andrzaj Nowak, Andy Graham, Andy Sweet & Nancy Rainwater, Andy Symington, Andy van den Dobbelsteen, Andy Walters, Angela Gow, Angela Grimm, Anita Gallagher, Anita Gibbings, Anke Dehne, Ann Marie Scanlan, Anna Genet, Annabel Falk, Annabelle Daoust, Annabelle Lyon, Ann-Birte Krueger, Anne Bierman & Dirk de Kleuver, Anne Hammersbad & Adam Roberts, Anne Lise Opsahl & Kristin Bolenc & Nina Kyelby, Anneliese Lehmann, Anne-Marie Eischen, Annette Jacobs, Annick Donkers, Antonio Postigo, Arnaud Mariani, Arnold Joost & Annemieke Wevers, Arnold Parzer, Arnoud Troost & Fenna den Hartog, Arun Mucherjee, Ashley Booth, Gaia Ben-Zvi, Will Kumar & Simone McIsacre, Avi Ben-david, B Muldrow, B Laliberte, BA Rix, Banzon Christoffel, Barbara Spycher, Barbara Terpin, Barry Zeve, Bart Vandeputte, Bas Derksen, Bas Oank & Eppo Beertema, Beat Frauenfelder, Ben Bellows, Bernarda Mejia, Bernie & Jill Mcclean, Bertha Dawang, Beth Fridinger, Bill Klynnk, Björn Schroth, Bob Elner, Bob Gillis, Bob Packard, Bob Redlinger, Bram Bloemers, Brent C Brolin, Brent J Wexler, Brent Jones, Brent Matsuda, Brian & Lorna Lewis, Brian Alan Luff, Brian Ambrosio, Brian Morgan, Brian R Semelski, Brianne Musser, Bruno Jelk, Cameron Hutchison, Carine Attias, Carine Stevens, Carla Plate, Carlyn Ritzen, Carol Damm, Carol Oshana, Carol Outwater, Carol Pollack, Cassandra Garcia, Catherine Stewart & Lee Hallam, CB Denning, Charles Gutnaud, Charles Haley, Charles W Stansfield, Charlotte Blixt & Dirk Schwensen, Charlotte Grimbert, Cherise Miller, Chris Benenilts & Lucy Taylor, Chris Dawson, Chris O'Connell, Chris Olin, Christa Finsterer, Christian Darr, Christian Huettner, Christian Keil, Christian Silkenath, Christiane Hanstein, Christien Klaufus, Christien van Meurs, Christine Byron, Christine Karrer, Christine Lee, Christoph Richter, Christoph Willie, Claudette Laundry, Claudius Jstier, Cliff Hilpert, Clive Jones, Clive Walker, Colette Venderick, Colin Harvey, Colin Lewis, Colleen Nicholson, Connie Hughes, Craig P McVicar, Curtis Alan Clark, D Good, Dairne Fitzpatrick & Cherie Anderson, Dan Grady & Julie Gorshe, Dana Marshall, Daniel Boag, Daniel Drazan, Daniela Gerson, Darine Riem, Dave Dodge, Dave Fuller, Dave Kramer, Dave Lefkowitz, Dave Redmond, David Clapham & Alison Hoad, David Coultas, David Dolan, David Morris, David Ryan, David Wood & Nicole Sweeney, Davis Lee, Dawn & Kevin Hopkins, Deborah Rohrer, Demian & Sabrena San Miguel, Denise & Malcolm McDonaugh, Diana Kirk, Diane Bergeron, Diane De Pooter & Herman Claeys, Diane Hession, Diane V Corbett, Diego Ribetto, Dieter Bratschi, DN Griffiths, Dominique Pfeifer, Donald Koolisch & Pat Glowa, Dorianne Agius, Eban Namer, Edith McDowell Edson, Edith Nowak, Edmund Muller, Ekelijn Gerritsen, Elaine Mowat, Eleasha Gall, Eliana Samaniego, Eliane de Nicolini, Elisabeth & Bjornulf Haakenrud, Elise Richards, Elly & Aukje, Emily Sadigh, Eric Schwartz, Erica Blatchford, Erica Ryberg & Zach Brittsan, Erich Voegtli, Erik De Ryk, Erik Futtrup, Erik Munk Ballegaard & family, Erika Malitzky, Erika Spencer, Erin K Neff, Erith French, Erran Gilad, ES de Jong & HN Koomen, Esther Hofstede, Esther Hurwitz, ET Nance, Jr, Etain O'Carroll, EV Schofield, Eva Schmidt & Martin Rettenmayr, Eve Jansen, F Dizer, Fabrice Gendre, Fabrizzio Trivino, Felicia Beavar, Felix Bartelke, Ferdinand Höng, Fern Thomas, Fernando Sanchez-Heredero Gonzalez, Folke Andersson & Freddy Irusta, Fouad G Azzam, Fran Saporito, Francis J DiGiacomo, Francisco Frias, François Panchard, Frank Connor, Frank Murillo, Frank Verheggen, Franky Verdickt, Franz Schiemer, Fred Kockelbergh, Frederic Francken, Fredrik Anderson, Fritz Woldt, Frixos Michael, Gaby Raynes & Sam Scott, Galit Zadok, Gary B Smith, Gary Kaiser, Gary Kris, Gary Plamer, Gary Smith, Gavin Tanguay, Gemma Leighton, Geoff Copeland, George Lee, George

Majercak, Geraldine Hodgkins, Gerard Cornelissen & Marie Hesselink, Gerhard Kratz, Gert van Lancker & Sandra van Henste, Gianni Fortuna, Sandra Zaramella & Claudio Binotto, Gigi Hoeller, Gil Salomon, Giuseppe Piacentino, Giver Emmanuel, Gonda Bres, Gordon Kuper, Gordon Thompson, Gösta Hoffmann, Graham Disney, Greg Middleton, Guillaume Bouche, HB Kwa, Hanni Matt, Hansjoerg Maier, Hartmut Köhler, Heather Atwood & Richard Forrest, Heather Brown, Heather Cantwell, Heather Sutherland, Heidi Dietrich, Helen Haugh, Helen Morgan, Helen Newton, Helena Toctaquiza-van Maanen & Medardo Toctaquiza, Helga Hartsema-Bartelds, Helge Olav Svela, Helle Pederson, Henriette Jansen, Henrik & Pernille, Hermann-Josef Lohle, Hilde & Isabelle Bygdevoll, Hilde Sleurs, Hoger & Astrid Müller, Hugh Carroll, Ian & Lynn Grout, Ian Coeur, Ian Dean, Ian Mackley, Ian Munro, Ian Samways, Ilse Mayer, Ina Park, Ine Frijters, Inge Lights, Inge Pool, Ingrid de Vries, Ingrid Rudolf, Ingvild W Andersen, Ir Moshe, Irheen de Vries, Isaac Sylvander, Isabel Liao, Isabelle Lochet, Issy Gershon, JM Reid, Jaap Koerce, Jacek & Anna Czarnoccy, Jack Woy, Jacky Upson & Martin Scott, Jacob Massoud, Jacquelyn Shaw, Jacques Gauguin, Jake Jones, James Lombardino, James McLaughlin, James Miller, James Watson, Jamie Monk, Jamie Murray, Jan Tenzer, Jan Timmer, Jane A Lyons de Perez & Vinicio Perez, Jane Brodthagen, Jane Kelly, Jane Letham, Jane Mercer, Janet & Doug Phillops, Janine Abbate, Jarand Felland, Jaroslav Lébl, Jason Song, Jasper Jacobs, Jayne & Nicholas Hird, JC Le Berre, Jean Brown, Jean Sinclair RN (for useful medical as well as other travel info), Jean Stevens, Jeff Holt, Jelle Burma, Jennifer Haefeli, Jennifer Yantz, Jens Thoben, Jens Udsen & Signe Steninge, Jesper Lemmich, Jesper Nissen & Mettine Due, Jessica Hastings, Jessica Kennedy, Jill Wenke, Jilles & Slavica van Werkhoven, Joanna Luplin, Joanna Newton, Jochen Graff & Martina Becker, Jody Madala, John Beeken, John Beswetherick, John Dickinson, John Heidema, John Murby, John Parks, John Taylor, Jonathan Smith, Jorg Manser, Jörg Münzenberg, Jorge Samaniego, Joris & Joyce Snijders, Jorn Griesse, Jos Louwer & Uwe Schröder, Josiane Rompteau de Mulier, Josie Cali & Emmanuel Espino, Juan Galvan D, Judith M Night, Judith Slot, Judy Gabriel, Julia Fleminger, Julia Hinde, Julia Krasevec, Julianne Power, Julie & Jennifer Vick, Julie & Spiras Pappas, Julie Campbell, Julie Harris, Julie Levy, Julie Overnell, Julio Molineros, June MacDonald, Jürgen Buhr, K Sooby, Karen Fredericks, Karen Oorthuijs, Karen Talley, Karen van Duijnhoven, Karen Watts, Karin Donner, Karsten Seeber, Kath Jones, Katherine Hollis, Kathleen Mantel, Kathleen Taylor, Kathryn Elmer, Katja Lehmberg, Katy Foster, Kay Waefler, Keith Taylor, Kelly Hann, Ken Bail, Kennedy & Catherine Somerton, Kerry Mullen, Kevin Golde, Kirsteen Campbell, Kirsty & Dave Brien, Koen Westrik, Kristjan Markusson, Lachlan Mackenzie, Lara Giavi, Lara ten Bosch, Larry & Sue McCoy, Larry Moss, Lars Bech, Lars Terje Holmaas, Laura Anderson, Laura Grefa, Laura Terborgh, Laurens C Philippo, Lawrence Wilmshurst, Leah Berg, Lee Van Dixhorn, Leen Klaassen, Lena Tvede, Lenden Webb, Leonor Vodoz, Lesley Strauss, Liam Schubel, Liliana Nikolic, Lina McCain, Linda Mendelson, Lisa & Jim Grace, Lisbeth Allemann, Liz Smeeton, Liza Richards, Lois Bowman, Lorena Pozzo, Lori Willocks, Lothar Herb, Lou Neal, Louise Campbell, Louise Forrest, Louise Pabe, Lue Bas & Ann Jochems, Luc St-Pierre, Luce Lamy, Lucy Stockbridge, Lucy Wardle, Luis Carbo, Luis Pereira, Lukas Paterek, Lynn Kohner, M Graff, Maaiken Vander Plaetse, Manel Castello, Manfred Bader, Marc De Vries, Marcel Hermans, Marcia & Ralph Johnson, Marco Vitali, Margaret Roemer, Margies Kaag, Maria Dolores Diaz, Maria Nordstedt & Ann Christofferson & Anita Frohlin, Maria Smith, Marilyn Flax, Marilyn Ream & Fred Runkel, Mariusz Biela, Mark Thurber, Markus J Low, Marleen Brils, Martin Dillig, Martin Stead, Martin Webber, Martina Wiede, Mary Bell, Mary Cox, Mat Sumner, Mathew Gore, Matthew Burtch, Matthew Hunt, Matthew Woodley, Matthias Von Der Tann, Maureen Dooley, Mauricio Bergstein, Max Friedman, MC Whirter, Meinrad Tschann, Mélanie Walsh, Melissa Edwards, Melissa Madden, Meyer Jerome, Mia Huysmans, Michael Chewter, Michael Cunningham, Michael Fassbender, Michael Giacometti, Michael Hilburn, Michael Jaksch & Susanne Speidel, Michael Taylor, Michael Wheelahon, Michele Mattix, Michiel Osterveld, Miguel Angel Valera Arnanz, Miguel Falck, Mike Laing, Mike McCarty, Mike Missle, Mike Rahill, Mike Wolfe, Mikkel Levelt, Missy Cormier, Misty Ellis, Mollie Dobson, Monique Reeves, Morag Chase, Nadav Shashar, Nancy Watts, Naomi Eisenstein, Natalie Vial, Nathalie Bridley & Michel Leseigneur, Nathalie Pollier, Neal Teplitz, Nestor Barrero, Neville Antonio, Nici Andhlam-Gardiner, Nick Branch, Nick Lansdowne, Nick Prihoda, Nick

Rowlands, Nick Water, Nicolien Bredenoord & Jitske Jettinghoff, Nienke Bobbert & Jacqueline Casteleins, Nienke Groen, Nigel WR Cox, Nikki Kroan, Niklas Erixon, Nina Tool & Remco de Weerd, Noaz Harel, Oda Karen Kvaal, Olav Østrem, Oliver & Marjolijn von Garczynski, Oliver Maurath, Ondrej Frye, Otto Sluiter, P Maler, Pablo Prado, Padi Selwyn, Paige Newman, Palle Laursen, Pamela Ewasink, Pamela Shriman, Paolo Notarantonio, Patricia A Fitzpatrick, Patricia Pache, Patrick Garland, Patrick O'Bryan, Patrick O'Donnell, Patrick Shearer, Patrick Smith, Paul & Maria Offermans, Paul & Sarah Fretz, Paul Bouwman, Paul Brown, Paul Cook, Paul Goldberg, Paul Hofman, Paul Sinclair, Paul Toms, Perry Beebe, Perry Judd, Peter & Janet Flatley, Peter & Nathalie Bultinck-Brimmel, Peter Foster, Peter Fraser, Peter from Belgium, Peter Hausken, Peter Vanquaille, Peter Walla, Peter Wouter & Suzan Peeters, Petra Mueller, Phil Knoll, Philip Groth, Philip P Chen, Philippe Gillet, Philippe Theys, Phillip Andrus, Pien Wakkerman, Piero Boschi, Piero Ciccarelli, Pieter Nuiten, R Samuelson, Rachel Bentley & Shannon Lee-Rutherford, Rachel de Grey, Rachel Guthrie & Andrew Zybenko, Rafael Nakash, Rafael Pfaffen, Rafael Plonka, Rakesh Patel, Ralf Reinecke, Ralph Cook, Ralph Tomlinson, Ramsey Hart, Ranald & Su Coyne, Randal Henley, Raymond Dommanschet, RD Wicks, Rebecca Lush & Tim Allman, Regina Marchi & Ignacio Ochoa, Reinhard Baumann, Richard Marshall, Richard McCabe, Richard van Kruchten, Richard Ward, Rick Rhodes, Rini de Weijze, Robert Ayers, Robert Kirk, Robert Peeterse, Roberto Burocco, Robin Doudna, Robon Cook, Robyn Christie & Mark Dellar, Rodrigo Mora, Ron Vermaas, Rosa Comas, Rose Lea, Ruth & Geoff Erickson, SL Martin, Sally Blaser, Sally Vergette, Sam Whitley, Samantha Wilson, Sandro Marchesi, Santiago Herrera, Sara Beesley, Sara Tizard & Pat Coleman, Sayo Aoki, Schira Lineen, Schmid Karlheinz, Scott Harris, Sebastian Schaefer, Sebastien Masson, Seymore Schwartz, Shakeel Chaudhry, Shalin Smith, Sharon Shook, Sheila Webb & Steve Job, Shelly Selin, Sherry A Richardson, Sherry Doucette, Shomron Ben-Horin, Shuli Passow, Silke Stappen, Simon Meyer, Simone Ludwig, Simone Yurasek & Salvador Guerra, Siri Ardal, Sonya Lipsett-Rivera & Sergio Rivera Alaya, Sophie Verhagen, Stacy Gery, Stefan Kuhle, Stefan Ott, Stefan Westmeier, Stefany & Paul Brown, Steffen Rossel, Stephan Bollen & Denise Loykens, Stephane Scheyven, Stephanie Spivack, Stephen B Bergren, Stephen Scott, Steve Kohler, Steven Kusters, Stian Tangen, Sue Harvey, Sue Sterling, Sue Turner, Sumana Reddy, Susan Garcia, Susan Twombly, Susan Vetrone, Susanne Hrinkov, Susanne Ritz, Susie Krott, Suzyn Allens, Sylvia Meichsner, Tamar Adelaar & Robin Bollweg, Tamir Horesh, Tatiana Chausson & Philippe Lafon, Ted & Connie Ning, Terry Grant, Tessa Katesmark, Thomas Dietsche, Thomas Mader, Thomas Wilhelm, Thomas Winter, Thore Berg, Thorun Werswick, Tierza Davis, Tim Bollans, Tim Gagan, Tim Phipps, Tim Roden, Timothy Nevin, Tino Socher, Toby Roeoesli, Toby Stephens, Todd Schulz, Tom & Colleen Alspaugh, Tom Groeneveld, Tom Walsh, Ton Paardekooper, Tony Kuchler, Townsend Bancroft, Tracy Masters, Trish Lister, Twid McGrath & Colin Harvey, Ulf Lindén, Vandeputte Bart, Vanessa Teplin, Varnilis Zibus, Vera Cooley, Vera Donk, Veronica Birley, Vicki Irvine, Viktor Håkansson, Vilma Rychener, Volker Sauer, Walt Fraser, Ward Hobert, Wendy Zwaan, Werner Joos, Weze McIntosh, Wigolf & Lele Huss, Willie Gunn, Wim Van Rompay, Winfrid Ottmers, Wojciech Dabrowski, Ximena Alfaro, Ying Xiong Richard Cody, Yoav Yanir & Tamar Bar-El, Yorka Bosisio, Yvonne Morales, Zbynek Dubsky

LONELY PLANET

Guides by Region

Lonely Planet is known worldwide for publishing practical, reliable and no-nonsense information in our guides and on our Web site. The Lonely Planet list covers just about every accessible part of the world. Currently there are 16 series: Travel guides, Shoestring guides, Condensed guides, Watching Wildlife guides, Pisces Diving & Snorkeling guides, City Maps, Road Atlases, Out to Eat, World Food, Journeys travel literature and Pictorials.

AFRICA Africa on a shoestring • Cairo • Cape Town • Cape Town City Map • East Africa • Egypt • Egyptian Arabic phrasebook • Ethiopia, Eritrea & Djibouti • Ethiopian (Amharic) phrasebook • The Gambia & Senegal • Healthy Travel Africa • Kenya • Malawi • Morocco • Moroccan Arabic phrasebook • Mozambique • Read This First: Africa • South Africa, Lesotho & Swaziland • Southern Africa • Southern Africa Road Atlas • Swahili phrasebook • Tanzania, Zanzibar & Pemba • Trekking in East Africa • Tunisia • Watching Wildlife East Africa • Watching Wildlife Southern Africa • West Africa • World Food Morocco • Zimbabwe, Botswana & Namibia
Travel Literature: Mali Blues: Traveling to an African Beat • The Rainbird: A Central African Journey • Songs to an African Sunset: A Zimbabwean Story

AUSTRALIA & THE PACIFIC Auckland • Australia • Australian phrasebook • Australia Road Atlas • Bushwalking in Australia • Cycling New Zealand • Fiji • Fijian phrasebook • Healthy Travel Australia, NZ and the Pacific • Islands of Australia's Great Barrier Reef • Melbourne • Melbourne City Map • Micronesia • New Caledonia • New South Wales & the ACT • New Zealand • Northern Territory • Outback Australia • Out to Eat – Melbourne • Out to Eat – Sydney • Papua New Guinea • Pidgin phrasebook • Queensland • Rarotonga & the Cook Islands • Samoa • Solomon Islands • South Australia • South Pacific • South Pacific phrasebook • Sydney • Sydney City Map • Sydney Condensed • Tahiti & French Polynesia • Tasmania • Tonga • Tramping in New Zealand • Vanuatu • Victoria • Watching Wildlife Australia • Western Australia
Travel Literature: Islands in the Clouds: Travel in the Highlands of New Guinea • Kiwi Tracks: A New Zealand Journey • Sean & David's Long Drive

CENTRAL AMERICA & THE CARIBBEAN Bahamas, Turks & Caicos • Baja California • Bermuda • Central America on a shoestring • Costa Rica • Costa Rica Spanish phrasebook • Cuba • Dominican Republic & Haiti • Eastern Caribbean • Guatemala • Belize, Guatemala & Yucatán: La Ruta Maya • Healthy Travel Central & South America • Jamaica • Mexico • Mexico City • Panama • Puerto Rico • Read This First: Central & South America • World Food Mexico • Yucatán
Travel Literature: Green Dreams: Travels in Central America

EUROPE Amsterdam • Amsterdam City Map • Amsterdam Condensed • Andalucía • Austria • Baltic States phrasebook • Barcelona • Barcelona City Map • Berlin • Berlin City Map• Britain • British phrasebook • Brussels, Bruges & Antwerp • Budapest • Budapest City Map • Canary Islands • Central Europe • Central Europe phrasebook • Corfu & the Ionians • Corsica • Crete • Crete Condensed • Croatia • Cycling Britain • Cycling France • Cyprus • Czech & Slovak Republics • Denmark • Dublin • Dublin City Map • Eastern Europe • Eastern Europe phrasebook • Edinburgh • Estonia, Latvia & Lithuania • Europe on a shoestring • Finland • Florence • France • Frankfurt Condensed • French phrasebook • Georgia, Armenia & Azerbaijan • Germany • German phrasebook • Greece • Greek Islands • Greek phrasebook • Hungary • Iceland, Greenland & the Faroe Islands • Ireland • Istanbul • Italian phrasebook • Italy • Krakow • Lisbon • The Loire • London • London City Map • London Condensed • Madrid • Malta • Mediterranean Europe • Mediterranean Europe phrasebook • Moscow • Munich • Norway • Out to Eat – London • Paris • Paris City Map • Paris Condensed • Poland • Portugal • Portuguese phrasebook • Prague • Prague City Map • Provence & the Côte d'Azur • Read This First: Europe • Romania & Moldova • Rome • Russia, Ukraine & Belarus • Russian phrasebook • Scandinavian & Baltic Europe • Scandinavian Europe phrasebook • Scotland • Sicily • Slovenia • South-West France • Spain • Spanish phrasebook • St Petersburg • St Petersburg City Map • Sweden • Switzerland • Trekking in Spain • Tuscany • Ukrainian phrasebook • Venice • Vienna • Walking in Britain • Walking in France • Walking in Ireland • Walking in Italy • Walking in Spain • Walking in Switzerland • Western Europe • Western Europe phrasebook • World Food France • World Food Ireland • World Food Italy • World Food Spain
Travel Literature: Love and War in the Apennines • The Olive Grove: Travels in Greece • On the Shores of the Mediterranean • Round Ireland in Low Gear • A Small Place in Italy

INDIAN SUBCONTINENT Bangladesh • Bengali phrasebook • Bhutan • Delhi • Goa • Healthy Travel Asia & India • Hindi/Urdu phrasebook • India • Indian Himalaya • Karakoram Highway • Kerala • Mumbai (Bombay) •

LONELY PLANET

Mail Order

Lonely Planet products are distributed worldwide. They are also available by mail order from Lonely Planet, so if you have difficulty finding a title please write to us. North and South American residents should write to 150 Linden St, Oakland, CA 94607, USA; European and African residents should write to 10a Spring Place, London NW5 3BH, UK; and residents of other countries to Locked Bag 1, Footscray, Victoria 3011, Australia.

Nepal • Nepali phrasebook • Pakistan • Rajasthan • Read This First: Asia & India • South India • Sri Lanka • Sri Lanka phrasebook • Tibet • Trekking in the Indian Himalaya • Trekking in the Karakoram & Hindukush • Trekking in the Nepal Himalaya
Travel Literature: The Age of Kali: Indian Travels and Encounters • Hello Goodnight: A Life of Goa • In Rajasthan • A Season in Heaven: True Tales from the Road to Kathmandu • Shopping for Buddhas • A Short Walk in the Hindu Kush • Slowly Down the Ganges

ISLANDS OF THE INDIAN OCEAN Madagascar & Comoros • Maldives • Mauritius, Réunion & Seychelles

MIDDLE EAST & CENTRAL ASIA Bahrain, Kuwait & Qatar • Central Asia • Central Asia phrasebook • Dubai • Hebrew phrasebook • Iran • Israel & the Palestinian Territories • Istanbul • Istanbul City Map • Istanbul to Cairo on a shoestring • Jerusalem • Jerusalem City Map • Jordan • Lebanon • Middle East • Oman & the United Arab Emirates • Syria • Turkey • Turkish phrasebook • World Food Turkey • Yemen
Travel Literature: Black on Black: Iran Revisited • The Gates of Damascus • Kingdom of the Film Stars: Journey into Jordan

NORTH AMERICA Alaska • Boston • Boston City Map • California & Nevada • California Condensed • Canada • Chicago • Chicago City Map • Louisiana & the Deep South • Florida • Hawaii • Hiking in Alaska • Hiking in the USA • Las Vegas • Los Angeles • Miami • Miami City Map • New England • New Orleans • New York City • New York City City Map • New York City Condensed • New York, New Jersey & Pennsylvania • Oahu • Pacific Northwest • Puerto Rico • Rocky Mountains • San Francisco • San Francisco City Map • Seattle • Southwest • Texas • USA • USA phrasebook • Vancouver • Virginia & the Capital Region • Washington, DC • Washington, DC City Map • World Food Deep South, USA
Travel Literature: Caught Inside: A Surfer's Year on the California Coast • Drive Thru America

NORTH-EAST ASIA Beijing • Cantonese phrasebook • China • Hiking in Japan • Hong Kong • Hong Kong City Map • Hong Kong Condensed • Hong Kong, Macau & Guangzhou • Japan • Japanese phrasebook • Korea • Korean phrasebook • Kyoto • Mandarin phrasebook • Mongolia • Mongolian phrasebook • Seoul • South-West China • Taiwan • Tokyo
Travel Literature: In Xanadu: A Quest • Lost Japan

SOUTH AMERICA Argentina, Uruguay & Paraguay • Bolivia • Brazil • Brazilian phrasebook • Buenos Aires • Chile & Easter Island • Colombia • Ecuador & the Galapagos Islands • Healthy Travel Central & South America • Latin American Spanish phrasebook • Peru • Quechua phrasebook • Read This First: Central & South America • Rio de Janeiro • Rio de Janeiro City Map • Santiago de Chile • South America on a shoestring • Trekking in the Patagonian Andes • Venezuela
Travel Literature: Full Circle: A South American Journey

SOUTH-EAST ASIA Bali & Lombok • Bangkok • Bangkok City Map • Burmese phrasebook • Cambodia • Hanoi • Healthy Travel Asia & India • Hill Tribes phrasebook • Ho Chi Minh City • Indonesia • Indonesian phrasebook • Indonesia's Eastern Islands • Jakarta • Java • Lao phrasebook • Laos • Malay phrasebook • Malaysia, Singapore & Brunei • Myanmar (Burma) • Philippines • Pilipino (Tagalog) phrasebook • Read This First: Asia & India • Singapore • Singapore City Map • South-East Asia on a shoestring • South-East Asia phrasebook • Thailand • Thailand's Islands & Beaches • Thailand, Vietnam, Laos & Cambodia Road Atlas • Thai phrasebook • Vietnam • Vietnamese phrasebook • World Food Thailand • World Food Vietnam

ALSO AVAILABLE: Antarctica • The Arctic • The Blue Man: Tales of Travel, Love and Coffee • Brief Encounters: Stories of Love, Sex & Travel • Chasing Rickshaws • The Last Grain Race • Lonely Planet Unpacked • Not the Only Planet: Science Fiction Travel Stories • On the Edge: Extreme Travel • Sacred India • Travel with Children • Travel Photography: A Guide to Taking Better Pictures

Mail Order

Index

Text

```
        Barnes & Noble Bookseller
              23-80 Bell Blvd
            Bayside, NY 11360
              (718) 224-1083
        12-03-02 S02562 R006


TEACHER/EDUCATOR

Ecuador and the Galapago        15.99
0864427611
DISCOUNT        19.99   4.00

SUB TOTAL                       15.99
SALES TAX                        1.32
TOTAL                           17.31
AMOUNT TENDERED
CASH                            20.06

TOTAL PAYMENT                   20.06
CHANGE                           2.75
        Thank you for Shopping at
        Barnes & Noble Booksellers
   Shop online 24 hours a day www.bn.com
   #57574  12-03-02 11:22A annett

          Booksellers since 1873
```

Full refund issued for new and unread books and unopened music within 30 days with a receipt from any Barnes & Noble store.
Store Credit issued for new and unread books and unopened music after 30 days or without a sales receipt. Credit issued at <u>lowest sale price</u>.
We gladly accept returns of new and unread books and unopened music from bn.com with a bn.com receipt for store credit at the bn.com price.

Full refund issued for new and unread books and unopened music within 30 days with a receipt from any Barnes & Noble store.
Store Credit issued for new and unread books and unopened music after 30 days or without a sales receipt. Credit issued at <u>lowest sale price</u>.
We gladly accept returns of new and unread books and unopened music from bn.com with a bn.com receipt for store credit at the bn.com price.

Full refund issued for new and unread books and unopened music within 30 days with a receipt from any Barnes & Noble store.
Store Credit issued for new and unread books and unopened music after 30 days or without a sales receipt. Credit issued at <u>lowest sale price</u>.
We gladly accept returns of new and unread books and unopened music from

Bold indicates maps.

Bold indicates maps.

Boxed Text

Bold indicates maps.

MAP LEGEND

ROUTES

City	Regional	
		Primary Road
		Secondary Road
		Tertiary Road
		Primary Dirt
		Secondary Dirt
		Tertiary Dirt

Pedestrian Mall
Steps
Tunnel
Trail
Walking Tour
Path

TRANSPORTATION

Train
Tram
Bus Route
Ferry

BOUNDARIES

International
Provincial
County
Disputed

HYDROGRAPHY

River; Creek
Canal
Lake
Spring; Rapids
Waterfalls
Dry; Salt Lake

AREAS

Beach
Building
Campus
Cemetery
Forest
Garden; Zoo
Marine Park
Park
Plaza
Reservation
Sports Field
Swamp; Mangrove

POPULATION SYMBOLS

| ✪ NATIONAL CAPITAL | National Capital | ● Large City | Large City | ● Small City | Small City |
| ◉ PROVINCIAL CAPITAL | Provincial Capital | ● Medium City | Medium City | ● Town; Village | Town; Village |

MAP SYMBOLS

| ■ | Place to Stay | ▼ | Place to Eat | ● | Point of Interest |

	Airfield		Church		Museum		Skiing - Downhill
	Airport		Cinema		Observatory		Stately Home
	Archeological Site; Ruin		Dive Site		Park		Surfing
	Bank		Embassy; Consulate		Parking Area		Synagogue
	Baseball Diamond		Footbridge		Pass		Tao Temple
	Battlefield		Gas Station		Picnic Area		Taxi
	Bike Trail		Hospital		Police Station		Telephone
	Border Crossing		Information		Pool		Theater
	Bus Station; Terminal		Internet Café		Post Office		Toilet - Public
	Bus Stop		Lighthouse		Pub; Bar		Tomb
	Café		Lookout		RV Park		Trailhead
	Campground		Mine		Shelter		Train Station
	Castle		Mission		Shipwreck		Tram Stop
	Cathedral		Monument		Shopping Mall		Transportation
	Cave		Mountain		Skiing - Cross Country		Volcano

Note: not all symbols displayed above appear in this book

LONELY PLANET OFFICES

Australia
Locked Bag 1, Footscray, Victoria 3011
☎ 03 8379 8000 fax 03 8379 8111
email talk2us@lonelyplanet.com.au

USA
150 Linden Street, Oakland, California 94607
☎ 510 893 8555, TOLL FREE 800 275 8555
fax 510 893 8572
email info@lonelyplanet.com

UK
10a Spring Place, London NW5 3BH
☎ 020 7428 4800 fax 020 7428 4828
email go@lonelyplanet.co.uk

France
1 rue du Dahomey, 75011 Paris
☎ 01 55 25 33 00 fax 01 55 25 33 01
email bip@lonelyplanet.fr
www.lonelyplanet.fr

World Wide Web: www.lonelyplanet.com *or* AOL keyword: lp
Lonely Planet Images: lpi@lonelyplanet.com.au